MARVELOUS STORIES
from
THE PERFECTION OF WISDOM

The publication of this book has been enabled by
a generous donation from Sunny Lou.

A NOTE ON THE PROPER CARE OF DHARMA MATERIALS

Traditional Buddhist cultures treat books on Dharma as sacred. Hence it is considered disrespectful to place them in a low position, to read them when lying down, or to place them where they might be damaged by food or drink.

MARVELOUS STORIES
from
THE PERFECTION OF WISDOM

130 Didactic Stories from Ārya Nāgārjuna's
Exegesis on the Great Perfection of Wisdom Sutra

By the Great Indian Buddhist Patriarch
Ārya Nāgārjuna
(*ca* 200 CE)

Translation by Bhikshu Dharmamitra

KALAVINKA PRESS
Seattle, Washington
WWW.KALAVINKAPRESS.ORG

KALAVINKA PRESS
8603 39th Ave SW
Seattle, WA 98136 USA

WWW.KALAVINKAPRESS.ORG / WWW.KALAVINKA.ORG

Kalavinka Press is associated with the Kalavinka Dharma Association, a non-profit organized exclusively for religious educational purposes as allowed within the meaning of section 501(c)3 of the Internal Revenue Code. Kalavinka Dharma Association was founded in 1990 and gained formal approval in 2004 by the United States Internal Revenue Service as a 501(c)3 non-profit organization to which all donations are tax deductible.

Donations to KDA are accepted by mail and on the Kalavinka website where numerous free Dharma translations and excerpts from Kalavinka publications are available in digital format.

PUBLISHER'S CATALOGING-IN-PUBLICATION DATA

Nagarjuna, 2nd c.
  [Da zhi du lun / Mahaprajñāpāramitā Upadeśa. English translation.]
  Marvelous Stories from the Perfection of Wisdom. 130 Didactic Stories from Arya Nagarjuna's Exegesis on the Great Perfection of Wisdom Sutra.
  Translated by Bhikshu Dharmamitra. – 1st ed. – Seattle, WA: Kalavinka Press, 2009.

    p. ; cm.
    ISBN: 978-1-935413-07-3
    Includes: facing-page Chinese source text in both traditional and simplified scripts.

  1. Mādhyamika (Buddhism)—Early works to 1800. 2. Bodhisattvas. 3. Spiritual life—Mahayana Buddhism. I. Title
                                                    2009920875
                                                         0902

Cover and interior designed and composed by Bhikshu Dharmamitra.

Dedicated to the memory of the selfless and marvelous life of the
Venerable Dhyāna Master Hsuan Hua, the Weiyang Ch'an Patriarch
and the very personification of the Bodhisattva Path.

DHYĀNA MASTER HSUAN HUA

宣化禪師

1918–1995

ACKNOWLEDGMENTS

The accuracy and readability of these first ten books of translations have been significantly improved with the aid of extensive corrections, preview comments, and editorial suggestions generously contributed by Bhikkhu Bodhi, Jon Babcock, Timothy J. Lenz, Upāsaka Feng Ling, Upāsaka Guo Ke, Upāsikā Min Li, and Richard Robinson. Additional valuable editorial suggestions and corrections were offered by Bhikshu Huifeng, and Bruce Munson.

The publication of the initial set of ten translation volumes has been assisted by substantial donations to the Kalavinka Dharma Association by Bill and Peggy Brevoort, Freda Chen, David Fox, Upāsaka Guo Ke, Chenping and Luther Liu, Sunny Lou, Jimi Neal, and "Leo L." (a.k.a. *Camellia sinensis folium*). Additional helpful donations were offered by Doug Adams, Diane Hodgman, Bhikshu Huifeng, Joel and Amy Lupro, Richard Robinson, Ching Smith, and Sally and Ian Timm.

Were it not for the ongoing material support provided by my late guru's Dharma Realm Buddhist Association and the serene translation studio provided by Seattle's Bodhi Dhamma Center, creation of this translation would have been immensely more difficult.

Most importantly, it would have been impossible for me to produce this translation without the Dharma teachings provided by my late guru, the Weiyang Ch'an Patriarch, Dharma teacher, and exegete, the Venerable Master Hsuan Hua.

CITATION AND ROMANIZATION PROTOCOLS

Kalavinka Press *Taisho* citation style adds text numbers after volume numbers and before page numbers to assist rapid CBETA digital searches.

Romanization, where used, is Pinyin with the exception of names and terms already well-recognized in Wade-Giles.

THE CHINESE TEXT

This translation is supplemented by inclusion of Chinese source text on verso pages in both traditional and simplified scripts. Taisho-supplied variant readings from other editions are presented as Chinese endnotes.

This Chinese text and its variant readings are from the April, 2004 version of the Chinese Buddhist Electronic Text Association's digital edition of the Taisho compilation of the Buddhist canon.

Those following the translation in the Chinese should be aware that Taisho scripture punctuation is not traceable to original editions, is often erroneous and misleading, and is probably best ignored altogether.

GENERAL TABLE OF CONTENTS

STORIES DIRECTORY

Translator's Introduction

Marvelous Stories from the Perfection of Wisdom is a collection of stories drawn from the massive and encyclopedic *Exegesis on the Great Perfection of Wisdom Sutra* (*Mahāprajñāpāramitā Upadeśa* / 大智度論) composed by the Indian monastic patriarch Ārya Nāgārjuna (*ca* 200 CE), a renowned and pivotal figure in the doctrinal clarification and popularization of Mahāyāna Buddhism. The English translations presented here were made from the sole extant edition of the *Exegesis* as it is preserved in the Chinese Buddhist canon. This is the Sanskrit-to-Chinese translation created by the great translator-monk Kumārajīva in approximately 400 CE.

The selections included here vary markedly in length and character. Some are simply abbreviated versions of anecdotes found elsewhere in the scriptures of Southern and/or Northern School Buddhism. Others are much longer tales which may or may not be directly based on sutras. Some stories probably do have a factual basis whereas others roam freely into the realm of the unbelievable. Hyperbolic-description of this sort is quite common in Indian religious texts prioritizing sublime ideals and principles while being much less concerned with prosaic issues like plausibility.

This is not an ordinary story book wherein stories are related primarily for entertainment value. (Though many *are* fascinating.) Rather, it is a collection of tales set forth by Nāgārjuna for the express purpose of delivering important teachings on Dharma.

I have organized the story collection into seven chapters. The first six are associated with the "six perfections" that are standard in Mahāyāna Buddhism: giving, moral virtue, patience, vigor, meditative discipline, and wisdom. The stories in these six chapters correspond to those tales contained within Nāgārjuna's very long serial discussion of the six perfections in Chapters 17 through 30 of the *Exegesis*. The seventh chapter consists of stories on "various topics" found elsewhere in Nāgārjuna's immense work.

My arrangement of the stories according to the above schema may be slightly misleading, for the "perfections stories" often deal not just with the perfections themselves, but also with topics ranging beyond the scope of the perfection purportedly being treated in the corresponding chapter. Conversely, a fair number of the stories supposedly dealing with "various topics" happen to deal most directly with one or another of the six perfections.

I should mention that this volume is not exhaustively inclusive of every last story found in the *Exegesis*, but rather is a selective collection. Nearly all of the stories collected here are "framed" by brief doctrinal observations or discussions included by Nāgārjuna for the purpose of clarifying or amplifying a doctrinal meaning or lesson implicit in the story itself.

I was influenced to create this collection of stories not solely on account of a conviction that others would appreciate them as much as I have. I have found when giving talks on Buddhism to lay audiences that including stories along with the teachings makes "Dharma talks" more engaging, more memorable, and hence more useful. I realized early on that other Dharma teachers would likely be assisted by the ready availability of a collection of didactic stories helpful in setting forth instruction for Dharma students. Hence this realization became a primary rationale for preparation and publication of *Marvelous Stories from the Perfection of Wisdom*.

As with all Kalavinka Press translations, I have included the source text in both traditional and short-form scripts on the *verso* page. This was done in order to facilitate use of this work in the teaching of Sino-Buddhist Classical Chinese and was also done with an eye toward facilitating study by specialists and bilingual native readers of the Chinese language unfamiliar with classical Chinese Buddhist technical terms. "Source Text Variant Readings" from other editions are included as an appendix. The digital text used in this book is the 2004 edition of *CBETA*.

My apologies to those who justifiably would have expected copious annotation. Unfortunately, failing health precludes inclusion notes other than the few endnotes included in the initial draft translation.

I hope this work will be entertaining and useful for both Dharma students and teachers. As with all of my translations, corrections and suggestions for improvement are much appreciated. They may be forwarded via KALAVINKA.ORG website email.

Bhikshu Dharmamitra
September 6, 2008

Part One:

Nāgārjuna's Stories on Giving

复次以七宝人民车乘金银灯烛房舍香华布施故。得作转轮王七宝具足。复次施得时故。报亦增多。如佛说。施远行人远来人。病人看病人。风寒众难时施。是为时施。复次布施时随土地所须施故。得报增多。复次旷路中施故。得福增多。常施不废故。得报增多。如求者所欲施故。得福增多。施物重故。得福增多。如以精舍园林浴池等若施善人故。得报增多。若施僧故。得报增多。若施者受者俱有德故。[23]（丹注云如菩萨及佛慈心布施是为施者若施佛及菩萨阿罗汉辟支佛是为受者故)得报增多。种种将迎恭敬受者故。得福增多。难得物施故。得福增多。

復次以七寶人民車乘金銀燈燭房舍香華布施故。得作轉輪王七寶具足。復次施得時故。報亦增多。如佛說。施遠行人遠來人。病人看病人。風寒眾難時施。是為時施。復次布施時隨土地所須施故。得報增多。復次曠路中施故。得福增多。常施不廢故。得報增多。如求者所欲施故。得福增多。施物重故。得福增多。如以精舍園林浴池等若施善人故。得報增多。若施僧故。得報增多。若施者受者俱有德故。[23]（丹注云如菩薩及佛慈心布施是為施者若施佛及菩薩阿羅漢辟支佛是為受者故)得報增多。種種將迎恭敬受者故。得福增多。難得物施故。得福增多。

简体字

正體字

The Painter Who Gave Away His Savings

Nāgārjuna's Preamble: Karmically-Rewarding Forms of Giving

Furthermore, on account of making gifts of the seven precious things, workers, carriages, gold, silver, lamps, candles, buildings, incense and flowers, one is able to become a wheel-turning monarch possessing an abundance of his seven types of treasures.

Additionally, through making gifts with timely appropriateness, one's resulting karmic reward is increased. This is as explained by the Buddha when he said, "If one gives to a person about to travel far, to a person come from afar, to a sick person, to a person caring for the sick, or if one gives to assist with manifold difficulties arising from storms or cold, this qualifies as timely giving."

Again, if one gives in a way which accords with what is most needed in a particular place, one reaps an increased karmic reward from that.

Also, if one performs an act of giving on the road in a wilderness area, one thereby gains an increased measure of merit.

If one continues giving constantly and without neglecting that practice, one gains from that an increased karmic reward.

If one gives a gift which accords with what the solicitor desires, one gains from that an increased measure of merit.

If one gives gifts which are valuable, one gains an increased measure of merit.

If one gives monastic dwellings, parks, forests, bathing ponds, and so forth—provided that those gifts are bestowed upon people who are good—one gains an increased karmic reward on that account.

If one gives gifts to the Sangha, one thereby gains an increased karmic reward.

If both the benefactor and the recipient are possessed of virtue, an increased karmic reward is gained as a result of that.

(Chinese textual note: "The notes in red read, 'Take for example bodhisattvas and buddhas who give with a mind of compassion. This is what is intended with respect to the benefactor. Giving for example to buddhas, bodhisattvas, arhats, or pratyekabuddhas—this is what is intended in regard to the recipient.'")

When one extends all manner of welcoming courtesies out of respect for the recipient, one gains from this an increased measure of merit.

If one gives that which was difficult to come by, one gains an increased amount of merit.

随所有物尽能布施故。得福增多。譬如大月氏弗迦罗城中有一画师。名千那。到东方多[24]刹[25]陀罗国。客画十二年得三十两金。持还本国于弗迦罗城中。闻打鼓作大会声。往见众僧。信心清净即问维那。此众中几许物。得作一日食。维那答曰。三十两金足得一日食。即以所有三十两金付维那。为我作一日食。我明日当来。空手而归。其妇问曰。十二年作得何等物。答言。我得三十两金。即问三十两金今在何所。答言。已在福田中种。妇言。何等福田。答言施与众僧。妇便缚[26]其夫送官治罪断事。大官问。以何事故。妇言我夫 [142a] 狂痴。十二年[1]客作得三十两金。不怜愍妇儿尽以与他人。依如官制辄缚送来。大官问其夫。汝何以不供给妇儿。乃以与他。

简体字

隨所有物盡能布施故。得福增多。譬如大月氏弗迦羅城中有一畫師。名千那。到東方多[24]刹[25]陀羅國。客畫十二年得三十兩金。持還本國於弗迦羅城中。聞打鼓作大會聲。往見眾僧。信心清淨即問維那。此眾中幾許物。得作一日食。維那答曰。三十兩金足得一日食。即以所有三十兩金付維那。為我作一日食。我明日當來。空手而歸。其婦問曰。十二年作得何等物。答言。我得三十兩金。即問三十兩金今在何所。答言。已在福田中種。婦言。何等福田。答言施與眾僧。婦便縛[26]其夫送官治罪斷事。大官問。以何事故。婦言我夫 [142a] 狂癡。十二年[1]客作得三十兩金。不憐愍婦兒盡以與他人。依如官制輒縛送來。大官問其夫。汝何以不供給婦兒。乃以與他。

正體字

Story: The Painter who Gave Away his Savings

If one is able to give all that one has, one gains thereby an increased amount of merit. This principle is illustrated by the case of a painter named Karṇa from the city of Puṣkarāvatī in the state of Greater Tokharestan. He had traveled to the east to the state of Takṣaśilā where he served as a painter to that court for a period of twelve years.

He received payment of thirty two-ounce pieces of gold for his work and took it back with him when he journeyed back to the city of Puṣkarāvatī in his home state. He chanced to hear the sound of a drum beating to convene a great assembly. He went there and saw an assembly of the Sangha. With a mind of pure faith he asked the Karmadāna, "How much would be required to provide a day's feast for this assembly?"

The Karmadāna replied, "Thirty two-ounce pieces of gold would be adequate to supply food for one day." At this point, he immediately brought forth the entire sum of thirty two-ounce pieces of gold and entrusted it to the Karmadāna saying, "Prepare on my behalf a day's feast [for this entire assembly]. I will return here tomorrow." He then went back to his home empty-handed.

His wife asked him, "Well, what did you earn for your twelve years of work?"

He replied, "I earned thirty two-ounce pieces of gold."

She immediately asked, "Where are the thirty two-ounce pieces of gold now?"

He replied, "They have already been planted in the merit field."

The wife asked, "What merit field?"

He replied, "I gave them to the assembly of the Sangha." His wife then had him detained and sent before a judge that his crime could be dealt with and the matter properly adjudicated. The Grand Judge asked, "Why is it that we are convened here?"

The wife replied, "My husband has become crazy and deluded. He worked in royal service in a foreign country for twelve years and earned thirty two-ounce pieces of gold. He had no compassionate regard for his wife or child and so gave away the entire sum to other people. Thus, wishing him to be dealt with by judicial decree, I quickly moved to have him detained and brought forth."

The Grand Judge then asked her husband, "Why did you not share it with your wife and child, preferring instead to give the gold away to others?

答言。我先世不行功德。今
世贫穷受诸辛苦。今世遭遇
福田。若不种福后世复贫。
贫贫相续无得脱时。我今欲
顿舍贫穷。以是故尽以金施
众僧。大官是优婆塞信佛清
净。闻是语已赞言。是为甚
难。懃苦得此少物尽以施
僧。汝是善人。即脱身璎珞
及所乘马并一聚落以施贫
人。而语之言。汝始施众
僧。众僧未食是为谷子未
种。[2]牙已得生。大果方在
后[3]身以是故言。难得之物
尽用布施其福最多。

答言。我先世不行功德。今
世貧窮受諸辛苦。今世遭遇
福田。若不種福後世復貧。
貧貧相續無得脫時。我今欲
頓捨貧窮。以是故盡以金施
眾僧。大官是優婆塞信佛清
淨。聞是語已讚言。是為甚
難。懃苦得此少物盡以施
僧。汝是善人。即脫身瓔珞
及所乘馬并一聚落以施貧
人。而語之言。汝始施眾
僧。眾僧未食是為穀子未
種。[2]牙已得生。大果方在
後[3]身以是故言。難得之物
盡用布施其福最多。

简体字   正體字

He replied, "In previous lives I did not cultivate merit. In the present life I am poor and so have undergone all manner of bitter suffering. Now, in this life I have encountered the field of merit. If I do not plant merit, in later lives I will still be poor, and so poverty will follow upon poverty continuously, such that there will be no time when I am able to escape it. I now wish to immediately relinquish this state of poverty. It is for this reason that I took all of the gold and gave it to the Sangha community."

The Grand Judge happened to be an *upāsaka*[1] who maintained a pure faith in the Buddha. When he heard these words, he praised him, saying, "This is an extremely difficult thing to have done. You applied yourself diligently and underwent hardship in order to obtain such a small material reward, and then you were able to take it all and give it to the Sangha. You are a good man."

He then took off the strand of jewels around his neck and gave it to the poor man along with his horse and the income which he received from the taxes on an entire village. He then declared to him, "At the beginning, when you had already made the gift to an assembly of the Sangha, but that assembly of Sangha members had still not partaken of that food, it was a case of the seed still not really having been planted. But now a sprout has already come forth from it. The great fruit of this will come forth in the next life."

Conclusion

It is for reasons such as this that it is said that one gains the most merit if one is able to give entirely of that which has been hard to come by.

Notes

1. An *upāsaka* (feminine: *upāsikā*) is a Buddhist layman, the minimum qualification for which is having formally received from duly-ordained clergy (usually a bhikshu with at least five years full ordination) the Three Refuges: refuge in the Buddha; refuge in the Dharma; and refuge in the Ārya Sangha. ("Ārya" is a reference to those who have realized the path of seeing or above.) Although pledging adherence to specific moral norms is not a prerequisite to obtain the Refuges and become formally "Buddhist," the universal ethical standard for the Buddhist layperson consists in the five precepts which prohibit: killing; stealing; sexual misconduct; false speech; intoxicants.

简体字	正體字
复次不为众生。亦不为知诸法实相故施。但求脱生老病死。是为声闻檀。为一切众生故施。亦为知诸法实相故施。是为诸佛菩萨檀。于诸功德不能具足。[7]但欲得少许分。是为声闻檀。一切诸功德欲具足满。是为诸佛菩萨檀。畏老病死故施。是为声闻檀。为助佛道为化众生不畏老病死。是为诸佛菩萨檀。是中应说菩萨本生经。如说阿婆陀那经中。昔阎浮提中有王。名婆[8]萨婆。尔时有婆罗门菩萨。名韦罗摩。是国王师。教王作转轮圣王法。韦罗摩财富无量珍宝具足。作是思惟。人谓我为贵[9]人财富无量。饶益众生今正是时应当大施。富贵虽乐一切无常。五家所共令人心散轻[10]泆不定。譬如猕猴不能暂住。人命逝速疾于电灭。人身无常众苦之薮。以是之故应行布施。	復次不為眾生。亦不為知諸法實相故施。但求脫生老病死。是為聲聞檀。為一切眾生故施。亦為知諸法實相故施。是為諸佛菩薩檀。於諸功德不能具足。[7]但欲得少許分。是為聲聞檀。一切諸功德欲具足滿。是為諸佛菩薩檀。畏老病死故施。是為聲聞檀。為助佛道為化眾生不畏老病死。是為諸佛菩薩檀。是中應說菩薩本生經。如說阿婆陀那經中。昔閻浮提中有王。名婆[8]薩婆。爾時有婆羅門菩薩。名韋羅摩。是國王師。教王作轉輪聖王法。韋羅摩財富無量珍寶具足。作是思惟。人謂我為貴[9]人財富無量。饒益眾生今正是時應當大施。富貴雖樂一切無常。五家所共令人心散輕[10]泆不定。譬如獼猴不能暫住。人命逝速疾於電滅。人身無常眾苦之藪。以是之故應行布施。

The Fabulous Giving of Velāma Bodhisattva

Nāgārjuna's Preamble: Śrāvaka *Dāna* versus Bodhisattva *Dāna*

Moreover, if it is not done for the sake of beings, if it is not done for the sake of realizing the true character of dharmas,[1] and if it is done solely for the sake of gaining liberation from birth, old age, sickness, and death, this is the *dāna* of the Śrāvaka Disciples.[2] If one gives for the sake of all beings and if one does so for the sake of realizing the true character of dharmas, this is the *dāna* of the Buddhas and the Bodhisattvas.

If one is unable to make one's giving replete with every manner of meritorious quality, but rather desires only to gain a minor measure thereof, this is the *dāna* of the Śrāvaka Disciples. If one wishes to make it entirely replete with every manner of meritorious quality, this is the *dāna* of the Buddhas and the Bodhisattvas.

If one gives out of a fear of old age, sickness, and death, this is the *dāna* of the Śrāvaka Disciples. If it is done to assist the realization of the Buddha Path, if it is done for the sake of transforming beings, and if it is not done out of fear of old age, sickness, and death, this is the *dāna* of the Buddhas and the Bodhisattvas.

Story: The Fabulous Giving of Velāma Bodhisattva

In this connection one ought to draw upon *The Sutra of the Past Lives of the Bodhisattva*. As discussed in *The Avadāna Sutra*, in the past, in Jambudvīpa, there was a king named Vāsava. At that time there was a brahman bodhisattva named Velāma who served as the teacher of the King. He taught the King the method for becoming a wheel-turning sage king.[3]

Velāma's own wealth was immeasurable. He possessed an abundance of precious jewels. He had these thoughts: "People look upon me as a noble man possessed of immeasurable wealth. If I am to be of benefit to beings, now is precisely the right time. I should perform a great act of giving. Although being wealthy and noble is blissful, everything is impermanent. This wealth, held in common with five types of agents (the King, thieves, fire, flood, and bad sons), causes a man's mind to be so scattered, agitated and unfocused as to make it like a monkey which is unable to remain still. A person's life passes more quickly than the disappearance of a lightning bolt. A person's body is impermanent and is a thicket of the manifold sufferings. On account of these things, one ought to practice giving."

如是思惟已自作手疏。普告
阎浮提诸婆罗门及一切出家
人。愿各屈德来集我舍。欲
设大施满十二岁。饭汁行船
以酪为池。米面为山[11]苏油
为渠。衣服饮食卧具汤药。
皆令极妙过十二岁。欲以布
施。八万四千白象犀甲金饰
珞。以名宝建大金幢。四宝
庄严。八万四千马。亦以犀
甲金饰。四宝[12]交络。八
万四千车。皆以金银琉璃颇
梨宝饰。覆以师子虎豹之
皮。若白剑婆罗宝[13][车*
宪]杂饰以为庄严。八万四
千四宝床。杂色绲綖种种茵
蓐柔软细滑以为挍饰。丹枕
锦被置床两头。妙衣盛服皆
亦备有。八万四千金钵盛满
银粟。银钵盛金粟。琉璃钵
盛[14]颇梨粟。颇梨钵盛琉璃
粟。八万四千乳牛。牛出乳
一斛。金饰其[15][跳-兆+甲]
角衣以白[16]叠。八万四千美
女端正福德。皆以白珠名宝
璎珞其身。略举其要如是。
种种不可胜记。尔时婆罗婆
王及八万四千[17]诸小国王。
并诸臣民豪杰

如是思惟已自作手疏。普告
閻浮提諸婆羅門及一切出家
人。願各屈德來集我舍。欲
設大施滿十二歲。飯汁行船
以酪為池。米麵為山[11]蘇油
為渠。衣服飲食臥具湯藥。
皆令極妙過十二歲。欲以布
施。八萬四千白象犀甲金飾
珞。以名寶建大金幢。四寶
莊嚴。八萬四千馬。亦以犀
甲金飾。四寶[12]交絡。八
萬四千車。皆以金銀琉璃頗
梨寶飾。覆以師子虎豹之
皮。若白劍婆羅寶[13][車*
憲]雜飾以為莊嚴。八萬四
千四寶床。雜色綩綖種種茵
蓐柔軟細滑以為挍飾。丹枕
錦被置床兩頭。妙衣盛服皆
亦備有。八萬四千金鉢盛滿
銀粟。銀鉢盛金粟。琉璃鉢
盛[14]頗梨粟。頗梨鉢盛琉璃
粟。八萬四千乳牛。牛出乳
一斛。金飾其[15][跳-兆+甲]角
衣以白[16]疊。八萬四千美女
端正福德。皆以白珠名寶瓔
珞其身。略舉其要如是。種
種不可勝記。爾時婆羅婆王
及八萬四千[17]諸小國王。并
諸臣民豪傑

简体字   正體字

After having these thoughts he wrote out a personal declaration in which he announced to all of the brahmans and monastics throughout Jambudvīpa, "We pray that each shall condescend to come and gather at our estate as we desire to present a great offering lasting for a period of twelve years during which boats will cruise on streams of rice consommé and there will be ponds filled with curds. There will be mountains made of rice and noodles and canals created of *perilla* oil. There will be robes, food, drink, bedding, and medicines. Everything will be of the most supremely marvelous quality for over a dozen years during which time we desire to make offerings in this way."

There were eighty-four thousand[4] white elephants girded in gold-adorned rhinoceros hide armor. Rare gems were strung together to create a huge gold pavilion ornamented with four kinds of precious things. There were eighty-four thousand horses also clad in gold-adorned rhinoceros hide armor and caparisoned with strands of the four kinds of precious things.

There were eighty-four thousand carriages, each adorned with gold, silver, beryl, and crystal, shaded with the skins of lions, tigers, and leopards, draped with curtains of *pāṇḍukambala* gems and ornamented with various embellishments.

There were eighty-four thousand precious thrones fitted and adorned with multicolored cushions which were soft and smooth. Arranged at each end of the thrones were crimson pillows and embroidered blankets. Marvelous garments and flowing robes were supplied in abundance. There were eighty-four thousand gold bowls filled with silver nuggets, silver bowls filled with gold nuggets, beryl bowls filled with crystals, and crystal bowls filled with beryl gems.

There were eighty-four thousand dairy cattle. The cows each produced an abundant measure of milk. The horns of the bulls were adorned with gold. They were each dressed in white blankets.

There were eighty-four thousand beautiful women of refined appearance and endowed with meritorious qualities. Their bodies were draped in strands of white pearls and precious gems.

This represents only a summary recital of the main features. There were all manner of other arrangements which one could never succeed in detailing.

At that time, King Vāsava and eighty-four thousand kings of lesser states, together with their ministers, national heroes, and

长者。各以十万旧金钱赠遗
劝助。设此法祠具足施已。
释提婆那民来语韦罗摩菩
萨。说此偈言天地难得物能
喜悦一切汝今皆[18]以得为佛
道布施[0142c18]　尔时净居诸
天现身而赞。说此偈言开门
大布施汝所为者是怜愍众生
故为之求佛道[0142c21]　是时诸
天作是思惟。我当闭其金瓶
令水不下。所以者何。有施
者无福田故。是时魔王语净
居天。此诸婆罗门。皆出家
持戒清净入道。何以[19]故乃
言无有福田。净居天言。是
菩萨为佛道故布施。今此诸
人皆是邪见。是故我言无有
福田。魔王语天言。云何知
是人为佛道故布施。是时净
居天化作婆罗门身。持金瓶
执金杖。至韦罗摩菩萨所语
言。汝大布施难舍能舍欲求
何等。欲作转轮圣王七宝千
子王四天下耶。菩萨答言。
不求此事。

简体字

長者。各以十萬舊金錢贈遺
勸助。設此法祠具足施已。
釋提婆那民來語韋羅摩菩
薩。說此偈言天地難得物能
喜悅一切汝今皆[18]以得為佛
道布施[0142c18]　爾時淨居諸
天現身而讚。說此偈言開門
大布施汝所為者是憐愍眾生
故為之求佛道[0142c21]　是時諸
天作是思惟。我當閉其金瓶
令水不下。所以者何。有施
者無福田故。是時魔王語淨
居天。此諸婆羅門。皆出家
持戒清淨入道。何以[19]故乃
言無有福田。淨居天言。是
菩薩為佛道故布施。今此諸
人皆是邪見。是故我言無有
福田。魔王語天言。云何知
是人為佛道故布施。是時淨
居天化作婆羅門身。持金瓶
執金杖。至韋羅摩菩薩所語
言。汝大布施難捨能捨欲求
何等。欲作轉輪聖王七寶千
子王四天下耶。菩薩答言。
不求此事。

正體字

Your wisdom has become detached and unobstructed.
Your realization of buddhahood cannot be far off.

At that time the gods rained down a profusion of blossoms as an offering to the Bodhisattva. The gods of the Pure Dwelling Heaven who had stopped up the water from the vase then disappeared from sight.

The Bodhisattva then went before the most senior ranked among the brahmans and attempted to pour forth the water from the gold vase [and thus formally endow them as recipients of his offerings]. However, the water remained stopped up and would not flow out. The members of the assembly were then overcome with doubt and consternation and wondered, "All of these various kinds of great giving are replete in every way and the benefactor's meritorious qualities are also immense. Why then does the water now fail to flow forth from the vase?"

The Bodhisattva thought to himself, "This circumstance could be due to nothing other than one of these factors: Have I freed my mind of all impurity? Have I achieved a situation where there are no deficiencies in the gifts? What could have brought this about?" He personally contemplated the sixteen parts of the *Classic on Giving* and found that all preparations were pure and free of defects.

At this time the gods spoke to the Bodhisattva, saying, "Do not become overcome by doubt and regret. There is nothing which you have failed to accomplish. It is because these brahmans are characterized by unwholesomeness, error, and impurity." They then uttered a verse, saying,

These men are caught in the net of erroneous views.
Their afflictions have brought on destruction of right wisdom.
They have abandoned purity in the observance of moral precepts.
They indulg useless asceticism and fall into unorthodox paths.

"It is for these reasons that the water is stopped up and will not pour forth."

Having said this, they suddenly disappeared. The gods of the Six Desire Heavens then emitted many different kinds of light which illuminated the entire assembly and then spoke to the Bodhisattva, proclaiming in a verse:

Practices from within the sea of error and unwholesomeness
Do not accord with your orthodox path.
Among the recipients of your gifts,
There are none who can compare with you.

[0143b09] 说是语已忽然不现。是时菩萨闻说此偈自念。会中实自无有与我等者。水闭不下其将为此[7]乎。即说偈言若有十方天地中诸有好人清净者我今归命稽首礼右手执瓶灌左手而自立愿我一人应受如是大布施[0143b15] 是时瓶水[8]踊在虚空从上来下而灌其左手。是时[9]婆[10]萨婆王。见是感应心生恭敬。而说偈言大婆罗门主清琉璃色水从上流注下来堕汝手中[0143b20] 是时大婆罗门众恭敬心生。合手作礼归命菩萨。菩萨是时说此偈言今我所布施不求三界福为诸众生故以用求佛道[0143b24] 说此偈已。一切大地山川树木皆六[11]返震动。韦罗摩本谓此众应受供养故与。既知[12]此众无堪受者。今以怜愍故。以所受物施之。如是种种檀本生因缘。是中应广说。是为外布施。

[0143b09] 說是語已忽然不現。是時菩薩聞說此偈自念。會中實自無有與我等者。水閉不下其將為此[7]乎。即說偈言若有十方天地中諸有好人清淨者我今歸命稽首禮右手執瓶灌左手而自立願我一人應受如是大布施[0143b15] 是時瓶水[8]踊在虛空從上來下而灌其左手。是時[9]婆[10]薩婆王。見是感應心生恭敬。而說偈言大婆羅門主清琉璃色水從上流注下來墮汝手中[0143b20] 是時大婆羅門眾恭敬心生。合手作禮歸命菩薩。菩薩是時說此偈言今我所布施不求三界福為諸眾生故以用求佛道[0143b24] 說此偈已。一切大地山川樹木皆六[11]返震動。韋羅摩本謂此眾應受供養故與。既知[12]此眾無堪受者。今以憐愍故。以所受物施之。如是種種檀本生因緣。是中應廣說。是為外布施。

简体字   正體字

After speaking in this way, they suddenly disappeared. After the Bodhisattva had listened to this verse, he then thought to himself, "If it were actually the case that there was no one in the assembly who could serve as my equal, the water would indeed be stopped up and so would not flow forth. Could it actually be then that it is on account of this?" He then uttered a verse:

Throughout the ten directions, in the heavens or on earth,
Wherever there are good and pure people—
I now take refuge in them and, in reverence, make obeisance.
With the vase in the right hand, I pour an ablution on the left hand,

I now swear that I, this one person,
Should accept on their behalf such a great offering as this.

The water from the vase then straightaway spouted forth into the air, descended from above, and came down as an ablution upon his left hand. Then, when King Vāsava had witnessed this marvelous response, his mind became filled with reverence and he uttered a verse, saying:

Great Lord of the Brahmans,
This clear beryl-hued water
Has flowed on down from above
And, falling, has come to rest in your hand.

At that time, there arose thoughts of reverence in the minds of those brahmans in the great assembly. They placed their palms together, made obeisance, and took refuge in the Bodhisattva. At this time, the Bodhisattva uttered this verse, saying:

That which I have now given
Is not in quest of any blessings in the sphere of the three realms.[6]
It is for the sake of all beings,
And is to be employed in seeking the path of the Buddhas.

After he had spoken this verse, the entire earth with its mountains, rivers, and trees quaked and moved in six ways. Velāma had originally been of the opinion that this assembly should be the recipient of the offering and so gave it. Even though he realized there was no one in the assembly worthy to accept it, he now, out of pity, gave to them all those things which he had himself accepted.

Ideally, one would proceed at this point into an extensive discussion of all sorts of similar past-life causes and conditions associated with *dāna* (giving). The foregoing was an example of "outward giving."

Notes

1. "True character of dharmas" (諸法實相) is my translation of Kumārajīva's loose Chinese rendering of the Sanskrit *dharmatā* ("dharmas as they really are"). It is simply a reference to the "genuine character" or "actual nature" of dharmas (i.e. "phenomena") in their very essence as seen in accordance with ultimate truth (*paramārtha-satya*). It is simply a reference to phenomena as seen in the absence of even the most subtle discriminations and imputations. The implications of this definition would not seem to amount to a particularly earth-shaking revelation but for the fact that no ordinary common person actually sees phenomena in this way. Only āryas (those who have at least reached "the path of seeing") actually behold phenomena as they really are. In the dialectic of the *Exegesis*, this level of understanding is repeatedly identified both implicitly and explicitly with non-dual emptiness, nirvāṇa, and an utter absence of inherent existence, all non-nihilistic and non-affirming emblematic Mādhyamika expressions of the highest truth.

2. For the benefit of those unfamiliar with the terminology, "Śrāvakas" (lit. "Hearers") refers to those Buddhists who strive only to gain the relatively rapid individual liberation of the arhat. Generally speaking, they do not wish to involve themselves in the extremely long training period required to become a buddha. The Bodhisattvas, on the other hand, do not fear even eons of working equally for themselves and equally for the liberation of other beings, all of this in preparation for their goal of realizing the utmost, right, and perfect enlightenment of a fully-enlightened buddha.

3. This refers to a *cakravartin*, a universal monarch possessed of personal qualities, powers, reign duration, and dominion vastly beyond those possessed by any royalty who have ever held sway in recorded human history.

4. "Eighty-four thousand" is, in Indian Buddhist literature, similar to the American vernacular use of "millions" which actually just means "lots," or, in more formal terms: "numerous."

5. Just as a fertile field planted with good seed yields abundant crops, so, too, a "field of merit" (*puṇya-kṣetra*) in the form of an adequately virtuous recipient, yields karmic fruits for the benefactor. The problem about which these celestial beings are so concerned is one of planting a marvelously potent karmic seed (in the form of this extravagant generosity) in a barren field. They are worried that the seed will be wasted.

6. "The three realms" is synonymous with all of existence and refers to the three progressively more refined zones of reincarnation coursed

through by beings stranded in cyclic birth-and-death: the desire realm (home of hell-dwellers, animals, hungry ghosts, humans, demi-gods, and the lesser gods); the form realm; and the formless realm.

Both of these latter zones may be entered in the deeper levels of meditative absorption, but also comprise the abodes of the higher and highest classes of god realms, each of which is itself comprised of a number of different subsidiary levels of celestial existence. Even though they involve immensely long lifetimes and freedom from suffering, because these celestial existences are impermanent and bound to eventually be fallen from, even the gods are seen in Buddhism to be not only not spiritually liberated, but also tragically-enmeshed in karma-bound suffering, no less enmeshed in fact than the denizens of the lowest purgatorial existences.

云何名内布施。不惜身命施
诸众生。如本生因缘说。释
迦文佛本为菩萨为大国王
时。世无佛无法无比丘僧。
是王四出求索佛法。了不能
得。时有一婆罗门言。我知
佛偈。供养我者当以与汝。
王即问言。索何等供养。答
[13]言。汝能就汝身上。破
肉为灯炷供养我者。当以与
汝。王心念言。今我此身危
脆不净。世世受苦不可复
数。未曾为法今始得用甚不
惜也。如是念已唤旃陀罗。
遍割身上以作灯炷。而以白
[*]叠缠肉酥油灌之。一时遍
烧举身。火燃。乃与一偈。
又复释迦文佛本作一鸽在雪
山中。时大雨雪。有一人失
道穷厄辛苦。饥寒并至命在
须臾。鸽见此人即飞求火。
为其聚薪然之。又复以身投
火施此饥人。如是等头目髓
脑给施众生。种种本生因缘
经此中应广说。如是等种种
是名内布施。

简体字

云何名内布施。不惜身命施
諸眾生。如本生因緣說。釋
迦文佛本為菩薩為大國王
時。世無佛無法無比丘僧。
是王四出求索佛法。了不能
得。時有一婆羅門言。我知
佛偈。供養我者當以與汝。
王即問言。索何等供養。答
[13]言。汝能就汝身上。破
肉為燈炷供養我者。當以與
汝。王心念言。今我此身危
脆不淨。世世受苦不可復
數。未曾為法今始得用甚不
惜也。如是念已喚旃陀羅。
遍割身上以作燈炷。而以白
[*]疊纏肉酥油灌之。一時遍
燒舉身。火燃。乃與一偈。
又復釋迦文佛本作一鴿在雪
山中。時大雨雪。有一人失
道窮厄辛苦。飢寒并至命在
須臾。鴿見此人即飛求火。
為其聚薪然之。又復以身投
火施此飢人。如是等頭目髓
腦給施眾生。種種本生因緣
經此中應廣說。如是等種種
是名內布施。

正體字

Two Jātaka Tales of Shākyamuni's Sacrificing His Life

What is meant by "inward giving"? It refers to not stinting even in sacrificing one's own life as one gives for the sake of beings.

Story: The Buddha's Past-life Sacrifice of His Body for Dharma

It is as discussed in the [stories of the Buddha's] past-life causes and conditions at a time when, as a bodhisattva, Shākyamuni Buddha was serving as the king of a great country. The world had no buddha, no Dharma, and no sangha of bhikshus. This king searched in the four directions for the Dharma of the Buddha, but was finally unable to find it.

At that time, there was a brahman who said, "I know a verse uttered by the Buddha. If an offering is made to me, I will give it to you."

The King then asked, "What sort of offering are you seeking?"

He replied, "If you are able to break open your flesh and turn it into a torch as an offering to me, then I shall give it to you."

The King then thought to himself, "This body of mine is fragile and impure. The amount of suffering which I have undergone on its behalf in life after life is incalculable. It has never been for the sake of Dharma. Only now does it begin to be truly useful. It is certainly not to be spared now."

After reflecting thus, he called forth a *caṇḍāla* and ordered him to scrape the surface of his entire body so that it might serve as a torch. Then the *caṇḍāla* wrapped the King's flesh in white cloth, drenched it in ghee, and set fire to his entire body. Only once the fire had been lit did the brahman bestow on him that single verse.

Story: The Buddha's Past Life as a Pigeon

Additionally, in a previous life, Shākyamuni Buddha was a pigeon in the snowy mountains. One time there was a great blizzard. There was a man who had lost his way. He was poor and in miserable straits, undergoing bitterness and suffering. Hunger and cold were both upon him and at that moment his life hung in the balance. The pigeon saw this man and immediately flew in search of fire, piling up twigs and then lighting them. He then additionally cast his body upon the fire as a gift to this starving man.

In just such a manner, he gave up his head, eyes, marrow, and brains for beings. Ideally, one would cite here many comparable instances from the *Sutra on the Causes and Conditions of Previous Lives*. All sorts of similar cases show what is meant by "inward" giving.

复次非但言说名为法施。常以净心善[2]思。以教一切是名法施。譬如财施不以善心不名福德法施亦尔。不以净心善思则非法施。复次说法者。能以净心善思赞叹三宝。开罪福门示四真谛。教化众生令入佛道。是为真净法施。复次略说法有二种。一者不恼众生善心慈愍。是为佛道因缘。二者观知诸法真空。是为涅盘道因缘。在大众中兴愍哀心说此二法。不为名闻利养恭敬。是为清净佛道法施。如说。阿输伽王一日作八万佛图。虽未见道于佛法中少有信乐。日日请诸比丘入宫供养。日日次第留法师说法。

復次非但言說名為法施。常以淨心善[2]思。以教一切是名法施。譬如財施不以善心不名福德法施亦爾。不以淨心善思則非法施。復次說法者。能以淨心善思讚歎三寶。開罪福門示四真諦。教化眾生令入佛道。是為真淨法施。復次略說法有二種。一者不惱眾生善心慈愍。是為佛道因緣。二者觀知諸法真空。是為涅槃道因緣。在大眾中興愍哀心說此二法。不為名聞利養恭敬。是為清淨佛道法施。如說。阿輸伽王一日作八萬佛圖。雖未見道於佛法中少有信樂。日日請諸比丘入宮供養。日日次第留法師說法。

简体字　　　　　　　　　　　　　　正體字

The Monk with the Fragrant Breath

Nāgārjuna's Preamble: The Defining Bases of Dharma Giving

Moreover, the giving of Dharma does not consist solely in words and speech. The giving of Dharma consists in constantly employing a pure mind and wholesome thoughts in the offering of instruction to everyone. Just as it is with the giving of material gifts wherein there is no measure of blessings or virtue associated with it if one fails to maintain a wholesome mind, so too it is with the giving of Dharma: If one fails to maintain a pure mind and wholesome thoughts, then it is not the case that this qualifies as the giving of Dharma.

Then again, if the speaker of Dharma is able to maintain a pure mind and wholesome thought as he praises the Three Jewels, opens the door to understanding offenses and blessings, explains the four truths, and so goes about teaching and transforming beings so that they are caused to enter the Buddha Path, this qualifies as true and pure Dharma giving.

Looked at another way, generally speaking, the Dharma [to be given] is of two types: The first consists in refraining from afflicting beings while also maintaining a wholesome mind, loving-kindness, and sympathy. This constitutes the causal basis for the path to buddhahood. The second consists in contemplating and realizing that all dharmas are truly empty. This constitutes the causal basis for the path to nirvāṇa.

If, while in the midst of the Great Assembly, one lets flourish a deeply compassionate mind as one sets forth these two types of Dharma, and if in doing so it is not done for the sake of garnering fame, offerings, or expressions of reverence, this constitutes pure Dharma giving rooted in the Buddha Path.

Story: The Monk with the Fragrant Breath

This concept is illustrated in a story told in connection with King Aśoka who in a single day was responsible for the creation of eighty-thousand buddha images. Although he had not yet achieved the stage of "the path of seeing,"[25] still, he did maintain a minor degree of faith and bliss in the Dharma of the Buddha. Every day he invited bhikshus to enter the palace to receive offerings. Every day he retained one Dharma Master by order of seniority to speak the Dharma.

有一三藏年少法师。聪明端
正次应说法。在王边坐。口
有异香。王甚疑怪谓为不
端。欲以香气动王宫人。语
比丘言。口中何等开口看
之。即为开口了无所有。与
水令漱香气如故。王问。大
德新有此香旧有之耶。比丘
答言。如此久有非适今也。
又问有此久如。[3]比丘以偈
答[*]言迦叶佛时集此香法如
是久久常若新出[0144a25]　　王
言。大德略说未解。为我广
演。答[*]言。王当一心善听
我说。我昔于迦叶佛法中作
说法比丘。常在大众之中欢
喜演说。迦叶世尊无量功德
诸法实相。无量法门慇懃赞
[4]叹教诲一切。自是以来常
有妙香从口中出。世世不绝
恒如今日。而说此偈

有一三藏年少法師。聰明端
正次應說法。在王邊坐。口
有異香。王甚疑怪謂為不
端。欲以香氣動王宮人。語
比丘言。口中何等開口看
之。即為開口了無所有。與
水令漱香氣如故。王問。大
德新有此香舊有之耶。比丘
答言。如此久有非適今也。
又問有此久如。[3]比丘以偈
答[*]言迦葉佛時集此香法如
是久久常若新出[0144a25]　　王
言。大德略說未解。為我廣
演。答[*]言。王當一心善聽
我說。我昔於迦葉佛法中作
說法比丘。常在大眾之中歡
喜演說。迦葉世尊無量功德
諸法實相。無量法門慇懃讚
[4]歎教誨一切。自是以來常
有妙香從口中出。世世不絕
恒如今日。而說此偈

简体字　　　　　　　　　　正體字

One day there was a young Dharma Master, a master of the Tripiṭaka, who was intelligent and handsome and next in order to speak the Dharma. He sat down next to the King. His mouth exuded an exotic fragrance. The King was filled with extreme doubt and suspicion. He was of the opinion that this constituted a deliberate impropriety arising from a desire to employ a fragrant scent to influence the retinue in the royal palace.

The King asked the bhikshu, "What do you have in your mouth? Open your mouth so I can see into it." [The bhikshu] then opened his mouth for [the King] and it turned out that there was nothing whatsoever therein. He was ordered to rinse out his mouth with water after which the fragrance remained just as before. The King asked, "Venerable One, is this fragrance newly manifest or has it abided with you for a long time?"

The bhikshu replied, saying, "It has been like this for a long time. It is not the case that it is just manifesting now."

[The King] continued to inquire, "How long has it been this way?"

The bhikshu replied in verse, saying:

It was at the time of Kāśyapa Buddha
That I gathered the Dharma underlying this fragrance.
It has remained so like this for a very long time,
And has always been fresh as if newly arisen.

The King said, "Venerable One, I do not yet understand this brief explanation. Pray, expound on it more extensively for me."

He replied by saying, "The King should listen well and single-mindedly to my explanation. In the past, during the time of Kāśyapa Buddha's Dharma, I was a Dharma-proclaiming bhikshu who, in the midst of the Great Assembly, constantly took pleasure in expounding on the immeasurable qualities of Kāśyapa, the Bhagavān , on the true character of dharmas, and on an incalculable number of methods to access Dharma.

I conscientiously and earnestly set forth praises and offered instruction to everyone. From this time on forward to the present I have always had a marvelous fragrance coming forth from my mouth. This has been the case in life after life without cease. It has constantly been just as it is this very day." He then spoke forth a verse:

草木诸华香此香气超绝能悦
一切心世世常不灭[0144b04]
[5]于时国王愧喜交集。白比
丘言。未曾有也。说法功德
大果乃尔。比丘言。此名为
华。未是果也。王言其果云
何愿为演说。答言。果略说
有十。王谛听之。即为说偈
[6]言大名闻端[7]政得乐及恭
敬威光如日[8]月为一切所爱
辩才有大智能尽一切结苦灭
得涅盘如是名为十[0144b12]
王言。大德。赞佛功德云何
而得如是果报。尔时比丘以
偈答曰赞佛诸功德令一切普
闻以此果报故而得大名誉赞
佛实功德令一切欢喜以此功
德故世世常端正为人说罪福
令得安乐所以此之功德受乐
常欢豫赞佛功德力令一切心
伏以此功德故常获恭敬报

草木諸華香此香氣超絕能悅
一切心世世常不滅[0144b04]
[5]于時國王愧喜交集。白比
丘言。未曾有也。說法功德
大果乃爾。比丘言。此名為
華。未是果也。王言其果云
何願為演說。答言。果略說
有十。王諦聽之。即為說偈
[6]言大名聞端[7]政得樂及恭
敬威光如日[8]月為一切所愛
辯才有大智能盡一切結苦滅
得涅槃如是名為十[0144b12]
王言。大德。讚佛功德云何
而得如是果報。爾時比丘以
偈答曰讚佛諸功德令一切普
聞以此果報故而得大名譽讚
佛實功德令一切歡喜以此功
德故世世常端正為人說罪福
令得安樂所以此之功德受樂
常歡豫讚佛功德力令一切心
伏以此功德故常獲恭敬報

简体字   正體字

The fragrance from flowers on shrubs and on trees
Is utterly surpassed by this incense-like fragrance.
It is able to please the minds of all people.
In life after life it abides without ceasing.

At this time the King was filled with a mixture of shame and delight. He said to the bhikshu, "This is such as has never been before. The merit of speaking the Dharma brings such a great fruition as this."

The bhikshu said, "This may be thought of as merely the blossom. It is not yet the fruit."

The King asked, "What then is its fruit? Pray, expound upon this for me."

He replied, "Briefly speaking, the fruits are tenfold. May the King listen earnestly." He then set forth a verse for his sake:

There is a grand reputation and finely-formed features.
One experiences bliss and is the object of reverence.
There shines awesome brilliance like sunshine and moonlight.
So thus one becomes a man loved by all people.

There is eloquence and also there is prodigious wisdom.
One is able to end then the grip of the fetters.
One ceases all suffering and reaches nirvāṇa.
And so in this manner the count reaches to ten.

The King asked, "Venerable One, How is it that one gains such a reward as a result of praising the qualities of the Buddha?"

The bhikshu then replied in verse, saying:

If one praises the qualities possessed by the Buddha
And causes this to be heard everywhere by all people,
On account of results which come forth as reward,
One comes to be known by a grand reputation.

If one praises the genuine qualities of Buddha
And causes all people to experience delight,
On account of the [force] which is born from this merit,
In life after life features always are fine.

If one explains for people offenses and blessings,
Allowing them to reach a place of peace and delight,
On account of the merit which is thus produced,
One experiences bliss and is always content.

The powers of praising the merits of Buddha
Cause everyone hearing to have minds made humble.
On account of the power produced by this merit,
One eternally garners men's reverence as reward.

显现说法灯照悟诸众生以此
之功德威光如日曜种种赞佛
德能悦于一切以此功德故常
为人所爱巧言赞佛德无量无
穷已以此功德故辩才不可尽
赞佛诸妙法一切无过者以此
功德故大智慧清净赞佛功德
时令人烦恼薄以此功德故结
尽诸垢灭二种结尽故涅盘身
已[9]证譬如澍大雨火[10]尽无
馀热[0144c05]　　重告王言。若
有未悟今是问时。当以智箭
破汝疑军。王白法师。我心
悦悟无所疑也。大德福人善
能赞佛。如是等种种因缘说
法度人。名为法施。

顯現說法燈照悟諸眾生以此
之功德威光如日曜種種讚佛
德能悅於一切以此功德故常
為人所愛巧言讚佛德無量無
窮已以此功德故辯才不可盡
讚佛諸妙法一切無過者以此
功德故大智慧清淨讚佛功德
時令人煩惱薄以此功德故結
盡諸垢滅二種結盡故涅槃身
已[9]證譬如澍大雨火[10]盡無
餘熱[0144c05]　　重告王言。若
有未悟今是問時。當以智箭
破汝疑軍。王白法師。我心
悅悟無所疑也。大德福人善
能讚佛。如是等種種因緣說
法度人。名為法施。

简体字　　　　　　　　正體字

Displaying the lamp of the speaking of Dharma
Illumining and wakening all of the people —
On account of the power produced by this merit,
One's awesome bright brilliance shines forth like the sun.

If in many a fashion one praises Buddha's merits
And delights thus the hearts of all [by those words],
On account of the power produced by this merit,
One is ever the object of people's affection.

If with clever discourse one praises Buddha's merits
Which cannot be measured and cannot be exhausted,
On account of the power produced by this merit,
One's eloquent speech is never brought to an end.

If one praises the marvelous dharmas of Buddha
Which are such as no one can ever surpass,
On account of the power produced by this merit,
One possesses great wisdom which is pure in its nature.

When one praises the qualities possessed by the Buddha,
One causes afflictions of men to be scant.
On account of the power produced by this merit,
Fetters are cut off and defilements destroyed.

Because both kinds of fetters are brought to an end,
Nirvāṇa in this body has already been achieved,
As when torrents of rain pour down from the sky
All fires are extinguished and no embers remain.

Once again he addressed the King, saying, "If there still remains anything to which you've not awakened, now is the time to bring questions forth. The arrows of wisdom should be used to smash your armor of doubts."

The King replied to the Dharma master, "My mind has been both delighted and awakened such that now there remain no more objects of doubt. The Venerable One is a blessed man well able to speak forth the praises of Buddha."

When one speaks forth the Dharma in accord with the various causes and conditions discussed above and so brings about the deliverance of beings, this qualifies then as the giving of Dharma.

[0145a15] [3]【论】问曰。云何名檀波罗[4]蜜[5]满。答曰。檀义如上说。波罗(6)秦言彼岸)蜜([*]秦言到)是名渡布施河得到彼岸。问曰。云何名不到彼岸。答曰。譬如渡河未到而还。名为不到彼岸。如舍利弗。于六[7]十劫中行菩萨道。欲渡布施河。时有乞人来乞其眼。舍利弗言。眼无所[8]任。何以索之。若须我身及财物者当以相与。答言。不须汝身及以财物。唯欲得眼。若汝实行檀者以眼见与。尔时舍利弗。出一眼与之。乞者得眼。于舍利弗前[9]嗅之。嫌臭唾而弃地。又以脚蹋。舍利弗思惟言。如此弊人等难可度也。眼实无[10]用而强索之。既得而弃又以脚蹋。何弊之甚。如此人辈不可度也。不如自调早脱生死。思惟是已。于菩萨道退迴向小乘。是名不到彼岸。若能直进不退。成办佛道。名到彼岸。

简体字

[0145a15] [3]【論】問曰。云何名檀波羅[4]蜜[5]滿。答曰。檀義如上說。波羅(6)秦言彼岸)蜜([*]秦言到)是名渡布施河得到彼岸。問曰。云何名不到彼岸。答曰。譬如渡河未到而還。名為不到彼岸。如舍利弗。於六[7]十劫中行菩薩道。欲渡布施河。時有乞人來乞其眼。舍利弗言。眼無所[8]任。何以索之。若須我身及財物者當以相與。答言。不須汝身及以財物。唯欲得眼。若汝實行檀者以眼見與。爾時舍利弗。出一眼與之。乞者得眼。於舍利弗前[9]嗅之。嫌臭唾而棄地。又以腳蹋。舍利弗思惟言。如此弊人等難可度也。眼實無[10]用而強索之。既得而棄又以腳蹋。何弊之甚。如此人輩不可度也。不如自調早脫生死。思惟是已。於菩薩道退迴向小乘。是名不到彼岸。若能直進不退。成辦佛道。名到彼岸。

正體字

Śāriputra Retreats from the Bodhisattva Path

Nāgārjuna's Preamble: The "Fulfillment" of *Dāna* pāramitā

Question: What is meant by the fulfillment of *dāna* pāramitā?

Response: The meaning of *dāna* is as discussed above. As for [the Sanskrit antecedent for "perfection," namely] *"pāramitā,"* it refers here to being able to cross beyond the river of [imperfect] giving and to succeed in reaching its far shore. (Ch. text notes: As for *"pāra-,"* this means "the other shore." As for *"-mi,"* this means "to reach.")

Question: What is meant by failing to reach the far shore?

Response: It is analogous to crossing over a river but returning before having arrived. This is what is meant by failing to reach the far shore.

Story: Śāriputra Retreats from the Bodhisattva Path

For example, Śāriputra cultivated the Bodhisattva path for a period of sixty kalpas, desiring to cross over the river of giving. At that time there was a beggar who came along and demanded that he give him one of his eyes. Śāriputra said, "The eye would then be useless. What do you want it for? If you need to put my body to use or if you want any valuables I own, then I'll give those to you."

The beggar replied, "I've got no use for your body and I don't want any valuables you might own. I just want an eye, that's all. If you were truly a cultivator of the practice of giving, then I would receive an eye from you."

At that time Śāriputra pulled out one of his eyes and gave it to him. The beggar got the eye and then right there in front of Śāriputra he sniffed it, cursed, "It stinks," spat, and then threw it down on the ground. Then, in addition, he smashed it beneath his foot.

Śāriputra thought to himself, "It's a difficult task to cross over such base people as this. He actually had no use for the eye and yet he forcefully demanded it. Having gotten it, he not only threw it away, he even smashed it with his foot. How extremely base! People of this sort cannot be crossed over to liberation. Far better that I just concentrate on disciplining myself so as to gain an early liberation from the cycle of birth and death."

Having thought this to himself he then turned from the Bodhisattva Path and directed himself to the Small Vehicle. This is what is meant by "failing to reach the other shore." If one is able to advance directly, avoid retreating, and complete the Buddha Path, this is what qualifies as "reaching the far shore."

复次于事成办亦名到彼岸。（天竺俗法凡造事成办皆言到彼岸）复次此岸名悭贪檀名河中。彼岸名佛道。复次有无见名此岸。破有无见智慧名彼岸。懃修布施是名河中。复次檀有二种。一者魔檀二者佛檀。若为结使贼所夺忧恼怖畏。是为魔檀。名曰此岸。若有清净布施。无结使贼无所怖畏得至佛道。是为佛檀。名曰到彼岸。是为波罗蜜。如佛说毒蛇喻经中。有人得罪于王。王令掌护一箧。箧中有四毒蛇。王勅罪人令看视养育。此人思惟。四蛇难近。近则害人。一犹叵养。而况于四。[11]便弃箧而走。王令五人拔刀追之。复有一人口言附顺。

復次於事成辦亦名到彼岸。（天竺俗法凡造事成辦皆言到彼岸）復次此岸名慳貪檀名河中。彼岸名佛道。復次有無見名此岸。破有無見智慧名彼岸。懃修布施是名河中。復次檀有二種。一者魔檀二者佛檀。若為結使賊所奪憂惱怖畏。是為魔檀。名曰此岸。若有清淨布施。無結使賊無所怖畏得至佛道。是為佛檀。名曰到彼岸。是為波羅蜜。如佛說毒蛇喻經中。有人得罪於王。王令掌護一篋。篋中有四毒蛇。王勅罪人令看視養育。此人思惟。四蛇難近。近則害人。一猶叵養。而況於四。[11]便棄篋而走。王令五人拔刀追之。復有一人口言附順。

简体字   正體字

The Analogy of the Poisonous Snakes

Nāgārjuna's Preamble: The Meaning of Perfect Giving

Then again, to succeed in completing any endeavor is also referred to as "reaching to the far shore." (In the common parlance of India, whenever one takes up a task and then completes it, it is referred to as "reaching the far shore.")

Additionally, one may say that "this shore" refers to being miserly, *dāna* refers to being in the midst of the river, and "the far shore" refers to the Buddha Path.

Also, one may say that holding a view which insists on "existence" or "nonexistence" is what is meant by "this shore." The wisdom which refutes views insisting on "existence" or "nonexistence" constitutes "the far shore" whereas the diligent cultivation of giving corresponds to being in the middle of the river.

Then again, one may also say that there are two kinds of *dāna*, the first being the *dāna* of demons and the second being the *dāna* of the Buddhas. If in this practice one is being robbed by the thieves of the fetters such that one is afflicted by worries and abides in fearfulness, this constitutes the *dāna* of the demons and exemplifies what is meant by "this shore."

Where there is pure giving in which there is an absence of the thieves of the fetters and in which there is nothing of which one is fearful, one succeeds thereby in arriving at the Buddha Path. This constitutes the *dāna* of the Buddhas and exemplifies what is meant by "reaching to the far shore." This is "pāramitā."

Story: The Analogy of the Poisonous Snakes

By way of illustration, in *The Buddha Speaks the Analogy of the Poisonous Snakes Sutra*, there once was a man who had offended the King. The King ordered that he be required to carry around a basket and look after it. Inside the basket there were four poisonous snakes. The King ordered the criminal to look after them and raise them.

This man thought to himself, "It's a difficult thing to have to draw close to four snakes. If one grows close to them they bring harm to a person. I could not raise even one of them, how much the less could I do that for four of them." And so he cast aside the basket and ran away.

The King ordered five men carrying knives to chase after him. There was yet another man who tried to persuade him to obey. [This

心欲中伤而语之言。养之以
理此亦无苦。其人觉之驰走
逃命。至一空聚有一善人方
便语之。此聚虽空是贼所止
处。汝今住此必为贼害慎勿
住也。于是复去至一大河。
河之彼岸即是异国。其国安
乐坦然清净无诸患难。于是
集众草木缚以为[12]栰进。
以手足竭力求渡。既到彼岸
安乐无患。王者魔王。箧者
人身。四毒蛇者四大。[13]五
拔刀贼者五[14]众。一人口
善心恶者。是[15]染着空聚是
六情。贼是六尘。一人愍而
语之是为善师。大河是爱。
栰是八正道。手足懃渡是精
进。此岸是世间。彼岸是涅
盘。度者漏尽阿罗汉。菩萨
法中亦如是。若施有三碍。
我与彼受所施者财。是为堕
魔境界未离众难。如菩萨布
施三种清净无[16]此三碍[17]得
到

心欲中傷而語之言。養之以
理此亦無苦。其人覺之馳走
逃命。至一空聚有一善人方
便語之。此聚雖空是賊所止
處。汝今住此必為賊害慎勿
住也。於是復去至一大河。
河之彼岸即是異國。其國安
樂坦然清淨無諸患難。於是
集眾草木縛以為[12]栰進。
以手足竭力求渡。既到彼岸
安樂無患。王者魔王。篋者
人身。四毒蛇者四大。[13]五
拔刀賊者五[14]眾。一人口
善心惡者。是[15]染著空聚是
六情。賊是六塵。一人愍而
語之是為善師。大河是愛。
栰是八正道。手足懃渡是精
進。此岸是世間。彼岸是涅
槃。度者漏盡阿羅漢。菩薩
法中亦如是。若施有三礙。
我與彼受所施者財。是為墮
魔境界未離眾難。如菩薩布
施三種清淨無[16]此三礙[17]得
到

简体字   正體字

other man] had it in mind to bring him harm and so said to him, "Just raise them in a sensible fashion. There will be no suffering in that." But the man became wise to this and so ran off, fleeing for his life. When he came to an empty village there was a good man who assisted him by telling him, "Although this village is empty, it is a place that is frequented by thieves. If you now take up residence here you will certainly be harmed by the thieves. Be careful. Don't dwell here."

At this point he took off again and next arrived at a great river. On the other side of the river there was a different country. That country was a peaceful, blissful, and easeful place. It was a pure place devoid of any form of calamity or adversity. Then he gathered together a mass of reeds and branches and bound them into the form of a raft. He moved it along with his hands and feet. He exerted all of his strength in seeking to make a crossing. When he had reached the other shore he was at peace, happy, and free of distress.

The King represents the demon king. The basket represents the human body. The four poisonous snakes represent the four great elements. The five knife-wielding thieves represent the five aggregates. The man of fine speech but evil mind represents defiled attachment. The empty village represents the six sense faculties. The thieves represent the six sense objects. The one man who took pity on him and instructed him represents the good [spiritual] teacher.

The great river represents love. The raft represents the eightfold right path. The hands and feet earnestly applied to making a crossing represent vigor. This shore represents this world. The far shore represents nirvāṇa. The man who crossed over represents the arhat who has put an end to outflow impurities. This is just the same in the dharma of the bodhisattva.

Conclusion

If in giving there exist the three hindrances of an "I" who gives, an "other" who receives, and a valuable object which is given, then one falls into a demonic mental state wherein one has not yet left behind multiple difficulties.

In the case of giving as performed by the bodhisattva, it is characterized by three kinds of purity in which there is an absence of these three hindrances and in which one has succeeded in reaching

简体字	正體字
彼岸。为诸佛所赞。是名[18]檀波罗蜜。以是故名到彼岸。此六波罗蜜能令人渡悭贪等烦恼染着大海到于彼岸。以是故名波罗蜜。	彼岸。為諸佛所讚。是名[18]檀波羅蜜。以是故名到彼岸。此六波羅蜜能令人渡悭貪等煩惱染著大海到於彼岸。以是故名波羅蜜。

to the far shore. It is such as is praised by the Buddhas. This is what is meant by *dāna* pāramitā. On account of this it is referred to as having reached the far shore.

These six pāramitās are able to cause a person to cross beyond miserliness and the other afflictions—beyond the great sea of defiled attachment—so that one reaches to the far shore. It is for this reason that they are referred to as "pāramitās."

复次菩萨有二种身。一者结
业生身。二者法身。是二种
身中檀波罗蜜满。是名具足
檀波罗蜜。问曰。云何名结
业生身檀波罗蜜满。答曰。
未得法身结使未尽。能以一
切宝物头目髓脑国财妻子内
外所有。尽以布施心不动
转。如须[3]提拏太子[4]（秦
言好爱）以其二子布施婆罗
门。次以妻施其心不转。又
如萨婆达王[5]（秦言一切施）
为敌国所灭。身窜穷林。见
有远国婆罗门来欲从己乞。
自以国破家亡一身藏窜。愍
其辛苦故。从远来而无所
得。语婆罗门言。我是萨婆
达王。新王募人求我甚重。
即时自缚以身施之。送与新
王大得财物。亦如月光太子
出行游观。癞人见之要车白
言。我身重病辛苦

简体字

正體字

The Giving of King Sarvada and Prince Candraprabha

Nāgārjuna's Preamble: Perfect *Dāna* in Two Body Types

Additionally, the bodhisattva possesses two kinds of bodies. The first is the body produced from the karma of the fetters. The second is the Dharma body. Fulfillment of *dāna* pāramitā in both of these bodies is what is intended by perfectly fulfilling *dāna* pāramitā.

Question: What is meant by fulfillment of *dāna* pāramitā within the body produced from the karma of the fetters (*saṃyojana*)?

Response: This refers to when one has not yet gained the Dharma body and to when the fetters have not yet been brought to an end. One becomes able to give completely of all that one possesses, both inwardly and outwardly, including all manner of precious objects, and including one's head, eyes, marrow, brain, country, wealth, wives, and sons, doing so without one's mind moving or turning away from it. Take for instance Prince Sudinna who made a gift of his two sons to a brahman. (Chinese textual note: In our language, this [Sudinna] means "fine fondness.") Next, he relinquished his wife, and even then, his mind still did not turn away from continuing on with this practice.

Story: King Sarvada Turns Himself In

This is also exemplified by King Sarvada (Chinese textual note: In our language, this ["Sarvada"] means "giving everything.") who was vanquished by an enemy country and who then fled and hid in the furthest reaches of the forests. He encountered a brahman from a faraway country who sought to receive alms from him. As for himself, his country had been crushed, his family had been wiped out, and he had been forced to flee alone and go into hiding.

Because he felt pity for [the brahman's] hardship in having come from afar and yet having gotten nothing, he said to the brahman, "I am King Sarvada. The new king has sent men out who are trying very hard to find me." He then immediately tied himself up and gave himself to [the brahman] who then gave him over to the new king and received great wealth and valuables [in reward].

Story: Prince Candraprabha Sacrifices Himself

This is also illustrated by [the story of] Prince Candraprabha who had gone out sightseeing when a leper noticed him, presented himself at the carriage and addressed him, saying, "My body has come down with a serious disease which causes intense suffering and

懊恼。太子嬉游独自欢耶。
大慈愍念愿见救疗。太子闻
之以问诸医。医言当须从生
长大无瞋之人血髓。涂而饮
之。如是可愈。太子念言。
设有此人贪生惜寿何可得
耶。自除我身无可得处。即
命旃陀罗。令除身肉破骨出
髓以涂病人以血饮之。如是
等种种身。及妻子施而无恡
如弃草木。观所施物知从缘
有。推求其实都无所得。一
切清净如涅盘相。乃至得无
生法忍。是为结业生身行檀
波罗蜜满。

懊惱。太子嬉遊獨自歡耶。
大慈愍念願見救療。太子聞
之以問諸醫。醫言當須從生
長大無瞋之人血髓。塗而飲
之。如是可愈。太子念言。
設有此人貪生惜壽何可得
耶。自除我身無可得處。即
命旃陀羅。令除身肉破骨出
髓以塗病人以血飲之。如是
等種種身。及妻子施而無恡
如棄草木。觀所施物知從緣
有。推求其實都無所得。一
切清淨如涅槃相。乃至得無
生法忍。是為結業生身行檀
波羅蜜滿。

简体字　　　　　　正體字

causes me to be grievously tormented. The prince is traveling about for pleasure. Will he only bring happiness to himself? May he bring forth great loving-kindness and bring pity to mind. Pray, may I receive a cure that will rescue me?"

When the Prince heard him, he asked the physicians about this matter. The physician replied, "It would be necessary to obtain the blood and marrow of a man who from the time of birth had grown up without any hatred. It would be topically applied and also drunk. If one proceeded in this fashion, then he could be cured."

The Prince thought to himself, "If there is such a person, he is desirous of living and cherishes his own life. How could such a person be obtained? Aside from myself, there is no place where he could be found." He then issued an order for a *caṇḍāla* to come and instructed him to strip away flesh from his body, break his bones, extract his marrow, smear it on the body of the sick man, and then take his blood and provide it as a drink for him.

Conclusion of Fetter-Generated Body Discussion

In this very manner one gives up all sorts of different physical bodies and gives up even one's own wives and sons and yet does not stint at all, treating these sacrifices as if they amounted only to only casting away some grass or some wood. One contemplates those things which are given and realizes that they exist merely on the basis of conditions. When one pursues this and seeks to find their reality, it can never be found. Everything is characterized by being pure and like nirvāṇa. And so this proceeds until one realizes the unproduced-dharmas patience (*anutpattikadharmakṣānti*). This is what is meant by fulfillment of *dāna* pāramitā while abiding in a body produced from the karma of the fetters.

云何法身菩萨行檀波罗蜜满。菩萨末后肉身得无生法忍。舍肉身得法身。于十方六道中。变身应适以化众生。种种珍宝衣服饮食给施一切。又以头目髓脑国财妻子内外所尽以布施。譬如释迦文佛。曾为六牙白象。猎者[6]伺便以毒箭射之。诸象竞至欲来蹈杀猎者。白象以身捍之。拥护其人愍之如子。[7]谕遣群象徐问猎人。何故射我。答曰。我须汝牙。即时以六牙内石孔中血肉俱出。以鼻举牙授与猎者。虽曰象身用心如是。当知此象非畜生行报。阿罗汉法中都无此心。当知此为法身菩萨。有时阎浮提人不知礼敬。[8]耆旧有德。以言化之未可得度。

简体字

云何法身菩薩行檀波羅蜜滿。菩薩末後肉身得無生法忍。捨肉身得法身。於十方六道中。變身應適以化眾生。種種珍寶衣服飲食給施一切。又以頭目髓腦國財妻子內外所有盡以布施。譬如釋迦文佛。曾為六牙白象。獵者[6]伺便以毒箭射之。諸象競至欲來蹈殺獵者。白象以身捍之。擁護其人愍之如子。[7]諭遣群象徐問獵人。何故射我。答曰。我須汝牙。即時以六牙內石孔中血肉俱出。以鼻舉牙授與獵者。雖曰象身用心如是。當知此象非畜生行報。阿羅漢法中都無此心。當知此為法身菩薩。有時閻浮提人不知禮敬。[8]耆舊有德。以言化之未可得度。

正體字

Two Stories of Bodhisattvas Manifesting as Animals

Nāgārjuna's Preamble: Dharma-body *Dāna* Pāramitā

How does the Dharma-body bodhisattva cultivate *dāna* pāramitā to fulfillment? In his very last fleshly body, the bodhisattva achieves the unproduced-dharmas patience. He relinquishes the fleshly body and gains the Dharma body.[1] In the six destinies and throughout the ten directions, he transformationally creates bodies in response to what is appropriate, and thereby goes about transforming beings. He provides all sorts of precious jewels, clothing, drink, and food as gifts to everyone and additionally gives exhaustively of everything he inwardly or outwardly possesses, including his head, his eyes, his marrow, his brain, his country, wealth, wives, and sons.

Story: Buddha's Past Life as an Elephant

A case in point is that of Shākyamuni Buddha when he once was a six-tusked white elephant. A hunter had ambushed him and shot him with poison arrows. The herd of elephants stampeded towards him with the intention of trampling the hunter to death. The white elephant used his own body to defend him, protecting that man and having pity upon him just the same as if he was his own son. He ordered the herd of elephants away and then calmly asked the hunter, "Why did you shoot me?"

He replied, "I need your tusks." Immediately then, blood and flesh spontaneously pushed forth all six tusks from their sockets. He then used his trunk to pick up the tusks and give them to the hunter.

Although this was described as the [animal] body of an elephant, in a case where the mind is used in this manner, one should realize that this elephant could not have come into existence as retribution for the karmic actions typical of animals. Nowhere among the dharmas of those [on the path of the] arhat are there mental practices of this sort. One should realize that this was a Dharma-body bodhisattva.

Story: The Elephant, the Monkey, and the Kapiñjala Bird

There once was a time when people in Jambudvīpa did not know enough to render proper reverence and respect to those who are older and those who are virtuous. At that time they had not been able to be crossed over to liberation through the use of words alone in teaching them.

是时菩萨自变其身。作迦频阇罗鸟。是鸟有二亲友。一者大象二者猕猴。共在必钵罗树下住。自相问言。我等不知谁应为[9]长。象言。我昔见此树在我腹下。今大如是以此推之我应为长。[10]猕猴言。我曾蹲地手[11]挽树头以[12]是推之我应为长。鸟言。我于必钵罗林中食此树果。子随粪出此树得生。以是推之我应最[*]长。[13]鸟复说言先生宿旧礼应供养。即时大象背负猕猴。鸟在猴上。周游而行。一切禽兽见而问之。何以如此。答曰。以此恭敬供养长老。禽兽受化皆行礼敬。不侵民田不害物命。众人疑怪一切禽兽不复为害。猎[14]者入林见象负猕猴[15]猕猴戴鸟。行敬化物物皆修善传告国人。人各庆曰。时将太平鸟兽而仁。人亦效之。皆行礼敬。自古及今化流万世。当知是为法身菩萨。

简体字

是時菩薩自變其身。作迦頻阇羅鳥。是鳥有二親友。一者大象二者獼猴。共在必鉢羅樹下住。自相問言。我等不知誰應為[9]長。象言。我昔見此樹在我腹下。今大如是以此推之我應為長。[10]獼猴言。我曾蹲地手[11]挽樹頭以[12]是推之我應為長。鳥言。我於必鉢羅林中食此樹果。子隨糞出此樹得生。以是推之我應最[*]長。[13]鳥復說言先生宿舊禮應供養。即時大象背負獼猴。鳥在猴上。周遊而行。一切禽獸見而問之。何以如此。答曰。以此恭敬供養長老。禽獸受化皆行禮敬。不侵民田不害物命。眾人疑怪一切禽獸不復為害。獵[14]者入林見象負獼猴[15]獼猴戴鳥。行敬化物物皆修善傳告國人。人各慶曰。時將太平鳥獸而仁。人亦效之。皆行禮敬。自古及今化流萬世。當知是為法身菩薩。

正體字

At that time, a bodhisattva manifest as a *kapiñjala* bird. This bird had two close friends. The first was a great elephant and the second was a monkey. They all lived together around the base of a pipal tree. They were inquiring of one another, wondering, "We don't know who among us ought to be accorded the status of 'elder.'"

The elephant said, "In the past I viewed this tree when it was shorter than the height of my belly. Now it is so huge. From this we can deduce that I ought to be known as the eldest."

The monkey said, "In the past I've squatted down and plucked with my hand at the top of the tree. From this we can deduce that I should be recognized as the eldest."

The bird said, "In the past I fed on the fruit of such trees in the pipal forest. The seed then passed out with my feces and as a result this tree grew forth. It can be deduced from this that I ought to be recognized as the eldest." The bird continued, saying, "As a matter of propriety, the first born, being the eldest, ought to be the recipient of offerings."

The great elephant immediately took the monkey on his back and the bird then rode on the back of the monkey. They traveled all around in this fashion. When all of the birds and beasts observed this, they asked them, "Why are you going about like this?"

They replied, "We mean by this an expression of reverence and offerings to the one who is the eldest." The birds and the beasts all accepted this teaching and all practiced such reverence. They no longer invaded the fields of the people and no longer brought harm to the lives of other animals. The people were all amazed that all of the birds and beasts no longer engaged in harmful activities.

The hunters went into the forest and observed that the elephant bore the monkey on his back, that the monkey carried along the bird, and that they so transformed the creatures through cultivating respectfulness that the creatures all cultivated goodness. They passed this on to the people of the country. The people all celebrated this and remarked, "The times are growing peaceful. Though they are but birds and beasts, still, they are possessed of humanity."

And so the people as well modeled themselves on this. They all cultivated propriety and respectfulness. From ancient times until the present, this transformative teaching has flowed down through a myriad generations. One should know that this was brought about by a Dharma-body bodhisattva.

复次法身菩萨一时之顷。化作无央数身。供养十方诸佛。一时能化无量财宝给足众生。能随一切上中下声一时之顷。普为说法。乃至坐佛树下。如是等种种名为法身菩萨行檀波罗蜜满。	復次法身菩薩一時之頃。化作無央數身。供養十方諸佛。一時能化無量財寶給足眾生。能隨一切上中下聲一時之頃。普為說法。乃至坐佛樹下。如是等種種名為法身菩薩行檀波羅蜜滿。
简体字	正體字

Conclusion of Dharma-body *Dāna* Discussion

Additionally, the Dharma-body bodhisattva, in a single moment, can transformationally produce countless bodies with which he makes offerings to the Buddhas of the ten directions. He is able in a single moment to transformationally create an immeasurable number of valuable jewels which he supplies in abundance to beings. He is able in a single moment, in accordance with all of the different superior, middling and inferior voices, to universally speak Dharma for them. And so he proceeds on in this fashion until he comes to sit at the base of the bodhi tree.

All sorts of examples such as these constitute what is meant by the Dharma-body bodhisattva's fulfillment of the practice of *dāna* pāramitā.

Notes

1. Generally speaking, a "Dharma-body bodhisattva" refers to a bodhisattva who has at least reached the first bodhisattva ground, a level which may sound rather elementary but which, on the contrary, is already the culmination of countless lifetimes of preparatory practice on the Bodhisattva Path.

復次有人于他物中我心生。
如外道坐禅人。用地一切入
观时。见地则是我我则是
地。水火风空亦如是。颠倒
故于他身中亦计我。复次有
时于他身生我。如有一人受
使远行。独宿空舍。夜中有
鬼担一死人来着其前。复有
一鬼逐来瞋骂前鬼。是死人
是我物。汝何以担来。先鬼
言是我物我自持来。后鬼言
是死人实我担来。二鬼各捉
一手争之。前鬼言[13]此有
人可问。后鬼即问。是死人
谁担来。是人思惟。此二鬼
力大。若实语亦当死。若妄
语亦当死。俱不免死何为妄
语。[14]语言。前鬼担来。后
鬼大瞋。捉人手拔出着地。
前鬼取死人一臂[15]拊之即
着。如是两臂两脚头胁

復次有人於他物中我心生。
如外道坐禪人。用地一切入
觀時。見地則是我我則是
地。水火風空亦如是。顛倒
故於他身中亦計我。復次有
時於他身生我。如有一人受
使遠行。獨宿空舍。夜中有
鬼擔一死人來著其前。復有
一鬼逐來瞋罵前鬼。是死人
是我物。汝何以擔來。先鬼
言是我物我自持來。後鬼言
是死人實我擔來。二鬼各捉
一手爭之。前鬼言[13]此有
人可問。後鬼即問。是死人
誰擔來。是人思惟。此二鬼
力大。若實語亦當死。若妄
語亦當死。俱不免死何為妄
語。[14]語言。前鬼擔來。後
鬼大瞋。捉人手拔出著地。
前鬼取死人一臂[15]拊之即
著。如是兩臂兩腳頭胁

简体字　　　　　　　正體字

The Traveler and the Ghosts

Nāgārjuna's Preamble

Then again, there *are* people who *do* have the idea of a self arise in relation to other phenomena. Take for example certain non-Buddhists who sit in dhyāna meditation. When they employ the "earth" universal-basis (*kṛtsnāyatana*) contemplation and thus perceive the [pervasive] existence of the earth element, they may then think, "The earth is me and I am the earth." They may also be prone to do this in regard to water, fire, wind or space. Thus, on account of inverted views, they may then also reckon the self as existing within another person's body.

Story: The Traveler and the Ghost

Additionally, there are times when someone generates the idea that his self inhabits another person's body. Take for example the case of a man who had been given a mission whereby he was compelled to travel a great distance. He spent the night alone in a vacant dwelling. In the middle of the night a ghost carried in a man's corpse and laid it down in front of him. Then there was another ghost who chased along behind and angrily castigated the first ghost, yelling, "This corpse is mine! Why did you carry it in here?"

The first ghost said, "It belongs to me! I carried it in here myself!"

The second ghost retorted, "The fact of the matter is, *I* am the one who carried this corpse in here!" Then each of the ghosts grabbed one of the hands of the corpse and tried to pull it away from the other. Thereupon the first ghost said, "There's a man here. We can ask *him* to settle this."

The ghost who had come in later then asked the traveler, "Well, who was it that carried this corpse in here?"

The traveler thought to himself, "Both of these ghosts are very strong. If I report the facts, I'm bound to die. If I lie, I'm also bound to die. So, since I can't avoid being killed in either case, what's the point in lying about it?" And so he replied, "It was the first ghost who carried in the corpse."

The second ghost flew into a rage, grabbed one of the man's hands, tore the limb off, and then threw it down on the ground. At this, the first ghost pulled off one of the arms from the corpse and attached it as a replacement. They then proceeded in this fashion with both arms, both feet, the head, the two sides, and so forth

举身皆易。于是二鬼共食所
易人身拭口而去。其人思
惟。我[16]人母生身眼见二鬼
食尽。今我此身尽是他肉。
我今定有身耶。为无身耶。
若以为有尽是他身。若以为
无今现有身。如是思惟。其
心迷闷。譬如狂人。明朝寻
路而去。到前国土见[17]有佛
塔众僧。不论[18]馀事但问
己身为有为无。诸比丘问。
汝是何人。答言。我亦不自
知是人非人。即为众僧广说
上事。诸比丘言。此人自知
无我易可得度。而语之言。
汝身从本已来恒自无我。非
适今也。但以四大和合故计
为我身。如[19]汝本身与今无
异。诸比丘度之为道断诸烦
恼。即得阿罗汉是为有时他
身亦计为我。不可以有彼此
故谓有[20]我。复次是[*]我实
性决定不可得。若常相非常
相

舉身皆易。於是二鬼共食所
易人身拭口而去。其人思
惟。我[16]人母生身眼見二鬼
食盡。今我此身盡是他肉。
我今定有身耶。為無身耶。
若以為有盡是他身。若以為
無今現有身。如是思惟。其
心迷悶。譬如狂人。明朝尋
路而去。到前國土見[17]有佛
塔眾僧。不論[18]餘事但問
己身為有為無。諸比丘問。
汝是何人。答言。我亦不自
知是人非人。即為眾僧廣說
上事。諸比丘言。此人自知
無我易可得度。而語之言。
汝身從本已來恒自無我。非
適今也。但以四大和合故計
為我身。如[19]汝本身與今無
異。諸比丘度之為道斷諸煩
惱。即得阿羅漢是為有時他
身亦計為我。不可以有彼此
故謂有[20]我。復次是[*]我實
性決定不可得。若常相非常
相

until the traveler's entire body had been switched. The two ghosts then proceeded to devour the body which they had gotten from the exchange. When they had finished, they wiped off their mouths and departed.

At that point the traveler thought to himself, "With my very own eyes I saw those two ghosts entirely devour the body born of my mother! This body which I now have here is composed entirely of someone else's flesh! Do I really still have a body now? Or is it the case that I have no body at all? If I hold the view that I *do* indeed have a body—that body is actually somebody else's entirely. If I hold that I *don't* have one—still, there *is* a body here right now!" He continued to ponder like this until his mind became so confused and distressed that he became like a man gone mad.

The next morning, he went off down the road. When he reached the neighboring country, he saw that there was a buddha stupa and a group of monks. He couldn't talk about anything else. He could only keep asking whether his body was existent or nonexistent. The bhikshus asked him, "Just who are you, anyway?"

The traveler replied, "Well, as for me, I don't know myself whether I'm a person or a non-person." He then described in detail the events which had transpired.

The bhikshus remarked, "This man has a natural understanding of the nonexistence of a self. He could easily gain deliverance." And so they offered an explanation, saying, "From its origin on up until the present, your body has always naturally been devoid of a self. It's not something that just happened now. It is merely on account of an aggregation of the four great elements that one conceives of it as '*my*' body. In this respect, your original body and this one you now have are no different."

Thus the bhikshus precipitated the traveler's deliverance to the Path, whereupon he cut off all afflictions and immediately realized arhatship. This illustrates the occasional instance of reckoning the existence of one's self in the body of some other person.

One cannot hold the view that a self exists based on its being there or here.

Conclusion: Refutation of any Valid Characteristics of a Self

Moreover, the actual nature of the "self" most definitely cannot be gotten at. And whether it be the characteristic of permanency, the characteristic of being impermanent, the characteristic of being

自在相不自在相作相不作相色相非色相。如是等种种皆不可得。若有相则有法。无相则无法。[*]我今无相则知无[*]我。	自在相不自在相作相不作相色相非色相。如是等種種皆不可得。若有相則有法。無相則無法。[*]我今無相則知無[*]我。
简体字	正體字

inherently existent, the characteristic of not being inherently existent, the characteristic of being compounded, the characteristic of not being compounded, the characteristic of being form, or the characteristic of being formless, all such characteristics as these cannot be gotten at.

If a characteristic exists, then a dharma exists. If there is no corresponding characteristic, then there is no associated dharma. Because it is now the case that this "self" is devoid of any characteristics, one knows consequently that there is no self.

云何菩萨布施生尸[15]罗波罗蜜。菩萨思惟众生不[16]布施故。后世贫穷。以贫穷故劫盗心生。以劫盗故而有杀害。以贫穷故不足于色。色不足故而行邪婬。又以贫[17]穷故为人下贱。下贱畏怖而[18]生妄语。如是等贫穷因缘故。行十不善道。若行布施生有财物。有财物故不为非法。何以故五[19]尘充足无所乏短故。如提婆达。本生曾为一蛇。与一虾蟇一龟在一池中共结亲友。其后池水竭尽。饥穷困乏无所控告。时蛇遣龟以呼虾蟇。虾蟇说偈[20]以遣龟言

　若遭贫穷失本心
　不惟本义食为先
　汝持我声以语蛇
　虾蟇终不到汝边

云何菩薩布施生尸[15]羅波羅蜜。菩薩思惟眾生不[16]布施故。後世貧窮。以貧窮故劫盜心生。以劫盜故而有殺害。以貧窮故不足於色。色不足故而行邪婬。又以貧[17]窮故為人下賤。下賤畏怖而[18]生妄語。如是等貧窮因緣故。行十不善道。若行布施生有財物。有財物故不為非法。何以故五[19]塵充足無所乏短故。如提婆達。本生曾為一蛇。與一蝦蟇一龜在一池中共結親友。其後池水竭盡。飢窮困乏無所控告。時蛇遣龜以呼蝦蟇。蝦蟇說偈[20]以遣龜言

　若遭貧窮失本心
　不惟本義食為先
　汝持我聲以語蛇
　蝦蟇終不到汝邊

简体字　　　　　正體字

The Snake, the Turtle, and the Frog

Nāgārjuna's Preamble: *Dāna* Pāramitā Generates *Śīla* Pāramitā; Failing to Give Generates Ten Bad Karmas

How is it that the bodhisattva's practice of giving can generate *śīla* pāramitā? The bodhisattva reflects, "Beings become poor and destitute in later lives on account of not practicing giving. On account of becoming poor and destitute, the thought of stealing arises in them. On account of engaging in stealing, killing occurs. On account of being poor and destitute, one may be sexually unsatisfied. On account of being sexually unsatisfied, one may engage in sexual misconduct. Additionally, on account of being poor and destitute, one may be treated as of low social station by others. On account of the fearfulness associated with being of low social station, one may engage in false speech.

"On account of causes and conditions such as these which are associated with being poor and destitute one courses along the path of the ten unwholesome deeds. If, however, one practices giving, then when one is reborn, one possesses valuable goods. Because one has valuable goods, one does not engage in that which is not Dharma. Why is this the case? It is because the five objects of the senses are abundant and there is nothing which one lacks."

Story: The Snake, the Turtle, and the Frog

This is exemplified by the case of Devadatta in a previous life when he was a snake who dwelt together with a frog and a turtle in a pond. They had all become close friends. Later, the water of the pond dried up. They were hungry, poor, in desperate straits, and lacking in any other resources. At that time, the snake dispatched the turtle to call forth the frog. The frog then sent back the turtle by uttering a verse:

> If one encounters poverty, he may stray from his original intent.
> Failing to regard original principles, eating becomes foremost.
> You should take my words and tell them to that snake:
> "This frog will never come on over and show up at your side."

[0150c10] 若修布施后生有福无所短乏。则能持戒无此众恶。是为布施能生尸罗波罗蜜。复次布施时能令破戒诸结使薄。益持戒心令得坚固。是为布施因缘增益于戒。复次菩萨布施。常于受者生慈悲心。不着于财自物不惜。何况劫盗。慈悲受者何有杀意。如是等能遮破戒。是为[21]施生戒。若能布施以破悭心。然后持戒忍辱等易可得行。如文殊师利。在昔过去久远劫时。曾为比丘入城乞食。得满钵百味欢喜丸。城中一小儿追而从乞不即与之。乃至佛图手捉二丸而要之言。汝若能自食一丸。以一丸施僧者当以施汝。即相然可。以一欢喜丸布施众僧。然后于文殊师利许受戒发心作佛。

简体字

[0150c10] 若修布施後生有福無所短乏。則能持戒無此眾惡。是為布施能生尸羅波羅蜜。復次布施時能令破戒諸結使薄。益持戒心令得堅固。是為布施因緣增益於戒。復次菩薩布施。常於受者生慈悲心。不著於財自物不惜。何況劫盜。慈悲受者何有殺意。如是等能遮破戒。是為[21]施生戒。若能布施以破慳心。然後持戒忍辱等易可得行。如文殊師利。在昔過去久遠劫時。曾為比丘入城乞食。得滿鉢百味歡喜丸。城中一小兒追而從乞不即與之。乃至佛圖手捉二丸而要之言。汝若能自食一丸。以一丸施僧者當以施汝。即相然可。以一歡喜丸布施眾僧。然後於文殊師利許受戒發心作佛。

正體字

Mañjuśrī Teaches a Beggar Child

Nāgārjuna's Preamble: Giving's Generation of Virtue

If one cultivates giving, in later lives one will possess merit and have nothing which one lacks. If this is the case, then one will be able to uphold the precepts and will be free of these manifold ills. This is how giving is able to bring forth *śīla* pāramitā.

Additionally, when one gives, one is able to bring about a scarcity of all of the fetters associated with the breaking of precepts while also being able to strengthen the resolve to uphold the precepts, causing it to become solid. This constitutes the causal basis associated with giving's ability to bring about increase in moral precept cultivation.

Moreover, when the bodhisattva practices giving he constantly brings forth thoughts of loving-kindness and compassion for the recipient. He is not attached to valuables and does not cherish his own goods. How much the less would he engage in stealing. When one feels loving-kindness and compassion for the recipient, how could one maintain any thought of killing? In ways such as these he is able to block off the breaking of precepts. This constitutes the practice of giving bringing forth precepts.

If one is able to carry out giving while employing a mind which destroys miserliness, then afterwards he will easily succeed in practicing the upholding of precepts, patience, and so forth.

Story: Mañjuśrī Teaches a Beggar Child

This principle is illustrated by the case of Mañjuśrī when he was a bhikshu long ago in the past in a far distant kalpa. Having gone into the city to seek alms, he received a bowl full of "hundred-flavored delightful dumplings." There was a young child in that city who followed along after him, begging. [Mañjuśrī] did not immediately give anything to him.

Then, when they had reached a Buddha stupa, [the monk] picked up two of the dumplings in his hand and required of the child, "If you are able to eat only one of the dumplings yourself, while taking one of the dumplings and giving it to the Sangha, I will give these to you."

The child immediately agreed and so then took one of the delightful dumplings and presented it to the Sangha community. Later, he obtained Mañjuśrī's consent to receive the precepts and subsequently brought forth the aspiration to become a buddha.

如是布施能令受戒发心作佛。是为布施生尸罗波罗蜜。复次布施之报得四事供养好国善师无所乏少。故能持戒。又布施之报其心调柔。心调柔故能生持戒。能生持戒故从不善法中能自制心。如是种种因缘。从布施生尸罗波罗蜜。

如是布施能令受戒發心作佛。是為布施生尸羅波羅蜜。復次布施之報得四事供養好國善師無所乏少。故能持戒。又布施之報其心調柔。心調柔故能生持戒。能生持戒故從不善法中能自制心。如是種種因緣。從布施生尸羅波羅蜜。

简体字   正體字

Conclusion: How Giving Brings Forth Moral Virtue

In this fashion the practice of giving is able to cause one to take on the precepts and to bring forth the aspiration to become a buddha. This illustrates how the practice of giving brings forth *śīla* pāramitā.

Furthermore, it is as a karmic reward for giving that one subsequently receives offerings of the four requisites, lives in a fine country, finds a good spiritual master, and has nothing in which he is lacking. One is therefore able to uphold the moral precepts. Additionally, it is as a karmic reward for giving that one's mind becomes well-regulated and supple. Because one's mind becomes well-regulated and supple, one is able to observe the precepts. Because one is able to observe the moral precepts, one is able to control one's own mind even from within the midst of unwholesome dharmas. All sorts of causes and conditions such as these demonstrate the bringing forth of *śīla* pāramitā on the basis of the practice of giving.

云何布施生毘梨耶波罗蜜。菩萨布施时常行精进。何以故。菩萨初发心时功德未大。尔时欲行二施充满一切众生之愿。以物不足故。懃求财法以给足之。如释迦文尼佛本身。作大医王疗一切病不求名利。为怜愍众生故。病者甚多力不周救。忧念一切而不从心。懊恼而死即生忉利天上。自思惟言。我今生天。但食福报无所长益。即自方便自取灭身。舍此天寿生[1]婆[2]迦陀龙王宫中为龙太子。其身长大父母爱重。欲自取死就金翅鸟王。鸟即取此龙子。于舍摩利树上吞之。父母[3]嚖啕啼哭懊恼。龙子既死生阎浮提中。为大国王太子。名曰能施。生而能言。问诸左右。今此国中有何等物。尽皆持来以用布施。

云何布施生毘梨耶波羅蜜。菩薩布施時常行精進。何以故。菩薩初發心時功德未大。爾時欲行二施充滿一切眾生之願。以物不足故。懃求財法以給足之。如釋迦文尼佛本身。作大醫王療一切病不求名利。為憐愍眾生故。病者甚多力不周救。憂念一切而不從心。懊惱而死即生忉利天上。自思惟言。我今生天。但食福報無所長益。即自方便自取滅身。捨此天壽生[1]婆[2]迦陀龍王宮中為龍太子。其身長大父母愛重。欲自取死就金翅鳥王。鳥即取此龍子。於舍摩利樹上吞之。父母[3]嚖咷啼哭懊惱。龍子既死生閻浮提中。為大國王太子。名曰能施。生而能言。問諸左右。今此國中有何等物。盡皆持來以用布施。

简体字 正體字

The Buddha's Past-Life Giving & His Perfection of Vigor

Nāgārjuna's Preamble: How *Dāna* Generates *Vīrya* Pāramitā

How is it that giving brings forth *vīrya* pāramitā? When the bodhisattva engages in the practice of giving, he constantly cultivates vigor. Why is this? When the bodhisattva first brings forth the aspiration [to achieve buddhahood], his merit is not yet vast. At that time he is desirous of cultivating the two kinds of giving in order to fulfill the aspirations of all beings. Because of a shortage of things to give, he earnestly seeks for valuables and Dharma in order to be able to provide for them adequately.

Story: The Buddha's Past Giving Generating His Perfection of Vigor

This is illustrated by the case of Shākyamuni Buddha in a previous lifetime when he was a great king of physicians who worked to cure every manner of disease without any concern for fame or profit. It was done out of pity for all beings. The sick were extremely numerous and so his powers were inadequate to rescue everyone. He was concerned about and mindful of everyone and yet matters did not correspond in their outcome to his aspirations. He became so distressed and agitated that he died.

He was then reborn in the Trāyastriṃśa Heaven. He thought to himself, "Now, I've been reborn in the heavens. All I'm doing here is consuming my reward of blessings without any sort of progress arising thereby." He then used an expedient means to put an end to that personal existence.

Having relinquished this long life in the heavens, he was next reborn as a dragon prince in the palace of Sāgara, the Dragon King. His body grew to full maturity. His parents were extremely attached in their love for him. But he desired to die, and so he went to the king of the golden-winged [*garuḍa*] birds. The bird immediately seized this young dragon and devoured him in the top of a *śālmalī* tree. His father and mother then wailed and cried in grief-stricken distress.

Having died, the young dragon was then reborn in Jambudvīpa as a prince in the house of the king of a great country. He was named "Able to Give." From the moment he was born he was able to speak. He asked all of the retainers, "Now, what all does this country contain? Bring it all forth so that it can be used to make gifts."

众人[4]怪畏皆舍之走。其母
怜爱独自守之。语其母言。
我非罗刹众人何以故走。我
本宿命常好布施。我为一切
人之檀越。母闻其言以语众
人。众人即还母好养育。及
年长大自身所有尽以施尽。
至父王所索物布施。父与其
分复以施尽。见阎浮提人贫
穷辛苦。思[5]欲给施而财物
不足。便自啼泣问诸人言。
作何方便当令一切满足于
财。诸宿人言。我等曾闻有
如意宝珠。若得此珠则能随
心所索无不必得。菩萨闻是
语已白其父母。欲入大海求
龙王头上如意宝珠。父母报
言。我唯有汝一儿耳。若入
大海众难难度。一旦失汝我
等亦当何用活为。不须去
也。我今藏中犹亦有物当以
给汝。儿言。藏中有限。我
意无量。我欲以财充满一切
令无乏短。愿见听许。得遂
本心使阎浮提人一切充足。
父母知其志大。不敢制之。
遂放令去。是时五百贾客。

众人[4]怪畏皆捨之走。其母
憐愛獨自守之。語其母言。
我非羅剎眾人何以故走。我
本宿命常好布施。我為一切
人之檀越。母聞其言以語眾
人。眾人即還母好養育。及
年長大自身所有盡以施盡。
至父王所索物布施。父與其
分復以施盡。見閻浮提人貧
窮辛苦。思[5]欲給施而財物
不足。便自啼泣問諸人言。
作何方便當令一切滿足於
財。諸宿人言。我等曾聞有
如意寶珠。若得此珠則能隨
心所索無不必得。菩薩聞是
語已白其父母。欲入大海求
龍王頭上如意寶珠。父母報
言。我唯有汝一兒耳。若入
大海眾難難度。一旦失汝我
等亦當何用活為。不須去
也。我今藏中猶亦有物當以
給汝。兒言。藏中有限。我
意無量。我欲以財充滿一切
令無乏短。願見聽許。得遂
本心使閻浮提人一切充足。
父母知其志大。不敢制之。
遂放令去。是時五百賈客。

简体字　　　　　正體字

Everyone was struck with amazement and became fearful. They all withdrew from him and ran off. His mother, however, felt kindness and love for him and so looked after him by herself. He said to his mother, "I am not a *rākṣasa* ghost. Why has everyone run off? In my previous lives I have always taken pleasure in giving and thus have been a benefactor to everyone."

When his mother heard his words, she reported them to everyone else. The other people all returned. The mother thenceforth took pleasure in raising him. By the time he had grown older, he had given away everything he owned. He then went to his father, the King, and requested things to give. His father gave him his share. Again, he gave it all away. He observed that the people of Jambudvīpa were all poverty-stricken and lived lives of intense hardship. He thought to supply them all with gifts, but the valuables were inadequate. He then began to weep and inquired of everyone, "How will I be able to cause everyone to become completely supplied with valuables?"

The wise elders said, "We have heard of the existence of a precious wish-fulfilling pearl. If you were able to obtain this pearl then, no matter what your heart desired, there would be nothing which would not be obtained with certainty."

When the Bodhisattva had heard these words he spoke to his mother and father, saying, "I desire to go out upon the great sea and seek the precious wish-fulfilling pearl worn on the head of the Dragon King."

His father and mother replied, "We have only you, our one son. If you go out upon the great sea the many difficulties will be difficult to overcome. If ever we were to lose you, what use would we have for going on living? It is not necessary for you to go. We do still have other things in our treasury with which we will be able to supply you."

The son said, "There is a limit to the contents of the treasury. My intentions are measureless. I wish to bestow enough wealth to satisfy everyone so that they will never be found wanting. I pray that you will give your permission so that I may fulfill my original aspiration to cause everyone in Jambudvīpa to be completely provided for."

His parents knew that his determination was immense. They did not dare to restrain him and so subsequently relented and allowed him to go. At that time, there were five hundred merchants who,

以其福德大。人皆乐随从。
知其行日集海道口。菩萨先
闻婆伽陀龙王头上有如意宝
珠。问众人言。谁知水道
至彼龙宫。有一盲人名陀
舍。曾以七反入大海中具知
海道。菩萨即命共行。答[6]
曰。我年既老两目失明。
曾虽数入今不能去。菩萨[7]
语言。我今此行不自为身。
普为一切求如意宝珠。欲给
足众生令身无乏。[8]次以道
法因缘而教化之。汝是智人
何得辞耶。我愿得成岂非汝
力。陀舍闻其要言。欣然同
怀语菩萨言。我今共汝俱入
大海我必不[9]全。汝当安我
尸骸着大海之中金沙洲上。
行事都集断第七绳。船去如
驼到众宝渚。众贾竞取七宝
各各已足。语菩萨言。何以
不取。菩萨报言。我所求者
如意宝珠。此有尽物我不须
也。汝等各当知足知量无令
船重不自[10]免也。是时众贾
白菩萨言。大德。为我咒愿
令得安隐。于是辞去。

简体字

以其福德大。人皆樂隨從。
知其行日集海道口。菩薩先
聞婆伽陀龍王頭上有如意寶
珠。問眾人言。誰知水道
至彼龍宮。有一盲人名陀
舍。曾以七反入大海中具知
海道。菩薩即命共行。答[6]
曰。我年既老兩目失明。
曾雖數入今不能去。菩薩[7]
語言。我今此行不自為身。
普為一切求如意寶珠。欲給
足眾生令身無乏。[8]次以道
法因緣而教化之。汝是智人
何得辭耶。我願得成豈非汝
力。陀舍聞其要言。欣然同
懷語菩薩言。我今共汝俱入
大海我必不[9]全。汝當安我
尸骸著大海之中金沙洲上。
行事都集斷第七繩。船去如
駝到眾寶渚。眾賈競取七寶
各各已足。語菩薩言。何以
不取。菩薩報言。我所求者
如意寶珠。此有盡物我不須
也。汝等各當知足知量無令
船重不自[10]免也。是時眾賈
白菩薩言。大德。為我呪願
令得安隱。於是辭去。

正體字

because his special qualities were so extraordinary, took pleasure in following him wherever he went. They happened to know the day when he was due to depart and so they gathered there at the port.

The Bodhisattva had heard earlier that Sāgara, the Dragon King, had a precious wish-fulfilling pearl. He inquired of everyone, "Who knows the route across the sea to his dragon palace?" There was a blind man named Dāsa who had been to sea seven times and who knew all of the sea routes. The Bodhisattva instructed him to travel along with him.

He replied, "As I have grown old, both of my eyes have lost their acuity. Although I have been to sea many times, I cannot go this time."

The Bodhisattva said, "In going forth this time, I do not do it for my own sake. I seek the precious wish-fulfilling pearl for the universal benefit of everyone. I desire to completely supply all beings so that they are caused to never again be found wanting for anything at all. Then I wish to instruct them in the causes and conditions of the Dharma of the Path. You are a wise man. How can you withdraw? How, in the absence of your efforts, could my vow possibly succeed?"

When Dāsa heard his entreaty, he then happily shared the Bodhisattva's aspiration and said to him, "I'll now go out with you onto the great sea. However, I certainly will not survive. You should lay my body to rest on the island of gold sands out in the middle of the ocean."

When the provisions for the journey had all been loaded, they loosened the last of the seven lines. The ship set forth like a camel and arrived at the island of numerous gems. The host of merchants all tried to outdo each other in gathering up the seven precious jewels. When they had all satisfied themselves, they asked the Bodhisattva, "Why do you not gather them, yourself?"

The Bodhisattva replied, "It is the precious wish-fulfilling pearl which I seek. I have no use for these things which can be used up You all should know when enough is enough and should realize the limits so as to avoid overloading the ship and failing to prevent self-destruction."

At this time the group of merchants said to the Bodhisattva, "Virtuous One, please invoke a spell for us to insure our safety." They then withdrew.

陀舍是时语菩萨言。别留艇
舟当随是别道而去。待风七
日。[11]博海南岸至一险处。
当有绝崖枣林枝皆覆水。大
风吹船[12]船当摧覆。汝当
仰[13]板枣枝可以自济。我身
无目于此当死。过此隘岸当
有金沙洲。可以我身置此沙
中。金沙清净是我愿也。即
如其言。风至而去。既到绝
[14]崖。如陀舍语。菩萨仰
[*]板枣枝得以自[15]免。置陀
舍尸安厝金地。于是独去如
其先教。深水中浮七日。[16]
至[17]坌咽水中行七日。坌腰
水中行七日。坌膝水中行七
日。[18]泥中行七日。见好
莲华鲜洁柔软。自思惟言。
此华软脆当入虚空三昧。自
轻其身行莲华上七日。见诸
毒蛇念言。含毒之虫甚可畏
也。即入慈心三昧。行毒蛇
头上七日。蛇皆擎头授与菩
萨令蹈上而过。过此难已见
有七重宝城。有七重堑。堑
中皆满毒蛇有[19]三大龙守
门。龙见菩萨形容端[*]政相
好严仪。能度

陀舍是時語菩薩言。別留艇
舟當隨是別道而去。待風七
日。[11]博海南岸至一險處。
當有絕崖棗林枝皆覆水。大
風吹船[12]船當摧覆。汝當
仰[13]板棗枝可以自濟。我身
無目於此當死。過此隘岸當
有金沙洲。可以我身置此沙
中。金沙清淨是我願也。即
如其言。風至而去。既到絕
[14]崖。如陀舍語。菩薩仰
[*]板棗枝得以自[15]免。置陀
舍屍安厝金地。於是獨去如
其先教。深水中浮七日。[16]
至[17]坌咽水中行七日。坌腰
水中行七日。坌膝水中行七
日。[18]泥中行七日。見好
蓮華鮮潔柔軟。自思惟言。
此華軟脆當入虛空三昧。自
輕其身行蓮華上七日。見諸
毒蛇念言。含毒之蟲甚可畏
也。即入慈心三昧。行毒蛇
頭上七日。蛇皆擎頭授與菩
薩令蹈上而過。過此難已見
有七重寶城。有七重塹。塹
中皆滿毒蛇有[19]三大龍守
門。龍見菩薩形容端[*]政相
好嚴儀。能度

简体字   正體字

At this point Dāsa instructed the Bodhisattva, "Hold aside the dinghy. We will want to go off on this other route. When we have been driven by the wind for seven days, we will arrive at a treacherous place on the southern shore of the vast sea. There should be a steep cliff with branches from a date tree forest overhanging the water. If a strong wind blows, the ship will be overturned and capsized. By reaching up and grabbing hold of the date branches, you may be able to save yourself. As I have no sight, I will likely die at that point. Beyond this precipitous shoreline there will be the isle of gold sand. You can take my body and lay it to rest in the midst of those sands. Those gold sands are pure. This is my desire."

And so it was just as he had foretold. The wind came and they set off. Having come to the steep cliffs, it was just as Dāsa had described. The Bodhisattva reached up, grabbed onto the date branches and so avoided disaster. He interred Dāsa's body in the ground of gold. From this point, he went on alone according to Dāsa's earlier instructions. He floated in deep water for seven days. He then walked for seven days in water the depth of his throat. Then he moved for seven days through water up to his waist. After that he walked for seven days through water up to his knees. Then he walked through mud for seven days.

Next, he came upon marvelous lotus flowers which were fresh and pure and soft. He thought to himself, "These blossoms are so soft and fragile. I should enter into the empty space samādhi." And so he made his body light and then walked upon the lotus blossoms for another seven days.

Next, he came upon poisonous snakes and thought to himself, "These poisonous serpents are extremely fearsome." He then entered the samādhi of loving kindness and proceeded to walk upon the heads of the poisonous snakes for seven days. As he did this, the snakes all extended their heads up to receive the Bodhisattva, thus allowing him to tread upon them as he passed.

After he had passed through this difficulty he saw that up ahead there was a jeweled city protected by seven sets of city walls. There were seven successive moats. Each of the moats was filled with poisonous snakes and there were three huge dragons guarding the gates.

The dragons saw that the Bodhisattva was possessed of a handsome and fine appearance, that he was a bearer of refined features and solemn deportment, and that he had been able to successfully

众难得来至此念言。此非凡
夫必是菩萨大功德人。即听
令前逐得入宫。龙王夫妇丧
儿未久犹故哀泣。见菩萨来
龙[20]王妇有神通。知是其
子。两乳[21]汁流出。命之令
坐。而问之言。汝是我子。
舍我命终生在何处。菩萨亦
自识宿命。知是父母而答母
言。我生阎浮提上。为大国
王太子。怜愍贫人饥寒勤苦
不得自在故。来至此欲求如
意宝珠。母言。汝父头上有
此宝珠以为首饰。难可得
也。必当将汝入[1]诸宝藏。
随汝所欲必欲与汝。汝当报
言。其馀杂宝我不须也。唯
欲大王头上宝珠。若见怜愍
愿以与我。如此可得。即
往见父。父大悲喜[2]欢庆无
量。愍[3]念其子远涉艰难乃
来至此。指示妙宝随意与汝
须者取之。菩萨言。我从远
来愿见大王。求王头上如意
宝珠。若见怜愍当以与我。
若不见与不须馀物。

简体字 正體字

pass through numerous difficulties in arriving at this place. They thought to themselves, "It is not the case that this is an ordinary man. It is certainly the case that he is a bodhisattva, a man possessed of much merit." They then immediately allowed him to advance directly to enter the palace.

It was not so long ago that the Dragon King and his mate had lost their son and so they continued as before to grieve and weep. They had observed the arrival of the Bodhisattva. The Dragon King's mate possessed the superknowledges and so, realizing that this was her son, milk spontaneously flowed forth from her two breasts. She gave the order allowing him to sit down and then spoke to him, "You are my son. After you left me and then died, where were you reborn?"

The Bodhisattva was also able to know his previous lives. He knew that these were his parents and so replied to his mother, "I was reborn on the continent of Jambudvīpa as a prince to the king of a great country. I felt pity for the poverty-stricken people afflicted by the intense hardship of hunger and cold who thus are unable to enjoy their own unrestrained freedom. It is because of this that I have come here seeking to obtain the precious wish-fulfilling pearl."

His mother replied, "Your father wears this precious pearl as an adornment on his head. It is a difficult thing to acquire. Surely he will take you into the treasury of jewels where he will certainly wish to give you whatever you desire. You should reply by saying, 'I have no need of the various other jewels. I only desire the precious pearl atop the head of the Great King. If I may receive such kindness, I pray that you will bestow it upon me.' It may be that you can acquire it in this way."

He then went to see his father. His father was overcome with nostalgia and delight and experienced boundless rejoicing. He thought with pity on his son's coming from afar, having to undergo extreme difficulties, and now arriving at this place. He showed him his marvelous jewels and said, "I will give you whatever you want. Take whatever you need."

The Bodhisattva said, "I came from afar wishing to see the Great King. I am seeking to obtain the precious wish-fulfilling pearl on the King's head. If I may receive such kindness, may it be that you will bestow it upon me. If I am not given that, then I have no need of any other thing."

龙王报言。我唯有[4]此一珠常为首饰。阎浮提人薄福下贱不应见也。菩萨白言。我以此故。远涉艰难冒死远来。为阎浮提人薄福贫贱。欲以如意宝珠济其所愿。然后以佛道因缘而教化之。龙王与珠而要之言。今以此珠与汝。汝既去世当以还我。答曰。敬如王言。菩萨得珠飞腾虚空。如屈伸臂顷到阎浮提。人王父母见儿吉还。欢悦踊跃[5]抱而问言。汝得何物。答[6]言。得如意宝珠。问言。今在何许。白言。在此衣角里中。父母言。何其[7]泰小。白言。在其神德不在大也。白父母言。当勅城中内外扫灑烧香。悬缯幡盖持斋受戒。明日清旦以长木为表以珠着上。菩萨是时自立誓愿。若我当成佛道度脱一切者。珠当如我意愿出一切宝物。随人所[8]须尽皆备有。是时阴云普遍雨种种宝物。衣服饮食

龍王報言。我唯有[4]此一珠常為首飾。閻浮提人薄福下賤不應見也。菩薩白言。我以此故。遠涉艱難冒死遠來。為閻浮提人薄福貧賤。欲以如意寶珠濟其所願。然後以佛道因緣而教化之。龍王與珠而要之言。今以此珠與汝。汝既去世當以還我。答曰。敬如王言。菩薩得珠飛騰虛空。如屈伸臂頃到閻浮提。人王父母見兒吉還。歡悅踊躍[5]抱而問言。汝得何物。答[6]言。得如意寶珠。問言。今在何許。白言。在此衣角裏中。父母言。何其[7]泰小。白言。在其神德不在大也。白父母言。當勅城中內外掃灑燒香。懸繒幡蓋持齋受戒。明日清旦以長木為表以珠著上。菩薩是時自立誓願。若我當成佛道度脫一切者。珠當如我意願出一切寶物。隨人所[8]須盡皆備有。是時陰雲普遍雨種種寶物。衣服飲食

简体字　　　　　　　正體字

The Dragon King replied, saying, "I have only this single pearl which I always wear as crown. The people of Jambudvīpa possess only scant merit and are of such base character that they should not be allowed even to see it."

The Bodhisattva replied, "It is on this account that I have come from afar, experiencing extreme difficulties and risking death. It is for the sake of the people of Jambudvīpa who have only scant merit, who are poverty-stricken, and who are possessed of base character. I wish to use the precious wish-fulfilling pearl to provide for them everything they desire so that I may then use aspects of the Buddha Path to teach and transform them."

The Dragon King gave him the pearl and placed a condition on it by saying, "I will now give you this pearl. But when you are about to depart from the world, you must first return it to me."

He replied, "With all respect, it shall be as the King instructs." When the Bodhisattva had acquired the pearl, he flew up into space and, in the time it takes to withdraw or extend one's arm, he straightaway arrived in Jambudvīpa.

When the [Bodhisattva's] human royal parents observed his auspicious return they were delighted and danced about with joy. They hugged him and then asked, "Well, what did you acquire?"

He replied, "I have obtained the precious wish-fulfilling pearl."

They asked, "Where is it now?"

He told them, "It's in the corner of my robe."

His parents said, "How could it be so small?"

He explained, "Its power resides in its supernatural qualities. It is not a function of its size." He told his parents, "It should be ordered that, both inside and outside of the city, the grounds are to be swept clean and incense is to be burned. Banners should be hung and canopies set up. Everyone should observe the standards of pure diet and take on the moral precepts."

The next morning at dawn he set up a tall wooden pillar as a display pedestal and attached the pearl up on the very top of it. The Bodhisattva then swore an oath, "If it is the case that I am to be able to complete the Buddha Path and bring everyone to deliverance, then this pearl should, in accordance with my vow, bring forth all kinds of precious things so that, whatever anyone needs, it will manifest in utter repletion."

At that time, dark clouds covered the entire sky and rained down every type of precious thing, including clothes, drink, food,

卧具汤药。人之所须一切具
足。至其命尽常尔不绝。如
是等名为菩萨布施生精进波
罗蜜。

臥具湯藥。人之所須一切具
足。至其命盡常爾不絕。如
是等名為菩薩布施生精進波
羅蜜。

简体字   正體字

bedding, and medicines. Whatever people needed was amply available. This was constantly the case, never ceasing until the end of his life.

Instances such as this illustrate what is meant by a bodhisattva's practice of giving coincidentally serving as the means to bring forth the pāramitā of vigor.

云何菩萨布施生禅波罗蜜。
菩萨布施时能除悭贪。除悭
贪已因此布施而行一心渐除
五盖。能除五盖是名为禅。
复次心依布施入于初禅。乃
至灭定禅。云何为依。若施
行禅人时心自念言。我以此
人行禅定故。净心供养。我
今何为自替于禅。即自[9]歘
心思惟行禅。若施贫人念此
宿命。作诸不善不求一心不
修福业今世贫穷。以是自勉
修善一心以入禅定。如说。
喜见转轮圣王八万四千小王
来朝。皆持七宝妙物来献。
王言我不须也。汝等各可自
以修福。诸王自念。大王虽
不肯取。我等亦复不宜自
用。即共造工立七宝殿。[10]
殖七宝行树作七宝浴池。于
大殿中造八万四千七宝[11]
楼。楼中皆有七宝床座。杂
色被枕置床两头。

云何菩薩布施生禪波羅蜜。
菩薩布施時能除慳貪。除慳
貪已因此布施而行一心漸除
五蓋。能除五蓋是名為禪。
復次心依布施入於初禪。乃
至滅定禪。云何為依。若施
行禪人時心自念言。我以此
人行禪定故。淨心供養。我
今何為自替於禪。即自[9]歘
心思惟行禪。若施貧人念此
宿命。作諸不善不求一心不
修福業今世貧窮。以是自勉
修善一心以入禪定。如說。
喜見轉輪聖王八萬四千小王
來朝。皆持七寶妙物來獻。
王言我不須也。汝等各可自
以修福。諸王自念。大王雖
不肯取。我等亦復不宜自
用。即共造工立七寶殿。[10]
殖七寶行樹作七寶浴池。於
大殿中造八萬四千七寶[11]
樓。樓中皆有七寶床座。雜
色被枕置床兩頭。

简体字   正體字

Sudarśana, the Wheel-Turning Sage-King

Nāgārjuna's Preamble: *Dāna's* Generation of Dhyāna Pāramitā

How is it that the bodhisattva's practice of giving generates the pāramitā of dhyāna? When the bodhisattva gives, he is able to eliminate stinginess. Having gotten rid of stinginess, he is further able on account of this giving to devote himself to single-minded practice and the gradual elimination of the five hindrances (*nīvaraṇa*). It is the ability to eliminate the five hindrances which in itself constitutes [the basis for success in] dhyāna.[1]

Then again, it is on account of giving that the mind enters into the first dhyāna and so forth on up to the dhyāna of the extinction-samādhi. How is it that it is "on account of" giving? Perhaps when one gives to a practitioner of dhyāna, one reflects, "It is because of this person's cultivation of dhyāna absorption that I make an offering with a pure mind. Why do I settle for only a vicarious experience of dhyāna?" And so one then restrains his mental discursion and takes up the cultivation of dhyāna himself.

Then again, it could be that on giving to a poverty-stricken person, one reflects on this person's previous lives in which he engaged in all manner of unwholesomeness, failed to seek single-mindedness, failed to cultivate works generating karmic blessings and then consequently became poverty-stricken in this life. On account of this, one may provoke himself to cultivate skillful single-mindedness, thus enabling himself to enter the dhyāna absorptions.

Story: Sudarśana, the Wheel-Turning Sage-King

According to the story about Sudarśana, a wheel-turning sage-king, eighty-four thousand of the lesser kings came to his court, all bringing marvelous things made of the seven treasures which they presented as offerings. The King declared, "I do not need them. You may each use them yourselves to cultivate blessings."

Those kings thought to themselves, "Although the great King cannot bring himself to take them, still, it wouldn't be appropriate for us to take them for our own use." And so together they constructed a seven-jeweled pavilion. They planted rows of seven-jeweled trees and created bathing pools made of the seven jewels. Within the great pavilion, they built eighty-four thousand multi-storied halls of the seven jewels.[2]

Within each of the multi-storied halls, there was a seven-jeweled throne with multi-colored cushions at each end of the throne.

悬缯幡盖香熏涂地。众事备
已。白大王言。愿受法殿宝
树浴池。王默然受之。而自
念言。我今不应先处新殿以
自娱乐。当求善人诸沙门婆
罗门等先入供养。然后我当
处之。即集善人先入宝殿。
种种供养微妙具足。诸人出
已王入宝殿登金楼坐银床。
念布施除五盖摄六情却六尘
受喜乐入初禅。次登银楼坐
金床入二禅。次登毘琉璃楼
坐[12]颇梨宝床入三禅。次
登颇梨宝楼坐毘琉璃床入四
禅。独坐思惟终竟三月。玉
女宝后与八万四千诸侍女
俱。皆以白珠名宝璎珞其
身。来白[13]大王。久违亲
觐。敢来问讯。王告诸妹。
汝等各当端心。当[14]为知识
勿为我怨。玉女宝后垂泪而
言。[*]大王何为谓我为妹。
必有异心愿闻其意。云何见
勅当为知识勿为我怨。

简体字　　　　　　正體字

Decorated canopies were suspended above and the ground was sprinkled with fragrances. After all of these preparations had been made, they addressed the King, saying, "We pray that his majesty will accept this Dharma pavilion with its bejeweled trees and bathing pools."

The King indicated his acceptance by remaining silent and then thought to himself, "I ought not to indulge myself with the pleasure of being the first to dwell within this new pavilion. I should invite good people such as the Śramaṇas and the Brahmans to first enter here to receive offerings. After that, I may go ahead and dwell in it." He then gathered together those good personages and had them be the first to enter the jeweled pavilion. There they were provided an abundance of all manner of fine and marvelous offerings.

After those people had all left, the King entered the jeweled pavilion, ascended into the multi-storied hall of gold, and then sat down upon the silver throne. There he reflected upon giving, dispensed with the five hindrances, withdrew the six sense faculties, did away with the six sense objects, and, experiencing joy and bliss, entered into the first dhyāna.

Next, he ascended into the multi-storied hall of silver, sat down upon the throne of gold, and then entered into the second dhyāna. Next he ascended into the multi-storied hall of beryl, sat down upon the crystal throne, and then entered into the third dhyāna. And then, finally, he ascended into the multi-storied jeweled hall of crystal, sat down upon the beryl throne, and entered into the fourth dhyāna. He sat there alone in contemplation for a total of three months.

The jade ladies, the precious queen, and eighty-four thousand female retainers all draped their bodies in strands of pearls and rare jewels and then came to see the King, saying, "As His Majesty has for so long now withdrawn from intimate audiences, we have dared to come and offer our greetings."

The King announced to them, "Sisters, each of you should maintain a mind imbued with correctness. You should serve me as friends. Don't act as my adversaries."

The jade ladies and the precious queen then began to weep and, as their tears streamed down, they inquired, "Why does the Great King now refer to us as 'sisters'? Surely, he must be thinking of us in a different way now. Pray, may we hear his intent? Why do we now receive the remonstrance: 'You should serve me as friends. Don't act as my adversaries.'?"

王告之言。汝若以我为世因缘。共行欲事以为欢乐。是为我怨。若能觉悟非常知身如幻。修福行善绝去欲情。是为知识。诸玉女言敬如王勅。说此语已各遣令还。诸女出已王登金楼坐银床行慈三昧。登银楼坐金床行悲三昧。登毘琉璃楼坐颇梨床行喜三昧。登颇梨宝楼坐毘琉璃床行舍三昧。是为菩萨布施生禅波罗蜜。

王告之言。汝若以我為世因緣。共行欲事以為歡樂。是為我怨。若能覺悟非常知身如幻。修福行善絕去欲情。是為知識。諸玉女言敬如王勅。說此語已各遣令還。諸女出已王登金樓坐銀床行慈三昧。登銀樓坐金床行悲三昧。登毘琉璃樓坐頗梨床行喜三昧。登頗梨寶樓坐毘琉璃床行捨三昧。是為菩薩布施生禪波羅蜜。

简体字   正體字

The King instructed them, saying, "If you look upon me as a mere worldly entity with whom to indulge desires and thus abide in bliss, this amounts to acting as my adversary. If, however, you are able to awaken to the fact of impermanence, realize that the body is like an illusion, cultivate blessings, practice goodness, and cut away desire-laden affections—it is this which amounts to serving me as a friend."

The jade ladies responded, "We shall adhere respectfully to the dictates of the King." After they had spoken these words, they were sent back to their quarters.

After the women had gone, the King ascended into the multi-storied hall of gold and sat down upon the silver throne where he immersed himself in the samādhi of loving-kindness. He then ascended into the multi-storied hall of silver, sat down upon the throne of gold, and immersed himself in the samādhi of compassion. Next, he ascended into the multi-storied hall of beryl, sat down upon the crystal throne, and immersed himself in the samādhi of sympathetic joy. Finally, he ascended into the multi-storied jeweled hall of crystal and sat down upon the throne of beryl where he immersed himself in the samādhi of evenmindedness. This is an instance of the bodhisattva's practice of giving generating the pāramitā of dhyāna.

Notes

1. The five hindrances are: desire; ill-will; lethargy-and-sleepiness; excitedness-and-regretfulness; and doubt. Nāgārjuna explains them in Fascicle Seventeen of the *Exegesis* early in his discussion of the perfection of dhyāna meditation.

2. Perhaps it bears repeating here that "eighty-four thousand" is not to be taken literally in the context of Indian Buddhist literature. At the conservative end of its interpretation, it is akin to the American colloquial exaggeration "millions" which really just means "impressively many."

Part Two:

Nāgārjuna's Stories on Moral Virtue

[0153c16] 人虽贫贱。而能持戒胜于富贵。而破戒者华香木香不能远闻。持戒之香周遍十方。持戒之人具足安乐。名声远闻天人敬爱。现世常得种种快乐。若欲天上人中富贵长寿。取之不难。持戒清净所愿皆得。复次持戒之人。见破戒人刑狱[23]考掠种种苦恼。自知永离此事以为欣庆。若持戒之人。见善人得誉名闻快乐。心自念言。如彼得誉。我亦有分。持戒之人寿终之时刀风解身筋脉断绝。自知持戒清净心不怖畏。如偈说

大恶病中	戒为良药
大恐怖中	戒为守护
死暗冥中	戒为明灯
于恶道中	戒为桥梁
死海水中	戒为大船

简体字

[0153c16] 人雖貧賤。而能持戒勝於富貴。而破戒者華香木香不能遠聞。持戒之香周遍十方。持戒之人具足安樂。名聲遠聞天人敬愛。現世常得種種快樂。若欲天上人中富貴長壽。取之不難。持戒清淨所願皆得。復次持戒之人。見破戒人刑獄[23]考掠種種苦惱。自知永離此事以為欣慶。若持戒之人。見善人得譽名聞快樂。心自念言。如彼得譽。我亦有分。持戒之人壽終之時刀風解身筋脈斷絕。自知持戒清淨心不怖畏。如偈說

大惡病中	戒為良藥
大恐怖中	戒為守護
死闇冥中	戒為明燈
於惡道中	戒為橋樑
死海水中	戒為大船

正體字

The Man with the Marvelous Vase

Nāgārjuna's Preamble: The Good Fortune from Observing Precepts

Although one may be poor and of low social station, still, if one is able to uphold the precepts, this is superior to being wealthy or of noble status while yet being a breaker of the precepts.

The fragrance of flowers and the fragrance of the trees is such that one is unable to smell them from afar. The fragrance from upholding the precepts universally pervades throughout the ten directions. The person who upholds the precepts perfects peacefulness and bliss. His name is heard in faraway quarters and he is revered and cherished by both men and gods. In the present life he always achieves all manner of happiness. If he desires wealth, nobility, and long life in the heavens or among people, it is not difficult for him to obtain it. If one is pure in upholding the precepts, he gains whatever he wishes.

Moreover, a person who upholds the precepts observes the precept breaker's suffering and affliction through undergoing punishment, confinement, beating and flogging, knows with respect to himself that he has eternally transcended such vulnerabilities, and is overjoyed on that account.

If a person who upholds the precepts sees a good person gaining a good name, fame, and happiness, in his own mind, he thinks to himself, "In just the same fashion as he has come by a good reputation, I too am bound to gain a measure of that same circumstance." When the life of a person who upholds the precepts comes to an end, when the knife-like wind cuts loose the body, and when the sinews and blood vessels are severed, because he knows that he has upheld the precepts purely, his mind is free of fearfulness. This situation is as described in a verse:

> Amidst the disease of great evil,
> The precepts are a fine medicine.
> In the midst of great fearfulness,
> The precepts are a guardian protector.

> Within the darkness of death,
> The precepts are a bright lamp.
> Amidst the wretched destinies,
> The precepts serve as a bridge.

> Within the waters of the sea of death,
> The precepts are a great ship.

[0154a01]　復次持戒之人。常
得今世人所敬養心樂不悔。
衣食無乏。死得生天後得佛
道。持戒之人無事不得。破
戒之人一切皆失。譬如有人
常供養天。其人貧窮一心供
養滿十二歲求索富貴。天愍
此人自現其身而問之曰。汝
求何等。答言。我求富貴。
欲令心之所願一切皆得。天
與一器名曰德瓶。而語之
言。所須之物從此瓶出。其
人得已應意所欲無所不得。
得如意已具作好舍象馬車
乘。七寶具足。供給賓客事
事無乏。客問之言。汝先貧
窮。今日[1]所由得如此富。
答言。我得天瓶。瓶能出此
種種眾物故富如是。客言。
出瓶見示并所出物。即為出
瓶。瓶中引出種種眾物。其
人憍泆立瓶上舞。瓶即破
壞。一切眾物亦一時滅。

正體字

Furthermore, the person who upholds the precepts always succeeds in being revered and supported by people of the present era. His mind is blissful and does not experience regret. He has no shortage of either clothing or food. When he dies, he is born in the heavens and then, later, he gains the Buddha Path. For the person who upholds the precepts, there is no matter in which he is not successful. For a person who breaks the precepts, everything is lost.

Story: The Man with the Marvelous Vase

This situation is analogous to that of the man who constantly made offerings to a god. As this man was poverty-stricken, for twelve full years he single-mindedly made offerings seeking to gain wealth and nobility. The god felt pity for this man, manifest himself before him, and asked, "What is it that you seek?"

The man replied, "I'm seeking to gain wealth and nobility. I desire to have it occur that I may obtain everything I wish for."

The god then gave him a vessel known as "the vase of virtue" and told the man, "Everything you need will come forth from this vase."

After the man got it, there was nothing which he wished for that he did not gain. After he acquired the ability to get anything he wished for, he built himself a fine house complete with elephants, horses, and carriages and also came to possess an abundance of the seven kinds of jewels. He gave generously to all of his guests so that they were never wanting in any respect.

One of his guests inquired of him, "You used to be poverty-stricken. How is it that now you have come by such wealth as this?"

The man replied, "I received this celestial vase. The vase is able to put forth all of these different kinds of things. It's on account of this that I have gained such wealth."

The guest asked, "Would you show me the vase and something which it has put forth?"

He immediately brought out the vase. From within the vase, he drew forth all manner of objects. Then, in prideful carelessness, he began to dance about on the top of the vase. The vase was immediately shattered. At the very same time, all of the different sorts of things which it had produced all simultaneously disappeared.

持戒之人亦复如是。种种
妙乐无愿不得。若人破戒
憍泆[2]自恣亦如彼人破瓶失
[3]物。复次持戒之人名称之
香。今世后世[4]周满天上及
在人中。复次持戒之人。人
所乐施不惜财物。不修世利
而无所乏得生天上。十方佛
前入三乘道而得解脱。唯种
种邪见。持戒后无所得。复
次若人虽不出家。但能修行
戒法。亦得生天。若人持戒
清净[5]行禅智慧。欲求度脱
老病死苦此愿必得。持戒之
人虽无兵仗众恶不加。持戒
之财无能夺者。持戒亲亲虽
死不离。持戒庄严胜于七
宝。以是之故。当护于戒如
护身命如爱宝物。

持戒之人亦復如是。種種
妙樂無願不得。若人破戒
憍泆[2]自恣亦如彼人破瓶失
[3]物。復次持戒之人名稱之
香。今世後世[4]周滿天上及
在人中。復次持戒之人。人
所樂施不惜財物。不修世利
而無所乏得生天上。十方佛
前入三乘道而得解脫。唯種
種邪見。持戒後無所得。復
次若人雖不出家。但能修行
戒法。亦得生天。若人持戒
清淨[5]行禪智慧。欲求度脫
老病死苦此願必得。持戒
之人雖無兵仗眾惡不加。持
戒之財無能奪者。持戒親親
雖死不離。持戒莊嚴勝於七
寶。以是之故。當護於戒如
護身命如愛寶物。

简体字　　　　　　　　　正體字

Conclusion

One who upholds the precepts is just like this. He receives all manner of marvelous bliss and there is no wish which he does not realize. If, however, a person breaks the precepts—if he becomes pridefully careless and gives free reign to willfulness—he will become just like this man who broke the vase and lost everything.

Amplifying Discussion on the Good Fortune of the Morally Virtuous

Furthermore, the fragrance of the name of the person who upholds the precepts pervades both the heavens and the human realm in this and later lives. Additionally, the person who upholds the precepts is one to whom people enjoy making gifts, not stinting in giving even their valuable possessions. He does not cultivate worldly profit and yet there is nothing with which he is inadequately supplied. He succeeds in being born in the heavens. He enters the way of the Three Vehicles in the presence of the Buddhas of the ten directions and so achieves liberation. It is only in a case where all manner of erroneous views figure in one's upholding of precepts that there might be nothing gained later.

Then again, although a person may not have left the home life, if he is able only to cultivate and practice the dharma of the precepts, he too will succeed in being reborn in the heavens. If a person is pure in his upholding of the precepts while also cultivating dhyāna and wisdom, and if he seeks thereby to cross himself over to liberation from the suffering of aging, sickness, and death, this wish will certainly be realized. Although a person who upholds the precepts may not have the protection of military weapons, still, awful events will not befall him.

The wealth of upholding precepts is such that none can steal it away. The upholding of precepts is the most intimate of intimates. Although one dies, one is still not separated from it. The adornment furnished by the upholding of precepts is superior to that of the seven precious things. For these reasons one should be protective of the precepts just as one is protective of one's own body and life and just as one cherishes precious things.

复次假令后世无罪。不为善人所诃怨家所嫉。尚不应故夺他命。何以故。善相之人所不应行。何况[17]两世有罪弊恶果报。复次杀为罪中之重。何以故人有死急不惜重宝。但以活命为先。譬如贾客[18]入海采宝。垂出大海其船卒坏珍宝失尽。而自喜庆举手而言。几失大宝。众人怪言。汝失财物裸形得脱。云何喜言几失大宝。答言。一切宝中人命第一。人为命故求财。不为财故求命。以是故。佛说十不善道中杀[19]罪最在初。五戒中亦最在初。若人种种修诸福德。而无不杀生戒则无所益。何以故。虽在富贵处生势力豪强。而无寿命谁受此乐。以是故知。诸馀罪中杀罪最重。诸功德中不杀第一。世间中

復次假令後世無罪。不為善人所訶怨家所嫉。尚不應故奪他命。何以故。善相之人所不應行。何況[17]兩世有罪弊惡果報。復次殺為罪中之重。何以故人有死急不惜重寶。但以活命為先。譬如賈客[18]入海採寶。垂出大海其船卒壞珍寶失盡。而自喜慶舉手而言。幾失大寶。眾人怪言。汝失財物裸形得脫。云何喜言幾失大寶。答言。一切寶中人命第一。人為命故求財。不為財故求命。以是故。佛說十不善道中殺[19]罪最在初。五戒中亦最在初。若人種種修諸福德。而無不殺生戒則無所益。何以故。雖在富貴處生勢力豪強。而無壽命誰受此樂。以是故知。諸餘罪中殺罪最重。諸功德中不殺第一。世間中

简体字

正體字

The Merchant Who Lost All but the Most Precious Jewel

Nāgārjuna's Preamble: Contemplations to Restrain Killing

Then again, even if one were able to cause there to be no karmic retributions in later lives, no denunciation by good people, and no detestation by enemies, still, one should not deliberately take another's life. Why? This is a thing which should not be done by those who are good. How much the more is this the case where, in both this life and the next, one encounters the resulting retribution arising from the baseness and evil of one's own offenses.

Furthermore, killing constitutes the most serious of offenses. Why? When a person encounters a life-threatening situation, he will not be sparing of even the most valuable treasures. He takes simply being able to survive as what is primary.

Story: The Merchant Who Lost All but the Most Precious of Jewels

This is exemplified by the case of the merchant who went to sea to gather jewels. When he had just about gotten back from the great sea, his boat suddenly broke apart and the precious jewels were all lost. And yet, he was overjoyed and exultant, throwing up his hands and exclaiming, "I almost lost a great jewel!"

Everyone thought this strange and said, "You lost all your valuable possessions and escaped without even any clothes on your back. How can you joyfully exclaim, "I almost lost a great jewel"?

He replied by saying, "Among all the jewels, a person's life is foremost. It is for the sake of their lives that people seek wealth. It is not that they seek to live for the sake of wealth."

Conclusion: How Killing is the Worst and Not Killing is Finest

It is for this reason that the Buddha said that among the ten bad karmic actions, the offense of killing is listed first. It is also the first among the five precepts. Even if a person cultivates all sorts of merit, if he still fails to uphold the precept against taking life, there is nothing to be gained from it. Why? Although one may be born into a place of blessings and nobility while also being possessed of strength and the power of an aristocratic background, if, [as retribution for killing], his future lives are not long, who would be able to experience this bliss?

For these reasons, one knows that, among all of the offenses, the offense of killing is the most serious and, among all of the meritorious practices, refraining from killing is foremost. In the world, it

惜命为第一。何以知之。一切世人甘受刑罚[20]刑残[*]考掠以护寿命。	惜命為第一。何以知之。一切世人甘受刑罰[20]刑殘[*]考掠以護壽命。
简体字	正體字

is the preserving of one's own life which is the primary concern. How do we know this? Every person in the world would agree to undergo the physical cruelty of corporeal punishment, including even beating and flogging, in order to spare his own life.

问曰。不侵我者杀心可息。
若为侵害强夺逼迫。是当云
何。答曰。应当量其轻重。
若人杀己先自思惟。 [26]全
戒利重[*]全身为重。破戒为
失丧身为失。如是思惟已。
知持戒为重[*]全身为轻。若
苟免[*]全身身何所得。是身
名为老病死薮。必当坏败。
若为持戒失身其利甚重。又
复思惟。我前后失身世世无
数。或作恶贼禽兽之身。但
为财利诸不善事。今乃得为
持净戒故。不惜此身舍命持
戒。胜于毁禁[*]全身。百千
万[1]倍不[2]可为喻。如是定
心应当舍身。以护净戒。如
一须陀洹人。生屠杀家年向
成人。应当修其家业而不肯
杀生。父母与刀并一口羊闭
着屋中。而语之言。若不杀
羊。不令汝出

問曰。不侵我者殺心可息。
若為侵害強奪逼迫。是當云
何。答曰。應當量其輕重。
若人殺己先自思惟。 [26]全
戒利重[*]全身為重。破戒為
失喪身為失。如是思惟已。
知持戒為重[*]全身為輕。若
苟免[*]全身身何所得。是身
名為老病死藪。必當壞敗。
若為持戒失身其利甚重。又
復思惟。我前後失身世世無
數。或作惡賊禽獸之身。但
為財利諸不善事。今乃得為
持淨戒故。不惜此身捨命持
戒。勝於毀禁[*]全身。百千
萬[1]倍不[2]可為喻。如是定
心應當捨身。以護淨戒。如
一須陀洹人。生屠殺家年向
成人。應當修其家業而不肯
殺生。父母與刀并一口羊閉
著屋中。而語之言。若不殺
羊。不令汝出

简体字　　　　　　　　　　　正體字

Story: The Butcher's Son Refuses to Kill

Nāgārjuna's Preamble: The Primacy of the Precepts

Question: If it is not a case of my being attacked, then the thought of killing may be put to rest. If, however, one has been attacked, overcome by force, and is then being coerced by imminent peril, what should one do then?

Reply: One should weigh the relative gravity of the alternatives. If someone is about to take one's life, one should first consider whether the benefit from preserving the precept is more important or whether the benefit from preserving one's physical life is more important and whether breaking the precept constitutes a loss or whether physical demise constitutes a loss.

After having reflected in this manner, one realizes that maintaining the precept is momentous and that preserving one's physical life is a minor matter. If, in avoiding peril, one is able only to succeed in preserving one's body, then what advantage is gained with the body? This body is the swamp of senescence, disease and death. It will inevitably deteriorate and decay. If, however, it is for the sake of upholding the precept that one loses one's body, the benefit of it is extremely consequential.

Furthermore, one should consider thus: "From the past on up to the present, I have lost my life an innumerable number of times. At times, I have incarnated as a malevolent brigand, as a bird, or as a beast where I have lived merely for the sake of wealth or profit, or else have engaged in all manner of unworthy pursuits.

"Now I have encountered a situation where it might be for the sake of preserving the precepts of purity. To not be stinting of this body and to sacrifice my life to uphold the precepts would be a billion times better than—and in fact incomparable to—merely safeguarding my body at the expense of violating the prohibitions." In this manner, one decides that one should forsake the body in order to protect the integrity of the pure precepts.

Story: The Butcher's Son Refuses to Kill

For example, there once was a man, a *srota-āpanna*,[2] who had been reborn into the family of a butcher. He had grown to the threshold of adulthood. Although he was expected to pursue his household occupation, he was unwilling to kill animals. His father and mother gave him a knife and shut him up in a room with a sheep, telling him, "If you do not kill the sheep, we will not allow you to come

简体字	正體字
得见日月生活饮食。儿自思惟言。我若杀此一羊。便当终为此业。岂以身故为此大罪。便以刀自杀。父母开户见。羊在一面立儿已命绝。当自杀时即生天上。若如此者是为不惜寿命[*]全护净戒。	得見日月生活飲食。兒自思惟言。我若殺此一羊。便當終為此業。豈以身故為此大罪。便以刀自殺。父母開戶見。羊在一面立兒已命絕。當自殺時即生天上。若如此者是為不惜壽命[*]全護淨戒。

out and see the sun or the moon, or to have the food and drink to survive."

The son thought to himself, "If I kill this sheep, then I will be compelled to pursue this occupation my entire life. How could I commit this great crime simply for the sake of this body?" Then he took up the knife and killed himself. The father and mother opened the door to look. The sheep was standing to one side whereas the son was laying there, already deceased.[2]

At that time, when he killed himself, he was reborn in the heavens. If one is like this, then this amounts to not sparing [even one's own] life in safeguarding the integrity of the pure precepts.

Notes

1. A *srota-āpanna* is a "stream-enterer," or "first-stage arhat."

2. One should understand that taking one's own life is a matter not to be taken lightly. For most of us, it would involve psychically depressed circumstances attended by deeply-afflicted and intensely emotional influences. These are conditions which tend to conduce to less fortunate rebirth circumstances. The situation of the *srota-āpanna* was quite different: Because he was a "stream-enterer," he had already gained the Path at a level where his liberation was guaranteed. He had already moved beyond being affected significantly by the afflictions and he was no longer subject to falling into lower states of rebirth. Because most of us do not enjoy such spiritually-advanced circumstances, it would be better for us to forego taking our own lives while also refusing to kill the sheep.

问曰。妄语有何等罪。答曰。妄语之人。先自诳身然后诳人。以实为虚以虚为实。虚实颠倒不受善法。譬如覆瓶水不得入。妄语之人心无惭愧。闭塞天道涅盘之门。观知此罪。是故不作。复次观知实语其利甚广。实语之利自从己出甚为易得。是为一切出家[5]人[6]力。如是功德居家出家人共有此利。善人之相。复次实语之人其心端直。其心端直易得免苦。譬如稠林曳木直者易出。问曰。若妄语有如是罪。人何以故妄语。答曰。有人愚痴少智。遭事苦厄妄语求脱不知事发。今世得罪不知后世有大罪报。复有人虽知妄语罪。悭贪瞋恚愚痴多故而作妄语。复有人虽不贪恚。而妄证人罪心谓实尔。死堕地狱

问曰。妄語有何等罪。答曰。妄語之人。先自誑身然後誑人。以實為虛以虛為實。虛實顛倒不受善法。譬如覆瓶水不得入。妄語之人心無慚愧。閉塞天道涅槃之門。觀知此罪。是故不作。復次觀知實語其利甚廣。實語之利自從己出甚為易得。是為一切出家[5]人[6]力。如是功德居家出家人共有此利。善人之相。復次實語之人其心端直。其心端直易得免苦。譬如稠林曳木直者易出。問曰。若妄語有如是罪。人何以故妄語。答曰。有人愚癡少智。遭事苦厄妄語求脫不知事發。今世得罪不知後世有大罪報。復有人雖知妄語罪。慳貪瞋恚愚癡多故而作妄語。復有人雖不貪恚。而妄證人罪心謂實爾。死墮地獄

简体字　　　　正體字

Kokālika's Slanderous Offense

Nāgārjuna's Preamble: The Inherent Faults in False Speech

Question: What faults are there in false speech?

Response: The person who commits false speech first deceives himself and later deceives others. He takes that which is real as false and that which is false as real. He turns false and real upside down and does not accept good dharmas. He is comparable to an inverted vase into which water cannot flow.

The mind of a person who commits false speech is devoid of a sense of shame or a sense of blame. He blocks off the way to the heavens and the gate to nirvāṇa. One contemplates and realizes the existence of these disadvantages and therefore refrains from engaging in it.

Additionally, one contemplates and realizes that the benefits of true speech are extremely vast. The benefits of true speech naturally come forth from one's self and are extremely easily gained. This is the power of all who have left the home life. Both householders and those who have left the home life possess the benefits of this sort of merit. It is the mark of a good person.

Moreover, the mind of a person whose words are true is correct and straight. Because his mind is correct and straight, it is easy for him to succeed in avoiding suffering. It is just as when pulling forth logs from a dense forest. The straight ones come forth easily.

Question: If false speech entails disadvantages such as these, why then do people engage in false speech?

Response: There are those who are foolish and deficient in wisdom who, when they encounter anguishing difficulties, tell lies as a stratagem to escape them. They do not recognize the manner in which matters unfold. When they commit a transgression in this present life, they do not realize that in a later life there will be an immense retribution resulting from that transgression.

Then again, there are people who, although they are aware of the fact that false speech entails a transgression, nonetheless engage in the telling of lies due to an abundance of greed, hatred or delusion.

Story: Kokālika's Slanderous Offense

Additionally, there are people who, although they are not afflicted with greed or hatred, nonetheless falsely testify to another man's transgression because, in their own minds, they are of the opinion that this is truly the case. When they die, they fall into the hells in

如提婆达多弟子俱伽离。常求舍利弗目揵连过失。是时二人夏安居竟。游行诸国值天大雨。到陶作家宿盛陶器舍。此舍中先有一女人在暗中宿。二人不知。此女人其夜梦失不净。晨朝趣水澡[7]洗。是时俱伽离偶行见之。俱伽离能相知人交会情状。而不知梦与不梦。是时俱伽离顾语弟子。此女人昨夜与人情通。即问女人汝在何处卧。答言。我在陶师屋中寄宿。又问共谁。答言。二比丘。是时二人从屋中出。俱伽离见已。又以相验之。意谓二人必为不净。先怀嫉妒既见此事。遍诸城邑聚落告之。次到[8]只洹唱此恶声。于是中间梵天王来欲见佛。佛入静室寂然三昧。诸比丘众亦各闭房三昧。皆不可觉。即自思惟。我[9]故来见佛。佛入三昧且欲还去。即复念言。佛从定起亦将不久。于是小住。到俱伽离房前。扣其户而言。俱伽离俱伽离。舍利弗目揵连心

如提婆達多弟子俱伽離。常求舍利弗目揵連過失。是時二人夏安居竟。遊行諸國值天大雨。到陶作家宿盛陶器舍。此舍中先有一女人在闇中宿。二人不知。此女人其夜夢失不淨。晨朝趣水澡[7]洗。是時俱伽離偶行見之。俱伽離能相知人交會情狀。而不知夢與不夢。是時俱伽離顧語弟子。此女人昨夜與人情通。即問女人汝在何處臥。答言。我在陶師屋中寄宿。又問共誰。答言。二比丘。是時二人從屋中出。俱伽離見已。又以相驗之。意謂二人必為不淨。先懷嫉妒既見此事。遍諸城邑聚落告之。次到[8]祇洹唱此惡聲。於是中間梵天王來欲見佛。佛入靜室寂然三昧。諸比丘眾亦各閉房三昧。皆不可覺。即自思惟。我[9]故來見佛。佛入三昧且欲還去。即復念言。佛從定起亦將不久。於是小住。到俱伽離房前。扣其戶而言。俱伽離俱伽離。舍利弗目揵連心

简体字　　　　　　　　　　　正體字

the same manner as did Kokālika, a disciple of Devadatta. He constantly sought to find fault with Śāriputra and Maudgalyāyana. At that time, those two men had just come to the end of the summer retreat and so they proceeded to travel about and journey to the various states. Having encountered a great rain storm, they arrived at the home of a potter where they spent the night in a building full of pots.

Before they arrived, unbeknownst to these two, a woman had already gone in and fallen asleep in a darkened part of the building. That night, this woman had an orgasm in her dreams. In the early morning, she went to get water with which to bathe. At this time Kokālika happened to be walking by and took notice of her. Kokālika possessed the ability to know about a person's sex life by observing the countenance. However, he couldn't deduce whether the activity had taken place in a dream state or while awake.

At this time, Kokālika told a disciple, "This woman had sex with someone last night." Then he asked the woman, "Where did you spend the night?"

She replied, "I spent the night in the pottery building."

Next, he asked, "Together with whom?"

She replied, "With a couple of bhikshus." At this time, the two men happened to come out from within the building. After Kokālika had noticed them, he examined their countenances and became convinced in his own mind that the two men were definitely not pure. He had formerly nurtured jealousy toward them. Having now observed this situation, he then proceeded to spread it all about in all of the cities, villages and hamlets. Next, he went to the Jeta Grove where he loudly proclaimed this evil news.

At this time, Brahmā, the King of the Gods, had come wishing to have an audience with the Buddha. The Buddha had entered into a silent room where he was very still, immersed in samādhi. All of the bhikshus, too, had each closed their doors and entered into samādhi. None of them could be roused. Then he thought to himself, "I originally came to see the Buddha. The Buddha has entered samādhi."

He was about to return when he had another thought, "It won't be long before the Buddha arises from meditative absorption. I'll wait here for a little while longer." He then went to the entrance to Kokālika's room, knocked on the door, and then called out, "Kokālika! Kokālika! The minds of Śāriputra and Maudgalyāyana

净柔软。汝莫谤之而长夜受
苦。俱伽离问言。汝是何
人。答言。我是梵天王。问
言。佛说汝得阿那含道。汝
何以故来。梵王心念而说偈
言。无量法欲量。不应以相
取。无量法欲量。是[10]野
人覆没。[0157b29]　说[11]此偈
已。到佛所具说其[12]事。
佛言。善哉善哉。快说此
偈。尔时世尊复说此偈。无
量法欲量。不应以相取。
无量法欲量。是[*]野人覆
没。[0157c04]　梵天王听佛说
已。忽然不现即还天上。尔
时俱迦离到佛所。头面礼佛
足却住一面。佛告俱伽离。
舍利弗目揵连心净柔软。汝
莫谤之而长夜受苦。俱伽离
白佛言。我于佛语不敢不
信。但自目见了了。定知二
人实行不净。佛如是三呵。
俱伽离亦三不受。即从坐起
而去。还其房中举身生疮。
始如芥子渐大如豆如枣如[13]
奈。转大如苽。翕然烂坏

净柔软。
简体字

淨柔軟。汝莫謗之而長夜受
苦。俱伽離問言。汝是何
人。答言。我是梵天王。問
言。佛說汝得阿那含道。汝
何以故來。梵王心念而說偈
言。無量法欲量。不應以相
取。無量法欲量。是[10]野
人覆沒。[0157b29]　說[11]此偈
已。到佛所具說其[12]事。
佛言。善哉善哉。快說此
偈。爾時世尊復說此偈。無
量法欲量。不應以相取。
無量法欲量。是[*]野人覆
沒。[0157c04]　梵天王聽佛說
已。忽然不現即還天上。爾
時俱迦離到佛所。頭面禮佛
足却住一面。佛告俱伽離。
舍利弗目揵連心淨柔軟。汝
莫謗之而長夜受苦。俱伽離
白佛言。我於佛語不敢不
信。但自目見了了。定知二
人實行不淨。佛如是三呵。
俱伽離亦三不受。即從坐起
而去。還其房中舉身生瘡。
始如芥子漸大如豆如棗如[13]
奈。轉大如苽。翕然爛壞

正體字

are pure and pliant. Do not slander them or you will spend the long night [of your future lifetimes] undergoing suffering."

Kokālika asked, "Who are you?"

He replied, "I am Brahmā, the King of the Gods."

He asked, "The Buddha has said that you have realized the path of the *anāgāmin* (third-stage arhat, lit. "never-returner"). Why then have you returned here?"

Brahmā, the King of the Gods, thought for a moment and then uttered a verse, saying:

> In wishing to fathom immeasurable dharmas,
> One shouldn't then seize on what is mere appearance.
> In wishing to fathom immeasurable dharmas,
> A boor such as this then will capsize and drown.

After he had spoken this verse, he went to where the Buddha was and set forth the entire matter. The Buddha said, "Good indeed. Good indeed. This verse should be proclaimed straightaway." At that time, the Bhagavān himself repeated the verse:

> In wishing to fathom immeasurable dharmas,
> One shouldn't then seize on what is mere appearance.
> In wishing to fathom immeasurable dharmas,
> A boor such as this then will capsize and drown.

After Brahmā, the King of the Gods, had heard the Buddha proclaim this, he suddenly disappeared and immediately returned to the heavens.

At that time, Kokālika went to where the Buddha was, prostrated in reverence before the Buddha, and then stood off to one side. The Buddha told Kokālika, "The minds of Śāriputra and Maudgalyāyana are pure and pliant. Do not slander them or you will spend the long night [of future lifetimes] undergoing suffering."

Kokālika addressed the Buddha, saying, "I don't dare disbelieve the words of the Buddha. However, I saw this clearly with my own eyes. I know definitely that these two men have actually committed impure acts."

The Buddha rebuked him in this way three times and Kokālika three times refused to accept it. He then got up from his place, left, and then returned to his room. His entire body then broke out in sores. At first they were the size of sesame seeds. Gradually then, they became as big as beans, as big as dates, as big as mangoes, and finally, as big as melons. Then, they all simultaneously broke open,

如大火烧。叫唤[14]嗥哭其夜
即死。入大莲华地[15]狱。有
一梵[16]天夜来白佛。俱伽离
已死复有一梵天言。堕大莲
华地狱。其夜过已佛命僧集
而告之言。汝等欲知俱伽离
所堕地狱寿命长短不。诸比
丘言。愿乐欲闻。佛言。有
六十斛胡麻。有人过百岁取
一胡麻。如是至尽。阿浮陀
地狱中寿故未尽。二十阿浮
陀地狱中寿。为一尼罗浮陀
地狱中寿。如二十尼罗浮陀
地狱中寿为一[17]阿罗逻地狱
中寿。二十[*]阿罗逻地狱中
寿。为一[*]阿婆婆地狱中寿。
二十[*]阿婆婆地狱中寿。为一
休休地狱中寿。二十休休地
狱中寿。为一沤波罗地狱中
寿。二十沤波罗地狱中寿。
为一分陀梨迦地狱中寿。二
十分陀梨迦地狱中寿。为一
摩呵波头摩地狱中寿。俱伽
离堕是摩呵波头摩地狱中。
出其大舌以[18]百钉钉之。五
百具犁耕之。尔时世尊说此
偈言。[1]夫士之生。斧在口
中。所以斩身。由其恶言。
应呵而赞。应赞而呵。口集
诸恶终不见乐。心口业生恶
堕尼罗浮狱。具满百千世受
诸[2]毒苦痛。若生阿浮陀具满
三[3]十六

如大火燒。叫喚[14]嗥哭其夜
即死。入大蓮華地[15]獄。有
一梵[16]天夜來白佛。俱伽離
已死復有一梵天言。墮大蓮
華地獄。其夜過已佛命僧集
而告之言。汝等欲知俱伽離
所墮地獄壽命長短不。諸比
丘言。願樂欲聞。佛言。有
六十斛胡麻。有人過百歲取
一胡麻。如是至盡。阿浮陀
地獄中壽故未盡。二十阿浮
陀地獄中壽。為一尼羅浮陀
地獄中壽。如二十尼羅浮陀
地獄中壽為一[17]阿羅邏地獄
中壽。二十[*]阿羅邏地獄中
壽。為一[*]阿婆婆地獄中壽。
二十[*]阿婆婆地獄中壽。為一
休休地獄中壽。二十休休地
獄中壽。為一漚波羅地獄中
壽。二十漚波羅地獄中壽。
為一分陀梨迦地獄中壽。二
十分陀梨迦地獄中壽。為一
摩呵波頭摩地獄中壽。俱伽
離墮是摩呵波頭摩地獄中。
出其大舌以[18]百釘釘之。五
百具犁耕之。爾時世尊說此
偈言。[1]夫士之生。斧在口
中。所以斬身。由其惡言。
應呵而讚。應讚而呵。口集
諸惡終不見樂。心口業生惡
墮尼羅浮獄。具滿百千世受
諸[2]毒苦痛。若生阿浮陀具滿
三[3]十六

简体字   正體字

leaving him looking as if he had been burned by a great fire. He wailed and wept. Then, that night, he died and entered the Great Lotus Blossom Hell. A Brahma Heaven god came and informed the Buddha, "Kokālika has already died."

Another Brahma Heaven god said, "He has fallen into the Great Lotus Blossom Hell." After that night had passed, the Buddha ordered the Sangha to assemble, and then asked, "Do you all wish to know the length of the life in that hell into which Kokālika has fallen?"

The Bhikshus replied, "Pray, please tell us. We wish to hear it."

The Buddha said, "It is as if there were sixty bushels of sesame seeds and then a man came along only once every hundred years and took away but a single sesame seed. If this went on until all of the sesame seeds were gone, the lifespan endured in the Arbuda Hells would still not have come to an end. Twenty Arbuda Hell lifespans equal the lifespan in the Nirarbuda Hells. Twenty Nirarbuda Hell lifespans equal the lifespan in the Aṭaṭa Hells. Twenty Aṭaṭa Hell lifespans equal the lifespan in the Hahava Hells. Twenty Hahava Hell lifespans equal the lifespan in the Huhuva Hells. Twenty Huhuva Hell lifespans equal the lifespan in the Utpala Hells. Twenty Utpala Hell lifespans equal the lifespan in the Puṇḍarīka Hells. Twenty Puṇḍarīka Hell lifespans equal the lifespan in the Mahāpadma Hells. Kokālika has fallen into these Mahāpadma Hells. His tongue is drawn forth and nailed down with a hundred nails where it is plowed by five hundred plows." At that time the Bhagavān set forth this verse, saying:

When a person takes rebirth here,
Hatchets are plunged into his mouth.
The reason for the body's being hacked
Is found in his utterance of evil words.

What should be criticized, he nonetheless has praised.
What should be praised, he nonetheless has criticized.
The mouth thus piles up all manner of evil deeds,
With the result that one is never able to experience any bliss.

The actions of mind and mouth generate evil.
One plummets then into the Nirarbuda Hells.
For a term of fully a hundred thousand lifetimes,
He endures there all manner of excruciating pain.

When one takes rebirth into the Arbuda Hells,
He is bound to endure it for a full thirty-six lives,

別更有[4]五世。皆受诸苦
毒。心依邪见。破贤圣
语。如竹生实。自毁其[5]
形。[0158a10]　如是等心生疑
谤。遂至决定亦是妄语。妄
语人乃至佛语而不信受。受
罪如是。以是故不应妄语。

別更有[4]五世。皆受諸苦
毒。心依邪見。破賢聖
語。如竹生實。自毀其[5]
形。[0158a10]　如是等心生疑
謗。遂至決定亦是妄語。妄
語人乃至佛語而不信受。受
罪如是。以是故不應妄語。

简体字　　　　　　　　　正體字

And then suffer for yet another additional five lives,
Where in all of them he suffers all manner of suffering anguish.

The mind comes to rely upon erroneous views,
And speaks then in a way destroying the Worthies and Āryas.
In this, it is like that bamboo which, in putting forth its fruit,
Thereby brings on the destruction of its very own physical form.

Conclusion

In just such a manner, the mind generates doubts and slanders. Once they have become rigidly established, they also become manifest in false speech. Thus a person who courses in false speech refuses to believe in or accept even the words of the Buddha. He becomes bound then to undergo punishments just such as these. It is for these reasons that one must refrain from engaging in false speech.

复次如佛子罗睺罗。其年幼稚未知慎口。人来问之。世尊在不。诡言不在。若不在时。人问罗睺罗。世尊在不。诡言佛在。有人语佛。佛语罗睺罗。澡[6]盘取水与吾洗足。洗足已。语罗睺罗。覆此澡[*]盘。如勅即覆。佛言。以水注之。注已问言。水入中不。答言。不入。佛告罗睺罗。无惭愧人妄语覆心道法不入。亦复如是。如佛说。妄语有十罪。何等为十。一者口气臭。二者善神远之非人得便。三者虽有实语人不信受。四者智人[7]语议常不参豫。五者常被诽谤。丑恶之声周闻天下。六者人所不敬。虽有教勅人不承用。七者常多忧愁。八者种诽谤业因缘。九者身坏命终当堕地狱。十者若出为人常被诽谤。

復次如佛子羅睺羅。其年幼稚未知慎口。人來問之。世尊在不。詭言不在。若不在時。人問羅睺羅。世尊在不。詭言佛在。有人語佛。佛語羅睺羅。澡[6]槃取水與吾洗足。洗足已。語羅睺羅。覆此澡[*]槃。如勅即覆。佛言。以水注之。注已問言。水入中不。答言。不入。佛告羅睺羅。無慚愧人妄語覆心道法不入。亦復如是。如佛說。妄語有十罪。何等為十。一者口氣臭。二者善神遠之非人得便。三者雖有實語人不信受。四者智人[7]語議常不參豫。五者常被誹謗。醜惡之聲周聞天下。六者人所不敬。雖有教勅人不承用。七者常多憂愁。八者種誹謗業因緣。九者身壞命終當墮地獄。十者若出為人常被誹謗。

简体字　　　　　　　正體字

Rāhula's Lesson About False Speech

Then again, a case in point is that of the Buddha's son Rāhula who, being in years but a child, had still not yet understood the importance of taking care with his words. When people would come and ask him, "Is the Bhagavān here, or not?" he would deceive them by saying, "He's not here."

If in fact he was not present, when others would ask Rāhula, "Is the Bhagavān here or not?" he would deceive them by saying, "The Buddha is here."

Someone informed the Buddha about this. The Buddha then told Rāhula, "Get a wash basin, fill it with water, and wash my feet for me." After his feet had been washed, he instructed Rāhula, "Cover this wash basin."

Then, obeying the command, he immediately covered it. The Buddha then said, "Take water and pour it in." After it had been poured, he asked, "Did the water go in or not?"

Rāhula replied, "It did not go in."

The Buddha told Rāhula, "The lies of a person who has no sense of shame or blame cover over his mind so that, in just the same manner, the Dharma of the Path does not enter into it."

Conclusion: Ten Karmic Effects of False Speech

As stated by the Buddha, false speech has ten karmic retributions. What are the ten?

The first is that the breath always smells bad.

The second is that the good spirits depart far from him, whereas the non-humans get their way with him.

The third is that, although he may have instances in which he speaks the truth, people nonetheless do not believe or accept it.

The fourth is that he can never take part in discussions with those who are wise.

The fifth is that he is always slandered and his ugly and foul reputation is heard throughout the land.

The sixth is that he is not respected by others. Although he may issue instructions and orders, people do not accept or follow them.

The seventh is that he is always afflicted with much worry.

The eighth is that he plants the karmic causes and conditions for being slandered.

The ninth is that when his body deteriorates and his life comes to an end, he will then fall into the hells.

The tenth is that if he emerges and becomes a person, he is always slandered.

不取不舍乃应行法。是名
为难。若出家离俗绝诸[2]纷
乱。一向专心行道为易

[0161a06]　　复次居家愦閙多事
多务。结使之根众恶之府。
是为甚难。若出家者。譬如
有人出在空野无人之处而一
其心。无思无虑内想既除。
外事亦去。如偈说

闲坐林树间　寂然灭众恶
恬澹得一心　斯乐非天乐
人求富贵利　名衣好床褥
斯乐非安隐　求利无厌足
纳衣行乞食　动止心常一
自以智慧眼　观知诸法实
种种法门中　皆以等观入
解慧心寂然　三界无能及

[0161a18] 以是故知出家修戒行
道为易。复次出家修戒。得
无量善律仪。一切具足满。
以是故

簡体字

不取不捨乃應行法。是名
為難。若出家離俗絕諸[2]紛
亂。一向專心行道為易

[0161a06]　　復次居家愦閙多事
多務。結使之根眾惡之府。
是為甚難。若出家者。譬如
有人出在空野無人之處而一
其心。無思無慮內想既除。
外事亦去。如偈說

閑坐林樹間　寂然滅眾惡
恬澹得一心　斯樂非天樂
人求富貴利　名衣好床褥
斯樂非安隱　求利無厭足
納衣行乞食　動止心常一
自以智慧眼　觀知諸法實
種種法門中　皆以等觀入
解慧心寂然　三界無能及

[0161a18] 以是故知出家修戒行
道為易。復次出家修戒。得
無量善律儀。一切具足滿。
以是故

正體字

Three Stories on Lay Versus Monastic Life

Nāgārjuna's Preamble: Lay Life Versus Monasticism

If one neither seizes upon anything nor relinquishes anything, it is then and only then that one acts in correspondence with the practice of Dharma. This is renowned for its difficulty. However, if one leaves the home life, separates from the world of the layperson, cuts off all of the complexity and chaos, and then, with singular purpose, focuses the mind, then cultivating the Path becomes easy.

Moreover, the befuddlement and boisterousness of the householder's life involves many endeavors and much responsibility. It is the root of the fetters and the repository of the manifold ills. This is an extremely difficult situation.

If, however, one leaves the home life, it is analogous to a person being able to go forth into the unpopulated empty wilderness to unify his mind. He is then able to become free of immersion in ideation and mental discursion. Once the inward thoughts have been gotten rid of, the outward matters depart as well. This is as described in a verse:

Leisurely sitting within the forest,
In a state of stillness, one extinguishes the manifold ills.
Calmly and contentedly, one gains unity of mind.
This sort of bliss is not the bliss of the heavens.

People seek after the benefit of wealth and noble status,
For fame, robes, and for fine furnishings.
This sort of pleasure is not peaceful or secure.
One seeks after benefit, but finds no satiation.

The one of patchwork robes travels about seeking alms,
Whether moving or still, his mind is always unified.
He spontaneously employs the eye of wisdom
To contemplate and know the reality of all dharmas.

Among all the different types of Dharma methods,
All are entered through equanimitous contemplation.
With understanding and wisdom, the mind abides in stillness.
Throughout the three realms, nothing is able to equal this.

For these reasons, one should know that, having left the home life, cultivating the precepts and practicing the Path become easy.

Additionally, if one leaves the home life and cultivates the precepts, one achieves the complete perfection of an incalculable number of aspects of good moral conduct. For these reasons, members

白衣等应[3]当出家受[4]具足
戒。复次佛法中出家法第一
难修。如阎浮呿提梵志问舍
利弗。于佛法中何者最难。
舍利弗答曰。出家为难。
又问。出家[5]有何等难。答
曰。出家乐法为难。既得乐
法复何者为难。修诸善法
难。以是故应出家。复次若
人出家时。魔王惊[6]愁言。
此人诸结使欲薄。必得涅盘
堕僧宝数中。复次佛法中出
家人。虽破[7]戒堕罪。罪毕
得解脱。如[8]优钵罗华比丘
尼本生经中说。佛在世时。
此比丘尼得六神通阿罗汉。
入贵人舍常赞出家法。语诸
贵人妇女言。姊妹可出家。
诸贵妇女言。我等少壮容色
盛美持戒为难。或当破戒。
比丘尼言。但出家破戒便
破。

简体字

白衣等應[3]當出家受[4]具足
戒。復次佛法中出家法第一
難修。如閻浮呿提梵志問舍
利弗。於佛法中何者最難。
舍利弗答曰。出家為難。
又問。出家[5]有何等難。答
曰。出家樂法為難。既得
樂法復何者為難。修諸善法
難。以是故應出家。復次若
人出家時。魔王驚[6]愁言。
此人諸結使欲薄。必得涅槃
墮僧寶數中。復次佛法中出
家人。雖破[7]戒墮罪。罪畢
得解脫。如[8]優鉢羅華比丘
尼本生經中說。佛在世時。
此比丘尼得六神通阿羅漢。
入貴人舍常讚出家法。語諸
貴人婦女言。姊妹可出家。
諸貴婦女言。我等少壯容色
盛美持戒為難。或當破戒。
比丘尼言。但出家破戒便
破。

正體字

of the lay community should leave the home life and take the complete precepts.

Story: Jambukhādaka's Questions to Śāriputra on Monasticism

Then again, within the Dharma of the Buddha, the particular dharma of leaving the home life is the one which is the most difficult to cultivate. This is as alluded to in the questions of the brahmacārin Jambukhādaka to Śāriputra, wherein he asked, "What is most difficult within the Buddha's Dharma?"

Śāriputra replied, "Leaving behind the home life is difficult."

He also asked, "What are the difficulties involved in leaving the home life?"

He replied, "To leave behind the home life and find bliss in Dharma is difficult."

"If one succeeds in finding bliss in Dharma, then what beyond this is difficult?"

"To cultivate all good dharmas is difficult."

For these reasons, one should leave behind the home life. Moreover, when one leaves behind the home life, the king of the demons becomes frightened and worried, saying, "The fetters of this man are about to become scant. He will certainly gain nirvāṇa and thus fall in among the members of the Sangha Jewel."

Story: The Bhikshuni Utpalavarṇā's Promotion of Monasticism

Also, although among those persons who have left the home life in the Dharma of the Buddha there are those who may happen to break the precepts and fall into offenses, when those offenses are done away with, they will then succeed in gaining liberation. This is as discussed in *The Sutra on the Jātaka of Bhikshuni Utpalavarṇā.*

When the Buddha was in the world, this bhikshuni gained the six superknowledges and arhatship. She made a practice of going into the households of the aristocracy where she constantly praised the tradition of leaving the home life. She spoke to the wives and daughters of the nobility, saying, "Sisters, you could leave behind the home life."

The aristocratic wives and daughters would reply, "We are young and strong. Our countenances and physical forms are full and beautiful. It would be difficult to uphold the precepts. It might happen that we would break the precepts."

The Bhikshuni replied, "Just go ahead and leave the home life, anyway. If it happens that you end up breaking the precepts, then so it is: You break them."

问言。破戒当堕地狱。云何
可破。答言。堕地狱便堕。
诸贵妇[9]女笑之言。地狱受
罪云何可堕。比丘尼言。我
自忆念本宿命。时作戏女着
种种衣服而说旧语。或时着
比丘尼衣以为戏笑。以是因
缘故。迦叶佛时作比丘尼。
自恃贵姓端[*]政。心生憍慢
而破禁戒。破戒罪故堕地狱
受种种罪。受罪毕竟值释迦
牟尼佛。出家得六神通阿罗
汉道。以是故知。出家受
戒。虽复破戒以戒因缘故。
得阿罗汉道。若但作恶无戒
因缘不得道也。我乃昔时世
世堕地狱。地狱出为恶人。
恶人死还入地狱都无所得。
今以此证知出家受戒。虽复
破戒以是因缘可得道果。复
次如佛在[10]只洹。有一醉婆
罗门。来到佛所

简体字

問言。破戒當墮地獄。云何
可破。答言。墮地獄便墮。
諸貴婦[9]女笑之言。地獄受
罪云何可墮。比丘尼言。我
自憶念本宿命。時作戲女著
種種衣服而說舊語。或時著
比丘尼衣以為戲笑。以是因
緣故。迦葉佛時作比丘尼。
自恃貴姓端[*]政。心生憍慢
而破禁戒。破戒罪故墮地獄
受種種罪。受罪畢竟值釋迦
牟尼佛。出家得六神通阿羅
漢道。以是故知。出家受
戒。雖復破戒以戒因緣故。
得阿羅漢道。若但作惡無戒
因緣不得道也。我乃昔時世
世墮地獄。地獄出為惡人。
惡人死還入地獄都無所得。
今以此證知出家受戒。雖復
破戒以是因緣可得道果。復
次如佛在[10]祇洹。有一醉婆
羅門。來到佛所

正體字

They responded, "If we break the precepts, we'll fall into the hells. How could it be conceivable that they might be broken?"

She replied, "If it happens that you end up falling into the hells, then you fall."

The wives and daughters of the nobility all laughed at this, saying, "When one falls into the hells, one undergoes punishments. How could one even contemplate a situation where one might fall?"

The Bhikshuni replied, "I recall that in a previous life I was an actress who put on all sorts of costumes and played traditional parts. There were times when I would put on the robes of a bhikshuni in order to amuse the audience. On account of this causal basis, at the time of Kāśyapa Buddha I was actually able to become a bhikshuni. However, on account of my aristocratic birth and beauty, I became arrogant and then broke the restrictive prohibitions. On account of the offenses of breaking the precepts, I fell into the hells wherein I underwent all manner of punishment as retribution.

"When I had finished undergoing retribution for those offenses, I was able to encounter Shakyamuni Buddha and leave the home life again, whereupon I gained the six superknowledges and the way of the arhat. For this reason, one should be aware that if one leaves home and takes the precepts, although one may happen to break the precepts, still, on account of the causal basis inhering in taking the precepts, one is bound to succeed in gaining the way of arhatship.

"However, if one merely does evil things, but yet does not have the causal basis of having taken the precepts, then one will not gain the Path. Thus, in the past, I have fallen into the hells in many lifetimes. Then, upon coming forth from the hells, I would become an evil person, and when this evil person died, I would go right back into the hells again. Thus, in every one of those instances, I gained nothing whatsoever as a result."

Now, on account of this, we can verify and thus realize that if one merely leaves home and takes the precepts, although one may eventually break the precepts, still, on account of this causal basis, one eventually becomes able to gain the fruits of the Path.

Story: An Inebriated Brahman Becomes a Monk

Then again, this is exemplified by that time when the Buddha dwelt in Jetavana and a drunken brahman came to the Buddha and

求作比丘。佛勅阿难与剃头着法衣。醉酒既醒惊怪己身忽为比丘即便走去。诸比丘问佛。何以听此醉婆罗门作比丘。佛言。此婆罗门无量劫中初无出家心。今因醉故暂发微心。以是因缘故 [11] 后当出家得道。如是种种因缘。出家之利功德无量。以是故白衣虽有五戒不如出家。

简体字

求作比丘。佛勅阿難與剃頭著法衣。醉酒既醒驚怪己身忽為比丘即便走去。諸比丘問佛。何以聽此醉婆羅門作比丘。佛言。此婆羅門無量劫中初無出家心。今因醉故暫發微心。以是因緣故 [11] 後當出家得道。如是種種因緣。出家之利功德無量。以是故白衣雖有五戒不如出家。

正體字

requested to become a bhikshu. The Buddha ordered Ānanda to administer tonsure and outfit the man in Dharma robes. When the brahman awoke from his inebriation, he was startled and amazed that he had suddenly turned into a bhikshu. He immediately ran off.

The other bhikshus then inquired of the Buddha, "Why did the Buddha permit this drunken brahman to become a bhikshu?"

The Buddha replied, "Even in innumerable eons, this brahman has never thought to leave the home life. Now, due to his inebriation, he briefly generated a feeble intention to do so. On account of this causal basis, he will later be able to leave behind the home life and succeed in gaining the Path."

Concluding Statement on Lay Life versus Monasticism

For causal reasons such as these, one can see that the benefits of leaving the home life involve incalculable merit. Hence, although the members of the lay community do possess the five precepts, they cannot be compared to leaving the home life.

[0162a08] 问曰。已知尸罗相。云何为尸罗波罗蜜。答曰。有人言。菩萨持戒宁自失身不毁小戒。是为尸罗波罗蜜。如[2]上苏陀苏摩王经中说。不惜身命以[3]全禁戒。如菩萨本身曾作大力毒龙。若众生在前。身力弱者眼视便死。身力强者气[4]往而死。是龙受一日戒。出家求静入林树间。思惟坐久疲懈而睡。龙法睡时形状如蛇。身有文章七宝杂色。猎者见之惊喜言曰。以此希有难得之皮。献上国王以为[5]服饰不亦宜乎。便以杖[6]按其头以刀剥其皮。龙自念言。我力如意。倾覆此国其如反掌。此人小物岂能困我。我今以持戒故不计此身当从佛语。于是自忍[7]眠目不视。闭气不息怜愍此人。为持戒故一心

[0162a08] 問曰。已知尸羅相。云何為尸羅波羅蜜。答曰。有人言。菩薩持戒寧自失身不毀小戒。是為尸羅波羅蜜。如[2]上蘇陀蘇摩王經中說。不惜身命以[3]全禁戒。如菩薩本身曾作大力毒龍。若眾生在前。身力弱者眼視便死。身力強者氣[4]往而死。是龍受一日戒。出家求靜入林樹間。思惟坐久疲懈而睡。龍法睡時形狀如蛇。身有文章七寶雜色。獵者見之驚喜言曰。以此希有難得之皮。獻上國王以為[5]服飾不亦宜乎。便以杖[6]按其頭以刀剝其皮。龍自念言。我力如意。傾覆此國其如反掌。此人小物豈能困我。我今以持戒故不計此身當從佛語。於是自忍[7]眠目不視。閉氣不息憐愍此人。為持戒故一心

简体字   正體字

Buddha's Dragon Life as the Perfection of Moral Virtue

Nāgārjuna's Preamble: Śīla Pāramitā Defined

Question: We are already aware of the characteristics of śīla. What is it that constitutes śīla pāramitā?

Response: There are those who say that when the bodhisattva upholds the precepts and would rather lose his physical life than damage minor precepts, it is this which constitutes śīla pāramitā. As described in the previously-cited Sutra of King Sutasoma, one does not spare even one's own physical life in order to preserve the integrity of the restrictive precepts.

Story: Buddha's Past Life as a Dragon

For example, in a former life the Bodhisattva was a greatly powerful poisonous dragon. Whenever any being came to stand before him, in the case of those who were physically weak, if he so much as gazed upon them, they would die on the spot. As for those who were physically strong, if he breathed on them, they would die.

This dragon had taken the one-day precepts. He left his dwelling seeking quietude and had gone into the forest. He had been sitting in contemplation for a long time, became tired and lax, and then had fallen asleep. It is the way of dragons that when they fall asleep their bodies become in appearance like a snake. His body had patterns on it which were composed of the various colors of the seven precious things.

Hunters noticed him and, both startled and delighted, said, "Wouldn't it be appropriate to take this skin, so rare and difficult to come by, and then offer it up to the King of our country that he might use it as an adornment for his robes?" They then held its head down with a staff and used a knife to strip away its skin.

The dragon thought to himself, "My strength is such that, were I only to wish it, turning this entire country upside down would be as easy as turning over one's hand. These people are but little things. How could they be able to put me in difficult straits? Because I am now upholding the precepts, I shall relinquish all regard for this body. I should just follow along with the instructions of the Buddha."

And so he remained patient while this was going on, kept his eyes as if asleep, and refrained from gazing upon them. He held his breath and, out of pity for these men, kept himself from breathing. For the sake of upholding the precepts, he single-mindedly endured

受剥不生悔意。既以失皮赤肉在地。时日大热宛转土中欲趣大水。见诸小虫来食其身。为持戒故不复敢动。自思惟言。今我此身以施诸虫。为佛道故今以肉施以充其身。后成佛时当以法施以益其心。如是誓已身乾命[8]绝。即生第二忉利天上。尔时毒龙释迦文佛是。[9]是时猎者提婆达等六师是也。诸小虫辈。释迦文佛初转法轮八万诸天得道者是。菩萨护戒不惜身命。决定不悔。其事如是。是名尸罗波罗蜜。复次菩萨持戒。为佛道故作大要誓。必度众生不求今世后世之乐。不为名闻[10]虚誉法故。亦不自为早求涅盘。但为众生没在长流。恩爱所欺愚惑所误。我当度之令到彼岸。一心持戒为生善处。生善处故见善人。见善人故生[11]智慧。生[*]智慧故得行六波罗蜜。[12]得

简体字

受剥不生悔意。既以失皮赤肉在地。時日大熱宛轉土中欲趣大水。見諸小蟲來食其身。為持戒故不復敢動。自思惟言。今我此身以施諸蟲。為佛道故今以肉施以充其身。後成佛時當以法施以益其心。如是誓已身乾命[8]絕。即生第二忉利天上。爾時毒龍釋迦文佛是。[9]是時獵者提婆達等六師是也。諸小蟲輩。釋迦文佛初轉法輪八萬諸天得道者是。菩薩護戒不惜身命。決定不悔。其事如是。是名尸羅波羅蜜。復次菩薩持戒。為佛道故作大要誓。必度眾生不求今世後世之樂。不為名聞[10]虛譽法故。亦不自為早求涅槃。但為眾生沒在長流。恩愛所欺愚惑所誤。我當度之令到彼岸。一心持戒為生善處。生善處故見善人。見善人故生[11]智慧。生[*]智慧故得行六波羅蜜。[12]得

正體字

the peeling away of his skin, and did not develop any thoughts of regret.

Then, having lost his skin, his bare flesh rested directly on the ground. It was in a season where the sun was very hot. He slithered along through the dirt desiring to make his way to a large body of water. He then observed all of the little insects which came to eat his body. At that point, for the sake of upholding the precepts, he did not dare to move any more.

He thought to himself, "Now I'll make a gift to the insects of this body. For the sake of the Buddha Path, I will now make a gift of this flesh so as to fill up their bodies. Later, when I have achieved buddhahood, I will employ the giving of Dharma to benefit their minds."

After he had made this vow, his body dried up and his life was cut off. He was then immediately reborn in the second of the Trāyastriṃśa heavens. At that time, the poisonous dragon was Shakyamuni Buddha. In the present era, those hunters manifest as Devadatta and the six [non-Buddhist] masters. The little insects were the eighty-thousand gods who gained the Path when Shakyamuni Buddha first turned the wheel of Dharma.

Conclusion: Extended Explanation of the Perfection of Moral Virtue

The bodhisattva guards the precepts and does not spare even his own physical life in doing so. He is decisive in this and has no regrets. When his endeavors are of this sort, this constitutes *śīla pāramitā*.

Then again, when the bodhisattva upholds the precepts, for the sake of the Buddha Path, he makes a great vow, "I will certainly cross over beings, will not seek the pleasures of this or later lives, will not do it for the sake of fame or the dharmas of an empty reputation, and will not do it for the sake of seeking an early nirvāṇa for myself. I will do it solely for the sake of beings who are submerged in the long-continuing flow [of the river of cyclic existence], who are cheated by affection, and who are deceived by their own delusion. I will cross them over and cause them to reach the other shore."

He single-mindedly upholds the precepts and so is reborn in a good place. Because he is reborn in a good place, he meets good people. Because he meets good people, he develops wisdom. Because he develops wisdom, he succeeds in practicing the six pāramitās. Because he succeeds in practicing the six pāramitās, he gains the

行六波罗蜜故得佛道。如是
持戒名为尸罗波罗蜜。复次
菩萨持戒心乐善清净。不为
畏恶道。亦不为生天。但求
善[13]净以戒[14]熏心令心乐
善。是为尸罗波罗蜜。复次
菩萨以大悲心持戒得[15]至佛
道。是名尸罗波罗蜜。

简体字

行六波羅蜜故得佛道。如是
持戒名為尸羅波羅蜜。復次
菩薩持戒心樂善清淨。不為
畏惡道。亦不為生天。但求
善[13]淨以戒[14]熏心令心樂
善。是為尸羅波羅蜜。復次
菩薩以大悲心持戒得[15]至佛
道。是名尸羅波羅蜜。

正體字

Buddha Path. When one upholds the precepts in this manner, it is this which constitutes *śīla* pāramitā.

Moreover, when the bodhisattva upholds the precepts, that mind which takes pleasure in goodness is pure. It is not motivated by fear of the wretched destinies nor by a desire to be reborn in the heavens. He seeks to achieve purity characterized by goodness. Through causing the precepts to permeate his mind, he influences his mind to find pleasure in goodness. It is this which constitutes *śīla* pāramitā.

Moreover, the bodhisattva employs the mind of great compassion in his upholding of the precepts and thus succeeds in arriving at the Buddha Path. It is this which constitutes *śīla* pāramitā.

云何持戒而生精进。持戒之
人除去放逸。自力勠修习无
上法。舍世间乐入于善道。
志求涅盘以度一切。大心不
懈以求佛为本。是为持戒能
生精进。复次持戒之人疲厌
世苦老病死患。心生精进必
[22]求自脱。亦以度人。譬
如野干在林树间。依随师子
及诸虎豹。求其残肉以自存
活。[23]有时空乏夜半逾城深
入人舍。求肉不得[24]屏处睡
息不觉夜竟惶怖无计。走则
虑不自免。住则惧畏死痛。
便自定心诈死在地众人来见
有一人言。我须野干耳即便
截取。野干自念。截耳虽痛
但令身在。次有一人言。我
须野干尾便复截去。野干复
念。截尾虽痛犹是小事。

A Coyote Makes His Escape

Nāgārjuna's Preamble: Śīla's Generation of Renunciation

How is it that if one upholds the precepts one then produces vigor? The person who upholds the precepts gets rid of negligence (*pramāda*). Through one's own power, one earnestly cultivates the unsurpassed dharma. One relinquishes the pleasures of the world and enters into the path of goodness. One resolves to seek nirvāṇa for the sake of all. One possesses a great mind and is not lazy and so takes seeking buddhahood as what is fundamental. This is how upholding the precepts is able to produce vigor.

Moreover, the person who upholds the precepts becomes weary and abhorrent of the sufferings of the world and the calamities of aging, sickness, and death. His mind generates vigor and the resolve that he will certainly seek his own liberation while also bringing about the deliverance of others.

Story: A Coyote Makes His Escape

This is analogous to the case of the coyote who lived in the forest and, as a means of surviving, relied on following along after the lions, tigers and leopards, seeking after the meat from their leftover carcasses. There was a period of time when there was a shortage of food for him and so in the middle of the night he slipped into the city and made his way deep into a man's household. He was seeking for meat but did not find any.

He fell asleep in a screened-off spot and, unaware that the night had already ended, awoke, startled, frightened, and at a loss for what to do. If he tried to run out, he figured he would be unable to save himself, but if he remained, he feared he would fall victim to the pain of death. He then fixed his mind on laying there on the ground, pretending to be dead.

Many people came to see. There was one man who said, "I have need of the ears of a coyote." He then cut them off and took them away.

The coyote thought to himself, "Although it hurts to have one's ears cut off, still, the body is allowed to survive."

Next, there was a man who said, "I have need of the tail of a coyote." He then cut that off as well and then departed.

The coyote next thought, "Although it hurts to have one's tail cut off, still, it's a minor matter."

次有一人言。我须野[1]干牙。野干心念。取者转多傥取我头则无活路。即从地起奋其智力。绝踊[2]间關径得自济。行者之心求脱苦难亦复如是。若老至时犹故自宽。不能慇懃决断精进。病亦如是。以有[3]差期未能决计。死欲至时自知无冀。便能自勉果敢慇懃大修精进。从死地中[4]毕至涅盘。

简体字

次有一人言。我須野[1]干牙。野干心念。取者轉多儻取我頭則無活路。即從地起奮其智力。絕踊[2]間關徑得自濟。行者之心求脫苦難亦復如是。若老至時猶故自寬。不能慇懃決斷精進。病亦如是。以有[3]差期未能決計。死欲至時自知無冀。便能自勉果敢慇懃大修精進。從死地中[4]畢至涅槃。

正體字

Next, there was a man who said, "I have need of a coyote's teeth."

The coyote thought, "The scavengers are becoming more numerous. Suppose they were to take my head. If they did, I would have no way to survive." He then sprang up off the ground and, arousing his intelligence and strength, suddenly bolted for a narrow exit, thereby straightaway succeeding in saving himself.

Conclusion: The Practitioner's Self-Exhortation to Realize the Path

In seeking liberation from the trials of suffering, the mind of the practitioner is just like this. When old age arrives, he may still find reason to forgive himself and may still be unable to be diligent, earnest, and decisive in the application of vigor. It may be just the same when encountering sickness. Because there is still hope for a cure, he may still be unable to be resolute in carrying out his strategy.

But when death is about to arrive, he realizes that there is no further hope. He is able to dare to be decisive and diligent in devoting himself mightily to the cultivation of vigor. Then, escaping from the spot where death is upon him, he finally succeeds in reaching nirvāṇa.

问曰。定有众生。何以故言
无。五众因缘有众生法。譬
如五指因缘[29]拳法生。 答
曰。此言非也。若五众因缘
有众生法者。除五众则别有
众生法然不可得。眼自见色
耳自闻声鼻嗅香舌知味身知
触意知法空无我法。离此六
事更无众生。诸外道辈倒见
故。言眼能见色是为众生。
乃至意能知法是为众生。又
能忆念能受苦乐是为众生。
但作是见不知众生实。譬如
一长老大德比丘。人谓是阿
罗汉多致供养。其后病死。
诸弟子惧失供养故。夜盗出
之。于其卧处安施被枕。令
如师在其[1]状如卧。人来问
疾师在何许。诸弟子言。汝
不见床上被枕耶。愚者不审
察之。谓师病卧大送供养而
去。如是非一。

問曰。定有眾生。何以故言
無。五眾因緣有眾生法。譬
如五指因緣[29]拳法生。 答
曰。此言非也。若五眾因緣
有眾生法者。除五眾則別有
眾生法然不可得。眼自見色
耳自聞聲鼻嗅香舌知味身知
觸意知法空無我法。離此六
事更無眾生。諸外道輩倒見
故。言眼能見色是為眾生。
乃至意能知法是為眾生。又
能憶念能受苦樂是為眾生。
但作是見不知眾生實。譬如
一長老大德比丘。人謂是阿
羅漢多致供養。其後病死。
諸弟子懼失供養故。夜盜出
之。於其臥處安施被枕。令
如師在其[1]狀如臥。人來問
疾師在何許。諸弟子言。汝
不見床上被枕耶。愚者不審
察之。謂師病臥大送供養而
去。如是非一。

简体字   正體字

A Deceased Guru Disguised

Nāgārjuna's Preamble: On the Nonexistence of Beings

Question: It is definitely the case that beings exist. Why do you say that they are nonexistent? It is based on the causes and conditions of the five aggregates that the dharma of a being exists. This is analogous to the case of the causes and conditions of the five fingers generating the dharma of a fist.

Response: This statement is wrong. If the dharma of a being exists in the causes and conditions of the five aggregates, then, aside from the five aggregates themselves, there exists some separate "being" dharma. However, no such thing can be found. The eye itself sees forms. The ear itself hears sounds. The nose smells fragrances. The tongue knows flavors. The body knows tangibles. The intellectual mind faculty knows dharmas as objects-of-mind. They are all empty and devoid of the dharma of a self. Apart from these six [sense-based] phenomena, there is no additional "being."

On account of inverted views, the non-Buddhists claim that when the eye is able to see forms, this involves a being and so forth until we come to when the mind is able to know dharmas, this involves a being. Additionally, they claim that when one remembers and when one is able to undergo suffering and pleasure, these circumstances involve a being. However, they simply create this view. They do not have any direct knowledge of anything genuine associated with this "being."

Story: A Deceased Guru Disguised

This is analogous to the case of an old, senior, and very venerable bhikshu. People were of the opinion that he was an arhat. They brought many offerings. Later on, he became ill and then died. Because the disciples were alarmed that they would lose the offerings, they surreptitiously removed him during the night and in that place where he had been laying down, they arranged blankets and pillows, causing it to appear as if their master was present, but merely lying down. People came and asked about his illness, inquiring "Where is the Master?"

The disciples replied, "Don't you see the blankets and pillows on the bed?" The gullible ones did not investigate into it. They believed that the master was lying down with illness, went ahead and presented large offerings, and then left. This happened more than once.

复有智人来而问之。诸弟子
亦如是答。智人言。我不问
被枕床褥。我自求人发被求
之竟无人可得。除六事相更
无我人。知者见者亦复如
是。

復有智人來而問之。諸弟子
亦如是答。智人言。我不問
被枕床褥。我自求人發被求
之竟無人可得。除六事相更
無我人。知者見者亦復如
是。

简体字　　　　　　　　　　　　　正體字

Next, there was a wise person who came and asked about him. The disciples replied in the same way. The wise person said, "I did not ask about blankets, pillows, beds, or cushions. As for myself, I'm looking for a person." He then threw back the covers, looking for the master. In the end, there was no person who could be found.

Conclusion

Apart from the characteristic features of the six [sense-based] phenomena, there is no additional self or person beyond that. This [absence of genuine reality] is equally true in the case of a "knower" or a "perceiver."

Part Three:

NĀGĀRJUNA'S STORIES ON PATIENCE

问曰。云何[11]名生忍。答
曰。有二种众生来向菩萨。
一者恭敬供养。二者瞋骂打
害。尔时菩萨其心能忍。不
爱敬养众生不瞋加恶众生。
是名生忍。问曰。云何恭敬
供养。名之为忍。答曰。有
二种结使。一者属爱结使。
二者属恚结使。恭敬供养虽
不生恚令心爱着。是名[12]
软贼。是故于此应当自忍不
着不爱。云何能忍。观其无
常是结使生处。如佛所说利
养[13]疮深。譬如断皮至肉断
肉至骨断骨至髓。人着利养
则破持戒皮。断禅定肉。破
智慧骨。失微妙善心髓。如
佛初游迦毗罗婆国。与千二
百五十比丘俱。悉是梵志之
身。供养火故。形容憔悴。

問曰。云何[11]名生忍。答
曰。有二種眾生來向菩薩。
一者恭敬供養。二者瞋罵打
害。爾時菩薩其心能忍。不
愛敬養眾生不瞋加惡眾生。
是名生忍。問曰。云何恭敬
供養。名之為忍。答曰。有
二種結使。一者屬愛結使。
二者屬恚結使。恭敬供養雖
不生恚令心愛著。是名[12]
軟賊。是故於此應當自忍不
著不愛。云何能忍。觀其無
常是結使生處。如佛所說利
養[13]瘡深。譬如斷皮至肉斷
肉至骨斷骨至髓。人著利養
則破持戒皮。斷禪定肉。破
智慧骨。失微妙善心髓。如
佛初遊迦毗羅婆國。與千二
百五十比丘俱。悉是梵志之
身。供養火故。形容憔悴。

简体字　　　　　　　　　　　　正體字

Devadatta's Ruination Through Affection for Offerings

Nāgārjuna's Preamble

Question: What is meant by patience with respect to beings?

Response: There are two kinds of beings who come and approach the bodhisattva: The first are those who are respectful and who contribute offerings. The second are those who are hateful, who scold, and who may even bring injury through blows. At such times, the mind of the bodhisattva is able to be patient. He does not feel affection for the beings who contribute offerings, nor does he hate those beings who heap evil upon him. This constitutes patience with respect to beings.

Question: How is it that one can speak of "patience" with regard to respectfulness and the giving of offerings?

Response: There are two kinds of fetters (samyojana): The first are the fetters which belong to the sphere of affection. The second are those fetters which belong to the sphere of hatefulness. Although respectfulness and the giving of offerings do not generate hatefulness, they cause the mind to become affectionately attached. These are known as the soft thieves. Hence one should cause himself to be patient with these things so that he does not become attached and is not moved by affection.

How is one able to be patient? One contemplates that these situations are impermanent and that they constitute a point for the potential arising of the fetters. As stated by the Buddha, the wounds which occur through offerings go deep. It is as if they cut through the skin and reach the flesh, cut through the flesh and reach the bone, and then break through the bones and reach the marrow. When a person becomes attached to offerings, then he breaks through the skin of upholding the precepts, cuts into the flesh of dhyāna absorption, breaks through the bones of wisdom, and brings about loss of the marrow of the subtle and marvelous mind of goodness.

Story: Devadatta's Ruination Through Affection for Offerings

This principle is exemplified by a case which began when the Buddha first roamed to the state of Kapilavastu. He went together with twelve hundred and fifty bhikshus, all of whom had the physical appearance of brahmacārins. Because they had previously been involved in making offerings to fire, their form and appearance were haggard. Because they had previously been engaged in

绝食苦行故。肤体瘦黑。净
饭王心念言。我子侍从虽复
心[14]净清洁竝无容貌。我当
择取累重多子孙者。家出一
人为佛弟子。如是思惟已。
勅下国中。[15]简择诸释贵
[16]戚子弟。应书之身皆令
出家。是时斛饭王子提婆达
多。出家学道诵六万法聚。
精进修行满十二年。其后为
供养利故来至佛所。求学神
通。佛告憍[17]昙。[18]汝观
五阴无常可以得道。亦得神
通。而不为说取通之法。出
求舍利弗目揵连乃至五百阿
罗汉。皆不为说言。汝当观
五阴无常。可以得道可以得
通。不得所求涕泣不乐。到
阿难所求学神通。是时阿难
未得他心智。[19]敬其兄故如
佛所言以授提婆达多。[20]
受学通法入山不久便得五
神通。得五神通已自念。谁
当与我作檀越者。如王子阿
阇世。有大王相。欲与为亲
厚。到天上取天食。还到欎
[21]旦罗越。取自然粳米。至
阎浮

絕食苦行故。膚體瘦黑。淨
飯王心念言。我子侍從雖復
心[14]淨清潔竝無容貌。我當
擇取累重多子孫者。家出一
人為佛弟子。如是思惟已。
勅下國中。[15]簡擇諸釋貴
[16]戚子弟。應書之身皆令
出家。是時斛飯王子提婆達
多。出家學道誦六萬法聚。
精進修行滿十二年。其後為
供養利故來至佛所。求學神
通。佛告憍[17]曇。[18]汝觀
五陰無常可以得道。亦得神
通。而不為說取通之法。出
求舍利弗目揵連乃至五百阿
羅漢。皆不為說言。汝當觀
五陰無常。可以得道可以得
通。不得所求涕泣不樂。到
阿難所求學神通。是時阿難
未得他心智。[19]敬其兄故如
佛所言以授提婆達多。[20]
受學通法入山不久便得五
神通。得五神通已自念。誰
當與我作檀越者。如王子阿
闍世。有大王相。欲與為親
厚。到天上取天食。還到欎
[21]旦羅越。取自然粳米。至
閻浮

正體字

简体字

the ascetic practice of fasting, their skin and flesh were emaciated and black.

King Śuddhodana thought to himself, "Although my son's retinue is pure in mind and pure in conduct, they are utterly lacking as regards their appearance. I should select from among those families with many sons and grandsons and have each send one man to become a disciple of the Buddha." After he had this thought, he issued an edict throughout the country so as to be able to select from among the sons of the Śākyan nobility. Those who came forth in response to the official declaration were all ordered to leave the home life.

At this time, Devadatta, the son of King Droṇadana, left the home life, studied the Path, and memorized the sixty-thousand [verse] Dharma collection. He was vigorous in his cultivation for a full twelve years. Afterwards, for the sake of the benefit of offerings, he came to the place where the Buddha was and sought to study the superknowledges. The Buddha told him, "Gautama, if you contemplate the impermanence of the five aggregates, you can succeed in gaining the Path and will also gain the superknowledges." But he did not instruct him in the method of obtaining the superknowledges.

Devadatta left and sought this same thing from Śāriputra, from Maudgalyāyana, and eventually from five hundred arhats. None of them would explain it to him, saying instead, "You should contemplate the impermanence of the five aggregates. You can thereby gain the Path and can also gain the superknowledges."

He did not get what he was seeking and so wept and felt unhappy. He went to where Ānanda was and sought to study the superknowledges. At this time Ānanda had not yet achieved the knowledge of others' thoughts. Out of respect for his elder brother, he passed these techniques on to Devadatta as they had been explained to him by the Buddha. Having gotten the method for studying the superknowledges, he went into the mountains and before long gained the five superknowledges.

After he had gained the five superknowledges, he thought to himself, "Who should become my *dānapati?*[1] There is, for instance, Prince Ajātaśatru. He possesses the features of a great king." Seeking to become his close intimate, he went up to the heavens and acquired heavenly food. Returning by way of Uttaravatī, he obtained some "spontaneous" rice. Finally, he went to the jambū

林中取阎浮果。与王子阿阇世。或时自变其身。作象宝马宝以惑其心。或作[22]婴孩坐其膝上。王子抱之鸣[23]啀与唾。时时自说己名令太子知之。种种变态以动其心。王子意惑。于[24]奈园中[25]大立精舍。四种供养并种种杂供无物不备。以给提婆达多。日日率诸大臣。自为送五百釜羹饭。提婆达多大得供养而徒众尠少。自念。我有三十相减佛未几。直以弟子未集。若大众围绕与佛何异。如是思惟已生心破僧得五百弟子。舍利弗目犍连说法教化。僧还和合。尔时提婆达多便生恶心推山压佛。金刚力士以金刚杵而遥掷之。碎石迸来伤佛足指。华色比丘尼呵之。复以[*]拳打尼。尼即时眼出而死。作三逆罪。与恶邪师富兰那外道等为亲厚。断诸善根心无愧悔。复以恶毒着指[1]爪中。欲因礼佛以中伤佛。

林中取閻浮果。與王子阿闍世。或時自變其身。作象寶馬寶以惑其心。或作[22]嬰孩坐其膝上。王子抱之鳴[23]啀與唾。時時自說己名令太子知之。種種變態以動其心。王子意惑。於[24]奈園中[25]大立精舍。四種供養并種種雜供無物不備。以給提婆達多。日日率諸大臣。自為送五百釜羹飯。提婆達多大得供養而徒眾尠少。自念。我有三十相減佛未幾。直以弟子未集。若大眾圍繞與佛何異。如是思惟已生心破僧得五百弟子。舍利弗目犍連說法教化。僧還和合。爾時提婆達多便生惡心推山壓佛。金剛力士以金剛杵而遙擲之。碎石迸來傷佛足指。華色比丘尼呵之。復以[*]拳打尼。尼即時眼出而死。作三逆罪。與惡邪師富蘭那外道等為親厚。斷諸善根心無愧悔。復以惡毒著指[1]爪中。欲因禮佛以中傷佛。

简体字

正體字

forest, got some jambū fruit (*eugenia jambolana*),[2] and then presented these as gifts to Prince Ajātaśatru.

Sometimes he would transform himself into a precious elephant or into a precious horse so as to play tricks on the Prince's mind. At other times he would become an infant and sit on his knee. The Prince would cradle him in his arms and he would coo and gurgle and drool. Each time he did this, he would utter his own name thereby causing the Prince to become aware of it.

He manifested all sorts of unusual appearances in order to move the Prince's mind. The Prince's mind was tricked by this. In Ambavana Park he built an immense *vihāra*.[3] He prepared the four kinds of offerings as well as all sorts of other assorted gifts. There was nothing not present in abundance. He provided them all to Devadatta. Each day he brought along all of the great officials and personally presented five hundred dishes of fine foods with rice.

Devadatta received offerings in great measure and yet his following of disciples was very small in number. He thought to himself, "I possess thirty of the marks of a great man, only slightly less than the Buddha. It is only that I have not yet had disciples gathering around me. If I was surrounded by a great assembly, how would I be any different from the Buddha?" After having had thoughts like this, he developed the idea to break up the Sangha and so gain five hundred disciples. Śāriputra and Maudgalyāyana spoke Dharma and provided instruction. As a result the Sangha became harmonious and united again.

Devadatta then had the evil idea to push down [a boulder] from the mountain to crush the Buddha. A *vajra*-bearing stalwart intervened from a distance by throwing his *vajra* cudgel [to deflect it]. A broken piece of the boulder rolled up and injured the Buddha's toe. Floral Appearance Bhikshuni[4] rebuked Devadatta who responded by striking the bhikshuni with his fist. The bhikshuni's eyes popped out [from the force of the blow] and she immediately died.

He committed three of the mortal (*ānantarya*) transgressions[5] and drew close to such evil and fallacy-promoting non-Buddhist masters as Pūraṇa. He severed all roots of goodness and his mind became devoid of a sense of shame or regret. Additionally, he imbedded a noxious poison under his fingernails, wishing to take the occasion of bowing to the Buddha to injure the Buddha through poisoning.

欲去未[2]到王舍城中。地自
然破裂火车来迎生入地狱。
提婆达多身有三十相。而不
能忍伏其心。为供养利故而
作大罪。生入地狱。以是故
言利养[*]疮深破皮至髓[3]应
当除却爱供养人心。是为菩
萨忍心不爱着供养恭敬人。

欲去未[2]到王舍城中。地自
然破裂火車來迎生入地獄。
提婆達多身有三十相。而不
能忍伏其心。為供養利故而
作大罪。生入地獄。以是故
言利養[*]瘡深破皮至髓[3]應
當除却愛供養人心。是為菩
薩忍心不愛著供養恭敬人。

He was about to proceed, but had not yet arrived when the ground in the city of Kings' Abode (Rājagṛha) spontaneously split open and a fiery carriage came forth. It took him on board and transported him, still alive, down into the hells.

Devadatta's body possessed thirty of the marks of a great man and yet he was unable to resist and overcome his own mind. For the sake of the benefits of offerings, he created great offenses and entered the hells even while still alive. It is for this reason that it is said that the wounds inflicted by offerings go deep, breaking through the skin and reaching even to the marrow.

One should cast off and get rid of the mind which feels affection for those persons who make offerings. This is what is meant by the bodhisattva's mind of patience not becoming affectionately attached to those persons who make offerings or demonstrate respect.

Notes

1. A *dānapati* is a layperson who provides support to the monastic community.

2. A species of rose apple.

3. A *vihāra* is a monastic dwelling.

4. "Floral Appearance" (Utpalavarṇā) was a nun who had gained arhatship.

5. The five mortal (*ānantarya*) transgressions are: patricide; matricide; killing an arhat; creating a schism in a harmoniously-dwelling community of the monastic Sangha; and spilling the blood of a buddha. The Sanskrit term connotes immediacy, unavoidability, and relentlessness of hell-bound retribution. These transgressions are discussed in Vasubandhu's *Abhidharma Kośa Bhāṣyam*, Ch. 4.

复次供养有三种。一者先世因缘福德故。二者今世功德修戒禅定智慧故[4]为人敬养。三者虚妄欺惑内无实德外如清白。以诳时人而得供养。于此三种供养中。心自思惟。若先世因缘懃修福德今得供养。是为懃身作之而自得耳。何为于此而生贡高。譬如春种秋获。自以力得何足自憍。如是思惟已。忍伏其心不着不憍。若今世故功德而得供养当自思[5]惟。我以智慧。若知诸法实相。若能断结。以此功德故。是人供养于我无事。如是思惟已。自伏其心不自憍高。此实爱乐功德不爱我也。譬如罽宾三藏比丘。行阿兰若法至一王寺。寺设大会。守门人见其衣服尩弊遮门

復次供養有三種。一者先世因緣福德故。二者今世功德修戒禪定智慧故[4]為人敬養。三者虛妄欺惑内無實德外如清白。以誑時人而得供養。於此三種供養中。心自思惟。若先世因緣懃修福德今得供養。是為懃身作之而自得耳。何為於此而生貢高。譬如春種秋穫。自以力得何足自憍。如是思惟已。忍伏其心不著不憍。若今世故功德而得供養當自思[5]惟。我以智慧。若知諸法實相。若能斷結。以此功德故。是人供養於我無事。如是思惟已。自伏其心不自憍高。此實愛樂功德不愛我也。譬如罽賓三藏比丘。行阿蘭若法至一王寺。寺設大會。守門人見其衣服尩弊遮門

The Kashmiri Tripiṭaka Master

Nāgārjuna's Preamble

Moreover, there are three kinds of offerings: The first are those which come on account of the causes and conditions associated with past-life merit. The second are those where one receives respect and offerings from people on account of the present life's merit associated with cultivating the precepts, dhyāna absorption, and wisdom. The third are those where one gains offerings through falseness and pretense by deceiving others at the time when, although one is inwardly devoid of actual meritorious qualities, one makes it appear outwardly as if one is utterly pure.

With respect to these three kinds of offerings, one should consider to oneself, "If one now obtains offerings through the causes and conditions of former lives wherein one diligently cultivated merit, this is just something which has been created through personal diligence and thus is naturally obtained. What would be the point in becoming haughty over something like this? This is just like planting in the spring and reaping in the fall. This is something gained for oneself through the application of one's own efforts. What in it is sufficient cause for arrogance?" After one has reflected in this manner, he is able to endure and overcome his own mind so that he is able to refrain from becoming attached or prideful.

If on account of efforts in the present life, one generates merit and so consequently obtains offerings, one should think to oneself, "This comes to me on account of wisdom, whether through understanding the true character of dharmas or whether through being able to cut off the fetters. It is on account of this associated merit. When this person makes offerings, it has nothing to do with me." After having reflected in this fashion, one is able to overcome his own thoughts and refrain from arrogance or condescension. He realizes, "Truly, this is just a case of people having a fondness for merit. It is not that they are fond of me."

Story: The Kashmiri Tripiṭaka Master

This is comparable to the case of the Kashmiri tripiṭaka master bhikshu who cultivated the dharma of the aranya[1] and who went one day to one of the King's temples. The temple had set up a great convocation. The person who guarded the door observed the coarse and low-quality nature of his robes and so blocked the door and did not allow him to go on ahead. In this manner, time and time

不前。如是数数以衣服弊故
每不得前。便作方便假借好
衣而来。门家见之听前不
禁。既至会坐得种种好食。
先以与衣。众人问言。何以
尔也。答言。我比数来每不
得入。今以衣故得在此坐得
种种好食。实是衣故得之。
故以与衣。行者以修行功德
持戒智慧故而得供养。自念
此为功德非为我也。如是思
惟能自伏心是名为忍。若虚
妄欺伪而得供养。是为自害
不可近也。当自思惟。若我
以此虚妄而得供养。与恶贼
劫盗得食无异。是为堕欺妄
罪。如是于三种供养人中心
不爱着亦不自高。是名生
忍。

不前。如是數數以衣服弊故
每不得前。便作方便假借好
衣而來。門家見之聽前不
禁。既至會坐得種種好食。
先以與衣。眾人問言。何以
爾也。答言。我比數來每不
得入。今以衣故得在此坐得
種種好食。實是衣故得之。
故以與衣。行者以修行功德
持戒智慧故而得供養。自念
此為功德非為我也。如是思
惟能自伏心是名為忍。若虛
妄欺偽而得供養。是為自害
不可近也。當自思惟。若我
以此虛妄而得供養。與惡賊
劫盜得食無異。是為墮欺妄
罪。如是於三種供養人中心
不愛著亦不自高。是名生
忍。

简体字   正體字

again, on account of his robes being of low quality, he was never allowed to go on forward.

He then employed the skillful means of borrowing a fine robe before coming. The doorman observed this and permitted him to go forward without restriction. Having arrived at a seat in the convocation he obtained all manner of fine foods. Before eating, he first made an offering of it to his robes. Everyone asked him, "Why do you do that?"

He replied, "I have of late been coming here repeatedly and on every occasion have been unable to gain entry. Now, on account of wearing these robes, I have been allowed to sit in this seat and obtain all kinds of fine food. It is actually on account of the robes that I have obtained it. It is for this reason that I present it to the robes."

When one obtains offerings on account of the merit of cultivation, on account of upholding the precepts and on account of wisdom, the practitioner should think to himself, "This is on account of merit. It is not the case that it is on account of me." When one contemplates in this fashion and is then able to overcome his own thoughts, this qualifies as patience.

If one were to gain offerings through falseness and deception, this would be tantamount to self-destruction and thus it is a behavior to which one cannot draw near. One should consider to himself, "If I were to employ this falseness and then obtain offerings as a result, it would be no different from an evil thief committing a robbery to get his food. This would be a case of falling into the offense of deception."

When in this fashion one's mind refrains from becoming affectionately attached to the three types of offering-bearing persons while also refraining from arrogance, this qualifies as patience with respect to beings.

Notes

1. An *araṇya* is a secluded hermitage.

复次若有女人来欲娱乐诳惑
菩萨。菩萨是时当自伏心忍
不令起。如释迦文尼佛在菩
提树下。魔王忧愁遣三[11]玉
女。一名乐见。二名悦彼。
三名渴爱。来现其身作种种
姿态欲坏菩萨。菩萨是时心
不倾动目不暂视。三女念
言。人心不同好爱[12]各异。
或有好少或爱中年或好长好
短[13]好黑好白。如是众好各
有所爱。是时三女各各化作
五百美女。[14]一一化女作
无量变态从林中出。譬如黑
云电光暂现。或扬眉顿[15]睐
娑媟细视。作众伎乐种种姿
媚。来[16]近菩萨欲以态身触
[17]逼菩萨。尔时密迹金刚力
士瞋目叱之。此是何人而汝
妖媚敢来触娆。尔时密迹说
偈呵之
汝不知天[18]命　失好而黄髯
大海水清美　今日尽苦醎

復次若有女人來欲娛樂誆惑
菩薩。菩薩是時當自伏心忍
不令起。如釋迦文尼佛在菩
提樹下。魔王憂愁遣三[11]玉
女。一名樂見。二名悅彼。
三名渴愛。來現其身作種種
姿態欲壞菩薩。菩薩是時心
不傾動目不暫視。三女念
言。人心不同好愛[12]各異。
或有好少或愛中年或好長好
短[13]好黑好白。如是眾好各
有所愛。是時三女各各化作
五百美女。[14]一一化女作
無量變態從林中出。譬如黑
雲電光暫現。或揚眉頓[15]睞
娑媟細視。作眾伎樂種種姿
媚。來[16]近菩薩欲以態身觸
[17]逼菩薩。爾時密迹金剛力
士瞋目叱之。此是何人而汝
妖媚敢來觸嬈。爾時密迹說
偈呵之
汝不知天[18]命　失好而黃髯
大海水清美　今日盡苦醎

简体字　　　　　　　　　正體字

Māra's Daughters and Buddha at the Bodhi Tree

Furthermore, if it happens that women come who are desirous of sensual pleasures and who seek to seduce the bodhisattva, at such times the bodhisattva should overcome his own thoughts, have patience and not allow them to arise.

This situation is comparable to that of Shakyamuni Buddha beneath the bodhi tree. The king of the demons was distressed and so sent three of his "jade" daughters. The first was named "Blissful to Behold." The second was named "Pleasurable to Others." The third was named "Lust." They came, revealed their bodies, and assumed various poses, desiring to destroy the Bodhisattva. At this time the mind of the Bodhisattva did not move for even a moment and he did not lay eyes upon them for even a moment.

The three maidens thought to themselves, "The minds of people are not the same. That which they are fond of is different in each case. Some are fond of the young, some are fond of the middle-aged. Some are fond of those who are tall and some are fond of those who are short. Some are fond of those who are black and some are fond of those who are white. There are many preferences like these. Everyone has that of which he is fond."

At this time the three maidens each transformed themselves into five hundred beautiful maidens. Each of the transformation-ally-produced maidens assumed innumerable unusual poses as they emerged from the forest, like flashes of lightning appearing momentarily from the midst of black clouds. Some displayed their eyebrows and fluttered their eyelids, or posed alluringly, or offered subtle gazes. They made many sorts of music and showed all kinds of seductive mannerisms. They drew close to the Bodhisattva, desiring with posed bodies to touch and pressure the Bodhisattva.

At that time the secret *vajra*-bearing stalwarts bellowed and glowered hatefully at them, "Who do you think this is that you dare to approach him seductively to touch and bother him?" At that time those secret stalwarts uttered a verse in which they scolded them:

You are unaware of the fate of the gods.
They lose what is fine and their beards turn yellow.
The waters of the great sea which were clear and beautiful,
Today have become entirely bitter and salty.

汝不知[19]日减　婆薮诸天堕
火本为天口　而今一切噉
[0165c09] 汝不知此事。敢轻此
圣人。是时众女逡巡小退。
语菩萨言。今此众女端严无
比可自娱意。端坐何为。菩
萨言。汝等不净臭秽可恶去
勿妄谈。菩萨是时即说偈言
是身为秽薮　不净物腐积
是实为行厕　何足以乐意
[0165c15]　女闻此偈自念。此
人不知我等清净天身而说此
偈。即自变身还复本形。光
曜[20]昱烁照林树间作天伎
乐。语菩萨言。我身如是有
何可呵。菩萨答言。时至自
知。问曰。此言何谓。以偈
答言
诸天园林中　七宝莲华池
天人相娱乐　失时汝自知
是时见无常　天人乐皆苦
汝当厌欲乐　爱乐正真道
[0165c24] 女闻偈已心念。此人
大智无量。天乐清净犹知其
恶

简体字

汝不知[19]日減　婆藪諸天墮
火本為天口　而今一切噉
[0165c09] 汝不知此事。敢輕此
聖人。是時眾女逡巡小退。
語菩薩言。今此眾女端嚴無
比可自娛意。端坐何為。菩
薩言。汝等不淨臭穢可惡去
勿妄談。菩薩是時即說偈言
是身為穢藪　不淨物腐積
是實為行廁　何足以樂意
[0165c15]　女聞此偈自念。此
人不知我等清淨天身而說此
偈。即自變身還復本形。光
曜[20]昱爍照林樹間作天伎
樂。語菩薩言。我身如是有
何可呵。菩薩答言。時至自
知。問曰。此言何謂。以偈
答言
諸天園林中　七寶蓮華池
天人相娛樂　失時汝自知
是時見無常　天人樂皆苦
汝當厭欲樂　愛樂正真道
[0165c24] 女聞偈已心念。此人
大智無量。天樂清淨猶知其
惡

正體字

You are unaware that your days are diminishing.
All of the Vasu gods are bound to fall away.[11]
Fire is originally the mouth [consuming] the heavens.
And so now everything therein is bound to be devoured.

You remain unaware of all these matters.
Thus it is that you dare to slight this ārya.

At this time the crowd of maidens suddenly retreated a little and spoke to the Bodhisattva, saying, "Now these numerous maidens are beautiful and adorned beyond compare. They could serve to delight your mind. Why do you just sit there so uprightly?"

The Bodhisattva said, "You all are impure, foul-smelling, filthy and detestable. Depart from here and cease this deceptive discourse." At this time the Bodhisattva then spoke forth a verse, saying,

This body is a thicket of filthiness.
It is but a collection of decaying matter.
This truly is a walking toilet.
What in it is sufficient to please the mind?

When the maidens heard this verse, they thought to themselves, "This man is unaware of our pure heavenly bodies and thus utters this verse." They then immediately transformed their bodies, returning to their original forms. They radiated light which shimmered and illuminated the forest and proceeded to make heavenly music. They then spoke to the Bodhisattva, saying, "Since our bodies are like this, what is there to criticize?"

The Bodhisattva replied, saying, "When the time comes you will realize this for yourselves."

They asked, "What do you mean by these words?"

He replied with a verse:

In the parks and forests of the heavens,
And in the seven-jeweled lotus blossom pools,
The gods enjoy with one another the pleasures of the senses,
When that is lost, you will realize this for yourself.

At this time, you will observe impermanence.
And realize the pleasures of the gods are all wedded to suffering.
You should renounce the pleasures of desire
And cherish the Path that is right and true.

When the maidens had heard this verse, they thought to themselves, "This man is possessed of a great wisdom which is measureless. He realizes the ills inherent even in the pure pleasures of the

不可当也。即时灭去。菩萨如是观婬欲乐。能自制心忍不[21]倾动。	不可當也。即時滅去。菩薩如是觀婬欲樂。能自制心忍不[21]傾動。
简体字	正體字

gods. He is not one who can be obstructed." They then immediately disappeared.

The bodhisattva contemplates in this fashion the pleasures involved in sexual desire. He is able to control his own mind. His patience is such that he is not even slightly moved.

如说国王有女名曰拘牟头。有捕鱼师名[13]述婆伽。随道而行。遥见王女在高楼上窗中见面。想像染着心不暂舍。弥历日月不能饮食。母问其故以情答母。我见王女心不能忘。母谕儿言。汝是小人。王女尊贵不可得也。儿言。我心愿乐不能暂忘。若不如意不能活也。母为子故入王宫中。常送肥鱼[14]美肉以遗王女而不取价。王女怪而问之欲求何愿。母白王女。愿却左右当以情告。我唯有一子敬慕王女情结成病。命不云远。愿垂愍念赐其生命。王女言。汝去月十五日于某甲天祠中住天像后。母还语子。汝愿已得告之如上。沐浴新衣在天像后住。王女至时白其父王。我有不吉须至天祠以求吉福。王言大善。即严车五百乘出至天祠。既到勅诸从者。

如說國王有女名曰拘牟頭。有捕魚師名[13]述婆伽。隨道而行。遙見王女在高樓上窗中見面。想像染著心不暫捨。彌歷日月不能飲食。母問其故以情答母。我見王女心不能忘。母諭兒言。汝是小人。王女尊貴不可得也。兒言。我心願樂不能暫忘。若不如意不能活也。母為子故入王宮中。常送肥魚[14]美肉以遺王女而不取價。王女怪而問之欲求何願。母白王女。願卻左右當以情告。我唯有一子敬慕王女情結成病。命不云遠。願垂愍念賜其生命。王女言。汝去月十五日於某甲天祠中住天像後。母還語子。汝願已得告之如上。沐浴新衣在天像後住。王女至時白其父王。我有不吉須至天祠以求吉福。王言大善。即嚴車五百乘出至天祠。既到勅諸從者。

简体字　　　　　　　正體字

The Fisherman's Burning Desire for the King's Daughter

There once was a king who had a daughter named Kumuda. There was a fisherman named Śubhakara. He was walking along the road when he looked from afar and saw the princess's face in the window of a tall building. In his imagination, he developed thoughts of defiled attachment which he could not relinquish for even a moment. He went through days and months during which he was unable to drink or eat properly. His mother asked him the reason and he revealed his feelings to his mother, "I saw the daughter of the King. My mind is unable to forget her."

The mother explained to her son, saying, "You are a man of lesser station. The daughter of the King is an honored member of the nobility. She is unobtainable."

The son said, "My mind prays for this bliss and is unable to forget it for even a moment. If I cannot have it as I will it, then I will be unable to go on living."

For the sake of her son, the mother entered the palace of the King, constantly providing gifts of fat fish and fine meats which she left for the daughter of the King without asking any remuneration. The Princess thought this strange and so asked her what wish she was seeking to fulfill.

The mother addressed the Princess, "Pray, dismiss the retainers. I must relate a personal matter." [She then continued], "I have only one son. He cherishes a respectful admiration for the daughter of the King. His feelings have taken hold in a way that has caused him to become ill. He is not likely to survive much longer. I pray that you will condescend to have pity on him and give him back his life."

The Princess said, "On the fifteenth of the month have him go into such-and-such a deity's shrine and stand behind the image of the deity."

The mother returned and told her son, "Your wish has already been fulfilled." She then described what had transpired. He bathed, put on new clothes, and stood behind the image of the deity.

When the time came, the Princess told her father, the King, "I have something inauspicious which has come up. I must go to the shrine of the deity and seek for auspiciousness and blessings."

The King replied, "That is very good." He then immediately had five hundred carriages nicely adorned and had them escort her to the shrine of the deity. Having arrived, she ordered her retainers to

齐门而止独入天祠。天神思惟。此不应尔。王为[15]世主不可令此小人毁辱王女。即厌此人令睡不觉。王女既入见其睡。重推之不悟。即以璎珞直十万两金遗之而去。去后此人得觉见有璎珞。又问众人知王女来。情愿不遂忧恨懊恼。婬火内发自烧而死。

齊門而止獨入天祠。天神思惟。此不應爾。王為[15]世主不可令此小人毀辱王女。即厭此人令睡不覺。王女既入見其睡。重推之不悟。即以璎珞直十萬兩金遺之而去。去後此人得覺見有璎珞。又問眾人知王女來。情願不遂憂恨懊惱。婬火內發自燒而死。

简体字　　　　　　　　　　　正體字

close the doors and wait as she entered the shrine alone.

The shrine's celestial spirit thought, "This should not be this way. The King is the lord of the land. I cannot allow this petty man to destroy and dishonor the Princess." He then cast a spell on the man, causing him to fall into a deep sleep from which he could not awaken. Having entered, the Princess saw him sleeping. She shook him very hard and yet he did not awaken. She then left him a necklace worth a hundred thousand double-ounces of gold and went away.

After she had left, this man was able to awaken and see that the necklace was there. Next, he asked a person in the crowd. He then knew that the King's daughter had come. Because he was unable to follow up on his infatuation, he became distressed, full of regret, and overcome with the affliction of grief. The fire of lust broke loose within him. He was burned up by it, and then died.

云何瞋恼人中而得忍辱。当自思惟。一切众生有罪因缘更相侵害。我今受恼亦本行因缘。虽非今世所作。是我先世恶报。我今偿之。应当甘受何可逆也。譬如负债。债主索之应当欢喜偿债不可瞋也。复次行者常行慈心。虽有恼乱逼身必能[16]忍受。譬如羼提仙人。在大林中修忍行慈。时迦利王将诸婇女入林游戏。饮食既讫王小睡息。诸婇女辈[17]游花林间。见此仙人加敬礼拜在一面立。仙人尔时为诸婇女赞说慈忍。其言美妙听者无厌。久而不去。迦利王觉不见婇女拔剑追踪。见在仙人前立。憍妒隆盛。瞋目奋剑而问仙人。汝作何物。仙人答言。我今在此修忍行慈。

云何瞋惱人中而得忍辱。當自思惟。一切眾生有罪因緣更相侵害。我今受惱亦本行因緣。雖非今世所作。是我先世惡報。我今償之。應當甘受何可逆也。譬如負債。債主索之應當歡喜償債不可瞋也。復次行者常行慈心。雖有惱亂逼身必能[16]忍受。譬如羼提仙人。在大林中修忍行慈。時迦利王將諸婇女入林遊戲。飲食既訖王小睡息。諸婇女輩[17]遊花林間。見此仙人加敬禮拜在一面立。仙人爾時為諸婇女讚說慈忍。其言美妙聽者無厭。久而不去。迦利王覺不見婇女拔劍追蹤。見在仙人前立。憍妒隆盛。瞋目奮劍而問仙人。汝作何物。仙人答言。我今在此修忍行慈。

简体字　　正體字

The Patience-Cultivating Rishi

Nāgārjuna's Preamble

How does one succeed in being patient in the midst of people who are hateful and tormenting? One should consider to oneself, "All beings possess the causes and conditions associated with transgressions and thus alternate in attacking and harming one another. That I now undergo torment is also owing to causes and conditions from my own actions in previous lives.

"Although this is not something I have committed in this present life, it is the retribution for evil committed in a previous life. I am now paying for it. I should accept it agreeably. How could I go against it?" This is analogous to the circumstances surrounding indebtedness. When the lender asks for it, one ought to repay it happily. One can't legitimately get angry over it.

Moreover, the practitioner constantly implements thoughts of loving-kindness. Although there may be torment and chaos forced on his person, he must certainly be able to have patience and undergo it.

Story: The Patience-Cultivating Rishi

This is exemplified by the rishi who practiced *kṣānti*. He dwelt in a great forest where he cultivated patience and practiced kindness. At that time King Kali brought his courtesans along with him as he entered the forest to wander and sport about. Having finished his refreshments and meal, the King took a short nap.

The courtesans wandered off amongst the flowers and trees and then saw this rishi. They offered their reverential respects and then stood off to one side. At that time, for the sake of the courtesans, he spoke in praise of kindness and patience. His words were so fine and marvelous that the listeners could not get enough. They remained a long time and would not leave.

King Kali woke up and failed to see his courtesans and so picked up his sword and followed along behind so as to catch up with them. He saw them standing before the rishi. He became filled up with arrogance and jealousy. With hate-filled glowering, he brandished his sword and demanded of the rishi, "Just what are you doing?!"

The rishi replied, saying, "I'm abiding here in the cultivation of patience and the practice of kindness."

王言。我今试汝。当以利剑截汝耳鼻斩汝手足。若不瞋者知汝修忍。仙人言任意。王即拔剑截其耳鼻斩其手足。而问之言。汝心动不。答言。我修慈忍心不动也。王言。汝一身在此无有势力。虽口言不动谁当信者。是时仙人即作誓言。若我实修慈忍血当为乳。即时血变为乳。王大惊喜。将诸婇女而去。是时林中龙神为此仙人雷电霹雳。王被毒害没不还宫。以是故言于恼[18]乱中能行忍辱。

王言。我今試汝。當以利劍截汝耳鼻斬汝手足。若不瞋者知汝修忍。仙人言任意。王即拔劍截其耳鼻斬其手足。而問之言。汝心動不。答言。我修慈忍心不動也。王言。汝一身在此無有勢力。雖口言不動誰當信者。是時仙人即作誓言。若我實修慈忍血當為乳。即時血變為乳。王大驚喜。將諸婇女而去。是時林中龍神為此仙人雷電霹靂。王被毒害沒不還宮。以是故言於惱[18]亂中能行忍辱。

| 简体字 | 正體字 |

The King said, "I'm now going to put you to the test. I'm going to take a sharp sword and slice off your ears and nose. I'm going to chop off your hands and feet. If you don't get angry, then we'll know that you cultivate patience."

The rishi said, "Do what you will."

The King immediately drew forth his sword, sliced off his ears and nose, and then chopped off his hands and feet. He then asked, "Has your mind moved or not?"

He replied, "I cultivate loving-kindness and compassion. The mind has not moved."

The King said, "You are just a single person here. You have no power in this situation. Although you claim that you have not moved, who would believe it?"

The rishi then straightaway made a vow, "If I truly cultivate loving-kindness and patience, the blood ought to turn into milk." The blood immediately transformed into milk.

The King was both greatly frightened and delighted. He then left, leading away the courtesans with him. On account of his actions toward this rishi, the dragons and spirits of the forest then set loose a cataclysmic storm with thunder and lightning bolts. The King was mortally wounded by it and, sinking away, was unable even to return to the palace.

Thus it is that it is said that one should be able to practice patience even in the midst of torment and chaos.

复次瞋恚之人。譬如虎狼难可共止。又如恶疮易发易坏。瞋恚之人譬如毒蛇人不憙见。积瞋之人。恶心渐大至不可至。杀父杀君恶意向佛。如拘睒弥国比丘。以小因缘瞋心转[12]大分为二部。若欲断当终竟三月犹不可了。佛来在众举相[13]轮手遮而[14]告言

[15]汝诸比丘　勿起斗诤
恶心相续　苦报甚重
汝求涅盘　弃舍世利
在善法中　云何瞋诤
世人忿诤　是犹可恕
出家之人　何可诤斗
出家心中　怀毒自害
如冷云中　[16]火出烧身

[0167c04] 诸比丘白佛言。佛为法王愿小默然。是辈侵我不可不答。

復次瞋恚之人。譬如虎狼難可共止。又如惡瘡易發易壞。瞋恚之人譬如毒蛇人不憙見。積瞋之人。惡心漸大至不可至。殺父殺君惡意向佛。如拘睒彌國比丘。以小因緣瞋心轉[12]大分為二部。若欲斷當終竟三月猶不可了。佛來在眾舉相[13]輪手遮而[14]告言

[15]汝諸比丘　勿起斗諍
惡心相續　苦報甚重
汝求涅槃　棄捨世利
在善法中　云何瞋諍
世人忿諍　是猶可恕
出家之人　何可諍斗
出家心中　懷毒自害
如冷雲中　[16]火出燒身

[0167c04] 諸比丘白佛言。佛為法王願小默然。是輩侵我不可不答。

简体字　　　　　　　　正體字

The Contentious Kauśāmbī Monks

Nāgārjuna's Preamble

Again, a person who is possessed by hatred, like a tiger or a wolf, is difficult to remain together with. He is also like a purulent sore which readily exudes discharges and easily decays. The person who is full of hatred is like a venomous snake. People take no delight in encountering him. The evil mind of the person who accumulates hatreds becomes gradually greater so that he ends up doing what one cannot do, killing even his father, killing even his ruler, and even developing evil intentions towards the Buddha.

Story: The Contentious Kauśāmbī Monks

This idea is well illustrated by the case of the bhikshus in the state of Kauśāmbī. For relatively minor reasons, their hateful thoughts for each other became so severe that they split into two factions. If they had wished to come to a breaking off of relations, they should ordinarily have had to wait to the end of their three-month retreat. But they remained unable to put their differences to rest. The Buddha eventually came and, in the midst of the Assembly, raised up his wheel-marked hand to quiet them. He then told them:

> All of you bhikshus—
> Don't generate such disputation.
> When evil thoughts continue on,
> The bitter retribution grows extremely severe.

> You are seeking to gain nirvāṇa.
> Cast off and relinquish worldly benefits.
> When abiding in the dharmas of goodness,
> How could you be so hateful and full of disputation?

> When worldly men become angry and contentious,
> This is something one might yet forgive.
> But with men who have left the home life,
> How can it be that they dispute and struggle?

> When in the mind of one who has left the home life,
> One cherishes venomousness, this brings harm on oneself.
> It is as if from a cool cloud
> Lightning struck forth and burned the body.

The Bhikshus addressed the Buddha, saying, "The Buddha is the king of Dharma. But pray, may he remain silent for a moment. This group assailed us. We cannot but respond."

佛念是人不可度也。于众僧中凌虚而去。入林树间寂然三昧。瞋罪如是乃至不受佛语。以是之故应当除瞋修行忍辱。复次[17]能修忍辱慈悲易得。得慈悲者则至佛道。

佛念是人不可度也。於眾僧中凌虚而去。入林樹間寂然三昧。瞋罪如是乃至不受佛語。以是之故應當除瞋修行忍辱。復次[17]能修忍辱慈悲易得。得慈悲者則至佛道。

简体字

正體字

The Buddha thought, "These men cannot be crossed over." From the midst of the group of those Sanghans, he soared aloft and disappeared. He went into the forest where he remained still in samādhi.

In just this manner, the offense of hatred is such that, at its extreme, one does not accept even the words of the Buddha. It is for this reason that one should get rid of hatred and cultivate patience.

Moreover, when one is able to cultivate patience, it is easy to gain loving-kindness and compassion. If one has gained loving-kindness and compassion, one succeeds in reaching the Buddha Path.

问曰。云何内心法中能忍。
答曰。菩萨思惟。我虽未得
道诸结未断。若当不忍与凡
人不异。非为菩萨。复自思
惟。若我得道断诸结使则无
法可忍。复次。饥渴寒热。
是外魔军。结使烦恼。是内
魔贼。[2]我当破此二军。以
成佛道。若不尔者。佛道不
成。如说。佛苦行六年。魔
王来言。刹利贵人。汝千分
生中正有一分活耳。速起还
国布施修福。可得今世后世
人中天上之乐道。不可得汝
唐勤苦。汝若不受[*]软言守
迷不起。我当将大军众来击
破汝。菩萨言。我今当破汝
大力内军。何况外军。魔
言。何等是我内军。答曰

欲是汝初军　忧愁为第二
饥渴第三军　渴爱为第四
睡眠第五军　怖畏为第六
疑[3]悔第七军　瞋恚为第八

简体字

The Demon King Confronts the Buddha

Nāgārjuna's Preamble

Question: How is one able to be patient with respect to the dharmas in one's mind?

Response: The bodhisattva reflects, "Although I have not yet gained the Path and have not yet cut off the fetters, if I do not maintain patience, then I am no different from a common person and it is not the case that I am a bodhisattva."

He additionally considers to himself, "If I gain the Path and cut off all of the fetters, then there will be no dharmas remaining with which one must be able to be patient. Additionally, hunger, thirst, cold, and heat are the outward demon armies. The afflictions of the fetters are the inward demon insurgents. I should break these two armies and thereby perfect the Buddha Path. If it is not done in this way, then the Buddha Path will not be perfected."

Story: The Demon King Confronts the Buddha

This is as told of the Buddha when he was cultivating ascetic practices for a period of six years. The demon king came and said, "Noble man of the *kṣatriya* lineage. Of a thousand parts of your life, you have only a single part left to live. Hurry, get up and return to your country, perform acts of giving and cultivate blessings. You will be able to gain the path of bliss among men and in the heavens in the present life and in later lives. It is unacceptable that you uselessly subject yourself to intense suffering. If you don't yield to these gentle words, but instead continue this confusion and so fail to get up, I will lead forth a great mass of troops which will come and strike and break you."

The Bodhisattva replied, "I am now going to break even your extremely powerful inward army, how much the more so your outward army."

The demon said, "What is it that makes up my internal army?" He replied:

Desire is the first among your armies,
Worry is the second.
Hunger and thirst are the third army.
Craving is the fourth.

Drowsiness is the fifth of the armies.
Fearfulness is number six.
Doubt and regret are the seventh army.
Hatred and anger are the eighth.

利养虚称九　　自高[4]蔑人十 如是等军众　　厌没出家人 我以禅智力　　破汝此诸军 得成佛道已　　度脱一切人 [0169a26]　　菩萨于此诸军虽未能破。着忍辱铠捉智慧剑执禅定[5]楯。遮诸烦恼箭。是名内忍。	利養虛稱九　　自高[4]蔑人十 如是等軍眾　　厭沒出家人 我以禪智力　　破汝此諸軍 得成佛道已　　度脫一切人 [0169a26]　　菩薩於此諸軍雖未能破。著忍辱鎧捉智慧劍執禪定[5]楯。遮諸煩惱箭。是名內忍。
简体字	正體字

Beneficial support and an empty reputation are the ninth.
Elevating oneself and belittling others is the tenth.
Such a company of armies as these
Vanquishes those people who have left the home life.

I employ the power of dhyāna and wisdom
To break these armies of yours and,
After perfecting the Buddha Path,
Deliver everyone to liberation.

Although the bodhisattva is not yet able to break all of these armies, he dons the armor of patience, takes up the sword of wisdom, holds onto the shield of dhyāna absorption and deflects the arrows of the afflictions. This is what is meant by inward patience.

复次于十四[1]难不答法中。有常无常等。观察无碍不失中道。是法能忍是为法忍。如一比丘。于此十四难思惟观察。不能通达心不能忍。持衣钵至佛所白佛言。佛能为我解[2]此十四难。使我意了者当作弟子。若不能解我当更求馀道。佛告痴人汝本共我要誓。若答十四难汝作我弟子耶。比丘言不也。佛言。汝痴人今何以言。若不答我不作弟子。我为老病死人说法济度。此十四难是鬪诤法。于法无益但是戏论。何用问为。若为[3]汝答汝心不了。至死不解不能得脱生老病死。譬如有人身被毒箭。亲属呼医欲为出箭涂药。便言未可出箭。我先当知汝姓字亲里父母年岁。次欲知箭出在何山何木何羽。

復次於十四[1]難不答法中。有常無常等。觀察無礙不失中道。是法能忍是為法忍。如一比丘。於此十四難思惟觀察。不能通達心不能忍。持衣鉢至佛所白佛言。佛能為我解[2]此十四難。使我意了者當作弟子。若不能解我當更求餘道。佛告癡人汝本共我要誓。若答十四難汝作我弟子耶。比丘言不也。佛言。汝癡人今何以言。若不答我不作弟子。我為老病死人說法濟度。此十四難是鬪諍法。於法無益但是戲論。何用問為。若為[3]汝答汝心不了。至死不解不能得脫生老病死。譬如有人身被毒箭。親屬呼醫欲為出箭塗藥。便言未可出箭。我先當知汝姓字親里父母年歲。次欲知箭出在何山何木何羽。

简体字

正體字

The Bhikshu Impatient with the Fourteen Imponderables

Nāgārjuna's Preamble

Furthermore, with respect to the unanswered dharmas associated with the fourteen difficult questions such as permanence, impermanence, and so forth, he finds no obstacle to investigating them but still does not lose the Middle Way. When one is able to have patience with these dharmas this constitutes patience with respect to dharmas.

Story: The Bhikshu Impatient With the Fourteen Imponderables

A related case is that of the bhikshu who contemplated and investigated into these fourteen difficult questions, found that he was so unable to break through them that his mind was unable to endure it. He took up his robe and bowl and went to where the Buddha was and addressed the Buddha, saying, "If the Buddha is able to explain these fourteen difficult questions for me so that my mind is caused to completely understand them, then I will continue to be a disciple. If he is unable to explain them, then I will seek after another path."

The Buddha told him, "You foolish man. Are you not basically presenting me with an ultimatum whereby only if I reply to the fourteen difficult questions will you continue to be my disciple?"

The bhikshu replied, "No."

The Buddha said, "You foolish man. Why then do you now say, 'If you don't answer these for me, I will not remain as a disciple? I explain Dharma for the rescue and deliverance of persons who are subject to aging, sickness and death. These fourteen difficult questions are dharmas of disputation. They possess no benefit for the Dharma. They are only frivolous dialectics. What is the point of inquiring into them? If I were to offer an answer for your sake, your mind would not completely comprehend it. You would go to your dying day without being able to understand and would be unable to gain liberation from birth, aging, sickness, and death.

"This is analogous to a man who has been shot by a poison arrow. His relatives call a physician who is about to extract the arrow for him and then apply medications. But he then says, 'You can't take the arrow out yet. I must first know your first and last name, the village from whence you come as well as the ages of your father and mother. Next, I wish to know from which mountain this arrow came, from which tree it is made, from what sort of feathers it is fletched,

作箭镞者为是何人是何等铁。复欲知弓何山木何虫角。复[4]欲知药是何处生是何种名。如是等事尽了了知之。然后听汝出箭涂药。佛问比丘此人可得知此众事然后出箭不。比丘言。不可得知。若待尽知此则已死。佛言。汝亦如是。为邪见箭爱毒涂已入汝心。欲拔此箭作我弟子。而不欲出箭。方欲求尽世间常无常边无边等。求之未得则失慧命。与畜生同死。自投黑暗。比丘惭愧深识佛语。即得阿罗汉道。复次菩萨。欲作一切智人。应推求一切法。知其实相。于十四难中不滞不碍。知其是心重病。能出能忍。是名法忍。

作箭鏃者為是何人是何等鐵。復欲知弓何山木何蟲角。復[4]欲知藥是何處生是何種名。如是等事盡了了知之。然後聽汝出箭塗藥。佛問比丘此人可得知此眾事然後出箭不。比丘言。不可得知。若待盡知此則已死。佛言。汝亦如是。為邪見箭愛毒塗已入汝心。欲拔此箭作我弟子。而不欲出箭。方欲求盡世間常無常邊無邊等。求之未得則失慧命。與畜生同死。自投黑闇。比丘慚愧深識佛語。即得阿羅漢道。復次菩薩。欲作一切智人。應推求一切法。知其實相。於十四難中不滯不礙。知其是心重病。能出能忍。是名法忍。

简体字   正體字

who the arrowhead maker is and from which sort of metal it is cast. I wish also to know from which wood and on what mountain the bow was manufactured as well as what animal's horns were used. Additionally, I wish to know where the poison was produced and what type it is. After I have completely understood all sorts of other such matters I shall give my permission for you to extract the arrow and apply medications.' "

The Buddha asked the bhikshu, "Would it be possible for this man to come to know all these many matters and only later extract the arrow or not?"

The bhikshu said, "He would not be able to succeed in knowing them. If he waited to completely understand this then he would already have died."

The Buddha said, "You are just like this. You have been shot by the arrow of erroneous views smeared with the poison of love and it has already entered your heart. It was out of a desire to extricate this arrow that you became my disciple, and yet now, you do not wish to pull out the arrow, but instead next wish to find out in its entirety whether the world is eternal or non-eternal, bounded or unbounded, and so forth. Before you have succeeded in finding these things out you will have lost your wisdom life and will have died in a fashion identical with the beasts. You hereby cast yourself into darkness."

The bhikshu felt ashamed, deeply understood the words of the Buddha, and then immediately gained the path of arhatship.

Conclusion: The Bodhisattva Transcends the Fourteen Imponderables

Furthermore, the bodhisattva desires to become a person possessed of omniscience. He should pursue investigations into all dharmas and understand their true character. He should not be bogged down in or obstructed by the fourteen difficult questions and so should know that they are a severe illness of the mind. When he is able to transcend them and is able to endure them, this constitutes possessing patience with respect to dharmas.

Part Four:

Nāgārjuna's Stories on Vigor

复次如阿难。为诸比丘说七
觉[8]意。至精进觉意。佛问
阿难。汝说精进觉意耶。阿
难言说精进觉意。如是三问
三答。佛即从坐起告阿难。
人能爱乐修行精进。无事不
得得至佛道终不虚也。如是
种种因缘。观精进利而得增
益。如是精进。佛有时说为
[9]欲。或时说精进。有时说
不放逸。譬如人欲远行。初
欲去时是名为欲。发行不住
是为精进。能自劝励不令行
事稽留。是为不放逸。以是
故知欲生精进。精进生故不
放逸。不放逸故能生诸法。
乃至得成佛道。复次菩萨欲
脱生老病死[10]亦欲度脱众
生。常应精进一心不放逸。
如人擎油钵行大众中。现前
一心不放逸故大得名利。又
如偏阁嶮道若[11]悬绳若[12]乘
山[13]羊。此诸恶道以

復次如阿難。為諸比丘說七
覺[8]意。至精進覺意。佛問
阿難。汝說精進覺意耶。阿
難言說精進覺意。如是三問
三答。佛即從坐起告阿難。
人能愛樂修行精進。無事不
得得至佛道終不虛也。如是
種種因緣。觀精進利而得增
益。如是精進。佛有時說為
[9]欲。或時說精進。有時說
不放逸。譬如人欲遠行。初
欲去時是名為欲。發行不住
是為精進。能自勸勵不令行
事稽留。是為不放逸。以是
故知欲生精進。精進生故不
放逸。不放逸故能生諸法。
乃至得成佛道。復次菩薩欲
脫生老病死[10]亦欲度脫眾
生。常應精進一心不放逸。
如人擎油鉢行大眾中。現前
一心不放逸故大得名利。又
如偏閣嶮道若[11]懸繩若[12]乘
山[13]羊。此諸惡道以

简体字   正體字

The Buddha's Proclamation on the Power of Vigor

Then again, for example, when Ānanda was discoursing on the seven limbs of enlightenment (*bodhyaṅga*) for the sake of the Bhikshus, he came to the "vigor" limb of enlightenment whereupon the Buddha then asked Ānanda, "Are you explaining the vigor limb of enlightenment?"

Ānanda replied, "I *am* explaining the vigor limb of enlightenment."

And so this continued with three such inquiries and three such responses, whereupon the Buddha got up from where he had been sitting and spoke to Ānanda, saying, "If a person is able to cherish and take pleasure in cultivating vigor, there is no endeavor in which he will not be successful. He will succeed in arriving at the Buddha Path and in the end, his efforts will not have been in vain."

Based on all sorts of causes and conditions such as these, one contemplates the benefits of vigor and succeeds in making it increase.

Concluding Discussion on the Nature and Aspects of Vigor

Vigor of this sort was referred to by the Buddha at some times as being "zeal" (*chanda*), at some times as being "vigor" (*vīrya*), and at some times as being "non-negligence" (*apramāda*). This may be exemplified by the case of man who is about to travel far. At the beginning when he is desirous of leaving, this is referred to as "zeal." When, having begun his journey, he does not stop, this constitutes "vigor." When he is able to exhort himself and so not allow his journey's endeavors to be delayed, this constitutes "non-negligence."

From this, one can know that zeal generates vigor. Because vigor has been brought forth, one remains non-negligent. Because one is non-negligent, one is able to bring forth all dharmas up to and including the Buddha Path.

Furthermore, the bodhisattva who wishes to gain liberation from birth, aging, sickness, and death while also desiring to cross over beings to liberation should constantly be vigorous and should be single-minded in his non-negligence. He should be like the man who was able to carry a bowl of oil through a great crowd [without spilling a drop]. Because he was able to manifest single-mindedness and non-negligence, he gained great fame and benefit.

This is also just like when traveling on an extremely precipitous and difficult route: Whether one uses suspended ropes or rides on a mountain goat, on all such bad pathways as these, it is on account

一心不放逸故。身得安隐。今世大得名利。求道精进亦复如是。若一心不放逸所愿皆得。	一心不放逸故。身得安隱。今世大得名利。求道精進亦復如是。若一心不放逸所願皆得。
简体字	正體字

of being single-minded and non-negligent that one succeeds in preserving one's physical safety while also being able in this very life to gain great fame and benefit.

The vigor employed in seeking the Path is just the same. If one is single-minded and non-negligent, he gains everything he seeks.

复次譬如水流能决大石。不放逸心亦复如是。专修方便。常行不废。能破烦恼诸结使山。复次菩萨有三种思惟。若我不作不得果报。若我不自作不从他来。若我作者终不失。如是思惟当必精进。为佛道故懃修专精而不放逸。如一小阿兰若。独在林中坐禅而生懈怠。林中有神是佛弟子。入一死尸骨中。歌儛而来。说此偈言

林中小比丘　何以生懈废
昼来若不畏　夜复如是来

[0174a03]　是比丘惊怖起坐内自思惟。中夜复睡。是神复现十头口中出火牙爪如剑眼赤如炎。顾语将从捉此懈怠比丘。此处不应懈怠。何以故尔。[1]是比丘大怖即起思惟。专精念法得阿罗汉道。是名自强精进不放逸力能得道果。

简体字

復次譬如水流能決大石。不放逸心亦復如是。專修方便。常行不廢。能破煩惱諸結使山。復次菩薩有三種思惟。若我不作不得果報。若我不自作不從他來。若我作者終不失。如是思惟當必精進。為佛道故懃修專精而不放逸。如一小阿蘭若。獨在林中坐禪而生懈怠。林中有神是佛弟子。入一死屍骨中。歌儛而來。說此偈言

林中小比丘　何以生懈廢
晝來若不畏　夜復如是來

[0174a03]　是比丘驚怖起坐內自思惟。中夜復睡。是神復現十頭口中出火牙爪如劍眼赤如炎。顧語將從捉此懈怠比丘。此處不應懈怠。何以故爾。[1]是比丘大怖即起思惟。專精念法得阿羅漢道。是名自強精進不放逸力能得道果。

正體字

A Lazy Monk Discovers the Value of Vigor

Nāgārjuna's Preamble: On the Value of Vigor

Then again, just as flowing water is able to cut through a huge boulder, so to it is with the non-negligent mind. If one engages in focused cultivation of skillful means which one constantly carries forward and does not desist from, then one will be able to smash the mountain of the afflictions and fetters.

Moreover, the bodhisattva engages in three sorts of analyses: "If I do not do this, then I will not gain the resultant reward. If I don't do it myself, then it shall not come from someone else. If I do accomplish this, then it will never be lost." When one contemplates in this way, then he will certainly become vigorous and, for the sake of the Buddha Path, shall diligently cultivate, shall remain focused and attentive to detail, and shall avoid falling into negligence.

Story: A Lazy Monk Discovers the Value of Vigor

This is exemplified by the case of a minor *araṇya* (hermitage) dweller who sat alone in dhyāna meditation in the forest and became lazy. There was a spirit in the forest who was a disciple of the Buddha who entered the skeleton of a corpse and came forth singing and dancing and then uttered this verse:

> Little bhikshu in the forest,
> Why have you become lazy and neglectful?
> If when I come in the daytime, you do not fear me,
> I will come again like this at night.

This bhikshu was shocked and frightened, took up his sitting again, and then carried on with his internal contemplation. In the middle of the evening he fell back to sleep. This spirit manifested again with ten heads each spewing fire from its mouth, each with fangs like swords, and each with eyes as red as flames. He spoke gravely, followed after, and then seized this lazy bhikshu, saying, "You should not be lazy in this place! Why are you being this way?"

This bhikshu was filled with great terror and immediately resumed his contemplations. He became focused and precise in his mindfulness of the Dharma and consequently gained the path of arhatship.

Concluding Discussion on the Nature and Value of Vigor

This is what is meant by forcing oneself to become vigorous. Through the power of being non-negligent one is able to gain the fruition of the Path.

复次是精进不自惜身而惜
果报。于身四仪坐卧行[2]住
常勲精进。宁自失身不废
道业。譬如失火以瓶水[3]投
之。唯存灭火而不惜瓶。如
仙人师教弟子说偈言
决定心悦豫　如获大果报
如愿事得时　乃知此最妙
[0174a15] 如是种种因缘。观精
进之利。能令精进增益。

復次是精進不自惜身而惜
果報。於身四儀坐臥行[2]住
常勲精進。寧自失身不廢
道業。譬如失火以瓶水[3]投
之。唯存滅火而不惜瓶。如
仙人師教弟子說偈言
決定心悅豫　如獲大果報
如願事得時　乃知此最妙
[0174a15] 如是種種因緣。觀精
進之利。能令精進增益。

简体字   正體字

Moreover, in this practice of vigor, one does not cherish his own body but rather cherishes the resultant retribution. One is constantly diligent and vigorous in the four physical postures of sitting, lying down, walking, and standing. One would rather lose his own body than diminish the quality of his path-associated karma.

This is analogous to when a fire has gotten out of control and one throws a vase full of water at it. One only bears in mind the idea of putting out the fire and so does not continue to cherish the vase. This principle is also exemplified in the verse spoken by a rishi in instructing his disciple:

> The mind which is resolute experiences pleasure.
> It's just as when garnering great rewards
> Or when something wished for is finally gained.
> It is then that one realizes this is the most marvelous thing.

Focusing on all sorts of reasons such as these, one contemplates the benefits of vigor and is able thereby to cause one's vigor to increase and become enhanced.

[0174a29] 问曰。云何名精进相。答曰。于事必能起发无难。志意坚强心无疲惓所作究竟。[5]以此五事为精进相。复次如佛所说。精进相者。身心不息故。譬如释迦[6]牟尼佛。先世曾作贾客主。将诸贾人入嶮难处。是中有罗刹鬼。以手遮之言。汝住莫动不听汝去。贾客主即以右拳击[*]之。拳即着鬼挽不可离。复[7]以左拳击之亦不可离。以右足蹴之足复粘着。复以左足蹴之亦复如是。以头冲之头即复着。鬼问言。汝今如是欲作何等心[8]休息未。答言。虽复五事被系。我心终不为汝[9]息也。当以精进力。与汝相击要不懈退。鬼时欢喜心念。此人胆力极大。即语人言。汝精进力大。必不休息放汝令去。行者如是。于善法中初夜中夜后夜诵经坐禅求诸法实相。

简体字

[0174a29] 問曰。云何名精進相。答曰。於事必能起發無難。志意堅強心無疲惓所作究竟。[5]以此五事為精進相。復次如佛所說。精進相者。身心不息故。譬如釋迦[6]牟尼佛。先世曾作賈客主。將諸賈人入嶮難處。是中有羅剎鬼。以手遮之言。汝住莫動不聽汝去。賈客主即以右拳擊[*]之。拳即著鬼挽不可離。復[7]以左拳擊之亦不可離。以右足蹴之足復粘著。復以左足蹴之亦復如是。以頭衝之頭即復著。鬼問言。汝今如是欲作何等心[8]休息未。答言。雖復五事被繫。我心終不為汝[9]息也。當以精進力。與汝相擊要不懈退。鬼時歡喜心念。此人膽力極大。即語人言。汝精進力大。必不休息放汝令去。行者如是。於善法中初夜中夜後夜誦經坐禪求諸法實相。

正體字

The Buddha's Past Life as a Fiercely Vigorous Guide

Nāgārjuna's Preamble: On the Five Characteristics of Vigor

Question: What are the characteristics of vigor?

Response: With regard to endeavors, one has the attitude that he is certainly able to succeed. In taking them up, one finds no difficulty. One's determination and intentions are solid and strong. One's mind is free of weariness. Whatever is engaged in is carried through to the end. These five factors constitute the characteristics of vigor.

Then again, according to what the Buddha said, the marks of vigor consist in the body and mind not resting.

Story: The Buddha's Past Life as a Fiercely Vigorous Guide

This is as exemplified by Shakyamuni Buddha in a previous life when he was the leader of a group of merchants. He led the merchants into a precipitous and difficult place. There was a *rākṣasa* ghost there who blocked their way with his hands, saying, "You must stop. Don't move. I will not permit you to go."

The leader of the merchants then hit him with his right fist. The fist immediately stuck to the ghost such that he was unable to pull it away. Next, he hit it with his left fist and was also unable to pull it away. He kicked him with his right foot and it, too, became stuck. Next he kicked it with his left foot and then the same thing happened. He used his head to butt it, whereupon it immediately became stuck in just the same way.

The ghost asked, "Now that you are in this fix, what do you propose to do now? Has your mind given up or not?"

He replied, "Although I continue to be bound up in these five ways, my mind will never be forced to cease by you. I will use the power of vigor to carry on the fight with you. I'm determined not to retreat."

At that point the ghost felt delighted and thought, "This man's really got guts." He then told the man, "Your power of vigor is immense. You definitely won't give up. I'll turn you loose and allow you to leave."

Concluding Discussion on the Characteristics of Vigor

The practitioner is just like this. With respect to good dharmas, in the beginning, middle, and end of the night he recites scriptures, sits in dhyāna meditation, and seeks [realization of] the true character

不为诸结使所覆身心不懈。是名精进相。	不為諸結使所覆身心不懈。是名精進相。
简体字	正體字

of dharmas. He is not covered over by the fetters and he does not become lazy in either body or mind. These are the characteristics of vigor.

[0178b07]　复次一切法中皆能成办不惜身命。是为身精进。求一切禅定智慧时心不懈惓。是为心精进。复次身精进者。受诸勲苦终不[8]懈废。如说。波罗奈国梵摩达王。游猎于[9]野林中见二鹿群。群各有主。一主有五百群鹿。一主身七宝色。是释迦[10]牟尼菩萨。一主是提婆达多。菩萨鹿王见[11]人王大众杀其部党。起大悲心迳到王前。王人竞射飞矢如雨。王见此鹿直进趣已无所忌惮。勅诸从人摄汝弓[12]矢无得断其来意。鹿王既至跪白[13]人王。君以嬉游逸乐小事故。群鹿一时皆受死苦。若以供膳[14]辄当差次日送一鹿以供王厨。王善其言听如其[15]意。于是二鹿群主大集差次各当一日[16]送应次者。是[17]时提婆达多鹿群中。有一鹿怀[18]子来白其主。

[0178b07]　復次一切法中皆能成辦不惜身命。是為身精進。求一切禪定智慧時心不懈惓。是為心精進。復次身精進者。受諸勲苦終不[8]懈廢。如說。波羅奈國梵摩達王。遊獵於[9]野林中見二鹿群。群各有主。一主有五百群鹿。一主身七寶色。是釋迦[10]牟尼菩薩。一主是提婆達多。菩薩鹿王見[11]人王大眾殺其部黨。起大悲心逕到王前。王人競射飛矢如雨。王見此鹿直進趣已無所忌憚。勅諸從人攝汝弓[12]矢無得斷其來意。鹿王既至跪白[13]人王。君以嬉遊逸樂小事故。群鹿一時皆受死苦。若以供膳[14]輒當差次日送一鹿以供王廚。王善其言聽如其[15]意。於是二鹿群主大集差次各當一日[16]送應次者。是[17]時提婆達多鹿群中。有一鹿懷[18]子來白其主。

简体字　　　　　　　　　　　正體字

The Buddha's Past Life as King of a Deer Herd

Nāgārjuna's Introduction

Then again, when with respect to all dharmas, one is able to succeed in bringing them to completion while not stinting one's body or life, this constitutes vigor on the part of the body. While seeking to develop all of the types of dhyāna absorptions and wisdom, one's mind refrains from indulging any laziness or weariness, this constitutes vigor on the part of the mind.

Story: The Buddha's Past Life as King of a Deer Herd

Moreover, as for vigor on the part of the body, one takes on all manner of hardship through diligence yet never succumbs to laziness or diminishment of one's endeavors. This is as told [in the *jātaka* tale of] Brahmadatta, the king of the state of Vārāṇasī. He was roaming and hunting in the wilderness forests where he saw two deer herds. The herds each had a ruler and each herd had five hundred deer.

One of the rulers [of the deer] was in color like the seven jewels. This was Shakyamuni as a bodhisattva. One ruler [of the deer] was Devadatta. The bodhisattva deer king observed a great mass of followers of the human king killing his clan, brought forth the mind of great compassion, and went directly before the King.

The King's men sought to shoot it [as it drew closer]. The flying arrows fell like rain. After the King saw that this deer was advancing fearlessly straight toward him he ordered all of his followers, "Halt your bows and arrows. Don't interfere with his intentions in coming forth."

When the king of the deer had arrived, he knelt and addressed the king of the humans, saying, "On account of what for your Lordship is but a minor matter of unrestrained pleasure in the enjoyment of sport, the [entire] herd of deer at once becomes vulnerable to the suffering of death. How would it be if instead we regularly offered for his meals, in accord with our own sequence, one deer each day as an offering to the kitchen of the King?" The King approved of his words and permitted it to be as he intended.

At this point the two rulers of the deer herds convened a great meeting to determine the order by which they would be sent. Each took responsibility for insuring that one of their herd would be sent forth each day in accord with the proper order.

Within the deer herd of Devadatta there was at this time a doe pregnant with a fawn which came and addressed her ruler, saying,

我身今日[19]当应送死。而我
怀子子非次也。乞垂料理使
死者得次生者不滥。鹿王怒
之言。谁不惜命。次来但去
何得辞也。鹿母思惟。我王
不仁不以理恕不察我辞。横
见瞋怒不足告也。即至菩萨
王所以情具白。王问此鹿。
汝主何言。鹿曰。我主不
仁。不见料理而见瞋怒。大
王仁及一切故来归命。如我
今日天地虽旷无所控告。菩
萨思惟。此甚可愍。若我不
理抂杀其子。若非次更差次
未及之。如何可遣。唯有我
当代之思。之[20]既定。即自
送身遣鹿母还。我今代汝汝
勿忧也。鹿王逐到王门。众
人见之怪其自来以事白王。
王亦怪之而命令前问言。诸
鹿尽耶。汝何以来。鹿王
言。大王仁及群鹿人无犯
者。但有滋茂何有尽时。我
以异部群中有一鹿怀子。以
子垂产

我身今日[19]當應送死。而我
懷子子非次也。乞垂料理使
死者得次生者不濫。鹿王怒
之言。誰不惜命。次來但去
何得辭也。鹿母思惟。我王
不仁不以理恕不察我辭。橫
見瞋怒不足告也。即至菩薩
王所以情具白。王問此鹿。
汝主何言。鹿曰。我主不
仁。不見料理而見瞋怒。大
王仁及一切故來歸命。如我
今日天地雖曠無所控告。菩
薩思惟。此甚可愍。若我不
理抂殺其子。若非次更差次
未及之。如何可遣。唯有我
當代之思。之[20]既定。即自
送身遣鹿母還。我今代汝汝
勿憂也。鹿王逕到王門。眾
人見之怪其自來以事白王。
王亦怪之而命令前問言。諸
鹿盡耶。汝何以來。鹿王
言。大王仁及群鹿人無犯
者。但有滋茂何有盡時。我
以異部群中有一鹿懷子。以
子垂產

简体字   正體字

"Today I personally should be sent forth to die. However I am pregnant with a fawn. It is not the case that it is the fawn's turn to go. I beg that you will dispense your calculations in a way whereby whosoever dies does so in proper order while still preventing the unborn from becoming involved."

The King of that herd of deer became angry at her and said, "Who does not cherish his own life? When the sequence comes up, one just goes. How could there be any withdrawing from it?"

The mother deer thought, "My king is not humane. He does not extend empathy in accord with principle. He will not countenance my withdrawal and so suddenly becomes enraged. He is not worthy of hearing my case." She then immediately went to the bodhisattva [deer] king and laid out completely her sentiments.

The [deer] king asked this doe, "What did your lordship say?"

The doe said, "My lord is not humane. He has not seen fit to apply his imagination to managing this matter but rather has become enraged at me. Because the great king's humanity extends to everyone, I came here to seek refuge. Although heaven and earth are vast, today those such as myself have no place to present our case."

The bodhisattva [deer] thought, "This is extremely pitiable. If I do not bring order to this matter, there will be the unprincipled slaughter of her fawn. If it is not done according to sequence and through a change in order [death] were to fall upon one whose turn has not yet come, how could such a one be sent off? There is only myself who would be appropriate to take her place." When his consideration of the matter had been decided, he immediately went along himself, dispatching the mother deer to return [to the herd], saying, "I am now going to substitute for you. You have nothing to worry about."

The deer king went directly to the gate of the King. When the group of people there saw him they were amazed that he himself had come and so told the King of this matter. The King, too, was amazed at it and so ordered that he be brought forward. He then inquired, "Have the deer all come to an end? Why is it that you yourself have come?"

The deer king said, "The humanity of the great King has extended to the entire herd of deer. Among men there are none who have transgressed it. There is only flourishing. How could there be a time when they would come to an end?

"I have come because there is a doe pregnant with fawn within the other herd. As the fawn is due to be born soon, when this doe

身当[21]俎割子亦[22]并命。归
告于我我以愍之。非分更差
是亦不可。若归而不救无异
木石。是身不久必不免死。
慈救苦厄功德无量。若人无
慈[23]与虎狼[24]无异。王闻是
言即从坐起。而说偈[25]言
我实是畜[26]兽名曰人头鹿
汝虽是鹿身名为鹿头人
以理而言之非以形为人
若能有慈惠虽兽实是人
我从今日始不食一切肉
我以无畏施且可安汝意
[0178c20]　　　诸鹿得安王得仁
信。

简体字

身當[21]俎割子亦[22]併命。歸
告於我我以愍之。非分更差
是亦不可。若歸而不救無異
木石。是身不久必不免死。
慈救苦厄功德無量。若人無
慈[23]與虎狼[24]無異。王聞是
言即從坐起。而說偈[25]言
我實是畜[26]獸名曰人頭鹿
汝雖是鹿身名為鹿頭人
以理而言之非以形為人
若能有慈惠雖獸實是人
我從今日始不食一切肉
我以無畏施且可安汝意
[0178c20]　　　諸鹿得安王得仁
信。

正體字

should be put to death, the fawn, too, would share the same fate. She took refuge in me, telling me of her plight. It is on account of this that I took pity on her.

"Nor could I allow a change in the sequence such that it would fall on one who should have no part in it. If she were to take refuge in me and I were to fail to rescue [her fawn], I would be no different from a tree or a stone. This body will not endure long [in any case]. It is certain that one cannot avoid death.

"To bring forth loving-kindness and rescue one from suffering and misery results in measureless merit. If a person has no loving-kindness, then he is no different from a tiger or a wolf."

When the King heard these words he immediately arose from his throne and uttered a verse, saying:

In truth it is I who am the beast
Who may be called a deer with the head of a man.
Although you have the body of a deer,
You may be called a man with the head of a deer.

To speak of it according to the principle,
It is not by one's form that one is human.
If one is able to possess loving-kindness and generosity,
Although one may be a beast, in truth one is a human.

For my own part, beginning with this very day,
I shall no longer eat any sort of flesh.
I will make a gift of fearlessness,
And so shall be able to put your mind at peace.

The deer gained a state of peacefulness and the King gained humanity and trustworthiness.

复次如[27]爱法梵志。十二岁
遍阎浮提。求知圣法而不能
得。时世无佛佛法亦尽。有
一婆罗门言。我有圣法一偈
若实爱法当以与汝。答言。
实爱法。婆罗门言。若实爱
法当以汝皮为纸以身骨为笔
以血书之。当以与汝。即如
其言破骨剥皮以血写[28]偈
如法应修行非法不应受
今世[29]亦后世行法者安隐

復次如[27]愛法梵志。十二歲
遍閻浮提。求知聖法而不能
得。時世無佛佛法亦盡。有
一婆羅門言。我有聖法一偈
若實愛法當以與汝。答言。
實愛法。婆羅門言。若實愛
法當以汝皮為紙以身骨為筆
以血書之。當以與汝。即如
其言破骨剝皮以血寫[28]偈
如法應修行非法不應受
今世[29]亦後世行法者安隱

简体字　　　　　　　　正體字

The Brahmacārin's Great Sacrifice from Love for Dharma

Then again, this is exemplified by the case of the *brahmacārin* known as "Lover of Dharma." For twelve years, he went everywhere in Jambudvīpa searching for knowledge of the Dharma of the Āryas but still was unable to find it. At that time there was no buddha in the world. The Dharma of the Buddha had disappeared as well. There was a brahman who said, "I possess one verse of the Dharma of the Āryas. If you are truly one who loves the Dharma, I will give it to you.

He replied, "I truly *do* love the Dharma."

The Brahman said, "If you truly do love the Dharma, then you ought to use your skin as paper and, using the bones of your body as a pen, you should use your blood to write it down. Then I will give it to you." He then acted in accord with this instruction, breaking his bones, stripping off his skin and writing this verse down in blood:

That which accords with Dharma, one should cultivate.
That which is non-Dharma, one should not accept.
In the present life and in the future life as well,
He who practices Dharma finds peaceful security.

[0178c29]　复次昔野火烧林。
林中有一雉慇身自力。飞入
水中渍其毛羽来灭大火。火
大水少往来疲乏不以为苦。
是时天帝释来问之言。汝作
何等。答言。我救此林愍众
生故。此林荫育处广清凉
快乐。我诸种类及诸宗亲并
诸众生皆依仰此。我有身力
云何懈怠而不救之。天帝问
言。汝乃精慇当至几时。雉
言。以死为期。天帝言。汝
心虽尔谁证知者。即自立
誓。我心至诚信不虚者火即
当灭。是时净居天。知菩萨
弘誓。即为灭火。自古及今
唯有此林。[1]常独蔚茂不为
火烧。如是等种种。宿世所
行难为能为。不惜身命国财
妻子象马七珍头目[2]骨髓慇
施不惓。如说。菩萨为诸众
生。一日之中千死千生如檀
尸忍禅。般若波罗蜜中所行

[0178c29]　復次昔野火燒林。
林中有一雉慇身自力。飛入
水中漬其毛羽來滅大火。火
大水少往來疲乏不以為苦。
是時天帝釋來問之言。汝作
何等。答言。我救此林愍眾
生故。此林蔭育處廣清涼
快樂。我諸種類及諸宗親并
諸眾生皆依仰此。我有身力
云何懈怠而不救之。天帝問
言。汝乃精慇當至幾時。雉
言。以死為期。天帝言。汝
心雖爾誰證知者。即自立
誓。我心至誠信不虛者火即
當滅。是時淨居天。知菩薩
弘誓。即為滅火。自古及今
唯有此林。[1]常獨蔚茂不為
火燒。如是等種種。宿世所
行難為能為。不惜身命國財
妻子象馬七珍頭目[2]骨髓慇
施不惓。如說。菩薩為諸眾
生。一日之中千死千生如檀
尸忍禪。般若波羅蜜中所行

简体字　　　　　　　　　　正體字

The Bird Who Tried to Save a Burning Forest

Then again, in the past there was a wildfire which was burning the forest. Within that forest there was a pheasant which with intensely strenuous physical efforts used his own strength to fly into the water, soaked his feathers and then flew forth attempting to extinguish the great blaze. The fire was great and water was but little. It flew back and forth and though it became exhausted it did not find that to be suffering. At that time the celestial lord Śakradevendra came and asked it, "What is it that you are doing?"

It replied, "I am [attempting to] save this forest out of pity for the beings in it. The area nurtured by the shade of this forest is vast, refreshingly cool, and blissful. All of our species—all of our lineages and relatives as well as all of the other beings rely upon and look to this [forest]. As long as I have the physical strength, how could I be lazy and so fail to attempt to rescue it."

The celestial lord then asked it, "As for your being so energetic and diligent, how much longer can you continue?"

The pheasant said, "I take death as the appointed time."

The celestial lord said, "Although your intentions may be so, who would be able to verify such a thing?"

It then immediately proclaimed a vow, "My mind is ultimately sincere. If its trustworthiness is not false, then the fire should immediately be extinguished." At this time the gods of the Pure Dwelling Heaven knew of the bodhisattva's vow and then immediately extinguished the fire for its sake.

From ancient times on up to the present, this forest alone has always been growing luxuriantly and remained unburned by fire.

Concluding Discussion

Numerous other cases of this sort illustrate that in past-life practices, [the Bodhisattva] has been able to do what is difficult to do. He has not stinted in sacrificing even his own body and life, his country, wealth, wives, sons, elephants, horses, the seven precious things, his head, eyes, bones, or his marrow. He has been diligent in giving without weariness.

As the saying goes, "For the sake of beings, the bodhisattva would undergo in a single day even a thousand deaths and a thousand births." Just as with *dāna*, the practices undertaken in perfecting the pāramitās of *śīla*, patience, dhyāna and prajñā are undertaken in this same way. The characteristic features of what is intended

如是。菩萨本生经中种种因缘相。是为身精进。于诸善法修行。信乐不生疑悔而不懈怠。从一切贤圣。下至凡[3]人求法无厌。如海吞流。是为菩萨心精进。

如是。菩薩本生經中種種因緣相。是為身精進。於諸善法修行。信樂不生疑悔而不懈怠。從一切賢聖。下至凡[3]人求法無厭。如海吞流。是為菩薩心精進。

简体字   正體字

by "physical vigor" are as illustrated by all sorts of causal circumstances described in the *Sutra on the Past Lives of the Bodhisattva.*

The carrying on of cultivation in all good dharmas while maintaining faith and happiness, while not generating doubts or regrets,
while not falling into laziness, and while continuing to seek the
Dharma insatiably from all of the Worthies, the Āryas, and everyone on down even to the common people, doing so in a manner
comparable to the sea's swallowing up of everything flowing into
it—it is this which constitutes the bodisattva's "mental vigor."

简体字	正體字
复次菩萨精进。遍行五波罗蜜。是为精进波罗蜜。问曰。若行戒波罗蜜时。若有人来乞三衣鉢[11]盂。若与之则毁戒。[12]何以故佛不听故。若不与则破檀波罗蜜。精进云何遍行五事。答曰。若新行菩萨。则不能一世一时遍行五波罗蜜。如菩萨行檀波罗蜜时。见饿虎饥急欲食其子。菩萨是时兴大悲心即以身施。菩萨父母以失子故。忧愁懊恼两目失明。虎杀菩萨亦应得罪而不筹量。父母忧苦虎得杀罪。但欲满檀自得福德。又如持戒比丘。随事轻重摈。诸犯法。被摈之人愁苦懊恼。但欲持戒不愍其苦。或时行世俗般若息慈悲心。如释迦[13]牟尼菩萨。宿世	復次菩薩精進。遍行五波羅蜜。是為精進波羅蜜。問曰。若行戒波羅蜜時。若有人來乞三衣鉢[11]盂。若與之則毀戒。[12]何以故佛不聽故。若不與則破檀波羅蜜。精進云何遍行五事。答曰。若新行菩薩。則不能一世一時遍行五波羅蜜。如菩薩行檀波羅蜜時。見餓虎飢急欲食其子。菩薩是時興大悲心即以身施。菩薩父母以失子故。憂愁懊惱兩目失明。虎殺菩薩亦應得罪而不籌量。父母憂苦虎得殺罪。但欲滿檀自得福德。又如持戒比丘。隨事輕重擯。諸犯法。被擯之人愁苦懊惱。但欲持戒不愍其苦。或時行世俗般若息慈悲心。如釋迦[13]牟尼菩薩。宿世

The Buddha's Past Life as a Doubting Prince

Nāgārjuna's Preamble on Concurrent Practice of Perfections

Furthermore, the vigor of the bodhisattva is universally active throughout the other five pāramitās. It is this which constitutes the pāramitā of vigor.

Question: When one is practicing the pāramitā of moral virtue, if someone comes and begs one's three robes and bowl, were one to go ahead and give them to him, one would thereby break the precepts. Why? Because the Buddha did not permit that. But if one fails to give, one thereby destroys the pāramitā of giving. How then can vigor be universally active in the other five endeavors?

Response: If one is a bodhisattva who is new in his practice, he will be unable to make [vigor] universally and simultaneously active in the other five pāramitās throughout that one single lifetime. This is illustrated by that time when the Bodhisattva was practicing the pāramitā of vigor and observed a starving tigress whose hunger had become so urgent that she was about to eat her own cubs.

At that time, the Bodhisattva let flourish the mind of great compassion and immediately made a gift of his body. Because the Bodhisattva's father and mother had lost their son, their distress and grief were such that they lost the vision in both eyes. Also, it should be the case that the tigress would have incurred a karmic transgression in killing the Bodhisattva.

Still, he did not take into account the grief-induced suffering on the part of his parents nor did he reckon the tigress's incurring of the killing offense. He wished only to perfect *dāna* and gain the associated meritorious qualities associated with this act.

This is also exemplified by the bhikshu who upholds the precepts. No matter what the situation, whether it might involve a minor or a major regulation, he rejects anyone with whom a transgression might occur. Even though the person who is rejected might experiences the anguish of distress and grief [at his refusal to accede to precept-threatening conduct], he strives only to uphold the precepts and does not take pity on the sufferings of others which might arise as a consequence.

Story: The Buddha's Past Life as Doubting Prince

It may be then that one practices the common prajñā of the world and so puts to rest the mind of loving-kindness and compassion. This is exemplified by the past-life case of Shakyamuni as a bodhisattva

为大国王太子。父王有梵志
[14]师不食[15]五谷。众[16]人
敬信以为奇特。太子思惟人
有四体[17]必资五谷。而此人
不食必是曲取人心非[18]真法
也。父母告子此人精进不食
[19]五谷是世希有。汝何愚甚
而不敬之。太子答言。愿小
留意。此人不久证验自出。
是时太子求其住处至林树
间。问林中牧牛人。此人何
所食噉。牧牛者答言。此人
夜中少多服[20]酥以自全命。
太子知已还宫欲出其证验。
即以种种诸下药草熏青莲
华。清旦梵志入宫坐王边。
太子手执此花来供养之拜已
授与。梵志欢喜自念。王及
夫人内外大小皆服事我。唯
太子不见敬信。今日以好华
供养甚善无量。得此好华敬
所来处。举以向鼻嗅之。华
中药气入腹。须臾腹内药作
欲求下处。

為大國王太子。父王有梵志
[14]師不食[15]五穀。眾[16]人
敬信以為奇特。太子思惟人
有四體[17]必資五穀。而此人
不食必是曲取人心非[18]真法
也。父母告子此人精進不食
[19]五穀是世希有。汝何愚甚
而不敬之。太子答言。願小
留意。此人不久證驗自出。
是時太子求其住處至林樹
間。問林中牧牛人。此人何
所食噉。牧牛者答言。此人
夜中少多服[20]酥以自全命。
太子知已還宮欲出其證驗。
即以種種諸下藥草熏青蓮
華。清旦梵志入宮坐王邊。
太子手執此花來供養之拜已
授與。梵志歡喜自念。王及
夫人內外大小皆服事我。唯
太子不見敬信。今日以好華
供養甚善無量。得此好華敬
所來處。舉以向鼻嗅之。華
中藥氣入腹。須臾腹內藥作
欲求下處。

简体字   正體字

who was a prince, the son of a great country's king. His father, the King, had a spiritual guru, a *brahmacārin* who abstained from eating any of the five types of grains. The masses of people revered him, had faith in him, and took him to be marvelously special.

The Prince thought, "Men possess [a body with] four limbs. They must sustain it with the five types of grains, and yet this man [supposedly] does not eat. It must certainly be the case that he has seized the minds of the people through deviousness. He must not be one who is possessed of the genuine Dharma."

His father and mother told their son, "This man is intensely vigorous [in his spiritual practice]. He does not eat the five types of grains and thus is a person only rarely encountered in this world. How can you be so extremely foolish that you do not respect him?"

The Prince replied by saying, "I pray that you may withhold judgment for a little while. It will not be long before this man's verifying evidence will naturally emerge." At that time the Prince then sought out [the guru's] dwelling place, went into the forest there, and asked the cowherds of the woodland, "Just what does this fellow eat?"

The cowherds replied, "At night, this man eats a greater or lesser measure of curds, relying on this as the means to sustain his life."

When the Prince realized this, he returned to the palace with the desire to bring forth the evidence. He then put to use all sorts of purgative medicinal herbs, causing them to completely permeate some blue lotus blossoms.

In the early morning, the Brahmacārin entered the palace and sat at the side of the King. The Prince then took up these flowers in his hands and came forward to make an offering to him. After having bowed, he then presented them to him.

The Brahmacārin was delighted and thought to himself, "The King, his wife, those inside and outside [the palace], those of high and low rank—they all make obeisance to me and serve me. It was only from the Prince that I had not yet received reverence and faith. Today he presents me with an offering of beautiful flowers. This is extremely fine, immeasurably so."

Having received these beautiful flowers, out of respect for benefactor, he raised them to his nose and inhaled their fragrance. As he did so, the medicinal vapors within the blossoms entered his belly. In but an instant, the medicine began to have an effect in his belly, whereupon he sought to find a place to stoop down.

太子言。梵志不食何缘向
厕。急捉之须臾便吐王边。
吐中纯[*]酥。证验现已。王
与夫人乃知其诈。太子言。
此人真贼求名故以诳一国。
如是行世俗般若。但求满
智。寝怜愍心不畏人瞋。或
时菩萨行出世间般若。于持
戒布施心不染着。何以故施
者受者所施财物。于罪不罪
于瞋不瞋。于进于怠摄心散
心不可得故。复次菩萨行精
进波罗蜜。于一切[21]法不生
不灭非常非无常非苦非乐非
空非实非我非无我非一非异
非有非无。尽知一切诸法因
缘和合。但有名字实相不可
得。菩萨作如是观。知一切
有为皆是虚诳心息无为。欲
灭其心唯以寂灭为安隐。尔
时念本愿怜愍众生故。还行
菩萨法集诸功德。菩萨自念
我虽知诸法虚诳。众生不知
是事。于五道中受诸苦痛。
我今当具足行六波罗蜜。

简体字

太子言。梵志不食何緣向
廁。急捉之須臾便吐王邊。
吐中純[*]酥。證驗現已。王
與夫人乃知其詐。太子言。
此人真賊求名故以誑一國。
如是行世俗般若。但求滿
智。寢憐愍心不畏人瞋。或
時菩薩行出世間般若。於持
戒布施心不染著。何以故施
者受者所施財物。於罪不罪
於瞋不瞋。於進於怠攝心散
心不可得故。復次菩薩行精
進波羅蜜。於一切[21]法不生
不滅非常非無常非苦非樂非
空非實非我非無我非一非異
非有非無。盡知一切諸法因
緣和合。但有名字實相不可
得。菩薩作如是觀。知一切
有為皆是虛誑心息無為。欲
滅其心唯以寂滅為安隱。爾
時念本願憐愍眾生故。還行
菩薩法集諸功德。菩薩自念
我雖知諸法虛誑。眾生不知
是事。於五道中受諸苦痛。
我今當具足行六波羅蜜。

正體字

The Prince said, "But the Brahmacārin does not even eat. Why then does he now move towards the toilet?" [The Prince] then held him tightly whereupon, in but another moment, he defecated and vomited at the side of the King. The vomit turned out to be composed entirely of curds.

When this evidence had been revealed, the King and his wife became aware of his deception. The Prince said, "This man is truly a thief. Out of a desire for fame, he has cheated an entire country."

Concluding Discussion on the Bodhisattva's Practice of Vigor

It was in this fashion that he practiced common worldly prajñā. Seeking only to perfect his wisdom, he put to rest the mind of sympathy and pity and thus did not fear incurring the hatred of others.

At other times, as the bodhisattva practices supramundane prajñā, in his upholding of the precepts and in his bestowing of gifts, his mind is not subject to defiling attachment. Why? Because the benefactor, the recipient, the valuable gift, offense, non-offense, hatred, non-hatred, vigor, laziness, the focused mind and the scattered mind—none of them can be gotten at.

Moreover, in his practice of the pāramitā of vigor, the bodhisattva takes all dharmas to be neither produced nor destroyed, neither eternal nor non-eternal, neither suffering nor blissful, neither empty nor real, neither self nor non-self, neither singular nor different, and neither existent nor nonexistent. He knows completely that all dharmas are a conjunction of causes and conditions. They possess only names. No reality can be found in them.

The bodhisattva carries on this sort of contemplation and realizes that everything which is conditioned is false and deceptive. He lets his mind rest in the unconditioned and desires to cause his thoughts to cease, [knowing that] it is only by resort to quiescent cessation that there is peacefulness and security. At that very time, he calls to mind his original vows and, on account of sympathy and pity for beings, returns to the practice of the dharmas of the bodhisattva and so accumulates every sort of meritorious quality.

The bodhisattva thinks to himself, "Although I realize that all dharmas are false and deceptive, beings still remain unaware of this matter. Throughout the five destinies, they endure all manner of suffering and pain. Thus I should now completely perfect the practice of the six pāramitās."

Part Five:

NĀGĀRJUNA'S STORIES ON MEDITATION

禅为守智藏　功德之福田
禅为清净水　能洗诸欲尘
禅为金[21]刚铠　能遮烦恼箭
虽未得无馀　涅盘分已得
得金刚三昧　摧碎结使山
得六神通力　能度无量人
嚣尘蔽天日　大雨能[22]淹之
觉观风散心　禅定能灭之
[0180c26] 复次禅定难得。行者
一心专求不废乃[23]当得之。
诸天及神仙[24]犹尚不能得。
何况凡夫懈怠[25]心者。如佛
在尼拘卢树下坐禅。魔王三
女。说偈问言
独坐林树间　六根常寂默
有若失重宝　无援愁苦[1]毒
容[2]颜世无比　而常闭目坐
我等心有疑　何求而在此
[0181a05] 　尔时世尊。以偈答
曰
我得涅盘味　不乐处染爱

简体字

禪為守智藏　功德之福田
禪為清淨水　能洗諸欲塵
禪為金[21]剛鎧　能遮煩惱箭
雖未得無餘　涅槃分已得
得金剛三昧　摧碎結使山
得六神通力　能度無量人
囂塵蔽天日　大雨能[22]淹之
覺觀風散心　禪定能滅之
[0180c26] 復次禪定難得。行者
一心專求不廢乃[23]當得之。
諸天及神仙[24]猶尚不能得。
何況凡夫懈怠[25]心者。如佛
在尼拘盧樹下坐禪。魔王三
女。說偈問言
獨坐林樹間　六根常寂默
有若失重寶　無援愁苦[1]毒
容[2]顏世無比　而常閉目坐
我等心有疑　何求而在此
[0181a05] 　爾時世尊。以偈答
曰
我得涅槃味　不樂處染愛

正體字

Māra's Daughters Confront the Buddha

Nāgārjuna's Introduction

Dhyāna is the treasury for the retaining of wisdom
And the field of merit for qualities which are worthy.
Dhyāna serves as the waters which are pure.
It is able to wash away the dusts of the desires.

Dhyāna is the armor made of adamant.
It's able to ward off the arrows of affliction.
Although one's not yet reached the [nirvāṇa] "without residue",
A share in nirvāṇa nonetheless has been attained.

One acquires then the coursing in adamantine samādhi,
Smashes then and shatters the mountain of the fetters.
One attains the power of six superknowledges,
And is able to deliver a number of people beyond count.

Dust raised by tumult may obscure the sky and sun,
Yet a heavy rain can soak it all away.
The winds of ideation (*vitarka*) and deliberation (*vicāra*) scatter the
     mind,
But dhyāna absorption can extinguish them.

Furthermore, dhyāna absorption is difficult to attain. Only if the
practitioner single-mindedly and exclusively strives without stint
will he attain it. Even the gods and spirits and rishis are unable to
attain it, how much the less lazy-minded ordinary fellows.

Story: Māra's Daughters Confront the Buddha

When the Buddha was sitting in dhyāna beneath the *nyagrodha* tree
the three daughters of the King of the Māras set forth a question in
verse, saying:

Sitting alone amongst the forest trees,
The six fold faculties always still and quiet.
It seems as if you've lost a precious jewel,
But have no pain of worry or distress.

In all the World your visage has no peer,
And yet you always sit with your eyes closed.
The thoughts of each of us possess a doubt:
"What do you seek by dwelling in this place?"

At that time the Bhagavān replied with a verse:

As I have found the flavor of nirvāṇa,
I don't find pleasure dwelling in tainted love.

内外贼[3]已除　汝父亦灭退 我得甘露味　安乐坐林间 恩爱之众生　为之起[4]慈心 [0181a10] 是时三女。心生惭愧 而自说言。此人离欲不可动 也。即灭去不现。	内外賊[3]已除　汝父亦滅退 我得甘露味　安樂坐林間 恩愛之眾生　為之起[4]慈心 [0181a10] 是時三女。心生慚愧 而自說言。此人離欲不可動 也。即滅去不現。
简体字	正體字

Within, without, the thieves have been expelled.
Your father too: destroyed and sought retreat.

I have discovered the flavor of sweet dew (*amṛta*),
In peace and bliss I sit within the forest.
The many beings immersed in fondness and love—
For all their sakes I raise compassionate thoughts.

At this time the three daughters felt ashamed and said to themselves, "This man has transcended desire and cannot be moved." They then disappeared and showed themselves no more.

此五欲者得之转剧。如火炙疖。五欲无益如狗齩骨。五欲增[9]諍如鸟竞肉。五欲烧人如逆风执炬。五欲害人如践恶蛇。五欲无实如梦所得。五欲不久如假借须臾。世人愚惑贪着五欲至死不舍。为之后世受无量苦。譬如愚人贪着好果。上树食之不肯时下。人伐其树树倾乃堕身首毁坏痛恼而死。又此五欲得时须臾。乐失时为大苦。如蜜涂刀舐者。贪甜不知伤舌。五欲法者与畜生共。有智者识之能自远离。如说。有一优婆塞。与众估客远出治生。是时寒雪夜行失伴。在一石窟中住。时山神变为一女。来欲试之。说此偈言

白雪覆山地鸟兽皆隐藏
我独无所恃[10]惟愿见愍伤

此五欲者得之轉劇。如火炙疖。五欲無益如狗齩骨。五欲增[9]諍如鳥競肉。五欲燒人如逆風執炬。五欲害人如踐惡蛇。五欲無實如夢所得。五欲不久如假借須臾。世人愚惑貪著五欲至死不捨。為之後世受無量苦。譬如愚人貪著好果。上樹食之不肯時下。人伐其樹樹傾乃墮身首毀壞痛惱而死。又此五欲得時須臾。樂失時為大苦。如蜜塗刀舐者。貪甜不知傷舌。五欲法者與畜生共。有智者識之能自遠離。如說。有一優婆塞。與眾估客遠出治生。是時寒雪夜行失伴。在一石窟中住。時山神變為一女。來欲試之。說此偈言

白雪覆山地鳥獸皆隱藏
我獨無所恃[10]惟願見愍傷

简体字　　　　　　　正體字

The Mountain Spirit Tests the Traveling Layman

Nāgārjuna's Preamble: On the Shortcomings of the Desires

As for these five desires, one obtains them and they become more severe. This is just as when one uses fire to cauterize an itch. Pursuing the five desires is a useless endeavor comparable to a dog's gnawing away at a bone. Pursuing the five desires increases disputation just as when birds fight with each other over carrion. The five desires burn people in the same way as happens when carrying a torch into an opposing wind. The five desires harm a person just as when one steps on a poisonous snake. The five desires are insubstantial like something obtained in a dream. [Satisfaction from] the five desires is short-lived and is as if borrowed [for only] an instant. Worldly people deludedly lust for and attach to the five desires, not forsaking them [even] unto death. On account of them, in later lives, they undergo immeasurable suffering.

This is analogous to a stupid person greedily attached to a type of fine fruit who climbs up the tree and feasts upon them, but cannot bring himself to descend in time. Someone then chops down the tree, causing the tree to tilt over whereupon he falls, his body and head are mangled, and he then dies an agonizing death.

Moreover, these five desires, when attained, are blissful [only] for a moment. When lost, there is great suffering. This is comparable to when a person licks away at a honey smeared blade. In his greed for the sweetness, he is unaware of injuring his tongue. The rituals involved in pursuing the five desires are held in common with animals. One who is wise is well aware of this and thus is naturally able to distance himself from them.

Story: The Mountain Spirit Tests the Traveling Layman

This is illustrated by the tale told of an *upāsaka* who together with a group of traders traveled afar in the course of their business. At this time it was cold and snowy. Traveling at night he lost touch with his companions and took shelter in a stone cave. At that time a mountain spirit transformed into a maiden who came to him desiring to test him. She spoke this verse, saying:

> The white snow covers the mountainous ground.
> The birds and beasts all hide themselves away.
> I alone have no one to indulge my needs.
> I pray only to experience your kindness in my plight.

[0181b01]　　优婆塞两手掩耳。
而答偈言
无羞弊恶人[11]说此不净言
水漂火烧去不欲闻[12]汝声
有妇心不欲何况造邪婬
诸欲乐甚浅大苦患甚深
诸欲得无厌失之为大苦
未得愿欲得得之为所恼
诸欲乐甚少忧苦毒甚多
为之失身命如蛾赴灯火
[0181b10]　　山神闻此偈已。即擎此人送至伴中。是为智者呵欲不可。[13]着五欲者。名为妙色声香味触。欲求禅定皆应弃之。云何弃色。观色之患。若人着色诸结使火。尽皆炽然烧害人身。如火烧金银。煮沸热蜜虽有色味烧身烂口。急应舍之。若人染着妙色美味亦复如是。

[0181b01]　　優婆塞兩手掩耳。
而答偈言
無羞弊惡人[11]說此不淨言
水漂火燒去不欲聞[12]汝聲
有婦心不欲何況造邪婬
諸欲樂甚淺大苦患甚深
諸欲得無厭失之為大苦
未得願欲得得之為所惱
諸欲樂甚少憂苦毒甚多
為之失身命如蛾赴燈火
[0181b10]　　山神聞此偈已。即擎此人送至伴中。是為智者呵欲不可。[13]著五欲者。名為妙色聲香味觸。欲求禪定皆應棄之。云何棄色。觀色之患。若人著色諸結使火。盡皆熾然燒害人身。如火燒金銀。煮沸熱蜜雖有色味燒身爛口。急應捨之。若人染著妙色美味亦復如是。

简体字　　　　　　　　正體字

The *upāsaka* covered his ears with his two hands and replied with a verse in which he said:

You shameless and base person.
You speak these impure words.
Would that water could rinse or fire burn them away.
I have no desire to further hear your voice.

I have a wife but my mind does not course in desire.
How much the less would I engage in sexual misconduct.
The bliss afforded by all desires is extremely shallow,
The calamity brought by its great suffering is extremely profound.

All the desires, once gained, then bring no satiation.
When one loses them, this makes for great suffering.
When not yet obtained, one prays that one might obtain them.
Once one's obtained them, one becomes tormented by them.

The bliss afforded by all of the desires is extremely slight.
The poison of distress and suffering is so very much.
For the sake of them, one may lose one's body and life.
Just like the moth which casts itself into the lantern fire.

When the mountain spirit had listened to this verse, she immediately lifted him up in her arms and transported him back into the midst of his companions.

Concluding Exegesis Passage

This is a case of one with wisdom renouncing desires [and realizing that] they cannot be attached to.

As for the five desires, they refer to fine [visible] forms, sounds, smells, tastes, and touchables. All who desire to seek dhyāna absorptions should reject them. How does one reject forms? One contemplates the calamity inherent in [the pursuit of] form. If a person becomes attached to form, the fire of all the fetters blazes up furiously, burning and injuring his body.

This is just as when one uses fire to melt gold and silver or as when one brings hot honey to the boil. Although they possess [the normal] appearance and flavor, they burn the body and ruinously scald the mouth. Then one must immediately cast them aside. If a person has developed a defiling attachment to marvelous forms and fine flavors, the circumstance is just the same.

云何呵声。声相不停暂闻即
灭。愚痴之人不解声相无常
变失故。于音声中妄生好
乐。于已过之声念而生着。
如五百仙人在山中住。甄陀
罗女于雪山池中浴。闻其歌
声即失禅定。心醉狂逸不能
自持。譬如大风吹诸林树。
闻此细妙歌声柔软清净。生
邪念想。是故不觉心狂。今
世失诸功德。后世当堕恶
道。有智之人观声。[15]念念
生灭前后不俱。无相及者。
作如是知则不生染着。若斯
[16]人者诸天音乐尚不能乱。
何况人声。

云何呵聲。聲相不停暫聞即
滅。愚癡之人不解聲相無常
變失故。於音聲中妄生好
樂。於已過之聲念而生著。
如五百仙人在山中住。甄陀
羅女於雪山池中浴。聞其歌
聲即失禪定。心醉狂逸不能
自持。譬如大風吹諸林樹。
聞此細妙歌聲柔軟清淨。生
邪念想。是故不覺心狂。今
世失諸功德。後世當墮惡
道。有智之人觀聲。[15]念念
生滅前後不俱。無相及者。
作如是知則不生染著。若斯
[16]人者諸天音樂尚不能亂。
何況人聲。

简体字   正體字

A *Kinnara* Maiden's Singing Disturbs the Rishis

Nāgārjuna's Preamble: On Sound and Attachment Thereto

Why must one renounce sounds? It is the characteristic of sounds that they do not abide. One hears them only momentarily and then they immediately disappear. Because foolish people do not understand a sound's characteristic of being impermanent and disappearing, they erroneously develop fondness for and pleasure in sounds. They retain in their minds sounds which have already passed and generate attachment to them.

Story: A *Kinnara* Maiden's Singing Disturbs the Rishis

This is illustrated by the case of the five hundred rishis who dwelt in the mountains. The *kinnara* maiden was bathing in a pool in the Snow Mountains. When they heard the sound of her singing, they immediately lost their dhyāna absorptions. Their minds became drunken, crazed, and so unrestrained that they were unable to control themselves. It was as if a great wind had begun to blow through the trees in the forest. When they heard this subtle and marvelous singing voice so soft and pure, they began to think indecent thoughts. On account of this, without their even being aware of it, their minds became deranged.

Thus it is that one may lose one's meritorious qualities in the present life and even become bound in later lives to fall into the wretched destinies.

Concluding Exegesis Passage on Sound and Avoiding Attachment

A person possessed of wisdom contemplates sounds and perceives that, in every new thought-moment, they are produced and destroyed, that the prior and latter sounds are not mutually inclusive, and that they do not even extend to reach each other. If one is able to develop such an understanding, then one does not develop defiling attachments [rooted in imputing meaning onto adjacent but unrelated sound vibrations]. Whoever becomes like this is unable to become disoriented even by the music of the gods, how much the less by the voices of humans.

云何呵香。人谓着香少罪。
染爱于香开结使门虽复百岁
持戒能一时坏之。如[17]一
阿罗汉。常入龙宫食已以钵
授[18]与沙弥令洗。钵中有
残饭数粒。沙弥嗅之大香。
食之甚美。便作方便入师绳
床下。两手捉绳床脚。其师
[19]至时与绳床俱入龙宫。
龙言。此未得道何以将来。
师言。不觉。沙弥得饭食
[20]之。又见龙女身体端正
香妙无比心大染着。即作要
愿。我当作福夺此龙处居其
宫殿。龙言。后莫将此沙弥
来。沙弥还已一心布施持
戒。专求所愿。愿早作龙。
是时遶寺足下水出。自知必
得作龙。

云何呵香。人謂著香少罪。
染愛於香開結使門雖復百歲
持戒能一時壞之。如[17]一
阿羅漢。常入龍宮食已以鉢
授[18]與沙彌令洗。鉢中有
殘飯數粒。沙彌嗅之大香。
食之甚美。便作方便入師繩
床下。兩手捉繩床腳。其師
[19]至時與繩床俱入龍宮。
龍言。此未得道何以將來。
師言。不覺。沙彌得飯食
[20]之。又見龍女身體端正
香妙無比心大染著。即作要
願。我當作福奪此龍處居其
宮殿。龍言。後莫將此沙彌
來。沙彌還已一心布施持
戒。專求所願。願早作龍。
是時遶寺足下水出。自知必
得作龍。

简体字

正體字

Fragrances Pull a Novice Away from the Path

Nāgārjuna's Preamble: On Fragrance and Attachment Thereto

Why must one renounce fragrances? People are of the opinion that having an attachment to fragrances is but a minor offense. A defiling attachment to fragrances opens the door to the fetters. Although one may have accumulated a hundred years in the observance of the moral precepts, one is nonetheless able to ruin it all in a single moment.

Story: Fragrances Pull a Novice Away from the Path

Take for instance the arhat who regularly entered the dragon palace. After eating, he took his bowl and gave it to his śramaṇera [attendant], ordering him to wash it. There were a few leftover grains of rice in the bowl. The śramaṇera smelled them, found them magnificently fragrant, and then ate them, finding them to be extremely delectable.

He then devised a clever technique through which he inserted himself in the under part of his master's rope-mesh [sedan] chair. By gripping the legs of the rope-mesh [sedan] chair with his two hands, when his master went forth, he entered the dragon palace right along with the rope-mesh [sedan] chair.

The Dragon asked him, "Why did you bring along this person who has not yet realized the Path?"

The Master said, "I was unaware [that he had come along with me]."

The śramaṇera obtained some of the rice and ate it. He also saw the daughter of the dragon whose body was beautiful and whose perfume was incomparably marvelous. His mind developed an immense defiling attachment [for her]. He then immediately made a vow, "I should create [enough] merit that I will be able to seize this dragon's dwelling and then live here myself."

The Dragon requested, "In the future, when you come here, do not bring this śramaṇera along with you."

After the śramaṇera had returned, he single-mindedly devoted himself to the practice of giving and to observance of the moral precepts. He sought exclusively to bring about that result which he had vowed to obtain. He wished to soon become a dragon. Then, whenever he performed his circumambulations in the monastery, water gushed forth from beneath his feet. He knew that he would certainly succeed in becoming a dragon.

[21]径至师本入处大池边。以袈裟覆头而入。即死变为大龙。福德大故即杀彼龙举池尽赤。未尔之前诸师及僧呵之。沙弥言。我心已定心相已出。[22]时师将诸众僧就池观之。如是因缘由着香故。

[21]徑至師本入處大池邊。以袈裟覆頭而入。即死變為大龍。福德大故即殺彼龍舉池盡赤。未爾之前諸師及僧呵之。沙彌言。我心已定心相已出。[22]時師將諸眾僧就池觀之。如是因緣由著香故。

简体字

正體字

He next went directly to the place alongside the great pond where his master had originally entered it. He then covered his head with his *kāṣāya* robe and plunged in. He immediately died and changed into a great dragon. Because his [accumulated] merit was so abundant, he [was able to] quickly slay the other dragon. At that point, the entire pond turned red in color.

Before the situation had come to this, all of his masters and the other members of the Sangha had scolded him. He had replied, "My mind has already become fixed on this and the characteristic features [of the desired result] have already begun to manifest in my mind."

At this time the Master led the Sangha assembly to the [edge of] the pool to observe this. Causal circumstances such as these may be brought about on account of an attachment to fragrances.

复次有一比丘。在林中莲华
池边经行。闻莲华香[23]其心
悦乐过而心爱。池神语[*]之
言。汝何以[24]故舍彼林[25]下
禅净坐处而偷我香。以着香
故诸结使卧者[26]皆起。时更
有一人来入池中。多取其花
掘挽根茎狼籍而去。池神默
无所言。比丘言。此人破汝
池取汝花。汝都无言。我但
池岸边行。便见呵骂[27]言偷
我香池神言。世间恶人常在
罪垢粪中不净没头。我不共
语也。汝是禅行好人。而着
此香破汝好事。是故呵汝。
譬如白[1]叠鲜净。而有黑物
点污众人皆见。彼恶人者。
譬如黑衣点墨人所不见。谁
问之者。

復次有一比丘。在林中蓮華
池邊經行。聞蓮華香[23]其心
悅樂過而心愛。池神語[*]之
言。汝何以[24]故捨彼林[25]下
禪淨坐處而偷我香。以著香
故諸結使臥者[26]皆起。時更
有一人來入池中。多取其花
掘挽根莖狼籍而去。池神默
無所言。比丘言。此人破汝
池取汝花。汝都無言。我但
池岸邊行。便見呵罵[27]言偷
我香池神言。世間惡人常在
罪垢糞中不淨沒頭。我不共
語也。汝是禪行好人。而著
此香破汝好事。是故呵汝。
譬如白[1]疊鮮淨。而有黑物
點污眾人皆見。彼惡人者。
譬如黑衣點墨人所不見。誰
問之者。

简体字　　　　　　正體字

A Spirit Criticizes a Bhikshu's Enjoyment of Flowers

Additionally, there was a bhikshu who was walking next to a lotus pool in the forest. When he smelled the fragrance of the lotus blossoms, his mind was pleased and so experienced a feeling of enjoyment. Having passed on by, his mind developed a fondness for it.

The pond spirit then spoke to him, saying, "Why is it that you have forsaken that spot beneath the trees where you sit purely in dhyāna meditation, preferring instead to come forth and steal these fragrances of mine? Through attachment to fragrances, dormant fetters may be influenced to arise again."

Then, yet another person came along. He went right into the pool and pulled up many of its flowers. He then started digging, pulling forth roots and stems, created a disorderly mess, and then left. The pond spirit remained silent, not saying anything at all.

The Bhikshu then said, "This person destroyed your pond and took your flowers. You didn't say anything at all to him. However, I merely passed by the bank of the pond whereupon I suffered your rebuke and a scolding in which you claimed I had stolen your fragrances."

The pond spirit said, "The evil people of the world constantly immerse their heads in the excrement of offense-related defilement. I do not even bother to speak to them. You, however, are a fine person who engages in the practice of dhyāna meditation. Thus, when you become attached to these fragrances, it destroys your fine endeavors. This is why I scolded you.

"This is analogous to a white cloth which is fresh and pure but then gets a spot where it has become stained by something black. Everyone observes it. In the case of those who are evil persons, it is comparable to an already-black robe becoming spotted with ink. It is such as people would not even notice. So, who would even bother to bring it up?"

云何呵味。当自觉悟。我但以贪着美味故当受众苦。洋铜灌口噉烧铁丸。若不观食[2]法嗜心坚着。堕不净虫中。如一沙弥心常爱酪。诸檀越饷僧酪。时沙弥每得残分。心中爱着乐喜不离。命终之后生此残酪瓶中。沙弥师得阿罗汉道。僧分酪时语言。徐徐莫伤此爱酪沙弥。诸人言。[3]此是虫何以言爱酪沙弥。答言。此虫本是我沙弥但坐贪爱残酪故生此瓶中。师得酪分虫在中来。师言。爱酪人汝何以来。即以酪与之。

简体字

云何呵味。當自覺悟。我但以貪著美味故當受眾苦。洋銅灌口噉燒鐵丸。若不觀食[2]法嗜心堅著。墮不淨虫中。如一沙彌心常愛酪。諸檀越餉僧酪。時沙彌每得殘分。心中愛著樂喜不離。命終之後生此殘酪瓶中。沙彌師得阿羅漢道。僧分酪時語言。徐徐莫傷此愛酪沙彌。諸人言。[3]此是虫何以言愛酪沙彌。答言。此虫本是我沙彌但坐貪愛殘酪故生此瓶中。師得酪分虫在中來。師言。愛酪人汝何以來。即以酪與之。

正體字

A Novice Falls Away through Attachment to Flavors

Nāgārjuna's Introduction

Why must one renounce tastes? One ought to realize that, "Solely on account of desirous attachment to fine flavors, I may be bound to undergo a multitude of sufferings, may have molten copper poured down my throat, and may be forced to consume burning hot iron pellets."

If one fails to observe the Dharma in its applications to eating, and if one's thoughts of particular fondness become solidly attached, one may even fall down amongst the worms which abide in the midst of impurities.

Story: A Novice Falls Away through Attachment to Flavors

Such a situation is exemplified by the case of a particular *śrāmaṇera* whose mind became obsessively fond of curds. Whenever the *dānapati* benefactors made an offering to the Sangha of curds, the portion which was left over would always be passed on to that *śrāmaṇera*. His thoughts became affectionately attached to its flavor, taking such pleasure and delight that he was unable to let go of it.

When his life came to an end, he was reborn in this vase which held the leftover curds. The guru of that *śrāmaṇera* had gained the way of arhatship. When the Sangha divided up the curds, he said to them, "Be careful, be careful. Don't injure the curd-loving śrāmaṇera."

Everyone said, "But this is just a worm. Why do you refer to it as 'the curd-loving *śrāmaṇera*'?"

He replied, "Originally, this worm was my *śrāmaṇera*. Because he only sat there immersed in a gluttonous affection for leftover curds, he came to be reborn in this vase. When the master received his share of the curds, the worm came along with it. The master said, "Curd-loving fellow. Why did you come here?" He then gave it the curds.

238   *Marvelous Stories from the Perfection of Wisdom*

复次如一[4]国王名月分王。有太子爱着美味。王守园者日送好菓。园中有一大树。树上有鸟养子。[5]常飞至香山中。取好香果以养其子。众子争之一果堕地。守园人晨朝见之。奇[6]其非常即送与王。王珍此果香色殊异。太子见之便索。王爱其子即以与之。太子食果得其气味。染心深着日日欲得。王即召园人问其所由。守园人言。此果无种从地得之。不知所由来也。太子啼[7]哭不食。王催责园人仰汝得之。园人至得果处。见有鸟巢知鸟衔来。翳身树上伺欲取之。鸟母来时即夺得果送。日日如是。鸟母怒之于香山中取毒果。其香味色全似前者。园人夺得输王。王与太子。食之未久身肉烂坏而死。[8]着味如是有失身之苦。如是等种种因缘。是名呵着味欲。

復次如一[4]國王名月分王。有太子愛著美味。王守園者日送好菓。園中有一大樹。樹上有鳥養子。[5]常飛至香山中。取好香果以養其子。眾子爭之一果墮地。守園人晨朝見之。奇[6]其非常即送與王。王珍此果香色殊異。太子見之便索。王愛其子即以與之。太子食果得其氣味。染心深著日日欲得。王即召園人問其所由。守園人言。此果無種從地得之。不知所由來也。太子啼[7]哭不食。王催責園人仰汝得之。園人至得果處。見有鳥巢知鳥銜來。翳身樹上伺欲取之。鳥母來時即奪得果送。日日如是。鳥母怒之於香山中取毒果。其香味色全似前者。園人奪得輸王。王與太子。食之未久身肉爛壞而死。[8]着味如是有失身之苦。如是等種種因緣。是名呵著味欲。

简体字　　　　　正體字

A Prince's Fatal Attachment to Fine Flavors

This [issue of attachment to fine flavors] is also illustrated by the case of a king known as "Partial Moon King" (Candrabhāga). He had a son who was a prince affectionately attached to delectable flavors. Every day the royal gardener brought fine fruits. There was a large tree within the garden. Up in the top of the tree, there was a bird carrying on with raising its young. It often flew off into the Fragrant Mountains from which it brought back a type of fine, aromatic fruit as nourishment for its young. The clutch of young birds happened to struggle over one of them so much that a fruit came tumbling on down to the ground.

Early in the morning, the gardener noticed it, was amazed by how unusual it was, and so immediately took it to the King. The King valued this fruit for its unusual fragrance and appearance. The Prince noticed it and asked to have it. The King loved his son and so immediately gave it to him. The Prince ate the fruit, experienced its bouquet and flavor, and was overcome with tainted thoughts of profound attachment. Thus he sought to receive it again, day after day. The King immediately summoned the gardener and asked into its origins. The gardener said, "This fruit has no seed. It was obtained from off of the ground. I do not know from whence it came." The Prince wailed and cried and stopped eating. The King forced upon the gardener the responsibility for this, saying, "We look to you to find more of it."

The gardener went to where he had found the fruit, saw there was a bird's nest, and realized the bird had carried it hence. He camouflaged himself up in the tree and waited with the intention of seizing one [of the fruits]. When the mother bird arrived, he immediately forcibly seized one of the fruits so as to deliver it forth.

This happened every day in the same way. The mother bird became furious at this and so returned with a poisonous fruit from the Fragrant Mountains which in fragrance, flavor, and appearance was identical to the earlier previously delivered variety. The gardener seized it and took it forth as tribute to the King. The King gave it to the Prince. Not long after [the prince] had eaten it, the flesh of his body rotted away and he died.

In just such a manner, attachment to tastes possesses the [potential] to precipitate the suffering of losing one's life. All sorts of causal circumstances such as these illustrate what is meant by renouncing the desire involved in attachment to tastes.

云何呵触。此触是生诸结使
之[9]火因。系缚心之根本。
何以故。馀四情[10]则各当其
分。此则遍满身识。生处广
故多生染着。此着难离。何
以知之。如人着色。观身不
净三十六种则生[11]厌心。若
于触中生着虽知不净。贪其
细软观[12]不净无所益。是
故难离。复次以其难舍故。
为之常作重罪。若堕地狱。
地狱有二部。一名寒冰二名
焰火。此二狱中皆以身触受
罪苦毒万端。此触名为大黑
暗处。危难之险道也。复次
如罗睺罗母本生经中说。释
迦文菩萨有二夫人。一名[13]
劬毘耶。二名耶输陀罗。耶
输陀罗罗睺罗母也。[*]劬毘
耶是宝女故不孕子。耶输陀
罗以菩萨出家夜。自觉[14]
妊身。菩萨出家六年苦行。
耶输陀罗[15]亦六年怀[*]妊不
产。诸释诘之。菩萨出家[16]
何由有此。耶输陀罗言。我
无他罪。我所怀子实是太子
体胤。

云何呵觸。此觸是生諸結使
之[9]火因。繫縛心之根本。
何以故。餘四情[10]則各當其
分。此則遍滿身識。生處廣
故多生染著。此著難離。何
以知之。如人著色。觀身不
淨三十六種則生[11]厭心。若
於觸中生著雖知不淨。貪其
細軟觀[12]不淨無所益。是
故難離。復次以其難捨故。
為之常作重罪。若墮地獄。
地獄有二部。一名寒冰二名
焰火。此二獄中皆以身觸受
罪苦毒萬端。此觸名為大黑
闇處。危難之險道也。復次
如羅睺羅母本生經中說。釋
迦文菩薩有二夫人。一名[13]
劬毘耶。二名耶輸陀羅。耶
輸陀羅羅睺羅母也。[*]劬毘
耶是寶女故不孕子。耶輸陀
羅以菩薩出家夜。自覺[14]
妊身。菩薩出家六年苦行。
耶輸陀羅[15]亦六年懷[*]妊不
產。諸釋詰之。菩薩出家[16]
何由有此。耶輸陀羅言。我
無他罪。我所懷子實是太子
體胤。

简体字　　　　　　　　正體字

Yaśodharā's Difficult Pregnancy

Nāgārjuna's Preamble: On the Nature and Perils of Touch

Why must one renounce touch? This touch is the cause for the production of the fire of the fetters and is the root of the bondage of the mind. How is this so? The other four sense faculties each occupy their own particular area. This one, however, involves a consciousness which pervades the entire body. Because the area from which it may arise is extensive, it more commonly [serves as the basis for] generating defiled attachment.

This attachment is difficult to separate from. How does one know this? Take for example a person attached to [sensual] forms. [Ordinarily], if one contemplates the impurity of the thirty-six parts of the body, one develops a mind of renunciation. If, however, one has become attached to touch, even though one is aware of the impurity, one may continue to crave its [sensations of] subtle tenderness. At this point, contemplation of impurity may not provide any benefits. It is for this reason that it is difficult to relinquish.

Additionally, because it is so difficult to relinquish, one may continue on this account to regularly generate grave karmic transgressions. If one falls into the hells, those hells have two regions: The first is known as "cold ice." The second is known as "blazing fire." In both of these hells, [sensations associated with] physical touch are employed to cause one to undergo punishments inflicting a myriad forms of the poison of suffering. This "touch" is known as the place of the great darkness. It is a precipitous path attended by danger and difficulty.

Story: Yaśodharā's Difficult Pregnancy

Then again, this is as described in the *Sutra on the Previous Lives of Rāhula's Mother*. As the Bodhisattva, Shakyamuni had two consorts. The first was named Gopiyā. The second was named Yaśodharā. Yaśodharā was the mother of Rāhula. Because Gopiyā was a barren woman, she did not become pregnant with child. It was on the night that the Bodhisattva left behind the home life that Yaśodharā realized that she was pregnant.

The Bodhisattva [Shakyamuni] engaged in ascetic practices for six years. For six full years, Yaśodharā remained pregnant without giving birth. All of the Shakyans inquired of her, "The Bodhisattva has left behind the home life. How is it that this could occur?"

Yaśodharā said, "I have committed no offenses with others. The child with which I am pregnant is truly a scion of the Prince."

诸释言。何以久而不产。答言。非我所知。诸释集议。闻王欲如法治罪。[*]劬毘耶白王。愿宽恕之。我常与耶输陀罗共住。我为其证知其无罪。待其子生知似父不治之无晚。王即宽置。佛六年苦行既满。初成佛时其夜生罗睺罗。王见其似父爱乐忘忧。语群臣言。我儿虽去今得其子。与儿在无异。耶输陀罗。虽免罪黜恶声满国。耶输陀罗欲除恶名。佛成道已。还迦毘罗婆度诸释子。时净饭王及耶输陀罗。常请佛入宫食。是时耶输陀罗持[17]一[18]鉢百味欢喜丸。与罗睺罗令持上佛。是时佛[19]以神力。变五百阿罗汉。[20]皆如佛身无有别异。罗睺罗以七岁身持欢喜丸。径至佛前奉进世尊。是时佛摄神力。诸比丘身复如故。皆空鉢而坐。唯佛鉢中盛满欢喜丸。耶输陀罗即白王言。以此证验我无罪也。

The Shakyans said, "How is it then that it has now been so long and yet it still has not been born?"

She replied, "Not even I understand this matter."

The Shakyans assembled and conferred on the matter. When she heard that the King wished to carry out a lawful punishment of offenses, Gopiyā addressed the King, "I pray that, out of sympathy for her, you will be lenient. I have dwelt together with Yaśodharā constantly. I can certify for her that I know she is free of transgressions. Wait for her child to be born. Then you will be able to know if it resembles the father or not. It would not be too late then to carry out punishments."

The King then allowed leniency. When the Buddha's six years of ascetic practices had been fulfilled, on the very night when he achieved buddhahood, she gave birth to Rāhula. The King observed that he resembled his father, felt affection and delight, and forgot his worries. He spoke to the group of ministers, saying, "Although my son has gone away, I have now gained his son. It is no different than if my son was here."

Although Yaśodharā had avoided the punishment of being cast out, she had nonetheless acquired a bad reputation which spread throughout the country. Yaśodharā wished to get rid of the stain on her reputation.

After the Buddha had gained realization of the Path, he returned to Kapilavastu in an attempt to cross over the sons of the Shakyans to liberation. At that time the Pure Rice King and Yaśodharā regularly invited the Buddha to come to the palace for meals. At one such time Yaśodharā took a bowl of "hundred-flavored delightful dumplings," handed it to Rāhula, and then directed him to take it up and offer them to the Buddha.

The Buddha then resorted to his spiritual powers to transform all five hundred arhats so that they all appeared identical to the Buddha, showing no differences at all. The seven-year-old Rāhula carried the delightful dumplings forward, went straight before the Buddha himself and offered them up to the Bhagavān .

[The Buddha] then withdrew his spiritual powers whereupon all of the bhikshus were restored to their original physical appearance. They were all sitting there with empty bowls. Only the Buddha's bowl was full of delightful dumplings. Yaśodharā then addressed the King, saying, "Let this serve as verification that I have remained free of any transgressions."

耶输陀罗即问佛言。我有何
因缘怀[*]妊六年佛言。汝子
罗睺罗。过去久远世时曾作
国王。时有一五通仙人来入
王国。语王言。王法治贼请
治我罪。王言。汝有何罪。
答言。我入王国犯不与取。
辄饮王水用王杨枝。王言。
我以相与何罪之有。我初登
王位。皆以水及杨枝施于一
切。仙人言。王虽已施我心
疑悔罪不除也。愿今见治无
令后罪。王言。若必欲尔。
小停待我入还。王入宫中六
日不出。此仙人在王园中六
日饥渴。仙人思惟。此王正
以此治我。王过六日而出辞
谢仙人。我便相忘莫见咎
也。以是因缘故。受五百世
三恶道罪。五百世常六年在
母胎中。以是证故。耶输陀
罗无有罪也。

简体字

耶輸陀羅即問佛言。我有何
因緣懷[*]妊六年佛言。汝子
羅睺羅。過去久遠世時曾作
國王。時有一五通仙人來入
王國。語王言。王法治賊請
治我罪。王言。汝有何罪。
答言。我入王國犯不與取。
輒飲王水用王楊枝。王言。
我以相與何罪之有。我初登
王位。皆以水及楊枝施於一
切。仙人言。王雖已施我心
疑悔罪不除也。願今見治無
令後罪。王言。若必欲爾。
小停待我入還。王入宮中六
日不出。此仙人在王園中六
日飢渴。仙人思惟。此王正
以此治我。王過六日而出辭
謝仙人。我便相忘莫見咎
也。以是因緣故。受五百世
三惡道罪。五百世常六年在
母胎中。以是證故。耶輸陀
羅無有罪也。

正體字

The Origins of Yaśodharā's Difficult Pregnancy

Yaśodharā inquired of the Buddha, "What is the causal basis behind my remaining pregnant for a period of six years?"

The Buddha said, "Long ago, in a lifetime far off in the past, your son Rāhula was the king of a country. There was a rishi possessed of the five superknowledges who came at that time and entered that king's country. He spoke to the King, saying, "It is the royal law to punish thieves. I request that you punishing me for my offenses."

The King said, "But what offenses have you committed?"

He replied, "I entered the King's country and transgressed by taking what had not been given. I have repeatedly drunk the King's water and used the King's willow branches [as tooth brushes]."

The King said, "But I have already given those things [to the people]. What transgression could there be in this? When I first ascended to the position of king, I bestowed the use of both water and willow branches universally on everyone."

The Rishi said, "Although the King has already made a gift of them, my mind is nonetheless afflicted by doubts and regrets. Thus the offense is not yet expiated. I pray that I will now undergo corrective measures so as to prevent being subjected to [karmic] punishments later.

The King said, "If you must insist, wait a little bit for me to go on in and come back out again."

The King then entered the palace. Even after six days, he still had not emerged again. The Rishi stayed in the King's garden enduring hunger and thirst for those six days. The Rishi thought to himself, "This King is just now using this situation to punish me."

After six days had gone by, the King came out and released the Rishi, saying, "I completely forgot about this. Do not hold it against me." On account of this causal circumstance, he underwent five hundred lifetimes of punishment in the three wretched destinies and then for five hundred lifetimes always remained in his mother's womb for a period of six years. On account of this verifying evidence, [we should realize that] Yaśodharā was free of transgressions.

是时世尊。食已出去。耶输陀罗心生悔恨。如此好人世所希有。我得遭遇而今永失。世尊坐时谛视不眴。世尊出时寻后观之远没乃止。心大懊恨。每一思至躄地气绝。傍人以水灑之乃得苏息。常独思惟。天下谁能善为呪术。能转其心令复本意欢乐如初。即以七宝名珠着金[21]盘上以持募人。有一梵志应之言。我能呪之令其意转。当作百味欢喜丸。以药草和之。以呪语禁之。其心便转必来无疑。耶输陀罗受其教法。遣人请佛。愿与圣众俱屈威神。佛入王宫。[1]耶输陀罗即[2]遣百味欢喜丸着佛钵中。佛既食之。耶输陀罗冀想如愿欢娱如初。佛食无异心[3]目澄静。耶输陀罗言。今不动者药力未行故耳。药势发时必如我愿。佛饭食讫

简体字

是時世尊。食已出去。耶輸陀羅心生悔恨。如此好人世所希有。我得遭遇而今永失。世尊坐時諦視不眴。世尊出時尋後觀之遠沒乃止。心大懊恨。每一思至躄地氣絕。傍人以水灑之乃得蘇息。常獨思惟。天下誰能善為呪術。能轉其心令復本意歡樂如初。即以七寶名珠著金[21]槃上以持募人。有一梵志應之言。我能呪之令其意轉。當作百味歡喜丸。以藥草和之。以呪語禁之。其心便轉必來無疑。耶輸陀羅受其教法。遣人請佛。願與聖眾俱屈威神。佛入王宮。[1]耶輸陀羅即[2]遣百味歡喜丸著佛鉢中。佛既食之。耶輸陀羅冀想如願歡娛如初。佛食無異心[3]目澄靜。耶輸陀羅言。今不動者藥力未行故耳。藥勢發時必如我願。佛飯食訖

正體字

Yaśodharā's Attempt to Bring Back the Buddha

At this time, after he had finished his meal, the Bhagavān departed. Yaśodharā's thoughts were full of regret, "Such a fine man as this, rare in all the world—I succeeded in encountering him, but now have lost him forever."

When the Bhagavān sat down, she gazed at him intently without even blinking. When the Bhagavān departed, her gaze followed along after him so intently that only when he sank away on the horizon did she desist. Her thoughts were full of grief and regret. Every time she thought of it, she would collapse and go into a faint. Her attendants would sprinkle her with water. Only then did she revive and breath normally again.

She constantly remained alone, pondering, "Who in all the world is so good at the skill of casting spells that they might be able to turn his mind around and cause him to return to his original state of mind, thus allowing us to once again be just as delighted and happy as before?" She then placed the seven precious things and other rare jewels into a tray made of gold and, taking it up, went forth to enlist the services of someone [who could help her do this].

There was one brahmacarin who responded to her by saying, "I am able to cast a spell upon him which will cause his mind to turn back. You must make hundred-flavored delightful dumplings in which you mix together herbs. Use the phrases of the spell to capture him. His mind will then turn around and he will certainly come. Of this there is no doubt."

Yaśodharā followed his instructions and sent others to invite the Buddha, saying, "Pray may you, together with the assembly of Āryas, deign to bend down from your [heights of] awesome spirituality [and honor us with your presence]." The Buddha then came and entered into the King's palace. Yaśodharā immediately sent forth the hundred-flavored delightful dumplings and had them placed in the Buddha's bowl. When the Buddha had eaten them, Yaśodharā hoped that, in accordance with her wish, they would be able to share joy together again just as before. The Buddha ate them but appeared no different, his mind and eyes remaining clear and quiet.

Yaśodharā said, "That he does not now move is just because the power of the potion has not yet become active, that's all. Once the strength of the potion has taken effect, events will certainly turn out just as I have wished." When the Buddha had finished his

而呪愿已从座起去。耶输陀
罗冀药力晡时日入当发必还
宫中。佛食如常身心无异。
诸比丘明日食时。着衣持钵
入城乞食。具闻此事增益恭
敬。佛力无量神心难测不可
思议。耶输陀罗药欢喜丸其
力甚大。而世尊食之身心无
异。诸比丘食已出城。以是
事具白世尊。

而呪願已從座起去。耶輸陀
羅冀藥力晡時日入當發必還
宮中。佛食如常身心無異。
諸比丘明日食時。著衣持鉢
入城乞食。具聞此事增益恭
敬。佛力無量神心難測不可
思議。耶輸陀羅藥歡喜丸其
力甚大。而世尊食之身心無
異。諸比丘食已出城。以是
事具白世尊。

简体字

正體字

meal and the spell had already been cast, he arose from his seat and left. Yaśodharā hoped that the power of the potion would take effect in the late afternoon and that it would then become active, certainly causing him to return then to the palace. However, the Buddha remained then the same as ever, no different in either body or mind.

When it came time on the next day for the Bhikshus to take their meal, they put on their robes, took up their bowls, and then went forth into the city to seek alms. They all then heard of this event and were thus moved to increased reverence, thinking, "The powers of the Buddha are immeasurable. His spirit and mind are difficult to fathom. They are inconceivable and indescribable. The power of Yaśodharā's delightful dumplings was extremely great and yet the Bhagavān ate them with no change being wrought on either his body or his mind."

When the Bhikshus had finished eating and had gone forth from the city, they reported the entire matter to the Bhagavān.

佛告諸比[4]丘。此耶輸陀羅。非但今世以歡喜丸惑我。乃往過去世時。亦以歡喜丸惑我。爾時世尊。為諸比丘說本生因緣。過去久遠世時。[5]婆羅奈國山中有仙人。以仲[6]春之月於澡[*]槃中小便。見鹿麚麂合會。婬心即動精流[*]槃中。麂鹿飲之即時有[7]娠。滿月生子形類如人。唯頭有一角其足似鹿。鹿當產時至仙人[8]菴邊而產。見子是人。以付仙人而去。仙人出時見此鹿子。自念本緣。知是己兒取已養育。及其年大懃教學問。通十八種大經。又學坐禪行四無量心[9]即得五神通。一時上山值大雨。泥滑其足不便。躄地破其[10]鍕持。又傷其足。便大瞋恚。以[*]鍕持盛水呪令不雨。仙人福德諸龍鬼神皆為不雨。不雨故五穀五果盡皆不生。人民窮乏無復生路。[*]婆羅奈[11]國王憂愁懊惱。命諸大[12]官集議雨事。明者議言。我[13]曾傳聞。仙人山中有一角仙人。以足不便故。上山躄地傷足

简体字   正體字

Buddha's Past Life as a One-horned Rishi

The Buddha told the Bhikshus, "As for this Yaśodharā, it is not just in this present life that she has used the delightful dumplings [in an attempt] to confuse me." The Bhagavān then described the past life causes and conditions behind this, saying, "In a time long ago and far off in the past, there was a rishi in the mountains of the state of Benares who, in the early spring was relieving himself into a basin when he observed a buck and a doe mating. Lustful thoughts suddenly arose in him, whereupon his semen flowed into the basin.

The doe happened to drink from that basin and became pregnant. When the months of pregnancy were complete, she gave birth to a fawn with the appearance of a man. There were only [the differences of] a single horn on the head and feet like those of a deer. When the deer was about to fawn, she went to a place alongside the rishi's hut and gave birth. She saw that her fawn was a person and so entrusted it to the rishi and left.

When the rishi came out, he saw this progeny of the deer, recalled to himself the original conditions, knew that it was his own son, and so took him and raised him. As [the son] grew to adulthood, he was diligent in instructing him in the topics of study so that he was able to penetrate the eighteen great classics. Additionally, he studied sitting in dhyāna meditation, practiced the four immeasurable minds, and then immediately gained the five superknowledges.

Once, he was climbing up the mountain and encountered a great rainstorm. The mud became slippery, causing him to lose his footing, fall to the ground, break his ewer, and injure his foot. He became greatly enraged. With a ewer full of water, he then cast a spell intended to cause all rains to cease. Due to the influence of the meritorious qualities possessed by this rishi, the dragons, ghosts, and spirits acted on his behalf to prevent any further rain.

Because it did not rain, the five types of grains and the five types of fruit all failed to grow. The populace became impoverished, destitute, and without any way whereby they might go on living. The king of the state of Benares was distressed, worried, and tormented by grief. He ordered all of the great officials to convene and discuss the rainfall situation.

One of the intelligent ones among them offered an opinion, saying, "I have heard it rumored that up in the Rishi Mountains there is a one-horned rishi who, on account of losing his footing, fell down as he ascended the mountain, injuring his foot. He cast a

瞋呪此雨令十二年不墮。王思惟言。若十二年不雨我國了矣。無復人民。王即開募。其有能令仙人失五通。屬我為民者。當與分國半治。是[*]婆羅奈國有婬女。名曰扇陀。端正[14]無雙。來應王募問諸人言。此是人非[15]人。眾人言。是人耳。仙人所生。婬女言。若是人者我能壞之。作是語已取金[*]槃盛好寶物。語[*]國王言。我當騎此仙人項來。婬女即時求五百乘車載五百美女。[16]五百鹿車載種種歡喜丸。皆以眾[17]藥和之。以[18]眾彩畫之令似雜果及持種種大力美酒色味如水。服樹皮衣草[19]衣。行林樹間[20]以像仙人。於仙人[*]菴邊作草庵而住。一角仙人遊行見之。諸女皆出迎逆。好華[21]好香供養仙人。仙人大喜。諸女[22]皆以美言敬辭問訊仙人。將入房中坐好床蓐。與好[23]淨酒以為淨水。與歡喜丸以為果蓏。食飲飽已語諸女言。我從生已來初未得如此好果好水。

简体字

瞋呪此雨令十二年不墮。王思惟言。若十二年不雨我國了矣。無復人民。王即開募。其有能令仙人失五通。屬我為民者。當與分國半治。是[*]婆羅奈國有婬女。名曰扇陀。端正[14]無雙。來應王募問諸人言。此是人非[15]人。眾人言。是人耳。仙人所生。婬女言。若是人者我能壞之。作是語已取金[*]槃盛好寶物。語[*]國王言。我當騎此仙人項來。婬女即時求五百乘車載五百美女。[16]五百鹿車載種種歡喜丸。皆以眾[17]藥和之。以[18]眾彩畫之令似雜果及持種種大力美酒色味如水。服樹皮衣草[19]衣。行林樹間[20]以像仙人。於仙人[*]菴邊作草庵而住。一角仙人遊行見之。諸女皆出迎逆。好華[21]好香供養仙人。仙人大喜。諸女[22]皆以美言敬辭問訊仙人。將入房中坐好床蓐。與好[23]淨酒以為淨水。與歡喜丸以為果蓏。食飲飽已語諸女言。我從生已來初未得如此好果好水。

正體字

hateful spell on these rains whereby he caused them to not fall for a period of twelve years."

The King thought to himself, "If it goes twelve years without raining, my country will surely be finished. There will be no people left at all." The King then issued an appeal, stating, "Could it be that there is someone who is able to cause a rishi to lose his five superknowledges who will instruct me in this for the sake of the population? I will divide the country so that we might each rule half."

In this country of Benares, there was a courtesan by the name of Śāntā who was incomparably beautiful. She came in response to the King's appeal and asked everyone there, "Is this a man or one who is not a man?"

Everyone replied, "He is a man, that's all. He was born to a rishi."

The courtesan said, "If he is a man, I will be able to destroy him." After she had said this, she took up a tray made of gold filled up with fine and precious objects, and told the king of the country, "I will come back here mounted on the neck of this rishi."

The courtesan then immediately sought to assemble five hundred carriages carrying five hundred beautiful maidens and five hundred deer-carts carrying all sorts of delightful morsels all of which had been admixed with many herbs. She used many different hues to color them so that they appeared like various kinds of fruits and then took all sorts of greatly powerful fine liquors which, in appearance and flavor, were identical to water.

They dressed in tree bark clothing and grass clothing and traveled into the forest, appearing thereby as if they were rishis themselves. They set up grass huts off to one side of the rishi's hut and then took up residence there. The one-horned rishi was wandering about and observed them. The maidens all came out and welcomed him. They used beautiful flowers and fine incenses as offerings to the rishi. The rishi was greatly delighted.

All of the maidens used lovely words and respectful phrases in greeting the rishi. They took him on into their quarters and sat with him on fine bedding. They gave him fine clear liquor which he took to be pure water. They gave him delightful morsels which he took to be fruit. After he had feasted and drunk his fill, he told the maidens, "From the time of my birth on up to the present, this is a first. I have never yet had such fine fruit and such fine water."

諸女言。我[24]以一心行善故天與我。願得此[25]好果好水。仙人問諸女。汝何以故膚色肥盛。答言。我曹食此好果。飲此美水故肥[26]盛如此。女白仙人言。汝何以不在此間住。答曰。亦可住耳。女言。可共澡洗即亦可之。女手柔軟觸之心動。便復與諸[27]美女更互相洗。欲心轉生遂成婬事。即失神通天為大雨七日七夜。令得歡[28]喜飲食。七日[29]已後酒[30]果皆盡。繼以山水木果。其味不美更索前者。答言。已盡今當共行。去此不遠有可得處。仙人言。隨意。即便共出。[31]婬女知去城不遠。女便在道中臥言。我極不能復行。仙人言。汝不能行者。騎我項上當[32]項汝去。女先遣信白王。王可觀我智能。王勅嚴駕出而觀之。問言。何由得爾。

諸女言。我[24]以一心行善故天與我。願得此[25]好果好水。仙人問諸女。汝何以故膚色肥盛。答言。我曹食此好果。飲此美水故肥[26]盛如此。女白仙人言。汝何以不在此間住。答曰。亦可住耳。女言。可共澡洗即亦可之。女手柔軟觸之心動。便復與諸[27]美女更互相洗。欲心轉生遂成婬事。即失神通天為大雨七日七夜。令得歡[28]喜飲食。七日[29]已後酒[30]果皆盡。繼以山水木果。其味不美更索前者。答言。已盡今當共行。去此不遠有可得處。仙人言。隨意。即便共出。[31]婬女知去城不遠。女便在道中臥言。我極不能復行。仙人言。汝不能行者。騎我項上當[32]項汝去。女先遣信白王。王可觀我智能。王勅嚴駕出而觀之。問言。何由得爾。

简体字 　 正體字

The maidens said, "It is because we have been single-minded in our practice of goodness that the gods fulfill our wishes to obtain these fine fruits and fine water."

The rishi asked the maidens, "How is it that your complexions and bodies are so full and flourishing?"

They replied, saying, "It is because we eat these fine fruits and drink this marvelous water that our bodies are so full and flourishing as this." The maidens addressed the rishi, saying, "Why don't you come and live here among us?"

He replied, saying, "I, too, could abide here."

The maidens said, "We could even bathe together." He then assented to that as well. The hands of the maidens were soft and tender. When they touched him, his mind moved. He then continued to bathe together with the beautiful maidens. Desirous thoughts began to develop and consequently he engaged in sexual intercourse. He immediately lost his superknowledges, whereupon the heavens made a great downpour of rain which went on for seven days and seven nights allowing them the opportunity to devote themselves to the delights of food and drink.

After the seven days had passed, the liquor and fruit were all gone, whereupon they continued to supply their needs with the waters of the mountain and the fruits from the trees. However, their flavors were not so marvelous, and so he sought more of what they had before.

She replied to him, saying, "They are already used up. We must now go together to a place, not far from here, where they can be gotten."

The rishi said, "We can do as you wish." They then went off together. The courtesan knew when they had come to a spot not far off from the city. The maiden then lay down in the middle of the road and said, "I'm exhausted. I can't walk any further."

The rishi said, "If it's the case that you cannot walk, sit up on my shoulders and I will carry you forth."

The maiden had already sent along beforehand a letter to the King in which she told the King, "The King will be able to observe my intelligence and abilities."

The King ordered up his official carriage and went forth to observe them. He asked, "How did you manage to bring this about?"

女白王言。我以方便力故今
已如此。無所復能。令住城
中好供養恭敬之。[33]足五
所欲。拜為大臣住城少日。
身轉羸瘦。念禪定心樂厭此
世欲。王問仙人。汝何不樂
身轉羸瘦。仙人答王。我雖
得五欲。常自憶念林間閑靜
諸仙遊處不能去心。王自思
惟。若我強違其志。違志為
苦苦極則死。本以求除旱
患。今已得之。當復何緣強
奪其志。即發遣之。既還山
中精進不久還得五通。佛告
諸比丘。一角仙人我身是
也。婬女者耶輸陀羅是。爾
時以歡喜丸惑我。我未斷結
為之所惑。今復欲以藥歡喜
丸惑我不可得也。以是事故
知。細軟觸法能動仙人。何
況愚夫。如是種種因緣。是
名呵細滑欲。如是呵五欲

女白王言。我以方便力故今
已如此。無所復能。令住城
中好供養恭敬之。[33]足五
所欲。拜為大臣住城少日。
身轉羸瘦。念禪定心樂厭此
世欲。王問仙人。汝何不樂
身轉羸瘦。仙人答王。我雖
得五欲。常自憶念林間閑靜
諸仙遊處不能去心。王自思
惟。若我強違其志。違志為
苦苦極則死。本以求除旱
患。今已得之。當復何緣強
奪其志。即發遣之。既還山
中精進不久還得五通。佛告
諸比丘。一角仙人我身是
也。婬女者耶輸陀羅是。爾
時以歡喜丸惑我。我未斷結
為之所惑。今復欲以藥歡喜
丸惑我不可得也。以是事故
知。細軟觸法能動仙人。何
況愚夫。如是種種因緣。是
名呵細滑欲。如是呵五欲

简体字   正體字

The maiden addressed the King, saying, "It is on account of the power of skillful means that I have now already caused the situation to develop in this way. I have no abilities beyond this. Order him to live within the city. Make fine offerings to him and pay respects to him. Keep him satisfied with the five objects of desire."

The King honored him with the status of a great official. He had dwelt in the city for only a short span of days when his body became haggard and emaciated. He remembered the mental bliss of dhyāna absorptions and so grew disgusted with these worldly desires. The King asked the rishi, "How is it that you have become so unhappy that your body is now so haggard and emaciated?"

The rishi replied to the King, "Although I have gained the five desires, I constantly recall to mind the leisure and stillness in the forest, the wandering place of all the rishis. I cannot get it out of my mind."

The King thought to himself, "If I force him to go against his aspirations, such a going against one's aspirations is suffering. If the suffering reaches an extreme, then he will die. Originally, this was on account of seeking to get rid of the calamity of drought. Now I have already succeeded in that. Why should I continue to forcibly keep him from his aspirations?" He then released him.

After he had returned to the mountains, he had not applied himself vigorously for long before he regained the five superknowledges.

The Buddha told the Bhikshus, "The one-horned rishi was myself. The courtesan was Yaśodharā. At that time she deceived me with the delightful dumplings. I had not yet cut off the fetters and so was tricked by her. Now she again wished to use the delightful dumplings to trick me but was unable to succeed."

On account of this matter one knows that the dharma of subtle and tender touch is able to move even a rishi, how much the more would this be so of any foolish common person. All sorts of causes and conditions such as these illustrate what is meant by renouncing the desire for [sensations of] subtle smoothness. In this fashion one renounces the five desires.

复次外道声闻菩萨皆得禅定。而外道禅中有三种患。或味着或邪见或憍慢。声闻禅中慈悲薄。于诸法中[8]不以利智贯达诸法实相。独善其身断诸佛种。菩萨禅[9]中无此事。欲集一切诸佛法故。于诸禅中不忘众生。乃至[10]昆虫常加慈念。如释迦文尼佛。本为螺[11]髻仙人。名尚阇[12]利。常行第四禅。出入息断在一树下坐[13]兀然不动。鸟见如此谓之为木。即于髻中生卵。是菩萨从禅觉知[14]头上有鸟卵。即自思惟。若我起动鸟母必不复来。鸟母不来鸟卵必坏。即还入禅。至鸟子飞去尔乃起。

復次外道聲聞菩薩皆得禪定。而外道禪中有三種患。或味著或邪見或憍慢。聲聞禪中慈悲薄。於諸法中[8]不以利智貫達諸法實相。獨善其身斷諸佛種。菩薩禪[9]中無此事。欲集一切諸佛法故。於諸禪中不忘眾生。乃至[10]昆蟲常加慈念。如釋迦文尼佛。本為螺[11]髻仙人。名尚闍[12]利。常行第四禪。出入息斷在一樹下坐[13]兀然不動。鳥見如此謂之為木。即於髻中生卵。是菩薩從禪覺知[14]頭上有鳥卵。即自思惟。若我起動鳥母必不復來。鳥母不來鳥卵必壞。即還入禪。至鳥子飛去爾乃起。

简体字　　　　　　　　　　　　　正體字

The Buddha's Past Life as Śaṅkhācārya, the Rishi

Nāgārjuna's Preamble

Additionally, non-Buddhists, the Śrāvaka Disciples, and the Bodhisattvas all achieve dhyāna absorption. However there are three sorts of calamities within the dhyāna of the non-Buddhists: In some cases, they are attached to its delectability. In some cases, they hold erroneous views. In some cases, they are afflicted with arrogance and pride. Within the dhyāna of the Śrāvaka Disciples, loving-kindness and compassion are scant. They do not employ sharp wisdom to penetrate through to the true character of dharmas. They exclusively benefit their own persons and sever the lineage of the Buddhas. The dhyāna of the bodhisattva is free of such issues. Because they wish to accumulate the Dharma of all Buddhas, even in the midst of the dhyānas, they do not forget beings and constantly retain a lovingly-kind mindfulness for even the smallest insects.

Story: The Buddha's Past Life as Śaṅkhācārya, the Rishi

This is illustrated by Shakyamuni Buddha who, in a previous life, was the conch-haired rishi by the name of Śaṅkhācārya who constantly cultivated the fourth dhyāna. His respiration had become cut off . He was sitting, erect and unmoving, beneath a tree. A bird saw him like this, took him to be a tree, and then laid its eggs in his hair. This bodhisattva came out of his dhyāna [absorption] and realized that there were bird's eggs laid on his head. He then thought to himself, "If I get up and move about, the mother bird will certainly not come back again. If the mother bird does not return, the bird's eggs will certainly be ruined." He then went back into dhyāna again. [He remained there] until the young birds had flown away. Then and only then did he get up [from his meditation spot].

复次菩萨观一切法。若乱若定皆是不二相。馀人[30]除乱求定。何以故。以乱法中起瞋想。于定法中生着想。如欝陀罗伽仙人。得五通日日飞到[1]国王宫中食。王大夫人如其国法[2]捉足而礼。夫人手触即失神通。从王求车乘驾而出。还其本处入林树间。更求五通一心专至。垂当得时有鸟在树上。急鸣以乱其意。舍树至水边求定。复闻鱼鬭动水之声。此人求禅不得。即生瞋恚。我当尽杀鱼鸟。此人久后思惟得定。生非有想非无想处。于彼寿尽下生作飞狸。杀诸鱼鸟作无量罪堕三恶道。是[3]为禅定[4]中着心因缘。

復次菩薩觀一切法。若亂若定皆是不二相。餘人[30]除亂求定。何以故。以亂法中起瞋想。於定法中生著想。如欝陀羅伽仙人。得五通日日飛到[1]國王宮中食。王大夫人如其國法[2]捉足而禮。夫人手觸即失神通。從王求車乘駕而出。還其本處入林樹間。更求五通一心專至。垂當得時有鳥在樹上。急鳴以亂其意。捨樹至水邊求定。復聞魚鬭動水之聲。此人求禪不得。即生瞋恚。我當盡殺魚鳥。此人久後思惟得定。生非有想非無想處。於彼壽盡下生作飛狸。殺諸魚鳥作無量罪墮三惡道。是[3]為禪定[4]中著心因緣。

简体字　　　　　　　　　　正體字

The Downfall of Udraka, the Rishi

Nāgārjuna's Preamble: The Bodhisattva's Contemplation

Additionally, as the bodhisattva contemplates all dharmas, whether they be [dharmas associated with mental] scatteredness or whether they be [dharmas associated with] the absorptions, in every case [he realizes that] they are non-dual in character. Other persons apply themselves to getting rid of mental scatteredness and seeking the absorptions. Why is this? It is because, in the midst of dharmas associated with scatteredness, their thoughts are freighted with hatefulness whereas, in the midst of dharmas associated with the absorptions, they develop thoughts characterized by attachment.

Story: The Downfall of Udraka, the Rishi

This is illustrated by the case of Udraka, the rishi. He had gained the five superknowledges. Every day he flew to the palace of the King where he took his meal.

[One day] according with the traditions of her country, the King's wife made obeisance to him, grasping his feet as she did so. When the wife's hands touched him, he immediately lost his spiritual powers. He [was forced to] seek a carriage from the King. He got into the carriage and left, returning to his original dwelling place.

He then went into the forest and again sought the five super-knowledges, applying himself to the endeavor single-mindedly and exclusively. Just when he was about to gain them again, there was a bird up in a tree which started calling out urgently, thus causing his mind to become scattered.

He then left that tree behind and went to the shore of a body of a lake and sought absorption there. He then repeatedly heard the splashing sound of a fish jumping. This man was then unsuccessful in seeking to enter dhyāna and so became enraged, swearing "I ought to kill every one of the fish and the birds, too!"

Much later, this man's cultivation of contemplative thought resulted in his gaining the absorptions. He was reborn in the station of neither perception nor non-perception. When that lifetime came to an end, he fell down into rebirth as a flying fox which killed birds and fish thus creating an incalculable number of karmic offenses.

As a result, he fell into rebirth in the three wretched destinies.

This is a set of causal circumstances associated with a mind attached to the dhyāna absorptions.

佛弟子中亦有一比丘。得四
禅生增上慢谓得四道。得初
禅时谓是须陀洹。第二禅时
谓是斯陀含。第三禅时谓是
阿那含。第四禅时谓得阿罗
汉。恃是而止不复求进。命
欲尽时见有四禅中阴相来。
便生邪见。谓无涅盘佛为欺
我。恶邪生故失四禅中阴。
便见阿鼻泥[5]犁中阴相。命
终即生阿鼻地狱。诸比丘问
佛。某甲比丘阿兰若命终生
何处。佛言。是人生阿鼻泥
[*]犁中。诸比丘皆大惊怪。
此人坐禅持戒所由尔耶。佛
言。此人增上慢。得四禅时
谓得四道故。临命终时见四
禅中阴相。便生邪见谓无涅
盘。我是阿罗汉今还复生。
佛为虚诳。是时即见阿鼻泥
[*]犁中阴相。命终即生阿鼻
地狱中。是时佛说偈言

简体字

佛弟子中亦有一比丘。得四
禪生增上慢謂得四道。得初
禪時謂是須陀洹。第二禪時
謂是斯陀含。第三禪時謂是
阿那含。第四禪時謂得阿羅
漢。恃是而止不復求進。命
欲盡時見有四禪中陰相來。
便生邪見。謂無涅槃佛為欺
我。惡邪生故失四禪中陰。
便見阿鼻泥[5]犁中陰相。命
終即生阿鼻地獄。諸比丘問
佛。某甲比丘阿蘭若命終生
何處。佛言。是人生阿鼻泥
[*]犁中。諸比丘皆大驚怪。
此人坐禪持戒所由爾耶。佛
言。此人增上慢。得四禪時
謂得四道故。臨命終時見四
禪中陰相。便生邪見謂無涅
槃。我是阿羅漢今還復生。
佛為虛誑。是時即見阿鼻泥
[*]犁中陰相。命終即生阿鼻
地獄中。是時佛說偈言

正體字

A Bhikshu Brought Down Over Pride in His Meditation

Among the disciples of the Buddha there was also a bhikshu who had gained the fourth dhyāna and had developed such extreme arrogance he assumed he had gained the four-fold path [of the arhats]. When he had gained the first dhyāna, he thought it was [the stage of] the *srota-āpanna*. When he gained the second dhyāna, he thought it was [the stage of] the *sakṛdāgāmin*. When he gained the third dhyāna, he thought it was [the stage of] the *anāgāmin*. When he gained the fourth dhyāna, he thought he had gained arhatship.

Based on this, he stopped applying himself and did not seek to advance any further. When his life was about to come to an end, he saw the signs of the arrival of the intermediary aggregates [bringing rebirth in] the fourth dhyāna [heavens]. He reacted to this with a wrong view whereby he thought, "There is no such thing as nirvāṇa. The Buddha has cheated me." On account of generating this maliciously perverse idea, he lost the intermediary aggregates [leading to rebirth in] the fourth dhyāna [heavens] and next saw the signs of the arrival of the intermediary aggregates associated with the Avīci [hells]. [As a consequence], when his life came to an end, he was immediately reborn in the Avīci hells. The Bhikshus asked the Buddha, "When bhikshu so-and-so, the *araṇya* hermitage dweller died, where was he reborn?"

The Buddha said, "This man was reborn in the Avīci hells."

The Bhikshus were all greatly startled and amazed, "This man sat in dhyāna meditation and upheld the precepts. Could this be the basis for such a circumstance?"

The Buddha said, "This man was extremely arrogant. This happened because when he gained the four dhyānas, he believed he had actually gained the four-fold path [of the arhats]. Then, when his life was coming to its end, he saw the signs of the fourth dhyāna intermediary aggregates and generated a wrong view, thinking, 'There is no such thing as nirvāṇa. I am an arhat [and yet] I am now returning to be born yet again. The Buddha's [teachings] are false and deceptive.'

"At this very time, he immediately saw the signs of the intermediary aggregates of the Avīci hells. When his life ended, he was immediately reborn in the Avīci hells." The Buddha then uttered a verse, saying:

多闻持戒禅　　未得无漏法
虽有此功德　　此事不可信
[0189a28] 是比丘受是恶道苦。
是故知。取乱相能生瞋等烦
恼。取定相能生着。菩萨不
取乱相。亦不取禅定相。乱
定相一故是名禅波罗蜜。

多聞持戒禪　　未得無漏法
雖有此功德　　此事不可信
[0189a28] 是比丘受是惡道苦。
是故知。取亂相能生瞋等煩
惱。取定相能生著。菩薩不
取亂相。亦不取禪定相。亂
定相一故是名禪波羅蜜。

简体字

正體字

One may have much learning, uphold the precepts, and be adept at
  dhyāna,
While not yet having gained the dharma beyond outflow impurities.
Although one may possess these meritorious qualities,
This situation is one in which one cannot have faith.

Concluding Exegesis Discussion

This bhikshu underwent this suffering in the wretched destinies.
One may realize from this that if one grasps at the characteristic
features of scatteredness, one may develop hate-filled thoughts and
other such afflictions. If one seizes upon the characteristics associated with the absorptions, then one develop attachments based on
this.

The bodhisattva does not seize upon the characteristics associated with mental scatteredness nor does he seize upon the characteristics associated with the dhyāna absorptions. This is because
the characteristics of scatteredness and absorption are singular in
character. It is this [realization] which qualifies as [concordant with]
the pāramitā of dhyāna.

Part Six:

NĀGĀRJUNA'S STORIES ON WISDOM

问曰。若辟支佛道亦如是者。云何分别声闻辟支佛。答曰。道虽一种而用智有异。若诸佛不出佛法已灭。是人先世因缘故。独出智慧不从他闻。自以智慧得道。如一国王出在园中游戏。清朝见林树华菓蔚茂甚可爱乐。王食已而卧。王诸夫人婇女。皆共取华毁折林树。王觉已见林毁坏而自觉悟。一切世间无常变坏皆亦如是。思惟是已无漏道心生断[13]诸结使得辟支佛道。具六神通即飞到闲静林间。如是等因缘。先世福德愿行果报。今世见少因缘。成辟支佛道如是为异。

問曰。若辟支佛道亦如是者。云何分別聲聞辟支佛。答曰。道雖一種而用智有異。若諸佛不出佛法已滅。是人先世因緣故。獨出智慧不從他聞。自以智慧得道。如一國王出在園中遊戲。清朝見林樹華菓蔚茂甚可愛樂。王食已而臥。王諸夫人婇女。皆共取華毀折林樹。王覺已見林毀壞而自覺悟。一切世間無常變壞皆亦如是。思惟是已無漏道心生斷[13]諸結使得辟支佛道。具六神通即飛到閑靜林間。如是等因緣。先世福德願行果報。今世見少因緣。成辟支佛道如是為異。

简体字   正體字

The King Enlightened by Damaged Gardens

Nāgārjuna's Introduction

Question: If it is the case that the path of a pratyekabuddha is the same [as that of an arhat], how then is one able to distinguish between the Śrāvaka Disciples and the Pratyekabuddhas?

Response: Although their paths are of a single type, still, their uses of wisdom have their differences. In a case where buddhas have not come forth [into the world] or the Dharma of any given buddha has already become extinct, this person, on account of causal factors associated with previous lifetimes, brings forth wisdom on his own and does not do so based on hearing it [directly, in this life], from anyone else. On his own, he employs wisdom to realize the Path.

Story: The King Enlightened by Damaged Gardens

This is illustrated by an instance in which the king of a country had gone out into his gardens to wander about and enjoy himself. In the very early morning he observed the trees in the grove, the flowers, and the fruit. They were extremely lovely and pleasurable. After the King had eaten, he then lay down to take a nap. Meanwhile, the wives and female entertainers of the King all went about picking flowers and, in the process, damaged the trees by breaking off branches.

After the King awoke, he observed the destruction in the grove and became spontaneously enlightened to the fact that all worlds are impermanent and bound to destruction in just this same way. After he had contemplated this, the mind of the path of no outflow impurities arose in him, he cut off the fetters, gained the way of the pratyekabuddha, perfected the six superknowledges, and flew off into an unoccupied and quiet area of the forest.

Concluding Exegesis Passage

On account of causal circumstances such as these which arise as retribution for previous-life meritorious deeds, vows, and practices, one may need in this life only to observe a minor cause or condition and then be able to perfect the path of the pratyekabuddha as a result. It is factors such as these which constitute the difference [between the paths of a pratyekabuddha and an arhat].

问曰。佛处处说观有为法无常苦空无我令人得道。云何言无常堕邪见。答曰。佛处处说无常。处处说不灭。如摩诃男释王来至佛所白佛言。是迦毘罗人众殷多。我或值奔车逸马狂象鬪人时。便失念佛心。是时自念。我今若死当生何处。佛告摩诃男。汝勿怖勿畏。汝是时不生恶趣必至善处。譬如树常东向曲。若有斫者必当东倒。善人亦如是。若身坏死时。善心意识长夜以信戒闻施慧熏[1]心故。必得利益上生天上。若一切法念念生灭无常。佛云何言诸功德[2]熏心故[3]必得上生。以是故知非无常性。

問曰。佛處處說觀有為法無常苦空無我令人得道。云何言無常墮邪見。答曰。佛處處說無常。處處說不滅。如摩訶男釋王來至佛所白佛言。是迦毘羅人眾殷多。我或值奔車逸馬狂象鬪人時。便失念佛心。是時自念。我今若死當生何處。佛告摩訶男。汝勿怖勿畏。汝是時不生惡趣必至善處。譬如樹常東向曲。若有斫者必當東倒。善人亦如是。若身壞死時。善心意識長夜以信戒聞施慧熏[1]心故。必得利益上生天上。若一切法念念生滅無常。佛云何言諸功德[2]熏心故[3]必得上生。以是故知非無常性。

简体字

正體字

King Mahānāman's Worries About Rebirth

Nāgārjuna's Introduction

Question: In place after place, the Buddha instructed one to contemplate conditioned dharmas as impermanent, suffering, empty, and devoid of self, thus causing people to gain the Path. How then can you state that, when one posits the reality of "impermanence," that constitutes an erroneous view?

Response: In place after place, the Buddha spoke of impermanence and in place after place, he spoke of [certain factors] "not being destroyed."

Story: King Mahānāman's Worries about Rebirth

Take for instance when the Shākyan King, Mahānāman, came to where the Buddha dwelt and addressed the Buddha, saying, "The population of Kapilavastu is huge. Sometimes when I encounter a speeding chariot, a runaway horse, a crazed elephant or battling people, I lose the thought focused on mindfulness of the Buddha. At these times, I think to myself, "If I died now, where would I be reborn?"

The Buddha told Mahānāman, "You should not be frightened. Do not fear. At such a time, you would not be reborn in one of the wretched destinies. You would certainly proceed to a good place. This is analogous to a tree which has always leaned well to the east. If there is someone who cuts it down, it will certainly fall toward the east.

"The situation is identical in the case of a person who is good. When the body deteriorates and one then dies, because throughout the long night [of time], the mental consciousness of the wholesome mind has imbued the mind with faith, moral virtue, learning, giving, and wisdom, one will certainly gain the benefit of it and thus achieve rebirth in the heavens."

Concluding Exegesis Discussion

If it was the case that all dharmas are impermanent by virtue of being produced and destroyed in every thought moment, why did the Buddha say that, because all of the meritorious qualities permeate the mind, one will certainly gain a superior rebirth? On account of this, one should realize that [dharmas] are not impermanent by nature.

问曰。若无常不实。佛何以
说无常。答曰。佛随众生所
应而说法。[4]破常颠倒故说
无常。以人不知不信后世
故。说心去后世上生天上。
罪福业因缘百千万劫不失。
是对治悉檀。非第一义悉
檀。诸法实相非常非无常。
佛亦处处说诸法空。诸法空
中亦无无常。以是故说世间
无常是邪见。是故名为法
空。

問曰。若無常不實。佛何以
說無常。答曰。佛隨眾生所
應而說法。[4]破常顛倒故說
無常。以人不知不信後世
故。說心去後世上生天上。
罪福業因緣百千萬劫不失。
是對治悉檀。非第一義悉
檀。諸法實相非常非無常。
佛亦處處說諸法空。諸法空
中亦無無常。以是故說世間
無常是邪見。是故名為法
空。

简体字   正體字

Question: If impermanence is not actually the case, why did the Buddha speak of impermanence?

Response: The Buddha accorded with what was appropriate for [particular] beings and so spoke that dharma for their sakes. It was in order to refute the inverted view [which imagines] permanence that he spoke of impermanence.

[In the opposite case], because people were unaware of or did not believe in later existences, he spoke of the mind going on into a later existence and being reborn in the heavens, [explaining that] the karmic causes and conditions of offenses and merit are not lost even in a million kalpas.

These are instances of the counteractive *siddhānta* (doctrinal perspective). They do not reflect [the ultimate truth of] the supreme meaning *siddhānta*. The true character of dharmas does not involve either the concept of permanence or the concept of impermanence. Then, too, the Buddha spoke in place after place of the emptiness of dharmas. In the emptiness of dharmas, impermanence is nonexistent. It is for these reasons that it is stated here that to claim that the world is impermanent is an erroneous view. Hence one refers to the emptiness of dharmas.

复次毘耶离梵志名论力。诸
[5]梨昌等大[6]雇其宝物令与
佛论。取其[7]雇已。即以其
夜思撰五百难。明旦与诸
[*]梨昌至佛所。问佛言。一
究竟道为众多究竟道。佛
言。一究竟道无众多也。梵
志言。佛说一道。诸外道师
各各有究竟道。是为众多非
一。佛言。是虽[8]各有众多
皆非实道。何以故。一切皆
以邪见着故。不名究竟道。
佛问梵志。鹿头梵志得道
不。答言。一切得道中是为
第一。是时长老鹿头梵志比
丘在佛后扇佛。佛问梵志。
汝识是比丘不。梵志识之惭
愧低头。是时佛说义品偈

各各谓究竟　而各自爱着
各自是非彼　是皆非究竟
是人入论众　辩明义理时
各各相是非　胜负怀忧喜

简体字

復次毘耶離梵志名論力。諸
[5]梨昌等大[6]雇其寶物令與
佛論。取其[7]雇已。即以其
夜思撰五百難。明旦與諸
[*]梨昌至佛所。問佛言。一
究竟道為眾多究竟道。佛
言。一究竟道無眾多也。梵
志言。佛說一道。諸外道師
各各有究竟道。是為眾多非
一。佛言。是雖[8]各有眾多
皆非實道。何以故。一切皆
以邪見著故。不名究竟道。
佛問梵志。鹿頭梵志得道
不。答言。一切得道中是為
第一。是時長老鹿頭梵志比
丘在佛後扇佛。佛問梵志。
汝識是比丘不。梵志識之慚
愧低頭。是時佛說義品偈

各各謂究竟　而各自愛著
各自是非彼　是皆非究竟
是人入論眾　辯明義理時
各各相是非　勝負懷憂喜

正體字

Vivādabala Attempts to Debate the Buddha

Additionally, [there is the case of] the brahmacārin from Vaiśali known as "Power of Debate" (Vivādabala) The Liccavis had given him many precious things to obtain his services so that he was caused to go and debate with the Buddha. After he had entered their employ, that night he thought over and selected five hundred challenging questions [as debate topics] and early the next morning went with the Liccavis to the place where the Buddha dwelt. He asked the Buddha, "Is there one ultimate path or are there many ultimate paths?"

The Buddha replied, "There is one ultimate path. There are not many."

The Brahmacārin said, "The Buddha claims that there is one path, yet all of the non-Buddhist masters each have an ultimate path. These constitute 'many,' not just 'one.'"

The Buddha said, "Although each has his own and there are many of them, in every case they are not the actual path. Why? It is because all of them are attached to erroneous views that they do not qualify as the ultimate path."

The Buddha then asked the Brahmacarin, "Has Deer Head (Mṛgaśiras) Brahmacārin realized the Path or not?"

He replied, "That individual is the one foremost among all who have realized the path."

It just so happened that the elder Deer Head Brahmacārin was standing as a bhikshu behind the Buddha at that very time, fanning the Buddha. The Buddha then asked the Brahmacārin, "Do you recognize this bhikshu here or not?" The Brahmacārin then recognized him and, struck with shame, lowered his head. The Buddha then uttered this verse found in the *Categories of Meaning* (the *Arthavarga*):

> Everyone is of the opinion that he [possesses] the ultimate,
> And so each is affectionately self-attached.
> Each sees himself as right and attributes fault to others.
> These in every case are not the ultimate.
>
> These people enter into the debate assembly.
> As they then engage in making clear distinctions among meanings
>   and principles,
> Each [speaks of] the rights and wrongs of the other.
> The victor and the defeated cherish distress and delight.

胜者堕憍坑　　负者[9]堕忧狱
是故有智者　　不随此二法
论力汝当知　　我诸弟子法
无虚亦无实　　汝欲何所求
汝欲坏我论　　终已无此处
一切智难胜　　适足自毁坏

[0193c01] 如是等处处声闻经中说诸法空。摩诃衍空门者。一切诸法性常自空。不以智慧方便观故空。如佛为须菩提说色。色自空受想行识识[10]自空。十二入十八界十二因缘三十七品十力四无所畏十八不共法大慈大悲萨婆若乃至阿耨多罗三藐三菩提皆自空。

勝者墮憍坑　　負者[9]墮憂獄
是故有智者　　不隨此二法
論力汝當知　　我諸弟子法
無虛亦無實　　汝欲何所求
汝欲壞我論　　終已無此處
一切智難勝　　適足自毀壞

[0193c01] 如是等處處聲聞經中說諸法空。摩訶衍空門者。一切諸法性常自空。不以智慧方便觀故空。如佛為須菩提說色。色自空受想行識識[10]自空。十二入十八界十二因緣三十七品十力四無所畏十八不共法大慈大悲薩婆若乃至阿耨多羅三藐三菩提皆自空。

简体字　　　　　　　　　　　正體字

The victor falls into the pit of arrogance.
The loser falls into the hell of distress.
Therefore, in a case where there is one who is wise,
He does not go along with either of these two dharmas.

"Power of Debate," you ought to know that,
Among my disciples and my Dharma,
There is nothing "false" nor is there anything "real."
What then is it that you are now seeking?

If you are wishing to destroy my discourse [on doctrine],
This is ultimately impossible endeavor.
It is difficult to succeed in vanquishing the knowledge of all modes,
And, in any case, it would be tantamount to destroying even your
    very own [doctrine].

Concluding *Exegesis* Discussion

In place after place within the sutras of the Śrāvaka Disciples there are discussions such as this about the emptiness of all dharmas. As for the Mahāyāna entryway to emptiness, all dharmas, by their very nature, are eternally inherently empty. It is not on account of a contemplation based on expedient means associated with wisdom that they are found to be empty.

This is illustrated by the Buddha's explanation to Subhūti about form: "Form is inherently empty. Feeling, perception, karmic formative factors, and each of the consciousnesses are inherently empty. The twelve sense bases, the eighteen sense realms, the twelve causes and conditions, the thirty seven wings of enlightenment, the ten powers, the four fearlessnesses, the eighteen exclusive dharmas, the great loving-kindness, the great compassion, *sarvajñāna* (omniscience), and so forth until we come to *anuttarasamyaksaṃbodhi* (perfect enlightenment)—they are all entirely inherently empty."

复次观[5]真空人。先有无量布施持戒禅定。其心柔软。诸结使薄。然后得真空。邪见中无此事。但欲以忆想分别邪心取空。譬如田舍人。初不识盐。见[6]贵人以盐着种种肉菜中而食。问言。何以故尔。语言此盐能令诸物味美故。此人便念此盐能令诸物美自味必多。便空抄盐满口食之醎苦伤口。而问言。汝何以言盐能作美。[*]贵人言。痴人。此当筹量多少和之令美。云何纯食盐。无智人闻空解脱门不行诸功德。但欲得空。是为邪见断诸善根。如是等义名为空门。若人入此三门则知佛法义不相违背。能知是事即是般若波罗蜜力。于一切法无所罣碍。

復次觀[5]真空人。先有無量布施持戒禪定。其心柔軟。諸結使薄。然後得真空。邪見中無此事。但欲以憶想分別邪心取空。譬如田舍人。初不識鹽。見[6]貴人以鹽著種種肉菜中而食。問言。何以故爾。語言此鹽能令諸物味美故。此人便念此鹽能令諸物美自味必多。便空抄鹽滿口食之醎苦傷口。而問言。汝何以言鹽能作美。[*]貴人言。癡人。此當籌量多少和之令美。云何純食鹽。無智人聞空解脫門不行諸功德。但欲得空。是為邪見斷諸善根。如是等義名為空門。若人入此三門則知佛法義不相違背。能知是事即是般若波羅蜜力。於一切法無所罣礙。

简体字   正體字

The Uncultured Rustic Discovers Salt

Nāgārjuna's Preamble

Furthermore, a person who contemplates true emptiness has first gone through an incalculable amount of giving, upholding of precepts, and dhyāna absorption. His mind is soft and pliant and his fetters are but scant. Afterwards, he gains [the realization of] true emptiness. In the case of [one who clings to] erroneous views, there have been none of these endeavors. He simply wishes to seize upon emptiness by resort to erroneous thoughts associated with speculations and discriminations.

Story: The Uncultured Rustic Discovers Salt

This is comparable to the man of rural origins who had never before seen salt. He happened to observe a man of noble status flavoring various meat and vegetable dishes with salt before eating them. He asked, "Why is it that you do that?"

The other man replied, "It is because this salt is able to make everything taste delectable."

This man thought, "If salt is able to cause everything to taste delectable, its own flavor must be even more delicious." He then foolishly scooped up salt, filled his mouth, and swallowed it. The intensity of the saltiness injured his mouth whereupon he said, "Why did you claim that salt is able to make for delectability?"

The man of noble background said, "You fool. With something like this, you must carefully calculate how much to mix in to cause [the food] to be delectable. How could you even contemplate just eating salt by itself?"

Concluding Exegesis Discussion

One deficient in wisdom hears of the emptiness gateway to liberation but fails to also cultivate all manner of meritorious qualities. He wishes only to realize emptiness. This is tantamount to the cutting off one's roots of goodness by resorting to erroneous views.

Principles such as these illustrate what is meant by the gateway of emptiness. If one enters into these three gateways [of emptiness, signlessness, and wishlessness], then he will realize that the principles contained in the Dharma of the Buddha are not mutually contradictory. The origin of one's ability to realize this concept is just the power of *prajñāpāramitā*. As a result, one has no hang-ups or obstructions with respect to any dharma.

复次断结有二种。一者断三
毒。心不着人天中五欲。二
者虽不着人天中五欲。于菩
萨功德果报五欲。未能舍
离。如是菩萨应行般若波罗
蜜。譬如长老阿泥卢豆。在
林中坐禅时。净爱天女等。
以净妙之身来试阿泥卢豆。
阿泥卢豆言。诸姊作青色来
不用杂色。欲观不净不能得
观。黄赤白色亦复如是。时
阿泥卢豆。闭目不视。语
言。诸姊远去。是时天女即
灭不现。天[9]福报形犹尚如
是。何况菩萨无量功德果报
五欲。

復次斷結有二種。一者斷三
毒。心不著人天中五欲。二
者雖不著人天中五欲。於菩
薩功德果報五欲。未能捨
離。如是菩薩應行般若波羅
蜜。譬如長老阿泥盧豆。在
林中坐禪時。淨愛天女等。
以淨妙之身來試阿泥盧豆。
阿泥盧豆言。諸姊作青色來
不用雜色。欲觀不淨不能得
觀。黃赤白色亦復如是。時
阿泥盧豆。閉目不視。語
言。諸姊遠去。是時天女即
滅不現。天[9]福報形猶尚如
是。何況菩薩無量功德果報
五欲。

简体字   正體字

Aniruddha and the Heavenly Maidens

Nāgārjuna's Introduction

Furthermore, "cutting off the fetters" is of two types. In the case of the first, one cuts off the three poisons. One's mind does not attach to the objects of the five desires among men and gods. In the case of the second, although one does not attach to the objects of the five desires among men and gods, one has still not yet been able to transcend the objects of the five desires which manifest as a consequence of the bodhisattva's merit. A bodhisattva of this sort should practice the *prajñāpāramitā*.

Story: Aniruddha and the Heavenly Maidens[1]

This was exemplified by the venerable Aniruddha. When he was dwelling in the forest sitting in dhyāna meditation, the heavenly maiden "Pure Love" and others manifest in their pure and marvelous bodies and came to test Aniruddha. Aniruddha said, "Sisters, make yourselves blue when you come here. Don't appear in a variety of colors. I wish to contemplate impurity and am not otherwise able to carry out the contemplation." They then turned yellow, then red, and then white. At that time Aniruddha closed his eyes and would not look, saying, "Sisters, go away from here." At that time the heavenly maidens disappeared. If even the physical forms gained as meritorious reward by the gods are of this sort, then how much the more so are the objects of the five desires which manifest as a consequence of the bodhisattva's immeasurable merit.

Notes

1. This story and the next do not come from the Perfection of Wisdom section of the *Exegesis* proper, but rather from Nāgārjuna's six perfections introductory discussion in which he defines the perfection of wisdom.

又如甄陀罗王。与八万四千
甄陀罗。来到佛所弹琴歌颂
以供养佛。尔时须弥山王及
诸山树木。人民禽兽一切皆
舞。佛边大众乃至大迦叶。
皆于座上不能自安。是时天
[10]须菩萨。问长老大迦叶。
耆年旧宿行十二头陀法之第
一。何以在座不能自安。大
迦叶言。三界五欲不能动
我。是菩萨神通功德果报力
故。令我如是。非我有心不
能自安也。譬如须弥山四边
风起不能令动。至大劫尽时
毘蓝风起如吹烂草。以是事
故知。二种结中一种未断。
如是菩萨等应行般若波罗
蜜。[11]是阿毘昙中。[12]如是
说。

又如甄陀羅王。與八萬四千
甄陀羅。來到佛所彈琴歌頌
以供養佛。爾時須彌山王及
諸山樹木。人民禽獸一切皆
舞。佛邊大眾乃至大迦葉。
皆於座上不能自安。是時天
[10]須菩薩。問長老大迦葉。
耆年舊宿行十二頭陀法之第
一。何以在座不能自安。大
迦葉言。三界五欲不能動
我。是菩薩神通功德果報力
故。令我如是。非我有心不
能自安也。譬如須彌山四邊
風起不能令動。至大劫盡時
毘藍風起如吹爛草。以是事
故知。二種結中一種未斷。
如是菩薩等應行般若波羅
蜜。[11]是阿毘曇中。[12]如是
說。

简体字   正體字

Mahākāśyapa and the Kinnara King

This is also illustrated by the instance when the *kinnara* king came together with eighty-four thousand other *kinnaras* to where the Buddha dwelt. They strummed their lutes and sang verses as an offering to the Buddha. At that time, Sumeru, the king among mountains, as well as the trees on the mountains, the people, the birds, and the beasts all danced. The members of the great assembly which surrounded the Buddha, even including Mahākāśyapa, were all unable to make themselves remain still. At that time the Bodhisattva Heavenly Imperative asked the venerable Mahākāśyapa, "You are of senior years and have long abided as foremost in the cultivation of the dharma of twelve *dhūta* (ascetic) practices. How is it that you are unable to remain still in your seat?"

Mahākāśyapa replied, "The five desires within the sphere of the three realms are unable to move me. It is on account of the power of this bodhisattva's superknowledges manifesting as a consequence of his merit that I am caused to be in this state. It is not that I have any thoughts whereby I can't remain still."

This is just as with Mount Sumeru which when the four directions' winds arise cannot be shaken, but which, when the *vairambhaka* winds arise at the end of a great kalpa, is blown flat like a blade of dead grass. We can know from these cases that one of the two kinds of fetters has not yet been cut off. A bodhisattva of this sort should practice the *prajñāpāramitā*. The Abhidharma explains the matter in this fashion.

Part Seven:

Nāgārjuna's Stories on Various Topics

复次菩萨初生时。放大光明
普遍十方。行至七步[4]四顾
观察。作师子吼。而说偈言
我生胎分尽　是最末后身
我已得解脱　当复度众生
[0058a16]　　作是誓已身渐长
大。欲舍亲属[5]出家修[6]无
上道。中夜起观见诸伎直[7]
后妃婇女状若臭尸。即命车
匿令[8]被白马。夜半逾城行
十二由旬。到[9]跋伽婆仙人
所住林中。以刀剃发。[10]以
上妙宝衣贸麁布僧伽梨。于
[11]泥连禅河侧六年苦行。
日食一麻或食一米等。而自
念言。是处非道。尔时菩萨
舍苦行处。到菩提树下坐金
刚处。魔王将十八亿万众来
坏菩萨。菩萨以智慧功德力
故。降魔众已。即得阿耨多
罗三藐三菩提。是时三千大
千世界主梵天王名式弃。及
色界诸天等。释提桓因。及
欲界诸天等。并四天王。皆
诣佛所劝请世尊初转法轮。
亦是[12]菩萨念本[13]所愿及大
慈大悲故。受请说法。

復次菩薩初生時。放大光明
普遍十方。行至七步[4]四顧
觀察。作師子吼。而說偈言
我生胎分盡　是最末後身
我已得解脫　當復度眾生
[0058a16]　　作是誓已身漸長
大。欲捨親屬[5]出家修[6]無
上道。中夜起觀見諸伎直[7]
后妃婇女狀若臭屍。即命車
匿令[8]被白馬。夜半踰城行
十二由旬。到[9]跋伽婆仙人
所住林中。以刀剃髮。[10]以
上妙寶衣貿麁布僧伽梨。於
[11]泥連禪河側六年苦行。
日食一麻或食一米等。而自
念言。是處非道。爾時菩薩
捨苦行處。到菩提樹下坐金
剛處。魔王將十八億萬眾來
壞菩薩。菩薩以智慧功德力
故。降魔眾已。即得阿耨多
羅三藐三菩提。是時三千大
千世界主梵天王名式棄。及
色界諸天等。釋提桓因。及
欲界諸天等。并四天王。皆
詣佛所勸請世尊初轉法輪。
亦是[12]菩薩念本[13]所願及大
慈大悲故。受請說法。

简体字　　　　　　　　　　正體字

Early Life of the Buddha

Moreover, when the Bodhisattva was first born, he radiated a great brilliance which extended universally throughout the ten directions. He walked seven steps, surveyed the four quarters, and, roaring the lion's roar, he uttered a verse, proclaiming:

Birth from the womb for me is now ended.
This is the very last physical form.
Already I have achieved liberation
And shall moreover bring deliverance to beings.

After pronouncing this pledge, in the course of time he grew to adulthood. He sought to relinquish his relatives and retinue, to leave behind the home life, and to cultivate the unsurpassed path. He arose in the night and, surveying the sleeping forms of his female entertainers and attendants, his wife and his consorts, beheld them as resembling decaying corpses.

He instructed Chaṇḍaka to saddle his white steed. At midnight they traversed the city wall, rode for twelve yojanas, and arrived at the forest inhabited by Bhārgava, the rishi. He then took up a knife, cut off his hair, and exchanged his wonderfully bejeweled raiments for a coarsely-woven *saṅghāṭī* robe.

On the banks of the Nairañjanā River he cultivated bitterly ascetic practices for six years, eating only a sesame seed or a grain of rice each day. He thought to, "This method contradicts the Path."

At that time the Bodhisattva left behind the place where he had cultivated such ascetic practices and went and sat at the adamantine place beneath the bodhi tree. The demon king brought a throng of his minions numbering eighteen myriads of *koṭīs* in an attempt to devastate the Bodhisattva. Because of the power of his wisdom and merit, the Bodhisattva overcame the demon hordes and afterwards achieved *anuttarasamyaksaṃbodhi* (perfect enlightenment).

At that time the ruler of the trichiliocosm , the Brahma Heaven king named Śikhin, the gods of the form realm, Śakradevendra, and the gods of the desire realm as well as the four Heavenly Kings, all came to pay their respects to the Buddha and to encourage and request the Bhagavān to commence the turning of the wheel of Dharma. Because of this, the Bodhisattva recalled his original vow, and also because of his great kindness and great compassion, he acceded to the request and proclaimed the Dharma.

复次佛初生时堕地行七步。口自发言。言竟便默。如诸婴孩不行不语。乳[2]哺三[3]岁。诸母养育渐次长大。然佛身无数过诸世间。为众生故现如凡人。凡人生时身分诸根及其意识未成就故。身四威仪坐卧行住言谈语默。种种人法皆悉未了。日月岁过渐渐习学[4]能[5]具人法。今佛云何生。便能语能行。后更不能[6]以此致怪。但为此故以方便力现行人法如人威仪。令诸众生信于深法。若菩萨生[7]时便能行[8]能语。世人当作是念。今见此人世未曾有。必是天龙鬼神。其所学法必非我等所及。何以故。我等生死肉身为结使业所牵不得自在。如此深法谁能及之。以此自绝不得成贤圣法器。为是人故。于岚毘尼[9]园中生。虽即能至菩提树下成佛。以方便力故。而现作孩[10]童幼[11]小年少成人。于诸时中次第而受嬉戏术艺服御五欲。

简体字

復次佛初生時墮地行七步。口自發言。言竟便默。如諸嬰孩不行不語。乳[2]餔三[3]歲。諸母養育漸次長大。然佛身無數過諸世間。為眾生故現如凡人。凡人生時身分諸根及其意識未成就故。身四威儀坐卧行住言談語默。種種人法皆悉未了。日月歲過漸漸習學[4]能[5]具人法。今佛云何生。便能語能行。後更不能[6]以此致怪。但為此故以方便力現行人法如人威儀。令諸眾生信於深法。若菩薩生[7]時便能行[8]能語。世人當作是念。今見此人世未曾有。必是天龍鬼神。其所學法必非我等所及。何以故。我等生死肉身為結使業所牽不得自在。如此深法誰能及之。以此自絕不得成賢聖法器。為是人故。於嵐毘尼[9]園中生。雖即能至菩提樹下成佛。以方便力故。而現作孩[10]童幼[11]小年少成人。於諸時中次第而受嬉戲術藝服御五欲。

正體字

Nāgārjuna's Discussion of the Buddha's Life

Furthermore, when the Buddha was first born, he dropped to the ground, strode seven steps, and spontaneously uttered words. After speaking, he then fell silent and, like other infants, neither walked nor talked. He was nursed to the age of three. His [step]mothers raised him and he gradually grew to maturity.

Now, although the bodies of the Buddha are countless and exceed in number the sum of all the worlds, for the sake of beings, he manifested like an ordinary person. Because the faculties of the body as well as the intellectual consciousness of ordinary people are not yet completely developed when they are born, the four types of deportment: sitting, lying down, walking and standing, as well as speaking, silence, and all manner of other human qualities—all of these are not yet perfected. As the days, months and years pass, one gradually practices, studies, and then is able to refine the various aspects of being a person.

Now, how was it that the Buddha, upon birth, was immediately able to speak and walk whereas, afterwards, he was no longer able to do so? One finds this astonishing. One should know that it is solely by dint of the power of skillful means that the Buddha manifests involvement in human endeavors, and comports himself as people do, thus influencing beings to believe in the profound Dharma.

If, when the Bodhisattva was born, he was then able from that point on to walk and talk, ordinary people of the world would think, "Now we behold this man such as has never existed in the world before. Certainly he is a god, a dragon, a ghost or a spirit. That dharma which he studies is certainly not such that people like us might accomplish it. Why is that? Our fleshly bodies, bound to birth and death, are dragged about by the karma of the fetters. We are unable to gain freedom. Who would be able to approach such a profound dharma as this?" In this manner they would cut themselves off so that they could not become receptacles for the Dharma of the Worthies and Āryas. It was for the sake of these very people that he was born in the Lumbini gardens.

Although he was capable of proceeding immediately to the Bodhi Tree and achieving buddhahood, because of the power of skillful means, he then manifest instead as an infant, as a youth, as a young man, and as a grown man, and in each phase sequentially took on the corresponding activities of playing, becoming skilled in the arts, having resort to the objects of the five desires, and consummately

具足人法。[12]后渐见老病死苦生厌患心。于夜中半逾城出家。到郁特伽阿罗[13]洛仙人所。现作弟子而不行其法。[14]虽常用神通自念宿命。迦叶佛时持戒行道。而今现修苦行六年求道。菩萨虽主三千大千世界[15]而现破魔军成无上道。随顺世法故现[16]是众变。今于般若波罗蜜中。[17]现大神通智慧力故。诸人当知。佛身无数过诸世间。

具足人法。[12]後漸見老病死苦生厭患心。於夜中半踰城出家。到鬱特伽阿羅[13]洛仙人所。現作弟子而不行其法。[14]雖常用神通自念宿命。迦葉佛時持戒行道。而今現修苦行六年求道。菩薩雖主三千大千世界[15]而現破魔軍成無上道。隨順世法故現[16]是眾變。今於般若波羅蜜中。[17]現大神通智慧力故。諸人當知。佛身無數過諸世間。

简体字　　　　　　　　　　　　　正體字

perfecting human endeavors. Subsequently, he gradually perceiving the suffering of senescence , disease, and death and finally generated thoughts of aversion and distress which led to his traversing the city wall in the middle of the night, leaving behind the home life, and going to the location of the hermits Udraka and Ārāḍa. He gave the appearance of becoming a disciple, but did not practice their dharmas.

Although, on account of constant use of his superknowledges, he recalled his previous lives wherein at the time of Kāśyapa Buddha he upheld the prohibitions and cultivated the Path, still, he now manifest in the role of cultivating ascetic practices for six years in search of the Path .

Although the Bodhisattva was already the sovereign of the great trichiliocosm, he nonetheless demonstrated the capacity of demolishing the demon armies and realizing the unsurpassed Path. In order to go along with the dharmas of the world, he displayed these various transformations. Because in the *prajñāpāramitā* he now demonstrates the great power of superknowledges and wisdom, people ought to know that the Buddha's bodies are innumerable and surpass in number the sum of all worlds.

復次欲令長[45]爪梵志等大論
議師。於佛法中生信故。說
是摩訶般若波羅蜜經。有梵
志[46]號名長[*]爪。更有名先
尼婆蹉衢多羅。更有名薩遮
[47]迦摩揵提等。是[48]等閻浮
提大論議師輩言。一切論可
破。一切語可壞。一切執可
轉。故無有實法可信可恭敬
者。如舍利弗本末經中說。
舍利弗舅摩訶俱絺羅。與姊
舍利論議不如。俱絺羅思惟
念言。非姊力也。必懷智人
寄言母口。未生乃爾。及生
長大當如之何。思[49]惟已
生憍慢心。為廣論議故出家
作梵志。入南天竺國始讀經
書。諸人問言。汝志何求。
學習何經。長[*]爪答[50]言。
十八種大經盡欲讀之。諸人
語言。盡汝壽命猶不能知
一。何況能盡。長爪自念。
昔作憍慢為姊所勝。今此諸
人復見輕辱。為[51]是二事
故。自作誓言我不剪爪。要
讀十八

復次欲令長[45]爪梵志等大論
議師。於佛法中生信故。說
是摩訶般若波羅蜜經。有梵
志[46]號名長[*]爪。更有名先
尼婆蹉衢多羅。更有名薩遮
[47]迦摩揵提等。是[48]等閻浮
提大論議師輩言。一切論可
破。一切語可壞。一切執可
轉。故無有實法可信可恭敬
者。如舍利弗本末經中說。
舍利弗舅摩訶俱絺羅。與姊
舍利論議不如。俱絺羅思惟
念言。非姊力也。必懷智人
寄言母口。未生乃爾。及生
長大當如之何。思[49]惟已
生憍慢心。為廣論議故出家
作梵志。入南天竺國始讀經
書。諸人問言。汝志何求。
學習何經。長[*]爪答[50]言。
十八種大經盡欲讀之。諸人
語言。盡汝壽命猶不能知
一。何況能盡。長爪自念。
昔作憍慢為姊所勝。今此諸
人復見輕辱。為[51]是二事
故。自作誓言我不剪爪。要
讀十八

簡体字　　　　　　　　　　正體字

Mahākauṣṭhila, the Long-Nailed Brahman

Translator's Note

This is a story from the introductory section of the *Exegesis* wherein Nāgārjuna explains the various reasons why the Buddha spoke the *Mahāprajñāpāramitā Sutra*.

The Story

Additionally, [the Buddha] spoke the *Mahāprajñāpāramitā Sutra* because he wished to cause the brahmacārin "Long Nails," and other great dialecticians like him to develop faith in the Dharma of the Buddha. [At that time], there was a brahmacārin named "Long Nails" as well as Śreṇika Vatsagotra, Satyaka Nirgranthīputra and others. The great dialectical masters of Jambudvīpa such as these claimed that all treatises can be demolished, all discourses can be devastated, all beliefs can be subverted, and that therefore there are no genuine dharmas in which one may have faith or towards which one may feel reverence.

As recounted in the *Sutra on the Life of Śāriputra*, Śāriputra's uncle, Mahākauṣṭhila, discovered that he could no longer match his own sister, Śāri, in debate. Kauṣṭhila cogitated upon this and thought to himself, "This cannot be due to my sister's own power. It must be that she is pregnant with a wise man who is conveying his words to his mother's mouth. If, before he is even born, he is already like this, what will he be like once he's born and grown?"

Having thought this over, he became afflicted with [hurt] pride and, for the sake of gaining extensive dialectical knowledge, left home and became a brahmacārin. He went to the south of India and began to study the classical texts. People asked him, "What have you set your mind on obtaining? Which classic do you wish to study?"

"Long Nails" replied, "I wish to exhaustively study all of the eighteen great classics."

Those people all said to him, "You could spend your entire lifetime studying and still would not be able to know even one. How much the less would you be able to know them all."

"Long Nails" thought to himself, "Before, my pride was hurt on account of being defeated by my sister. Now, yet again, I'm subjected to humiliation by these people." On account of these two events, he made a vow to himself, "I will not [even take time to] trim my fingernails. I must exhaustively study all of the eighteen

種經[52]書盡。人見爪長因號[53]為長爪梵志。是人以種種經書智慧力。種種譏刺是法是非法是應是不應是實是不實是有是無。破他論議。譬如大力狂象[54]唐突蹴踏無能制者。如是長爪梵志以論議力。摧伏諸論師已。還至摩伽陀國王舍城那羅聚落。至本生處問人言。我姊生子今在何處。有人語言。汝姊子者適生八歲。讀一切經書盡。至年十六論議勝一切人。有釋種道人姓[55]瞿曇。與作弟子。長爪聞之即起憍慢。生不信心而作是言。如我姊子聰明如是。彼以何術誘誆剃頭作弟子。說是語已直向佛所。爾時舍利弗初受戒半月。佛邊侍立以扇扇佛。長爪梵志見佛問訊訖。一面坐作是念。一切論可破一切語可壞。一切執可轉。是中何者是諸法實相。何者是第一義。何者性。何者相。不顛倒。如是思惟。譬如大海水[56]中欲盡其[57]涯底。求之既久不得一法實可以入心者。彼以何論議道。而得我姊子。

種經[52]書盡。人見爪長因號[53]為長爪梵志。是人以種種經書智慧力。種種譏刺是法是非法是應是不應是實是不實是有是無。破他論議。譬如大力狂象[54]唐突蹴踏無能制者。如是長爪梵志以論議力。摧伏諸論師已。還至摩伽陀國王舍城那羅聚落。至本生處問人言。我姊生子今在何處。有人語言。汝姊子者適生八歲。讀一切經書盡。至年十六論議勝一切人。有釋種道人姓[55]瞿曇。與作弟子。長爪聞之即起憍慢。生不信心而作是言。如我姊子聰明如是。彼以何術誘誆剃頭作弟子。說是語已直向佛所。爾時舍利弗初受戒半月。佛邊侍立以扇扇佛。長爪梵志見佛問訊訖。一面坐作是念。一切論可破一切語可壞。一切執可轉。是中何者是諸法實相。何者是第一義。何者性。何者相。不顛倒。如是思惟。譬如大海水[56]中欲盡其[57]涯底。求之既久不得一法實可以入心者。彼以何論議道。而得我姊子。

简体字　　　　　　　　　正體字

classics." People noticed his fingernails growing long. Because of this, they referred to him as the brahmacārin "Long Nails."

By using the power of wisdom derived from all types of classical texts, by using all manner of satirical barbs, [by maintaining that], "This is dharma," or that "This is non-dharma," "This is admissible," or "This is inadmissible," "This is true," or "This is not true," "This is existent," or "This is nonexistent," this man was able to refute other dialectical positions. He was like a mighty, crazed elephant which blocks and gores, kicks and tramples, and which none can bring under control.

After the brahmacārin "Long Nails" had employed his dialectical strength to smash and overcome all of the other dialecticians, he returned to the country of Magadha, to the city of Rājagṛha, to the community of Nara. He went to his birthplace and asked the people, "Where is that child born to my sister?"

Someone told him, "When your sister's son had reached the age of eight, he had already completely mastered all of the classical texts. When he reached the age of sixteen, he had overcome everyone in debate. There is a man of the Path from the Śākya clan named Gautama. [Your nephew] became his disciple."

When Long Nails heard this, he was overcome with arrogance and incredulousness and exclaimed, "What sort of trick could he have used to deceive and induce one so intelligent as my nephew to shave his head and become a disciple? Having said this, he proceeded directly to where the Buddha dwelt.

At this time Śāriputra had received the precepts [of monastic ordination] only a half-month before. He stood in service at the Buddha's side, using a fan to fan the Buddha.

The brahmacārin Long Nails went to see the Buddha and, having made salutations, sat off to one side and thought, "All treatises can be refuted, all discourse can be devastated, and all beliefs can be subverted. What is it in all of this that is the true character of dharmas? What is it that represents the ultimate meaning? What is it that constitutes the [true] nature? What are the characteristic features? And what is it that is not an inverted view?"

He continued reflecting in this manner: "[Resolving this quandary] is like seeking to completely reach the far shores and plumb the depths of a great ocean. Even though one may search for a long time, one can't find a single dharma actually admissible to the mind. What dialectical path could he have used to win over my nephew?"

作是思惟已[1]而語佛言。[*]瞿曇。我一切法不[2]受。佛問長爪。汝一切法不[*]受。是見[*]受不。佛[3]所質義。汝已飲邪見毒。[4]今出是毒氣。言一切法不[*]受。是[5]見汝[*]受不。爾時長爪梵志如好馬見鞭影[6]即覺便著正道。長爪梵志亦如是。得佛語鞭影入心。即棄捐貢高慚愧低頭。如是思惟。佛置我著[7]二處負門中。若我說是見我[*]受。是負處門麁。故[8]多人知。云何自言一切法不[*]受。今[9]受是見。[10]此是現前妄語。是麁負處門[*]多人所知。第二負處門細。[11]我[12]欲受之。以[13]不多人知故。作是念已。答佛言。[*]瞿曇。一切法不[14]受。是見亦不[*]受。佛語梵志。汝不[*]受一切法。是見亦不[*]受。則無所[15]受。與眾人無異。何用[16]自高而生憍慢如是。長爪梵志不能得答。自知墮負處。即於佛一切智中起恭敬生信心。自思惟。我墮負處。世尊不[17]彰我負。不言是非。不以為意。佛心柔[18]濡。[19]第一清[20]淨。

简体字

作是思惟已[1]而語佛言。[*]瞿曇。我一切法不[2]受。佛問長爪。汝一切法不[*]受。是見[*]受不。佛[3]所質義。汝已飲邪見毒。[4]今出是毒氣。言一切法不[*]受。是[5]見汝[*]受不。爾時長爪梵志如好馬見鞭影[6]即覺便著正道。長爪梵志亦如是。得佛語鞭影入心。即棄捐貢高慚愧低頭。如是思惟。佛置我著[7]二處負門中。若我說是見我[*]受。是負處門麁。故[8]多人知。云何自言一切法不[*]受。今[9]受是見。[10]此是現前妄語。是麁負處門[*]多人所知。第二負處門細。[11]我[12]欲受之。以[13]不多人知故。作是念已。答佛言。[*]瞿曇。一切法不[14]受。是見亦不[*]受。佛語梵志。汝不[*]受一切法。是見亦不[*]受。則無所[15]受。與眾人無異。何用[16]自高而生憍慢如是。長爪梵志不能得答。自知墮負處。即於佛一切智中起恭敬生信心。自思惟。我墮負處。世尊不[17]彰我負。不言是非。不以為意。佛心柔[18]濡。[19]第一清[20]淨。

正體字

After he had cogitated like this, he said to the Buddha, "Gautama, I do not accept any dharmas."

The Buddha asked Long Nails, "Your not accepting any dharmas, this view—do you accept it or not?" The Buddha's implicit meaning was, "You've already swallowed the poison of false views. Now get rid of this toxic influence." He said, "All dharmas—you say you don't accept them. But this poison of views: Do you accept it or not?"

At this time, the brahmacārin Long Nails was like a fine horse which, on merely seeing the shadow of the whip, immediately remembers to stay on the right track. The brahmacārin Long Nails, was also like this. The shadow of the whip of the Buddha's speech entered his mind. He immediately cast off his arrogance, was contrite, and lowered his head.

He then thought, "The Buddha has defeated me with a dilemma: If I say, 'I accept this view,' then this fallacy is obvious and most everybody will be aware of it. Why did I say, 'I don't accept any dharmas?' If I now say, 'As for this view—I accept it,' that would amount to a blatant error in discourse. It would be an obviously fallacious position. Most people would be aware of it.

"The alternative fallacious position is subtle. Since not that many people will be aware of it [as fallacious], I'll choose to accept that alternative."

Having pondered thus, he finally replied to the Buddha, "Gautama—this view that 'I don't accept any dharmas'—I don't accept it, either."

The Buddha said to the brahmacārin, "If you also don't accept your view that you don't accept any dharmas, then nothing is accepted. But, in this regard, you are no different from anyone else in this congregation. What then is the point in presenting in a haughty and arrogant manner like this?"

The brahmacārin Long Nails was unable to reply. He knew that he had fallen into a fallacious position. He then felt respect for and faith in the Buddha's omniscience. He thought to himself, "I did fall into a fallacious position and yet the Bhagavān did not reveal the fact that I had been defeated. He did not speak of right or wrong. He ignored it. The Buddha's mind is pliant. This is the ultimately pure stance. All rhetorical positions are extinguished in it. He has attained the extremely deep Dharma. This is a position which can be revered. He is supreme in the purity of his thought."

一切語論[21]處滅。 得[22]大
甚深法。 [23]是可恭敬處。
心淨第[24]一。 佛說法斷其
邪見故。 即於坐處得遠塵離
垢。[25]諸法中得法眼淨。 [26]
時舍利弗[27]聞是語得阿羅
漢。 是長爪梵[28]志出家作沙
門。 得大力阿羅漢。 [29]若
長爪梵志。 不聞般若波羅蜜
氣分離四句第一義相應法。
小信尚不得。 何況得出家道
果。 [30]佛欲導[31]引如是等大
論議師利根人故。 [32]說是般
若波羅蜜經。

简体字

一切語論[21]處滅。 得[22]大
甚深法。 [23]是可恭敬處。
心淨第[24]一。 佛說法斷其
邪見故。 即於坐處得遠塵離
垢。[25]諸法中得法眼淨。 [26]
時舍利弗[27]聞是語得阿羅
漢。 是長爪梵[28]志出家作沙
門。 得大力阿羅漢。 [29]若
長爪梵志。 不聞般若波羅蜜
氣分離四句第一義相應法。
小信尚不得。 何況得出家道
果。 [30]佛欲導[31]引如是等大
論議師利根人故。 [32]說是般
若波羅蜜經。

正體字

Because the Buddha's speaking of Dharma had caused him to cut off his false views, in the very place where he sat, he succeeded in distancing himself from the dust and leaving behind impurity. He achieved the purification of the Dharma eye with respect to all dharmas.

When Śāriputra heard this dialogue, he realized arhatship. This brahmacārin Long Nails then left the home life and became a *śramaṇa*. He gained the realization of the mighty arhat.

Nāgārjuna's Concluding Comments

If the brahmacārin Long Nails had not heard the spirit of the *prajñāpāramitā* which transcends the tetralemma and which is the Dharma corresponding to the ultimate meaning, he would not have developed even the faintest degree of faith, how much the less would he have been able to achieve the fruition of the way of the renunciant?

Thus it was also because the Buddha wished to lead forth such great dialectical masters and other such people of sharp faculties that he set forth this *Prajñāpāramitā Sutra*.

[15]佛言。若人有信。是人能入我大法海中。能得沙门果不空。剃头染[16]袈裟。若无信是人不能入我法海中。如枯树不生华实。不得沙门果。虽剃头染衣读种种经能难能答。于佛法中空无所得。以是故。如是义在佛法初。善信相故。复次佛法深远更有佛乃能知。人有信[17]者虽未作佛。[18]以信[19]力故能入佛法。如梵天王请佛初转法轮以偈[20]请佛

阎浮提先出　多诸不净法

愿开甘露门　[21]当说清净道

[0063a23] 佛以偈答

我法甚难得　能断诸结使

三有爱着心　[22]是人不能解

[0063a26] 梵天王白佛。大德。世界中智有上中下。善[23]濡直心者。易可得度。

简体字

[15]佛言。若人有信。是人能入我大法海中。能得沙門果不空。剃頭染[16]袈裟。若無信是人不能入我法海中。如枯樹不生華實。不得沙門果。雖剃頭染衣讀種種經能難能答。於佛法中空無所得。以是故。如是義在佛法初。善信相故。復次佛法深遠更有佛乃能知。人有信[17]者雖未作佛。[18]以信[19]力故能入佛法。如梵天王請佛初轉法輪以偈[20]請佛

閻浮提先出　多諸不淨法

願開甘露門　[21]當說清淨道

[0063a23] 佛以偈答

我法甚難得　能斷諸結使

三有愛著心　[22]是人不能解

[0063a26] 梵天王白佛。大德。世界中智有上中下。善[23]濡直心者。易可得度。

正體字

The Gods Request the Buddha to Speak the Dharma

Nāgārjuna's Preamble: On the Importance of Faith

The Buddha said, "If a person has faith, this person is able to enter the sea of my great Dharma, is able to obtain the fruit of the śramaṇa, and has not in vain shaven his head and donned the dyed robe. If one has no faith, this person is unable to enter the sea of my Dharma and is like a withered tree which produces neither flowers nor fruit. He will not obtain the fruit of the śramaṇa. Although he may have shaved his head, donned the dyed robe, studied all manner of scriptures, and may be able to pose and respond to difficult doctrinal questions, still, with respect to the Buddha's Dharma, his efforts are in vain, and he gains nothing whatsoever."

It is on account of this that the [true suchness] concept represented by "thus" [in "Thus I have heard, at one time..."] is situated at the beginning of the Buddha's [discourses on] Dharma. It signifies their worthiness as objects of wholesome faith.

Moreover, the Dharma of the Buddha is profound and far-reaching. Only another Buddha would be able to fathom it. If a person has faith, even though he has not yet realized buddhahood, he is nonetheless still able, by virtue of the power of faith, to gain entry into the Dharma of the Buddha.

Story: The Gods Request the Buddha to Speak Dharma

[This point was alluded to] when the King of the Brahma Heaven Gods requested the Buddha to begin the turning of the wheel of Dharma. He used a verse to entreat the Buddha:

There first have appeared in Jambudvīpa
The many and varied impure dharmas.
I pray you will open the sweet dew gateway
And will thus proclaim the path that is pure.

The Buddha replied with a verse:

My Dharma's profoundly difficult to master.
Yet able to sever all of the fetters.
Those in the three realms with love-bound minds—
Such persons as these cannot comprehend it.

The Brahma Heaven King addressed the Buddha, saying, "Venerable One. The wisdom encountered in the world may be superior, middling, or inferior. Those good people possessed of pliant and straightforward minds may easily obtain deliverance. If

是人若不闻法者。退堕诸恶
难中。譬如水中莲华。有生
有熟。有水中未出[24]者若
不得日光则不[25]能开。佛
亦如是。佛以大慈悲怜愍众
生故为说法。佛念过去未来
现在三世诸佛法。皆度众生
为说法。我亦应尔。如是思
惟竟。受梵天王等诸天请说
法。[26]尔时世尊以偈答曰

我今开甘露味门
若有信者得欢喜
于诸人中说妙法
非恼他故而为说

[0063b07] 佛此偈中不说布施
人得欢喜。亦不说多闻持戒
忍辱精进禅定智慧人得欢
喜。独说信人。佛意[27]如
是。[28]我第一甚深[29]法微妙
无量无数不可思议不动不[30]
猗不着无所得法。非一切智
人则不能解。是故佛法中信
力[31]为初。信力[32]能入。非
布施持戒[33]禅定智慧等能初
入佛法。如[34]说偈言

世间人心动　[35]爱好福[36]果
报

是人若不聞法者。退墮諸惡
難中。譬如水中蓮華。有生
有熟。有水中未出[24]者若
不得日光則不[25]能開。佛
亦如是。佛以大慈悲憐愍眾
生故為說法。佛念過去未來
現在三世諸佛法。皆度眾生
為說法。我亦應爾。如是思
惟竟。受梵天王等諸天請說
法。[26]爾時世尊以偈答曰

我今開甘露味門
若有信者得歡喜
於諸人中說妙法
非惱他故而為說

[0063b07] 佛此偈中不說布施
人得歡喜。亦不說多聞持戒
忍辱精進禪定智慧人得歡
喜。獨說信人。佛意[27]如
是。[28]我第一甚深[29]法微妙
無量無數不可思議不動不[30]
猗不著無所得法。非一切智
人則不能解。是故佛法中信
力[31]為初。信力[32]能入。非
布施持戒[33]禪定智慧等能初
入佛法。如[34]說偈言

世間人心動　[35]愛好福[36]果
報

简体字　　　　　　　　　　正體字

these people do not hear the Dharma, they shall retreat and fall away into dreadful adversity.

"They are like lotuses in the water of which some are undeveloped and others more mature. There are those still immersed in the water which have not yet come forth. If they do not encounter the radiance of the sun, then they shall be unable to blossom. The Buddha's present power is now just like that. May the Buddha employ the great kindness and compassion and, acting out of pity for beings, proclaim the Dharma for their sakes."

The Buddha brought to mind the Dharma of all Buddhas of the three period of time—the past, the future, and the present—recalling, "They all delivered beings to liberation through proclaiming the Dharma for their sakes. I ought to do so as well." After reflecting thus, he accepted the requests to proclaim the Dharma initiated by the Brahma Heaven King and the other gods. At that time the Bhagavān responded in verse:

> I'll open now the gates to the flavor of sweet dew ambrosia.
> If there be those with faith, then delight shall be theirs.
> Among all the people I'll speak wondrous Dharma.
> It's not to afflict others that I now speak for their sakes.

Concluding Exegesis Discussion on the Importance of Faith

The Buddha did not speak in this verse of those who practice giving as being those who would gain delight, nor did he refer to those who are learned, who uphold the moral precepts, who practice patience, who are vigorous, who cultivate dhyāna absorption, or who are wise as being those who would gain delight. He spoke only of those people who have faith.

The Buddha's intent was this: "Unless one is omniscient, one will not be able to fathom my dharmas which are supremely profound, subtle and wondrous, immeasurable and innumerable, inconceivable and ineffable, unmoving and nondependent, unattached and devoid of anything gained." Therefore, in the Dharma of the Buddha, it is the power of faith which is primary. It is by virtue of faith that one is able to gain entrance to it. It is not on account of giving, morality, dhyāna absorption, wisdom, and so forth that one gains initial entrance into the Buddha Dharma. This is as noted in a verse:

> The minds of people of the world all move
> From love for the rewards produced from merit.

而不好福[37]因求有不求灭
先闻邪见法心着而深入
我[38]此甚深法无信云何解

而不好福[37]因求有不求滅
先聞邪見法心著而深入
我[38]此甚深法無信云何解

简体字

正體字

And yet they are not fond of merit's causes,
They seek existence and favor not cessation.

At first they hear the dharmas of false views.
Their minds attach and then they enter deeply.
As for my Dharma which is extremely profound:
If one has no faith, how could he comprehend it?

[0066b21] 复次如是我闻。是阿难等佛大[44]弟子[45]辈说。入佛法相故名为佛法。如佛般涅盘时。于俱夷那竭国萨罗双树间。北首[46]卧将入涅盘。尔时阿难亲属爱未除未离欲故。心没忧海不能自出。尔时长老[47]阿泥卢豆语阿难。[48]汝守佛法藏[49]人。不应如凡人自没忧海。一切有为[50]法是无常相。汝[51]莫愁忧。又佛手付汝法。汝今愁闷失所[52]受事。汝当问佛。佛[53]般涅盘后我曹云何行道。谁当作师。恶口车匿云何共住。佛经[54]初作何等语。如是种种未来事应问佛。阿难闻是事。闷心小醒得念道力。助于佛末后卧床边。以此事问[55]佛。佛告阿难。若今现前。若我过去[56]后自依止法依止不[57]馀依止。云何比丘自依止法依止不[*]馀依止。[58]于是比丘[59]内观身。常[60]当一心智慧勤修精进。[61]除世间[62]贪忧。

简体字

[0066b21] 復次如是我聞。是阿難等佛大[44]弟子[45]輩說。入佛法相故名為佛法。如佛般涅槃時。於俱夷那竭國薩羅雙樹間。北首[46]臥將入涅槃。爾時阿難親屬愛未除未離欲故。心沒憂海不能自出。爾時長老[47]阿泥盧豆語阿難。[48]汝守佛法藏[49]人。不應如凡人自沒憂海。一切有為[50]法是無常相。汝[51]莫愁憂。又佛手付汝法。汝今愁悶失所[52]受事。汝當問佛。佛[53]般涅槃後我曹云何行道。誰當作師。惡口車匿云何共住。佛經[54]初作何等語。如是種種未來事應問佛。阿難聞是事。悶心小醒得念道力。助於佛末後臥床邊。以此事問[55]佛。佛告阿難。若今現前。若我過去[56]後自依止法依止不[57]餘依止。云何比丘自依止法依止不[*]餘依止。[58]於是比丘[59]內觀身。常[60]當一心智慧勤修精進。[61]除世間[62]貪憂。

正體字

Ānanda's Final Questions of the Buddha

"Thus I have heard" is a phrase spoken by Ānanda and other of the Buddha's great disciples. Because it signifies commencement of Dharma [spoken] by the Buddha, [scriptures beginning in this way] qualify thereby as the Dharma of the Buddha. This is as ordained at the time of the Buddha's *parinirvāṇa*. He was in the state of Kuśinigara, lying down between a pair of *sāla* trees with his head to the North and was about to enter nirvāṇa.

At that time because Ānanda had not yet transcended the realm of desire, he had not yet gotten rid of the affection felt for one's relatives. His mind was immersed in a sea of grief and he was powerless to pull himself out of it.

Then the Venerable Aniruddha instructed Ānanda, "You are the one responsible for guarding the treasury of the Buddha's Dharma. You should not be immersed in a sea of grief in the manner of an ordinary person. All conditioned dharmas are characterized by impermanence. Don't be sorrowful.

"Furthermore, the Buddha, with his own hand, has entrusted the Dharma to you. By now being so overcome with grief, you are neglecting the responsibility you have undertaken. You should ask the Buddha, 'After the Buddha's *parinirvāṇa*, how shall we cultivate the Path? Who shall serve as our teacher? How shall we dwell together with the harshly-speaking Chaṇḍaka? What phrases shall be placed at the beginning of the Buddha's scriptures?' You should inquire of the Buddha on all manner of topics such as these which deal with the future."

When Ānanda heard about these matters, his troubled mind revived somewhat, he regained the power of being mindful of the Path, and assisted alongside the Buddha's final resting place. He asked the Buddha about these matters whereupon the Buddha told Ānanda, "Whether right here and now or whether after I am gone, one should take refuge in oneself, should take refuge in the Dharma, and should not take refuge in anything else. How is it that a bhikshu should take refuge in himself, should take refuge in the Dharma, and should not take refuge in anything else? In this regard, a bhikshu should undertake [the station of mindfulness consisting in] the contemplation of his own body. He should constantly employ single-mindedness, wisdom, diligent cultivation, and vigor in getting rid of the woe of worldly desire.

"The contemplation of other's bodies and then simultaneously of

外身内外身观亦如是。受心
法念处亦复如是。是名比丘
自依止法依止不[*]馀依止。
从今日解脱戒经即是大师。
如解脱戒[63]经说。身业口业
应如是行。车匿比丘我涅盘
后。如[64]梵法治。若心濡[65]
伏者。应教[66]删陀迦旃延[67]
经。即可得道。[68]复次[69]我
三阿僧只劫所集法宝藏。是
[70]藏[71]初应作是说。如是
我闻一时佛在某方某国[72]土
某处[73]树林[74]中。何以故。
过去诸佛[75]经初。皆称是
语。未来诸佛[76]经初。亦称
是语。现在诸佛末后般涅盘
时。亦教称是语。今我般涅
盘后。经初亦应称如是我闻
一时。

外身內外身觀亦如是。受心
法念處亦復如是。是名比丘
自依止法依止不[*]餘依止。
從今日解脫戒經即是大師。
如解脫戒[63]經說。身業口業
應如是行。車匿比丘我涅槃
後。如[64]梵法治。若心濡[65]
伏者。應教[66]刪陀迦旃延[67]
經。即可得道。[68]復次[69]我
三阿僧祇劫所集法寶藏。是
[70]藏[71]初應作是說。如是
我聞一時佛在某方某國[72]土
某處[73]樹林[74]中。何以故。
過去諸佛[75]經初。皆稱是
語。未來諸佛[76]經初。亦稱
是語。現在諸佛末後般涅槃
時。亦教稱是語。今我般涅
槃後。經初亦應稱如是我聞
一時。

简体字 　　　　　　　　　 正體字

both his own and other's bodies should be taken up in like manner. The stations of mindfulness with regard to feelings, with regard to thoughts, and with regard to dharmas should each be taken up in this manner as well. This is what is meant by, 'A bhikshu should take refuge in himself, take refuge in the Dharma, and should not take refuge in anything else.'

"From this very day onwards, the *Scripture on the Liberating Precepts* is your great master. In one's physical actions and verbal actions, one should conduct himself in accord with the declarations of the *Scripture on the Liberating Precepts*.

"As for the bhikshu Chaṇḍaka, after my nirvāṇa, treat him according to the brahman method [of the silent treatment]. If his mind then becomes pliant and subdued, he should then be taught the *Saṃthakātyāyana Sutra*. He may then be able to realize the Path.

"As for the treasury of Dharma jewels which I have accumulated throughout the course of three *asaṃkhyeya* kalpas, one should place this phrase at the beginning of [the scriptures in] this treasury: 'Thus I have heard, at one time the Buddha was at such-and-such a state, in such-and-such a region, in such-and-such a location, dwelling in the forest....' Why? This phrasing has been spoken at the beginning of the scriptures of all of the Buddhas of the past. This phrase shall also be spoken at the beginning of the scriptures of all of the Buddhas of the future. All of the Buddhas of the present, at the very end, at the time of their *parinirvāṇa*—they, too, instruct that this phrase should be spoken. Now, after my *parinirvāṇa*—at the beginning of the scriptures—one should also declare, 'Thus I have heard at one time....'"

如集法經中[6]廣說。佛入涅槃時。地六種動諸河反流。疾風暴發黑雲四起。惡雷掣電雹雨驟墮處處星流師子[7]惡獸哮吼喚呼。諸天世人皆大號咷。諸[8]天人等皆發是言。佛取涅槃一何疾哉。世間眼滅。當是時[9]間。一切草木藥樹華[10]葉一時剖裂。諸須彌山王盡皆傾搖。海水波揚地大震動山[11]崖崩落。諸樹摧折四面煙起。甚大可畏。陂池江河盡皆[12]嬈濁。彗星晝出。諸人啼哭諸天憂愁。諸天女等郁伊[13]哽咽涕淚交流。諸學人等默然不樂。諸無學人。念有為諸法一切無常。如是天人夜叉羅剎犍[14]闥婆甄陀羅摩睺羅伽及諸龍等。皆大憂愁。諸阿羅[15]漢度老病死海。心念言

已渡凡[16]夫恩愛河

老病死券已裂破

見身篋中四大蛇

今入無餘滅涅槃

[0067a28]　　諸大阿羅漢。各各隨意於諸山林[17]流泉谿谷處處捨身而般涅槃。更有諸阿羅漢。

简体字

如集法經中[6]廣說。佛入涅槃時。地六種動諸河反流。疾風暴發黑雲四起。惡雷掣電雹雨驟墮處處星流師子[7]惡獸哮吼喚呼。諸天世人皆大號咷。諸[8]天人等皆發是言。佛取涅槃一何疾哉。世間眼滅。當是時[9]間。一切草木藥樹華[10]葉一時剖裂。諸須彌山王盡皆傾搖。海水波揚地大震動山[11]崖崩落。諸樹摧折四面煙起。甚大可畏。陂池江河盡皆[12]嬈濁。彗星晝出。諸人啼哭諸天憂愁。諸天女等郁伊[13]哽咽涕淚交流。諸學人等默然不樂。諸無學人。念有為諸法一切無常。如是天人夜叉羅剎犍[14]闥婆甄陀羅摩睺羅伽及諸龍等。皆大憂愁。諸阿羅[15]漢度老病死海。心念言

已渡凡[16]夫恩愛河

老病死券已裂破

見身篋中四大蛇

今入無餘滅涅槃

[0067a28]　　諸大阿羅漢。各各隨意於諸山林[17]流泉谿谷處處捨身而般涅槃。更有諸阿羅漢。

正體字

The Buddha's *Parinirvāṇa*

As extensively described in the *Compilation of the Dharma Sutra*, when the Buddha entered nirvāṇa, the earth pitched about in six different ways, the rivers flowed backwards, a fierce tempest struck violently, black clouds boiled up in the four directions, fearsome thunder boomed, lightning bolts crashed, and suddenly a storm of hail and rain came pouring down. Meteors streaked everywhere. Ferocious beasts bellowed and roared, yowled and shrieked. The deities and worldlings howled loudly. The gods all cried out, "Oh, why has the Buddha chosen nirvāṇa so swiftly?! The eyes of the World have perished!"

Then, all at the same time, the grasses and woods, herbs and trees, flowers and leaves, all split apart and burst open. The Sumerus, kings among mountains, tilted askew as they shook. The waters of the oceans roiled and heaved up billows. The earth shuddered and jolted mightily. The mountains and crags shattered and collapsed. The trees all splintered and split. From the four quarters smoke surged up into the sky.

These occurrences were enormously horrifying. The waters of the marshes and ponds, rivers and streams all began to churn and turned turbid. Comets appeared in the daytime. The people wailed and wept. The gods were overcome with sorrow. The heavenly maidens were overwhelmed with grief, choking and sobbing, with intertwining streams of tears flowing down.

Those still at the stage of study (*śaikṣa*)[1] were all silent and unhappy. Those beyond study (*aśaikṣa*)[2] remained mindful that all conditioned dharmas are impermanent. And so, in this manner, the gods, men, *yakṣas*, *rākṣasas*, *gandharvas*, *kinnaras*, *mahoragas* and dragons were all overcome with great grief. The arhats had been delivered from the sea of senescence, disease, and death and so thought to themselves:

> We've crossed already the river of the common man's affection and passion.
> The coil of aging, sickness, and death has been split apart and broken.
> We've seen the serpents of the four great elements within the bodily basket,[3]
> And now we shall enter the nirvāṇa of remainderless cessation.

In the mountains, forests, and valleys, among flowing springs and streams, all of the great arhats, each according to his will, shed his body and entered *parinirvāṇa*. Additionally, there were arhats

於虛空中飛騰而去。譬如鴈
王。現種種神力。令眾人心
信清淨。然後般涅槃。

於虛空中飛騰而去。譬如鴈
王。現種種神力。令眾人心
信清淨。然後般涅槃。

简体字

正體字

who flew straight up into the air like the king of geese and, in leaving, displayed all manner of spiritual powers, thus influencing the minds of many people towards faith and purity. Afterwards, they then entered *parinirvāṇa*.

Notes

1. This is a reference to the first three stages of arhatship.
2. This refers to those who have reached fourth-stage arhatship, the putative endpoint of the Śrāvaka-vehicle path.
3. This is a reference to a famous analogy for the treacherous nature of delusions regarding the body. It derives from the *Buddha Speaks the Analogy of the Poisonous Snakes Sutra* and may be found in *Marvelous Stories from the Perfection of Wisdom,* among the stories on the perfection of giving.

六欲[18]天乃至遍净天等。见诸阿罗汉[19]皆取灭度。各心念言。佛日既没种种禅定解脱智慧弟子[20]光亦[21]灭。是诸众生[22]有种种婬怒痴病。是法药师辈今疾灭度谁当治者。无量智慧大海中生。弟子莲华今已干枯。法树摧折法云散灭。[23]大智象王既逝象子亦随去。法商人过去。从谁求法宝。如偈说。

佛已永寂入涅盘。

诸灭结众亦过去。

世界如是空无智。

痴冥[24]遂增智[25]灯灭。

[0067b12]　尔时诸天礼摩诃迦叶足。说偈言。

耆年欲恚慢已除。

其形譬如紫金柱。

上下端严妙无比。

[26]目明清净如莲华。

[0067b15]　　如是赞已。白[27]大迦叶言。大德迦叶。仁者知不。[28]法[29]船欲破法城欲颓。法海欲竭法幢欲倒。法[*]灯欲灭说法人欲去。行道人渐少。恶人力转盛。当以大慈建立佛法。

[0067b19]　尔时大迦叶心如大海澄静不动。良久而答。汝等善说实如所言。

简体字

六欲[18]天乃至遍淨天等。見諸阿羅漢[19]皆取滅度。各心念言。佛日既沒種種禪定解脫智慧弟子[20]光亦[21]滅。是諸眾生[22]有種種婬怒癡病。是法藥師輩今疾滅度誰當治者。無量智慧大海中生。弟子蓮華今已乾枯。法樹摧折法雲散滅。[23]大智象王既逝象子亦隨去。法商人過去。從誰求法寶。如偈說。

佛已永寂入涅槃。

諸滅結眾亦過去。

世界如是空無智。

癡冥[24]遂增智[25]燈滅。

[0067b12]　爾時諸天禮摩訶迦葉足。說偈言。

耆年欲恚慢已除。

其形譬如紫金柱。

上下端嚴妙無比。

[26]目明清淨如蓮華。

[0067b15]　　如是讚已。白[27]大迦葉言。大德迦葉。仁者知不。[28]法[29]船欲破法城欲頹。法海欲竭法幢欲倒。法[*]燈欲滅說法人欲去。行道人漸少。惡人力轉盛。當以大慈建立佛法。

[0067b19]　爾時大迦葉心如大海澄靜不動。良久而答。汝等善說實如所言。

正體字

Gods Distressed at Dharma's Decline

The Gods, from the Six Desire Heavens on up to the Heaven of Universal Purity, observed all of the arhats opting for cessation, and each of them thought to himself, "Since the Buddha sun has set, the light of those disciples possessing all manner of dhyāna absorptions, liberations, and wisdom has gone out as well. All of these beings have all kinds of diseases arising from desire, anger and delusion. Now that these Dharma physicians have swiftly crossed into cessation, who shall treat them?

"Now, those lotus-blossom disciples, grown up within the great sea of immeasurable wisdom, have withered and dried up. The tree of Dharma has been smashed and split apart. The cloud of Dharma has scattered and vanished. Since the greatly wise king of the elephants has passed on, the offspring of the elephant have gone away as well. Now that the merchant of Dharma has moved on, from whom shall we seek jewels of Dharma?" This is as stated in a verse:

> The Buddha's achieved eternal quiescence and entered his nirvāṇa.
> That company which destroyed the fetters has also passed away.
> With this, the World is empty with none possessed of wisdom.
> The dark of ignorance has increased; the wisdom lamp's gone out.

At that point the Gods made obeisance at the feet of Mahākāśyapa and uttered a verse:

> This elder is already rid of desire, hatefulness, and arrogance.
> His figure stands before us here like a purple golden pillar.
> Above, below, in stately refinement, he's wondrous without peer.
> The brightness of his eyes is pure and like unto the lotus.

After having praised him in this manner, they addressed Mahākāśyapa, saying, "Venerable Mahākāśyapa, is the Humane One aware or is he not, that the ship of Dharma is about to break up, the city wall of Dharma is about to collapse, the sea of Dharma is about to dry up, the banner of Dharma is about to fall, the lamp of Dharma is about to die down, the proclaimers of Dharma are about to depart, the practitioners of Dharma are becoming fewer, and the power of the depraved is now waxing full? One ought to bring forth the great kindheartedness and establish here the Dharma of the Buddha."

At that time the mind of Mahākāśyapa was like a great sea, limpid, silent, and tranquil. After a goodly while, he responded, "You

简体字	正體字
世间不久无智盲冥。于是大迦叶默然受请。尔时诸天礼大迦叶足。忽然不现各自还去。	世間不久無智盲冥。於是大迦葉默然受請。爾時諸天禮大迦葉足。忽然不現各自還去。

have spoken well. Truly, it is as you describe. Before long, the world shall be devoid of wisdom, blind, and plunged in darkness."

With this, Mahākāśyapa silently acceded to their plea. At that point, the Gods made obeisance at the feet of Mahākāśyapa and suddenly disappeared, each returning whence he had come.

是时大迦叶[30]思惟。我今云
何使是三阿僧只劫难得佛法
而得久住。如是思惟竟。我
知是法可使久住。应当结集
修妬路阿毘昙毘[31]尼作三
法藏。如是佛法可得久住。
未来世人可得受行。所以
者何。佛世世勤苦慈愍众生
故。学得是法为人演说。我
曹亦应承用佛教宣扬开化。
是时大迦叶作是语竟。[32]住
须弥[33]山顶。挝铜[34]揵稚。
说此偈言。

　佛诸弟子　若念于佛。
当报佛恩　莫入涅盘。
[0067c04]　　　是揵[35]稚音大迦叶
语声。遍至三千大千世界。
皆悉闻知。诸有弟子得[36]神
力者。皆来集会大迦叶所。
尔时大迦叶告诸会者。佛法
欲灭。佛从三阿僧只劫。种
种勤苦慈愍众生[37]学得是
法。佛般涅盘已。诸弟子知
法持法诵法者皆亦随佛灭
度。法今欲灭。未来众生甚
可怜愍。失智慧眼

是時大迦葉[30]思惟。我今云
何使是三阿僧祇劫難得佛法
而得久住。如是思惟竟。我
知是法可使久住。應當結集
修妬路阿毘曇毘[31]尼作三
法藏。如是佛法可得久住。
未來世人可得受行。所以
者何。佛世世勤苦慈愍眾生
故。學得是法為人演說。我
曹亦應承用佛教宣揚開化。
是時大迦葉作是語竟。[32]住
須彌[33]山頂。撾銅[34]揵稚。
說此偈言。

佛諸弟子　若念於佛。
當報佛恩　莫入涅槃。
[0067c04]　　　是揵[35]稚音大迦葉
語聲。遍至三千大千世界。
皆悉聞知。諸有弟子得[36]神
力者。皆來集會大迦葉所。
爾時大迦葉告諸會者。佛法
欲滅。佛從三阿僧祇劫。種
種勤苦慈愍眾生[37]學得是
法。佛般涅槃已。諸弟子知
法持法誦法者皆亦隨佛滅
度。法今欲滅。未來眾生甚
可憐愍。失智慧眼

简体字

正體字

Mahākāśyapa Convenes a Dharma Council

At this time, Mahākāśyapa pondered, "How can I now cause this Buddha Dharma, obtained through such difficulty across the course of three *asaṃkhyeya* kalpas, to be preserved for a long time? After pondering like this, he said, "I know that this Dharma can be caused to remain a long time. We should collect together and compile the Sutras, the Abhidharma, and the Vinaya and make a threefold repository of Dharma. In this manner, the Buddha Dharma may be able to remain a long time. Thus people of future generations may be able to receive it and cultivate it.

"Why should we do this? It is because, in life after life, out of compassion and pity for beings, the Buddha was diligent and endured suffering to study and obtain this Dharma. He then expounded it for the sake of mankind. We, too, should undertake to put the Buddha's teaching to use, propagating it for the transformation of others."

After Mahākāśyapa had spoken these words, he went to the summit of Mount Sumeru and, striking a bronze *gaṇḍī* gong, uttered this verse:

All of you disciples of the Buddha,
If the Buddha now you do recall,
You should all repay the Buddha's kindness.
Do not now enter your nirvāṇa.

The sound of the *gaṇḍī* gong accompanied by the voice of Mahākāśyapa reached everywhere throughout the great trichiliocosm such that everyone heard and was aware of it. Of all of the disciples throughout the various realms of existence, those who had gained spiritual powers all came and assembled where Mahākāśyapa dwelt.

At that time Mahākāśyapa told all of those assembled there, "The Buddha's Dharma is about to become extinct. Out of compassion and pity for beings, the Buddha, for three *asaṃkhyeya* kalpas, was diligent and endured all manner of suffering in studying and obtaining this Dharma. After the Buddha's *parinirvāṇa*, those disciples who knew the Dharma, upheld the Dharma, and recited the Dharma proceeded to follow the Buddha, crossing on into cessation.

"Now, the Dharma itself is about to become extinct. The beings of the future are extremely pitiable, for they will have lost the eye

愚痴盲冥。佛大慈悲愍伤众
生。我曹应当承用佛教。须
待结集经藏竟。随意灭度。
诸来众会皆受教住。尔时大
迦叶选得千人。除[38]善阿
难。尽皆阿罗汉得六神通。
得共解脱无碍解脱。悉得三
明禅定自在。能逆顺行诸三
昧皆悉无碍。诵读三藏知内
外经书。诸外道家十八种大
经尽亦读知。皆能论议降伏
异学。

愚癡盲冥。佛大慈悲愍傷眾
生。我曹應當承用佛教。須
待結集經藏竟。隨意滅度。
諸來眾會皆受教住。爾時大
迦葉選得千人。除[38]善阿
難。盡皆阿羅漢得六神通。
得共解脫無礙解脫。悉得三
明禪定自在。能逆順行諸三
昧皆悉無礙。誦讀三藏知內
外經書。諸外道家十八種大
經盡亦讀知。皆能論議降伏
異學。

简体字 　　　正體字

of wisdom and shall be lost in the blindness and darkness of ignorance. With great kindness and compassion, the Buddha felt pity for beings. We, too, ought to undertake the work of putting the Buddha's teaching to use. We must wait until we have collected and compiled the repository of scriptures. After that, we may cross into cessation whenever we wish."

All of those who had assembled there accepted the instruction to remain. At that time Mahākāśyapa selected a thousand men. All of them except for Ānanda were arhats who had attained the six superknowledges, who were doubly-liberated (*ubhayato-bhāga-vimukta*),[1] and who had attained the unobstructed liberation (*asaṅga-vimokṣa*). They had all attained the three types of gnosis (*vidyā*)[2] and coursed freely in dhyāna samādhi. They were able to practice all of the samādhis in both ascending and descending order, and in all cases without hindrance. They could recite and had studied the three repositories of teachings and had knowledge of all the esoteric and exoteric scriptures. They had completely studied and understood the eighteen kinds of immense scriptures of the non-Buddhist schools of thought and were all able to debate and defeat the adherents of heterodox disciplines.

Notes

1. This refers to possessing liberation through both wisdom and meditative absorption.
2. This is a reference to knowledge of past lives of self and others, possession of the vision of the heavenly eye, and realization of the cessation of all outflow impurities (*āsrava*).

问曰。是时有如是等无数阿
罗汉。何以[39]故[40]正选取千
人不多取耶。答曰。[41]频婆
娑罗王得道。八万四千官属
亦各得道。是[42]时王教勅宫
中。常设饭食供养千[43]人。
阿阇[44]贳王不断是法。尔时
大迦叶思惟言。若我等常乞
食者。当有外道强来难问废
阙法事。今王舍城。常设饭
食供给千人。是中可住结集
经藏。以是故选[45]取千人。
不得[46]多取。

問曰。是時有如是等無數阿
羅漢。何以[39]故[40]正選取千
人不多取耶。答曰。[41]頻婆
娑羅王得道。八萬四千官屬
亦各得道。是[42]時王教勅宮
中。常設飯食供養千[43]人。
阿闍[44]貰王不斷是法。爾時
大迦葉思惟言。若我等常乞
食者。當有外道強來難問廢
闕法事。今王舍城。常設飯
食供給千人。是中可住結集
經藏。以是故選[45]取千人。
不得[46]多取。

简体字   正體字

Why Mahākāśyapa Chose One Thousand Arhats

Question: At this time there were innumerable arhats such as these. Why did he select only a thousand men and no more?

Response: When King Bimbasāra gained the Path, 84,000 other officials and subordinates also gained the Path. At that time the King instructed those in his palace to always prepare enough food to make offerings to a thousand people. King Bimbasāra did not suspend this practice.

At that time Mahākāśyapa thought, "If we are always having to go forth on the alms round, there will be non-Buddhists who insist on aggressively imposing themselves on us with objections and queries, causing inefficiency and lapses in our Dharma endeavors. Now, in the city of Rājagṛha, they always prepare food to donate to a thousand people. We shall be able to dwell here to collect and compile the repository of scriptures. It was on account of this that he selected one thousand men and was unable to choose more.

是时大迦叶与千人俱到王舍城耆阇崛山中。告语阿阇世王。给我等食日日送来。今我[1]曹[2]等结集经藏不得他行。是中夏安居三月初十五日说戒时。集和合僧。大迦叶入禅定。以天眼观今是众中谁有烦恼未尽。应逐出者。唯有阿难一人不尽。馀九百九十九人。诸漏已尽清净无垢。大迦叶从禅定起。众中手牵阿难出言。今清净众中结集经藏。汝结未尽不应住此。是时阿难惭耻悲泣而自念言。我二十五年。随侍世尊供给左右。未曾得如是苦恼。佛实大德慈悲含忍。念已白大迦叶言。我能有力久可得道。但诸佛法阿罗汉者。不得供给左右使令。以是故我留残结不尽断耳。大迦叶言。汝更有罪。佛意不欲听女人出家。[3]汝慇懃劝请[4]佛[5]听为道。以是故佛之正法五百岁而衰微。[6]是汝突吉罗[7]罪。阿难言。我怜愍瞿昙弥。又三世诸佛法皆有四部众。我释迦文佛[8]云何独[9]无。

是時大迦葉與千人俱到王舍城耆阇崛山中。告語阿阇世王。給我等食日日送來。今我[1]曹[2]等結集經藏不得他行。是中夏安居三月初十五日說戒時。集和合僧。大迦葉入禪定。以天眼觀今是眾中誰有煩惱未盡。應逐出者。唯有阿難一人不盡。餘九百九十九人。諸漏已盡清淨無垢。大迦葉從禪定起。眾中手牽阿難出言。今清淨眾中結集經藏。汝結未盡不應住此。是時阿難慚恥悲泣而自念言。我二十五年。隨侍世尊供給左右。未曾得如是苦惱。佛實大德慈悲含忍。念已白大迦葉言。我能有力久可得道。但諸佛法阿羅漢者。不得供給左右使令。以是故我留殘結不盡斷耳。大迦葉言。汝更有罪。佛意不欲聽女人出家。[3]汝慇懃勸請[4]佛[5]聽為道。以是故佛之正法五百歲而衰微。[6]是汝突吉羅[7]罪。阿難言。我憐愍瞿曇彌。又三世諸佛法皆有四部眾。我釋迦文佛[8]云何獨[9]無。

简体字   正體字

Ānanda's Banishment from the Dharma Council

At that time Mahākāśyapa arrived with a thousand men at the city of Rājagṛha on Mount Gṛdhrakūṭa. He informed King Ajātaśatru, "In providing food for us, have it brought to us each day. We are now in the process of compiling and collecting the repositories of scriptures and cannot be distracted by other activities." They dwelt therein for the three months of the summer retreat. During the initial fifteen days, at the time of the recitation of the prohibitions, they assembled the harmonious Sangha together.

Mahākāśyapa entered dhyāna absorption and, using the heavenly eye, surveyed the Assembly to see who still had afflictions which had not been brought to an end and thus who should be expelled therefrom. There was but one person, Ānanda, who had not put them to an end. The other nine hundred and ninety-nine had ended all outflow impurities, were pure, and thus were devoid of defilements.

Mahākāśyapa arose from dhyāna absorption and, from the midst of the Assembly, pulled Ānanda out by the hand, saying, "We are now engaged in collecting and compiling the repository of scriptures in the midst of the pure Assembly. Because your fetters have not yet been brought to an end, you should not remain here."

At this time, Ānanda was ashamed, wept sorrowfully, and thought to himself, "For twenty-five years I have followed along with and served the Bhagavān, providing him with assistance. Never before have I been so bitterly distressed! The Buddha was truly greatly virtuous, kind, compassionate and patient."

After he had this thought, he addressed Mahākāśyapa, saying, "The strength of my abilities is such that I could have realized the Path long ago. It's just that the arhats in the Buddha's Dharma wouldn't provide assistance or carry out directives. It is only because of this that I retain residual fetters which haven't yet been entirely cut off."

Mahākāśyapa said, "You still have offenses. The Buddha's intention was such that he did not wish to allow women to leave the home life. Because you so persistently petitioned, the Buddha allowed that they could take up the [monastic] Path. On account of this, after only five hundred years, the orthodox Dharma of the Buddha shall decline and diminish. In this you committed a *duṣkṛta* offense."

Ānanda said, "I felt pity for Gautamī. Moreover, the Dharma of all Buddhas of the three ages has had a fourfold community. Why then should only our Shakyamuni Buddha be without it?"

大迦叶复言。佛欲 [10]涅盘
时。近俱夷那竭城[11]脊痛。
四叠沤多罗僧敷卧。语汝
言。我须水。汝不供给。[12]
是汝突吉罗罪。阿难答言。
是时五百乘车截流而渡令水
浑浊。以是故不取。大迦叶
复言。正使水浊佛有大神力
能令大海浊水清净。汝何[13]
以不与。[14]是汝之罪。[15]
汝[16]去作突吉罗忏悔。大迦
叶复言。佛问汝。若有人四
神足好修。可住寿一劫若减
一劫。佛四神足好修。欲住
寿一劫若减一劫。汝默然不
答。问汝至三。汝故默然。
汝若答佛佛四神足好修。应
住一劫若减一劫。由汝故。
令佛世尊早入涅盘。[17]是汝
突吉罗[*]罪。阿难言。魔蔽我
心。是故无言。我非恶心而
不答佛。大迦叶复言。汝与
佛叠僧伽梨衣以足蹈上。是
[18]汝突吉罗[*]罪。阿难言。
尔时有大风起无人助。我捉
衣时风吹来堕我脚下。非不
恭敬故蹈佛衣。大迦叶[19]复
言。佛阴藏相般涅盘后以示
女人。是何可耻。

大迦葉復言。佛欲 [10]涅槃
時。近俱夷那竭城[11]脊痛。
四疊漚多羅僧敷臥。語汝
言。我須水。汝不供給。[12]
是汝突吉羅罪。阿難答言。
是時五百乘車截流而渡令水
渾濁。以是故不取。大迦葉
復言。正使水濁佛有大神力
能令大海濁水清淨。汝何[13]
以不與。[14]是汝之罪。[15]
汝[16]去作突吉羅懺悔。大迦
葉復言。佛問汝。若有人四
神足好修。可住壽一劫若減
一劫。佛四神足好修。欲住
壽一劫若減一劫。汝默然不
答。問汝至三。汝故默然。
汝若答佛佛四神足好修。應
住一劫若減一劫。由汝故。
令佛世尊早入涅槃。[17]是汝
突吉羅[*]罪。阿難言。魔蔽我
心。是故無言。我非惡心而
不答佛。大迦葉復言。汝與
佛疊僧伽梨衣以足蹈上。是
[18]汝突吉羅 [*]罪。阿難言。
爾時有大風起無人助。我捉
衣時風吹來墮我腳下。非不
恭敬故蹈佛衣。大迦葉[19]復
言。佛陰藏相般涅槃後以示
女人。是何可恥。

简体字   正體字

Mahākāśyapa replied, "When the Buddha was about to enter nirvāṇa and was approaching the town of Kuśinagara, his back began to hurt. He spread out the *uttarāsaṅga* robe, folded it in four layers, lay down, and said to you, 'I need water.' You did not provide it for him. In this you committed a *duṣkṛta* offense."

Ānanda responded, "At that time five hundred carts were passing through the current and their fording caused the water to become turbid and dirty. It was because of this that I did not get any."

Mahākāśyapa replied, "Even given that they had caused the water to become dirty, the Buddha has great spiritual power by which he is able to cause even a great ocean of polluted water to become pure. Why didn't you give it to him?. In this there was an offense committed by you. Go and perform the *duṣkṛta* repentance."

"Moreover," Mahākāśyapa said, "The Buddha, by way of prompting you, said, 'If there were a person who had well cultivated the four bases of psychic power, his lifetime could continue for a kalpa or somewhat less than a kalpa.' The Buddha had well cultivated the four bases of psychic power. He wished for his lifetime to continue for a kalpa or somewhat less than a kalpa. But you remained silent and made no reply. He placed this question before you three times, but you deliberately remained silent.

"If only you had replied to Buddha, 'The Buddha has well cultivated the four bases of psychic power. He should remain for a kalpa or perhaps somewhat less than a kalpa.' It was because of you that the Buddha, the Bhagavān, was caused to make an early entry into nirvāṇa. In this you committed a *duṣkṛta* offense."

Ānanda said, "Māra obscured my mind. It was because of this that I didn't say anything. It is not the case that I failed to reply to the Buddha on account of evil thoughts."

Mahākāśyapa responded, saying, "In your performing of the folding of the saṅghāṭī robe for the Buddha, you stepped on it. In this you committed a *duṣkṛta* offense."

Ānanda said, "At that time there was a big gust of wind which came up and nobody was assisting. When I picked up the robe, the wind blew it such that it came to fall under my foot. It is not the case that I was disrespectful and deliberately trod upon the Buddha's robe."

Mahākāśyapa replied, saying, "After the Buddha had entered *parinirvāṇa*, you revealed the Buddha's physical characteristic of genital ensheathement to women. How shameful this is! In this you

[*]是汝突吉罗[*]罪。阿难言。
尔时我思惟。若诸女人见佛
阴藏相者。便自羞耻女[20]人
形。欲得男子身修行佛相种
[21]福德根。以是故[22]我示
女人。不为无耻而故破戒。
大迦叶言。汝有六种突吉罗
[23]罪。尽应僧中[24]悔过。阿
难言诺。随长老大迦叶及僧
所教。是时阿难长跪合手。
偏袒右肩脱革[25]屣。六种突
吉罗罪忏悔。大迦叶于僧中
手牵阿难出。语阿难言。断
汝漏尽然后来入。残结未尽
汝勿来也。如是语竟便自闭
门。

[*]是汝突吉羅[*]罪。阿難言。
爾時我思惟。若諸女人見佛
陰藏相者。便自羞恥女[20]人
形。欲得男子身修行佛相種
[21]福德根。以是故[22]我示
女人。不為無恥而故破戒。
大迦葉言。汝有六種突吉羅
[23]罪。盡應僧中[24]悔過。阿
難言諾。隨長老大迦葉及僧
所教。是時阿難長跪合手。
偏袒右肩脫革[25]屣。六種突
吉羅罪懺悔。大迦葉於僧中
手牽阿難出。語阿難言。斷
汝漏盡然後來入。殘結未盡
汝勿來也。如是語竟便自閉
門。

简体字   正體字

committed a *duṣkṛta* offense."

Ānanda said, "At the time I thought, 'If women notice the Buddha's physical characteristic of genital ensheathement, then they might naturally come to feel chagrin regarding the female form and wish to gain rebirth in a male body whereby they might cultivate the characteristics of a Buddha and plant roots of merit.' It was because of this that I revealed this characteristic to women. It was not a deliberate breaking of the prohibitions arising from shamelessness."

Mahākāśyapa said, "You have committed six kinds of *duṣkṛta* offenses. For all of them you should repent your transgressions in the presence of the Sangha."

Ānanda said, "Alright, I shall accord with the instructions of the Venerable Mahākāśyapa and the Sangha." At this time Ānanda knelt, pressed his palms together, arranged his robe with the right shoulder bared, took off his sandals, and repented of six types of *duṣkṛta* offenses. From within the midst of the Assembly, Mahākāśyapa led Ānanda out by the hand and then said to Ānanda , "Completely cut off your outflow impurities and then afterwards you may come back in. As long as your residual fetters have not been brought to an end, you cannot come in." After he had said this, he secured the door.

尔时。诸阿罗汉[26]议[27]言。
谁能结集毘[*]尼法藏者。长
老[28]阿泥卢豆言。舍利弗是
第二[29]佛有好弟子。字憍梵
[30]波提[31]（秦言牛呞）柔[32]软
和雅常处闲居。住[33]心寂[34]
燕能知毘[*]尼法藏。今在天
上尸利沙[35]树园中住。遣使
请来。大迦叶语下坐比丘。
汝次应僧使。下坐比丘言。
僧有何使。大迦叶言。僧使
汝至天上尸利沙[*]树园[36]中
[37]憍梵[38]波提阿罗汉住处。
是比丘欢喜踊跃受僧勅命。
白大迦叶言。我到[*]憍梵[*]波
提阿罗汉所陈说何事。大迦
叶言。到已语[*]憍梵钵提。
大迦叶等漏尽阿罗汉。皆会
阎浮提。僧有大法事。汝可
疾来是。下坐比丘头面礼僧
右绕三匝。如金翅鸟飞腾虚
空。往到[*]憍梵波提所。头面
作礼。语[*]憍梵波提言。[*]软
善大德少欲知足常在禅定。
大迦叶问讯有[39]语。今僧有
大法事。可疾[40]下来观众宝
聚。是时[*]憍梵波提心[41]觉
生疑。语是比丘言。僧将无
鬪诤事唤我[42]来耶。无有破
僧者不。佛日灭度耶。

簡体字

爾時。諸阿羅漢[26]議[27]言。
誰能結集毘[*]尼法藏者。長
老[28]阿泥盧豆言。舍利弗是
第二[29]佛有好弟子。字憍梵
[30]波提[31]（秦言牛呞）柔[32]軟
和雅常處閑居。住[33]心寂[34]
燕能知毘[*]尼法藏。今在天
上尸利沙[35]樹園中住。遣使
請來。大迦葉語下坐比丘。
汝次應僧使。下坐比丘言。
僧有何使。大迦葉言。僧使
汝至天上尸利沙[*]樹園[36]中
[37]憍梵[38]波提阿羅漢住處。
是比丘歡喜踊躍受僧勅命。
白大迦葉言。我到[*]憍梵[*]波
提阿羅漢所陳說何事。大迦
葉言。到已語[*]憍梵鉢提。
大迦葉等漏盡阿羅漢。皆會
閻浮提。僧有大法事。汝可
疾來是。下坐比丘頭面禮僧
右繞三匝。如金翅鳥飛騰虛
空。往到[*]憍梵波提所。頭面
作禮。語[*]憍梵波提言。[*]軟
善大德少欲知足常在禪定。
大迦葉問訊有[39]語。今僧有
大法事。可疾[40]下來觀眾寶
聚。是時[*]憍梵波提心[41]覺
生疑。語是比丘言。僧將無
鬪諍事喚我[42]來耶。無有破
僧者不。佛日滅度耶。

正體字

Gavāṃpati After the Buddha's Nirvāṇa

At that time the Arhats began their discussions and asked, "Who is able to collect and compile the repository of the Vinaya Dharma?"

The Venerable Aniruddha said, "Śāriputra, second only to the Buddha, has a fine disciple named Gavāṃpati. He is one of supple mind and is both harmonious and refined. He always stays in a quiet place and abides in a feast of stillness of the mind. By his abilities, he has knowledge of the repository of the Vinaya Dharma. Now he is up in the heavens in the Śirīṣa Tree Gardens. Send a messenger requesting him to come."

Mahākāśyapa said to a subordinate bhikshu, "You are next in sequence to carry out the orders of the Sangha."

The subordinate bhikshu replied, "What directive does the Sangha have?"

Mahākāśyapa said, "The Sangha directs you to go to the Śirīṣa Tree Gardens up in the heavens to the place therein where Gavāṃpati, the arhat, dwells."

This bhikshu leaped up with delight, accepted the Sangha's command, and addressed Mahākāśyapa, asking, "When I reach the dwelling place of Gavāṃpati, the arhat, what matter should I set forth?"

Mahākāśyapa said, "After you arrive, tell Gavāṃpati, 'Mahākāśyapa and the other arhats who have put an end to outflow impurities have all assembled in Jambudvīpa. The Sangha has taken up a great matter of Dharma. You may come immediately.'"

The subordinate bhikshu made full reverential prostrations before the Sangha, circumambulated them three times and then, like the great golden-winged [garuḍa] bird, flew straight up into space, went to the dwelling place of Gavāṃpati, made full reverential prostrations, and said to Gavāṃpati, "Oh, supple, good, and greatly virtuous one who has but few desires, knows sufficiency, and constantly dwells in dhyāna absorption—Mahākāśyapa pays his respects and sends this message: 'Now the Sangha has taken up a great matter of Dharma. You may descend immediately to survey that congregation of a multitude of jewels.'"

At this time, doubts arose in Gavāṃpati's mind and he said to this bhikshu, "The generals of Dharma don't have any matters in dispute wherefore they summon me to come, do they? There isn't anyone causing a schism in the Sangha, is there? Has the Buddha, the Sun, crossed into cessation?"

是比丘言。实如所言。大师
佛已灭度。[*]憍梵波提言。佛
灭度[43]大疾。世间眼灭。能
逐佛转法[44]轮将[45]我[46]和上
舍利弗今在何所。答曰。先
入涅盘。[*]憍梵[*]波提言。大
师法将各自别离。当[47]可奈
何。摩诃目伽连今在何所。
是比丘言。是亦灭度。[*]憍梵
波提言。佛法欲散大人过去
众生可[48]愍。[49]问长老阿难
今何所作。是比丘言。长老
阿难佛灭度后。忧愁啼哭迷
[50]闷不能自喻。[*]憍梵波提
言。阿难懊[51]恼由有爱结别
离生苦。罗睺罗复云何。答
言。罗睺罗得阿罗汉故无忧
无愁。但观诸法无常相。[*]
憍梵波提言。难断爱已[52]断
无忧愁。[*]憍梵波提言。我
失离欲大师。于是[53]尸利沙
[*]树园中住。亦何所为。我[*]
和上大师皆已灭度。我今不
能复[54]下阎浮提。住此般涅
盘。说是言已入禅定中。踊
在虚空。身放光明。又出水
火。手摩日月现种种神变。
自心出火烧身。身中出水四
道流下。至大迦叶所。水中
有声。说此偈言。

简体字

正體字

This bhikshu said, "It is truly as you say. The Great Master, the Buddha, has already crossed into cessation."

Gavāṃpati said, "The Buddha has passed into cessation too swiftly. The eye of the World has perished. That Dharma-wheel-turning general capable of continuing on after the Buddha—my *upādhyāya*, Śāriputra—where is he now?"

He replied, "He has already entered nirvāṇa."

Gavāṃpati said, "The Dharma generals of the Great Master have each taken their leave. What can one do about this? Mahāmaudgalyāyana? Where is he now?"

The bhikshu said, "This one, too, has crossed into cessation."

Gavāṃpati said, "The Dharma of the Buddha is about to become scattered. The great men have passed on. Those beings who remain are to be pitied." He asked, "The Venerable Ānanda? what is he doing now?"

This bhikshu said, "After the Buddha crossed into cessation, the Venerable Ānanda was stricken with sorrow, weeping, and confusion-ridden desolation, so much so that he could not express himself clearly."

Gavāṃpati said, "Ānanda is so grief-stricken because he still possesses the fetters of affection and undergoes the suffering of separation. Rāhula? How was he?"

The reply: "Because Rāhula attained arhatship, he was neither sorrowful nor melancholy. He simply contemplated all dharmas as characterized by impermanence."

Gavāṃpati said, "When the affection which is difficult to cut off has been cut off, there is no sorrow or melancholy." Gavāṃpati continued, "I have lost the Great Master who transcended desire. Dwelling here in the Śirīṣa Tree Gardens—what point is there in that? My *upādhyāya* and the Great Master—they have all crossed into cessation. Now I can never again return to Jambudvīpa. I shall abide in this *parinirvāṇa*."

As he finished speaking these words, he entered dhyāna absorption and leapt up into space. His body radiated brilliant light and also shot forth water and fire. He touched the sun and moon with his hands and displayed all manner of spiritual transformations.

From his mind, he put forth fire which burned up his body. From his body, he gushed forth water which descended in four streams to the place of Mahākāśyapa. From within the water there came a voice which uttered this verse:

[*]憍梵鉢[1]提稽首礼。 妙众第一大德僧。 闻佛灭度我随去。 如大象去象子随。 [0069a07] 尔时下坐比丘。持衣鉢还僧。	[*]憍梵鉢[1]提稽首禮。 妙眾第一大德僧。 聞佛滅度我隨去。 如大象去象子隨。 [0069a07] 爾時下坐比丘。持衣鉢還僧。
简体字	正體字

"Gavāṃpati in reverence bows down before you,
The foremost wondrous assembly, the greatly virtuous Sangha.
I hear Buddha's crossed into cessation and so follow and depart.
As when the great elephant moves on, the young elephants follow
    too."

At that time the subordinate bhikshu took up [Gavāṃpati's] robe
and bowl and returned to the Sangha.

是时中间阿难思惟诸法求尽
残漏。其夜坐禅经行愍懃求
道。是阿难智慧多定力少。
是故不即得道。定智等者乃
可速得。后夜欲过疲极偃
息。却卧就枕头未至枕。廓
然得悟。如电光出暗者见
道。阿难如是入金刚定。破
一切诸烦恼山。得三明六[2]
神通[3]共解脱。作大力阿罗
汉。即夜到僧堂门[4]敲门而
唤。大迦叶问言。[*]敲门者
谁。答言。我是阿难。大迦
叶言。汝何以来。阿难言。
我今夜得尽诸漏。大迦叶
言。不与汝开门。汝从门[5]
钥孔中来。阿难答言。可
尔。即以神力从门[*]钥孔中
入。礼拜僧足忏悔。大迦叶
莫复见责。大迦叶手摩阿难
头言。我故为汝使汝得道。
汝无嫌恨。我亦如是以汝自
证。譬如手画虚空无所染
着。阿罗汉心亦如是。一切
法中得无所着。复汝本坐。

简体字

是時中間阿難思惟諸法求盡
殘漏。其夜坐禪經行愍懃求
道。是阿難智慧多定力少。
是故不即得道。定智等者乃
可速得。後夜欲過疲極偃
息。却臥就枕頭未至枕。廓
然得悟。如電光出闇者見
道。阿難如是入金剛定。破
一切諸煩惱山。得三明六[2]
神通[3]共解脫。作大力阿羅
漢。即夜到僧堂門[4]敲門而
喚。大迦葉問言。[*]敲門者
誰。答言。我是阿難。大迦
葉言。汝何以來。阿難言。
我今夜得盡諸漏。大迦葉
言。不與汝開門。汝從門[5]
鑰孔中來。阿難答言。可
爾。即以神力從門[*]鑰孔中
入。禮拜僧足懺悔。大迦葉
莫復見責。大迦葉手摩阿難
頭言。我故為汝使汝得道。
汝無嫌恨。我亦如是以汝自
證。譬如手畫虛空無所染
著。阿羅漢心亦如是。一切
法中得無所著。復汝本坐。

正體字

Ānanda's Return

During this time, Ānanda had been contemplating the nature of all dharmas and was seeking to bring his residual outflow impurities to an end. That night he sat in dhyāna contemplation and meditative walking, working diligently in his quest of the Path. This Ānanda was one whose wisdom was abundant but whose meditative power was scant. It was because of this that he did not immediately gain the Path. One whose absorptions and wisdom exist in equal measure may rapidly realize it.

When the final watch of the night was nearly over, his weariness was extreme and he was on the point of laying down to rest. In lying down, he took up the pillow. But, before his head reached the pillow, suddenly and expansively, he gained enlightenment. It was like when a flash of lightning appears: those immersed in darkness are able to see the road.

In this manner, Ānanda entered the *vajra* samādhi and shattered the mountain of all afflictions. He attained the three types of gnosis (*vidyā*), the six superknowledges, and the double liberation (*ubhayato-bhāga-vimukta*). He became an arhat possessed of great power. He then went in the night to the door of the Sangha hall, knocked upon the door, and called out. Mahākāśyapa asked, "Who's knocking at the door?"

The reply: "I'm Ānanda."

Mahākāśyapa queried, "Why have you come?"

Ānanda announced, "This very night I gained the ending of all outflow impurities."

Mahākāśyapa informed him, "We will not open the door for you. You come in through the keyhole."

Ānanda agreed: "It can be done that way." Then, using spiritual powers, he went in through the keyhole, prostrated himself in reverence at the feet of the Sangha, repented, and declared, "Mahākāśyapa, you need not censure me any more."

Mahākāśyapa rubbed the top of Ānanda's head with his hand and explained, "I deliberately and for your sake influenced you to gain the Path. You have no enmity. I too am thus. This is as you yourself have realized. This is like painting with the hand in empty space wherein there is no staining or adhering. The mind of the arhat is also like this. In the midst of all dharmas, one becomes such that there is nothing to which one clings. You may return to your original seat."

是时[6]僧[7]复议言。[*]憍梵[*]波提已取灭度。更有谁能结集[8]法藏。长老阿[9]泥卢豆言。是长老阿难。于佛[10]弟子常侍近佛。闻经能持佛常叹誉。是阿难能结集经藏。是时长老大迦叶摩阿难头言。佛嘱累汝令持法藏。汝应报佛恩。佛在何处最初说法。佛诸大弟子能守护法藏者皆以灭度。[11]唯汝一人在。汝今应随佛心怜愍众生。故集佛法藏。是时阿难礼僧已坐师子[12]床。时大迦叶说此偈言。

佛圣师子王　阿难是佛子。
师子座处坐　观众无有佛。
如是大德众　无佛失威神。
如[13]空无月时　[14]有宿而不严。
汝大智人说　汝佛子当演。
何处佛初说　今汝当布[15]现。

[0069b10] 是时长老阿难一心合[16]手。向佛涅盘方。如是说[17]言。

佛初说法时　尔时我不见。
如是展转闻　佛在波罗奈。

简体字

是時[6]僧[7]復議言。[*]憍梵[*]波提已取滅度。更有誰能結集[8]法藏。長老阿[9]泥盧豆言。是長老阿難。於佛[10]弟子常侍近佛。聞經能持佛常歎譽。是阿難能結集經藏。是時長老大迦葉摩阿難頭言。佛囑累汝令持法藏。汝應報佛恩。佛在何處最初說法。佛諸大弟子能守護法藏者皆以滅度。[11]唯汝一人在。汝今應隨佛心憐愍眾生。故集佛法藏。是時阿難禮僧已坐師子[12]床。時大迦葉說此偈言。

佛聖師子王　阿難是佛子。
師子座處坐　觀眾無有佛。
如是大德眾　無佛失威神。
如[13]空無月時　[14]有宿而不嚴。
汝大智人說　汝佛子當演。
何處佛初說　今汝當布[15]現。

[0069b10] 是時長老阿難一心合[16]手。向佛涅槃方。如是說[17]言。

佛初說法時　爾時我不見。
如是展轉聞　佛在波羅奈。

正體字

The First Dharma Council

At this time, the Sangha returned to its deliberations, whereupon a question arose: "Gavāṃpati has already opted to cross into cessation. Who else is there who is able to collect and compile the treasury of scriptures?" The Venerable Aniruddha said, "Among the Buddha's disciples, this Venerable Ānanda constantly assisted and was near to the Buddha. He heard the scriptures and is able to retain them. The Buddha always praised him, saying, 'This Ānanda is able to collect and compile the treasury of scriptures.'"

Then the Venerable Mahākāśyapa rubbed the top of Ānanda's head, saying, "The Buddha bequeathed this responsibility to you, ordering you to uphold the treasury of Dharma. You should repay the Buddha's kindness. Where did the Buddha speak Dharma the very first time? All of the Buddha's great disciples who have the ability to maintain and guard the treasury of Dharma have crossed into cessation. There is only you, one person, remaining. Now you ought to accord with the mind of the Buddha and, out of sympathy for beings, collect together the treasury of the Buddha's Dharma."

Ānanda then, after paying reverence to the Sangha, sat atop the lion's seat. At that time Mahākāśyapa uttered this verse:

The Buddha is the sovereign of all the ārya lions.
This Ānanda is a son unto the Buddha.
He now sits in that place upon the lion's throne.
Surveying this Assembly now without the Buddha.

Thus this congregation of the greatly virtuous,
In the absence of the Buddha, has lost its awesome spirit.
It now appears like a night without the brightness of the moon.
Though replete with constellations, it still is not majestic.

And now, you greatly wise one, it's time for you to speak.
You, scion of the Buddha, you ought now set it forth.
Just where did Buddha first expound it?
This now you should set forth and show.

Then, in a state of single-mindedness, the Venerable Ānanda pressed his palms together, faced the direction of the Buddha's nirvāṇa and spoke thus:

When first the Buddha spoke the Dharma,
It was at a time I did not see.
Like this I heard it roundabout that
The Buddha was at Vārāṇasī.

佛为五比丘　初开甘露门。
说四真谛法　苦[18]集灭道谛。
阿若憍陈如　最初得见道。
八万诸天众　皆亦入道迹。
[0069b18]　是千阿罗汉闻是语已。上升虚空高七多罗树。皆言[19]咄无常力大。如我等眼见佛说法。今乃言我闻。便说偈言。
我见佛身相　犹[20]如紫金山。
妙相众德灭　唯有名独存。
是故当方便　求出于三界。
勤集诸善[21]根　涅盘最[22]为乐。
[0069b25]　　尔时长老阿[*]泥卢豆。说[23]偈言。
咄世间无常　如水月芭蕉。
功德满三界　无常风所坏。
[0069b28]　尔时大迦叶。复说此偈。
无常力甚大　愚智贫富贵。
得道及未得　一切无能[24]免。
非巧言妙宝　非欺诳力净。
如火烧万物　无常相法尔。
[0069c04]　大迦叶语阿难。从转法轮经至大般涅盘。集作四阿含。增一阿含中阿含长阿含相应阿含。是名修[25]姤路

简体字

佛為五比丘　初開甘露門。
說四真諦法　苦[18]集滅道諦。
阿若憍陳如　最初得見道。
八萬諸天眾　皆亦入道迹。
[0069b18]　是千阿羅漢聞是語已。上昇虛空高七多羅樹。皆言[19]咄無常力大。如我等眼見佛說法。今乃言我聞。便說偈言。
我見佛身相　猶[20]如紫金山。
妙相眾德滅　唯有名獨存。
是故當方便　求出於三界。
勤集諸善[21]根　涅槃最[22]為樂。
[0069b25]　　爾時長老阿[*]泥盧豆。說[23]偈言。
咄世間無常　如水月芭蕉。
功德滿三界　無常風所壞。
[0069b28]　爾時大迦葉。復說此偈。
無常力甚大　愚智貧富貴。
得道及未得　一切無能[24]免。
非巧言妙寶　非欺誑力淨。
如火燒萬物　無常相法爾。
[0069c04]　大迦葉語阿難。從轉法輪經至大般涅槃。集作四阿含。增一阿含中阿含長阿含相應阿含。是名修[25]姤路

正體字

The Buddha for five bhikshus spoke it,
First opened there the sweet dew gate.
The four truths Dharma then he spoke.
Of suffering, origination, cessation and Path.

[It was an ascetic], Ājñāta Kauṇḍinya,
Was very first then to gain seeing of the Path.
A host, too, of gods, eighty-thousand in number,
All entered as well there the track of the Path.

After these one thousand arhats heard these words, they rose into the air to height of seven *tāla* trees and all said, "Alas! The power of impermanence is extreme. It is like when we saw the Buddha speaking Dharma. But now he says, 'I have heard!'" Then they uttered a verse:

We saw here once the marks of Buddha's body
It was just like seeing a purple golden mountain.
The wondrous marks and many virtues perish.
So now there's but a name alone remaining.

Hence therefore one should find a skillful method
To seek the exit from the triple world.
Diligently accumulate roots of goodness.
Nirvāṇa is the highest form of bliss.

At that time the Venerable Aniruddha also set forth a verse:

Alas! The World—there's nothing in it constant.
It's like the moon in water or plantain.
And though one's merits fill the Triple World,
They shall be destroyed by winds of change.

At that time Mahākāśyapa spoke another verse:

Impermanence—its power's very great.
The dull, the wise, the poor, the rich and noble—
Those who have gained the Path and those who have not—
Avoid it, none among them ever can.

Not with clever words or wondrous treasures,
Nor artifice, deception, strength, dispute.
It's like a fire which burns the myriad objects.
Dharmas marked by impermanence are just thus.

Mahākāśyapa said to Ānanda , "From the Turning the Dharma Wheel Scripture up to the great *parinirvāṇa*, we have collected and compiled the *Four Āgamas*: the *Item-Added Āgama*, the *Middle-Length Āgama*, the *Long Āgama*, and the *Connected Āgama*. These constitute the treasury of sutra Dharma."

法藏。诸阿罗汉更问。谁能明了集毗[*]尼法藏。皆言。长老[26]忧婆离于五百阿罗汉中持律第一。我等今请。即请言。起就师子座处坐[27]说。佛在何处初说毗[*]尼结戒。忧[*]婆离受[*]僧教。师子座处坐说。如是我闻一时佛在毗舍离。尔时须[28]提那迦兰陀长者子初作婬欲。以是因缘故结初大罪。二百五十戒[29]义作三部七法八法比丘尼毗[*]尼增一。忧[30]婆利问杂部善部。如是等八[31]十部作毗[*]尼藏。诸阿罗汉[32]复更思惟。谁能明了集阿毗昙藏。念言。长老阿难于五百阿罗汉[33]中。解修[*]妒路[34]义第一。我等今请。即请言。[35]起就师子座处坐。佛在何处初说阿毗昙。[36]阿难受僧教[37]师子座处坐说。如是我闻一时佛在舍[38]婆提城。尔时佛告诸比丘。诸有五怖五罪五怨不除不灭。是因缘故此生中身心受无量苦。[39]复后世堕恶道中。诸有无此五怖五罪五怨。是因缘故[40]于今生种种身心受乐。后世生天上乐处。何等五怖应远。一者[41]杀二者盗三者

简体字

法藏。諸阿羅漢更問。誰能明了集毗[*]尼法藏。皆言。長老[26]憂婆離於五百阿羅漢中持律第一。我等今請。即請言。起就師子座處坐[27]說。佛在何處初說毗[*]尼結戒。憂[*]婆離受[*]僧教。師子座處坐說。如是我聞一時佛在毗舍離。爾時須[28]提那迦蘭陀長者子初作婬欲。以是因緣故結初大罪。二百五十戒[29]義作三部七法八法比丘尼毗[*]尼增一。憂[30]婆利問雜部善部。如是等八[31]十部作毗[*]尼藏。諸阿羅漢[32]復更思惟。誰能明了集阿毗曇藏。念言。長老阿難於五百阿羅漢[33]中。解修[*]妒路[34]義第一。我等今請。即請言。[35]起就師子座處坐。佛在何處初說阿毗曇。[36]阿難受僧教[37]師子座處坐說。如是我聞一時佛在舍[38]婆提城。爾時佛告諸比丘。諸有五怖五罪五怨不除不滅。是因緣故此生中身心受無量苦。[39]復後世墮惡道中。諸有無此五怖五罪五怨。是因緣故[40]於今生種種身心受樂。後世生天上樂處。何等五怖應遠。一者[41]殺二者盜三者

正體字

The Arhats also asked, "Who is able to clearly understand and collect the treasury of the *Vinaya* Dharma?" They all agreed, "Among the five hundred Arhats, the Venerable Upāli is the foremost in upholding the moral precepts. Let us now request his assistance." They then summoned him, saying, "Arise. Go and sit upon the lion's seat and explain where the Buddha first spoke the *Vinaya* and formulated prohibitions."

Upāli accepted the instruction of the Sangha, sat in the lion's seat and declared, "Thus I have heard, at one time, the Buddha was at Vaiśālī. At that time Sudinna, son of Kalanda, first indulged in concupiscence. For this reason, the Buddha formulated the first major transgression. The explication of the meaning of the two hundred and fifty prohibitions constitutes three sections. Additionally there are the seven dharmas, the eight dharmas, the *Bhikshuni Vinaya*, the *Item-Added Section*, the *Inquiries of Upāli on Various Topics Section*, the *Miscellaneous Section*, and the *Goodness Section*. Topics such as these in eight categories and ten sections constitute the treasury of the *Vinaya*."

Again, the Arhats pondered further, "Who is able to clearly compile the treasury of the *Abhidharma*?" They thought, "Among the five hundred arhats, the Venerable Ānanda is foremost in the comprehension of the meaning of the sutras. Let us now request his assistance." They then summoned him, saying, "Arise. Go and sit upon the lion's seat. Where did the Buddha first set forth the *Abhidharma*?"

Ānanda accepted the instruction of the Sangha. He sat in the lion's seat and declared, "Thus I have heard, at one time, the Buddha was at the town of Srāvastī. At that time the Buddha told the Bhikshus, 'If throughout one's existences, five dreadables, five violations, and five loathables are not expelled and are not destroyed—then on account of these causes and conditions—during this very life, one's body and mind undergo immeasurable suffering. Moreover, in subsequent incarnations, one falls into the wretched destinies.

'If throughout one's existences, one does not have these five dreadables, five violations, five loathables—on account of these causes and conditions—during the present life, in body and in mind, one undergoes all manner of bliss. In subsequent incarnations, one is born in the blissful places in the heavens.

'What are the five dreadables from which one ought to distance oneself? The first is killing. The second is stealing. The third is

邪婬四者妄语五者饮酒。如
是等[42]名阿毗昙[43]藏。三法
藏[1]集竟。诸天鬼神诸龙天女
种种供养。雨天华香[2]幡盖天
衣。供养法故。于是说偈。
怜愍[3]世界故　集结三[4]藏
法。
十力一切智　说智无明灯。

邪婬四者妄語五者飲酒。如
是等[42]名阿毗曇[43]藏。三法
藏[1]集竟。諸天鬼神諸龍天女
種種供養。雨天華香[2]幡蓋天
衣。供養法故。於是說偈。
憐愍[3]世界故　集結三[4]藏
法。
十力一切智　說智無明燈。

简体字

正體字

sexual misconduct. The fourth is false speech. The fifth is the drinking of intoxicants.' Discourses such as these constitute the treasury of the Abhidharma."

When the treasuries of the three classes of Dharma were brought to completion, the gods, ghosts, spirits, dragons, and heavenly maidens presented all manner of offerings. There rained down celestial flowers, incense, banners, canopies and heavenly raiments as offerings to the Dharma. At that time those beings uttered a verse:

> Acting here from pity for the beings of the World.
> Now you have compiled all three treasuries of Dharma.
> Issued from the ten-fold powers and issued from omniscience,
> This spoken wisdom's a beacon amid ignorance's darkness.

复次[53]婆伽名破。婆名能。是[54]人能破婬怒痴故。称为[*]婆伽婆。问曰。如阿罗汉辟支佛。亦破婬怒痴与佛何异。答曰。阿罗汉[55]辟支佛虽破三毒。[56]气分不尽。譬如香在器中香虽[57]出馀气故在。[58]又如草木薪火烧烟出炭灰不尽。火力薄故。佛三毒永尽无馀。譬如劫尽火烧须弥山一切地都尽无烟无炭。如舍利弗瞋恚[59]气残。难陀婬欲[*]气残。[60]必陵伽婆[61]磋慢[*]气残。譬如人被[62]锁初脱时行犹不便。时佛从禅起经行。罗睺罗从佛经行。佛问罗睺罗。何以[63]羸瘦。罗睺罗说偈答佛

若人食油则得力

若食[64]酥者得好色

食麻[65]滓菜无色力

大德世尊自当知

復次[53]婆伽名破。婆名能。是[54]人能破婬怒癡故。稱為[*]婆伽婆。問曰。如阿羅漢辟支佛。亦破婬怒癡與佛何異。答曰。阿羅漢[55]辟支佛雖破三毒。[56]氣分不盡。譬如香在器中香雖[57]出餘氣故在。[58]又如草木薪火燒煙出炭灰不盡。火力薄故。佛三毒永盡無餘。譬如劫盡火燒須彌山一切地都盡無煙無炭。如舍利弗瞋恚[59]氣殘。難陀婬欲[*]氣殘。[60]必陵伽婆[61]磋慢[*]氣殘。譬如人被[62]鎖初脫時行猶不便。時佛從禪起經行。羅睺羅從佛經行。佛問羅睺羅。何以[63]羸瘦。羅睺羅說偈答佛

若人食油則得力

若食[64]酥者得好色

食麻[65]滓菜無色力

大德世尊自當知

简体字   正體字

Śāriputra's Unyielding Resolve

Nāgārjuna's Preamble: On Elimination of Residual Karma

Then again, [in the name *bhagavat*, one of the ten honorific names of the Buddha], *"bhāga"* may also mean "to destroy," whereas *"vat"* may also mean "able to." Because such a person is able to destroy sexual desire, anger, and delusion, he is called *"bhagavat."*

Question: Those such as the Arhats and the Pratyekabuddhas have also destroyed lust, anger, and delusion. How are they any different from the Buddha?

Response: Although arhats and pratyekabuddhas have destroyed the three poisons, residual traces have not been entirely brought to an end. This is analogous to the case of a vessel which has been used to store perfume. Even though the perfume has been emptied out, its residual traces still remain. This is also comparable to firewood from shrubs and trees which, after the fire has burned and the smoke has disappeared, the coals and ashes are still not completely gone. This is because the strength of the fire has been weak.

In the case of the Buddha, the three poisons have been eternally ended, leaving no residual traces. This is analogous to the case of the fire occurring at the end of the kalpa which entirely burns up Mount Sumeru and the entire earth, leaving neither smoke nor coals.

Take for example the remaining traces of hatred in the case of Śāriputra, the remaining traces of lust in the case of Nanda, and the remaining traces of arrogance in the case of Pilindavatsa. These instances are comparable to the circumstance of someone only recently freed from shackles who, in proceeding to walk again, does not move about with [normal] facility.

Story: Śāriputra's Unyielding Resolve

Once the Buddha arose from dhyāna and proceeded to walk along. Rāhula followed, walking with the Buddha.

The Buddha asked Rāhula, "Why are you so gaunt?" Rāhula replied to the Buddha in verse:

> If one partakes of foods with oils, then one gains in strength.
> And if one partakes of curds as food, then one gains in color.
> In eating leftover sesame vegetables, one gains no color or strength.
> The Venerable Bhagavān would naturally know such things.

[0070c16]　　佛问罗睺罗。是众中 [66]谁为上 [67]座。罗睺罗答。[*]和上舍利弗。佛言。舍利弗食不净食。尔时舍利弗 [68]转闻是 [69]语。即时吐食自作誓言。从今日不复受人请。是时波斯匿王长者须达多等。来诣舍利弗所。语舍利弗。佛不以无事而受人请。大德舍利弗复不受请。我等白衣云何当得大信清净。舍利弗言。我大师 [1]佛言。[2]舍利弗食不净 [3]食。今不得受人请。于是波斯 [4]匿等至佛所白佛言。佛不常受人请。舍利弗复不受请。我等云何心得大信。愿佛勅舍利弗还受人请。佛言。此人心坚不可移转。佛尔时 [5]引本生因缘。昔有一国王。[6]为毒蛇所噬。王时欲死呼 [7]诸良医令治蛇毒。时诸医言。还令蛇 [8]嗽毒气乃尽。是时诸医各设呪术。所噬王蛇即来王所。诸医积薪燃火勅蛇。还 [*]嗽汝毒。若不尔者当入此火。毒蛇思惟。我既吐毒云何还 [*]嗽。此事剧死。思惟 [9]心定即时入火。

[0070c16]　　佛問羅睺羅。是眾中 [66]誰為上 [67]座。羅睺羅答。[*]和上舍利弗。佛言。舍利弗食不淨食。爾時舍利弗 [68]轉聞是 [69]語。即時吐食自作誓言。從今日不復受人請。是時波斯匿王長者須達多等。來詣舍利弗所。語舍利弗。佛不以無事而受人請。大德舍利弗復不受請。我等白衣云何當得大信清淨。舍利弗言。我大師 [1]佛言。[2]舍利弗食不淨 [3]食。今不得受人請。於是波斯 [4]匿等至佛所白佛言。佛不常受人請。舍利弗復不受請。我等云何心得大信。願佛勅舍利弗還受人請。佛言。此人心堅不可移轉。佛爾時 [5]引本生因緣。昔有一國王。[6]為毒蛇所噬。王時欲死呼 [7]諸良醫令治蛇毒。時諸醫言。還令蛇 [8]嗽毒氣乃盡。是時諸醫各設呪術。所噬王蛇即來王所。諸醫積薪燃火勅蛇。還 [*]嗽汝毒。若不爾者當入此火。毒蛇思惟。我既吐毒云何還 [*]嗽。此事劇死。思惟 [9]心定即時入火。

简体字　　　　　　　　　　　　　　　　　正體字

The Buddha asked Rāhula, "Who is the most senior within this community?"

Rāhula replied, "It is the *upādhyāya*, Śāriputra."

The Buddha said, " Śāriputra consumes impure fare."[1]

Śāriputra came to hear of this pronouncement indirectly and immediately spat out his food and made a vow to himself, saying, "From this very day, I shall never again accept invitations."

At this time, King Prasenajit, Sudatta the Elder, and others came to pay a visit to Śāriputra and said to Śāriputra, "It is not without reason that the Buddha accepts people's invitations. If the greatly virtuous Śāriputra no longer accepts invitations, how shall we and other such laypeople be able to obtain the purification associated with great faith?"

Śāriputra said, "My great master, the Buddha, has said, 'Śāriputra consumes impure fare.' Now I can no longer bear to accept people's invitations."

At this, Prasenajit and the others went to the Buddha and addressed the Buddha, saying, "The Buddha does not often accept people's invitations. Śāriputra no longer accepts invitations. How shall the minds of [laypeople] such as us realize great faith? Pray, may the Buddha direct Śāriputra to continue to accept people's invitations."

The Buddha said, "This man's resolve is solid and it cannot be moved or deflected." Then the Buddha proceeded to recount the causes and conditions of an earlier lifetime:

"Formerly, there was a king who had been bitten by a poisonous snake. As that king was then on the verge of succumbing, he summoned the expert physicians and ordered them to treat the snake poisoning. Then the physicians said, "We must cause the snake to draw it out again. Then the poisonous effects shall cease."

At this time the physicians each performed incantational rituals. The snake which had bitten the King then came to the King's quarters. The physicians stacked up firewood, set it ablaze, and then commanded the snake, "Draw your poison back out again. If you don't, then you shall have to enter this fire."

The poisonous snake then thought, "Since I have already injected the poison, how can I draw it out again? This circumstance shall [inevitably] involve an agonizing death." Having reflected thus, his mind became fixed: He immediately slithered into the midst of the flames.

尔时毒蛇舍利弗是。世世心坚不可动也。	爾時毒蛇舍利弗是。世世心堅不可動也。
简体字	正體字

That poisonous snake was Śāriputra. In life after life, his mind has continued to be solid and immovable.

Notes

1. Śāriputra, by invitation, had led the monks to a prominent household where the senior monks were served a splendid meal while new ordinees and novices such as Rāhula were served only a two-week-old mixture of rice, sesame, and vegetables. Hence the Buddha's declaration that the discriminatory meal constituted "impure fare."

352 Marvelous Stories from the Perfection of Wisdom

复次长老[*]必陵伽婆蹉常患眼痛。是人乞食常渡恒水。到恒水边弹指言。小婢住莫流水。即两断得过乞食。是恒神到佛所白佛。佛弟子[*]必陵伽婆蹉。[10]常骂我言小婢住莫流[11]水。佛[12]告[*]必陵伽婆蹉。[13]忏谢恒神。[*]必陵伽婆蹉即时[14]合手语恒神言。小婢莫瞋今忏谢汝。是时大众笑[15]之。云何忏谢而复骂耶。佛语恒神。汝见[16]毕陵伽婆蹉[*]合手忏谢不。忏谢无慢而有此言。当知非恶。此人五百世来常生婆罗门家。常自憍贵轻贱馀人。本来所习口言而已。心无憍也。如是诸阿罗汉。虽断结使犹有[17]残气。如诸佛世尊。[18]若人以刀割一臂。

復次長老[*]必陵伽婆蹉常患眼痛。是人乞食常渡恒水。到恒水邊彈指言。小婢住莫流水。即兩斷得過乞食。是恒神到佛所白佛。佛弟子[*]必陵伽婆蹉。[10]常罵我言小婢住莫流[11]水。佛[12]告[*]必陵伽婆蹉。[13]懺謝恒神。[*]必陵伽婆蹉即時[14]合手語恒神言。小婢莫瞋今懺謝汝。是時大眾笑[15]之。云何懺謝而復罵耶。佛語恒神。汝見[16]畢陵伽婆蹉[*]合手懺謝不。懺謝無慢而有此言。當知非惡。此人五百世來常生婆羅門家。常自憍貴輕賤餘人。本來所習口言而已。心無憍也。如是諸阿羅漢。雖斷結使猶有[17]殘氣。如諸佛世尊。[18]若人以刀割一臂。

简体字

正體字

Pilindavatsa and the Ganges River Spirit

Translator's Note:

Following immediately on the earlier story of "Śāriputra's Unyielding Resolve," Nāgārjuna continues here to narrate instances of how, unlike the Buddha, arhats and pratyekabuddhas retain persistent residual traces of their previous afflictions even though they have indeed succeeded in cutting off the three poisons of attachment, aversion, and delusion.

The Story

The venerable Pilindavatsa was constantly afflicted with eye pain. During his alms round, this personage regularly forded the River Ganges. Upon reaching the shore of the Ganges, he would snap his fingers and call out, "Little servant! Stop! Don't flow!" The waters would then part and he would be free to cross and seek alms food. This Ganges River spirit went to where the Buddha dwelt and addressed the Buddha, [complaining], "The Buddha's disciple, Pilindavatsa, is forever insulting me, saying, 'Little servant! Stop! Don't flow!'"

The Buddha instructed Pilindavatsa to apologize to the Ganges spirit. Pilindavatsa immediately pressed his palms together and said to the Ganges spirit, "Little servant, don't be angry. I now apologize to you." At this moment, the Great Assembly laughed at this, [exclaiming], "How could you make an apology, and yet insult her once again as you do so?"

The Buddha said to the Ganges spirit, "As you look at Pilindavatsa, is he pressing his palms together and apologizing or not? In his apologizing, he remains free of arrogance and yet still speaks in this fashion. You should realize that this is not an instance of wickedness. For the last five hundred lifetimes, this man has always been born into brahman households and has always been haughty, esteeming himself while slighting and demeaning others. This is just the manner of speaking which he originally practiced, that's all. In his mind, there is no longer any haughtiness."

Concluding Exegesis Discussion: Buddha's Superior Transcendence

In just this way, although the Arhats have cut off the fetters, they still retain residual traces of them.

In the case of a Buddha, the Bhagavān, were someone to cut off one arm with a knife while someone else anointed the other arm

若人以栴檀香泥一臂。如左右眼心无憎爱。是以永无[*]残气。[19]栴闍婆罗门女。[20]木[21]杇谤佛于大众中言。汝使我有[22]娠。何以不忧与我衣食。为尔无羞誔惑馀人。是时五百婆罗门师等。皆举手唱言是[23]是。我曹知此事。是时佛无异色亦无惭色。此事即时彰露地为大动。诸天供养散众名华。赞叹佛德佛无喜色。复次佛食马麦亦无忧[24]戚。天王献食百味具足。不以为悦。一心无二。如是等种种饮食衣[25]被卧具。赞呵轻敬等种种事中心[26]无异也。譬如真金烧锻打磨都无增损。以是故阿罗汉虽断结得道。犹有[*]残气不得称婆伽婆。

若人以栴檀香泥一臂。如左右眼心無憎愛。是以永無[*]殘氣。[19]栴闍婆羅門女。[20]木[21]杇謗佛於大眾中言。汝使我有[22]娠。何以不憂與我衣食。為爾無羞誔惑餘人。是時五百婆羅門師等。皆舉手唱言是[23]是。我曹知此事。是時佛無異色亦無慚色。此事即時彰露地為大動。諸天供養散眾名華。讚歎佛德佛無喜色。復次佛食馬麥亦無憂[24]慼。天王獻食百味具足。不以為悅。一心無二。如是等種種飲食衣[25]被臥具。讚呵輕敬等種種事中心[26]無異也。譬如真金燒鍛打磨都無增損。以是故阿羅漢雖斷結得道。猶有[*]殘氣不得稱婆伽婆。

简体字   正體字

with sandalwood fragrance, no sooner would his mind entertain hatred or affection towards either of those persons than it would cherish preferential regard for either his own left or right eye. This is because he has become eternally free of residual traces [of the fetters].

In the midst of the Great Assembly, Ciñca, the brahman woman, wearing a bowl [beneath her clothes], slandered the Buddha, saying, "You got me pregnant! Why are you so unconcerned about this? You should provide me with clothing and food!" She acted that way, shamelessly deceiving and deluding others. At that time five hundred brahman leaders all raised up their arms, yelling, "It is so! It is so! We all have knowledge of this affair!"

At that time the Buddha had no change in countenance, nor did he possess any appearance of humiliation. This matter was immediately revealed [as fraudulent], for the earth quaked mightily and the gods made offerings, scattering a profusion of rare blossoms as they praised the virtues of the Buddha. The Buddha then made no expression of delight [at that, either].

Moreover, when the Buddha was once compelled to eat feed grain intended for horses, he was not disheartened by that. And when the King of the Gods offered up delicacies replete with the hundred flavors, he was not moved to pleasure on account of that. He was of a single mind and remained free of any duality-based thought. Amidst all kinds of food, drink, clothing, and bedding, and amidst all manner of praise, blame, slighting, and displays of reverence, his mind did not differ.

[His mind] is like pure gold, which can be smelted, forged, wrought, and polished, all without either increase or decrease. On account of [qualitative differences such as] these, although the Arhats have cut off the fetters, because they still retain residual traces [of the fetters], they are not deserving of the honorific appellation, *bhagavat*, [which signifies complete destruction of all traces of the fetters].

如放牛譬喻经中说。摩伽陀国王频婆娑罗请佛三月。及五百弟子。王须新乳酪[40]酥供养佛及比丘僧。[41]语诸放牛人来近处住。日日送新乳酪[*]酥。竟三月。王怜愍此放牛人语言。汝往见佛还出放牛。诸放牛人[42]往诣佛所。于道中自共论言。我[43]等闻人说。佛是一切智人。我等是下劣小人。[44]何能别知实有一切智[45]人。诸婆罗门[46]喜好[*]酥酪[47]故。常来[48]往诸放牛人所作亲厚。放牛人[49]由是闻婆罗门[50]种种经书名字故。言四[51]违[52]陀经中治病法鬪[53]战法星宿法祠天法歌舞论议难问法。[54]如是等六十四种世间[55]伎艺。净饭王子广学多闻。若知此事不足为难。其从生已来不放牛。我等以放牛秘法问之。若能解者实是一切智人。作是论已前入竹园。见佛光明照[56]于林间。进前觅佛见[57]坐树[58]下状似金山如[*]酥投火[59]其炎大明。有似[60]融金散竹林间上[61]紫金光色。视之无厌。心[62]大欢喜。自相谓言。

今此释师子　一切智有无。
见之无不喜

如放牛譬喻經中說。摩伽陀國王頻婆娑羅請佛三月。及五百弟子。王須新乳酪[40]酥供養佛及比丘僧。[41]語諸放牛人來近處住。日日送新乳酪[*]酥。竟三月。王憐愍此放牛人語言。汝往見佛還出放牛。諸放牛人[42]往詣佛所。於道中自共論言。我[43]等聞人說。佛是一切智人。我等是下劣小人。[44]何能別知實有一切智[45]人。諸婆羅門[46]喜好[*]酥酪[47]故。常來[48]往諸放牛人所作親厚。放牛人[49]由是聞婆羅門[50]種種經書名字故。言四[51]違[52]陀經中治病法鬪[53]戰法星宿法祠天法歌舞論議難問法。[54]如是等六十四種世間[55]伎藝。淨飯王子廣學多聞。若知此事不足為難。其從生已來不放牛。我等以放牛祕法問之。若能解者實是一切智人。作是論已前入竹園。見佛光明照[56]於林間。進前覓佛見[57]坐樹[58]下狀似金山如[*]酥投火[59]其炎大明。有似[60]融金散竹林間上[61]紫金光色。視之無厭。心[62]大歡喜。自相謂言。

今此釋師子　一切智有無。
見之無不喜

简体字   正體字

The Cowherds Test the Buddha's Omniscience

As described in the *Cowherding Analogies Sutra*, Bimbisāra, king of the state of Magadha, invited the Buddha and five hundred disciples to stay for three months. Because the King required fresh milk and yoghurt with which to make offerings to the Buddha and the Bhikshu Sangha he told the cowherds to come and dwell at a place close by. Every day, they delivered fresh milk and yoghurt. At the end of the three month period, the King, out of kindness for the cowherds, told them, "You may go to see the Buddha and then afterwards you may come back and look after the cows." All of the cowherds then set out to pay a visit to the Buddha. While on the road they had a discussion among themselves, saying, "We have heard people say that the Buddha is omniscient. We are all lesser fellows of inferior station. How would we be able to determine that an omniscient man actually exists?"

Because all of the Brahmans are fond of yoghurt, they were always coming and going at the cowherds' place and thus came to be quite friendly with them. Because of this, the cowherds had come to hear the names of all of the various Brahmanical scriptures.

They continued, "As for all the difficult questions about the teachings in the four Vedas on techniques of healing, fighting, astrology, sacrifices to the gods, singing, dancing, debating, and all of the other sixty-four kinds of worldly arts like these—because this son of King Śuddhodana has studied broadly and is very learned—if he were to know about all of these matters, it would not qualify as remarkably difficult. But he has never been a cowherd. We'll ask him about the secret methods involved in raising cows. If he is able to understand them, then he actually is an omniscient man."

After they had finished their discussion, they entered the bamboo gardens from the front and saw the light of the Buddha illuminating the forest. They moved forward, peeked at the Buddha, and saw him sitting beneath a tree, his shape like a mountain of gold. It was as when butter is thrown on the fire and its flames are intensely bright. It was as if molten gold had been showered all over the bamboo grove. They gazed insatiably upon his form as it radiated purple golden light. Their minds were greatly delighted and they said to themselves:

Now this lion of the Shakyan clan,
As to whether or not he possesses omniscience,
On seeing him no one fails to be delighted.
This matter alone would be sufficient as proof.

此事亦已足。
光明第一照　颜貌甚贵重。
身相威德备　与佛名相称。
相相[63]皆分明　威神亦满足。
福德自[64]缠络　见者无不爱。
圆光身处中　观者无厌足。
若有一切智　必[65]有是功德。
一切诸彩画　宝饰庄严像。
欲比此妙身　不可以为喻。
能满诸观者　令得第一乐。
见之发净信　必是一切智。

[0074a02]　　如是思惟已礼佛而坐。问佛言。放牛人有几法成就。能令牛群[1]番息。有几法不成就。令牛群不增不得安隐。佛答言。有十一法。放牛人能令牛群[*]番息。何等十一。知色知相知刮刷知覆[2]疮知作烟知好道知牛所宜处知好[3]度济知安隐处知留乳知养牛主。[4]若放牛人知此[5]十一法。能令牛群[*]番息。比丘亦如是。知十一法能增长善法。云何知色。知黑白杂色。比丘亦如是。知一切色

此事亦已足。
光明第一照　颜貌甚貴重。身相
威德備　與佛名相稱。相相[63]
皆分明　威神亦滿足。
福德自[64]纏絡　見者無不愛。
圓光身處中　觀者無厭足。
若有一切智　必[65]有是功德。
一切諸彩畫　寶飾莊嚴像。
欲比此妙身　不可以為喻。
能滿諸觀者　令得第一樂。
見之發淨信　必是一切智。

[0074a02]　　如是思惟已禮佛而坐。問佛言。放牛人有幾法成就。能令牛群[1]番息。有幾法不成就。令牛群不增不得安隱。佛答言。有十一法。放牛人能令牛群[*]番息。何等十一。知色知相知刮刷知覆[2]瘡知作煙知好道知牛所宜處知好[3]度濟知安隱處知留乳知養牛主。[4]若放牛人知此[5]十一法。能令牛群[*]番息。比丘亦如是。知十一法能增長善法。云何知色。知黑白雜色。比丘亦如是。知一切色

His light is the foremost illumination.
His countenance is extremely rare and precious.
The physical characteristics abound in awesome virtue.
They all measure up to the name of "Buddha."

Every characteristic is distinctly clear.
In awesome spirituality, he is utterly replete.
He is cloaked in meritorious qualities.
Of those who see him, none fail to adore him.

His body dwells amidst an orb of light.
Whoever looks upon him can never see enough.
If there is someone who possesses omniscience,
Certainly he would possess these meritorious qualities.

All of the paintings portrayed in various hues
And the images embellished with jeweled adornments
Might try to compare with this exquisite figure,
But could never succeed if even only by simile.

He is able to satisfy all who gaze upon him,
Causing them to develop the most supreme bliss.
Whoever looks upon him gains pure faith.
Certainly he is a man who's omniscient.

After having thought in this way, they paid reverence before the Buddha, sat down, and then asked, "What methods does a cowherd perfect that he is able to cause the herd to flourish and what methods might he fail to perfect that the herd thereby fails to grow and fails to become peaceful and secure?"

The Buddha replied, "There are eleven methods by which the cowherd is able to cause the herd to flourish. What are these eleven? They are: knowing the color; knowing the characteristics; knowing how to groom; knowing how to properly dress sores; knowing how to make smoke; knowing the good road; knowing the proper place for cattle; knowing the good place to ford; knowing the peaceful and secure place; knowing how to preserve the flow of milk; and knowing how to care for the lead bull.

"If the cowherd knows these eleven methods, he will be able to cause the herd to multiply. The bhikshu is also like this. If he knows eleven methods, he is able bring about increase and growth of wholesome dharmas.

"What is meant by 'knowing the color'? One is knowledgeable about the relative value of cattle which are black, white and various other colors. The bhikshu is also like this. He knows that all forms

皆是四大四大造。云何知
相。[6]知牛[7]吉不[*]吉相。
与他群合因相则识。比丘亦
如是。见善业相知是智人。
见恶业相知是愚人。云何刮
刷。[8]为诸[9]虫饮血则增长
诸[*]疮。刮刷[10]则除[11]害。
比丘亦如是。恶邪觉观虫饮
善根血增长心[*]疮。除则安
隐。云何覆[*]疮。[12]若衣若
草叶以防蚊[13]虻恶刺。比丘
亦如是。[14]念正[15]观法覆
六情[*]疮。不令烦恼贪欲瞋
恚恶虫刺�所伤。云何知作
烟除诸蚊[*]虻。牛[16]遥见烟
则来趣向屋舍。比丘亦[17]如
是。[18]如所闻而说除诸结
使蚊[*]虻。以说法烟[19]引众
生。入于无我实相空舍中。
云何知道。知[20]牛所行来
去好恶道。比丘亦如是。知
八圣道能至涅盘。离断常恶
道。云何知牛所宜处。能令
牛[21]番息少病。

皆是四大四大造。云何知
相。[6]知牛[7]吉不[*]吉相。
與他群合因相則識。比丘亦
如是。見善業相知是智人。
見惡業相知是愚人。云何刮
刷。[8]為諸[9]虫飲血則增長
諸[*]瘡。刮刷[10]則除[11]害。
比丘亦如是。惡邪覺觀虫飲
善根血增長心[*]瘡。除則安
隱。云何覆[*]瘡。[12]若衣若
草葉以防蚊[13]虻惡刺。比丘
亦如是。[14]念正[15]觀法覆
六情[*]瘡。不令煩惱貪欲瞋
恚惡虫刺herbs所傷。云何知作
煙除諸蚊[*]虻。牛[16]遙見煙
則來趣向屋舍。比丘亦[17]如
是。[18]如所聞而說除諸結
使蚊[*]虻。以說法煙[19]引眾
生。入於無我實相空舍中。
云何知道。知[20]牛所行來
去好惡道。比丘亦如是。知
八聖道能至涅槃。離斷常惡
道。云何知牛所宜處。能令
牛[21]番息少病。

简体字　　　　　　　　　　正體字

are themselves the four great elements or are composed of the four great elements.

"What is meant by 'knowing the characteristics'? One recognizes the characteristics of cattle which indicate auspiciousness and inauspiciousness. Whether or not a cow will be harmonious with another herd is known on the basis of its characteristics. The bhikshu is also like this. On seeing the characteristics of wholesome karma, he knows one is a wise person. On seeing the characteristics of bad karma, he knows one is a stupid person.

"What is meant by 'grooming'? When the blood of cattle is being sucked by insects, then there is an increase in sores as a result. By grooming, one gets rid of this harm and then the cow is happy and its hair is glossy. The bhikshu is also like this. When the insects of unwholesome and deviant initial and discursive thought drink the blood of one's roots of goodness, this increases the sores of the mind. When they are gotten rid of, one abides in peacefulness and security.

"What is meant by 'dressing sores'? This refers to employing dressings made from cloth or leaves of grasses in order to prevent the noxious bites of mosquitoes and biting flies. The bhikshu is also like this. He employs the dharmas of proper contemplation to cover up the sores of the six sense faculties and thus does not allow himself to be harmed by the stings of the noxious insects of afflictions such as desire and anger.

"What is meant by knowing how to create smoke in order to get rid of mosquitoes and biting flies? When from a distance, the cow sees smoke, then it will come towards the dwellings. The bhikshu is also like this. He speaks in strict accord with what he has heard and gets rid of all of the mosquitoes and biting flies of the fetters. He employs the [signal-fire] smoke of speaking Dharma in order to lead beings forth that they might enter into the dwelling of non-self, the the true character [of dharmas], and emptiness.

"What is meant by knowing the road? This refers to knowing the good and bad roads for having the cattle come and go. The bhikshu is also this way. He knows that the eight-fold path of the Āryas is able to take one to nirvāṇa and distances himself from the bad paths of annihilationism and eternalism.

"What is meant by knowing the appropriate location for cattle? When one knows the appropriate location for cows, one is able to cause the cattle to multiply and to have but little disease. The

比丘亦如是。说佛法时得清
净法喜。诸善根增盛。云何
[22]知济。知易入易[23]度无波
浪恶虫处。比丘亦如是。能
至多闻比丘所问法。说法者
知前[24]人心利钝烦恼轻重。
令[25]入[26]好济安隐得度。云
何知安隐处。知所住处无虎
狼师子恶虫毒兽。比丘亦如
是。[27]知四念处安隐无烦恼
恶魔毒兽。比丘入此则安隐
无患。云何留乳。犊母爱念
犊子故与乳。以留残乳故。
犊母欢喜则[28]犊子不竭。牛
主及放牛人。日日有益。比
丘亦如是。居士白衣给施衣
食。当知节量不令[29]罄竭。
则檀越欢喜信心不绝。受者
无乏。云何知养。牛主[30]诸
大[31]特牛能守牛群。故应养
护不令羸瘦。饮以麻油。饰
以璎珞。标以铁角摩刷[32]赞
誉称等。比丘亦如是。众僧
中有威德大人。护益佛法摧
伏外道。能令八众[33]得种诸
善根。

简体字

比丘亦如是。說佛法時得清
淨法喜。諸善根增盛。云何
[22]知濟。知易入易[23]度無波
浪惡虫處。比丘亦如是。能
至多聞比丘所問法。說法者
知前[24]人心利鈍煩惱輕重。
令[25]入[26]好濟安隱得度。云
何知安隱處。知所住處無虎
狼師子惡虫毒獸。比丘亦如
是。[27]知四念處安隱無煩惱
惡魔毒獸。比丘入此則安隱
無患。云何留乳。犢母愛念
犢子故與乳。以留殘乳故。
犢母歡喜則[28]犢子不竭。牛
主及放牛人。日日有益。比
丘亦如是。居士白衣給施衣
食。當知節量不令[29]罄竭。
則檀越歡喜信心不絕。受者
無乏。云何知養。牛主[30]諸
大[31]特牛能守牛群。故應養
護不令羸瘦。飲以麻油。飾
以瓔珞。標以鐵角摩刷[32]讚
譽稱等。比丘亦如是。眾僧
中有威德大人。護益佛法摧
伏外道。能令八眾[33]得種諸
善根。

正體字

bhikshu is also like this. When the Dharma of the Buddha is spoken, he gains a pure Dharma bliss and his roots of goodness increase thereby.

"What is meant by knowing where to ford? One knows the place where it is easy to enter, where it is easy to cross, where there are no waves or noxious pests. The bhikshu is also like this. He is able to go to the abode of a learned bhikshu and inquire about Dharma. The one who speaks Dharma is aware of the relative sharpness of mind and relative weight of afflictions possessed by the person before him. Thus he influences him to choose a good fording place and to succeed in making a safe crossing [from cyclic births and deaths to nirvāṇa].

What is meant by knowing a peaceful and secure place? One knows of a place to dwell which has no tigers, wolves, lions, noxious insects or venomous animal life. The bhikshu is also like this. He knows the peacefulness and security of the four stations of mindfulness where there are none of the noxious demons and venomous beasts of the afflictions. The bhikshu enters into these and thus is peaceful, secure and free of calamity.

What is meant by preserving the flow of milk? The cow produces milk out of affection for the calf. By leaving whatever milk is in excess of the need, the cow is happy and there continues to be an unexhausted supply. The lead bull as well as the cowherds benefit from this every day. The bhikshu is also like this. The laypeople donate clothing and food. One must know how to be conservative in the amount one accepts and thus one is able to prevent this resource from being exhausted. If this is the case, then the donors are happy and their faith is not cut short and yet the recipients have no shortage of essentials.

"What is meant by knowing how to care for the lead bull? If one protects the big bull, he will be able to guard the herd. Therefore one ought to care for it and protect it and not allow it to become gaunt. It should be given sesame oil to drink, provided with the adornment of a necklace and given the distinction of metal-covered horns. It should be kneaded and brushed and effusively praised. The bhikshu is also like this. When among the multitude of Sangha members, there is a great man possessed of awesome virtue who is able to protect and benefit the Buddha Dharma, is able to utterly defeat in debate non-Buddhists and is able to influence the eightfold assembly to succeed in planting roots of goodness, one should

随其所宜恭敬供养等。放牛人闻此语已如是思惟。我[34]等[35]所知不过三四事。放牛师辈远不过五六事。今闻此说叹未曾有。若知此事馀亦皆尔。实是一切智人。无复疑也。

随其所宜恭敬供養等。放牛人聞此語已如是思惟。我[34]等[35]所知不過三四事。放牛師輩遠不過五六事。今聞此說歎未曾有。若知此事餘亦皆爾。實是一切智人。無復疑也。

简体字

正體字

afford him respect and make offerings to him according to whatever he needs."

When the cowherds had heard these words, they thought to
themselves, "What we cowherds know doesn't go beyond three or
four of these subjects and the master cowherds at the very most
aren't familiar with more than five or six subjects." Now that they
had heard this discourse, they exclaimed over hearing what none of
them had heard before and agreed, "If he is aware of these matters,
then he must know all the rest as well. Truly, he is an omniscient
man." They then had no further doubts.

问曰。如舍婆提迦毘罗[3]婆波罗奈大城。皆有诸王舍。何以故独名此城为王舍。答曰。有人言。是摩伽陀国王有子。一头两面四臂。时人以为不祥。王即裂其身首弃之旷野。罗刹女鬼。名[4]梨罗。还合其身而乳养之。后大成人力能并兼诸国王。有天下取诸国[5]王万八千人。置此五山中。以大力势治阎浮提。阎浮提人因名此山。为王舍城。复次有人言。摩伽陀王先所住城。城中失火一烧一作。如是至七。国人疲役王大忧怖。集诸智人问其意故。有言[6]宜应易处。王即更求住处。见此五山周匝如城。即作宫殿于中止住。以是故名王舍城。

問曰。如舍婆提迦毘羅[3]婆波羅奈大城。皆有諸王舍。何以故獨名此城為王舍。答曰。有人言。是摩伽陀國王有子。一頭兩面四臂。時人以為不祥。王即裂其身首棄之曠野。羅刹女鬼。名[4]梨羅。還合其身而乳養之。後大成人力能并兼諸國王。有天下取諸國[5]王萬八千人。置此五山中。以大力勢治閻浮提。閻浮提人因名此山。為王舍城。復次有人言。摩伽陀王先所住城。城中失火一燒一作。如是至七。國人疲役王大憂怖。集諸智人問其意故。有言[6]宜應易處。王即更求住處。見此五山周匝如城。即作宮殿於中止住。以是故名王舍城。

简体字　　　　　　　　　　正體字

The City of the Kings' Abode

Translator's Note

Nāgārjuna brings up three stories here in the context of discussing the place wherein the Sutra was set forth. Rājagṛha, the town in India's Bihar State known today as "Rajgir" means literally: "Kings' Abode."

Exegesis Segue

Question: Cities such as Śrāvastī, Kapilavastu and Vārāṇasī each contain the domiciles of kings. Why then is this city [of Rājagṛha] alone referred to as "City of the Kings' Abode?"

Response: (See below.)

The First Story of Rājagṛha's Origins

There are people who say that the king of Magadha had a son who was born with a single head, but two faces and four arms. Because the people of the time took this to be inauspicious, the king sliced off the head from the body and then cast it aside in the wilderness. A female *rākṣasa* ghost named Līlā put his body back together again and then suckled and raised him. Later he grew into a great man whose power rivaled that of all of the kings of the neighboring states. He established sovereignty throughout the country, and sent all of the former kings, eighteen thousand in all, to dwell together in the area surrounded by these five mountains. He used his great power to rule over all of Jambudvīpa. Because of this, the people of Jambudvīpa named this mountain "City of the Kings' Abode."

The Second Story of Rājagṛha's Origins

Again, there are some people who say that the city where the king of Magadha formerly dwelt was subject to runaway fires. Each time the city burned, it was rebuilt. It happened like this seven times, after which the people were worn out from conscription and the king was greatly distressed and terrorized. He then assembled his advisors and solicited their opinions on the best course of action. There were those who came down in favor of the idea that the city should be moved to another place. The king then began to search for a new place to dwell. He saw these five mountains arranged in a circle like a city wall, built a palace in the area surrounded by them and then settled there. Because of this it came to be named "City of the King's Abode".

Marvelous Stories from the Perfection of Wisdom

复次往古世时。此国有王。
名婆薮。心厌世法出家作仙
人。是时居家婆罗门。与[7]
诸出家[8]仙人共论议。居家
婆罗门言。经书云。天祀中
应杀生噉肉。诸出家仙人
言。不应天祀中杀生噉肉。
共诤云云。诸出家婆罗门
言。此有大王出家作仙人。
汝等信不。诸居家婆罗门言
信。诸出家仙人言。我以此
人为证。后日当问。诸居家
婆罗门。即以其夜。先到婆
薮仙人所。种种问已。语婆
薮仙人。明日论议汝当助
我。如是明旦论时。诸出家
仙人问婆薮仙人。天祀中应
杀生噉肉不。婆薮仙人言。
婆罗门法天祀中应杀生噉
肉。诸出家仙人言。于汝实
心云何。应杀生噉肉不。婆
薮仙人言。为天祀故应杀生
噉肉。此生在天祀中死故得
生天上。诸出家仙人言。汝
大不是。汝大妄语。即唾之
言。罪人灭去。是时婆薮仙
人寻陷[9]入地没踝。是初开
大罪门故。诸出家仙人言。
汝应实语。

復次往古世時。此國有王。
名婆藪。心厭世法出家作仙
人。是時居家婆羅門。與[7]
諸出家[8]仙人共論議。居家
婆羅門言。經書云。天祀中
應殺生噉肉。諸出家仙人
言。不應天祀中殺生噉肉。
共諍云云。諸出家婆羅門
言。此有大王出家作仙人。
汝等信不。諸居家婆羅門言
信。諸出家仙人言。我以此
人為證。後日當問。諸居家
婆羅門。即以其夜。先到婆
藪仙人所。種種問已。語婆
藪仙人。明日論議汝當助
我。如是明旦論時。諸出家
仙人問婆藪仙人。天祀中應
殺生噉肉不。婆藪仙人言。
婆羅門法天祀中應殺生噉
肉。諸出家仙人言。於汝實
心云何。應殺生噉肉不。婆
藪仙人言。為天祀故應殺生
噉肉。此生在天祀中死故得
生天上。諸出家仙人言。汝
大不是。汝大妄語。即唾之
言。罪人滅去。是時婆藪仙
人尋陷[9]入地沒踝。是初開
大罪門故。諸出家仙人言。
汝應實語。

简体字

正體字

The Third Story of Rājagṛha's Origins

And then again, long ago in ancient times, this country had a king who was named Vasu. His mind became weary with worldly dharmas and as a result he left home and became a rishi. At this time the home-dwelling brahmans were involved in a doctrinal debate with the hermits who had left the home life. The home-dwelling brahmans insisted that the scriptures require that ritual offerings to the gods necessitate slaughtering animals and eating their flesh. The hermits who had left the home life insisted that one should not slaughter animals and eat their flesh in the course of making ritual offerings to the gods. They argued back and forth until finally the brahmans who had left the home life said, "Here we have a king who has left the home life and become a hermit. Do you all trust in him or not?"

The home-dwelling brahmans all said, "We trust in him."

The brahmans who had left the home life said, "We will use this man as an arbiter. Tomorrow we shall pose the question to him." Then, that very evening, the home-dwelling brahmans were first to pay a visit to the abode of Vasu the hermit. After having asked all manner of questions, they said to Vasu, the hermit, "In tomorrow's debate you must help us." The next morning at the appointed time for the discussion, the hermits who had left the home life asked Vasu the hermit, "In the course of performing ritual offerings to the gods, should one slaughter animals and eat their flesh or not?"

Vasu the hermit said, "According to the dharma of the Brahmans, during the course of performing ritual offerings to the gods, one should slaughter animals and eat their flesh."

The hermits who had left the home life said, "But what do you yourself actually think? Should one slaughter animals and eat their flesh?"

Vasu the hermit replied, "Because it is a sacrifice to the gods, one ought to slaughter animals and eat their flesh. Because these animals die in the course of a sacrifice made to the gods, they are able to be reborn in the heavens."

The hermits who had left the home life exclaimed, "You are utterly wrong! You have told a great lie!" Then they spat upon him and said, "Disappear, you criminal!" At this time Vasu the hermit sank into the ground up to the level of his ankles. Because he had only just opened for the first time the door to extreme offenses, the hermits who had left the home life said, " You ought to speak true

若故妄语者。汝身当陷入地中。婆薮仙人言。我知为天故杀[10]羊噉肉无罪。即复陷入地至膝。如是渐渐稍没至腰至[11]颈。诸出家仙人言。汝今妄语得现世报。更以实语者。虽入地下。我能出汝[12]令得[13]免罪。尔时婆薮仙人自思惟言。我贵[14]重人不应两种语。又婆罗门四[15]围陀法中。种种因缘赞祀天法。我一人死当何足计。一心言。应天祀中杀生噉肉无罪。诸出家仙人言。汝重罪人。[16]催去不用见汝。于是举身没地中。从是[17]以来乃至今日。常用婆薮仙人王法。于天祀中杀[*]羊。当下刀时言婆薮杀汝。婆[18]薮之子。名曰广车。[19]嗣位[20]为王。后亦厌世法而[21]复不能出家。如是思惟。我父先王出家生入地中。若治天下复作大罪。我今当何以自处。如是思惟时闻空中声言。汝若行见难值希有处。汝应是中作舍住。作是语已便不复闻声。未经几时王出田猎。见有一鹿走疾如风。王便逐之而不可及。遂逐不止。百官侍从无

若故妄語者。汝身當陷入地中。婆藪仙人言。我知為天故殺[10]羊噉肉無罪。即復陷入地至膝。如是漸漸稍沒至腰至[11]頸。諸出家仙人言。汝今妄語得現世報。更以實語者。雖入地下。我能出汝[12]令得[13]免罪。爾時婆藪仙人自思惟言。我貴[14]重人不應兩種語。又婆羅門四[15]圍陀法中。種種因緣讚祀天法。我一人死當何足計。一心言。應天祀中殺生噉肉無罪。諸出家仙人言。汝重罪人。[16]催去不用見汝。於是舉身沒地中。從是[17]以來乃至今日。常用婆藪仙人王法。於天祀中殺[*]羊。當下刀時言婆藪殺汝。婆[18]藪之子。名曰廣車。[19]嗣位[20]為王。後亦厭世法而[21]復不能出家。如是思惟。我父先王出家生入地中。若治天下復作大罪。我今當何以自處。如是思惟時聞空中聲言。汝若行見難值希有處。汝應是中作舍住。作是語已便不復聞聲。未經幾時王出田獵。見有一鹿走疾如風。王便逐之而不可及。遂逐不止。百官侍從無

简体字   正體字

words. If you deliberately lie, your body will sink into the earth."

Vasu the hermit said, "I know that because one slaughters the sheep and eats its flesh on behalf of the gods, there is no offense," whereupon he immediately sank farther into the earth up to the level of his knees. In this manner he gradually sank up to his waist and then up to his neck.

The hermits who had left the home life said to him, "You are now undergoing present and immediate retribution for your lying. However, if you change your ways and speak the truth, although you have sunken into the earth, we will still be able to get you out again and bring it about that your offense will be pardoned."

At that time Vasu the hermit thought to himself, "I am a noble and serious person and thus should not make two different, [contradictory] statements. Moreover, it is the dharma of the four Brahmanical Vedas to praise, for all manner of reasons, the methods for making offerings to the gods. If I, one single person, die [on account of this], how is that even worth reckoning? Then he single-mindedly stated, "It should be that there is no offense in slaughtering animals and eating them during the course of making offerings to the gods."

The hermits who had left the home life said, "You are man with heavy offenses. May you be pushed away. It's useless to even lay eyes on you." At this time his entire body sank into the earth. From that point on even until the present day, they have always used the method prescribed by Vasu, the hermit king, of slaughtering sheep in the course of making offerings to the gods. Jus as the knife is about to fall, they say, "It is Vasu who kills you."

The son of Vasu, named "Wide Chariot," assumed the throne. Later, he too grew weary of worldly dharmas, but was not also able to leave the home life. He thought to himself, "My father, the former king, left the home life, but even while still alive was swallowed up by the earth. However, to continue to rule the nation is to create more great offenses. How then should I now conduct myself?"

When he was thinking like this, he heard a voice from space, saying, "If when traveling, you see a place which is seldom seen and rare, you ought to build a home and live there." After it had made this statement, he no longer heard the voice.

It was not long after that the King ventured into the country to go hunting. He saw a deer that was running as fast as the wind. The King then chased after it but could not catch up to it. He pursued it without stopping. None of the hundred officials and

能及者。转前见有五山周匝峻固。其地平正生草细[22]软好华遍地。种种[23]林木华果茂盛。温泉[24]凉池皆悉清净其地庄严。处处有散天华天香闻天伎乐。尔时乾闼婆伎。适见王来各自还去。是处希有未曾所见。今我正当在是中作舍住。如是思惟已。群臣百官寻迹而到。王告诸臣。我前所闻空中声言。汝行若见希有难值之处。汝[25]应是中作舍住。我今见此希有之处。我应是中作舍住[*]即舍本城于此山中住。是王初始在[26]是中住。从是已后次第止住。是王[27]元起造立宫舍故。名王舍城。略说王舍城[28]本起竟。

能及者。轉前見有五山周匝峻固。其地平正生草細[22]軟好華遍地。種種[23]林木華果茂盛。溫泉[24]涼池皆悉清淨其地莊嚴。處處有散天華天香聞天伎樂。爾時乾闥婆伎。適見王來各自還去。是處希有未曾所見。今我正當在是中作舍住。如是思惟已。群臣百官尋跡而到。王告諸臣。我前所聞空中聲言。汝行若見希有難值之處。汝[25]應是中作舍住。我今見此希有之處。我應是中作舍住[*]即捨本城於此山中住。是王初始在[26]是中住。從是已後次第止住。是王[27]元起造立宮舍故。名王舍城。略說王舍城[28]本起竟。

简体字   正體字

retainers could keep up. As he traveled on farther ahead he saw a ridge of five mountains which ran in a steep and solid circle. The ground was flat and even. Delicate grasses which were fine and soft together with fine flowers covered the soil. All kinds of trees and flowers and fruits flourished there. The land was enhanced by pure-watered warm springs and bathing pools. Heavenly flowers and heavenly incense floated down everywhere and everywhere there was the sound of heavenly music. At that time the *gandharva* music-makers retreated on seeing the king approach.

He thought, "This place is rare and such as has never been seen before. Now I ought to build a home right in center of this area and live here." Just as he had finished this thought, the multitude of ministers and the hundred officials, following his tracks, arrived at the spot. The King told the ministers, "Formerly, the voice which I heard from empty space said, `If when traveling, you see a place which is seldom seen and rare, you ought to build a home and live there.' Now I have seen this rare place. I ought to build a home and live here." He then abandoned the original city and came to dwell amidst these mountains. This king was the first to dwell there. After that the succeeding kings each dwelt there as well. Because this king originally established his palace there, the place gained the name "City of the Kings' Abode."

This concludes the summary explanation of the origins of City of the Kings' Abode.

复次长老摩诃迦叶。[59]于
耆阇崛山。集三[60]法藏。
可度众生。度竟欲随佛入涅
盘。清朝着衣持钵入王舍城
乞食已。上耆阇崛山语诸弟
子。我今日入无馀涅盘。如
是语已入房结[61]加趺坐。诸
无漏禅定自[62]熏身。摩诃迦
叶诸弟子。入王舍城语诸贵
人。知不。尊者摩诃迦叶今
日入无馀涅盘。诸贵人闻是
语皆大愁忧言。佛已灭度。
摩诃迦叶持护佛法。今日复
欲入无馀涅盘。诸贵[63]人
诸比丘。晡时皆共集耆阇崛
山。长老摩诃迦叶。晡时从
禅[64]定起入众中坐。赞说无
常。[65]诸一切有为法因缘
生故无常。本无今有已有还
无故无常。因缘生故无常。
无常故苦。苦故无我。无我
故有智者不应着我[66]我所。
若着我[*]我所。得无量忧
[67]愁苦[68]恼一切[69]世间[70]
中。心应厌求离欲。如是种
种说[71]世界中苦。[72]开导
其心令入涅盘。说此语[73]
竟着从佛所得僧伽[74]梨。持
衣钵捉杖。如金翅鸟现[75]

简体字

復次長老摩訶迦葉。[59]於
耆闍崛山。集三[60]法藏。
可度眾生。度竟欲隨佛入涅
槃。清朝著衣持鉢入王舍城
乞食已。上耆闍崛山語諸弟
子。我今日入無餘涅槃。如
是語已入房結[61]加趺坐。摩
訶迦葉諸弟子。入王舍城語
諸貴人。知不。尊者摩訶迦
葉今日入無餘涅槃。諸貴人
聞是語皆大愁憂言。佛已滅
度。摩訶迦葉持護佛法。今
日復欲入無餘涅槃。諸貴[63]
人諸比丘。晡時皆共集耆闍
崛山。長老摩訶迦葉。晡時
從禪[64]定起入眾中坐。讚
說無常。[65]諸一切有為法
因緣生故無常。本無今有已
有還無故無常。因緣生故無
常。無常故苦。苦故無我。
無我故有智者不應著我[66]我
所。若著我[*]我所。得無量
憂[67]愁苦[68]惱一切[69]世間
[70]中。心應厭求離欲。如是
種種說[71]世界中苦。[72]開
導其心令入涅槃。說此語[73]
竟著從佛所得僧伽[74]梨。持
衣鉢捉杖。如金翅鳥現[75]

正體字

Mahākāśyapa and Mt. Gṛdhrakūṭa

Again, Mahākāśyapa, the elder, oversaw the compilation of the three-fold treasury of Dharma on Mt. Gṛdhrakūṭa. When all the beings which he was able to cross over to liberation had been crossed over, he wished to follow the Buddha by entering nirvāṇa. After he had risen in the early morning and had gone into The City of Kings' Abode to make his alms rounds, he ascended Mt. Gṛdhrakūṭa and told all of his disciples, "Today I shall enter the nirvāṇa without residue." After he had said this he went into his dwelling and sat in full lotus whereupon non-outflow dhyāna samādhi permeated his being.

The disciples of Mahākāśyapa went into the city of Kings' Abode and told all of the gentry, "Are you aware or not that the Honorable Mahākāśyapa is this very day going to enter the nirvāṇa without residue? When the various gentry folk heard these words, they became greatly saddened and distressed, saying, "The Buddha has already crossed into extinction. Mahākāśyapa maintains and protects the Dharma of the Buddha. Now, today, he too is about to enter the nirvāṇa without residue.

In the late afternoon, the various gentry folk and the bhikshus all assembled on Mt. Gṛdhrakūṭa. In the late afternoon Mahākāśyapa, the elder, arose from dhyāna, joined the assemblage and sat down. He spoke in praise of the teaching of impermanence, saying, "Because all composite dharmas are a product of causes and conditions, they are therefore impermanent. Because, formerly nonexistent, they now exist, and then pass again into nonexistence, they are therefore, impermanent. Because they are impermanent they do therefore conduce to suffering. Because they conduce to suffering, they are therefore not self. Because they are not self, he who is possessed of wisdom should not become attached to the concepts of `I' and `mine'." If one becomes attached to `I' and `mine,' then one becomes subject to an immeasurable amount of worry, distress, suffering and affliction. In all worldly spheres, one should abhor seeking and separate oneself from desire. In this fashion, he spoke in many ways about the suffering inherent in the World, leading forth his mind to cause it to enter nirvāṇa.

After he had delivered this discourse, he donned the *saṃghāṭī* robe obtained from the Buddha, and, taking hold of the robe and bowl and, grasping his staff, just like the golden-winged *garuḍa*, he rose up into space, appearing in the four different physical postures

上升虚空。四种身仪坐卧行
住。一身现无量身。满东方
世界。于无量身还为一身。
身上出火身下出水。身上出
水身下出火。南西北方亦如
是。众心厌世皆欢喜已。于
耆阇崛山头。与衣钵俱[1]作
是愿言。令我身不坏。弥勒
成佛。我是骨身还出。以此
因缘度众生。如是思惟已。
直[2]入山[3]头石内。如入[4]软
堲。入已山还合。后人寿八
万四千岁。身长八十尺。[5]
时弥勒佛[6]出。佛身长百六
十尺。佛面二十四尺。圆光
十里。是时众生闻弥勒佛出
[7]世。无量人[8]随佛出家。
佛在大众中。初说法时九十
九亿人得阿罗汉道。六通具
足。第二大会九十六亿人得
阿罗汉道。第三大会九十三
亿人得阿罗汉道。自是[9]已
后度无数[10]人。尔时人民
久后懈厌。弥勒佛见众[11]
人如是。以足指扣开耆阇崛
[12]山。是时长老摩诃迦叶
骨身。着僧伽梨而出礼弥勒
足。上升虚空现变如前。[13]
即于空中灭身[14]而般涅盘。

上昇虚空。四種身儀坐臥行
住。一身現無量身。滿東方
世界。於無量身還為一身。
身上出火身下出水。身上出
水身下出火。南西北方亦如
是。眾心厭世皆歡喜已。於
耆闍崛山頭。與衣鉢俱[1]作
是願言。令我身不壞。彌勒
成佛。我是骨身還出。以此
因緣度眾生。如是思惟已。
直[2]入山[3]頭石內。如入[4]軟
堲。入已山還合。後人壽八
萬四千歲。身長八十尺。[5]
時彌勒佛[6]出。佛身長百六
十尺。佛面二十四尺。圓光
十里。是時眾生聞彌勒佛出
[7]世。無量人[8]隨佛出家。
佛在大眾中。初說法時九十
九億人得阿羅漢道。六通具
足。第二大會九十六億人得
阿羅漢道。第三大會九十三
億人得阿羅漢道。自是[9]已
後度無數[10]人。爾時人民
久後懈厭。彌勒佛見眾[11]
人如是。以足指扣開耆闍崛
[12]山。是時長老摩訶迦葉
骨身。著僧伽梨而出禮彌勒
足。上昇虚空現變如前。[13]
即於空中滅身[14]而般涅槃。

简体字　　　　　　　　正體字

of sitting, lying down, walking and standing. His one body then manifest an immeasurable number of bodies which filled up the world to the east. Then these immeasurable number of bodies became one body again. From the top of his body he threw forth flames while from below he gushed forth water. Then, from the top of his body he gushed forth water while from below he threw forth flames. In the south, in the west, and in the north as well, it was also like this.

After the minds of those assembled had come to feel aversion for worldly existence and had been filled with delight, on the top of Mt. Gṛdhrakūṭa, complete with bowl and robe, he uttered an oath, "May my body be caused to not decay, so that when Maitreya becomes a Buddha, this skeleton of mine will appear once again, and on account of these causes and conditions, beings will be caused to obtain deliverance." After he had contemplated in this manner, he entered directly into the rock on the top of the mountain, just as if he were entering into soft mud. After he had entered, the mountain closed shut again behind him.

Later on, when the normal lifespan of people reaches 84,000 years and their normal height reaches eighty feet, Maitreya Buddha will appear. The Buddha's body will be one hundred and sixty feet tall and the Buddha's face will itself extend twenty-four feet while his nimbus will span several miles (lit. "ten *li*").

At that time when beings hear that Maitreya Buddha has appeared, countless people will follow the Buddha in leaving the home life. When the Buddha is in the midst of the great assembly and first speaks Dharma, ninety-nine *koṭīs* of people will gain the way of arhatship and will be replete with the six superknowledges. On the second day, ninety-six *koṭīs* of people will gain the way of arhatship. On the third day ninety-three *koṭīs* of people will gain the way of arhatship. From this time onward he will bring an innumerable number of people to deliverance.

Eventually, after a long time, the people will become lazy and reluctant. When Maitreya sees that the people in the assembly are like this, he will use his toe to split open Mt. Gṛdhrakūṭa. At that time Mahākāśyapa's skeleton, dressed in the *saṃghāṭī* robe will come forth and pay reverence at the feet of Maitreya. He will ascend into space and manifest again the various transformations described before. Then in the midst of space, he will make his body disappear as he enters *parinirvāṇa*.

尔时弥勒佛诸弟子怪而问言。此是何人。似人而小。身着法衣能作变化。弥勒佛言。此人是过去释迦[15]文尼佛弟子。名摩诃迦叶。行阿兰若少欲知足。行头陀比丘中第一。得六神通共解脱大阿罗[16]汉。彼时人寿百年少出多减。[17]以是小身。能办如是大事。汝等大身利根。云何不作如是功德。是时诸弟子皆惭愧发大厌心。弥勒佛随[18]众心。为说种种法。有人得阿罗汉阿那含斯陀含须陀洹。有种辟支佛善根。有得无生法忍不退菩萨。有得生天人中受种种福乐。以是故知。[19]是耆阇崛山福德吉处。[20]诸圣[21]人喜住处。[22]佛为诸圣人[23]主。是故佛多[24]住耆阇崛[25]山。

爾時彌勒佛諸弟子怪而問言。此是何人。似人而小。身著法衣能作變化。彌勒佛言。此人是過去釋迦[15]文尼佛弟子。名摩訶迦葉。行阿蘭若少欲知足。行頭陀比丘中第一。得六神通共解脫大阿羅[16]漢。彼時人壽百年少出多減。[17]以是小身。能辦如是大事。汝等大身利根。云何不作如是功德。是時諸弟子皆慚愧發大厭心。彌勒佛隨[18]眾心。為說種種法。有人得阿羅漢阿那含斯陀含須陀洹。有種辟支佛善根。有得無生法忍不退菩薩。有得生天人中受種種福樂。以是故知。[19]是耆闍崛山福德吉處。[20]諸聖[21]人喜住處。[22]佛為諸聖人[23]主。是故佛多[24]住耆闍崛[25]山。

简体字　　　　正體字

The disciples of Maitreya Buddha will then be astonished and will ask, "Who was that man who looked so like a person, but yet was so small? His body was wearing the Dharma robes and he was able to display these transformations."

Maitreya Buddha will say, "That was a disciple of the former Buddha, Shakyamuni. His name was Mahākāśyapa. He cultivated dwelling in an *araṇya* where he had but few desires and was easily contented. Among the bhikshus who cultivated the *dhūta* practices he was foremost. He was a great arhat who had obtained the six superknowledges and the two-fold liberation (*ubhayato-bhāga-vimukta*). At that time the lifespan of people was a hundred years, with a few exceeding it, but most not reaching it. If he, with such a small body, was able to succeed at such a great matter, why do not all of you, with such large bodies and sharp faculties, engage in such meritorious deeds as this?"

Then, all of his disciples will become repentant and will develop great renunciation. Maitreya Buddha, according with the minds of those beings, will speak all manner of dharmas for their sakes. There will be those who gain arhatship, the stage of the *anāgāmin*, the stage of the *sakṛd-āgāmin*, and the stage of the *srota-āpanna*. There will be those who plant the roots of goodness of the pratyekabuddha. There will be those who gain the stage of the non-retreating bodhisattva who has realized the unproduced-dharmas patience. There will be those who obtain rebirth in the heavens where they shall experience all manner of blessings and bliss.

Nāgārjuna's Concluding Comments

On account of this one should realize that Mt. Gṛdhrakūṭa is an auspicious place replete with meritorious qualities and is a place where āryas like to dwell. The Buddha is the lord of the Āryas. It is for this reason that the Buddha mostly dwelt at Mt. Gṛdhrakūṭa.

比丘名乞士。清净活命故名[57]为乞士。如经中说。舍利弗入城乞食。得已。向壁坐食。是[58]时有梵志女名净目。来见舍利弗。问舍利弗言。沙门汝食耶。答言食。净目言。汝沙门下口食耶。答言不[59]姊。仰口食[60]耶。不。方口食[*]耶。不。四维口食[*]耶。不。净目言。食法有四种。我问汝。汝言不。我不解。汝当[61]说。舍利弗[62]言。有出家人合药种[63]谷[64]殖树等不净活命者。是名下口食。有出家人观视星宿日月风雨雷电霹雳不净活命者。是名仰口食。有出家人曲媚豪势通使四方巧言多求不净活命者。是名方口食。有出家人学种种呪术卜[65]筮吉[66]凶如是等[67]种种

比丘名乞士。清淨活命故名[57]為乞士。如經中說。舍利弗入城乞食。得已。向壁坐食。是[58]時有梵志女名淨目。來見舍利弗。問舍利弗言。沙門汝食耶。答言食。淨目言。汝沙門下口食耶。答言不[59]姊。仰口食[60]耶。不。方口食[*]耶。不。四維口食[*]耶。不。淨目言。食法有四種。我問汝。汝言不。我不解。汝當[61]說。舍利弗[62]言。有出家人合藥種[63]穀[64]殖樹等不淨活命者。是名下口食。有出家人觀視星宿日月風雨雷電霹靂不淨活命者。是名仰口食。有出家人曲媚豪勢通使四方巧言多求不淨活命者。是名方口食。有出家人學種種呪術卜[65]筮吉[66]凶如是等[67]種種

简体字　　　　　　　　　　正體字

Śāriputra Explains Pure Sustenance

"Bhikshu" is a reference to one who relies on alms. It is on account of the purity of this means of sustaining one's life that [the Buddhist monk] is referred to as a "bhikshu." This point is illustrated by this story from the scriptures.

Śāriputra went into the city to make his alms rounds and having obtained his food sat down to eat, facing a wall. At this time, a brahmacarinī name Śucimukhī came along and saw Śāriputra and asked Śāriputra, "Śramaṇa, are you eating?"

He replied, "Yes, I'm eating."

Śucimukhī asked, "Do you *śramaṇas* eat with your attention directed downwards?"

He replied, "No, Sister."

"Do you eat with your attention directed upwards?"

"No."

"With your attention directed to the [four] directions?"

"No."

"With your attention directed to the four intermediary points?"

"No."

Śucimukhī said, "There are four methods employed in eating. I asked you about them and you said 'no' in every case. I don't understand. You ought to explain."

Śāriputra said, "There are those who have left the home life who blend herbs, sow grains, plant trees, or engage in other such forms of impure means of sustaining one's life. These methods are referred to as sustenance gained with one's attention directed downwards.

"There are those who have left the home life who observe the stars, the constellations, the sun, the moon, the wind, the rain, thunder and lightning, and lightning bolts, these impure means of sustaining one's life. These methods are referred to as sustenance gained with one's attention directed upwards.

"There are those who have left the home life who manipulate and flatter the noble and powerful, who deliver messages for them in all four directions, or who employ clever words and covetousness, these impure means of sustaining one's life. These methods are referred to as sustenance gained with one's attention directed in all directions.

"There are those who have left the home life who study all manner of incantational techniques, or who practice divination and calculation of auspiciousness and inauspiciousness and all kinds of

不净活命者。是名四维口食。姊。我不堕是四不净食中。我用[68]清净乞食活命。是时净[69]目闻说清净法食。欢喜信解。[70]舍利弗因为说法得须陀洹道。	不淨活命者。是名四維口食。姊。我不墮是四不淨食中。我用[68]清淨乞食活命。是時淨[69]目聞說清淨法食。歡喜信解。[70]舍利弗因為說法得須陀洹道。
简体字	正體字

other impure means of sustaining one's life such as these. These methods are referred to as sustenance gained with one's attention directed towards the intermediary points. Sister, I do not fall into any of these four types of impure means of sustaining one's life. I employ the pure alms round to sustain this life."

At this time, when Śucimukhī had heard the explanation of the dharma of pure sustenance, she was delighted and developed faith and understanding. Śāriputra, on account of having spoken Dharma for her, realized the path of the *srota-āpanna*.

须跋陀梵志年百二十岁。得
五神通。阿那跋达多池边
住。夜梦见一切人失眼裸形
冥中立。日堕地破大海水
竭。大风起吹须弥山破散。
觉已恐怖。思惟言。何以故
尔。我命欲尽。若天地主欲
[38]堕。犹豫不能自了。以有
此恶梦故。先世有善[39]知识
天。从上来下语须跋陀言。
汝莫恐怖。有一切智人名
佛。后夜半当入无馀涅盘。
是故汝梦。不为汝身。是时
须跋陀。明日到拘夷那竭国
树林中。见阿难经行。语阿
难言。我闻汝[40]师说[41]新
涅盘道。今日夜半当取灭
度。我心有疑。请欲见佛决
我所疑。阿难答言。世尊身
极。汝若难问劳扰世尊。须
跋陀如是重请至三。阿难答
如初。佛[42]遥闻之勒语阿
难。听须跋陀梵志来前自在
难问。是吾末后共谈。最后
得道弟子。是时须跋陀得前
见佛。问讯世尊已。于一面
坐。如是念。诸外道辈舍恩
爱财宝出家皆不得道。独瞿
昙沙门得道如是念竟。即问
佛言。是阎浮提地。六师辈
各自称言。我是一切智人。
是语实不。尔时世尊以偈答

简体字

須跋陀梵志年百二十歲。得
五神通。阿那跋達多池邊
住。夜夢見一切人失眼裸形
冥中立。日墮地破大海水
竭。大風起吹須彌山破散。
覺已恐怖。思惟言。何以故
爾。我命欲盡。若天地主欲
[38]墮。猶豫不能自了。以有
此惡夢故。先世有善[39]知識
天。從上來下語須跋陀言。
汝莫恐怖。有一切智人名
佛。後夜半當入無餘涅槃。
是故汝夢。不為汝身。是時
須跋陀。明日到拘夷那竭國
樹林中。見阿難經行。語阿
難言。我聞汝[40]師說[41]新
涅槃道。今日夜半當取滅
度。我心有疑。請欲見佛決
我所疑。阿難答言。世尊身
極。汝若難問勞擾世尊。須
跋陀如是重請至三。阿難答
如初。佛[42]遙聞之勒語阿
難。聽須跋陀梵志來前自在
難問。是吾末後共談。最後
得道弟子。是時須跋陀得前
見佛。問訊世尊已。於一面
坐。如是念。諸外道輩捨恩
愛財寶出家皆不得道。獨瞿
曇沙門得道如是念竟。即問
佛言。是閻浮提地。六師輩
各自稱言。我是一切智人。
是語實不。爾時世尊以偈答

正體字

Subhadra, the Brahmacārin

Subhadra, the brahmacārin, was one hundred and twenty years old and had obtained the five superknowledges. He dwelt on the shore of lake Anavatapta. One night, in a dream, he saw everyone blind and standing naked in the dark. The sun fell from the sky, the earth was broken, and the great oceans had all dried up. A great wind arose and blew away Mt. Sumeru. When he woke up he was frightened and thought, "Why was it like this? Is my life about to end or is the lord of heaven and earth about to fall? He was bewildered and unable to understand it. Because he had dreamt this terrible dream, a god who had been his spiritual guide in a former life descended from above and said to Subhadra, "Don't be frightened. There is a man possessed of omniscience known as the Buddha, who, tomorrow, in the middle of the night, will enter the nirvāṇa without residue. Therefore your dream had nothing to do with you."

Then, that very next day Subhadra went to the forest in the state of Kuśinagara and saw Ānanda walking along and said to Ānanda, "I have heard that your master describes a new path to nirvāṇa, and that this very day, in the middle of the night, he will choose to enter extinction. My mind is afflicted with doubts. Please, I wish to see the Buddha that he might resolve the cause of my doubts."

Ānanda replied, "The Bhagavān's body is exhausted. If you approach with difficult questions, it will weary and trouble the Bhagavān."

Subhadra repeated his request until he had asked three times. Each time Ānanda replied as before. The Buddha overheard this from a distance and ordered Ānanda, "Allow Subhadra the Brahmacārin to come forward and freely pose difficult questions. This will be my very last conversation and my very last disciple to gain the Path."

At this time Subhadra was able to have an audience with the Buddha. After he had greeted the Bhagavān, he sat down to one side and thought, "Although the followers of all of the non-Buddhist traditions renounce the ties of love and affection, of wealth and treasure, nonetheless they do not gain the Path. Only the Śramaṇa Gautama has found the Path." After he had finished this thought, he asked the Buddha, "Here in this land of Jambudvīpa, all of the Six Masters say of themselves, "I am possessed of all-knowledge. Is this talk true or not."

At this time, the Bhagavān, replied with a verse, saying:

[43]曰。
[44]我年一十九　出家学佛道。
我出家[45]已来　已过五十岁。
净戒禅智慧　外道无一分。
少分尚无有　何况一切智。
[0081a03] 若无八正道。是中无第一果第二第三第四果。若有八正道。是中有第一果第二第三第四果。须跋陀是我法中有八[1]正道。是中有第一道果第二第三第四道果。馀外道法皆空。无道无果无沙门无婆罗门。如是我大众中。实作师子吼。须跋陀梵志闻是法得阿罗汉道。思惟[2]言。我不应佛后般涅盘。如是思惟竟。在佛前结[3]加趺坐。自以神力身中出火烧身而取灭度。

[43]曰。
[44]我年一十九　出家學佛道。
我出家[45]已來　已過五十歲。
淨戒禪智慧　外道無一分。
少分尚無有　何況一切智。
[0081a03] 若無八正道。是中無第一果第二第三第四果。若有八正道。是中有第一果第二第三第四果。須跋陀是我法中有八[1]正道。是中有第一道果第二第三第四道果。餘外道法皆空。無道無果無沙門無婆羅門。如是我大眾中。實作師子吼。須跋陀梵志聞是法得阿羅漢道。思惟[2]言。我不應佛後般涅槃。如是思惟竟。在佛前結[3]加趺坐。自以神力身中出火燒身而取滅度。

简体字　　　　　　　　　　正體字

From the time I was twenty-nine years of age,
I left the home life and studied the way of the Buddha.
From the time I left home until now,
It has already been more than fifty years.

Of the pure precepts, dhyāna, and wisdom
The non-Buddhists possess not even a fraction.
If they do not possess even a minor fraction,
How much the less could they possess all-knowledge.

"If one does not possess the eight-fold correct path, then one does not possess the first fruit, the second, the third, nor the fourth fruit [of cultivating the Path]. If one possesses the eight-fold right path, then one possesses the first fruit, the second, the third, and the fourth fruit. Subhadra, here in my Dharma there exists the eight-fold right path. Herein there exists the first fruit of the Path, the second, the third, and the fourth fruit of the Path. The dharmas of the others, the non-Buddhists, are all empty. They have no path, no fruit, no *śramaṇas*, and no [genuine] brahmans. And so, like this, in the midst of the Great Assembly, I truly roar the lion's roar."

When Subhadra, the brahmacārin, heard this Dharma, he gained the way of the arhat. He thought to himself, "I should not enter *parinirvāṇa* after the Buddha." Having thought in this way, he arranged himself in full lotus before the Buddha and, resorting to his own spiritual powers, he generated fire from within his body which then burned up his body. He thereby thereupon chose to cross into cessation.

如摩犍提梵志弟子举其尸着床上。[34]与行城市中多人处唱言。若有眼见摩犍提尸者。是人皆得清净道。何况礼拜供养者。多有人信其言。诸比丘闻是语。白佛言。世尊。是事云何。佛说偈言。

小人眼见求清净。
如是无智无实道。
诸结烦恼满心中。
云何眼见得净道。
若有眼见得清净。
何用智慧功德宝。
[35]智慧功德乃为净。
[36]眼见求净无是事。

如摩犍提梵志弟子舉其屍著床上。[34]興行城市中多人處唱言。若有眼見摩犍提屍者。是人皆得清淨道。何況禮拜供養者。多有人信其言。諸比丘聞是語。白佛言。世尊。是事云何。佛說偈言。

小人眼見求清淨。
如是無智無實道。
諸結煩惱滿心中。
云何眼見得淨道。
若有眼見得清淨。
何用智慧功德寶。
[35]智慧功德乃為淨。
[36]眼見求淨無是事。

简体字   正體字

On Viewing Mākandika's Corpse

The disciples of Mākandika, the brahmacārin, placed his corpse in a litter, and holding it aloft, carried it through the city, with many of them calling out, "Whoever views the body of Mākandika will gain the way of purity. How much the more so if they pay reverence to it or make offerings." Many people believed what they said. The bhikshus heard this and asked the Buddha, "Bhagavān. What about this matter?"

The Buddha then uttered a verse in reply:

Men of lesser minds seek purification through what their eyes see.
People like these have no wisdom and have no actual path.
The afflictions of all the fetters fill up their minds.
How could they, merely by viewing, gain the way of purity?

If it were by the eye's seeing that one gained purity,
What use would there be in wisdom or the treasure of meritorious
    qualities?
Through wisdom and meritorious qualities, one then attains purity.
As for gaining purity through viewing with the eyes, there is no such
    thing.

问曰。大德阿难[25]名。以何因缘。是先世因缘。是父母作字。是依因缘立名。答曰。[26]是先世因缘亦父母作名亦依因缘立字。问曰。云何先世因缘。答曰。释迦文佛先世作瓦师。名大光明。尔时有佛名释迦文。弟子名舍利弗[27]目乾连阿难。佛与弟子俱到瓦师舍一宿。尔时瓦师。布施草坐灯明石蜜浆三事。供养佛及比丘僧。便发愿言。我于当来老病死恼五恶之世作佛。如今佛名释迦[28]文。我[29]佛弟子[30]名亦如今佛弟子[31]名。以佛愿故得字阿难。复次阿难世世立愿。我在释迦文佛弟子多闻众中。愿最第一字阿难。复次阿难世世忍辱除瞋。以是因缘故。生便端[*]正。父母以其端[*]正见者皆欢喜故字阿难。[32]（阿难者秦言欢喜）是为先世因缘字。云何父母作字。昔[33]有日种王。[34]名师子颊。其王有四子。[35]第一名净饭。二名白饭。三名斛饭。四名甘露饭。有一女名甘露味。净饭王有二子[36]佛难陀。白饭王有二子跋提提沙。

简体字

問曰。大德阿難[25]名。以何因緣。是先世因緣。是父母作字。是依因緣立名。答曰。[26]是先世因緣亦父母作名亦依因緣立字。問曰。云何先世因緣。答曰。釋迦文佛先世作瓦師。名大光明。爾時有佛名釋迦文。弟子名舍利弗[27]目乾連阿難。佛與弟子俱到瓦師舍一宿。爾時瓦師。布施草坐燈明石蜜漿三事。供養佛及比丘僧。便發願言。我於當來老病死惱五惡之世作佛。如今佛名釋迦[28]文。我[29]佛弟子[30]名亦如今佛弟子[31]名。以佛願故得字阿難。復次阿難世世立願。我在釋迦文佛弟子多聞眾中。願最第一字阿難。復次阿難世世忍辱除瞋。以是因緣故。生便端[*]正。父母以其端[*]正見者皆歡喜故字阿難。[32]（阿難者秦言歡喜）是為先世因緣字。云何父母作字。昔[33]有日種王。[34]名師子頰。其王有四子。[35]第一名淨飯。二名白飯。三名斛飯。四名甘露飯。有一女名甘露味。淨飯王有二子[36]佛難陀。白飯王有二子跋提提沙。

正體字

Why Ānanda was So Called

Question: What are the causal circumstances for the Venerable Ānanda receiving such a name? Was it as a result of causal circumstances from former lives? Was it a name given to him by his father and mother? Or was it based on particular causes and conditions that he was given this name?

Response: It was as a result of causal circumstances from former lives. It was also a name given to him by his father and mother. And it was also a name stemming from particular causes and conditions.

Question: What were the causal circumstances from former lives?

Response: In a former life, Shakyamuni Buddha was a potter named "Great Brilliance." At that time there was another Buddha also known as Shakyamuni who also had disciples named Śāriputra, Maudgalyāyana, and Ānanda. The Buddha went with his disciples and spent a night at the abode of the potter. At that time the potter made gifts of three things: grass sitting mats, lamp light, and rock-honey chutney. He presented them as offerings to the Buddha and the bhikshu sangha and then made a vow, saying, "May I become a buddha in the future in a world afflicted with ageing, sickness, death, and the five evils. May I also have the name Shakyamuni and may my disciples' names also be the same as these." Because of the vow of the Buddha, Ānanda is now so-named.

Additionally, in life after life, Ānanda made a vow, "May I be foremost among the learned disciples of Shakyamuni Buddha and may my name be Ānanda."

Furthermore, in life after life, Ānanda cultivated patience and ridding himself of anger. For this reason he was particularly handsome from birth. Because those who saw him were delighted on account of his handsomeness, his father and mother named him Ānanda [which means "delightful"]. These are the past life reasons for his name.

Why did his father and mother give him this name? In the past, there was a king of the Solar clan named "Lion Jaws." The king had four sons. The first was named "Pure Rice." The second was named "White Rice." The third was named "Bushel of Rice." The fourth was named "Ambrosia Rice." There was a daughter named "Ambrosia Flavor." The Pure Rice King had two sons, the Buddha and Nanda. The White Rice king had two sons, Badi and Tisha. The

斛饭王有二子提婆达多阿
难。甘露饭王有二子摩诃男
阿泥卢豆。甘露味女有一子
名施婆罗。是中悉达[37]陀菩
萨。渐渐长大弃转轮圣王[38]
位。夜半出家。[39]至沤楼鞞
罗国中尼连禅河边。六年苦
行。是时净饭王爱念子故。
常遣使问讯[40]欲知消息。我
子得道不。若病若[41]死。使
来白王。菩萨唯有皮骨筋相
连持[42]耳。命甚[43]微弱。若
今日若明日不复久也。王闻
其言甚大愁念没忧恼海。我
子既不作转轮王。又不得作
佛。一何衰苦无所得而死。
如是忧恼荒迷愦塞。是时菩
萨弃苦行处。食百味乳糜身
体充满。于[44]尼连禅水中洗
浴已。至菩提树下坐金刚[45]
座。而自誓言。要不破此结
[46]加趺坐成一切智。不得一
切智终不起也。是时魔王将
[47]十八亿众到菩萨所。敢与
菩萨决其得失。菩萨智慧力
故大破魔军。魔不如而退自
念。菩萨叵胜当恼其父。至
净饭王所诡言。汝子今日后
夜已[48]了。王闻此语惊怖堕
床。如热沙中鱼。王[49]时

简体字

斛飯王有二子提婆達多阿
難。甘露飯王有二子摩訶男
阿泥盧豆。甘露味女有一子
名施婆羅。是中悉達[37]陀菩
薩。漸漸長大棄轉輪聖王[38]
位。夜半出家。[39]至漚樓鞞
羅國中尼連禪河邊。六年苦
行。是時淨飯王愛念子故。
常遣使問訊[40]欲知消息。我
子得道不。若病若[41]死。使
來白王。菩薩唯有皮骨筋相
連持[42]耳。命甚[43]微弱。若
今日若明日不復久也。王聞
其言甚大愁念沒憂惱海。我
子既不作轉輪王。又不得作
佛。一何衰苦無所得而死。
如是憂惱荒迷憒塞。是時菩
薩棄苦行處。食百味乳糜身
體充滿。於[44]尼連禪水中洗
浴已。至菩提樹下坐金剛[45]
座。而自誓言。要不破此結
[46]加趺坐成一切智。不得一
切智終不起也。是時魔王將
[47]十八億眾到菩薩所。敢與
菩薩決其得失。菩薩智慧力
故大破魔軍。魔不如而退自
念。菩薩叵勝當惱其父。至
淨飯王所詭言。汝子今日後
夜已[48]了。王聞此語驚怖墮
床。如熱沙中魚。王[49]時

正體字

"Bushel-of-Rice King" had two sons, Devadatta and Ānanda. The Sweet Dew Rice King had two sons, Mahānāman and Aniruddha. The daughter, Ambrosia, had a son named Dānapāla.

It was in the midst of these circumstances that Siddharta Bodhisattva gradually grew up and rejected the station of the wheel-turning sage king. In the middle of the night, he left his home and went to the banks of the Nairañjanā River in the state of Uruvilvā. For six years, he cultivated ascetic practices. At that time because the pure Rice King lovingly remembered his son, he constantly sent messengers to ask after him as he desired to know the news: "Has my son gained the way or not?" "Has he become sick or has he died?"

The messengers came and addressed the king, saying, "The Bodhisattva only has skin and bones and ligaments holding them together., that's all." His life force is very fragile and weak. Whether it's today or whether it's tomorrow, he will not have much longer."

When the king heard their words, he was greatly distressed and his thoughts were sunken in a sea of worry and affliction. "My son not only failed to become the wheel-turning king, he was also unable to gain buddhahood. What utterly tragic suffering that he should gain nothing whatsoever and then die!" Thus he became afflicted with anguish, lost in desolation, and paralyzed with bewilderment. It was at that time that the Bodhisattva abandoned the site of his ascetic practices and partook of the many-flavored rice gruel with milk whereupon his body was restored to health. After bathing in the waters of the Nairañjanā, he proceeded to the bodhi tree and sat beneath it on the adamantine seat, vowing to himself, "Without breaking away from this full-lotus posture I must succeed in realizing omniscience. So long as I fail to realize omniscience, I shall never get up."

It was at this time that the king of the Māras led a multitude followers, eighteen *koṭis* in number, to the site where the bodhisattva sat, daring to test his attainment. On account of the power of the bodhisattva's wisdom, he utterly vanquished the demon armies. Māra was no match for him and in making his retreat, thought to himself, "As I can't overcome the Bodhisattva, I'll go afflict his father." He then went to the place of the Pure Rice King and, intending to deceive him, announced, "This very night, in the very last watch, your son was finally finished." When the king heard these words, he collapsed onto his bed, agonizing like a fish in hot sand.

悲哭而[50]说偈言。
阿夷陀虚言　瑞应亦无验。
得利之吉名　一切无所获。

[0083c24]　　是时菩提树神大欢喜。持天曼陀罗华。至净饭王所说偈言。

汝子已得道　魔众已破散。
光明如日出　普照十方[1]土。

[0084a03]　　王言。前有天来言。汝子已[2]了。汝今来言坏魔得道。二语相[3]违谁可信者。树神[4]又言。实不妄语。前[5]来天者诡言已[6]了。是魔怀嫉故来相恼。今日诸天龙神华香供养空中悬缯。汝子身出光明遍照天地。王闻其言于一切苦恼心得解脱。王言我子虽舍转轮圣王。今得法转轮王定得大利无所失也。[7]王心大欢喜。是时斛饭王家使来白净饭王。言。贵弟生男。王心欢喜言。今日大吉是欢喜日。语来使言。是儿当字为阿[8]难。是为父母作字。云何依因缘立名。阿难端[*]正清净如好明镜。老少好丑

悲哭而[50]說偈言。
阿夷陀虛言　瑞應亦無驗。
得利之吉名　一切無所獲。

[0083c24]　　是時菩提樹神大歡喜。持天曼陀羅華。至淨飯王所說偈言。

汝子已得道　魔眾已破散。
光明如日出　普照十方[1]土。

[0084a03]　　王言。前有天來言。汝子已[2]了。汝今來言壞魔得道。二語相[3]違誰可信者。樹神[4]又言。實不妄語。前[5]來天者詭言已[6]了。是魔懷嫉故來相惱。今日諸天龍神華香供養空中懸繒。汝子身出光明遍照天地。王聞其言於一切苦惱心得解脫。王言我子雖捨轉輪聖王。今得法轉輪王定得大利無所失也。[7]王心大歡喜。是時斛飯王家使來白淨飯王。言。貴弟生男。王心歡喜言。今日大吉是歡喜日。語來使言。是兒當字為阿[8]難。是為父母作字。云何依因緣立名。阿難端[*]正清淨如好明鏡。老少好醜

简体字　　　　　　　　　　正體字

The king wept pitifully and then uttered a verse:

Those spurious words pronounced by Ajita—
A propitious omen with no validation—
An auspicious entitlement assuring achievements—
But nothing whatsoever was finally gained.

At this time, the tree-spirit of the bodhi tree was in a state of great joy and taking heavenly *māndārava*, flowers he went to the place of the Pure Rice King and spoke forth a verse:

Your son has already gained the Path.
The hordes of demons have been broken and scattered.
His brilliant light shines like that of the rising sun
Which universally illumines the lands of the ten directions.

The King said, "Earlier, there was a deity who came and said, 'Your son is already finished.' Now you come and say that he has destroyed the demons and realized the Path. These two pronouncements are contradictory. Whose can be believed?"

The tree spirit continued, "These are true words, not false words. The 'deity' who came earlier and who attempted to deceive you by saying, 'He's finished' was a demon who came to afflict you because he was full of jealousy. Today, the gods, dragons, and spirits make offerings with flowers and incense and suspend celebratory banners in the sky. Your son's body is radiating light which illumines heaven and earth."

When the king heard these words, his mind gained liberation from all anguish and affliction. The King declared, "Although my son forsook the wheel-turning kingship, as he has now attained the Dharma-wheel-turning kingship, he has certainly gained great benefit and nothing has been lost." The King became greatly delighted in mind.

It was at this time that a messenger arrived from the abode of the Bushel-of-Rice King and addressed the Pure Rice King, saying, "Your highness's younger brother has fathered a son."

The King's mind was filled with great delight. He said, "Today is a greatly auspicious day. It is a day of rejoicing." He said to the messenger who had come, "This boy should be named 'Ānanda' ('joy')." This is how the name was given by the parents.

How was the giving of the name reliant upon particular causes and conditions? Ānanda's physique was as elegant and pure as a fine bright mirror. One's age, one's beauty, and the appearance of

容貌颜状。皆于身中现。其
身明净。女人见之欲心即
动。是故佛听阿难着覆肩
衣。是阿难能令他人见者心
眼欢喜故名阿难。于是造论
者赞言。

面如净满月　眼若[9]青莲华。
佛法大海水　流入阿难心。
能令人心眼　见者[10]大欢喜。
诸来求见佛　通现不失宜。

容貌顏狀。皆於身中現。其
身明淨。女人見之欲心即
動。是故佛聽阿難著覆肩
衣。是阿難能令他人見者心
眼歡喜故名阿難。於是造論
者讚言。

面如淨滿月　眼若[9]青蓮華。
佛法大海水　流入阿難心。
能令人心眼　見者[10]大歡喜。
諸來求見佛　通現不失宜。

简体字　　　　　　　　正體字

one's countenance are all reflected in the body. His body was bright and pure. When women looked upon him, they tended to be moved to thoughts of desire. It was on account of this that the Buddha permitted Ānanda to wear his robe with the shoulder covered. Thus it was because Ānanda was able to bring delight to the minds and eyes of those who gazed upon him that he was named Ānanda ("joy").

Nāgārjuna's Concluding Comments

At this point, the commentator offers words of praise:

His face was like the pure and full moon.
His eyes were like the blue lotus blossom.
The waters of the great sea of the Buddha Dharma
Flowed on into the mind of Ānanda

He was able to bring to the mind and eyes of any person
Who looked upon him a feeling of great joyfulness.
All who came seeking to see the Buddha—
He introduced them all with no loss in decorum.

問曰。菩薩几時能种三十二相。答曰。极迟百劫。极疾九十一劫。释迦牟尼菩萨。九十一大劫行办三十二相。如经中言。过去久远有佛名弗沙。时有二菩萨。一名释迦牟尼。一名弥勒。弗沙佛。欲观释迦牟尼菩萨心纯淑未。即观见之。知其心未纯淑。而诸弟子心皆纯淑。又弥勒菩萨心已纯淑。而弟子未纯淑。是时弗沙佛。如是思惟。一人之心易可速化。众人之心难可疾治。如是思惟竟。弗沙佛。欲使释迦牟尼菩萨疾得成佛。上雪山上。于宝窟中入[29]火定。是时释迦牟尼菩萨。作外道仙人。上山采药。见弗沙佛坐宝窟中入[*]火定放光明。见已心欢喜。信敬翘一脚立。叉手向佛一心而观。目未曾眴七日七夜。以一偈赞佛。

天上天下无如佛。
十方世界亦无比。
世界所有我尽见。
一切无有如佛者。

简体字

問曰。菩薩幾時能種三十二相。答曰。極遲百劫。極疾九十一劫。釋迦牟尼菩薩。九十一大劫行辦三十二相。如經中言。過去久遠有佛名弗沙。時有二菩薩。一名釋迦牟尼。一名彌勒。弗沙佛。欲觀釋迦牟尼菩薩心純淑未。即觀見之。知其心未純淑。而諸弟子心皆純淑。又彌勒菩薩心已純淑。而弟子未純淑。是時弗沙佛。如是思惟。一人之心易可速化。眾人之心難可疾治。如是思惟竟。弗沙佛。欲使釋迦牟尼菩薩疾得成佛。上雪山上。於寶窟中入[29]火定。是時釋迦牟尼菩薩。作外道仙人。上山採藥。見弗沙佛坐寶窟中入[*]火定放光明。見已心歡喜。信敬翹一腳立。叉手向佛一心而觀。目未曾眴七日七夜。以一偈讚佛。

天上天下無如佛。
十方世界亦無比。
世界所有我盡見。
一切無有如佛者。

正體字

The Bodhisattva Shakyamuni Encounters Puṣya Buddha

Question: How long does it take for the bodhisattva to be able to plant the causes for the thirty two marks [of a buddha's body]?

Response: The very slowest is one hundred kalpas. The very quickest is ninety-one kalpas. As a bodhisattva, Shakyamuni cultivated the thirty-two marks to completion in ninety one great kalpas. This is as described in a sutra:

Long ago and far away in the past there was a buddha named Puṣya. At that time there were two bodhisattvas. One was named Shakyamuni. One was named Maitreya. Puṣya Buddha wished to observe whether or not the mind of Shakyamuni Bodhisattva was completely still yet. He then contemplated and saw it. He knew that his mind was not yet completely still. And yet all of his disciples' minds were all completely still. Moreover Maitreya bodhisattva's mind was already completely still and yet the minds of his disciples were not yet completely still.

Puṣya Buddha then thought like this: "A single person's mind may easily be quickly transformed. The minds of a multitude of people, however, are difficult to treat so quickly. After he had thought in this manner, Puṣya Buddha wished to cause Shakyamuni Bodhisattva to quickly attain the realization of buddhahood. He ascended onto snow mountain and in the jeweled cave entered the fire samādhi.

At this time Shakyamuni Bodhisattva had manifest as a non-Buddhist rishi. He had ascended that very mountain to gather herbs. He chanced to observe Puṣya Buddha sitting in the jeweled cave having entered into the fire samādhi, radiating brilliant light. After he had laid eyes on Puṣya Buddha, his mind became so delighted that, as a demonstration of faith and reverence, he stood on one foot, pressed his palms together before that buddha and proceeded to contemplate him single-mindedly. For seven days and seven night he stood like this with his eyes without even blinking his eyes. Employing a verse, he praised the Buddha:

> Within and beneath the heavens, there are none like the Buddha.
> Throughout the world systems of the ten directions, there are none
> who can compare.
> Though I have seen completely everything throughout the world.
> Nowhere is there anyone who can compare to the Buddha.

[0087c13] 七日七夜谛观世尊目未曾眴。超越九劫于九十一劫中。得阿耨多罗三藐三菩提。	[0087c13] 七日七夜諦觀世尊目未曾眴。超越九劫於九十一劫中。得阿耨多羅三藐三菩提。

For seven days and seven nights, with eyes unblinking, he engaged in true contemplation of the Bhagavān. He thereby leapt over nine kalpas and thus was able to gain *anuttarasamyaksaṃbodhi* in a period of ninety-one kalpas.

问曰。[*]檀波罗蜜云何满。
答曰。一切能施无所遮碍。
乃至以身施时。心无所惜。
譬如尸毘王以身施鸽。释迦
牟尼佛本身作王。名尸毘。
是王得归命救护陀[1]罗尼。
大精进有慈悲心。视一切众
生如母爱子。时世无佛。释
提桓因命[2]尽欲[3]堕。自[4]
念言。何处有佛一切智人。
处处问难[5]不能断[6]疑。知
尽非佛。即还天上愁忧而
坐。巧变化师毘首羯磨天。
问曰。天主何以愁忧。答
曰。我求一切智人不可得。
以是故愁忧。毘首羯磨言。
有大菩萨。布施持戒禅定智
慧具足。不久当作佛。帝释
以偈答曰。

菩萨发大心　鱼子菴树华。
三事因时多　成果时甚少。

[0088a12]　毘首羯磨。答曰。
是优尸那种尸毘王。持戒精
进大慈大悲禅定智慧不久作
佛。释提桓因。语毘首羯
磨。当往试之。知有菩萨相
不。汝作鸽我作鹰。汝便
[7]佯怖入王[8]腋下。我当逐
汝。

The King Śibi Jātaka Tale

Question: How does one bring to perfect fulfillment *dāna* pāramitā (the perfection of giving)?

Response: One is able to give everything without reservation even to the point that when one gives of one's body, one's mind has no regrets. It is like the case of King Śibi who gave his body for the sake of pigeon. In a former life, Shakyamuni Buddha was a king who was named Śibi. This king had gotten the *dhāraṇī* of dedicating his life to rescuing and protecting [the helpless]. He possessed a mind of kindness and compassion which he invested with great vigor. He looked upon all beings in the same way that a mother looks with love upon her child.

At that time the world had no buddha. The life of [the god] Śakradevendra was coming to an end and he was about to fall. He thought to himself, "Where is there a buddha, an omniscient man?" He posed difficult questions everywhere and was unable to cut off his doubts. Realizing that none of them were buddhas, he returned to the heavens and sat down in a state of worry and distress. The god Viśvakarman, a master of clever transformations, asked him, "Why is the Lord of Heaven so worried and distressed?"

He replied, "I have been seeking after an omniscient man and have been unable to find one. It is because of this that I am worried and distressed."

Viśvakarman said, "There is a great bodhisattva who is perfect in giving, upholding the precepts, dhyāna samādhi, and wisdom. It will not be long before he becomes a buddha."

Śakra replied in verse:

Bodhisattvas who have brought forth the great resolve,
The eggs of fish, and blossoms of the [celestial] *āmrātaka* tree—
These three things are numerous at the time of initial causation,
But at the time of fruition, they are all extremely scarce.

Viśvakarman responded, "King Śibi of the Ushinar clan upholds the precepts, is vigorous, is greatly kind, greatly compassionate, is possessed of dhyāna samādhi and wisdom, and shall before long become a buddha."

Śakradevendra said to Viśvakarman, "We ought to go and test him. We shall know then whether or not he has the characteristics of a bodhisattva. You should change into a pigeon and I shall change into a falcon. Then you pretend to be frightened and fly into the armpit of the king. I'm going to pursue you."

毘首羯磨言。此大菩萨云何
以此事恼。释提桓因说偈
言。
我亦非恶心　如真金应试。
以此试菩萨　知其心定不。

[0088a20]　说此偈竟。毘首羯
磨。即自变身作一赤眼赤足
鸽。释提桓因。自变身[9]作
一鹰。急飞[10]逐鸽。鸽直来
入王[11]掖[12]底。举身战怖动
眼促声。
是时众多人　相与而语曰。
是王大慈仁　一切宜保[13]信。
如是鸽小鸟　归之如入舍。
菩萨相如是　[14]作佛必不久。

[0088a28] 是时鹰在近树上。语
尸毘王。还与我鸽此我所[15]
受。王时语鹰。我前受此非
是汝受。我初发意时。受此
一切众生皆欲度之。鹰言。
王欲度一切众生。我非一切
耶。何以独不见愍。而夺我
今日食。王答[16]言。汝须何
食。我作誓愿其有众生。来
归我者必救护之。汝须何食
亦当相给。鹰言。我须新杀
[17]热肉。王念言。如此难
得。自非杀生[18]无由得也。
我当云何杀一与一。

简体字

毘首羯磨言。此大菩薩云何
以此事惱。釋提桓因說偈
言。
我亦非惡心　如真金應試。
以此試菩薩　知其心定不。

[0088a20]　說此偈竟。毘首羯
磨。即自變身作一赤眼赤足
鴿。釋提桓因。自變身[9]作
一鷹。急飛[10]逐鴿。鴿直來
入王[11]掖[12]底。舉身戰怖動
眼促聲。
是時眾多人　相與而語曰。
是王大慈仁　一切宜保[13]信。
如是鴿小鳥　歸之如入舍。
菩薩相如是　[14]作佛必不久。

[0088a28] 是時鷹在近樹上。語
尸毘王。還與我鴿此我所[15]
受。王時語鷹。我前受此非
是汝受。我初發意時。受此
一切眾生皆欲度之。鷹言。
王欲度一切眾生。我非一切
耶。何以獨不見愍。而奪我
今日食。王答[16]言。汝須何
食。我作誓願其有眾生。來
歸我者必救護之。汝須何食
亦當相給。鷹言。我須新殺
[17]熱肉。王念言。如此難
得。自非殺生[18]無由得也。
我當云何殺一與一。

正體字

Viśvakarman said, "Why should we aggravate this great bodhi-sattva with this matter?"

Śakradevendra uttered a verse:

For my part I'm not of evil mind.
Just as with true gold, one ought to test it.
By this we shall test the bodhisattva
And know if his mind is resolute or not.

After he had spoken this verse, Viśvakarman acquiesced and then changed his body into that of a red-eyed, red-footed pigeon. Śakradevendra changed his body into that of a falcon which flew swiftly in pursuit of the pigeon. The pigeon straightaway came and flew into the armpit of the king. His entire body quivered in fright, his eyes moved about [anxiously] and let out cries of distress.

At this time many people
Gathered together and said,
"This king is greatly kind and humane.
Everyone rightfully testifies to his believability.

"Just so, this pigeon, a little bird,
Takes refuge in him as if entering his own abode.
The characteristics of the bodhisattva are just like this
It will certainly not be long before he becomes a buddha."

At this time the falcon was in a nearby tree. It called to King Śibi, "Give me back my pigeon. It belongs to me."

The King said to the falcon, "I took it in first. It's not the case that it belongs to you. When I first brought forth the resolve [to realize buddhahood], I took on responsibility for all of these beings and so wish to deliver them all to liberation."

The falcon said, "The King desires to bring deliverance to all beings. Am I not included within this "all beings"? How is it that I alone do not experience your pity so that you now take away my meal for today?"

The King replied, "What food do you require? I have made a vow that whatsoever being comes and takes refuge with me, I shall certainly rescue and protect it. Whatever food you require shall also be provided to you."

The falcon said, "I require freshly-killed warm flesh."

The King thought to himself, "It's difficult to obtain something like this. Unless one kills a being oneself there is no source from which to obtain it. How could I take the life of one so as to bestow

思惟心定即自说偈。
是我此身肉　恒属老病死。
不久当臭烂　彼须我当与。
[0088b11]　　如是思惟已。呼人持刀自割股肉与鹰。鹰语王言。王虽以[19]热肉与我。当用道理令肉轻重得与鸽等勿见欺也。王言持称来。以肉对鸽。鸽身转重王肉转轻。[20]王令人割二股亦轻不足。次割两[21][跳-兆+专]两[22]膞两乳[23]项脊。举身肉尽。鸽身犹重。王肉故轻。是时近臣内[24]戚。安施帐幔。却诸看人。王今如此无可观也。尸毗王言。勿遮诸人听令入看。而说偈言。
[25]天人阿修罗　一切来观我。
大心无上志　以求成佛道。
若有[26]求佛道　当忍此大苦。
不能坚固心　则当息其意。
[0088b24]　　是时菩萨。以血涂手攀[27]称欲上。定心以身尽以对鸽。鹰言。大王此事难办。何用如此以鸽还我。

思惟心定即自說偈。
是我此身肉　恒屬老病死。
不久當臭爛　彼須我當與。
[0088b11]　　如是思惟已。呼人持刀自割股肉與鷹。鷹語王言。王雖以[19]熱肉與我。當用道理令肉輕重得與鴿等勿見欺也。王言持稱來。以肉對鴿。鴿身轉重王肉轉輕。[20]王令人割二股亦輕不足。次割兩[21][跳-兆+專]兩[22]膞兩乳[23]項脊。舉身肉盡。鴿身猶重。王肉故輕。是時近臣內[24]戚。安施帳幔。却諸看人。王今如此無可觀也。尸毗王言。勿遮諸人聽令入看。而說偈言。
[25]天人阿修羅　一切來觀我。
大心無上志　以求成佛道。
若有[26]求佛道　當忍此大苦。
不能堅固心　則當息其意。
[0088b24]　　是時菩薩。以血塗手攀[27]稱欲上。定心以身盡以對鴿。鷹言。大王此事難辦。何用如此以鴿還我。

简体字　　　　　　　　　　　正體字

[life] on another?" After thinking like this, his mind became fixed
and he then spoke a verse to himself:

This, the flesh of this body of mine
Ever belongs to ageing, sickness and death.
It shall before long grow foul and rot.
As he requires it, I therefore shall give it.

After he had reflected in this way, he called a person to bring a
knife whereupon he cut flesh from his own thigh and gave it to the
falcon. The falcon said to the King, "Although the King has given
me warm flesh, he should be principled in doing so, thereby making sure that the weight of the flesh is equal to that of the pigeon.
Let's not countenance any cheating here."

The King ordered, "Bring some scales and balance this flesh
against the pigeon. The pigeon became heavier and the King's flesh
became lighter. The King ordered someone to carve the flesh from
the other thigh but it was still too light and hence not sufficient.
Then they successively carved the flesh extending on down to his
two feet, up to his two hips, from both sides of his chest, from his
neck and from along his spine. All of the flesh from his entire body
was gone. The body of the pigeon was still heavier. Just as before,
the flesh of the King was lighter.

The close officials and near relatives then set up a curtain and
sent away everyone who was watching, [saying], "With the King
in his present state, no one could bear to look upon him. King Śibi
said, "Don't block off the people. Allow them to enter and see." He
then spoke a verse:

The gods, men, and asuras
All may come and look at me.
With the great mind and the unsurpassed resolve.
One thereby seeks realization of the Buddha Path.

If one seeks to gain the Path of the Buddha,
He should be able to endure great suffering of this sort.
If one is unable to make his resolve solid,
His determination will then cease.

It was at this time that the bodhisattva, with blood-smeared
hands, grasped at the scales, wishing to climb up on it. He fixed his
mind on using his entire body to balance the weight of the pigeon.

The falcon said, "Great King, this matter is going to be difficult
to manage. What is the use in going about it like this? Just give the
pigeon back to me."

王言鸽来归我终不与汝。我
丧身无量于[28]物无益。今
欲以身求易佛道。以手攀[*]
称。[29]尔时菩萨。肉尽筋断
不能自制。欲上而堕自[30]责
心言。汝当自坚勿得迷闷。
一切众生堕忧苦大海。汝一
人立誓欲[31]度一切。何以[32]
怠闷。此苦甚少地狱苦多。
以此相比于十六分犹不及
一。我今有智慧精进持戒禅
定。犹患此苦。何况地狱中
人无智慧者。是时菩萨。一
心欲上复更攀[*]称。语人扶
我。是时菩萨。心定无悔。
诸天龙王阿修罗鬼神人民皆
大赞言。为[33]一小鸟乃尔。
是事希有。即时[34]大地为
六种[35]振动。大海波扬枯树
生华。天降香雨及散名华。
天女歌赞必得成佛。是时[36]
念我四方神仙皆来赞言。是
真菩萨必早成佛。鹰语鸽
言。[37]终试如此不惜身命。
是真菩萨。即说偈言。
慈悲地中生　一切智树牙。
我曹当[38]供养　不应施忧恼。

王言鵠來歸我終不與汝。我
喪身無量於[28]物無益。今
欲以身求易佛道。以手攀[*]
稱。[29]爾時菩薩。肉盡筋斷
不能自制。欲上而墮自[30]責
心言。汝當自堅勿得迷悶。
一切眾生墮憂苦大海。汝一
人立誓欲[31]度一切。何以[32]
怠悶。此苦甚少地獄苦多。
以此相比於十六分猶不及
一。我今有智慧精進持戒禪
定。猶患此苦。何況地獄中
人無智慧者。是時菩薩。一
心欲上復更攀[*]稱。語人扶
我。是時菩薩。心定無悔。
諸天龍王阿修羅鬼神人民皆
大讚言。為[33]一小鳥乃爾。
是事希有。即時[34]大地為
六種[35]振動。大海波揚枯樹
生華。天降香雨及散名華。
天女歌讚必得成佛。是時[36]
念我四方神仙皆來讚言。是
真菩薩必早成佛。鷹語鵠
言。[37]終試如此不惜身命。
是真菩薩。即說偈言。
慈悲地中生　一切智樹牙。
我曹當[38]供養　不應施憂惱。

简体字   正體字

The King said, "The pigeon came and sought refuge with me. I'll never give it to you. I've lost an innumerable number of bodies without providing any benefit to beings. Now I wish to employ my body in seeking to ease the way to buddhahood."

He grasped at the scales with his hands. At that time the bodhisattva's flesh was gone and his sinews were cut and he was unable to control his movement. He wished to rise up but fell back, thinking to himself self-critically, "You should make yourself strong. Don't allow yourself to become confused and depressed. All beings have fallen into the great seas of distress and anguish. You, one man, have made a vow whereby you desire to cross them all over to liberation. How can you allow yourself to lazily indulge in depression? This suffering is very slight. The suffering of the hells is greater. If you compare this to it, this still doesn't equal that of even one of the sixteen divisions of hell. I now have wisdom, vigor, the upholding of precepts, and dhyāna samādhi, and yet I am still beset with this suffering. How much the more so is this the case with people in hell who are devoid of wisdom."

The bodhisattva then single-mindedly desired to rise up and so again grasped at the scales. He asked the people, "Support me." The bodhisattva's mind was then fixed and devoid of any regret.

All of the gods, dragon kings, asuras, ghosts, spirits, and the ordinary people greatly praised him, saying, "He acts like this for the sake of a single small bird. This matter is rare."

It was then that the great earth quaked in six ways. The waves of the great sea churned up and withered trees brought forth flowers. The heavens let fall scented rain and then scattered rare blossoms. The heavenly maidens sang praises, "He will certainly achieve the realization of buddhahood."

Then the spirits and rishis from the four directions all came and praised him saying, "He is a true bodhisattva. He will certainly soon realize buddhahood."

The falcon said to the pigeon, "Finally, even when tested like this, he has not spared his body or life. He is a true bodhisattva. He then spoke forth a verse:

Produced from the soil of kindness and compassion,
He is a seedling growing forth of the tree of omniscience.
We should be making offerings to him
And should not give him such distress and affliction.

[0088c15]　毘首羯磨。语释提桓因言。天主汝有神力。可令此王身得平复。释提桓因言。不[39]须我也。[40]此王自作誓愿大心欢喜。不惜身命感发一切令求佛道。帝释语人王言。汝割肉辛苦心不恼没耶。王言。我心欢喜不恼不没。帝释言。谁当信汝心不没者。是时菩萨作实誓愿。我割肉血流不瞋不恼。一心不闷以求佛道者。我身当即平复如故。即出语时身复如本。人天见之皆大悲喜叹未曾有。此大菩萨必当作佛。我曹应当尽[41]心供养。愿令早成佛道。当念我等。[42]是时释提桓因毘首羯磨各还天上。如是等[43]种种相。[44]是檀波罗蜜满。

简体字

[0088c15]　毘首羯磨。語釋提桓因言。天主汝有神力。可令此王身得平復。釋提桓因言。不[39]須我也。[40]此王自作誓願大心歡喜。不惜身命感發一切令求佛道。帝釋語人王言。汝割肉辛苦心不惱沒耶。王言。我心歡喜不惱不沒。帝釋言。誰當信汝心不沒者。是時菩薩作實誓願。我割肉血流不瞋不惱。一心不悶以求佛道者。我身當即平復如故。即出語時身復如本。人天見之皆大悲喜歎未曾有。此大菩薩必當作佛。我曹應當盡[41]心供養。願令早成佛道。當念我等。[42]是時釋提桓因毘首羯磨各還天上。如是等[43]種種相。[44]是檀波羅蜜滿。

正體字

Viśvakarman said to Śakradevendra, "Lord of Heaven, you have the spiritual power. You can cause the body of this king to return to normal."

Śakradevendra said, "He has no need of me. This king has made a vow to himself with the joyfulness of the great mind that he will not spare his body or life in inspiring everyone and causing them to seek the Buddha Path."

Śakra asked the King, "With the bitter suffering of having your flesh carved away, didn't your mind become afflicted and sink into [discouragement]?"

The King said, "My mind remained joyful. It was neither afflicted nor sunken."

Śakra said, "Who could believe that your mind did not sink into discouragement?"

In response, the bodhisattva then made a "vow of truth," saying, "If while my flesh was carved away and my blood flowed forth I was neither angry nor afflicted, and if I remained single-minded and undiscouraged in seeking the Buddha Path, my body ought to immediately return to normal and become just as before." Having uttered these words his body immediately became once again just as it had been before.

When the men and gods witnessed this, they were all moved to great compassion and joy, exclaimed at this occurrence of what had never been before, and declared, "This great bodhisattva shall certainly become a buddha. We should make offerings to him from the very depths of our hearts. We pray that he will soon gain the realization of the Buddha Path and that, having done so, he will bring us to mind in the future."

At this time Śakradevendra and Viśvakarman each returned to the heavens. All manner of characteristics such as these illustrate what is involved in the fulfillment of *dāna* pāramitā.

问曰。尸罗波罗蜜云何满。
答曰。不惜身命护持净戒。
如须陀须摩王。以劫磨沙波
陀[45]大王故。[46]乃至舍命
不犯禁戒。昔有须陀须摩
王。是王精进持戒常依实[1]
语。晨朝乘车将诸婇女入园
游戏。出城门时有一婆罗门
来乞语王言。王是大福德人
我身贫穷。当见愍念赐[2]匃
少多。[3]王言[4]诺。敬如来
告当相布施须我出还。作此
语已入园[5]澡浴嬉戏。时有
两翅王名曰鹿足空中飞来。
于婇女中捉王将去。譬如金
翅鸟海中取龙。诸女啼哭号
[6]恸。一园[7]惊城内外搔扰
悲惶。鹿足负王腾跃虚空至
所住[8]止。置九十九[9]诸王
中。须陀须摩王涕零如雨。
鹿足[10]王语言。大刹利王汝
何以啼如小儿。人生有死合
会有离。须陀须摩王答言。
我不畏死[11]甚畏失信。我从
生[12]已来初不妄语。今日晨
朝出[13]门时有一婆罗门来从
我乞。我时许言还当

问曰。尸羅波羅蜜云何滿。
答曰。不惜身命護持淨戒。
如須陀須摩王。以劫磨沙波
陀[45]大王故。[46]乃至捨命
不犯禁戒。昔有須陀須摩
王。是王精進持戒常依實[1]
語。晨朝乘車將諸婇女入園
遊戲。出城門時有一婆羅門
來乞語王言。王是大福德人
我身貧窮。當見愍念賜[2]匃
少多。[3]王言[4]諾。敬如來
告當相布施須我出還。作此
語已入園[5]澡浴嬉戲。時有
兩翅王名曰鹿足空中飛來。
於婇女中捉王將去。譬如金
翅鳥海中取龍。諸女啼哭號
[6]慟。一園[7]驚城內外搔擾
悲惶。鹿足負王騰躍虛空至
所住[8]止。置九十九[9]諸王
中。須陀須摩王涕零如雨。
鹿足[10]王語言。大刹利王汝
何以啼如小兒。人生有死合
會有離。須陀須摩王答言。
我不畏死[11]甚畏失信。我從
生[12]已來初不妄語。今日晨
朝出[13]門時有一婆羅門來從
我乞。我時許言還當

King Sutasoma's Dedication to Truth

Question: What is meant by the fulfillment of *śīla* pāramitā (the perfection of moral virtue)?

Response: It consists in not even sparing one's own life in guarding and upholding the precepts of purity. A case in point is that of King Sutasoma who, on account of the Great King [of the *rākṣasa* ghosts,] Kalmāṣapāda, went so far as to give up his life to avoid transgressing the prohibitions.

In the past there was a king named Sutasoma. This king was assiduous in his upholding of the precepts and so always resorted to truth in speech. He got into his carriage one morning and, taking along his courtesans, set out to the gardens to roam about and enjoy himself. As he was leaving the city gates, he came upon a brahman who having come to request alms, said to the King, "The King is a great man endowed with many blessings whereas I am but a pauper. May it be that I receive compassionate consideration and a measure of offering in response to this entreaty?"

The King replied, "I'll consent to this. I respect the dictates of the Bhagavān that one should engage in giving. But it must wait until I return from this excursion." Having said this, he went on into the gardens where he bathed and enjoyed himself. Then, a two-winged king named Kalmāṣapāda[1] flew down from the sky, plucked up the King from amidst his courtesans and flew off with him. It was just like when the golden-winged [*garuḍa*] bird scoops up dragons from the sea. All of the women wept and wailed. Everyone in the gardens was in shock and everywhere inside and outside the city walls the people were in a commotion of grief and agitation. Kalmāṣapāda carried off the King, soared high up into the sky and then flew away to the mountain where he dwelt. There he kept the King together with ninety-nine other kings.

The tears of Sutasoma flowed down like raindrops. King Kalmāṣapāda inquired of him, "Oh great King of the *kṣatriya* lineage. Why is it that you cry like an infant? When a man is born, he is bound therefore to die. Whosoever comes together must eventually separate."

King Sutasoma replied, "I do not fear dying. I only regret the breach of trust. Even from the very time I was born, I have never uttered a falsehood. But when I was going out the gates this morning, there was a brahman who had come to request alms from me. At that time I consented and told him that, on my return, I would

布施。不虑无常[14]辜负彼
心自[15]招欺罪。是故啼耳。
鹿足王[16]言。汝意欲尔畏此
妄语。听汝还去七日布施婆
罗门讫便来还。若过七日不
还我有[17]两翅力取汝不难。
须陀须摩王得还本国恣意布
施。立太子为王。大会人民
忏谢之言。我智不周[18]物[19]
治不如法当见[20]忠恕。如我
今日身非已有正尔还去。举
国人民及诸亲戚叩头留之。
愿王留意慈荫此国。勿以鹿
足鬼王为虑也。当设铁舍奇
兵。鹿足虽神不畏之也。王
言不得尔也。而说偈言。
实语第一戒　实语升天梯。
实语[21]小而大　妄语入地狱。
我今守实语　宁弃身[22]寿命。
心无[23]有悔恨。
[0089b02]　　如是思惟已。王即
发去到[24]鹿足王所。[*]鹿足
遥见欢喜而言。汝是实语
人不失信要。一切人皆惜身
命。汝从死得脱还来

简体字

布施。不慮無常[14]辜負彼
心自[15]招欺罪。是故啼耳。
鹿足王[16]言。汝意欲爾畏此
妄語。聽汝還去七日布施婆
羅門訖便來還。若過七日不
還我有[17]兩翅力取汝不難。
須陀須摩王得還本國恣意布
施。立太子為王。大會人民
懺謝之言。我智不周[18]物[19]
治不如法當見[20]忠恕。如我
今日身非已有正爾還去。舉
國人民及諸親戚叩頭留之。
願王留意慈蔭此國。勿以鹿
足鬼王為慮也。當設鐵舍奇
兵。鹿足雖神不畏之也。王
言不得爾也。而說偈言。
實語第一戒　實語昇天梯。
實語[21]小而大　妄語入地獄。
我今守實語　寧棄身[22]壽命。
心無[23]有悔恨。
[0089b02]　　如是思惟已。王即
發去到[24]鹿足王所。[*]鹿足
遙見歡喜而言。汝是實語
人不失信要。一切人皆惜身
命。汝從死得脫還來

正體字

bestow some benefaction on him. I am not concerned about my own mortality. If I fail in my obligation to him, I shall naturally become guilty of deception. It is solely for this reason that I weep."

King Kalmāṣapāda said, "If in your mind you are so fearful of having uttered this falsehood, I will allow you to return. Having then made offerings to the brahman, you must then return within seven days. If after seven days you have still not returned, then, as I still possess the power of these two wings, it won't be difficult to seize you."

King Sutasoma was able to return to his native state where he was able to freely make offerings. He established the Prince as the King. At a great assembly of the citizenry he apologetically took leave of them, saying, "As my wisdom does not extend to all things, there are ways in which my rule has not accorded with Dharma. May we nonetheless continue to enjoy your loyalty and forgiveness. Now, in accordance with the fact that my person is no longer my own, it is only right that I return straightaway."

All of the citizens of the country and the relatives of the King bowed down and beseeched him to remain, pleading, "We pray that we may remain in the King's thoughts and that he will continue to offer this country the shade of his loving kindness. Don't make that Kalmāṣapāda, a king among the ghosts, the basis of your considerations. We will raise up an iron fortress and mount a surprise attack. Although Kalmāṣapāda may have supernatural powers, we need not fear him."

The King replied, "We cannot proceed in such a fashion." And then he uttered a verse, saying:

Truth in speech is the first among the precepts.
Truth in speech is the ladder to the heavens.
Truth in speech is minor yet major.
False speech is the means for entering the hells.

Now I in maintaining truth in speech,
Would rather cast aside my body and life.
In my thoughts, there are no regrets at all.

Having pondered the matter in this fashion the King immediately set out to the abode of King Kalmāṣapāda. When Kalmāṣapāda saw him in the distance he was delighted and said, "You are a man of true words. You do not fail in the essential of trustworthiness. Everyone cherishes his own life. Although you had been liberated from certain death you have come back again to attend to the matter

[25]赴信汝是大人。尔时须陀须摩王赞实语。[26]实语是为人非实语非人。如是种种赞实语呵妄语。[*]麁足闻之信心清净。语须陀须摩王言。汝好说此[27]今相放舍[28]汝既得脱。[29]九十九王亦布施汝。随意各还本国。如是语已[30]百王各得还去。如是等种种[31]本生中相是为尸罗波罗蜜满。

[25]赴信汝是大人。爾時須陀須摩王讚實語。[26]實語是為人非實語非人。如是種種讚實語呵妄語。[*]麁足聞之信心清淨。語須陀須摩王言。汝好說此[27]今相放捨[28]汝既得脫。[29]九十九王亦布施汝。隨意各還本國。如是語已[30]百王各得還去。如是等種種[31]本生中相是為尸羅波羅蜜滿。

简体字　　　　　　　　正體字

of trustworthiness. You are a great man."

At that time King Sutasoma spoke in praise of truth in speech, saying, "Truth in speech. This is what makes a man. As for one who utters words which are untrue, he is not a man." In this fashion, he spoke all manner of praises of truth and criticisms of falsehood.

As Kalmāṣapāda listened to this, thoughts of faithfulness became purified in him, whereupon he said to King Sutasoma, "You have spoken well about this. I am now releasing you and since you have gained your freedom, I am releasing the other ninety-nine kings as a gift to you. If you wish, they may each go back to their home country." After he had said this, all one hundred kings were able to return.

Nāgārjuna's Concluding Comments

All manner of characteristics such as these which are described in the *jātaka* tales describe what constitutes the fulfillment of the pāramitā of *śīla* (The perfection of moral virtue).

Notes

1. The Chinese frequently renders Kalmāṣapāda as "Deer Foot," which, for consistency, I have reconstructed throughout.

【经】如实巧[5]度

[0107a17] [*]【论】有外道法。虽度众生不如实度。[6]何以故。种种邪见结使残故[7]二乘虽有所度。不[8]如所应度。[9]何以故。无一切智方便心薄[10]故。唯有菩萨能如[11]实巧度。譬如渡师一人以浮囊草筏渡之。一人以[12]方舟而渡。二渡之中相降悬殊。菩萨巧渡众生亦如是。复次譬如治病苦药针灸痛而得差。如有妙药名苏陀扇陀。病人眼见众[13]病皆愈。除病虽同优劣法异。声闻菩萨教化度人亦复如是。苦行头陀初中后夜勤心[14]坐禅。观苦而得道声闻教也。

简体字

【經】如實巧[5]度

[0107a17] [*]【論】有外道法。雖度眾生不如實度。[6]何以故。種種邪見結使殘故[7]二乘雖有所度。不[8]如所應度。[9]何以故。無一切智方便心薄[10]故。唯有菩薩能如[11]實巧度。譬如渡師一人以浮囊草筏渡之。一人以[12]方舟而渡。二渡之中相降懸殊。菩薩巧渡眾生亦如是。復次譬如治病苦藥針灸痛而得差。如有妙藥名蘇陀扇陀。病人眼見眾[13]病皆愈。除病雖同優劣法異。聲聞菩薩教化度人亦復如是。苦行頭陀初中後夜勤心[14]坐禪。觀苦而得道聲聞教也。

正體字

The Bodhisattvas Prasannendriya and Agramati

Nāgārjuna's Preamble: On Reality-based Skillful Means

Sutra:

They were skillful in bringing about deliverance in accordance with reality.[1]

Exegesis:

There are dharmas propounded by non-Buddhists which, although they are able to bring about "deliverance" of beings, do so in a way which does not accord with reality. How is this so? It is because of the deficits inherent in all manner of erroneous views and fetters.

Although the followers of the Two Vehicles teachings do have those whom they bring to deliverance, they effect deliverance through inappropriate methods. How is this so? This is on account of the fact that, because they do not possess omniscience, the thought which they devote to skillful means is relatively shallow. Only the bodhisattvas are able to effect deliverance in accordance with reality. The difference here is analogous to that between two ferry men on a river, one of whom relies on a raft fashioned of reeds and floats, and the other of whom employs a ship. There is an obvious difference in the relative merits of the two approaches to ferrying people across. The bodhisattva's skillful deliverance of beings is just like this.

Then again, one might say that this is comparable to methods of healing disease. Bitter herbs, needles and cauterization induce pain in the process of effecting a cure. On the other hand, one may use a method of healing such as the miraculous medicine known as *śuddhaśāntā*[2] which the patient needs only lay eyes upon to effect the complete cure of a multitude of maladies. Although the two methods are the same in the sense that they both bring about the alleviation of disease, still, there is a difference as regards relative superiority of technique. The respective approaches employed by the Śrāvaka Disciples and the Bodhisattvas in the teaching and deliverance of people correspond to this analogy.

The teaching of the Śrāvaka Disciples consists in gaining the Path through the contemplation of suffering, resorting to the rigorous implementation of the *dhūta* practices,[3] and through sitting in dhyāna meditation, applying oneself with diligent mind in the beginning, middle and latter periods of the night. The teaching

观诸法相无缚无解心得清净
菩萨教也。如文殊师利本
缘。文殊师利白[15]佛。大
德。昔我先世过无量阿僧只
劫。尔时有佛名师子音王。
佛及众生寿十万亿那由他
岁。佛以三乘而度众生。国
名千光明。其国中诸树皆七
宝成。树出无量清净法音空
无相无作不生不灭无所有之
音。众生闻之心解得道。时
师子音王佛。初会说法九十
九亿人得阿罗汉道。菩萨众
亦复如是。是诸菩萨一切皆
得无生法忍。入种种法门。
见无量诸佛。恭敬供养能度
无量无数众生。得无量陀罗
尼门。[16]能得无量种种三
昧。初发心新入道门菩萨不
可称数。是[17]佛土无量庄严
说不可尽。时佛教化已讫。
入无馀涅盘。法住六万岁。
诸树法音亦不复出。尔时有
二菩萨比丘。一名喜根二名
胜意。

觀諸法相無縛無解心得清淨
菩薩教也。如文殊師利本
緣。文殊師利白[15]佛。大
德。昔我先世過無量阿僧祇
劫。爾時有佛名師子音王。
佛及眾生壽十萬億那由他
歲。佛以三乘而度眾生。國
名千光明。其國中諸樹皆七
寶成。樹出無量清淨法音空
無相無作不生不滅無所有之
音。眾生聞之心解得道。時
師子音王佛。初會說法九十
九億人得阿羅漢道。菩薩眾
亦復如是。是諸菩薩一切皆
得無生法忍。入種種法門。
見無量諸佛。恭敬供養能度
無量無數眾生。得無量陀羅
尼門。[16]能得無量種種三
昧。初發心新入道門菩薩不
可稱數。是[17]佛土無量莊嚴
說不可盡。時佛教化已訖。
入無餘涅槃。法住六萬歲。
諸樹法音亦不復出。爾時有
二菩薩比丘。一名喜根二名
勝意。

简体字　　　　　　　　正體字

of the bodhisattvas consists in achieving purification of the mind through contemplating the [true] character of all dharmas as being devoid of either that which binds or that which liberates. This is as illustrated in *The Origins of Mañjuśrī*.

Story: The Bodhisattvas Prasannendriya and Agramati

Mañjuśrī addressed the Buddha, saying, "Greatly Virtuous One, in the past, during the course of my previous lifetimes, innumerable *asaṃkhyeya* kalpas ago, there was at that time a Buddha named Siṃhanādarāja (lit. "King of the Lion's Roar"). The lifespan of that Buddha and the beings in that world was a hundred thousand *koṭīs* of *nayutas* of years. That Buddha employed the teaching of the Three Vehicles in delivering beings to liberation.

The name of that country was "Thousand Rays of Light." The trees in that country were made of the seven kinds of precious things. Those trees emitted innumerable pure sounds of Dharma, sounds proclaiming emptiness, signlessness, wishlessness, neither production nor extinction, and the non-existence of anything whatsoever. When beings heard these sounds, their minds became liberated and they succeeded in bringing the Path to realization.

At that time when the Buddha Siṃhanādarāja proclaimed the Dharma, during the first assembly, ninety-nine *koṭīs* of people gained the path of arhatship. Within the assembly of bodhisattvas, it was the same. All of these bodhisattvas gained the unproduced-dharmas patience They entered into all manner of dharma gateways and saw innumerable buddhas. They paid their respects to them, made offerings to them, and were able to bring countless beings to deliverance. They gained innumerable *dhāraṇī* gateways and became able to realize innumerable samādhis of all different kinds. Those bodhisattvas who had but recently established their resolve and who had newly entered the entrance to the Path were inexpressibly numerous. The innumerable adornments of this buddhaland exhausted the descriptive power of words.

At that time when that buddha had completed his teaching and transformation of beings, he entered upon the nirvāṇa without residue. His Dharma dwelt in the world for sixty thousand years. Eventually, the Dharma sound of those trees ceased to come forth. At that time there were two bodhisattva bhikshus, one of whom was named Prasannendriya (lit. "Joyous Faculty"), and the second of which was named Agramati (lit. "Superior Intellect").

是喜根法师。容仪质直不舍
世法。亦不分别善恶。喜根
弟子聪明乐法好闻深义。其
师不赞少欲知足。不赞戒行
头陀。但说诸法实相清净。
语诸弟子一切诸法婬欲相瞋
恚相愚痴相。此诸法相即是
诸法实相无所罣碍。以是方
便教诸弟子入一相智。时诸
弟子于诸人中无瞋无悔心[18]
不悔故得生忍。得生忍故[19]
则得法忍。于实法中不动如
山。胜意法师持戒清净。行
十二头陀。得四禅四无色
定。胜意诸弟子钝根。多[20]
求分别是净是不净。心即动
转。胜意异时入聚落中。至
喜根弟子家于坐处坐。赞说
持戒少欲知足行头陀[21]行闲
处禅寂。[22]訾毁喜根言。是
人说法教人入邪见中。

简体字

是喜根法師。容儀質直不捨
世法。亦不分別善惡。喜根
弟子聰明樂法好聞深義。其
師不讚少欲知足。不讚戒行
頭陀。但說諸法實相清淨。
語諸弟子一切諸法婬欲相瞋
恚相愚癡相。此諸法相即是
諸法實相無所罣礙。以是方
便教諸弟子入一相智。時諸
弟子於諸人中無瞋無悔心[18]
不悔故得生忍。得生忍故[19]
則得法忍。於實法中不動如
山。勝意法師持戒清淨。行
十二頭陀。得四禪四無色
定。勝意諸弟子鈍根。多[20]
求分別是淨是不淨。心即動
轉。勝意異時入聚落中。至
喜根弟子家於坐處坐。讚說
持戒少欲知足行頭陀[21]行閑
處禪寂。[22]訾毀喜根言。是
人說法教人入邪見中。

正體字

As for this Dharma Master Prasannendriya, in his comportment he was virtuous and in his character he was direct. However, he did not repudiate worldly dharmas, nor did he indulge in making discriminations as to what was good and what was bad. The disciples of Prasannendriya were intelligent, were pleased by Dharma, and were brought to delight through listening to the most abstruse levels of meaning.

Their master did not devote himself to praising the virtues of having but few desires and knowing when enough is enough, nor did he extol the merits of the prohibitions or cultivating the *dhūta* (ascetic) practices. He simply proclaimed that the true character of dharmas is [consistent with] purity. He told his disciples, "All dharmas, even if they are marked by sensual desire, marked by hatefulness, or marked by delusion—the marks of all of these dharmas are identical to the true character of dharmas. There is nothing therein which should serve to hang one up or obstruct one."[4]

He employed this skillful means to instruct his disciples and afford them entry into the "single-mark" wisdom. At that time his disciples came to have no more hatred or resentment with respect to other people. Because their thoughts were free of resentment, they gained the patience with regard to beings. Because they gained the patience with regard to beings, they were then able to realize the patience with regard to dharmas. They dwelt in the dharma of reality, remaining as unmoving as mountains.

The Dharma Master Agramati was pure in his observance of the prohibitions. He cultivated the twelve *dhūta* practices and gained the four dhyāna absorptions as well as the four formless samādhis. The disciples of Agramati were of dull faculties and were much inclined to make discriminations as to this being pure and that being impure. Thus their minds were easily moved and turned about.

There was a time when Agramati went into the town and, having arrived at the house of one of Prasannendriya's disciples, he sat down in the appointed seat and proceeded to extol the observance of the prohibitions, the limitation of desires, the knowing when enough was enough, the cultivating of the *dhūta* practices, and the taking up of dhyāna meditation and the cultivation of stillness in a quiet place. Additionally, he proceeded to disparage Prasannendriya, saying, "When this man speaks Dharma, he instructs people in a way which influences them to enter into erroneous views. He

是说婬欲瞋恚愚痴无所罣碍
相。是杂行人非纯清净。是
弟子利根得法忍。问胜意
言。大德。是婬欲法名何等
相。答言。婬欲是烦恼相。
问[*]言。是婬欲烦恼在内耶
在外耶。答言。是婬欲烦恼
不在内不在外。若在内不应
待外因缘生。若在外于我无
事不应恼我。居士言。若婬
[23]欲非内非外非东西南北
四维上下来。遍求实相不可
得。是法即不生不[24]灭。
若无生灭[25]相。空无所有。
云何能作[26]恼。胜意闻是
语已。其心不悦不能加答。
从座而起说如是言。喜根多
诳众人着邪道中。是胜意菩
萨未学音声陀罗尼。闻佛[27]
所说便欢喜。闻外道语便瞋
恚。闻三不善[28]则不欢[29]
悦。闻三善则大欢喜。闻说
生死则忧[30]闻涅盘则喜。

是說婬欲瞋恚愚癡無所罣礙
相。是雜行人非純清淨。是
弟子利根得法忍。問勝意
言。大德。是婬欲法名何等
相。答言。婬欲是煩惱相。
問[*]言。是婬欲煩惱在內耶
在外耶。答言。是婬欲煩惱
不在內不在外。若在內不應
待外因緣生。若在外於我無
事不應惱我。居士言。若婬
[23]欲非內非外非東西南北
四維上下來。遍求實相不可
得。是法即不生不[24]滅。
若無生滅[25]相。空無所有。
云何能作[26]惱。勝意聞是語
已。其心不悅不能加答。從
座而起說如是言。喜根多誑
眾人著邪道中。是勝意菩薩
未學音聲陀羅尼。聞佛[27]
所說便歡喜。聞外道語便瞋
恚。聞三不善[28]則不歡[29]
悅。聞三善則大歡喜。聞說
生死則憂[30]聞涅槃則喜。

简体字　　　　　　　正體字

speaks of lust, hatred, and delusion as being devoid of any characteristic features which should constitute an impediment. He is a man whose conduct is rather mixed. He is not entirely pure."

This disciple was one possessed of sharp faculties and who had achieved the patience with regard to dharmas. He asked Agramati, "Greatly Virtuous One, by what characteristic does one know this dharma of sensual desire?"

[Agramati] replied, "Sensual desire is characterized by afflictions."

He asked, "Do these desire-associated afflictions reside outwardly or do they reside inwardly?"

[Agramati] responded, "These desire-associated afflictions do not reside inwardly nor do they reside outwardly. If they resided inwardly, then it shouldn't be the case that they rely on outward causes and conditions for their arising. If they resided outwardly, then they should have nothing to do with oneself and should not therefore be able to afflict oneself."

The layperson then declared, "If it is the case that sensual desire does not come from the inside or from the outside or from the east or from the west or from the south or from the north or from any of the four midpoints or from above or below, and if it is the case that one can search everywhere and be entirely unable to find any real aspect in it, this dharma then is neither produced nor destroyed. If it is devoid of any mark of production or extinction, it is empty [of any inherent existence] and thus is entirely devoid of anything whatsoever which exists. How then can it be that it is able to be afflictive?"

After Agramati had listened to this declaration, he was not pleased and was unable to offer a reply. He got up from his seat and said words to this effect: "Prasannendriya has engaged in an extensive deception of many people and has influenced them to take up an erroneous path."

This Agramati Bodhisattva had not yet studied the dhāraṇī of sound. When he heard words which had been spoken by the Buddha, he was delighted. When he heard the doctrines of other paths, he was filled with aversion. When he heard of the three roots of unwholesomeness, then he would be displeased. When he heard of the three roots of wholesomeness, then he would be greatly delighted. When he heard of birth and death, then he would become worried. When he heard of nirvāṇa, then he would be happy.

从居士家至林树间入精舍
中。语诸比丘。当知。喜根
菩萨[31]是人虚诳多令人入恶
邪中。何以故。其言婬恚痴
相。及一切诸法皆[32]无碍
相。是时喜根作是念。此人
大瞋为恶业所覆当堕大罪。
我今当为说甚深[33]法。虽
今无所得。为作后世佛道因
缘。是时喜根集僧。[34]一心
说偈。

婬欲即是道　　恚痴亦如是。
如此三事中　　无量诸佛道。
若有人分别　　婬怒痴及道。
是人去佛远　　譬如天与地。
道及婬怒痴　　是一法平等。
若人闻怖畏　　去佛道甚远。
婬法不生灭　　不能令心恼。
若人计吾我　　婬将入恶道。
见有无法异　　是不离有无。
若知有无等　　超胜成佛道。

[0108a02] 说如是等七十馀偈。
时三万诸天子得无生法忍。
万八千声闻人。不着一切法
故。皆得解脱。是时胜意菩
萨。身[1]即陷入地狱[2]受

從居士家至林樹間入精舍
中。語諸比丘。當知。喜根
菩薩[31]是人虛誑多令人入惡
邪中。何以故。其言婬恚癡
相。及一切諸法皆[32]無礙
相。是時喜根作是念。此人
大瞋為惡業所覆當墮大罪。
我今當為說甚深[33]法。雖
今無所得。為作後世佛道因
緣。是時喜根集僧。[34]一心
說偈。

婬欲即是道　　恚癡亦如是。
如此三事中　　無量諸佛道。
若有人分別　　婬怒癡及道。
是人去佛遠　　譬如天與地。
道及婬怒癡　　是一法平等。
若人聞怖畏　　去佛道甚遠。
婬法不生滅　　不能令心惱。
若人計吾我　　婬將入惡道。
見有無法異　　是不離有無。
若知有無等　　超勝成佛道。

[0108a02] 說如是等七十餘偈。
時三萬諸天子得無生法忍。
萬八千聲聞人。不著一切法
故。皆得解脫。是時勝意菩
薩。身[1]即陷入地獄[2]受

简体字　　　　　　　　　　　正體字

[Agramati] departed from that layperson's house, went to the forest, entered the monastery, and announced to the Bhikshus, "You should all be aware that this Prasannendriya Bodhisattva has engaged in deceptions whereby he has extensively influenced people to engage in the unwholesome and the improper. How is this so? He has said, 'As for the characteristics of lust, anger and delusion as well as those of all other dharmas—they are all characterized by mutual non-obstruction.'"

At this time Prasannendriya thought, "This man is extremely hateful, is covered over by unwholesome karma, and is going to fall into committing a grave offense. I should now speak the most profound Dharma. Although he will gain nothing from it now, still, it will constitute for him a cause and condition for the path of buddhahood in a future age. Then Prasennendriya called an assembly of the Sangha and single-mindedly uttered a verse:

> One's sensual desire's identical with the Path.
> And so it is with hate and delusion.
> In just this way, amidst these three,
> One finds the Path of innumerable buddhas.

> So if a man discriminates
> 'Twixt lust and hate, delusion and Path,
> This man strays far away from Buddha,
> Just as heaven's far from earth.

> The Path, lust, hatred, and delusion
> Are all one dharma, all the same.
> Should one who hears this cringe in fear,
> He's far away from Buddha's Path.

> The dharma of lust's not born or destroyed,
> And cannot cause the mind affliction,
> But if one has a view of self,
> This lust leads forth to the wretched destinies.[5]

> Seeing dharmas of existence and nonexistence as different,
> One can't leave existence or nonexistence.
> But knowing existence and nonexistence as same,
> Transcending supremely, one achieves Buddha's Path.

[Prasannendriya] spoke more than seventy verses of this sort. At that time thirty thousand gods gained the unproduced-dharmas patience. Eighteen thousand Śrāvaka Disciples, because they did not cling to any dharmas, achieved liberation. At that time Agramati Bodhisattva fell into the hells where he underwent sufferings for

无量[3]千万亿岁[4]苦。出生
人中七十四万世常被诽谤。
无量劫中不闻佛名。是罪渐
薄得闻佛法。出家为道而复
舍戒。如是六万[5]三千世常
舍戒。无量世中作沙门。虽
不舍戒诸根暗钝。是喜根菩
萨于今东方。过十万亿佛
土作佛。其[6]土号宝严。佛
号光逾日明王。[7]文殊师利
[8]言。尔时胜意比丘我身是
也。我观尔时受是无量苦。
文殊师利[9]复白佛。若有人
求三乘道。不欲受诸苦者。
不应破诸法相而怀瞋恚。佛
问文殊师利。汝闻诸偈得何
等利。答[10]曰。我闻此偈得
毕众苦。世世得利根智慧。
能解深法巧说[11]深义。于
诸菩萨中最为第一。如是等
名巧说诸法相。是名如实巧
度。

無量[3]千萬億歲[4]苦。出生
人中七十四萬世常被誹謗。
無量劫中不聞佛名。是罪漸
薄得聞佛法。出家為道而復
捨戒。如是六萬[5]三千世常
捨戒。無量世中作沙門。雖
不捨戒諸根闇鈍。是喜根菩
薩於今東方。過十萬億佛
土作佛。其[6]土號寶嚴。佛
號光踰日明王。[7]文殊師利
[8]言。爾時勝意比丘我身是
也。我觀爾時受是無量苦。
文殊師利[9]復白佛。若有人
求三乘道。不欲受諸苦者。
不應破諸法相而懷瞋恚。佛
問文殊師利。汝聞諸偈得何
等利。答[10]曰。我聞此偈得
畢眾苦。世世得利根智慧。
能解深法巧說[11]深義。於
諸菩薩中最為第一。如是等
名巧說諸法相。是名如實巧
度。

简体字   正體字

an immeasurable period of ten million *koṭīs* of years. When he came out again and was born among men, for seven hundred and forty thousand existences, he was always slandered. He did not even hear the word "buddha" for an innumerable number of kalpas thereafter.

When [the karmic burden of] these offenses gradually became lighter he was able to hear the Buddha's Dharma. He then became able to leave the home life and become a monk for the sake of the Path, but, [even then], he relinquished the precepts (i.e. returned to lay life). In this manner, for sixty-three thousand existences, he always relinquished the precepts. Then, for an innumerable number of existences he was able to remain a *śramaṇa* but, although he no longer relinquished the precepts, his faculties remained dark and dull.

This Prasannendriya Bodhisattva is now a buddha far away to the east, one hundred thousand *koṭīs* of buddhalands away. His land is known as "Jeweled Adornment" and his buddha name is "Sun-Surpassing Brilliance King" (Sūryālokasamatikrāntarāja).

Mañjuśrī said, "At that time that bhikshu Agramati was myself. I observe that for just such a period of time I endured this immeasurable amount of suffering."

Mañjuśrī again addressed the Buddha, saying, "If there be a man who seeks the path of the Three Vehicles and who doesn't wish to undergo all manner of suffering, he should not [attempt to] discredit the [true] character of dharmas, cherishing hatefulness in doing so."

The Buddha asked Mañjuśrī, "What benefits did you gain from listening to those verses?"

He replied, "When I heard these verses, [they served as the causal basis for] my achieving the ending of the multitude of sufferings such that [eventually], in life after life, I gained sharp faculties and wisdom. I became able to understand the profound Dharma and became able to skillfully expound the profound meaning. I became foremost among the bodhisattvas in this regard."

Nāgārjuna's Concluding Comments

Examples such as these illustrate what is meant by "skillful explanation of the [true] character of dharmas." This is what is meant by "They were skillful in bringing about deliverance in accordance with reality."

Notes

1. The Sutra refers here to the bodhisattvas in attendance upon the Buddha when he delivered these teachings on the perfection of wisdom.

2. Transliteration per Lamotte.

3. This refers to twelve beneficial ascetic practices specifically recommended by the Buddha. They are to be distinguished from the *non*-beneficial ascetic practices specifically discouraged by the Buddha. The former include such practices as always sitting in meditation (i.e. never lying down), limiting one's indulgence in food to a single meal each day, limiting one's clothing to a single set of robes, dwelling in a quiet place distant from the hustle and bustle of civilization, etc.

4. For those unfamiliar with this teaching, it may be worth noting that it is not intended to endorse coursing in desire, hatefulness, or delusion. Its intention is simply to diminish fixed mental attachments by countering a tendency to make polarizing discriminations constituting obstacles to liberation. The teaching *does* presume an already clear awareness of the need to eliminate the three poisons from one's thoughts, words and actions.

5. The obvious conclusion from considering the flip-side of "But if one has a view of self, this lust leads forth to the wretched destinies," is that, since only the Āryas have transcended a view of self, failure to carefully observe the moral virtue precepts regarding sexual misconduct is virtually certain to lead to present and future suffering. One might think of this stanza as Prasannendriya's "warning label" on his very profound and very transcendent teaching.

如是诸烦恼。菩萨能种种方便自断。亦能巧方便断他人诸[11]烦恼。如佛在时三人。为伯仲[12]季。闻毘耶离国婬女人。名菴罗婆利。舍[13]婆提有婬女人。名须[14]曼那。王舍城婬女人。名优钵罗盘那。有三人各各闻人赞三女人端正无比。昼夜专念心着不舍。便于梦中梦与从事。觉已心念。彼女不[15]来我亦不往而婬事得办。因是而悟。一切诸法皆如是耶。于是往到颰陀婆罗菩萨所问是事。颰陀婆罗答言。诸法实尔。皆从念生。如是种种。为此三人方便巧说诸法空。是时三人即得阿鞞跋致。是诸菩萨亦复如是。为诸众生种种巧说法。断诸见缠烦恼。是名能断种种见缠及诸烦恼。

简体字

正體字

Three Brothers Become Enlightened

The Bodhisattva is able to employ all manner of skillful means to personally cut off all of these kinds of afflictions[1] and is also able to employ clever skillful means to bring about the cutting off of other people's afflictions. For example, when the Buddha was in the world, there were three men, an elder brother, second brother, and youngest brother who had heard that there was a courtesan in Vaiśālī named Āmrapālī, a courtesan in Śrāvastī named Sumanā, and a courtesan in Rājagṛha named Utpalavarṇā.

Each of the three men had heard people extol these three women as being incomparably lovely, so much so that, day and night, they were obsessed, could not put those women out of their thoughts, and then, in their dreams, dreamt that they had an affair with them. Upon awakening, they thought, "These women did not come to us, nor did we go to see them, and yet a sexual encounter was consummated." Because of this they experienced an awakening and wondered, "Could it be that all dharmas like this?" At this time they went to see the Bodhisattva Bhadrapāla to inquire about this matter.

Bhadrapāla replied, "Actually, all dharmas are precisely like this. In every case, they arise from thought." He continued to bring forth many instances like this and, for the benefit of these three men, employed skillful means whereby he cleverly explained the emptiness of all dharmas. At this time, these three men straightaway achieved the stage of the *avaivartika* (irreversibility).

Nāgārjuna's Concluding Comments

All of these bodhisattvas are like this. In all manner of ways, they cleverly explain dharma for the benefit of beings, influencing them to cut off all manner of views, entanglements and afflictions. This is what is meant when it is said, "They were able to cut off all views and entanglements as well as all afflictions."

Notes

1. This story occurs as commentary on the passage which reads, "They (the bodhisattvas) were able to cut off all kinds of views and entanglements as well as all afflictions."

问曰。恒河中沙为有几许。
答曰。一切算数所不能知。
唯有佛及法身菩萨能知其
数。佛及法身菩萨。一切阎
浮提中。微尘生灭多少皆能
数知。何况恒河沙。如佛在
只桓外林中树下坐。有一婆
罗门来到佛所。问佛。此树
林有几叶。佛即时便答有若
干数。婆罗门心疑谁证知
者。婆罗门去至一树边。取
一树上少叶藏。还问佛。此
树林定有几叶。即答今少若
干叶。如其所取语之。婆罗
门知已心大敬信。求佛出家
后得阿罗汉道。以是故知。
佛能知恒河沙数。

問曰。恒河中沙為有幾許。
答曰。一切算數所不能知。
唯有佛及法身菩薩能知其
數。佛及法身菩薩。一切閻
浮提中。微塵生滅多少皆能
數知。何況恒河沙。如佛在
祇桓外林中樹下坐。有一婆
羅門來到佛所。問佛。此樹
林有幾葉。佛即時便答有若
干數。婆羅門心疑誰證知
者。婆羅門去至一樹邊。取
一樹上少葉藏。還問佛。此
樹林定有幾葉。即答今少若
干葉。如其所取語之。婆羅
門知已心大敬信。求佛出家
後得阿羅漢道。以是故知。
佛能知恒河沙數。

简体字

正體字

The Buddha's Omniscience Converts a Brahman

Question: How many grains of sand are there in the Ganges River?[1]

Response: Their number is so great that it is unknowable by any numerical categories. Only the Buddhas and Dharma-body bodhisattvas are capable of knowing their number. Buddhas and Dharma-body bodhisattvas are even able to calculate how many atoms are arising and perishing throughout all of the continent of Jambudvīpa, how much the more so are they able to know the number of sands in the Ganges.

For example, once, when the Buddha was sitting beneath a tree in the forest beyond the Jeta Grove, a brahman arrived where the Buddha was and asked of the Buddha, "How many leaves are there on the trees of this forest?"

The Buddha immediately replied, stating a particular number of leaves. The Brahman thought doubtfully to himself, "Who would be able to corroborate this?" Then the Brahman went over to a tree and, removing a number of leaves, stashed them away and then returned to the Buddha, asking, "Precisely how many leaves are there in the forest, now?"

The Buddha then immediately replied that now the number of leaves had been reduced by a certain number, noting precisely the number of leaves which had been removed. When the Brahman realized this, his mind became filled with reverence and faith. He requested that the Buddha allow him to become a monk, after which he gained the path of the Arhat. We can know from this that the Buddha can know the number of sands in the Ganges.

Notes

1. The number of sands in the Ganges was commonly used by the Buddha in representing inconceivably large numbers. The question here is in response to such an instance.

[0115a04]　[*]【经】尔时世尊出广长舌相。遍覆三千大千世界。[3]熙怡[4]而笑。从其舌根出无量千万亿[5]光是一一光化成千叶金色宝华。是诸华上皆有化佛结[6]加趺坐。说六波罗蜜。众生闻者必得阿耨多罗三藐三菩提。复至十方如恒河沙等诸佛世界皆亦如是。

[0115a09]　[*]【论】问曰。如佛世尊大德尊重。何以故。出广长舌[7]似如轻相。答曰。上三种放光。照十方[8]众生令得度脱。今欲口说摩诃般若波罗蜜。摩诃般若波罗蜜甚深难解难知难可信受。是故出广长舌为证。舌相如是语必真实。如昔一时佛于舍[9]婆提国受岁竟。阿难从佛游行诸国。欲到婆罗门城。婆罗门城王。知佛神德能化众[10]人感动群心。今来到此谁复乐我便作

简体字

[0115a04]　[*]【經】爾時世尊出廣長舌相。遍覆三千大千世界。[3]熙怡[4]而笑。從其舌根出無量千萬億[5]光是一一光化成千葉金色寶華。是諸華上皆有化佛結[6]加趺坐。說六波羅蜜。眾生聞者必得阿耨多羅三藐三菩提。復至十方如恒河沙等諸佛世界皆亦如是。

[0115a09]　[*]【論】問曰。如佛世尊大德尊重。何以故。出廣長舌[7]似如輕相。答曰。上三種放光。照十方[8]眾生令得度脫。今欲口說摩訶般若波羅蜜。摩訶般若波羅蜜甚深難解難知難可信受。是故出廣長舌為證。舌相如是語必真實。如昔一時佛於舍[9]婆提國受歲竟。阿難從佛遊行諸國。欲到婆羅門城。婆羅門城王。知佛神德能化眾[10]人感動群心。今來到此誰復樂我便作

正體字

The Buddha, the Servant, and the Doubting Brahman

Nāgārjuna's Preamble: Why the Buddha Shows His Tongue

Sutra:

At that time the Bhagavān put forth his characteristically broad and long tongue, extending it so that it entirely covered the great trichiliocosm and then he smiled happily. From the root of his tongue he sent forth innumerable tens of millions of *koṭīs* of light rays. Each of these light rays transformed into a thousand-petalled golden-colored lotus blossom. Atop each of these blossoms, there sat a transformation buddha who had assumed the full-lotus posture and who was proclaiming the six pāramitās. Those beings who heard this became certain thereby to realize *anuttarasamyaksaṃbodhi*. Likewise, this [supernatural transformation] extended in the same manner to reach a Ganges-sands' number of buddhalands throughout the ten directions.

Exegesis:

Question: How is it that one of such great virtue, venerability and solemnity as the Buddha, the Bhagavān, would stick out his broad, long tongue? It seems rather like a mark of contemptuousness.

Response: In the above three instances of emitting light, the illumination reached to beings throughout the ten directions and caused them to gain liberation. Now, [the Buddha] wishes to speak the *mahāprajñāpāramitā*. The *mahāprajñāpāramitā* is extremely profound, difficult to understand, difficult to comprehend, and difficult to believe in and accept. For this reason, [the Buddha] extended his broad and long tongue as a form of certification [of believability]. Where one possesses a tongue with characteristics such as this, one's words are necessarily truthful.

Story: The Buddha, the Servant, and the Doubting Brahman

As an example, once, some time ago, when the Buddha had concluded the rains retreat in Śrāvastī, Ānanda followed the Buddha in traveling about from state to state. They were about to arrive at a particular brahman city. It happened that the king of that city was well aware of the Buddha's spiritual virtues, and that he was able to convert multitudes of people and influence the minds of the masses. [That king thought], "If now [the Buddha] comes here, who would find any further satisfaction with me?" He then issued

制限若有与佛食听佛语者。
输五百金钱。作制限后佛到
其国。将阿难持钵入城乞
食。城中众人皆闭门不应。
佛空钵而出。是时一家有一
老使人。持破瓦器盛臭[11]
［泳-永+(米*番)］淀出门弃
之。见佛世尊空钵而来。老
使人见佛相好金色白[12]毛
肉髻丈光钵空无食。见已思
惟。如此神人应食天厨。今
自降身持钵行乞。必是大慈
愍一切故。信心清净欲好供
养无由如愿。惭愧白佛。思
欲设供更不能得。今此弊食
佛须者可取。佛知其心信敬
清净。伸手以钵受其施食。
佛时即笑出五色光普照天
地。还从眉间相入。阿难合
掌长跪白佛。唯然世尊。今
笑因缘愿闻其意。

[0115b03]　佛告阿难。汝见老
女人信心施佛食不。阿难言
见。

制限若有與佛食聽佛語者。
輸五百金錢。作制限後佛到
其國。將阿難持鉢入城乞
食。城中眾人皆閉門不應。
佛空鉢而出。是時一家有一
老使人。持破瓦器盛臭[11]
［泳-永+(米*番)］淀出門棄
之。見佛世尊空鉢而來。老
使人見佛相好金色白[12]毛
肉髻丈光鉢空無食。見已思
惟。如此神人應食天廚。今
自降身持鉢行乞。必是大慈
愍一切故。信心清淨欲好供
養無由如願。慚愧白佛。思
欲設供更不能得。今此弊食
佛須者可取。佛知其心信敬
清淨。伸手以鉢受其施食。
佛時即笑出五色光普照天
地。還從眉間相入。阿難合
掌長跪白佛。唯然世尊。今
笑因緣願聞其意。

[0115b03]　佛告阿難。汝見老
女人信心施佛食不。阿難言
見。

简体字　　　　　　　正體字

a restrictive decree: "Whosoever donates food to the Buddha or listens to the words of the Buddha is thereby bound to pay a levy of five hundred gold pieces."

Having arrived in that jurisdiction after the restrictive decree had been laid down, the Buddha led Ānanda into the city to collect alms, the two of them proceeding with alms bowls in hand. The people of the city had all shut their doors and did not respond, whereupon the Buddha departed with his bowl still empty.

At that time one household's old servant came out the door carrying a cracked clay bowl brimming with spoiled gruel, intending to dispose of it. She noticed the Buddha, the Bhagavān, coming along with an empty bowl. The old servant observed the Buddha's major physical marks and his minor characteristics, his golden color, the white hair mark [between his eyebrows], the cowl [on the crown of his head], his ten-foot halo, his empty bowl, and realized that he had no food.

When she had seen this, she thought, "A person of such spiritual stature as this deserves to dine on the fare of the celestial kitchens. That he now voluntarily condescends to allow his body to appear carrying an alms bowl and walking along on alms rounds is certainly on account of his great loving-kindness and compassion for everyone." Her thoughts of faith were pure and, although she desired to present a fine offering to him, she had no means to accord with her wish. Feeling much abashed, she addressed the Buddha, saying, "Although I wish I could provide a suitable offering, I am unable to obtain anything more than this. If the Buddha has need of this lowly fare, he may take it."

The Buddha was aware that her thoughts were imbued with a pure faith and reverence and so extended his hand and accepted with his alms bowl the food which she had given. The Buddha thereupon smiled and emitted five-colored rays of light which everywhere illumined heaven and earth and then returned, entering through that characteristic feature on his brow.

Ānanda placed his palms together, knelt, and addressed the Buddha, "Pray, may the Bhagavān consent to explain the causes and conditions whereby he now smiles. I wish to hear his reasons."

The Buddha asked Ānanda, "Did you or did you not notice that this elderly woman, with a mind imbued with faith, made an offering of food to the Buddha?"

Ānanda said, "I did see that."

佛言。是老女人施佛食故。
十五劫中天上人间受福快乐
不堕恶道。后得男子身出家
学道。成辟支佛入无馀涅
盘。尔时佛边有一婆罗门。
立说[13]偈言。
汝是日种刹利姓。
净饭国王之太子。
而以食故大妄语。
如此臭食报何重。
[0115b10] 是时佛出广长舌覆面
上至发际。语婆罗门言。汝
见经书。颇有如此舌人而作
妄语不。婆罗门言。若人舌
能覆鼻言无虚妄。何况乃至
发际。我心信佛必不妄语。
不解小施报多如是。佛告婆
罗门。汝颇曾见世所希有难
见事不。婆罗门言见。我曾
共婆罗门道中行。见一尼拘
卢陀树荫覆贾客五百乘车。
荫犹不尽。是谓希有难见事
也。佛言。此树种子其形大
小。答言。大如芥子三分之
一。佛言。谁当信汝言者。
树大乃尔而种子[14]甚小。婆
罗门言。实尔世尊。我眼见
之

简体字

佛言。是老女人施佛食故。
十五劫中天上人間受福快樂
不墮惡道。後得男子身出家
學道。成辟支佛入無餘涅
槃。爾時佛邊有一婆羅門。
立說[13]偈言。
汝是日種刹利姓。
淨飯國王之太子。
而以食故大妄語。
如此臭食報何重。
[0115b10] 是時佛出廣長舌覆面
上至髮際。語婆羅門言。汝
見經書。頗有如此舌人而作
妄語不。婆羅門言。若人舌
能覆鼻言無虛妄。何況乃至
髮際。我心信佛必不妄語。
不解小施報多如是。佛告婆
羅門。汝頗曾見世所希有難
見事不。婆羅門言見。我曾
共婆羅門道中行。見一尼拘
盧陀樹蔭覆賈客五百乘車。
蔭猶不盡。是謂希有難見事
也。佛言。此樹種子其形大
小。答言。大如芥子三分之
一。佛言。誰當信汝言者。
樹大乃爾而種子[14]甚小。婆
羅門言。實爾世尊。我眼見
之

正體字

The Buddha said, "Because this elderly woman made an offering of food to the Buddha, she shall enjoy a period of fifteen kalpas in the heavens and among people wherein she shall be the recipient of blessings and bliss and shall not fall into the wretched destinies. Thereafter, she shall be reborn as a man, shall leave behind the home life, shall study the Path, shall realize pratyekabuddhahood, and shall enter the nirvāṇa without residue.

At that time there was a brahman standing close to the Buddha who then uttered a verse, saying:

> You Sir are [a scion] of the *kṣatriyan* Solar Clan
> And a prince of the house of the Pure Rice King,
> And yet, to gain food, you now tell a great lie.
> As reward for what crime do you reap such rank fare?

At that time the Buddha extended his broad and long tongue until it covered his face up to his hairline. He then asked the brahman, "In your perusal of the classical teachings, have you or have you not found any indication that a person could have a tongue like this and yet still tell a lie?"

The brahman replied, "If a person's tongue is capable of covering the nose alone, then there will be no falseness in his words, how much the less [could there be any false speech] in an instance where it can reach up to the hairline. Although, I now believe that the Buddha definitely does not speak falsely, still, I do not understand how such a small offering could have a retribution so great as this."

The Buddha asked the brahman, "Have you or have you not ever seen anything in this world which only rarely occurs and which is only seldom seen?"

The brahman replied, "I have indeed seen such a thing. I once was traveling on the road with other brahmans when I saw a single *nyagrodha* tree the shadow of which was still not used up even when shading a caravan of five hundred merchant wagons. This was a phenomenon which occurs but rarely and which is but rarely encountered."

The Buddha asked, "Is the seed of that tree large or is it small?"

He replied, "It is but one third the size of a mustard seed."

The Buddha asked, "But who could believe you when you say that there is a tree of such great size but which has a seed so extremely small?"

The brahman replied, "It is actually so, Bhagavān. I have seen it

非虛妄也。佛言。我亦如
是。见老女人净[15]信心施[16]
佛得大果报亦如此。树因少
报多。又是如来福田良美之
所致也。婆罗门心开意解。
五体投地悔过向佛。我心无
[17]状愚不信佛。佛为种种说
法。得初道果。即时举手大
发声言。一切众人甘露门开
如何不出。城中一切诸婆罗
门。皆送五百金钱。与王迎
佛供养。皆言得甘露味。谁
当惜此五百金钱。众人皆去
制限法破。是婆罗门王。亦
共臣民归命佛法。[18]城人一
切皆得净信。如是佛出广长
舌相。为不信者故。

非虛妄也。佛言。我亦如
是。見老女人淨[15]信心施[16]
佛得大果報亦如此。樹因少
報多。又是如來福田良美之
所致也。婆羅門心開意解。
五體投地悔過向佛。我心無
[17]狀愚不信佛。佛為種種說
法。得初道果。即時舉手大
發聲言。一切眾人甘露門開
如何不出。城中一切諸婆羅
門。皆送五百金錢。與王迎
佛供養。皆言得甘露味。誰
當惜此五百金錢。眾人皆去
制限法破。是婆羅門王。亦
共臣民歸命佛法。[18]城人一
切皆得淨信。如是佛出廣長
舌相。為不信者故。

简体字　　　　　　　　正體字

with my own eyes. This is not a falsehood."

The Buddha said, "So too it is that I have seen that this elderly woman by making a faithful offering to the Buddha thereby gains such a grand resultant retribution. It is just like the tree where the cause is minor but the effect is great and is a result brought about by the Tathāgata's magnificent field of merit.

The brahman's mind opened up and he understood. He made a full reverential prostration, casting the five parts of his body down to the ground and repenting of his error before the Buddha, saying, "My thoughts have been uncivil and thus I have stupidly failed to believe in the Buddha."

The Buddha spoke Dharma for him in various ways where-upon he gained the initial fruit of the Path (first-stage arhatship). He immediately raised his arm into the air and cried out loudly, "Everyone! The gate of sweet-dew ambrosia has been thrown open! Why don't you all come out?!"

Each of the brahmans in the city then remitted five hundred gold pieces to the king. They welcomed the Buddha and made offerings to him. They all exclaimed, "We have gained the flavor of sweet dew. Who would want to be sparing of five hundred gold pieces?" Then everyone came out, whereupon the restrictive decree became entirely unenforceable. This brahman king himself, together with his ministers and subjects, took refuge in the Buddha and the Dharma. All of the people of the city developed a pure faith. In just this fashion, the Buddha extended his characteristically broad and long tongue for the sake of those who did not yet believe.

如说南天竺国中有法师。高坐说五戒义。是众中多有外道来听。是时国王难曰。若如所说。有人施酒及自饮酒得[4]狂愚报。当今世人应狂者多正者少。而今狂者更少不狂者多。何以故尔。是时诸外道辈言善哉。斯难甚深。是秃高坐必不能答。以王利智故。是时法师以指指诸外道。而更说馀事。王时即解。诸外道语王言。王难甚深是不知答。耻所不知而但举指更说馀事。王语外道。高坐法师指答[5]已讫。将护汝故不以言说。向者指汝言。汝等是狂狂不少也。汝等以灰涂身裸形无耻。以人髑髅盛粪而食。拔头发卧刺上倒悬熏鼻。冬则入水夏则火炙。如是种种所行非道皆是狂相。

简体字

如說南天竺國中有法師。高坐說五戒義。是眾中多有外道來聽。是時國王難曰。若如所說。有人施酒及自飲酒得[4]狂愚報。當今世人應狂者多正者少。而今狂者更少不狂者多。何以故爾。是時諸外道輩言善哉。斯難甚深。是禿高坐必不能答。以王利智故。是時法師以指指諸外道。而更說餘事。王時即解。諸外道語王言。王難甚深是不知答。恥所不知而但舉指更說餘事。王語外道。高坐法師指答[5]已訖。將護汝故不以言說。向者指汝言。汝等是狂狂不少也。汝等以灰塗身裸形無恥。以人髑髏盛糞而食。拔頭髮臥刺上倒懸熏鼻。冬則入水夏則火炙。如是種種所行非道皆是狂相。

正體字

The Monk, the King and the Naked Ascetics

Once, in South India, there was a Dharma Master who was holding forth from the high seat on the meaning of the five moral virtue precepts. Within the Assembly, there were many followers of non-Buddhist paths who had come to listen. It happened that at this time the King himself challenged [the monk] with a difficult question, saying, "If it's really as you claim, then those who serve liquor to others as well as those who drink it themselves bring down upon themselves the retribution of being 'crazy' and dull-minded. [If that were so], then it ought to be the case that in this present age those who are crazy are in the majority whereas those who are normal are in the minority. However, those who are now crazy are very few, whereas those who are not crazy are the more numerous. Why is this the case?"

At this time, those followers of other paths [who had come to listen] chorused their approval, "Ah, good indeed! This difficulty is quite a profound one. On account of the King's incisive wisdom, this bald pate fellow in the high seat will definitely be unable to reply."

At that time the Dharma Master responded by simply raising his arm and pointing to those followers of non-Buddhist paths, whereupon he proceeded to discourse on an entirely different topic. Then the King immediately understood. But those followers of other paths reacted by exclaiming to the King, "The King's difficult question was extremely profound and this fellow didn't know any way to respond to it. He was embarrassed by knowing no answer and so just stuck up his finger and then changed the subject."

The King then addressed those followers of non-Buddhist paths, "The Dharma Master on the high seat gave his answer by pointing. Because he wished to spare all of you the embarrassment, he chose not to reply with words. He was pointing in your direction and indicating thereby that all of you are crazy, and that therefore the crazy ones are not in the minority.

"You all smear your bodies with ashes, go around naked and shameless, fill skulls with excrement which you then eat, pull out your hair, lie down on thorns, suspend your bodies upside down, subject your noses to smoke, plunge into the water in the winter, and then roast yourselves before a fire in the summer. All such things as these which you practice are contrary to the Path and are indications of mental derangement.

复次汝等法以卖肉卖盐即时失婆罗门法。于天祠中得牛布施。即时卖之自言得法。牛则是肉。是诳惑人岂非失耶。又言入吉河水中罪垢皆除。是为罪福无因无缘。卖肉卖盐此有何罪。入吉河水中言能除罪。若能除罪亦能除福。谁有吉者。[6]如此诸事无因无缘。强为因缘。是则为狂。如是种种狂相。皆是汝等法师将护汝故指而不说。

復次汝等法以賣肉賣鹽即時失婆羅門法。於天祠中得牛布施。即時賣之自言得法。牛則是肉。是誑惑人豈非失耶。又言入吉河水中罪垢皆除。是為罪福無因無緣。賣肉賣鹽此有何罪。入吉河水中言能除罪。若能除罪亦能除福。誰有吉者。[6]如此諸事無因無緣。強為因緣。是則為狂。如是種種狂相。皆是汝等法師將護汝故指而不說。

简体字 正體字

"Moreover, the practice which you all engage in of peddling meat and salt constitutes a direct miscarriage of brahmanical dharma. During the ceremonial offerings to the heavens, you receive cattle as donations and then immediately turn around and sell them off and yet say of yourselves that you are in accord with the Dharma. These cattle are [sold with the knowledge that they will be slaughtered and consumed as] meat. How could deceiving people in this way be anything but a transgression?

"What's more, you say that when one goes into the auspicious river, the filth of one's offenses is all gotten rid of. This amounts to claiming that there are no causal factors inherent in committing karmic offenses or engaging in meritorious deeds. What a crime it is to deal in beef and profiteer in salt! As for claiming that by going into the auspicious river one can get rid of one's offenses—if one is able to get rid of one's offenses that way, then one is also able to get rid of one's merit in that same way. Wherein does this auspiciousness lie?

"All such [supposedly efficacious] practices as these are devoid of [valid] causal factors and yet, by forced interpretation, you claim that these represent [effectual] causes and conditions. This all amounts to mental derangement. All such different indications of mental derangement apply to you. Because the Dharma Master wished to spare you embarrassment, he simply pointed at you and refrained from discussing the matter."

问曰。饥者得饱渴者得饮。
云何饥渴。答曰。福德薄
故。先世无因今世无缘。是
故饥渴。复次是人先世夺佛
阿罗汉辟支佛食及父母所亲
食。虽值佛世犹故饥渴。以
罪重故。问曰。今有恶世生
人得好饮食。值佛世生而更
饥渴。若罪人不应生值佛
世。若福人不应生恶世。何
以故尔。答曰。业报因缘各
各不同。或有人有见佛因
缘。无饮食因缘。或有饮食
因缘。无见佛因缘。譬如黑
蛇。而抱摩尼珠卧。有阿罗
汉人乞食不得。又如迦叶佛
时。有兄弟二人出家求

問曰。飢者得飽渴者得飲。
云何飢渴。答曰。福德薄
故。先世無因今世無緣。是
故飢渴。復次是人先世奪佛
阿羅漢辟支佛食及父母所親
食。雖值佛世猶故飢渴。以
罪重故。問曰。今有惡世生
人得好飲食。值佛世生而更
飢渴。若罪人不應生值佛
世。若福人不應生惡世。何
以故爾。答曰。業報因緣各
各不同。或有人有見佛因
緣。無飲食因緣。或有飲食
因緣。無見佛因緣。譬如黑
蛇。而抱摩尼珠臥。有阿羅
漢人乞食不得。又如迦葉佛
時。有兄弟二人出家求

简体字　　　　　　正體字

The Arhat, the Elephant, and Causality

Nāgārjuna's Preamble: On Causality

Question: As for [the Sutra's statement], "The hungry became satisfied and the thirsty were able to drink," what causal factors bring about hunger and thirst?

Response: They arise on account of a scarcity of merit . There is an absence of conducive causes originating in previous lives and an absence of conducive conditions in this present life. It is on account of this that one becomes afflicted with hunger and thirst. Then again, it may be that in previous lives this individual stole the food of buddhas, arhats, or pratyekabuddhas or else stole food which was reserved for the personal consumption by one's parents. Now, although one may take birth in an era where one might encounter the Buddha, still, on account of the gravity of one's offenses, he will continue to be afflicted by hunger and thirst.

Question: Nowadays we have people who, although they have taken birth in an evil age, they are still able to enjoy fine food and drink. There have also been individuals who have taken birth in an era where they could encounter the Buddha, but who have nonetheless been especially afflicted with hunger and thirst. If one is a person who has committed offenses, it should not be that one can take birth in an era where he might encounter the Buddha. If one is a person possessed of karmic blessings, it should not be that he could be born into an evil age. How is it that these circumstances could occur?

Response: The causes and conditions associated with each individual person's karmic retribution are different. Some people possess the causes and conditions for being able to see the Buddha but lack the causes and conditions requisite to adequacy in food and drink. Others possess the causes and conditions requisite to adequacy in food and drink but lack the causes and conditions for being able to see the Buddha. The situation of these latter individuals is analogous to that of a black snake who lies curled up around a [wish-granting] *mani* pearl. There are even cases of people who, although they have realized arhatship, are nonetheless still unable to be successful in searching for alms food.

Story: The Arhat, the Elephant, and Causality

We have in addition an illustrative case of two brothers who, at the time of Kāśyapa Buddha, left home [to become monks] in search

道。一人持戒诵经坐禅。一
人广求檀越修诸福业。至释
迦文佛出世。一人生长者
家。一人作大白象。力能破
贼。长者子出家学道。得六
神通阿罗汉。而以薄福乞食
难得。他日持钵入城乞食遍
不能得。到白象厩[8]中。见
王供象种种豐足。语此象
言。我之与汝俱有罪过。象
[9]即感结三日不食。守象人
怖求觅道人。见而问言。汝
作何[10]呪令王白象病不能
食。答言。此象是我先身时
弟。共于迦叶佛时出家学
道。我但持戒诵经坐禅不行
布施。弟但广求檀越作诸布
施。不持戒不学问。以其不
持戒诵经坐禅故今作此象。
大修布施故饮食备具种种豐
足。我但行道不修布施故。
今虽得道乞食不能得。

道。一人持戒誦經坐禪。一
人廣求檀越修諸福業。至釋
迦文佛出世。一人生長者
家。一人作大白象。力能破
賊。長者子出家學道。得六
神通阿羅漢。而以薄福乞食
難得。他日持鉢入城乞食遍
不能得。到白象厩[8]中。見
王供象種種豐足。語此象
言。我之與汝俱有罪過。象
[9]即感結三日不食。守象人
怖求覓道人。見而問言。汝
作何[10]呪令王白象病不能
食。答言。此象是我先身時
弟。共於迦葉佛時出家學
道。我但持戒誦經坐禪不行
布施。弟但廣求檀越作諸布
施。不持戒不學問。以其不
持戒誦經坐禪故今作此象。
大修布施故飲食備具種種豐
足。我但行道不修布施故。
今雖得道乞食不能得。

简体字   正體字

of the Path. One of them upheld the precepts, recited the Sutras, and sat in dhyāna meditation. The other brother sought extensive contacts with the *dānapatis* (lay benefactors) while also cultivating all manner of merit-generating karmic deeds. When it came to the time when Shakyamuni Buddha appeared in the World, one of the brothers was reborn into the household of an elder while the other brother was reborn as a great white elephant whose strength was such that he was able to smash the ranks of rebel insurgents. The son of that elder left home to study the Path and succeeded in gaining the six superknowledges and arhatship. However, on account of possessing only a scant amount of merit, whenever he sought alms food, it was difficult for him to come by any.

One day, [the arhat] took up his bowl and entered the city to seek alms food, but was unable to get any anywhere. He happened upon the stable of the white elephant and witnessed the King's providing to the elephant all manner of sustenance in great abundance. He then said to this elephant, "In comparing myself to you, [I see that] we both have committed offenses." The elephant was so moved by this comment that he became choked up and could not eat for three days. The elephant keeper panicked and sought out this man of the Path. Once he had found him, he inquired, "What spell did you cast that it caused the King's white elephant to become so ill that he can't eat?"

[The arhat] replied, "In a previous life this elephant was my younger brother. It was at the time of Kāśyapa Buddha that we left home together to study the Path as monks. I dedicated myself exclusively to upholding the precepts, reciting sutras and sitting in dhyāna meditation, but entirely neglected the practice of giving. My younger brother busied himself exclusively with extensively seeking contacts with *dānapatis* and all manner of giving, neglecting all the while to uphold the precepts or pursue his studies.

Because [my brother] did not uphold the precepts, recite sutras or sit in dhyāna meditation, he has now been reborn as this elephant. However, because he extensively cultivated the practice of giving, his food and drink are replete and marked by all manner of abundance. Because I only cultivated the Path and did not cultivate the practice of giving, although I have now gained the Path, whenever I seek alms food, I remain unable to come by any."

以是事故因缘不同。虽值佛世犹故饥渴。	以是事故因緣不同。雖值佛世猶故飢渴。
简体字	正體字

Nāgārjuna's Concluding Comments

On account of these circumstances, we can see that causes and conditions differ from case to case. Although one may take birth at a time when he might be able to see the Buddha, still, he might continue to be afflicted by hunger and thirst.

病者得愈。病有二种。先世
行业报故。得种种病。今世
冷热风发故。亦得种种病。
今世病有二种。一者内病。
五[11]藏不调结坚宿[12]疹。
二者外病。奔车逸马[13]塠压
坠落。兵刃刀[14]杖种种诸
病。问曰。以何因缘得病。
答曰。先世好行鞭杖拷掠闭
系种种恼故。今世得病。现
世病不知将身。饮食不节卧
起无常。以是事故得种种诸
病。如是有四百四病。以佛
神力故。令病者得愈。如
说。佛在舍[15]婆提国有一
居士。请佛及僧于舍饭食。
佛住精舍迎食有五因缘。一
者欲入定。二者欲为诸天
说法。三者欲游行观诸比丘
房。四者看诸病比丘。

简体字

病者得愈。病有二種。先世
行業報故。得種種病。今世
冷熱風發故。亦得種種病。
今世病有二種。一者內病。
五[11]藏不調結堅宿[12]疹。
二者外病。奔車逸馬[13]塠壓
墜落。兵刃刀[14]杖種種諸
病。問曰。以何因緣得病。
答曰。先世好行鞭杖拷掠閉
繫種種惱故。今世得病。現
世病不知將身。飲食不節臥
起無常。以是事故得種種諸
病。如是有四百四病。以佛
神力故。令病者得愈。如
說。佛在舍[15]婆提國有一
居士。請佛及僧於舍飯食。
佛住精舍迎食有五因緣。一
者欲入定。二者欲為諸天
說法。三者欲遊行觀諸比丘
房。四者看諸病比丘。

正體字

The Buddha Cares for a Sick Bhikshu

Nāgārjuna's Preamble: On the Origins of Illness[1]

(Nāgārjuna comments here on the line of sutra text which reads,"… those who were afflicted with illness were cured…"):

There are [basically] two categories of illness: [In the case of the first], one may become afflicted with all manner of sickness as retribution for karmic activities in former lives. [Secondly], one may also become afflicted with all manner of sickness in the present incarnation, this due to the influence of [such pathogenic factors as] coldness, heat, and wind.

Among the disorders originating in the present incarnation, there are two categories: The first consists of internal disorders wherein non-regulation of the five organs precipitates the arising of firmly-entrenched pathologies originating from former lives. The second consists of all manner of externally-arising disorders involving such phenomena as vehicular accidents, bolting horses, being crushed, falling down from a height, or [being afflicted with] a soldier's sword, a knife, or a club.

Question: What are the causes and conditions for becoming afflicted with physical maladies?

Exegesis: If in one's previous lives one took pleasure in inflicting all manner of cruelties involving lashing with a whip, beating with a club, imprisonment, and tying up, then in one's present life, one becomes afflicted with illness. [Then again,] if in this present life one is unaware of how to take care of one's body and so does not observe proper measure in eating and drinking or is irregular in one's sleeping habits, one may develop all manner of illnesses on account of this. And so there are four hundred and four categories of illness like these. On account of the Buddha's spiritual powers, those afflicted with illness were able to become cured.

Story: The Buddha Cares for a Sick Bhikshu

An exemplary case is told of the Buddha when he was in the state of Śrāvastī. There was a layman who had invited the Buddha and the Sangha to take their meal in his home. The Buddha had five reasons whereby [in some cases] he might choose to accept his meal while continuing to abide in the monastic dwelling: First, out of a wish to enter samādhi; second, out of a wish to speak Dharma for the gods; third, out of a desire to stroll about and inspect the dwellings of the bhikshus; fourth, to look in on the bhikshus who were

五者若未结戒欲为诸比丘结戒。是时佛[16]手[17]持户[18]排入诸比丘房。见一比丘。病苦无人瞻视。卧大小便。不能起居。佛问比丘。汝何所苦独无人看。比丘答言。大德。我性嬾。他人有病。初不看视。是故我病他亦不看。佛言。善男子我当看汝。时释提婆那民[19]盥水。佛以手摩其身。摩其身时。一切苦痛即皆除愈身心安隐。是时世尊安徐扶此病比丘起。将出房澡洗着衣。安徐将入更与敷褥令坐。佛语病比丘。汝久来不勤求。未得事令得。未到时令到。未识事令识。受诸苦患如是。[1]方当更有大[2]苦。比丘闻已心自思念。佛恩无量神力无数。以手摩我苦痛即除身心快乐。以是故佛以神力令病者得愈。形残者得具足。

五者若未結戒欲為諸比丘結戒。是時佛[16]手[17]持戶[18]排入諸比丘房。見一比丘。病苦無人瞻視。臥大小便。不能起居。佛問比丘。汝何所苦獨無人看。比丘答言。大德。我性嬾。他人有病。初不看視。是故我病他亦不看。佛言。善男子我當看汝。時釋提婆那民[19]盥水。佛以手摩其身。摩其身時。一切苦痛即皆除愈身心安隱。是時世尊安徐扶此病比丘起。將出房澡洗著衣。安徐將入更與敷褥令坐。佛語病比丘。汝久來不勤求。未得事令得。未到時令到。未識事令識。受諸苦患如是。[1]方當更有大[2]苦。比丘聞已心自思念。佛恩無量神力無數。以手摩我苦痛即除身心快樂。以是故佛以神力令病者得愈。形殘者得具足。

简体字

正體字

ill; and fifth, in instances where no prohibitions had been instituted, to formulate prohibitions for the benefit of the bhikshus.

At this time the Buddha, keys in hand, went in order from one door to the next, entering the rooms of the bhikshus. He observed a bhikshu who suffered from illness, but whom no one was looking after. [The monk] was lying there in his excrement and urine and was unable to rise from that position. The Buddha asked the bhikshu, "How is it that you are so afflicted with suffering and yet no one is looking after you?"

The bhikshu replied, "Bhagavat, I am, by nature, lazy. When others have fallen ill, I have never seen fit to look after them. Therefore, when it happened that I was taken ill, others have not bothered to look after me, either."

The Buddha said, "Son of good family, I shall look after you. At that time [the god] Shakra Devānām Indra bathed him with water and the Buddha rubbed his hands along the [bhikshu's] body. When he rubbed his body, all of the suffering and pain immediately disappeared and was cured. His body and mind became peaceful and restored. At this time the Bhagavān gently and slowly supported this sick bhikshu as he got up, took him outside of the dwelling, saw to his getting cleaned up, and to his dressing in [fresh] robes. Then he gently and slowly assisted him in going back in whereupon he provided him with a fresh sitting mat and allowed him to sit down.

The Buddha then said to the sick bhikshu, "For a long time now you have not been earnest in striving to gain what has not been gained, to arrive at what has not yet been reached, and to become aware of what has not yet been realized. Consequently you now undergo suffering and distress like this. [This being the case,] it may yet be that you are bound to undergo even greater suffering in the future."

When the bhikshu heard this he thought to himself, "The kindness of the Buddha is immeasurable and his spiritual powers are countless. When he used his hand to rub me, the anguish and pain immediately disappeared such that, in body and mind, I became filled with happiness."

Nāgārjuna's Concluding Comments

On account of this, [we can know that] the Buddha employs his spiritual power to cause those who are sick to be cured and those who are disfigured to become whole again.

Notes

1. Although Nāgārjuna explains that there *are* specific karmic causes behind the arising of many unfortunate circumstances such as sickness, disfigurement, and premature death, still, this in no way alters the need for all Buddhists to look upon all with equally genuine compassion entirely free of patronizing or cruel judgmentalism. In this connection, there is another important fact worthy of our consideration: We are all more-or-less equally possessed of an abundance of such disaster-generating causes in our past-life karmic history. Hence it is only a matter of time before the same fate (or even worse) befalls us, this unless we have the humility to use such examples of suffering as motivation to purify and thus neutralize our own karmic transgressions. Thus, even if one were tempted to fall into an attitude of condescension, cognizance of our shared karmic vulnerability should make the folly of such responses entirely obvious.

形残者得具足。云何名形残
[3]者。若有人先世破他[4]身
截其头斩[5]其手足。破种种
身分。或[6]破坏佛像毁佛像
鼻及诸贤圣形像。或破父母
形像。以是罪故受形多不具
足。

[0120a10] 复次不善法报受身丑
陋。若今世被贼或被刑戮。
种种因缘以[7]致残毁。或风
寒热病身生恶疮体分烂坏。
是名形残。蒙佛大恩皆得具
足。譬如只洹中奴。字[8]犍
抵。[9]（捷抵[10]秦言续[11]也）
是波斯匿王兄子。端正勇健
心性和善。王大夫人见之心
着。即微呼之欲令从己。[*]
犍抵不从。夫人大怒向王谗
之反[12]被其罪。王闻即节节
解之弃于冢间。命未绝顷其
夜虎狼罗刹来欲食之。[13]是
时佛到其边光明照之。身即

形殘者得具足。云何名形殘
[3]者。若有人先世破他[4]身
截其頭斬[5]其手足。破種種
身分。或[6]破壞佛像毀佛像
鼻及諸賢聖形像。或破父母
形像。以是罪故受形多不具
足。

[0120a10] 復次不善法報受身醜
陋。若今世被賊或被刑戮。
種種因緣以[7]致殘毀。或風
寒熱病身生惡瘡體分爛壞。
是名形殘。蒙佛大恩皆得具
足。譬如祇洹中奴。字[8]犍
抵。[9]（捷抵[10]秦言續[11]也）
是波斯匿王兄子。端正勇健
心性和善。王大夫人見之心
著。即微呼之欲令從己。[*]
犍抵不從。夫人大怒向王讒
之反[12]被其罪。王聞即節節
解之棄於塚間。命未絕頃其
夜虎狼羅刹來欲食之。[13]是
時佛到其邊光明照之。身即

简体字   正體字

Gaṇḍaka's Miraculous Restoration

Nāgārjuna's Preamble: On the Origins of Disfigurement[1]

(Nāgārjuna comments here on the line of sutra text which reads,"… those who's bodies were disfigured were made whole again…"):

What is meant by being "disfigured"? If there is a person who in a former life mangled someone's body or cut off someone's head or sliced off someone's hands or feet or mangled parts of someone's body or who perhaps destroyed images of the Buddha or broke the nose of a Buddha image or did these things to images of worthies or sages, or who perhaps destroyed images of his father or mother— on account of these offenses, he may take on a physical form which in many ways is not complete.

Moreover, it may be a retribution for unwholesome dharmas to take on a body that is ugly. If in this present life one is victimized by thieves or if one is subjected to capital punishment or if one encounters all manner of causes and conditions whereby one is caused to be disfigured, or if perhaps one becomes afflicted with wind-type, cold-type or heat-type diseases whereby one's body develops horrible sores or where parts of the body start to decay—this is what is meant [in this Sutra passage] by "disfigured."

Story: Gaṇḍaka's Miraculous Restoration

[And so it indicates in the Sutra passage that] they received the great kindness of the Buddha and were all made whole again. An exemplary case in point is that of a servant in the Jeta Grove named Gaṇḍaka. (Chinese textual note: In Chinese, "Gaṇḍaka" means "put together.") He was a nephew of King Prasenajit. He was handsome, brave, strong and possessed a mind which was harmonious and wholesome in nature. When the King's most senior consort saw him, she became attached to him and called to him softly, desiring thereby to influence him to go along with her intentions. But Gaṇḍaka did not go along with her and so the consort became greatly enraged and slandered him maliciously by accusing him of being guilty of what had been her own offense.

When the King heard this accusation, he had him sliced apart, joint after joint, and then had his body cast upon the charnel ground. That evening, at the moment just before his spirit was about to depart, the tigers, wolves and rākṣasa ghosts came around desiring to eat his body. At that moment the Buddha arrived at his side and let his light shine upon his body. His body suddenly became

平[14]复其心大喜。佛为说
法即得三道。佛牵其手将至
只[15]洹。是人言我身已破已
弃。佛续我身今当尽此形寿
以身布施佛及比丘僧。明日
波斯匿王闻如是事来至只[*]
洹语[*]犍抵言。向汝悔过。
汝实无罪枉相刑害。今当与
汝分国半治。[*]犍抵言我已
厌矣。王亦无罪。我宿世殃
咎罪报应尔。我今以身施佛
及僧不复还也。如是若有众
生形残不具足者。蒙佛光明
即时平[*]复。是故言乃至形
残皆得具足。蒙佛光明即时
平[*]复。

平[14]復其心大喜。佛為說
法即得三道。佛牽其手將至
祇[15]洹。是人言我身已破已
棄。佛續我身今當盡此形壽
以身布施佛及比丘僧。明日
波斯匿王聞如是事來至祇[*]
洹語[*]犍抵言。向汝悔過。
汝實無罪枉相刑害。今當與
汝分國半治。[*]犍抵言我已
厭矣。王亦無罪。我宿世殃
咎罪報應爾。我今以身施佛
及僧不復還也。如是若有眾
生形殘不具足者。蒙佛光明
即時平[*]復。是故言乃至形
殘皆得具足。蒙佛光明即時
平[*]復。

简体字　　　　　　正體字

as before and he became overjoyed. The Buddha then spoke the Dharma for his benefit whereupon he immediately realized the third stage of the path [of arhatship]. The Buddha then led him by the hand back to the Jeta Grove whereupon this man exclaimed, "My body had already been broken and had already been cast off. The Buddha put my body back together! Now I shall devote the rest of my life to serving with this body the Buddha and the Bhikshu Sangha."

The next day, when King Prasenajit heard of this matter, he came to the Jeta Grove and said to Gaṇḍaka, "I wish to repent to you for this transgression of mine. In truth you were blameless, but on false grounds, I subjected you to punitive injury. I am now going to present to you half of this country over which you may rule."

Gaṇḍaka replied, "I have already developed a revulsion [for worldly possessions]. As for the King, he is blameless. Disastrous mistakes from my former lives have made this event appropriate retribution for my offenses. I am now going to put my body to work in service to the Buddha and the Sangha and so will not be coming back again."

Nāgārjuna's Concluding Comments

[Instances] like this [illustrate what is meant when the Sutra records that] if there is a being who is disfigured and imperfect, when he is illumined by the Buddha's light, he is immediately restored to normalcy. And so it says, "Even all of those who were disfigured became whole. When illumined by the Buddha's light they were immediately restored to normalcy."

Notes

1. Please see note to previous story clarifying the concept of karmic origins of unfortunate present-life experiences.

佛在毘耶离国。是时佛语阿难。我身中热风气发。当用牛乳。汝持我鉢乞牛乳来。阿难持[4]佛鉢。晨朝入毘耶离。至一居士[5]门立。是时毘摩罗诘在是中行。见阿难持[6]鉢而立。问阿难。汝何以晨朝持鉢立此。阿难答[7]言。佛身小疾当用牛乳。故我到此。毘摩罗诘言。止止阿难。勿谤如来。佛为世尊已过一切诸不善法。当有何[8]疾。勿使外道闻此麁语。彼当轻佛便言。佛自疾不能救安能救人。阿难言。此非我意。面受佛勅当须牛乳。毘摩罗诘言。此虽佛勅是为方便。以今五恶之世故。以是像度脱一切。若未来世有诸病比丘。当从白衣求诸汤药。白衣言。汝自疾不能救。安能救馀人。诸比丘言。我等大师。犹尚有病。况我等身如艸芥能不病耶。以是事故诸白衣等。以诸汤药供给比丘。使得安隐坐禅行道。有外道仙人。能以药艸呪术除他人病。

佛在毘耶離國。是時佛語阿難。我身中熱風氣發。當用牛乳。汝持我鉢乞牛乳來。阿難持[4]佛鉢。晨朝入毘耶離。至一居士[5]門立。是時毘摩羅詰在是中行。見阿難持[6]鉢而立。問阿難。汝何以晨朝持鉢立此。阿難答[7]言。佛身小疾當用牛乳。故我到此。毘摩羅詰言。止止阿難。勿謗如來。佛為世尊已過一切諸不善法。當有何[8]疾。勿使外道聞此麁語。彼當輕佛便言。佛自疾不能救安能救人。阿難言。此非我意。面受佛勅當須牛乳。毘摩羅詰言。此雖佛勅是為方便。以今五惡之世故。以是像度脫一切。若未來世有諸病比丘。當從白衣求諸湯藥。白衣言。汝自疾不能救。安能救餘人。諸比丘言。我等大師。猶尚有病。況我等身如艸芥能不病耶。以是事故諸白衣等。以諸湯藥供給比丘。使得安隱坐禪行道。有外道仙人。能以藥艸呪術除他人病。

简体字   正體字

The Buddha's Skillful Means on Behalf of Monastics

The Buddha was abiding in the state of Vaiśālī when once he said to Ānanda, "There has developed within my body a type of hot wind energy for which it is appropriate to use cow's milk as a treatment. Take my bowl, beg for some milk and bring it forth."

Ānanda took up the Buddha's bowl and, early in the morning, went into Vaiśālī where, arriving at the door of a layman, he stood there. At that time [the layman] Vimalakīrti was walking by and noticed Ānanda standing there holding a bowl, whereupon he asked Ānanda, "Why is it that so early in the morning you stand here holding a bowl?"

Ānanda replied, "The Buddha's body is afflicted with a minor ailment for which one should use cow's milk as a treatment. And so it is that I have come to be here."

Vimalakīrti said, "Stop. Stop, Ānanda. Don't slander the Tathāgata. The Buddha is the Bhagavān. He has already gone beyond all unwholesome dharmas. What illness then could he possibly have? Don't allow non-Buddhists to hear such coarse speech. They will slight the Buddha and say, 'The Buddha can't even save himself from his own illnesses. How, then, could he save others?'"

Ānanda responded, "This was not my idea. It was face-to-face that I received the Buddha's order that he required cow's milk."

Vimalakīrti then said, "Although this was an order from the Buddha, it was but a skillful means. It is on account of this now being an age of the five evils that he employs this appearance for the sake of bringing everyone to deliverance. If in the future there are any bhikshus who are afflicted with illness they will have to seek medicines from the laity. [In such a case] the laity will say, 'You can't even save yourselves from your own illnesses. How could you save other people?' Those bhikshus then may say, "Even our great master was afflicted with illnesses. How much the less could the likes of us whose bodies are [as fragile] as reeds or sesame be able to escape affliction by illness?'

"On account of this situation, the laity and others will provide the bhikshus with medicines whereby they are allowed to peacefully and securely sit in dhyāna meditation and cultivate the Path. Even non-Buddhist rishis are able to employ herbs and incantations to get rid of the illnesses of others. How much the less could it be the case that the Tathāgata who possesses the virtue of omniscience would have an illness afflicting his own body which he couldn't

何況如來一切智德。自身有
病而不能除。汝且默然持鉢
取乳。勿令餘人異學得聞知
也。以是故知佛為方便非
實病也。諸罪因緣[9]皆亦如
是。

何況如來一切智德。自身有
病而不能除。汝且默然持鉢
取乳。勿令餘人異學得聞知
也。以是故知佛為方便非
實病也。諸罪因緣[9]皆亦如
是。

简体字

正體字

cure himself? It were better that you stand silently holding the bowl and so obtain the milk. Don't allow others of unorthodox persuasion to hear of this."

Nāgārjuna's Concluding Comments

On account of this we should know that the Buddha was acting this way merely as a skillful means and was not actually afflicted with illness. All of the other cases of his supposedly undergoing retribution were also of this sort.

佛言一事难值是佛世尊。又言九十一劫。三劫有佛馀劫皆空无佛甚可怜愍。佛为此重罪不种见佛善根人说言。佛世难值如优昙波罗树华时时一有。如是罪人轮转三恶道。或在人天中佛出世时。其人不见如说。舍卫城中九亿家。三亿家眼见佛。三亿家耳闻有佛而眼不见。三亿家不闻不见。佛在舍卫[11]国二十五年。而此众生不闻不见。何况远者。复次佛与阿难入舍卫城乞食。是时有一贫老母立在道头。阿难白佛。此人可愍佛应当度。佛语阿难。是[12]人无因缘。阿难言。佛往近之。此人见佛相好光明。发欢喜心为作因缘。

佛言一事難值是佛世尊。又言九十一劫。三劫有佛餘劫皆空無佛甚可憐愍。佛為此重罪不種見佛善根人說言。佛世難值如優曇波羅樹華時時一有。如是罪人輪轉三惡道。或在人天中佛出世時。其人不見如說。舍衛城中九億家。三億家眼見佛。三億家耳聞有佛而眼不見。三億家不聞不見。佛在舍衛[11]國二十五年。而此眾生不聞不見。何況遠者。復次佛與阿難入舍衛城乞食。是時有一貧老母立在道頭。阿難白佛。此人可愍佛應當度。佛語阿難。是[12]人無因緣。阿難言。佛往近之。此人見佛相好光明。發歡喜心為作因緣。

简体字　　　　正體字

The Buddha Attempts to Connect with an Old Woman

Nāgārjuna's Preamble: The Rarity of Meeting a Buddha

The Buddha said that there is one situation which is difficult to encounter. It is that of meeting up with a buddha, one of the Bhagavāns. He also said that in a period of ninety-one kalpas, only three kalpas have buddhas whereas the rest of the kalpas are all empty. They have no buddha. It is extremely lamentable.

The Buddha explained this circumstance for the sake of those who are burdened by severe karmic offenses and who have not planted the roots of goodness whereby they might see a buddha, stating, "The difficulty of encountering an age in which there is a buddha is like that of encountering the blossoms of the *udumbara* tree which appear only once in a great long time." People with karmic offenses such as these turn about in the three wretched destinies. Perhaps they may come to abide among men or gods at a time when a buddha appears in the world but, still, these people do not succeed in seeing him even then.

As it has been told, there were nine hundred thousand households in the city of Śrāvastī among whom three hundred thousand actually saw the Buddha, three hundred thousand heard of the existence of the Buddha but never saw him, and the remaining three hundred thousand neither heard of nor saw him. Although the Buddha dwelt in the state of Śrāvastī for twenty-five years, still, these beings neither heard of him nor saw him. How much the less did those who dwelt at a distance.

Story: The Buddha Attempts to Connect with an Old Woman

In addition, we have the exemplary case wherein the Buddha once went together with Ānanda into the city of Śrāvastī seeking alms food. At just that time there was a poverty-stricken old mother who was standing at the end of the street. Ānanda said to the Buddha, "This person is pitiable. The Buddha should bring her to deliverance."

The Buddha replied, "This person has no conducive causes and conditions."

Ānanda said, "Would that the Buddha would just go forth and approach her. When this person sees the Buddha's special characteristics and becomes aware of the light which he radiates, she will develop a delighted mind and will thereby create conducive causes and conditions."

佛往近之迴身背佛。佛从四边往。便四向背佛仰面上向。佛从上来低头下向。佛从地出两手覆眼不肯视佛。佛语阿难复欲作何因缘。有如是人无度因缘。不得见佛。以是故佛[13]言。佛难得值如优昙波罗树华。譬如水雨虽多处处易得。饿鬼常渴不能得饮。

佛往近之迴身背佛。佛從四邊往。便四向背佛仰面上向。佛從上來低頭下向。佛從地出兩手覆眼不肯視佛。佛語阿難復欲作何因緣。有如是人無度因緣。不得見佛。以是故佛[13]言。佛難得值如優曇波羅樹華。譬如水雨雖多處處易得。餓鬼常渴不能得飲。

简体字   正體字

The Buddha then went forth and approached her with the result that she turned her body so that her back was towards the Buddha. The Buddha then approached her from each of the four sides and in each case she turned her back towards the Buddha and raised her head so as to gaze upwards. And so the Buddha approached from above with the result that she then lowered her head so as to look downwards. The Buddha emerged from the ground beneath her, but she then covered her eyes with both hands and, even then, was unable to gaze at the Buddha. The Buddha then inquired of Ānanda, "Well, just what further causes and conditions would you wish to have created now?"

Nāgārjuna's Concluding Comments

There are people such as these who are lacking in the causes and conditions requisite to being brought to deliverance. They are unable to succeed in seeing the Buddha. It is for this reason that the Buddha said that the rarity of being able to encounter the Buddha is comparable to that of being able to see the blossoms of the *udumbara* tree. This is analogous to the situation of the hungry ghosts who, even when rainwater is abundant and easily found everywhere, still remain constantly thirsty and unable to find anything at all to drink.

复次诸佛大菩萨。有时众生
恐惧急难一心念。或时来度
之。如大月氏西佛肉髻住处
国。一佛图中有人癞风病。
来至遍吉菩萨像边。一心自
归念遍吉菩萨功德。愿除此
病。是时遍吉菩萨像。即以
右手宝磲光明。摩其身病即
除愈。复一国中有一阿兰若
比丘。大读摩诃衍。其国王
常布发令蹈上而过。有[15]
一比丘语王言。此人摩诃罗
不多读经。何以大供养如
是。王言我一日夜半欲见此
比丘。即往到其住处。见此
比丘在窟中读法华经。见一
金色[1]光明人骑白象合[2]手
供养。我转近便灭。我即问
大德以我来故。金色光明
人灭。比丘言。此即遍吉菩
萨。遍吉菩萨[3]自言。若有
人[4]诵读法华经者。我当

復次諸佛大菩薩。有時眾生
恐懼急難一心念。或時來度
之。如大月氏西佛肉髻住處
國。一佛圖中有人癩風病。
來至遍吉菩薩像邊。一心自
歸念遍吉菩薩功德。願除此
病。是時遍吉菩薩像。即以
右手寶磲光明。摩其身病即
除愈。復一國中有一阿蘭若
比丘。大讀摩訶衍。其國王
常布髮令蹈上而過。有[15]
一比丘語王言。此人摩訶羅
不多讀經。何以大供養如
是。王言我一日夜半欲見此
比丘。即往到其住處。見此
比丘在窟中讀法華經。見一
金色[1]光明人騎白象合[2]手
供養。我轉近便滅。我即問
大德以我來故。金色光明
人滅。比丘言。此即遍吉菩
薩。遍吉菩薩[3]自言。若有
人[4]誦讀法華經者。我當

简体字   正體字

Bodhisattvas Appearing in the World

Translator's Note

Nāgārjuna concludes a reply to a question as to why the Buddhas and the Bodhisattvas of the ten directions don't seem to manifest in the world by offering a few stories testifying to their actually having appeared in response to sincere believers.

The Leper Cured Through Devotion to Samantabhadra

There are times when the Buddhas and the great Bodhisattvas come and cross over beings who, frightened and in extreme difficulty, are single-minded in calling upon them. For instance, in the west of the state of Greater Tokharestan, in a place where the Buddha's summit-mark abides, there was a leper at a Buddha stupa who drew close to an image of Samantabhadra Bodhisattva. He then singlemindedly took refuge in him, bore in mind the meritorious qualities of Samantabhadra Bodhisattva, and prayed that he could get rid of this disease. At that time the image of Samantabhadra Bodhisattva poured forth a stream of light from the right hand which gently massaged across the [leper's] body, whereupon the disease disappeared entirely.

Samantabhadra Appears to a Bhikshu Reciting the *Lotus Sutra*

Then again, in one country, there was a bhikshu who dwelt in an *araṇya*[1] and specialized in the study of the Mahāyāna [teachings]. The king of his country would often lay down his hair in the path of the bhikshu that he might walk over it as he went by.[2] There was another bhikshu who spoke to the King, saying, "This man, O Great King, is not one who spends that much time reciting scriptures. Why is it that you make such great offerings in this fashion?"

The King replied, saying, "There was one day when, in the middle of the night, I wished to go and see this bhikshu. And so I immediately proceeded to where he dwells. I saw this bhikshu inside of his cave reciting the *Lotus Sutra*. At the same time, I observed a person made of gold-colored light sitting astride an elephant with his palms together as a sign of respect. As I grew closer, he disappeared. I then queried the greatly virtuous one as to how it was that, on account of my coming, the man of gold-colored light disappeared. The bhikshu then said to me, 'That was Samantabhadra Bodhisattva. Samantabhadra Bodhisattva himself has stated: "If there is anyone who recites the *Lotus Sutra*, I will come to him

乘白象来教导之。我诵法华[5]经故遍吉自来。（遍吉法华[6]经名为[7]普贤）复[8]有一国有[9]一比丘。诵阿弥陀佛经及摩诃般若波罗蜜。是人欲死时语弟子言。阿弥陀佛与彼大众俱来。即时动身自归。须臾命终。命终之后弟子积薪烧之。明日。灰中见舌不烧。诵阿弥陀佛经故。见佛自来。诵般若波罗蜜故。舌不可烧。此皆今世现事。如经中说。诸佛菩萨来者甚多。如是处处有人罪垢结薄。一心念佛信净不疑必得见佛。终不虚也。

乘白象來教導之。我誦法華[5]經故遍吉自來。（遍吉法華[6]經名為[7]普賢）復[8]有一國有[9]一比丘。誦阿彌陀佛經及摩訶般若波羅蜜。是人欲死時語弟子言。阿彌陀佛與彼大眾俱來。即時動身自歸。須臾命終。命終之後弟子積薪燒之。明日。灰中見舌不燒。誦阿彌陀佛經故。見佛自來。誦般若波羅蜜故。舌不可燒。此皆今世現事。如經中說。諸佛菩薩來者甚多。如是處處有人罪垢結薄。一心念佛信淨不疑必得見佛。終不虛也。

简体字　　　　　　　　　　　正體字

astride a white elephant in order to offer him instruction." It is
because I recite the *Lotus Sutra* that Samantabhadra Bodhisattva
himself comes here.'"

The Monk Who Saw Amitābha and Whose Tongue Would Not Burn

Additionally, in another country, there was a bhikshu who recited
the *Amitābha Buddha Sutra* and the *Mahāprajñāpāramitā*. When this
man was about to die, he spoke to his disciples, saying, "Amitābha
Buddha and his great assembly have all come. I shall depart forth-
with and return [to Amitābha's pureland]."

In just another instant, his life had come to an end. After he had
passed on, his disciples gathered firewood and cremated him. The
next day they found that his tongue had not been burned. Because
he had recited the *Amitābha Buddha Sutra*, he saw the Buddha himself come to him. Because he had recited the *Mahāprajñāpāramitā*,
his tongue could not be burned.

Nāgārjuna's Concluding Comments

These are all manifest events which have occurred in the present
era. As recorded in the scriptures, the instances of buddhas and
bodhisattvas coming are quite numerous. Everywhere there are
people such as these whose fetters arising from offenses and defilements are but slight. If they are single-minded in their mindfulness
of the Buddha and if there faith is pure and they have no doubts
they will certainly be able to see the Buddha. In the end, it will not
have been in vain.

Notes

1. An *araṇya* is an often solitary dwelling, usually for meditation or
    study, usually in a quiet place away from the city.
2. The intention being to cover rough or muddy places in the path and
    thus make a smoother path for the passing monk.

语密者。有人闻佛声一里。有闻十里百千万亿无数无量遍虚空中。有一会中或闻说布施。或有闻说持戒。或闻说忍辱精进禅定智慧。如是乃至十二部经。八万法[26]聚。各各随心所闻是名语密。是时目连心念。欲知佛声近远。即时以己神足力。[27]至无量千万亿佛[28]世界而息。闻佛音声如近不异。所息[29]世界其佛与大众方食。彼土人大。目连立其钵缘。彼佛弟子问其佛言。此人头虫从何所来。着沙门被服而行。其佛报言。勿轻此人。此是东方过无量佛[30]土。有佛名释迦牟尼。此是彼佛神足弟子。彼佛问目[31]度伽略子。汝何以来此。目连答言。我寻佛音声故来至此。彼佛告目连。汝寻佛声过无量亿劫。不能得其边际。

简体字

語密者。有人聞佛聲一里。有聞十里百千萬億無數無量遍虛空中。有一會中或聞說布施。或有聞說持戒。或聞說忍辱精進禪定智慧。如是乃至十二部經。八萬法[26]聚。各各隨心所聞是名語密。是時目連心念。欲知佛聲近遠。即時以己神足力。[27]至無量千萬億佛[28]世界而息。聞佛音聲如近不異。所息[29]世界其佛與大眾方食。彼土人大。目連立其鉢緣。彼佛弟子問其佛言。此人頭蟲從何所來。著沙門被服而行。其佛報言。勿輕此人。此是東方過無量佛[30]土。有佛名釋迦牟尼。此是彼佛神足弟子。彼佛問目[31]度伽略子。汝何以來此。目連答言。我尋佛音聲故來至此。彼佛告目連。汝尋佛聲過無量億劫。不能得其邊際。

正體字

Maudgalyāyana Seeks the Bounds of Buddha's Voice

Nāgārjuna's Preamble: On the Nature of Buddha's Voice

As for the esoteric aspect of the Buddha's speech, there are those who can hear the voice of the Buddha even at a distance of a third of a mile. There are those who can hear it at a distance of three miles, thirty-three miles, three hundred and thirty miles, three thousand, three hundred miles, thirty-three thousand miles, or even at a distance of innumerable and measureless miles, or even throughout all of empty space. It is also the case that, even in a single Dharma assembly, some people may hear a discussion of giving, others may hear a discussion of the moral precepts, and still others may hear a discussion of patience, of vigor, of dhyāna absorption, of wisdom, or of still other topics such as those from among the twelve categories of scriptural text or the eighty-thousand-fold collection of other dharmas. This phenomenon wherein different individuals may hear different [dharmas] matching differences in their own minds constitutes the esoteric aspect of the Buddha's speech.

Story: Maudgalyāyana Seeks the Bounds of Buddha's Voice

There was one time when Maudgalyāyana wished to discover the precise reach of the Buddha's voice and so immediately employed his own spiritual powers, traveling to and stopping in a place at a distance of immeasurable thousands of myriads of *koṭīs* of world systems away. He still heard the voice of the Buddha just as clearly as if he were right close by. In the world system where he stopped, there was a buddha who was eating together with his great assembly of followers. The people of that land were huge. Maudgalyāyana stood on the edge of one of their begging bowls, whereupon one of that buddha's disciples asked that buddha, "Where did this human-headed bug come from? He's walking around in the clothes of a *śramaṇa*. That buddha replied, "Don't slight this man. He is a [monk] possessed of spiritual powers who is a disciple of a buddha named Shakyamuni who dwells an immeasurable number of buddha lands off in the east."

That buddha then asked Maudgalyāyana, "Why have you come here?"

Maudgalyāyana replied, "It is because I am seeking to find how far the Buddha's voice can reach that I have come here."

That buddha told Maudgalyāyana, "Even if you were to follow the Buddha's voice for an immeasurable number of *koṭīs* of kalpas, you would still be unable to find the limit of its reach.

[0128a17] [*]【论】问曰。若诸佛持戒禅定智慧度人皆等。是普明菩萨何以欲来见释迦牟尼佛。答曰。诸菩萨常欲见佛无厌足。听法无厌足。见诸菩萨僧无厌足。诸菩萨于世间法皆以厌患。于上三事心无厌足。如手居士。从净居天来欲见佛。其身微细没失。譬如消苏不得立地。佛语手居士。汝化作麁身观此地相。居士即如佛言。化作麁身观念[7]此地相。头面礼佛足一面立。佛问居士。汝几事无厌生净居天。答言。我三事无厌生净居天。一见[8]诸佛供养无厌。二听法无厌。三供给僧无厌。如佛在

简体字

[0128a17] [*]【論】問曰。若諸佛持戒禪定智慧度人皆等。是普明菩薩何以欲來見釋迦牟尼佛。答曰。諸菩薩常欲見佛無厭足。聽法無厭足。見諸菩薩僧無厭足。諸菩薩於世間法皆以厭患。於上三事心無厭足。如手居士。從淨居天來欲見佛。其身微細沒失。譬如消蘇不得立地。佛語手居士。汝化作麁身觀此地相。居士即如佛言。化作麁身觀念[7]此地相。頭面禮佛足一面立。佛問居士。汝幾事無厭生淨居天。答言。我三事無厭生淨居天。一見[8]諸佛供養無厭。二聽法無厭。三供給僧無厭。如佛在

正體字

Hastaka's Three Insatiables

Translator's Note

Nāgārjuna relates the following story in commenting on a section of sutra text wherein the Bodhisattva Samantaraśmi (lit. "Universal Brightness") departs from the assembly of Ratnākara Buddha (lit. "Accumulation of Jewels") to pay his respects to Shakyamuni Buddha.

Nāgārjuna's Preamble: The Bodhisattva's Insatiability

Question: If the capacity of all buddhas is identical with respect to observance of the precepts, dhyāna absorptions, wisdom, and also with respect to the deliverance of beings, why is it that this Samantaraśmi Bodhisattva desires to come and pay his respects to Shakyamuni Buddha?

Response: The bodhisattvas are all always insatiable in their desire to see the Buddhas, insatiable in their desire to hear the Dharma, and insatiable in their desire to see the Bodhisattva Sangha. The Bodhisattvas are all weary of and abhor worldly dharmas.

Story: Hastaka's Three Insatiables

[The bodhisattva's] insatiability with respect to the above three matters is similar to the case of the layman Hastaka who came from the Pure Abode Heaven wishing to see the Buddha. His body was so fine and delicate that it verged on disappearance and, like melting frankincense resin (*taila*), it was unable to stand up on the ground.

The Buddha said to the layman Hastaka, "You should transformationally create a coarser body by contemplating the characteristic of the earth element." The layman Hastaka immediately accorded with the Buddha's instructions, bore in mind the characteristic of the element earth and then made obeisance at the feet of the Buddha and stood off to one side.

The Buddha then inquired of the layman, "With respect to how many things have you become insatiable that, as a result, you have gained rebirth in the Pure Abode Heaven?"

He replied, "It is on account of being insatiable with respect to three matters that I have been born in the Pure Abode Heaven: First, I have been insatiable in desiring to see the Buddhas and make offerings to them. Second, I have been insatiable in desiring to hear the Dharma. Third, I have been insatiable in making offerings to supply the needs of the Sangha. Just as, while the Buddha dwells

阎浮提。四部众常随逐佛听法问法。是我净居诸天。亦常从我听法问法。声闻犹尚听法无厌足。何况法性身菩萨。以是故普明菩萨。来见释迦牟尼佛。及见此间诸菩萨摩诃萨绍尊位者。

閻浮提。四部眾常隨逐佛聽法問法。是我淨居諸天。亦常從我聽法問法。聲聞猶尚聽法無厭足。何況法性身菩薩。以是故普明菩薩。來見釋迦牟尼佛。及見此間諸菩薩摩訶薩紹尊位者。

简体字　　　　正體字

in Jambudvīpa, the Four Assemblies constantly follow along after the Buddha for the purpose of hearing the Dharma and inquiring about Dharma, so too my fellow gods from the Pure Abode Heaven follow along with me in listening to the Dharma and in inquiring about the Dharma."

Nāgārjuna's Concluding Comment

Even the Śrāvaka Disciples are insatiable when it comes to listening to Dharma. How much the more so would this be the case with the Dharma-body bodhisattvas. It is for this reason that Samantaraśmi Bodhisattva came to see Shakyamuni Buddha and to also see the bodhisattvas and the *mahāsattvas* who abide here and who [in the future] will inherit the [Buddha's] honored position.

[128b09]如说诸佛要集经中。文殊尸利欲见佛集。不能得到。诸佛各还本处。文殊尸利到诸佛集处。有一女人近彼佛坐入三昧。文殊尸利入礼佛足已。白佛言。云何此女人得近佛坐而我不得。佛告文殊尸利。汝觉此女人令从三昧起。汝自问之。文殊尸利即弹指觉之。而不可觉。以大声唤亦不可觉。捉手牵亦不可觉。又以神足动三千大千世界。犹亦不觉。文殊尸利白佛言。世尊。我不能令觉。是时佛放大光明照下方世界。是中有一菩萨。名弃诸盖。即时从下方出。来到佛所头面礼佛足一面立。佛告弃诸盖菩萨。汝觉此女人。即时弹指此女从三昧起。文殊尸利白佛言。以何因缘。我动三千大千世界。不能令此女起。弃诸盖菩萨一弹指便从三昧起。佛告文殊尸利。汝因此女人。初发阿耨多罗三藐三菩提意。是女人因弃诸盖菩萨。初发阿耨多罗三藐三菩提意。以是故汝不能令觉。汝于诸佛三昧中功德未满。是诸菩萨三昧中得自在。佛三[128c]昧中少多入而未得自在故耳。

[128b09]如說諸佛要集經中。文殊尸利欲見佛集。不能得到。諸佛各還本處。文殊尸利到諸佛集處。有一女人近彼佛坐入三昧。文殊尸利入禮佛足已。白佛言。云何此女人得近佛坐而我不得。佛告文殊尸利。汝覺此女人令從三昧起。汝自問之。文殊尸利即彈指覺之。而不可覺。以大聲喚亦不可覺。捉手牽亦不可覺。又以神足動三千大千世界。猶亦不覺。文殊尸利白佛言。世尊。我不能令覺。是時佛放大光明照下方世界。是中有一菩薩。名棄諸蓋。即時從下方出。來到佛所頭面禮佛足一面立。佛告棄諸蓋菩薩。汝覺此女人。即時彈指此女從三昧起。文殊尸利白佛言。以何因緣。我動三千大千世界。不能令此女起。棄諸蓋菩薩一彈指便從三昧起。佛告文殊尸利。汝因此女人。初發阿耨多羅三藐三菩提意。是女人因棄諸蓋菩薩。初發阿耨多羅三藐三菩提意。以是故汝不能令覺。汝於諸佛三昧中功德未滿。是諸菩薩三昧中得自在。佛三[128c]昧中少多入而未得自在故耳。

简体字　　　　　　　　　正體字

The Limits of Mañjuśrī's Samādhi Power

As described in the *Assemblage of Buddhas Sutra*, Mañjuśrī wished to view that assemblage of Buddhas, but was unable to arrive for it. The Buddhas had all returned to their original places. When Mañjuśrī arrived at that place where the Buddhas had all come together, there was a woman close to that buddha's seat, immersed in samādhi. Mañjuśrī entered and, having bowed at the Buddha's feet, inquired of the Buddha, "Why has this woman been able to draw so close to the Buddha's seat whereas I have not?"

The Buddha told Mañjuśrī, "Rouse this woman, cause her to arise from her samādhi, and inquire of her yourself."

Mañjuśrī then snapped his fingers to rouse her but she was unable to be roused thereby. He yelled loudly but still she was unable to be roused by that. He then tugged her by the hand, but that couldn't rouse her either. Finally, he employed his psychic powers , shaking the entire great trichiliocosm, but still this did not succeed in rousing her. Mañjuśrī addressed the Buddha, saying, "I am unable to cause her to be roused."

At this time the Buddha emitted a great beam of light which illuminated the world system towards the nadir. There was therein a bodhisattva named Apahṛtanīvaraṇa (lit. "Dispeller of the Hindrances") who immediately emerged therefrom and who came to this Buddha's place, made reverential obeisance at the Buddha's feet, and then stood off to one side. The Buddha then instructed Apahṛtanīvaraṇa Bodhisattva, "Rouse this woman." Thereupon [that bodhisattva] snapped his fingers and this woman immediately arose from samādhi.

Mañjuśrī addressed the Buddha, inquiring, "Why is it that even though I shake the entire great trichiliocosm I am still unable to rouse this woman whereas Apahṛtanīvaraṇa Bodhisattva need only snap his fingers one time and so rouses her from samādhi?"

The Buddha told Mañjuśrī, "It was on account of this woman that you first set your resolve on *anuttarasamyaksaṃbodhi* whereas it was on account of Apahṛtanīvaraṇa Bodhisattva that this woman first set her resolve on *anuttarasamyaksaṃbodhi*. It is for this reason that you are unable to rouse her. You have not yet completely gained the meritorious qualities associated with the Buddhas' samādhis. This bodhisattva has achieved sovereign independence in the samādhis. It is on account of having entered to some degree the samādhis of the Buddhas while not yet having achieved sovereign independence in them that this situation is as it is.

问曰。如佛不求福德。何以故供养。答曰。佛从无量阿僧只劫中。修诸功德常行诸善。不但求报敬功德故而作供养。如佛在时有一盲比丘。眼无所见而以手缝衣时针[1]紩脱。便言。谁爱福德为我[*]紩针。是时佛到其所语比丘。我是爱福德人。为汝[*]紩[2]针来。是比丘识佛声。疾起着衣礼佛足白佛言。佛功德已满。云何言爱福德。佛报言。我虽功德已满。我深知功德[3]恩功德果报功德力。[4]令我于一切众生中得最第一。由此功德。是故我爱。佛为此比丘赞功德已。次为随意说法。是比丘得法眼净肉眼更明。复次佛虽功德已满更无所须。为教化弟子故。语之言。我[5]尚作功德汝云何不作。如伎家百岁老[6]翁而舞。有人呵之言。老[*]翁年已百岁何用是舞。[*]翁答。我不须舞。但欲教子孙故耳。佛[7]亦如是。功德虽满。为教弟子作功德故。而作供养。

简体字

問曰。如佛不求福德。何以故供養。答曰。佛從無量阿僧祇劫中。修諸功德常行諸善。不但求報敬功德故而作供養。如佛在時有一盲比丘。眼無所見而以手縫衣時針[1]紩脫。便言。誰愛福德為我[*]紩針。是時佛到其所語比丘。我是愛福德人。為汝[*]紩[2]針來。是比丘識佛聲。疾起著衣禮佛足白佛言。佛功德已滿。云何言愛福德。佛報言。我雖功德已滿。我深知功德[3]恩功德果報功德力。[4]令我於一切眾生中得最第一。由此功德。是故我愛。佛為此比丘讚功德已。次為隨意說法。是比丘得法眼淨肉眼更明。復次佛雖功德已滿更無所須。為教化弟子故。語之言。我[5]尚作功德汝云何不作。如伎家百歲老[6]翁而舞。有人呵之言。老[*]翁年已百歲何用是舞。[*]翁答。我不須舞。但欲教子孫故耳。佛[7]亦如是。功德雖滿。為教弟子作功德故。而作供養。

正體字

The Buddha's Love of Meritorious Deeds

Question: Given that beings such as the Buddha do not [have any further need to] seek karmic blessings, why does he persist in making offerings?

Response: For an immeasurable number of *asaṃkhyeyas* of kalpas, the Buddha has cultivated every type of merit and has constantly practiced all manner of good. It was not solely for the sake of seeking reward, respect, or merit that he has made offerings. For example, when the Buddha was still abiding in the World, there was a blind bhikshu who, although he could not see a thing with his eyes, still used his hands to sew his robe. When once his thread slipped out of the needle, he called out, "May whoever loves to generate merit come thither and assist me by threading my needle."

At that time the Buddha came to where he was and said to the bhikshu, "I am a man who loves to generate merit. I will assist you by threading the needle."

This bhikshu recognized the Buddha's voice, quickly got up, donned his robe, made obeisance at the Buddha's feet, and addressed the Buddha, saying, "The Buddha's merit is already complete. Why is it that he states that he loves to generate merit?"

The Buddha replied, "Although my merit is already complete, I am deeply aware of the causes of merit, of the resulting reward of merit, and of the power of merit. It is on account of this merit that I have become the most supreme among beings. It is for this reason that I love it." After the Buddha had praised the generation of merit for the sake of this bhikshu, he next spoke Dharma for him which accorded with his mind. The bhikshu then achieved the purification of the Dharma eye and the return of sight to his fleshly eyes.

Moreover, although the Buddha is already complete in merit and has nothing further which he needs, it is for the sake of teaching disciples that he says to them, "If even I still engage in the generation of merit, how can you fail to do so?"

This is like a 100-year-old dancer who, though a geriatric, still continued to dance only to be scolded by someone who said, "Old man, you're already a hundred years old. What use is it for you to continue to dance?"

The old man replied, "I have no need of dancing. It is solely because I wish to teach my children and grandchildren that I do so." The Buddha is just like this. Although his merit is already complete, it is for the sake of teaching disciples to generate merit that he himself engages in the making of offerings.

复次以人心多散如[24]狂如醉。一心敬慎则是诸功德初门。摄心得禅。便得实智慧。得实智慧便得解脱。得解脱便得尽苦。如是事皆从一心得。如佛般涅盘后一百岁有一比丘。名[25]优波毱。得六神通阿罗汉。当尔时世为阎浮提大导师。彼时有一比丘尼。年百二十岁。此比丘尼年[26]小时见佛。[*]优波毱来入其舍。欲问佛容仪。先遣弟子。弟子语比丘尼。我大师[*]优波毱。欲来见汝问佛容仪。是时比丘尼。以鉢盛满麻油着户扇下试之。知其威仪详审以不。[*]优波毱入徐排户扇麻油小弃。坐已问比丘尼。汝见佛不。容[27]仪何似。为我说之。比丘尼答。我尔时年[*]小见佛来入聚落。众人言佛来。我亦随众人出

復次以人心多散如[24]狂如醉。一心敬慎則是諸功德初門。攝心得禪。便得實智慧。得實智慧便得解脫。得解脫便得盡苦。如是事皆從一心得。如佛般涅槃後一百歲有一比丘。名[25]優波毱。得六神通阿羅漢。當爾時世為閻浮提大導師。彼時有一比丘尼。年百二十歲。此比丘尼年[26]小時見佛。[*]優波毱來入其舍。欲問佛容儀。先遣弟子。弟子語比丘尼。我大師[*]優波毱。欲來見汝問佛容儀。是時比丘尼。以鉢盛滿麻油著戶扇下試之。知其威儀詳審以不。[*]優波毱入徐排戶扇麻油小棄。坐已問比丘尼。汝見佛不。容[27]儀何似。為我說之。比丘尼答。我爾時年[*]小見佛來入聚落。眾人言佛來。我亦隨眾人出

简体字 正體字

The Arhat Upagupta Meets an Elderly Nun

Translator's Note

Nāgārjuna employed this story in reply to a question regarding the importance of "single-minded respectfulness and carefulness."

Nāgārjuna's Introductory Comments

Furthermore, [this single-minded respectfulness and carefulness is important] on account of the fact that people's minds are for the most part scattered as if they were either crazy or intoxicated. Being single-mindedly respectful and careful is the essential prerequisite for the development of all meritorious qualities. If one is able to focus one's mind, then one is able to succeed in dhyāna meditation and is thus then able to realize true wisdom. If one is able to develop true wisdom, then one is able to achieve liberation. If one is able to achieve liberation, then one is able to put an end to suffering. Matters such as these are all realized through single-mindedness.

The Story

For example, one hundred years after the Buddha's *parinirvāṇa*, there was a bhikshu named Upagupta who had become an arhat possessed of the six superknowledges. In the world at that time he was a great guiding master for the entire continent of Jambudvīpa. At that time there was a bhikshuni who was one hundred and twenty years old. When this bhikshuni was young she had seen the Buddha. Upagupta came with the intention of entering her dwelling as he wished to enquire about the Buddha's countenance and comportment. He sent a disciple on ahead of him. The disciple said to the bhikshuni, "My great master is Upagupta. He wishes to come and see you for the purpose of inquiring about the Buddha's countenance and comportment."

The bhikshuni then took a bowl filled to the brim with sesame oil and set it beneath the doorway so as to test him and thus evaluate whether or not he himself was possessed of the awesome comportment. When Upagupta entered he slowly pushed aside the door but still spilled a little of the sesame oil. Having sat down he asked the bhikshuni, "Did you actually see the Buddha or not? What were his countenance and comportment like? Describe them for me."

The bhikshuni replied, "I was young then. I saw the Buddha come and enter into the village. Everybody said, 'The Buddha has come!' I followed along with everyone else. When I went out and

见光明便礼。头上金钗堕地
在大暗[28]林下。佛光明照之
幽隐皆见即时得钗。我自是
后乃作比丘尼。[*]优波毱更
问。佛在世时比丘威仪礼法
何如。答曰。佛在时六群比
丘无羞无耻最是弊恶。威仪
法则胜汝。今日何以知之。
六群比丘入户不令油弃。此
虽弊恶[29]知比丘仪法。行住
坐卧不失法则。汝虽是六神
通阿罗汉不如彼也。[*]优波
毱闻是语大自惭愧。以是故
言一心敬慎。一心敬慎善人
相也。

見光明便禮。頭上金釵墮地
在大闇[28]林下。佛光明照之
幽隱皆見即時得釵。我自是
後乃作比丘尼。[*]優波毱更
問。佛在世時比丘威儀禮法
何如。答曰。佛在時六群比
丘無羞無恥最是弊惡。威儀
法則勝汝。今日何以知之。
六群比丘入戶不令油棄。此
雖弊惡[29]知比丘儀法。行住
坐臥不失法則。汝雖是六神
通阿羅漢不如彼也。[*]優波
毱聞是語大自慚愧。以是故
言一心敬慎。一心敬慎善人
相也。

简体字　　　　　　　正體字

saw the light, I bowed down, whereupon my gold hair clasp fell to the ground and slid underneath a large bench where it was very dark. The Buddha's light illuminated the darkness so that I could see everything. Thus I became immediately able to retrieve the hair clasp. It was starting from this very time that I became a bhikshuni."

Upagupta then asked, "When the Buddha was in the World, what were the comportment and manners of the bhikshus like?"

She replied, "When the Buddha was in the World there was one group of six bhikshus who were utterly shameless and the most poorly behaved. But their manner of displaying the awesome comportment was still superior to yours. How is it that one can know this today? When the six bhikshus entered a doorway they would not have caused the oil to spill. Although they were poorly behaved, they still knew how to carry forth with the awesome deportment of a bhikshu. Whether walking, standing, sitting, or lying down, they did not depart from the Dharma standards. Even though you are an arhat possessed of the six superknowledges, you are still not such as can be compared to them."

When Upagupta heard these words, he was greatly ashamed. And so it is for this reason that we refer to being possessed of single-minded respectfulness and carefulness. Being single-mindedly respectful and careful is the mark of a good person.

[0136a07] 　　[5]【论】问曰。般
若波罗蜜是菩萨摩诃萨法。
佛何以故告舍利弗而不告菩
萨。答曰。舍利弗于一切弟
子中智慧最第一。如佛偈
说。

一切众生智　唯除佛世尊。
欲比舍利弗　智慧及多闻。
于十六分中　犹尚不及一。

[0136a14] 复次舍利弗智慧多闻
有大功德。年始八岁诵十八
部经。通解一切经书义理。
是时摩伽陀国有龙王兄弟。
一名姞利二名阿伽[6]罗。降
雨以时国无荒年。人民感
之。常以仲春之月一切大集
至龙住处。为设大会作乐谈
义终此一日。自古及今斯集
未替。遂以龙名以名此会。
此日常法敷四高座。一为国
王。二为太子。三为大臣。
四为论士。尔时舍利弗以八
岁之身。问众人言。此四高
座为谁敷之。众人答[7]言。
为国王太子大臣论士。是时
舍利弗观察时人婆罗门等。
神情瞻向无胜己者。便升论
床结跏趺坐。众人

简体字

[0136a07] 　　[5]【論】問曰。般
若波羅蜜是菩薩摩訶薩法。
佛何以故告舍利弗而不告菩
薩。答曰。舍利弗於一切弟
子中智慧最第一。如佛偈
說。

一切眾生智　唯除佛世尊。
欲比舍利弗　智慧及多聞。
於十六分中　猶尚不及一。

[0136a14] 復次舍利弗智慧多聞
有大功德。年始八歲誦十八
部經。通解一切經書義理。
是時摩伽陀國有龍王兄弟。
一名姞利二名阿伽[6]羅。降
雨以時國無荒年。人民感
之。常以仲春之月一切大集
至龍住處。為設大會作樂談
義終此一日。自古及今斯集
未替。遂以龍名以名此會。
此日常法敷四高座。一為國
王。二為太子。三為大臣。
四為論士。爾時舍利弗以八
歲之身。問眾人言。此四高
座為誰敷之。眾人答[7]言。
為國王太子大臣論士。是時
舍利弗觀察時人婆羅門等。
神情瞻向無勝己者。便昇論
床結跏趺坐。眾人

正體字

The Life of Śāriputra

Nāgārjuna's Preamble: Śāriputra's Wisdom

Question: The *prajñāpāramitā* is a dharma associated with the Bodhisattvas and the Mahāsattvas. Why then is it that the Buddha addresses Śāriputra herein?

Response: Among all of the disciples, Śāriputra was foremost in wisdom. This is as indicated by a verse spoken by the Buddha:

If one were to take the wisdom of any being,
This with the exception of the Buddha,
And desired then to compare it to Śāriputra,
His wisdom and his knowledge are such that,
Supposing it consisted of sixteen parts,
That person would still not possess even one.

Story: The Life of Śāriputra

Also, Śāriputra was wise, knowledgeable, and possessed of great meritorious qualities. From the time he was eight years old he was able to recite from memory the eighteen classics and was able to penetratingly understand the principles of all of the classics and their related texts. At that time in the state of Magadha, there were two dragon-king brothers, one named Giri and the other named Agra. They sent down the rains in accord with the seasons so that there were no drought-afflicted years. The population was grateful to them and so always amassed at the abode of the dragons on the second full moon of spring to celebrate them with a grand festival. On these occasions, there would be music and philosophical debates which lasted the entire day. This had been the unchanging custom from ancient times on up to the present. Consequently this great festival came to be named after the dragons.

It was the custom on these occasions to set up four seats of honor, the first being reserved for the King, the second for the Prince, the third for the Prime Minister and the fourth for a master of dialectics. At that time the eight-year-old Śāriputra asked the assembled people there, "For whom are these four seats of honor prepared?"

Those people replied, "They have been prepared for the King, the Prince, the Prime Minister, and a master of dialectics."

Śāriputra then assessed the physiognomy of all of the brahmans and others who were present, observed that none of them were superior to himself, and so ascended the seat prepared for a master of dialectics, sitting down there in the full lotus posture. Those men

疑怪。或谓愚小无知。或谓智量过人。虽复嘉其神异。而犹各怀自矜。耻其年小不自与语。皆遣年少弟子传言问之。其答酬旨趣辞理超绝。时诸论师叹未曾有。愚智大小一切皆伏。王大欢喜即命有司。封一聚落常以给之。王乘象舆振铃告[8]告宣示一切十六大国六大城中无不庆悦。是时[9]告占师子名拘律陀。姓大目揵连。舍利弗友而亲之。舍利弗才明见[10]重。目揵连豪爽[11]最[12]贵。此二人者才智相比德行互同。行则俱游[13]住则同止。少长缱绻结要终始。后俱厌世出家学道作梵志弟子。[14]情求道门久而无徵。以问于师。师名删阇耶。而答之言。自我求道弥历年岁。不知为[15]有道果无耶。我非其人耶而亦不得。他日其师寝疾。舍利弗在头边立。大目连在足边立。喘喘然其命将终。

简体字

正體字

assembled there were struck with doubt and consternation and so thought to themselves that either this was just a little ignorant fool or else it might be one whose wisdom surpassed that of men.

Although they admired his extraordinary spiritual demeanor, each of them remained prideful of himself. Embarrassed by his youth, they did not speak to him directly, but rather each dispatched a young disciple as a surrogate to subject him to questioning. The import, phrasing, and principle behind each of his replies utterly surpassed the ken of ordinary men. At that time those dialecticians exclaimed at what they had never before encountered in their entire lives. The fool, the sage, the elder, and the young—all alike were humbled.

The King was extraordinarily delighted and so immediately ordered his officials to make a grant of [the taxes from] an entire village as perpetual support for him. The King ascended onto the platform atop his elephant, rang a bell, and proclaimed this. Thus there was no place throughout the sixteen great states and the six great cities where he did not become a celebrated figure.

At that time there lived a man, the son of a diviner, whose personal name was Kolita and whose family name was Mahāmaudgalyāyana. Śāriputra befriended and grew close to him. The talent and intelligence of Śāriputra were universally esteemed even while the extraordinary character of Maudgalyāyana was the most acclaimed. These two men were comparable in talent and wisdom and were peers in the practice of virtue. When traveling about, they kept each other's company, and when abiding in any place, they stayed in close proximity. They pledged a pact of lifelong friendship.

Later on, they both renounced the worldly life and left home to study the Path, each becoming disciples of a particular brahmacārin. They sought for the entry onto the Path, but even after a long time, they found no subtleties through their studies with him and so asked their guru about the matter. Their guru, one who was named Sañjaya, replied to them, saying, "I have sought the Path for many years now and still do not know whether or not I have reached the fruition of the Path. Could it be that I am not the man for it and thus, even [in spite of my efforts], I cannot be successful in this?"

Later, their guru was stricken ill. Śāriputra stood at the head of his bed while Maudgalyāyana stood at the foot of his bed. Struggling for breath, [the guru's] life was about to draw to an end when he sighed with sadness and then laughed. The two men simultaneously

乃憨尔而笑。二人同心俱问笑意。师答之言。世俗无眼为恩爱所侵。我见金地国王死。其大夫人自投火[卄/积]求同一处。而此二人行报各异生处殊绝。是时二人笔受师[16]语。欲以验其虚实。后有金地商人。远来摩伽陀国。二人以疏验之果如师语。乃怃然叹曰。我等非其人耶。为是师隐我耶。二人相与誓曰。若先得甘露要[17]毕同味。是时佛度迦叶兄弟千人。次游诸国到王舍城顿止竹园。二梵志师闻佛出世。俱入王舍城欲知消息。尔时有一比丘。名阿说示。（五人之一）着衣持钵入城乞食。舍利弗见其仪服异容诸根静默。就而问言。汝谁弟子师是何人。答言。释种太子厌老病死苦出家。学道得阿耨多罗三藐三菩提。是我师也。舍利弗言。汝师教授为我说之。即答偈曰。

简体字

乃憨爾而笑。二人同心俱問笑意。師答之言。世俗無眼為恩愛所侵。我見金地國王死。其大夫人自投火[卄/積]求同一處。而此二人行報各異生處殊絕。是時二人筆受師[16]語。欲以驗其虛實。後有金地商人。遠來摩伽陀國。二人以疏驗之果如師語。乃憮然歎曰。我等非其人耶。為是師隱我耶。二人相與誓曰。若先得甘露要[17]畢同味。是時佛度迦葉兄弟千人。次遊諸國到王舍城頓止竹園。二梵志師聞佛出世。俱入王舍城欲知消息。爾時有一比丘。名阿說示。（五人之一）著衣持鉢入城乞食。舍利弗見其儀服異容諸根靜默。就而問言。汝誰弟子師是何人。答言。釋種太子厭老病死苦出家。學道得阿耨多羅三藐三菩提。是我師也。舍利弗言。汝師教授為我說之。即答偈曰。

正體字

asked the meaning of the laugh, whereupon the guru replied to them, saying, "The common people of the world have no eyes. They have been laid waste by love. I can observe now that the King of Suvarṇabhūmi (lit. "Land of Gold") has died and that his wife has thrown herself on the funeral pyre, seeking thereby to be reborn together with him. But the actions and retributions of each of those two people are quite different and so their places of rebirth will be distantly separate."

The two men then recorded their guru's words wishing to look into whether they were false or true. Later on there arrived in Magadha a businessman from Suvarṇabhūmi. The two men inquired of him regarding that which they had recorded and, as it turned out, matters were in accord with the words of their guru. They then exclaimed disappointedly, "Could it be that we are not such as can succeed at this? Or could it be that our guru [deliberately] kept us in the dark?" The two men then vowed to each other that if either of them was first to gain the sweet-dew ambrosia, they must both finally share in its flavor.

At this time the Buddha had crossed over the Kāśyapa brothers and their thousand followers and had then proceeded next to travel throughout the neighboring states until he arrived at the City of the Kings' Abode (Rājagṛha) where he paused and remained at the Bamboo Grove. Meanwhile, our two brahmacārin masters had heard of the Buddha's coming forth into the world and so came together to the City of the Kings' Abode wishing to learn further news of him.

There was at that time a bhikshu named Aśvajit (one of the five bhikshus) who had donned his robes, had taken up his bowl, and had entered into the city for the purpose of obtaining alms. Śāriputra observed his deportment and attire, his extraordinary countenance, and the fact that all of his senses were still and quiet. Consequently he went up to him and inquired, "Whose disciple are you? Who is your guru?"

[The monk] replied, "He is the prince of the Śākyan clan who grew weary of the sufferings of old age, sickness, and death, and who consequently left behind the home life, studied the Path, and realized *anuttarasamyaksaṃbodhi*. It is he who is my guru."

Śāriputra asked, "That which your guru teaches and passes on to you—pray, explain it for me."

[The monk] immediately replied in a verse, saying,

简体字	正體字
我年既幼稚　[18]学日又初浅。 岂能[19]宣至真　广说如来义。 [0136c02]　　舍利弗言。略说其要。尔时阿说示比丘。说此偈言。 诸法因缘生　是法说因缘。 是法因缘尽　大师如是[20]说。 [0136c06]　　舍利[21]弗闻此偈已即得初道。还报目连。目连见其颜色和悦迎谓之言。汝得甘露味耶。为我说之。舍利弗即为其说向所闻偈。目连言。更为重说。即复为说。亦得初道。二师与二百五十弟子俱到佛所。佛遥见二人与弟子俱来。告诸比丘。汝等见此二人在诸梵志前者不。诸比丘言。已见。佛言。是二人者。是我弟子中智慧第一神足第一。弟子大众俱来以渐近佛。既到稽首在一面立俱白佛言。世尊。我等于佛法中欲出家受戒。佛言。善来比丘。即时须发自落法服着身。衣钵具足受成就戒。过半月后佛为长爪梵志说法。	我年既幼稚　[18]學日又初淺。 豈能[19]宣至真　廣說如來義。 [0136c02]　　舍利弗言。略說其要。爾時阿說示比丘。說此偈言。 諸法因緣生　是法說因緣。 是法因緣盡　大師如是[20]說。 [0136c06]　　舍利[21]弗聞此偈已即得初道。還報目連。目連見其顏色和悅迎謂之言。汝得甘露味耶。為我說之。舍利弗即為其說向所聞偈。目連言。更為重說。即復為說。亦得初道。二師與二百五十弟子俱到佛所。佛遙見二人與弟子俱來。告諸比丘。汝等見此二人在諸梵志前者不。諸比丘言。已見。佛言。是二人者。是我弟子中智慧第一神足第一。弟子大眾俱來以漸近佛。既到稽首在一面立俱白佛言。世尊。我等於佛法中欲出家受戒。佛言。善來比丘。即時鬚髮自落法服著身。衣鉢具足受成就戒。過半月後佛為長爪梵志說法。

Because in years I am so young,
And because my time in study has also been preliminary and shallow,
How could I proclaim what is ultimately true,
And broadly speak of the Tathāgata's meaning?

Śāriputra said, "Briefly speak of its essentials." The bhikshu
Aśvajit then spoke this verse, saying:

All dharmas are produced of causes and conditions.
These dharmas—he explains their causes and conditions.
These dharmas come to an end through causes and conditions.
The Great Guru explains it in just this way.

When Śāriputra heard this verse, he immediately realized the
initial stage of the Path. He returned to report of his experience to
Maudgalyāyana. Maudgalyāyana could see that [Śāriputra's] countenance was harmonious and blissful and so, in welcoming him,
asked him, "Have you gotten the flavor of the sweet-dew ambrosia?
Explain it for me!"

Śāriputra then uttered for him the verse he had heard.
Maudgalyāyana said, "Speak it for me again." He immediately
spoke it for him again whereupon [Maudgalyāyana], too, realized
the initial stage of the Path.

Thereupon those two masters went together to where the
Buddha dwelt, each bringing along his following of two hundred
and fifty disciples. When the Buddha observed from a distance that
these two men were coming together with their disciples, he asked
the Bhikshus [assembled at his side], "Do you all see or do you not
those two men at the head of all those brahmacārins?"

The Bhikshus replied, "Yes, we have observed them."

The Buddha said, "Of these two men, one is the foremost among
my disciples in wisdom and the other is foremost in the development of spiritual powers."

That great group of disciples came and slowly approached the
Buddha. Having arrived, they made obeisance, stood off to one
side, and then together asked the Buddha, saying, "Bhagavān, we
all desire to leave the home life and take up the precepts under the
auspices of the Buddha's Dharma."

The Buddha said, "Come well, O Bhikshus." Immediately their
hair and beards spontaneously fell away, they became complete
with robe and bowl, and they succeeded in taking on the moral
precepts. After only a half month, when the Buddha was speaking Dharma for the sake of the brahmacārin named "Long Nails"

时舍利弗得阿罗汉道。所以
半月后得道者。是人当作逐
佛转法轮[22]师。应在学地现
前自入诸法种种具知。是故
半月后得阿罗汉道。如是等
种种功德甚多。是故舍利弗
虽是阿罗汉。佛以是般若波
罗蜜甚深法。为舍利弗说。

時舍利弗得阿羅漢道。所以
半月後得道者。是人當作逐
佛轉法輪[22]師。應在學地現
前自入諸法種種具知。是故
半月後得阿羅漢道。如是等
種種功德甚多。是故舍利弗
雖是阿羅漢。佛以是般若波
羅蜜甚深法。為舍利弗說。

简体字

正體字

(Dīrghanakha), Śāriputra realized the path of arhatship.

Nāgārjuna's Concluding Comments:

As for his having realized the Path after only a half month, such a person was surely bound to become a master who would follow along after the Buddha in turning the wheel of Dharma. It should surely have been that, in the station of one on the path of learning, he had already naturally entered into all dharmas and had already gained a complete awareness with respect to many different varieties of them. Thus it was that, on account of this, only a half month [after becoming a monk], he succeeded in bringing the path of arhatship to realization. The meritorious qualities of these sorts which he possessed were extremely numerous. It was on account of this that, although Śāriputra was an arhat, the Buddha nonetheless chose to address Śāriputra as he proceeded with the explanation of the extremely profound Dharma of the *prajñāpāramitā*.

问曰。若尔者何以初少为舍利弗说。后多为须菩提说。若以智慧第一故应为[23]多说。[24]复何以为须菩提说。答曰。舍利弗佛弟子中智慧第一。须菩提于弟子中。得无诤三昧最第一。无诤三昧相常观众生不令心恼多行怜愍。诸菩萨者弘大誓愿以度众生怜愍相同。是故命说。

[0137a01] 复次是须菩提好行空三昧。如佛在忉利天夏安居受岁已还下阎浮提。尔时须菩提于石窟中住自思惟。佛从忉利天来下。我当至佛所耶。不至佛所耶。又念言。佛常说。若人以智慧眼观佛法身。则为见佛中最。是时以佛从忉利天下故。阎浮提中四部众集。诸天见人人亦见天。座中有佛及转轮圣王诸天大众。众会庄严先未曾有。须菩提心念。今此大众虽复殊特势不久停。

简体字

問曰。若爾者何以初少為舍利弗說。後多為須菩提說。若以智慧第一故應為[23]多說。[24]復何以為須菩提說。答曰。舍利弗佛弟子中智慧第一。須菩提於弟子中。得無諍三昧最第一。無諍三昧相常觀眾生不令心惱多行憐愍。諸菩薩者弘大誓願以度眾生憐愍相同。是故命說。

[0137a01] 復次是須菩提好行空三昧。如佛在忉利天夏安居受歲已還下閻浮提。爾時須菩提於石窟中住自思惟。佛從忉利天來下。我當至佛所耶。不至佛所耶。又念言。佛常說。若人以智慧眼觀佛法身。則為見佛中最。是時以佛從忉利天下故。閻浮提中四部眾集。諸天見人人亦見天。座中有佛及轉輪聖王諸天大眾。眾會莊嚴先未曾有。須菩提心念。今此大眾雖復殊特勢不久停。

正體字

Subhūti and Floral Appearance Bhikshuni

Nāgārjuna's Preamble: Why Subhūti Speaks Here

Question: Why then is it that it was only at the beginning and only briefly that [the Perfection of Wisdom] was addressed to Śāriputra whereas, later on, it was addressed in great measure to Subhūti? In a case where one takes being foremost in wisdom as the basis [as with Śāriputra], it should be addressed in great measure to him instead. What's more, why was it even addressed to Subhūti at all?

Response: Śāriputra was foremost in wisdom among the Buddha's disciples. Subhūti was foremost among the disciples in cultivation of the non-disputation samādhi. It is the characteristic of the non-disputation samādhi that one may constantly contemplate beings while not allowing one's mind to become agitated and while also primarily practicing compassion for them. The great bodhisattvas employ vast and magnanimous vows by which they cross over beings. In terms of compassion, he was much the same. It was on account of this that [the Buddha] ordered him to speak [the Perfection of Wisdom].

Story: Subhūti and Floral Appearance Bhikshuni

Additionally, this Subhūti took pleasure in the practice of the emptiness samādhi. For instance, at the conclusion of the period of the Summer retreat when the Buddha had been dwelling in the Trāyastriṃśa Heaven and was about to return to Jambudvīpa, Subhūti was dwelling in a rock cave and thought to himself, "The Buddha is descending from the Trāyastriṃśa Heaven. Should I go to where the Buddha is or should I not go to where the Buddha is?" He thought further, "The Buddha always says that, if one employs the wisdom eye to contemplate the Dharma body of the Buddha, then that is the most supreme manner in which to see the Buddha."

At this time, because the Buddha was descending from the Trāyastriṃśa Heaven, the four-fold community assembled. The gods were able to view people and people were also able to see the gods. Among the seats there were places for the Buddha as well as for a wheel-turning sage king and a great assembly of gods. The adornments of that assembly place were such as had never been before.

Subhūti thought to himself, "Although this great assembly is extraordinary and special, this situation will not abide for long.

[1]磨灭之法皆归无常。因此无常观之初门。悉知诸法空无有实。作是观时即得道证。尔时一切众人。皆欲求先见佛礼敬供养。有华色比丘尼。欲除[2]女名[3]之恶。便化为转轮圣王及七宝千子。众人见之皆避坐起去。化王到佛所已还复本身为比丘尼。最初礼佛。是时佛告比丘尼非汝初礼。须菩提最初礼我。所以者何。须菩提观诸法空是为见佛法身。得真供养供养中最。非以致敬生身为供养也。以是故言须菩提常行空三昧。与般若波罗蜜空相相[4]应。[5]以是故佛命令说般若波罗蜜。

[1]磨滅之法皆歸無常。因此無常觀之初門。悉知諸法空無有實。作是觀時即得道證。爾時一切眾人。皆欲求先見佛禮敬供養。有華色比丘尼。欲除[2]女名[3]之惡。便化為轉輪聖王及七寶千子。眾人見之皆避坐起去。化王到佛所已還復本身為比丘尼。最初禮佛。是時佛告比丘尼非汝初禮。須菩提最初禮我。所以者何。須菩提觀諸法空是為見佛法身。得真供養供養中最。非以致敬生身為供養也。以是故言須菩提常行空三昧。與般若波羅蜜空相相[4]應。[5]以是故佛命令說般若波羅蜜。

简体字　　　　正體字

Any dharma which is subject to deterioration is bound to revert to impermanence. It is on account of this that it is an elementary tenet of the contemplation of impermanence that all dharmas are empty and devoid of any substantiality." As he carried on this contemplation, he suddenly gained realization of the Path.

Everyone in the assembly sought at that time to be the first to see the Buddha, show reverence, and present offerings to him. There was a bhikshuni named "Floral Appearance" (Utpalavarṇā) who wished to escape the disadvantage of being seen then as just another woman. Thus she then transformed herself into the appearance of a wheel-turning sage king bringing the seven precious things and a thousand sons. When the members of the assembly saw this, they all retreated from their seats by getting up and standing aside. When the transformationally-created king reached the place where the Buddha was, it reverted to the original person of the bhikshuni who was then able to be first to pay respects to the Buddha.

The Buddha then said to the bhikshuni, "It is not the case that you were the first to pay your respects. Subhūti was the first to pay his respects to me. How was this so? Subhūti contemplated and realized that all dharmas are empty. This constitutes seeing the Dharma body of the Buddha. He was by this able to make a true offering, an offering which is the most supreme among offerings. It is not the case that the making of offerings is achieved by reverence before that body which is subject to birth."

Nāgārjuna's Concluding Comment
It is for this reason that it is said that Subhūti constantly cultivated the samādhi of emptiness. His practice corresponded to the emptiness attribute of the *prajñāpāramitā*. It was for this reason that the Buddha ordered him to speak forth the *prajñāpāramitā*.

問曰。何以名舍利弗為是父母所作字。為是依行功德立名。答曰。是父母所作名字。於閻浮提中。第一安樂有摩伽陀國。是中有大城名王舍。王名頻婆娑羅。有婆羅門論[7]議師。名摩陀羅。王以其人善能論故。賜封一邑去城不遠。是摩陀羅遂有居家婦生一女。眼似舍利鳥眼。即名此女為舍利。次生一男。膝骨麤大名拘[8]郗羅。拘[*]郗羅([9]秦言大膝[10]也)是婆羅門既有居家畜養男女。所學經書皆已[11]廢忘又不業新。是時南天竺有一婆羅門大論[*]議師字提舍。於十八種大經皆悉通利。是人入王舍城。頭上戴火以[12]銅鍱腹。人問其故。便言我所學經書甚多恐腹破裂。是故鍱之。又問。頭上何以戴火。答言。以大闇故。眾人言。日出照明何以言闇。答言。闇有二種。一[13]者日光不照。二者愚癡闇蔽。今雖有日明而愚癡猶黑。眾人言。汝但未見

简体字

問曰。何以名舍利弗為是父母所作字。為是依行功德立名。答曰。是父母所作名字。於閻浮提中。第一安樂有摩伽陀國。是中有大城名王舍。王名頻婆娑羅。有婆羅門論[7]議師。名摩陀羅。王以其人善能論故。賜封一邑去城不遠。是摩陀羅遂有居家婦生一女。眼似舍利鳥眼。即名此女為舍利。次生一男。膝骨麤大名拘[8]郗羅。拘[*]郗羅([9]秦言大膝[10]也)是婆羅門既有居家畜養男女。所學經書皆已[11]廢忘又不業新。是時南天竺有一婆羅門大論[*]議師字提舍。於十八種大經皆悉通利。是人入王舍城。頭上戴火以[12]銅鍱腹。人問其故。便言我所學經書甚多恐腹破裂。是故鍱之。又問。頭上何以戴火。答言。以大闇故。眾人言。日出照明何以言闇。答言。闇有二種。一[13]者日光不照。二者愚癡闇蔽。今雖有日明而愚癡猶黑。眾人言。汝但未見

正體字

The Story Behind Śāriputra's Name

Question: Why was he named "Śāriputra"? Was it a name made up by his parents or was it instead a name based upon his practice of virtue?

Response: It is a name created by his parents. The most blissful location in Jambudvīpa was the state of Magadha wherein there was a great city by the name of "Kings' Abode". The king at that time was Bimbasāra. There was a great dialectician by the name of Māṭhara. Because he was very capable in debate, the King had bestowed upon him the income from taxes on a village not far from the city. This Māṭhara subsequently came to settle into a home where he took a wife and gave birth to a daughter whose eyes resembled those of the *śāri* bird and who was then named "Śāri." Next, he produced a son whose knee bones were coarse and large who was named Kauṣṭhila. (Chinese textual note: "In Chinese, "Kauṣṭhila" means "big knees.") Because this brahman had taken up the life of a householder busy with the raising of a son and daughter, his expertise deteriorated and was lost as regards those classics and other texts he had studied earlier. What's more, he did not apply himself to further studies.

At this time there was a great brahman dialectician from south India known as Tiṣya. He had entirely penetrated and become acutely familiar with all of the eighteen great classics. This man entered into the city of Kings' Abode wearing a burning flame atop his head and girding his belly with brass plate mail. Someone asked him why he dressed this way to which he then replied, "The classics and other texts which I have studied are extremely many. I fear that my belly might burst and tear open. That's why I gird myself with mail."

He was also asked, "Why do you wear a burning flame atop your head?"

He replied, "It's on account of the great darkness."

A member of the crowd asked, "The sun has arisen and now illuminates clearly. Why do you speak of 'darkness'?"

He replied, "There are two kinds of darkness. The first is when the light of the sun does not shine. The second is when the darkness of stupidity brings about obscurity. Now, even though we do enjoy the brightness of the sun, still, stupidity continues to engender darkness."

A member of the crowd said, "It's just that you have not yet met

婆羅門摩陀羅。汝若見者腹當縮明當闇。是婆羅門逕至鼓邊打論[*]議鼓。國王聞之問是何人。眾臣答言。南天竺有一婆羅門名提舍大論[*]議師。欲求論處故打論鼓。王大歡喜即集眾人而告之曰。有能難者與之論[*]議。摩陀羅聞之自疑。我以[*]廢忘又不業新。不知我今能與論不。儴俛而來。於道中見二特牛方相觝觸。心中作想。此牛是我彼牛是彼。以此為占知誰得勝。此牛不如便大愁憂而自念言。如此相者我將不如。欲入眾時見有母人挾一瓶水正在其前躄地破瓶。復作是念。是亦不吉甚大不樂。既入眾中見彼論師。顏貌意色勝相具足。自知不如。事不獲已與共論[*]議。論[*]議既交便墮負處。王大歡喜。大智明人遠入我國。復欲為之封一聚落。諸臣[*]議言。一聰明人來便封一邑。功臣不賞

婆羅門摩陀羅。汝若見者腹當縮明當闇。是婆羅門逕至鼓邊打論[*]議鼓。國王聞之問是何人。眾臣答言。南天竺有一婆羅門名提舍大論[*]議師。欲求論處故打論鼓。王大歡喜即集眾人而告之曰。有能難者與之論[*]議。摩陀羅聞之自疑。我以[*]廢忘又不業新。不知我今能與論不。儴俛而來。於道中見二特牛方相觝觸。心中作想。此牛是我彼牛是彼。以此為占知誰得勝。此牛不如便大愁憂而自念言。如此相者我將不如。欲入眾時見有母人挾一瓶水正在其前躄地破瓶。復作是念。是亦不吉甚大不樂。既入眾中見彼論師。顏貌意色勝相具足。自知不如。事不獲已與共論[*]議。論[*]議既交便墮負處。王大歡喜。大智明人遠入我國。復欲為之封一聚落。諸臣[*]議言。一聰明人來便封一邑。功臣不賞

the brahman Māṭhara. If you were to encounter him, your belly would shrink and your brightness would become dim."

This brahman then went directly to the side of the drum and proceeded to beat upon the debating drum. When the King heard this, he asked, "Who is that?"

The assembly of officials replied, "There is a great dialectician from South India, a brahman named Tiṣya. It is because he seeks to issue a debate challenge that he has begun beating on the debate drum."

The King was delighted and so immediately called forth an assembly whereupon he announced to them, "As there is one who is capable of presenting a challenge, let there now be a debate with him."

When Māṭhara heard of this, he became seized by self-doubt, thinking, "Because I have lost all I knew and have not taken up further studies, I do not know whether or not I will now be able succeed in debate." But he forced himself to come forth. After he set forth, he observed two bulls in the street who proceeded to gore one another with their horns. He thought to himself, "This bull represents me. That other bull represents him. I can take this as an omen by which to know who will be victorious." The bull he had seen as representing himself was no match for the other and so he became greatly distressed and worried. He then thought to himself, "Given a sign such as this, it must be that I shall be no match for him."

When he was about to enter the assembly, he saw a mother carrying a vase of water who fell down and broke the vase directly in front of him. He thought to himself again, "This, too, is inauspicious." Consequently he felt extremely unhappy. When he had entered into the assembly he caught sight of that dialectician and saw that his countenance and look of confidence were replete with superior signs. As a result, he knew that he was no match for that man. After all this things had not gone his way, he went ahead and joined in the debate. After he became involved in the debate, he stumbled into a fallacious position [and so lost the debate].

The King was greatly delighted, exclaiming, "Such a greatly wise and intelligent man has come to my kingdom. In return, I want to grant him the tribute from an entire village."

The assembly of officials discussed it and said, "A single intelligent man comes and then you make a grant to him of the proceeds from an entire village while you fail to offer any reward to

但寵語論。恐非安國全家
之道。今摩陀[14]羅論[*]議不
如。應奪其封以與勝者。若
更有勝人復以與之。王用其
言即奪與後人。是時摩陀羅
語提舍言。汝是聰明人。我
以女妻汝。男兒相累今欲遠
出他國以求本志。提舍納其
[15]女為婦。其婦懷妊夢見一
人。身[16]被甲冑手執金剛。
摧破諸山而在大山邊立。覺
已白其夫言。我夢如是。提
舍言。汝當生男。摧伏一切
諸論[*]議師。唯不勝一人當
與作弟子。舍利懷妊。以
其子故。母亦聰明大能論[*]
議。其弟拘[*]郗羅與姊談論
每屈不如。[17]知所懷子必大
智慧。未生如是何況出生。
即捨家學問至南天竺[18]不剪
指[19]爪。讀十八種經書皆令
通利。是故時人[20]號為長
[*]爪梵志。姊子既生七日之
後。裹以白[21]疊以示其父。
其父思惟我名提舍。逐我名
字字為憂[22]波提舍。（憂波
秦言[23]逐提舍星名）是為父
母作字。眾人以其舍利所
生。皆共名之

简体字　　　　正體字

meritorious officials. If you only esteem those who debate, we fear that this is not the way to establish the state and succeed in preserving the [royal] house. The dialectician Māṭhara has now proved himself to be no match. It should be that his grant is taken away and awarded to the victor. If there comes to be yet another victor later, then it should be given to him in turn."

The King accepted their advice and so took [that grant] and gave it to the man who came later. Māṭhara then said to Tiṣya, "You are an intelligent man. I will give you my daughter as a wife. My son will come along with her. I want now to travel afar to another country so as to continue in the pursuit of my original aspirations."

Tiṣya took [Māṭhara's] daughter as a wife. When his wife became pregnant, she had a dream in which she saw a man whose body was girded in armor and who held a *vajra* in his hand. He smashed all of the mountains until he came to stand next to a huge mountain. When she woke up she told her husband, "I had a dream like this."

Tiṣya replied, "You will give birth to a male child who will smash all of the dialecticians in defeat. There will be only one man over which he will be unable to be victorious. He will become a disciple to him."

When Śāri was pregnant, on account of her son, she, too, became especially intelligent and well able to carry on in debate. Every time her younger brother Kauṣṭhila debated with her, he was overcome and was no match for her. He realized then that the son with whom she was pregnant must certainly be greatly wise and so thought that, if even before birth he was like this, how much the more so will it be the case once he is born.

Consequently, he immediately left behind his home and pursued his studies in South India where, [due to the intensity of his studying], he never even paused to trim his nails. He studied the eighteen types of classics as well as the related texts, doing so to the point where he developed a penetrating and sharp understanding of them all. It was on account of this that he came to be known by the people of the time as "The Long-nailed Brahmacārin."

Seven days after his sister gave birth, she swaddled the child in white cloth and showed it to the father. The father thought, "As I am named 'Tiṣya,' name him after me as 'Upatiṣya.'" (Chinese textual note: "In Chinese, *"upa"* means "following after" and "Tiṣya" is the name of a star.) This was the name created by the parents. Because he was born to Śāri, everybody came to refer to him as "Śāriputra".

為舍利弗。（[24]弗秦言[25]子）
復次舍利弗世世本願。於釋
迦文尼佛所作智慧第一弟
子。字舍利弗。是為本願因
緣名字。以是故名舍利弗。
問曰。若爾者何以不言憂波
提舍。而但言舍利弗。答
曰。時人貴重其母。於眾女
人中聰明第一。以是因緣故
稱舍利弗。

為舍利弗。（[24]弗秦言[25]子）
復次舍利弗世世本願。於釋
迦文尼佛所作智慧第一弟
子。字舍利弗。是為本願因
緣名字。以是故名舍利弗。
問曰。若爾者何以不言憂波
提舍。而但言舍利弗。答
曰。時人貴重其母。於眾女
人中聰明第一。以是因緣故
稱舍利弗。

简体字   正體字

(Chinese textual note: In Chinese, *"putra"* means "son.")

Moreover, in life after life Śāriputra had vowed to become the disciple foremost in wisdom to the Buddha Shakyamuni and to then be known as "Śāriputra." In this sense, "Śāriputra" is a name finding its origin in past life vows. It was for [all of] these reasons that he was named "Śāriputra".

Question: If it is as you have said, why was he not then known as "Upatiṣya," but was rather referred to simply as "Śāriputra"?

Response: The people of the time prized and esteemed his mother. She was foremost in intelligence among all the women. It is for this reason that he was known as "Śāriputra."

复次舍利弗非一切智。于佛智慧中。譬如小儿。如说阿婆檀那经中。佛在 [32]只洹住哺时经行。舍利弗从佛经行。是时有鹰逐鸽。鸽飞来佛边住。佛经行过之影覆鸽上。鸽身安隐怖畏即除不复作声。后舍利弗影到鸽。便作声[33]战怖如初。舍利弗白佛言。佛及我身俱无三毒。以何因缘佛影覆鸽。鸽便无声不复恐怖。我影覆上鸽便作声[34]战栗如[35]故。佛言。汝三毒习气未尽。以是故汝影覆时恐怖不除。汝观此鸽宿世因缘几世作鸽。舍利弗即时入宿命智三昧。观见此鸽从鸽中来。如是一二三世乃至八万大劫常作鸽身。过是已往不能复见。舍利弗从三昧起白佛言。是鸽八万大劫中常作鸽身。过是已前不能复知。

復次舍利弗非一切智。於佛智慧中。譬如小兒。如說阿婆檀那經中。佛在 [32]祇洹住哺時經行。舍利弗從佛經行。是時有鷹逐鴿。鴿飛來佛邊住。佛經行過之影覆鴿上。鴿身安隱怖畏即除不復作聲。後舍利弗影到鴿。便作聲[33]戰怖如初。舍利弗白佛言。佛及我身俱無三毒。以何因緣佛影覆鴿。鴿便無聲不復恐怖。我影覆上鴿便作聲[34]戰慄如[35]故。佛言。汝三毒習氣未盡。以是故汝影覆時恐怖不除。汝觀此鴿宿世因緣幾世作鴿。舍利弗即時入宿命智三昧。觀見此鴿從鴿中來。如是一二三世乃至八萬大劫常作鴿身。過是已往不能復見。舍利弗從三昧起白佛言。是鴿八萬大劫中常作鴿身。過是已前不能復知。

简体字   正體字

Śāriputra, the Buddha, and the Pigeon

Then again, it was not the case that Śāriputra himself was possessed of all-knowledge. When compared with the wisdom of the Buddha, his (own level of wisdom) was comparable to that of an infant. This is as described in the *Avadāna Sutra*:

The Buddha was dwelling in the Jeta Grove. When it came time for the meal, he proceeded to walk forth [on the alms round]. Śāriputra followed along behind the Buddha. At this time there was a hawk pursuing a pigeon. The pigeon flew towards the Buddha and stood alongside the Buddha. As the Buddha was walking past him, his shadow fell upon and covered the pigeon. The pigeon then became calm, its frightfulness immediately disappeared, and it ceased its squawking [in terror].

After this, Śāriputra came along, whereupon his shadow then fell upon and covered the pigeon. The pigeon then proceeded to squawk and tremble just the same as before.

Śāriputra then addressed the Buddha, saying, "The Buddha and I are both free of the three poisons. Why then is it that, when the shadow of the Buddha covered the pigeon, the pigeon became quiet and ceased to be filled with terror, whereas when my shadow fell upon the pigeon, he then began to squawk and tremble again, just as before?"

The Buddha replied, "In your case, the residual propensities associated with the three poisons have not all been brought to an end. It is for this reason that, when your shadow came to cover [the pigeon], its fearfulness would not go away.

"Now, when you contemplate the past-life causes and conditions associated with this pigeon, for how many lifetimes do you observe that it has been incarnating as a pigeon?"

Śāriputra immediately entered the "past-life-recall" samādhi, observed that this pigeon had come forth from a previous lifetime as a pigeon and, in this same manner, noted that for one, two, and three lifetimes, and so forth until we come to eighty thousand great kalpas, it had always incarnated in the body of a pigeon. Beyond this span of time, he was unable to see any farther back into the past.

Śāriputra arose from his samādhi and addressed the Buddha, saying, "This pigeon has always incarnated as a pigeon throughout the last eighty thousand kalpas. Beyond this, I am unable to know about any lifetimes previous to these."

佛言。汝若不能尽知过去
世。试观未来世此鸽何时当
脱。舍利弗即入愿智三昧。
观见此鸽一二三世乃至八万
大劫未脱鸽身。过是已往亦
不能知。从三昧起白佛言。
我见此鸽从一世二世乃至八
万大劫未免鸽身。过此已往
不复能知。我不知过去未来
齐限。不审此鸽何时当脱。
佛告舍利弗。此鸽除诸声闻
辟支佛所知齐限。复于恒河
沙等大劫中常作鸽身。罪讫
得出。轮转五道中后得为
人。经五百世中乃得利根。
是时有佛度无量阿僧只众
生。然后入无馀涅盘。遗法
在世是人作五戒优婆塞。从
比丘闻赞佛功德。于是初发
心愿欲作佛。然后于三阿僧
只劫。行六波罗蜜。十地具
足得作佛。度无量众生已而
入[1]无馀涅盘。是时舍利弗
向佛忏悔白佛言。我

佛言。汝若不能盡知過去
世。試觀未來世此鴿何時當
脫。舍利弗即入願智三昧。
觀見此鴿一二三世乃至八萬
大劫未脫鴿身。過是已往亦
不能知。從三昧起白佛言。
我見此鴿從一世二世乃至八
萬大劫未免鴿身。過此已往
不復能知。我不知過去未來
齊限。不審此鴿何時當脫。
佛告舍利弗。此鴿除諸聲聞
辟支佛所知齊限。復於恒河
沙等大劫中常作鴿身。罪訖
得出。輪轉五道中後得為
人。經五百世中乃得利根。
是時有佛度無量阿僧祇眾
生。然後入無餘涅槃。遺法
在世是人作五戒優婆塞。從
比丘聞讚佛功德。於是初發
心願欲作佛。然後於三阿僧
祇劫。行六波羅蜜。十地具
足得作佛。度無量眾生已而
入[1]無餘涅槃。是時舍利弗
向佛懺悔白佛言。我

简体字   正體字

The Buddha said, "Well, if you're unable to know completely the circumstances of the past, try contemplating this pigeon's future lifetimes, observing how long it will be before it succeeds in gaining liberation.

Śāriputra immediately entered the "seeking-knowledge-[of-the-future]" samādhi. He contemplated and observed that, even after one, two, three lifetimes, and so forth until we come to eighty-thousand kalpas of lifetimes, this pigeon would still not have become liberated from being reincarnated in the body of a pigeon. In this case, too, he was unable to see beyond this span of time.

He arose from samādhi and addressed the Buddha, saying, "I observed that this pigeon would still be unable to avoid incarnation in the body of a pigeon even after one lifetime, two lifetimes, and so forth until we come to eighty-thousand kalpas of lifetimes. I am unable to have knowledge of the circumstances beyond this period of time. I am unable to have knowledge extending to the very limits of past and future time. Thus I could not search out how long it will be before this pigeon succeeds in gaining liberation.

The Buddha then told Śāriputra, "The circumstances associated with this pigeon extend beyond the limits of what may be known by the Śrāvaka Disciples and the Pratyekabuddhas. For an additional Ganges sands' number of great kalpas, it will continue to always be reborn in the body of a pigeon. Then, after its karmic punishments have come to an end, it will finally succeed in escaping from this circumstance. After it has circulated about in the five destinies, it will then succeed in becoming a human. Then, after five hundred such lifetimes, it will succeed in developing sharp faculties.

"At that time there will be a buddha who will cross over to liberation countless *asaṃkhyeyas* of beings and will then enter the nirvāṇa without residue (*nirupadhiśeṣa-nirvāṇa*). When the Dharma which he leaves behind is still abiding in the world, this person will become a five-precept *upāsaka* who hears a bhikshu praising the meritorious qualities of the Buddhas. It will be at that very time that he will generate for the very first time the aspiration to become a buddha. Then, for a period of three *asaṃkhyeya* kalpas, he will cultivate the six pāramitās, perfect [the practices associated with] the ten grounds, and will then succeed in becoming a buddha. After he crosses countless beings over to liberation, he himself will then enter the nirvāṇa without residue."

Śāriputra then repented before the Buddha, saying, "I am unable

于一鸟尚不能知其本末。何况诸法。我若知佛智慧如是者。为佛智慧故。宁入阿鼻地狱。受无量劫苦不以为难。	於一鳥尚不能知其本末。何況諸法。我若知佛智慧如是者。為佛智慧故。寧入阿鼻地獄。受無量劫苦不以為難。
简体字	正體字

to know even the origins and destiny of a single pigeon. How much the less am I able to fathom all dharmas. If I was able to gain knowledge comparable to such wisdom as this which the Buddha possesses, then, as the price of gaining the Buddha's wisdom, I would not find it an inordinate hardship even to have to enter the hells and undergo countless kalpas of suffering."

复次佛定众具足。问曰。持戒以身口业清净故可知。智慧以分别说法能除众[2]生疑故可知。定者馀人修定尚不可知。何况于佛云何得知。答曰。大智慧具足故当知禅定必具足。譬如见莲华大必知池亦深大。又如灯明大者必知[3]苏油亦多。亦以佛神通变化力无量无比故。知禅定力亦具足。亦如见果大故知因亦必大。复次有时佛自为人说。我禅定相甚深。如经中说。佛在阿头摩国林树下坐入禅定。是时大雨雷电霹雳。有四特牛耕者二人。闻声怖死。须臾便晴。佛起经行。有一居士礼佛足已。随从佛后白佛言。世尊。向者雷电霹雳。	復次佛定眾具足。問曰。持戒以身口業清淨故可知。智慧以分別說法能除眾[2]生疑故可知。定者餘人修定尚不可知。何況於佛云何得知。答曰。大智慧具足故當知禪定必具足。譬如見蓮華大必知池亦深大。又如燈明大者必知[3]蘇油亦多。亦以佛神通變化力無量無比故。知禪定力亦具足。亦如見果大故知因亦必大。復次有時佛自為人說。我禪定相甚深。如經中說。佛在阿頭摩國林樹下坐入禪定。是時大雨雷電霹靂。有四特牛耕者二人。聞聲怖死。須臾便晴。佛起經行。有一居士禮佛足已。隨從佛後白佛言。世尊。向者雷電霹靂。
简体字	正體字

A Layman Witnesses Buddha's Concentration

Nāgārjuna's Preamble: Buddha's Accomplishment in Meditation

Furthermore, the Buddha's accumulation of the meditative absorptions is entirely perfect.

Question: As for [the Buddha's] upholding of precepts, one is able to know of this on account of the purity of his physical and verbal karma. As for his wisdom, one is able to know of it on account of his making distinctions in his explanations of Dharma and through his ability to dispel the doubts of beings. But, as for his meditative absorptions, one is not even able to know about this in the case of other persons, how much the less would one be able to know about it in the case of the Buddha?

Response: Because his great wisdom is perfect, one should know that his dhyāna absorptions must be entirely perfect. This is analogous to when one sees a lotus blossom which is huge: One necessarily knows that the pool [in which it grew] is both deep and large. It is also just as when there is a lamp whose brightness is great. One necessarily knows that it must also contain a lot of *perilla* oil. Also, because the power of the Buddha's superknowledges and spiritual transformations is incalculable and incomparable, one knows that the power of his dhyāna absorptions is also entirely perfect. This is also just as when one sees a result which is grand, one therefore knows that the cause must be great as well.

Story: A Layman Witnesses Buddha's Concentration

Furthermore, there are times when the Buddha himself has explained this matter for the sake of others, saying, "The qualities of my dhyāna absorptions are extremely profound." This is just as set forth in the scriptures where it is stated that the Buddha was once in the country of Ādumā, sitting beneath a tree in the forest, having entered into dhyāna absorption. At this very time there was a huge rainstorm attended by crashing thunder and lightning bolts. There happened to be a team of four bull oxen and two plowmen who all died from fright on hearing the sound, after which, in a just a brief moment, the sky became clear again. The Buddha then arose and began to walk about.

There was then a layman who, having bowed reverently at the feet of the Buddha, followed on along behind the Buddha and addressed the Buddha, saying, "Bhagavān, there was just now such a crashing of thunder and flashing of lightning bolts that a team of

有四特牛耕者二人闻声怖
死。世尊闻不。佛言。不
闻。居士言。佛时睡耶。佛
言不睡。[4]问曰。入无心想
定耶。佛言。不也。我有心
想但入定耳。居士言。未曾
有也。诸佛禅定大为甚深。
有心想在禅定。如是大声觉
而不闻。

有四特牛耕者二人聞聲怖
死。世尊聞不。佛言。不
聞。居士言。佛時睡耶。佛
言不睡。[4]問曰。入無心想
定耶。佛言。不也。我有心
想但入定耳。居士言。未曾
有也。諸佛禪定大為甚深。
有心想在禪定。如是大聲覺
而不聞。

简体字   正體字

four bull oxen and two plowmen all died from terror on hearing the sound. Did the Bhagavān hear it or not?"

The Buddha said, "I did not even hear it."

The layman said, "Was the Buddha sleeping during this time?"

The Buddha said, "No, I was not sleeping."

[The layman] asked, "Well, was it then a case of his having entered into the 'no-thought' absorption?"

The Buddha said, "No. I was still possessed of thought. It was just that I had entered into absorption, that's all."

The layman said, "This is something which has never been before."

Nāgārjuna's Concluding Comments

The greatness of a Buddha's dhyāna absorption is extremely profound. He may be possessed of thought and abiding in dhyāna absorption, whereupon there occurs such a great sound as this which, even while entirely awake, he nonetheless does not hear at all.

如馀经中。佛告诸比丘。佛入出诸定。舍利弗目捷连[5]尚不闻其名。何况能知何者是。如三昧王三昧师子游戏三昧等。佛入其中能令十方世界六种[6]震动。放大光明化为无量诸佛遍满十方。如阿难一时心生念。过去然灯佛时。时世好人寿长易化度。今释迦牟尼佛时世恶人寿短难教化。佛事未讫而入涅盘耶。清旦以是事白[7]佛。已日出。佛时入日出三昧。如日出光明照阎浮提。佛身如是毛孔普出光明。遍照十方恒河沙等世界。一一光中出七宝千叶莲华。一一华上皆有坐佛。一一诸佛皆放无量光明。一一光中皆出七宝千叶莲华。一一华上皆有坐佛。是诸佛等遍满十方恒河沙等世界教化众生。或有说法或有默然

如餘經中。佛告諸比丘。佛入出諸定。舍利弗目捷連[5]尚不聞其名。何況能知何者是。如三昧王三昧師子遊戲三昧等。佛入其中能令十方世界六種[6]震動。放大光明化為無量諸佛遍滿十方。如阿難一時心生念。過去然燈佛時。時世好人壽長易化度。今釋迦牟尼佛時世惡人壽短難教化。佛事未訖而入涅槃耶。清旦以是事白[7]佛。已日出。佛時入日出三昧。如日出光明照閻浮提。佛身如是毛孔普出光明。遍照十方恒河沙等世界。一一光中出七寶千葉蓮華。一一華上皆有坐佛。一一諸佛皆放無量光明。一一光中皆出七寶千葉蓮華。一一華上皆有坐佛。是諸佛等遍滿十方恒河沙等世界教化眾生。或有說法或有默然

简体字　　　　　　　　正體字

Ānanda Witnesses Buddha's Sunrise Samādhi

Nāgārjuna's Preamble

As noted in another scripture, the Buddha himself told the Bhikshus, "The meditative absorptions which the Buddha enters into and comes out of are such as Śāriputra and Maudgalyāyana have not even heard the names." So how much the less would they be able to know what they are all about. There are, for example, the Samādhi King Samādhi, the Lion's Sport Samādhi, and so forth. When the Buddha enters into them, he is able to cause the worlds of the ten directions to shake and move about in six ways. He emits a great brilliant light which transforms into an incalculable number of Buddhas which universally fill up the ten directions.

Story: Ānanda Witnesses Buddha's Sunrise Samādhi

As a case in point, Ānanda once thought to himself, "In the past, at the time of Burning Lamp Buddha, the world was a fine one, the lifespan of the people was long, and they were easy to teach and bring across to liberation. Now, in the time of Shakyamuni Buddha, the world is an evil one, the lifespan of the people is short, and they are difficult to teach. Will the Buddha nonetheless go ahead and enter nirvāṇa even though the Buddha's work will not have been completed?"

It was early in the morning when [Ānanda] expressed this concern to the Buddha. The sun had already risen. At that very time the Buddha then entered into the sunrise samādhi. Just as when the sun rises, its light illuminates all of Jambudvīpa, so, too, it was with the body of the Buddha. His hair pores all sent forth light which universally illuminated worlds throughout the ten directions as numerous as the sands of the Ganges.

Each and every one of the rays of light put forth a seven-jeweled thousand-petalled lotus blossom. Atop each and every one of the blossoms, there was a buddha seated there. Each and every one of those buddhas sent forth an incalculable number of light beams. From within each and every one of those rays of light there was put forth a seven-jeweled, thousand-petalled lotus blossom. Atop each and every one of those blossoms there was a seated buddha.

All of these buddhas universally filled up worlds throughout the ten directions as numerous as the sands of the Ganges and each of them carried forth with the teaching and transforming of beings. In some cases they spoke Dharma. In some cases they remained silent.

或以经行。或神通变化身出
水火。如是等种种方便。度
脱十方五道众生。阿难承佛
威神悉见是事。佛摄神足从
三昧起。告阿难。见是事
不。闻是事不。阿难言。蒙
佛威神已见已闻。佛言。佛
有如是力能究竟佛事不。阿
难言。世尊。若众生满十方
恒河沙等世界中。佛寿一日
用如[8]是力必能究竟施作佛
事。阿难叹言。未曾有也。
世尊。诸佛法无量不可思
议。以是故知佛禅定具足。

或以經行。或神通變化身出
水火。如是等種種方便。度
脱十方五道眾生。阿難承佛
威神悉見是事。佛攝神足從
三昧起。告阿難。見是事
不。聞是事不。阿難言。蒙
佛威神已見已聞。佛言。佛
有如是力能究竟佛事不。阿
難言。世尊。若眾生滿十方
恒河沙等世界中。佛壽一日
用如[8]是力必能究竟施作佛
事。阿難歎言。未曾有也。
世尊。諸佛法無量不可思
議。以是故知佛禪定具足。

简体字   正體字

In some cases they were walking along. In some cases they engaged in displays of the superknowledges wherein they transformed their bodies and poured forth from them either water or fire. In manners such as these they employed all sorts of skillful means whereby they crossed over to liberation beings throughout the ten directions who were immersed in the five destinies of rebirth.

On account of receiving assistance from the awesome spiritual power of the Buddha, Ānanda was able for a time to completely observe these phenomena. The Buddha then withdrew his manifestation of the fulfillment of spiritual power and then arose from samādhi, asking of Ānanda whether or not he had seen these phenomena and whether or not he had heard these phenomena.

Ānanda replied, "Having received the assistance of the Buddha's awesome spiritual power, I have indeed seen and I have indeed heard."

The Buddha asked, "Given that the Buddha possesses powers such as these, is he able to bring the Buddha's work to ultimate completion or is he not?"

Ānanda replied, "Bhagavān, even in a case where beings filled up worlds throughout the ten directions as numerous as the sands of the Ganges, if the Buddha were to employ powers such as these for just a single day of his life, he would still certainly be able to completely implement the work of the Buddha."

Ānanda exclaimed, "This is a matter such as I have never experienced before. Bhagavān, the Dharma of the Buddhas is immeasurable, inconceivable and ineffable."

Nāgārjuna's Concluding Comment

From this we can know that the Buddha has completely perfected the dhyāna absorptions.

复次行者应念僧。僧是我趣涅盘之真伴。一戒一见如是。应欢喜一心恭敬顺从无违。我先伴种种众恶妻子奴婢人民等。是入三恶道伴。[5]今得圣人伴安隐至涅盘。佛如医王法如良药僧如瞻病人。我[6]当清净持戒正忆念。如佛所说法药我当顺从。僧是我断诸结病中一因缘。所谓瞻病人。是故当念僧。复次僧有无量戒禅定智慧等具足。其德不可测量。如一富贵长者信乐僧。白僧执事。[7]我次第请僧于舍食。日日次请乃至沙弥。执事不听沙弥受请。诸沙弥言。以何意故不听沙弥。

復次行者應念僧。僧是我趣涅槃之真伴。一戒一見如是。應歡喜一心恭敬順從無違。我先伴種種眾惡妻子奴婢人民等。是入三惡道伴。[5]今得聖人伴安隱至涅槃。佛如醫王法如良藥僧如瞻病人。我[6]當清淨持戒正憶念。如佛所說法藥我當順從。僧是我斷諸結病中一因緣。所謂瞻病人。是故當念僧。復次僧有無量戒禪定智慧等具足。其德不可測量。如一富貴長者信樂僧。白僧執事。[7]我次第請僧於舍食。日日次請乃至沙彌。執事不聽沙彌受請。諸沙彌言。以何意故不聽沙彌。

简体字　　　　　　　　　　正體字

The Novices' Lesson to a Benefactor

Nāgārjuna's Preamble: Recollection of the Sangha

Furthermore, the practitioner should engage in recollection of the Sangha, [thinking], "The members of the Sangha are my true companions on the road to nirvāṇa. We all possess identical standards of moral virtue and we all possess identical views [of what constitutes right Dharma]. Thus I should be delighted and single-mindedly engage in respectful behavior, acquiescence, and non-contrariness [in relations with them]. My former companions include wives, sons, servants, citizenry, and other such persons who engage in much unwholesomeness of many varieties. These people were companions on the road to the three wretched destinies. Now, I have gained Āryas as companions with whom I may progress peacefully and securely [along the path] to nirvāṇa."

"The Buddha is comparable to the king of physicians. The Dharma is like excellent medicine. The members of the Sangha are like those who look after the sick. I should uphold the precepts purely, maintaining right mindfulness, and, in accord with manner in which the Buddha set explained the medicine of Dharma, I should comply and follow along with that.

"The Sangha are one of the causes and conditions conducing to my cutting off of the disease of the fetters. They are those so-called "nurses" of the sick. Therefore, I should engage in recollection of the Sangha."

Story: The Novices' Lesson to a Benefactor

Moreover, the Sangha is possessed of countless perfections in the sphere of the [three trainings]: moral-virtue precepts, the dhyāna absorptions, and wisdom. The depth of its meritorious qualities is unfathomable. This is illustrated by the case of a wealthy and noble elder who had faith in and took pleasure in the Sangha. He addressed the manager of Sangha affairs, saying, "I wish to issue invitations according to their proper order to the Sangha, so that they might come to my household for meals." Day after day, he invited them in proper order until the sequence extended on down to the Śrāmaṇeras (the novices). It was at that point that the manager of Sangha affairs did not permit the Śrāmaṇeras to accept the invitation.

The Śrāmaṇeras then inquired, "What is the reasoning behind not allowing the Śrāmaṇeras to go as well?"

答言。以檀越不喜请年少[8]故。便说偈言。

须发白如雪　齿落皮肉皱。
偻步形体羸　乐请如是辈。

[0224b04]　诸沙弥等皆是大阿罗汉。如打师子头欻然从坐起。而说偈言。

檀越无智人　见形不取德。
舍是[9]少年相　但取老瘦黑。

[0224b08]　上尊耆[10]年相者。如佛说偈。

所谓长老相　不必以年耆。
形瘦须发白　空老内无德。
能舍罪福果　精进行梵行。
已离一切法　是名为长老。

[0224b13]　是时诸沙弥复作是念。我等不应坐观。此檀越品量僧好恶。即复说偈。

赞叹呵骂中　我等心虽一。
是人毁佛法　不应不教诲。
当疾到其舍　以法教语之。
我等不度者　是则为弃物。

[0224b19]　即时诸沙弥自变其身皆成老年。须发白如雪秀眉垂

简体字

答言。以檀越不喜請年少[8]故。便說偈言。

鬚髮白如雪　齒落皮肉皺。
傴步形體羸　樂請如是輩。

[0224b04]　諸沙彌等皆是大阿羅漢。如打師子頭欻然從坐起。而說偈言。

檀越無智人　見形不取德。
捨是[9]少年相　但取老瘦黑。

[0224b08]　上尊耆[10]年相者。如佛說偈。

所謂長老相　不必以年耆。
形瘦鬚髮白　空老內無德。
能捨罪福果　精進行梵行。
已離一切法　是名為長老。

[0224b13]　是時諸沙彌復作是念。我等不應坐觀。此檀越品量僧好惡。即復說偈。

讚歎呵罵中　我等心雖一。
是人毀佛法　不應不教誨。
當疾到其舍　以法教語之。
我等不度者　是則為棄物。

[0224b19]　即時諸沙彌自變其身皆成老年。鬚髮白如雪秀眉垂

正體字

He replied, "It is because the Dānapati (the benefactor) doesn't enjoy inviting those who are still so young." He then uttered a verse, saying:

Those whose beard and hair are white like snow—
Those whose teeth are gone and whose skin is wrinkled—
Those with hunch-backed gait and emaciated form—
He enjoys inviting the ones who are of just this sort.

These Śrāmaṇeras happened to all be great arhats. Thus, just as if one had smacked a tiger on the head, they immediately got up from their seats and uttered a verse, saying:

This *dānapati* is a man who has no wisdom.
He looks at forms but does not fix on virtues.
He rejects these signs indicating youthful years,
And seizes only on the withered and dark complexions of the old.

As for revering the appearance of those of a venerable old age, it is just as explained by the Buddha in a verse:

As for the so-called marks of the venerable elder,
It's not necessarily through aging that one is deemed an "elder."
The form may be emaciated, the beard and hair white,
Whilst growing old has been in vain and within there's no virtue.

If able to relinquish effects of karmic offense and blessings—
If one is vigorous in the practice of the brahman conduct—
When one thus manages to transcend all dharmas—
This is what qualifies one as a venerable elder.

The Śrāmaṇeras then thought once again, "We shouldn't just sit by and observe this person of *dānapati* status indulging in calculations regarding the relative goodness of different members of the Sangha. They then uttered another verse:

Within the realm of praise and castigation,
Although our minds behold them all as one,
This person destroys the Dharma of the Buddha,
Hence we shouldn't fail to provide him some instruction.

We should swiftly go forth to his household,
And employ the Dharma to serve him with a lecture.
If we refrain from bringing him across to liberation,
Then this would amount to abandonment of beings.

The Śrāmaṇeras immediately transformed their bodies so that they all assumed the appearance of old age. Their beards and hair were white like snow. Their eyebrows grew long and draped down

覆眼。皮皱如波浪。其脊曲
如弓。两手负杖行。次第而
受请。举身皆振[11]掉。行止
不自安。譬如白[12]杨树随风
而动摇。檀越见此辈欢喜迎
入坐。坐已须臾顷还复年少
形。檀越惊怖言。

如是耆老相　还变成少身。
如服还年药　是事何由然。

[0224b27]　　诸沙弥言。汝莫[13]
生疑畏。我等非非人。汝欲
平量僧。是事甚可伤。我等
相怜愍故现如是化。汝当深
识之圣众不可量。如说。

譬如以蚊[14]嘴　犹可测海底。
一切天[15]与人　无能量僧者。
僧以功德[16]贵　犹尚不分别。
而汝以年岁　称量诸大德。
大小生于智　不在于老少。
有智懃精进　虽少而是老。
懈怠无智慧　虽老而是少。

[0224c08]　　汝今平量僧是则为
大失。如欲以一指测知大海
底。为智者之所笑。

覆眼。皮皺如波浪。其脊曲
如弓。兩手負杖行。次第而
受請。舉身皆振[11]掉。行止
不自安。譬如白[12]楊樹隨風
而動搖。檀越見此輩歡喜迎
入坐。坐已須臾頃還復年少
形。檀越驚怖言。

如是耆老相　還變成少身。
如服還年藥　是事何由然。

[0224b27]　　諸沙彌言。汝莫[13]
生疑畏。我等非非人。汝欲
平量僧。是事甚可傷。我等
相憐愍故現如是化。汝當深
識之聖衆不可量。如說。

譬如以蚊[14]嘴　猶可測海底。
一切天[15]與人　無能量僧者。
僧以功德[16]貴　猶尚不分別。
而汝以年歲　稱量諸大德。
大小生於智　不在於老少。
有智懃精進　雖少而是老。
懈怠無智慧　雖老而是少。

[0224c08]　　汝今平量僧是則為
大失。如欲以一指測知大海
底。為智者之所笑。

简体字　　　　　　　　　　正體字

over their eyes. Their skin became so creased as to appear like waves. Their spines became bent like bows. Their two hands grasped canes as they walked. And so, in proper order, they accepted the invitation. The entire body of each of them trembled and quavered so much so that, whether walking or standing, they remained unstable. They were like the white willow tree which, under the influence of the wind, moves and shakes.

When the Dānapati saw this group, he was delighted and welcomed them to come in and sit down. After they had sat down for only a moment, they instantly reverted in appearance to their youthful forms. The Dānapati was startled and alarmed and so said:

> "For a venerable old appearance like this
> To change back and become the body of a youth—
> It's as if you've drunk the elixir which turns back the years.
> Pray, what is the source of this matter being thus?"

The Śrāmaṇeras said, "Don't be overcome by doubts or fear. It is not the case that we are non-humans. You have aspired to engage in calculations regarding the quality of the Sangha. This is an endeavor which is bound to be extremely injurious. Because we felt pity for you, we manifest transformations of this sort. You should develop a profound understanding about this: The assembly of Āryas is not such as can be fathomed. This is as described herein:

> It's comparable to employing the beak of a mosquito,
> Assuming that one might still thus plumb the ocean's depths.
> Among all of the gods and all of the humans,
> There are none who can fathom those in the Sangha.

> The Sangha takes meritorious qualities as noble,
> And even then, they still make no distinctions.
> And yet you resort to a person's age in years
> In order to judge all who possess great virtue.

> Greatness or pettiness are a function of one's wisdom.
> They are not based on being either elderly or youthful.
> The wise ones earnestly bring forth their vigor
> And, although still young, are nonetheless elders.

> Those who are lazy are lacking in wisdom.
> Although in years aged, still, they are nonetheless young.

"That you now engage in judging the qualities of the Sangha is a grave error. It is as if one wished to use a single finger to plumb the very bottom of the great sea. Such an endeavor is laughed at by the wise.

汝不闻佛说四事虽小而不可
轻。太子虽小当为国王。是
不可轻。蛇子虽小毒能杀
人。亦不可轻。小火虽微能
烧山野。又不可轻[17]也。沙
弥虽小得圣神通最不可轻。
又有四种人。如菴罗果。生
而似熟熟而似生。生而似生
熟而似熟。佛弟子亦如是。
有圣功德成就。而威仪语言
不似善人。有威仪语言似善
人。而圣功德不成就。有威
仪语言不似善人。圣功德未
成就。有威仪语言似[18]善
人。而圣功德成就。汝云何
不念是言。而欲称量于僧。
汝若欲毁僧[19]是则为自毁。
汝为大失。己过事不可追。
方来善心除去诸疑悔。听我
所[20]说。
圣众不可量　难以威仪知。
不可以族姓　亦不以多闻。
亦不以威[21]德　又不以耆年。

汝不聞佛說四事雖小而不可
輕。太子雖小當為國王。是
不可輕。蛇子雖小毒能殺
人。亦不可輕。小火雖微能
燒山野。又不可輕[17]也。沙
彌雖小得聖神通最不可輕。
又有四種人。如菴羅果。生
而似熟熟而似生。生而似生
熟而似熟。佛弟子亦如是。
有聖功德成就。而威儀語言
不似善人。有威儀語言似善
人。而聖功德不成就。有威
儀語言不似善人。聖功德未
成就。有威儀語言似[18]善
人。而聖功德成就。汝云何
不念是言。而欲稱量於僧。
汝若欲毀僧[19]是則為自毀。
汝為大失。己過事不可追。
方來善心除去諸疑悔。聽我
所[20]說。
聖眾不可量　難以威儀知。
不可以族姓　亦不以多聞。
亦不以威[21]德　又不以耆年。

"Have you not heard the Buddha declare that there are four situations where although something is small, still, one cannot look on it lightly? Although a prince may be small, he will become the king of the country. This is one who cannot be slighted. A baby snake, although small, possesses poison which can kill a man and hence it, too, cannot be looked on lightly. A small fire, although still just faint, is nonetheless able to burn up the mountains and wilderness. It too cannot be looked upon lightly. A śrāmaṇera, although but small, may have obtained the superknowledges of the Ārya and thus he is the one who one most cannot slight.

"Furthermore, there are four kinds of people who are comparable to the *āmra* (mango) fruit: Those who are unripe and yet appear to be ripe; those who are ripe and yet appear to be unripe; those who are unripe and so do appear to be unripe; and those which are ripe and so do appear to be ripe.

"The disciples of the Buddha are just like this. There are those who have perfected the meritorious qualities of an ārya, and yet, as regards their deportment and speech, they do not seem to be good people. There are those who, by their deportment and speech, appear to be good persons, and yet they have not perfected the meritorious qualities of an ārya. There are those who, by their deportment and speech do not appear to be good persons, and who have not in fact perfected the meritorious qualities of an ārya. And then there are those who possess deportment and speech which appear like those of the good person and they have indeed perfected the meritorious qualities of an ārya.

"Why is it that you have not remained mindful of these words and so have desired to make judgments regarding the qualities of the Sangha? If it was your desire to destroy the Sangha, this then is actually just self-destruction. You have committed a grave error.

Those things which have already transpired cannot be pursued. However, in the future, if you bring forth a wholesome mind, you will be able to get rid of your doubts and regrets. You should listen to what we explain:

The assembly of the Āryas cannot be fathomed.
It would be difficult to judge on the basis of deportment.
One can't assess either by one's family or name.
Nor can one know on account of great learning.

One also can't know through the quality of awesomeness,
Nor can one deduce through one's elderly age.

简体字	正體字
亦不以严容　复不以辩言。	亦不以嚴容　復不以辯言。
圣众大海水　功德故甚深。	聖眾大海水　功德故甚深。
佛以百事赞是僧	佛以百事讚是僧
施之虽少得[22]报多。	施之雖少得[22]報多。
是第三宝声远闻。	是第三寶聲遠聞。
以是故应供养僧	以是故應供養僧
不应分别是老少。	不應分別是老少。
多知少闻及明暗。	多知少聞及明闇。
如人观林不分别。	如人觀林不分別。
伊兰瞻卜及萨罗。	伊蘭瞻蔔及薩羅。
汝欲念僧[1]当如是。	汝欲念僧[1]當如是。
不应以愚分别圣。	不應以愚分別聖。
摩诃迦叶出家时。	摩訶迦葉出家時。
纳衣价直十万金。	納衣價直十萬金。
欲作乞人下贱服。	欲作乞人下賤服。
更求麁弊不能得。	更求麁弊不能得。
圣众僧中亦如是。	聖眾僧中亦如是。
求索最下小福田。	求索最下小福田。
能[2]报施者十万倍。	能[2]報施者十萬倍。
更求不如不可得。	更求不如不可得。
众僧大海[3]水　结戒为畔际。	眾僧大海[3]水　結戒為畔際。
若有破戒者　终不在僧数。	若有破戒者　終不在僧數。
譬如大海水　不共死尸宿。	譬如大海水　不共死屍宿。
[0225a11]　　檀越闻是事。见是神通力身惊毛竖。合[4]掌白诸沙弥言。诸圣人。我今忏悔。我是凡夫[5]人心常怀罪。我有少疑今欲请问。而说偈言。	[0225a11]　　檀越聞是事。見是神通力身驚毛竪。合[4]掌白諸沙彌言。諸聖人。我今懺悔。我是凡夫[5]人心常懷罪。我有少疑今欲請問。而說偈言。
大德[6]已过疑　我今得遭遇。	大德[6]已過疑　我今得遭遇。
若复不谘问　则是愚中愚。	若復不諮問　則是愚中愚。

One cannot know either from a demeanor that is solemn.
And again, one cannot know through one's eloquent words.

The waters of the great sea of the assembly of Āryas
On account of their meritorious qualities, is extremely deep.

The Buddha praised this Sangha on one hundred bases.
A gift to them, though little, brings a reward which is much.
This third of the Jewels is famous even in distant quarters.
Thus for such reasons, one should make offerings to the Sangha.

One should not make discriminations based on either age or youth,
By much knowledge, scant learning, brilliance, or dullness.
Just as in viewing the forest, one does not distinguish
Which [tree] is *campaka*, which *eraṇḍa*, and which *śāla*.

If you wish to be mindful of Sangha, accord then with this:
One shouldn't so foolishly make discriminations regarding āryas.

When Mahākāśyapa left off the home life,
His monk's robe was worth a hundred thousand in gold.
He wished to take on the humble robes of an almsman,
And sought for more coarse ones but couldn't obtain them.

In the Sangha's assembly of Āryas, it is also like this:
One may seek for the least among the fields of merit.
Still, he rewards a donor a hundred thousand fold.
One might search for one who is inferior, but one cannot be found.

In the waters of the great sea of the assembly of the Sangha,
The formulation of precepts is what forms the line of its shore.
If there be one who has broken the precepts,
He finally isn't counted as being in the Sangha.

It's just as it is with the great ocean's waters,
Which does not abide with corpses [and so casts them ashore]."

The Dānapati listened to this matter. When he had observed the effect of these spiritual powers, he was so shocked that the hairs of his body stood on end. He pressed his palms together and addressed the Śrāmaṇeras, saying, "Āryas, I now repent. I am but a common person whose mind is constantly embracing offenses. Still, I have a minor doubt which I now wish to ask about." He then uttered a verse:

Those of great virtue have passed beyond doubt.
And now I myself have here managed to meet them.
But if once again I don't set forth a question,
This would be foolishness in the midst of foolishness."

[0225a17]　諸沙弥言。汝欲问者便问。我当以所闻答檀越问言。于佛宝中信心清净。于僧宝中信心清净。何者福胜。答[7]曰。我等初不见僧宝佛宝有增减。何以故。佛一时舍婆提乞食。有[8]一婆罗门姓婆罗埵逝。佛数数到其家乞食。心作是念。是沙门何以[9]来数数[10]如负其债。佛时说偈。

时雨数数堕　五谷数数成。
数数修福业　数数受果报。
数数受生法　故受数数死。
圣法数数成　谁数数生死。

[0225a28]　婆罗[11]门闻是偈已。作是念。佛大圣人具知我心。惭愧取钵入舍盛满美食以奉上佛。佛不受作是言。我为说偈故得此食我不食也。婆罗门言。是食当与谁。佛言。我不见天及人能消[12]是食者。汝持去置少草地[13]若无[14]虫水中。即如佛教持食着无虫水中。水即大沸烟火俱出。如投大热铁。婆罗门见已惊怖言未曾有也。乃至食中神力如是。

[0225a17]　諸沙彌言。汝欲問者便問。我當以所聞答檀越問言。於佛寶中信心清淨。於僧寶中信心清淨。何者福勝。答[7]曰。我等初不見僧寶佛寶有增減。何以故。佛一時舍婆提乞食。有[8]一婆羅門姓婆羅埵逝。佛數數到其家乞食。心作是念。是沙門何以[9]來數數[10]如負其債。佛時說偈。

時雨數數堕　五穀數數成。
數數修福業　數數受果報。
數數受生法　故受數數死。
聖法數數成　誰數數生死。

[0225a28]　婆羅[11]門聞是偈已。作是念。佛大聖人具知我心。慚愧取鉢入舍盛滿美食以奉上佛。佛不受作是言。我為說偈故得此食我不食也。婆羅門言。是食當與誰。佛言。我不見天及人能消[12]是食者。汝持去置少草地[13]若無[14]虫水中。即如佛教持食著無虫水中。水即大沸烟火俱出。如投大熱鐵。婆羅門見已驚怖言未曾有也。乃至食中神力如是。

簡体字　　　　　　　正體字

The Śrāmaṇeras responded, "Go ahead and inquire according to your wishes and we shall reply as befits the question.

The Dānapati asked, "Which situation is more supreme as regards merit: a pure faith in the Buddha Jewel or a pure faith in the Sangha Jewel?"

They replied, saying, "We have never perceived any relatively greater or lesser stature between the Sangha Jewel and the Buddha Jewel. Why is this?

Story within the Story: Buddha Refuses Bhāradvāja's Offering

"Once when the Buddha was making his alms rounds in Śrāvastī, he went repeatedly for alms to the household of a brahman named Bhāradvāja. This led the brahman to think, 'Why is it that this *śramaṇa* comes here time after time? It's as if I owe him some debt.'"

"At that point the Buddha uttered a verse:

'The seasonal rains fall time after time.
The five sorts of grain ripen time after time.
Time after time, one may cultivate meritorious karma.
Time after time, one receives the fruits in reward.

Time after time, one takes on the dharma of rebirth.
Thus, time after time, one's then bound to die.
The Dharma of the Ārya is perfected time after time.
Who then, time after time, goes through birth and then death?'

"After that brahman had listened to this verse, he had this thought, 'The Buddha is a great Ārya who knows my mind utterly.' He then felt ashamed, took the bowl, entered his house, and filled it with fine cuisine which he then offered up to the Buddha. The Buddha refused to accept it and then said, 'Because I gained this food through the utterance of a verse, I cannot eat it.'

"The Brahman said, 'Then to whom should I present this food?'

"The Buddha replied, 'I do not perceive that there is anyone, whether god or man, who can digest this food. You should take this food to a place of little vegetation or immerse it in water free of insects.'"

"Then, following the Buddha's instructions, he took the food and placed it in water free of insects, whereupon the water simultaneously boiled and poured forth smoke and fire. It was just as if he had thrown in intensely hot metal. When the brahman had observed this he was alarmed and frightened, exclaiming, 'This is unprecedented that even his food possesses such spiritual powers

还到佛所头面礼佛足。忏悔
乞出家受戒。佛言善来。即
时须发自堕便成沙门。渐渐
断结得阿罗汉道。复有摩诃
憍昙弥。以金色上下[15]宝
衣奉佛。佛知众僧堪能受用
告憍昙弥。以此上下衣与
众僧。以是故知佛宝僧宝福
无多少。檀越言。若为佛布
施。僧能消能受。何以故。
婆罗埵逝婆罗门食佛不教令
僧食。诸沙弥答[16]言。为显
僧大力故。若不见食在水中
有大神力者。无以知僧力为
大。若为佛施物而僧得受。
便知僧力为大。譬如药师欲
试毒药。先以与鸡鸡即时死
然后自服。乃知药[17]师威力
为大。是故檀越当知。
若人爱敬佛　　[18]亦当爱敬僧。
不当有分别　　同皆为宝故。
[0225b22]　　尔时檀越闻说[19]是
事欢喜言。我某甲从今日若
有入僧数中。若小若大一心
信

簡体字

還到佛所頭面禮佛足。懺悔
乞出家受戒。佛言善來。即
時鬚髮自墮便成沙門。漸漸
斷結得阿羅漢道。復有摩訶
憍曇彌。以金色上下[15]寶
衣奉佛。佛知眾僧堪能受用
告憍曇彌。以此上下衣與眾
僧。以是故知佛寶僧寶福無
多少。檀越言。若為佛布
施。僧能消能受。何以故。
婆羅埵逝婆羅門食佛不教令
僧食。諸沙彌答[16]言。為顯
僧大力故。若不見食在水中
有大神力者。無以知僧力為
大。若為佛施物而僧得受。
便知僧力為大。譬如藥師欲
試毒藥。先以與鷄鷄即時死
然後自服。乃知藥[17]師威力
為大。是故檀越當知。
若人愛敬佛　　[18]亦當愛敬僧。
不當有分別　　同皆為寶故。
[0225b22]　　爾時檀越聞說[19]是
事歡喜言。我某甲從今日若
有入僧數中。若小若大一心
信

正體字

as this.' He then returned to where the Buddha was, bowed down his head in reverence at the feet of the Buddha, repented, begged to leave the home life, and took on the moral precepts. The Buddha then said, 'Come forth well.' [Bhāradvāja's] beard and hair immediately fell away, whereupon he became a *śramaṇa*. He gradually cut off the fetters and succeeded in gaining the way of the arhat."

The Main Story Continues

"Additionally, there was the case wherein Mahāgautamī made an offering to the Buddha of precious gold-colored upper and lower robes. The Buddha knew that the assembled members of the Sangha were able to accept and use them. So he told Gautamī to give these upper and lower robes to the assembled members of the Sangha. One can know from this that there is no issue of greater or lesser merit between the Buddha Jewel and the Sangha Jewel."

The Dānapati then asked, "If it is the case that the Sangha is able to digest and is able to accept something given to the Buddha as a gift, why didn't the Buddha instruct that the monks be allowed to eat the food offered by the brahman Bhāradvāja?"

The Śrāmaṇeras replied, "This was done for the sake of displaying the great power of the Sangha. If he had not observed that such food placed in water possessed such great spiritual potency, he would have had no way of knowing that the power of the Sangha is so great. Because, [in the case of Mahāgautamī's offering], the Sangha was then deemed fit to accept something given to the Buddha, we know that the power of the Sangha is great.

"This is analogous to the process used by a master of herbal potions in his testing of toxic herbal potions. If he were to first give it to a chicken, causing the chicken to immediately die, and he were then to drink the potion himself, one would then know that the herb master possessed an awesome power which is great indeed. Therefore the Dānapati should realize:

If a person regards the Buddha with fondness and respect,
He should also regard the Sangha with fondness and respect.
One should not engage in making such distinctions,
For the both of them qualify as 'jewels.'"

At that time when the Dānapati had listened to this matter, he was delighted and said, "I, so-and-so, from this very day forward, whenever I might go among the ranks of the Sangha, whether they be young or old, I shall single-mindedly treat them with faith and

敬不敢分别。诸沙弥言。汝
心信敬[20]无上福田。不久当
得道。何以故。
多闻及持戒　智慧禅定者。
皆入僧数中　如万川归海。
譬如众药草　依止于雪山。
百谷诸草木　皆依止于地。
一切诸善人　皆在僧数中。

[0225c02] 复次汝等曾闻佛为长
鬼神将军赞三善男子阿泥卢
陀难提迦翅弥罗不。佛言。
若一切世间天及人。一心念
三善男子长夜得无量利益。
以是事故倍当信敬僧。是三
人不名僧。佛说念三人有如
是果报。何况一心清净念
僧。是故檀越当[21]任力念[22]
僧名。如说偈。
是诸圣人众　则为雄猛军。
摧灭魔王贼　是伴至涅盘。

[0225c11] 诸沙弥为檀越。种种
说僧圣功德。檀越闻已举家
大小皆见四谛得须陀洹道。
以是因缘故。应当一心念
僧。

敬不敢分別。諸沙彌言。汝
心信敬[20]無上福田。不久當
得道。何以故。
多聞及持戒　智慧禪定者。
皆入僧數中　如萬川歸海。
譬如眾藥草　依止於雪山。
百穀諸草木　皆依止於地。
一切諸善人　皆在僧數中。

[0225c02] 復次汝等曾聞佛為長
鬼神將軍讚三善男子阿泥盧
陀難提迦翅彌羅不。佛言。
若一切世間天及人。一心念
三善男子長夜得無量利益。
以是事故倍當信敬僧。是三
人不名僧。佛說念三人有如
是果報。何況一心清淨念
僧。是故檀越當[21]任力念[22]
僧名。如說偈。
是諸聖人眾　則為雄猛軍。
摧滅魔王賊　是伴至涅槃。

[0225c11] 諸沙彌為檀越。種種
說僧聖功德。檀越聞已舉家
大小皆見四諦得須陀洹道。
以是因緣故。應當一心念
僧。

简体字　　　　　　　　正體字

respect, and shall not dare to make any discriminations regarding them."

The Śrāmaṇeras said, "If your mind possesses a faithful respect in the unsurpassed field of blessings, you shall succeed before long in gaining the Path. Why?:

Those of much learning, observers of precepts,
The wise, and adepts in dhyāna absorption,
They all enter into the ranks of the Sangha,
As the myriad streams all return to the sea.

Just as the manifold herbs and the shrubs,
Have come to abide in the snow-mantled mountains,
And just as the hundred-fold crops, shrubs, and trees
All do depend on and rest on the earth,

Just so, all the persons who are graced with much goodness
All come to abide in the ranks of the Sangha.

"Furthermore, haven't you heard that, for the benefit of Dīrgha, a general among the ghosts and spirits, the Buddha praised three sons of good family, namely Aniruddha, Nandika, and Kimbila? The Buddha said, 'If all of the world's gods and humans became single-minded in their recollection of these three sons of good family, then, during the long night [of cyclic existence], they would gain incalculable benefits.'

"Because of this one ought to bring forth redoubled faith and reverence for the Sangha. These three men did not by themselves constitute the Sangha. Since the Buddha stated that recollection of just these three men brings such fruits as reward, how much the more so would such effects arise from single-minded pure recollection of the entire Sangha. Therefore, the Dānapati should invest the full extent of his powers in recollection of the name of the Sangha. This is as explained in a verse:

This community of all of the Āryas
Makes up a heroic and valiant army
Which crushes the demon king rebels.
These are companions on through to nirvāṇa."

The Śrāmaṇeras provided to this *dānapati* all manner of descriptions of the meritorious qualities of the Sangha's āryas. When the Dānapati had finished listening, his entire household, both young and old, all experienced the perception of the four truths and gained the path of a *śrota-āpanna*. For these reasons, one should single-mindedly engage in recollection of the Sangha.

复次财物[17]是种种烦恼罪
业因缘。若持戒禅定智慧种
种善法。是涅盘因缘。以是
故财物[18]尚应自弃。何况好
福田中[19]而不布施。譬如有
兄弟二人。各担十斤金行道
中更无馀伴。兄作是念我何
以不杀弟取金。此旷路中人
无知者。弟复生念欲杀兄取
金。兄弟各有恶心。语言视
[20]瞻皆异。兄弟即自悟还
生悔心。我等非人与禽兽何
异。同生兄弟而为少金故而
生恶心。兄弟共至深水边。
兄以金投着水中。弟言。善
哉善哉。弟寻复弃金水中。
兄复言。善哉善哉。兄弟[21]
更互相问。何以[22]故言善
哉。各[23]相答言。我以此金
故。生不善心欲相[24]危害
今得弃之故言善哉。二辞各
尔。

復次財物[17]是種種煩惱罪
業因緣。若持戒禪定智慧種
種善法。是涅槃因緣。以是
故財物[18]尚應自棄。何況好
福田中[19]而不布施。譬如有
兄弟二人。各擔十斤金行道
中更無餘伴。兄作是念我何
以不殺弟取金。此曠路中人
無知者。弟復生念欲殺兄取
金。兄弟各有惡心。語言視
[20]瞻皆異。兄弟即自悟還
生悔心。我等非人與禽獸何
異。同生兄弟而為少金故而
生惡心。兄弟共至深水邊。
兄以金投著水中。弟言。善
哉善哉。弟尋復棄金水中。
兄復言。善哉善哉。兄弟[21]
更互相問。何以[22]故言善
哉。各[23]相答言。我以此金
故。生不善心欲相[24]危害
今得棄之故言善哉。二辭各
爾。

简体字   正體字

Two Brothers Throw Away Their Gold

Nāgārjuna's Preamble

Furthermore, valuable material possessions constitute the causes and conditions for all sorts of afflictions and offense karma whereas observing the precepts, developing dhyāna absorption, and bringing forth wisdom and all of the many other sorts of good dharmas constitute the causal bases for the realization of nirvāṇa. Therefore one should constantly engage in the spontaneous riddance of valuable material possessions, how much the less should one fail to engage in giving even in the presence of an excellent field of blessings?

Story: Two Brothers Throw Away Their Gold

This is illustrated by the case of two brothers who, free of any escort, were traveling down the road, each carrying ten pounds of gold. The elder brother had this thought, "Why don't I just go ahead and kill my younger brother and take his gold? On such a deserted wilderness road as this, no one would know."

The younger brother also had thoughts wherein he wished to kill the elder brother and confiscate his gold. Thus, the elder and younger brothers were each entertaining evil thoughts, such that what they were saying and what they were envisioning were at odds.

The two brothers then suddenly and spontaneously came to their senses, felt remorse, and then thought, "We are inhuman! How are we any different from birds and beasts? We are brothers born of the same mother and yet now, just for the sake of a little gold, we begin to consider such evil thoughts."

The two brothers arrived at the edge of a deep river and then the elder brother threw his gold into the water, whereupon the younger brother exclaimed, "Good indeed! Good indeed!"

Next, the younger brother threw his gold into the water as well, whereupon the elder brother also exclaimed, "Good indeed! Good indeed!"

The two brothers then turned to each other and simultaneously asked, "Why did you say, 'Good indeed! Good indeed!'?"

They each replied, "On account of this gold, I contemplated unwholesome thoughts desirous of inflicting harm. Now, because I've gotten rid of it, I say, 'Good indeed!'." They each described it in this way.

以是故知财为恶心因缘常应 自舍。何况施得大福而[25]不 施。如[26]说。 施[27]名行宝藏　亦为善亲友。 [28]终始相利益　无有能坏者。 施为[1]好密盖　能遮饥渴雨。 施为坚牢船　能度贫穷海。 悭为凶衰相　为之生忧畏。 洗之以施水　则为[2]生福利。 悭惜不衣食　终身无欢乐。 虽云有财物　与贫困无异。 悭人之室宅　譬如丘冢墓。 [3]求者远避[4]之　终无有向 者。 如是悭贪人　智者所[5]摈弃。 命气虽未尽　与死等无异。 悭人无福慧　于施无坚要。 临当堕死坑　恋惜生懊恨。 涕泣当独去　忧悔火烧身。 好施者安乐　终无有是苦。	以是故知財為惡心因緣常應 自捨。何況施得大福而[25]不 施。如[26]說。 施[27]名行寶藏　亦為善親友。 [28]終始相利益　無有能壞者。 施為[1]好密蓋　能遮飢渴雨。 施為堅牢船　能度貧窮海。 慳為凶衰相　為之生憂畏。 洗之以施水　則為[2]生福利。 慳惜不衣食　終身無歡樂。 雖云有財物　與貧困無異。 慳人之室宅　譬如丘塚墓。 [3]求者遠避[4]之　終無有向 者。 如是慳貪人　智者所[5]擯棄。 命氣雖未盡　與死等無異。 慳人無福慧　於施無堅要。 臨當墮死坑　戀惜生懊恨。 涕泣當獨去　憂悔火燒身。 好施者安樂　終無有是苦。
简体字	正體字

Nāgārjuna's Concluding Discussion

From this, one knows that material wealth is a cause and condition for evil thoughts. One should constantly engage in spontaneous relinquishing of it, how much the more so should one avoid failure to give when such giving will cause one to obtain great karmic blessings. This is as illustrated in a verse:

A Verse in Praise of Giving

To give is the treasury of the jewels of practice,
It's also a good and an intimate friend,
Which, beginning to end, brings forth benefit and increase.
There's nothing whatever that's able to destroy it.

This giving is an excellent and well-sealed covering.
It's able to block rains of hunger and thirst.
This giving is a solid and durable vessel.
It's able to ferry across an ocean of poverty.

The miserly nature marks inauspiciousness and failure.
Because of it, one becomes anxious and fearful.
It's cleansed with the waters which flow forth from giving.
This then creates benefits linked to one's blessings.

Being miserly and sparing brings neither clothing nor food.
To the end of this life, there's no delight and no bliss.
Though one speaks of possessing such valuable artifacts,
This isn't any different from the misery of poverty.

The household dwelt in by the miserly person
Is aptly compared to a burial tomb site.
For any who would seek out one just avoid it at great distance.
In the end, there is no one inclined to go hence.

So any who are miserly and greedy like this,
Are such as the wise are inclined to reject.
Though energies of this life haven't yet been exhausted,
Still, he's no different at all from a man who has died.

A miserly man has no blessings or wisdom,
And for the practice of giving feels no firm commitment.
When about to plunge down in the chasm of death,
He's maudlin and clinging, feeling bitter distress.

He grievously weeps that he goes on alone.
The fires of sorrow burn throughout his whole being.
But those who love giving are peaceful and happy
And when their lives end, then they feel no such anguish.

人修布施者　名闻满十方。
智者所爱敬　入众无所畏。
命终生天上　久必得涅盘。

[0227a18]　如是等种种诃[6]悭贪赞布施。是名念财施。

人修布施者　名聞滿十方。
智者所愛敬　入眾無所畏。
命終生天上　久必得涅槃。

[0227a18]　如是等種種訶[6]悭貪讚布施。是名念財施。

简体字

正體字

The man who strives on in the practice of giving
Finds fame and renown throughout all ten directions.
He's loved and respected by those who are wise
So that entering any gathering, he's free of dismay.

At the end of this life, he's reborn in the heavens,
And then, in the long term, nirvāṇa is certain.

In all sorts of ways such as this, one criticizes miserliness and praises giving. This is what is meant by recollection of the giving of material wealth.

念死者。有二种死。一者自
死二者他因缘死。是二种死
行者常念。是身若他不杀必
当自死。如是有为法中。不
应弹指顷生信不死心。是身
一切时中皆有死不待老。不
应[1]恃是种种忧恼凶衰身。
生心望安隐不死。是心痴人
所生。身中四大各各相害。
如人持毒蛇箧。云何智人以
为安隐。若出气保当还入入
息保[2]出。睡眠[3]保复得还
觉。是皆难必。何以故。是
身内外多怨故。如说。
或有胎中死 　或有生时死。
或年壮时死 　或[4]老至时死。
亦如果熟时 　种种因缘堕。
当求[5]免离此 　死[6]怨之恶
贼。
是贼难可信 　[7]时舍则安隐。
假使大智人 　威德力无上。
无前亦无后 　于今无脱者。

念死者。有二種死。一者自
死二者他因緣死。是二種死
行者常念。是身若他不殺必
當自死。如是有為法中。不
應彈指頃生信不死心。是身
一切時中皆有死不待老。不
應[1]恃是種種憂惱凶衰身。
生心望安隱不死。是心癡人
所生。身中四大各各相害。
如人持毒蛇篋。云何智人以
為安隱。若出氣保當還入入
息保[2]出。睡眠[3]保復得還
覺。是皆難必。何以故。是
身內外多怨故。如說。
或有胎中死 　或有生時死。
或年壯時死 　或[4]老至時死。
亦如果熟時 　種種因緣墮。
當求[5]免離此 　死[6]怨之惡
賊。
是賊難可信 　[7]時捨則安隱。
假使大智人 　威德力無上。
無前亦無後 　於今無脫者。

简体字   正體字

The Buddha Questions Monks on Mindfulness of Death

Nāgārjuna's Preamble: Recollection of Death

As for "Recollection of Death," there are two sorts of death: death by natural causes and death due to other causal factors. The practitioner is constantly mindful of these two kinds of death and so bears in mind that this body, if not slain by another, will certainly die of its own accord. Among composite dharmas such as these, one shouldn't entertain a thought of belief that one might not die even for a moment as brief as a finger snap.

This body is constantly involved in dying and does not await the arrival of old age [for its occurrence]. One should not depend on this body, beset as it is by all manner of calamitous afflictions and by the fierce process of deterioration, hoping somehow that one might be able to remain secure and unaffected by death. Thoughts of this sort are entertained only by foolish people.

The four great elements within the body are engaged in mutual destruction. The situation is analogous to that of a person carrying around a basket of venomous snakes. How could a wise person see any peace or security in this? It is difficult to guarantee with any certainty that, breathing out, one will be able to breath in again, that breathing in, one will be able to breath out again, and, that falling asleep, one will be able to wake up again. Why is this? It is because this body, both inwardly and outwardly, is beset by many adversaries. This is as explained in a verse:

A Mindfulness of Death Verse

Perhaps one will die while still in the womb.
Perhaps one will die at the time of one's birth.
Perhaps one will die at the height of one's strength.
Perhaps one will die just as old age arrives.

This may also be compared to when a fruit ripens
And through many causes and conditions proceeds then to fall.

One might seek a means to leave this behind.
The hated thief, the evil of death
Such a thief is so hard to trust.
Only when abandoned will security be gained.

Even supposing one's a man of great wisdom,
With unsurpassed powers of awesome virtue,
Whose become free of the past and the future,
Still, in the present, none can escape it.

亦无巧辞谢　无请求得脱。
亦无捍挌处　可以得免者。
亦非持净戒　精进可以脱。
死贼无怜愍　来时无避处。

[0228a24]　是故行者不应于无常危脆命中而信望活。如佛为比丘说死[8]相义。有一比丘偏袒白[9]佛。我能修是死[*]相。佛言。汝云何修。比丘言。我不望过七岁活。佛言。汝为放逸修死[*]相。有比丘言。我不望过七月活。有比丘言七日。有言六五四三二一日活。佛言。汝等皆是放逸修死[10]相。有言从旦至食时。有言一食顷。佛言。汝等亦是放逸修死[*]相。一比丘偏袒白佛。我于出气不望入。于入气不望出。佛言。[11]是真修死相为不放逸。比丘。一切有为法念念生灭。住时甚少其犹如幻。欺诳无智行者。

亦無巧辭謝　無請求得脱。
亦無捍挌處　可以得免者。
亦非持淨戒　精進可以脱。
死賊無憐愍　來時無避處。

[0228a24]　是故行者不應於無常危脆命中而信望活。如佛為比丘說死[8]相義。有一比丘偏袒白[9]佛。我能修是死[*]相。佛言。汝云何修。比丘言。我不望過七歲活。佛言。汝為放逸修死[*]相。有比丘言。我不望過七月活。有比丘言七日。有言六五四三二一日活。佛言。汝等皆是放逸修死[10]相。有言從旦至食時。有言一食頃。佛言。汝等亦是放逸修死[*]相。一比丘偏袒白佛。我於出氣不望入。於入氣不望出。佛言。[11]是真修死相為不放逸。比丘。一切有為法念念生滅。住時甚少其猶如幻。欺誑無智行者。

简体字

正體字

Nor may one cleverly and politely decline.
There's no point in requesting to be set free.
Nor is there some place from which to fend it off
And thus thereby be able to avoid it.

Nor is it the case through observance of precepts
Or by practice of vigor one then might be freed.
The thief of death is devoid of pity.
When it comes, there's no place to avoid it.

Therefore the practitioner, ensconced in an impermanent and fragile life span, should not trust in or hope for survival.

Story: The Buddha Questions Monks on Mindfulness of Death

This point is illustrated by an instance when the Buddha was explaining for the Bhikshus the meaning of the reflection on death. There was one bhikshu who arranged his robes to one side, [baring his right shoulder], and then addressed the Buddha, "I am able to cultivate this reflection on death."

The Buddha asked, "How, then, does one cultivate it?"

The Bhikshu replied, "I cherish no hope to live beyond another seven years."

The Buddha declared, "You are negligent in your practice of the reflection on death."

There was another bhikshu who said, "I cherish no hope of living beyond another seven months." There was yet another bhikshu who spoke of living only another seven days, and others who spoke of but six, five, four, three, two, and a single day.

The Buddha responded, "All of you are negligent in your cultivation of the reflection on death." Then there was one who spoke of the period from dawn to mealtime and another who spoke of the space of a meal. To both of these, the Buddha replied, "You, too, are negligent in your cultivation of the reflection on death."

Then one more bhikshu arranged his robes to bare the right shoulder and addressed the Buddha, "When I exhale, I cherish no hope of being able to inhale again. When inhaling, I cherish no hope of being able to exhale again."

The Buddha then replied, "This does constitute a genuine cultivation of the reflection on death which reveals no negligence. Bhikshus, all composite dharmas are newly produced and destroyed in each successive moment. The duration of their abiding is so extremely brief that they are like a magical conjuration deceiving those practitioners deficient in wisdom."

如是观食则生厌想。因食厌故于五欲[15]中皆厌。譬如一婆罗门修净洁法。有事缘故到不净国。自[16]思我当云何得免此不净。唯当乾食可得清净。见一老母卖白[17]髓饼而语之言。我有因缘住此百日。常作此饼送来当多与价。老母日日作饼送之。婆罗门贪着饱食欢喜。老母作饼初时白净。后转无色无味。即问老母何缘尔[18]耶。母言痈疮差故。婆罗门[19]问。此言何谓。母言。我大家夫人隐处生痈。以面酥甘草拊之。痈熟脓出和合[*]酥饼。[20]日日如是。以此作饼与汝。是以饼好。今夫人痈差。我当何处更[21]得。婆罗门闻之两[22]拳打头[23]搥胸[24]吁呕。我当云何破此净法我为了矣。弃舍缘事驰还本国。

简体字

如是觀食則生厭想。因食厭故於五欲[15]中皆厭。譬如一婆羅門修淨潔法。有事緣故到不淨國。自[16]思我當云何得免此不淨。唯當乾食可得清淨。見一老母賣白[17]髓餅而語之言。我有因緣住此百日。常作此餅送來當多與價。老母日日作餅送之。婆羅門貪著飽食歡喜。老母作餅初時白淨。後轉無色無味。即問老母何緣爾[18]耶。母言癰瘡差故。婆羅門[19]問。此言何謂。母言。我大家夫人隱處生癰。以麵酥甘草拊之。癰熟膿出和合[*]酥餅。[20]日日如是。以此作餅與汝。是以餅好。今夫人癰差。我當何處更[21]得。婆羅門聞之兩[22]拳打頭[23]搥胸[24]吁嘔。我當云何破此淨法我為了矣。棄捨緣事馳還本國。

正體字

The Traveling Brahman's Quest for Pure Food

If one contemplates food in this manner [as prescribed by the correct contemplation on the nature of food], then one develops the reflection on its repulsiveness. Because of this revulsion with respect to food, one develops a disgust with all of the five objects of desire.

This is illustrated by the case of the Brahman who cultivated the dharma of maintaining purity. Because of a situation associated with his work, he traveled to a country noted for its lack of purity. He thought to himself, "How am I going to be able to avoid this defilement? It is solely through restricting myself to eating dry foods that I will be able to maintain purity."

Observing that there happened to be an elderly matron who was selling cakes with a white filling, he then told her, "I have encountered a situation requiring me to abide here for a hundred days. If you will continue to make these cakes and bring them to me, then I shall pay you a premium beyond their value." The elderly matron then made these cakes every day and delivered them to him. The Brahman became covetously attached to them. He would eat his fill and then abide in happiness.

When the elderly matron first made these cakes, they were completely white in their purity. Later on, however, they became colorless and lacking in flavor. He then asked the elderly matron, "Why have they now become like this?"

The matron replied, "It's because the open sore from the abscess has healed over."

The Brahman asked, "What do you mean by that?"

The matron explained, "The wife whom I serve in the great estate developed an abscess in the pelvic region which has been treated through the application of flour, ghee, and sweet grass. When the abscess came to a head, the pus began to flow out and was mixed in with ghee cakes. It's been like this day after day. I've been using this in making the cakes which I have presented to you. It's because of this that the cakes were so fine. But now, the lady's abscess has healed over. How could I succeed in finding any more?"

When the Brahman heard this, he beat his head with his two fists, hammered on his chest and began to groan and vomit, [exclaiming], "How could I have so violated this dharma of purity?! I'm doomed!"

He then forsook his responsibilities there and fled back to his home country.

行者亦如是。着是饮食欢喜
乐噉。见其[25]好色细滑香
美可口不观不净。后受苦报
悔将何及。若能观食本末如
是生恶厌心。因离食欲[26]四
欲皆舍。于欲界中乐悉皆舍
离断此五欲。于五下分结亦
断。如是等种种因缘恶罪不
复乐着。是名食厌想。

行者亦如是。著是飲食歡喜
樂噉。見其[25]好色細滑香
美可口不觀不淨。後受苦報
悔將何及。若能觀食本末如
是生惡厭心。因離食欲[26]四
欲皆捨。於欲界中樂悉皆捨
離斷此五欲。於五下分結亦
斷。如是等種種因緣惡罪不
復樂著。是名食厭想。

简体字   正體字

Nāgārjuna's Concluding Comments

The situation of the practitioner is just like this. He becomes attached to these beverages and foods, is delighted by them and takes pleasure in feasting upon them. He observes their fine appearance, subtle texture, magnificent fragrance, and delectability. He fails to contemplate their impurity. When later he undergoes a bitter retribution, what use will regret be then?

If one is able to contemplate that food is , from beginning to end, just like this, he will develop thoughts of aversion and disgust. On account of leaving behind the desire for food, all of the other four objects of desire will be relinquished. Then he will abandon all of the pleasures within the desire realm, will cut off these five types of desire and will also cut off the five inferior category fetters [comprised by desire, hatefulness, the view of the body as self, the seizing upon unprincipled prohibitions, and delusion-based doubtfulness]. On account of all sorts of causal factors such as these, one abhors karmic offenses and no longer courses in fond attachments. This is what is meant by the reflection on the repulsiveness of food.

欲无减者。佛知善法恩故。
常欲集诸善法故。欲无减。
修习诸善法。心无[6]厌足故
欲无减。譬如一长老比丘。
目暗自缝僧伽梨。针[7]紽
脱。语诸人[*]言。谁乐欲福
德者为我[*]紽针。尔时佛现
其前语言。我是乐欲福德
无[*]厌足人。持汝针来。是
比丘斐[8]亹见佛光明。又识
佛音声。白佛言。佛无量功
德海皆尽其边底。云何无厌
足。佛告比丘。功德果报甚
深。无有如我知恩分者。我
虽复尽其边底。我本以欲心
无厌足故得佛。是故今犹不
息。虽[9]更无功德可[10]得。
我欲心亦不休。诸天世人惊
悟。佛于功德尚无厌足。何
况馀人。佛为比丘说法。是
时肉眼即明慧眼成就。问
曰。如佛[11]尝断一切善法中
欲。今云何言欲无减。

欲無減者。佛知善法恩故。
常欲集諸善法故。欲無減。
修習諸善法。心無[6]厭足故
欲無減。譬如一長老比丘。
目闇自縫僧伽梨。針[7]紽
脫。語諸人[*]言。誰樂欲福
德者為我[*]紽針。爾時佛現
其前語言。我是樂欲福德
無[*]厭足人。持汝針來。是
比丘斐[8]亹見佛光明。又識
佛音聲。白佛言。佛無量功
德海皆盡其邊底。云何無厭
足。佛告比丘。功德果報甚
深。無有如我知恩分者。我
雖復盡其邊底。我本以欲心
無厭足故得佛。是故今猶不
息。雖[9]更無功德可[10]得。
我欲心亦不休。諸天世人驚
悟。佛於功德尚無厭足。何
況餘人。佛為比丘說法。是
時肉眼即明慧眼成就。問
曰。如佛[11]嘗斷一切善法中
欲。今云何言欲無減。

简体字　　　　　　　　正體字

The Buddha's Unceasing Zeal

As for [the Buddha's] "zeal is undiminished," it is because the Buddha knows the favorable aspects of good dharmas and thus is constant in his zeal to accumulate good dharmas that his zeal remains undiminished. It is because his mind is free of any sense of weariness or satiety in his cultivation of good dharmas that his zeal remains undiminished.

For example, there was once a venerable elder bhikshu who, with eyes dimmed [with age], was doing some sewing on his own saṅghāṭī robe when the thread slipped from the needle. He called out to the others, saying "Whoever delights in merit might care to help me thread this needle."

At that very moment, the Buddha manifest before him and called back, "I'm a man whose delight in merit is insatiable. Bring your needle over here."

The bhikshu's vision was struck by the stately brilliance of the Buddha's light at the same time that he recognized the Buddha's voice. He addressed the Buddha, saying, "The Buddha has already entirely exhausted the boundaries and depths of the immeasurable sea of merit. How then could it be that he is still insatiable in this?"

The Buddha told the bhikshu, "The resulting rewards from merit are extremely profound. No one knows as well as myself the favor it bestows. Although I have indeed exhausted its boundaries and depths, it is because I originally employed the mind of zeal insatiably that I have now succeeded in becoming a buddha. It is on account of this that, even now, I still do not desist. Although there is no further merit which I might be able to acquire, my mind of zeal remains unceasing."

The gods and worldly men were then startled and struck with the realization: "If even the Buddha remains insatiable in his pursuit of meritorious deeds, how much the more should this be the case with other people!" When the Buddha spoke Dharma for this bhikshu, his fleshly eyes immediately became clear and his wisdom eye became perfected as well.

Nāgārjuna's Concluding Discussion

Question: Those such as the Buddha have already cut off all zeal within the sphere of good dharmas. Why then does one now claim that his zeal is undiminished?

答曰。言断一切善法中欲者。是未得欲得。得已欲增。佛无如是欲。佛一切功德具足。无不得者亦无增益。今言欲者。如先说。佛虽具得一切功德。欲心犹不息。譬如马宝虽到至处去心不息至死不已。[12]佛宝亦如是。又如劫尽[13]大火。烧三千大千世界悉尽。火势故不息。佛智慧火亦如是。烧一切烦恼。照诸法已智慧相应欲亦不尽。复次佛虽一切善法功德满足。众生未尽故欲度不息。

简体字

答曰。言斷一切善法中欲者。是未得欲得。得已欲增。佛無如是欲。佛一切功德具足。無不得者亦無增益。今言欲者。如先說。佛雖具得一切功德。欲心猶不息。譬如馬寶雖到至處去心不息至死不已。[12]佛寶亦如是。又如劫盡[13]大火。燒三千大千世界悉盡。火勢故不息。佛智慧火亦如是。燒一切煩惱。照諸法已智慧相應欲亦不盡。復次佛雖一切善法功德滿足。眾生未盡故欲度不息。

正體字

Response: When one speaks of having already cut off all zeal within the realm of good dharmas, this properly refers to that zeal which strives to acquire something not yet acquired and, once having acquired it, zealously strives to accumulate even more of it.

The Buddha is completely free of all such forms of zeal. The Buddha has already perfected every form of merit. There is none which he has not already acquired and no such means by which he might accumulate yet more. When now we speak of "zeal," it is in accordance with the earlier statement wherein it was said that, although the Buddha has perfected the acquisition of every form of meritorious quality, his mind of zeal [for the nobility of] the endeavor still remains unceasing.

This is analogous to the case of the [wheel-turning sage king's] precious horse which, even when having reached the destination, still cherishes the aspiration to continue going forth and does so unceasingly, even on to its very death. So too it is with the Buddha Jewel.

This is also comparable to the great conflagration which occurs at the end of the kalpa. It completely burns up the entire trichiliocosm and then, due to the intense strength of its flames, it still does not cease. The wisdom fire of the Buddha is also just like this. It burns up all of the afflictions. Then, even after it has illuminated all dharmas, that zeal conforming to wisdom still does not cease.

Additionally, even though all of the good dharmas and meritorious qualities of the Buddha have already become completely perfected, because beings have still not all been liberated, his zeal to cross them all over to liberation continues on, unceasing.

复[17]次是精进诸佛所乐。如
释迦牟尼佛。精进力故超越
九劫。疾得阿耨多罗三藐三
菩提。复次如说一时佛告阿
难。汝为诸比丘说法。我背
痛小息。尔时世尊。四[18]
襵欝多罗僧敷下。以僧伽梨
枕头而卧。是时阿难说七觉
义。至精进觉佛惊起坐。告
阿难。汝赞精进义。阿难言
赞。如是至三。佛言。善哉
善哉。善修精进。乃至得阿
耨多罗三藐三菩提。何况馀
道。以是义故佛精进无减。
病时犹尚不息。何况不[1]
病。复次佛为度众生故。舍
甚深禅定乐。种种身种种语
言种种方便力度脱众生。或
时[2]遇恶险道。或时[3]食恶
食或时受寒热。或时值诸邪
难[4]闻恶口骂詈忍受不厌。
佛世尊虽于诸法中自在而行
是事。不生懈怠。

復[17]次是精進諸佛所樂。如
釋迦牟尼佛。精進力故超越
九劫。疾得阿耨多羅三藐三
菩提。復次如說一時佛告阿
難。汝為諸比丘說法。我背
痛小息。爾時世尊。四[18]
襵欝多羅僧敷下。以僧伽梨
枕頭而臥。是時阿難說七覺
義。至精進覺佛驚起坐。告
阿難。汝讚精進義。阿難言
讚。如是至三。佛言。善哉
善哉。善修精進。乃至得阿
耨多羅三藐三菩提。何況餘
道。以是義故佛精進無減。
病時猶尚不息。何況不[1]
病。復次佛為度眾生故。捨
甚深禪定樂。種種身種種語
言種種方便力度脫眾生。或
時[2]遇惡險道。或時[3]食惡
食或時受寒熱。或時值諸邪
難[4]聞惡口罵詈忍受不厭。
佛世尊雖於諸法中自在而行
是事。不生懈怠。

简体字　　　　　　　　　正體字

The Buddha Praises Vigor

Additionally, this "vigor" is a concept of which all Buddhas are fond. For example, in the case of Shakyamuni Buddha, he was able to overstep nine kalpas [cultivating the Path] on account of the power of his vigor. This allowed him to achieve rapid acquisition of *anuttarasamyaksaṃbodhi*.

Also, as it is told, there was one time when the Buddha instructed Ānanda, "You should proceed with the speaking of Dharma for the Bhikshus. Since my back is aching, I am going to take a short rest." Then the Bhagavān folded his *uttarasaṅga* robe in four layers, laid it on the ground, arranged the *saṅghāṭī* cloak as a pillow, and lay down.

Ānanda proceeded to discourse on the meaning of the seven limbs of bodhi. When he reached the "vigor" limb of bodhi, the Buddha, as if startled, rose to a sitting position and called over to Ānanda, asking "Are you praising the concept of vigor?"

Ānanda replied, "I am praising it."

This same [question-and-answer] then occurred a total of three times, whereupon the Buddha declared, "Good indeed! Good indeed! The skillful cultivation of vigor carries one all the way through even to *anuttarasamyaksaṃbodhi*, how much the more does it lead to acquisition of the other dharmas."

Nāgārjuna's Concluding Comments

And so it is based on this idea as well that the Buddha's vigor is held to be undiminished. Hence, even when afflicted with physical maladies, it was still unceasing. How much the more was this the case when he was free of maladies.

Furthermore, the Buddha set aside the bliss of his extremely deep dhyāna absorptions and, employing all sorts of physical forms, all sorts of language, and the power of all sorts of skillful means. strove to cross beings over to liberation. Sometimes he traveled fearsomely dangerous roads. Sometimes he consumed horrible meals. Sometimes he endured cold or heat. Sometimes he encountered all manner of perversely difficult challenging questions, abusive speech, scolding, and disparagement.

He endured it all without succumbing to disgust. Although the Buddha, the Bhagavān, was already sovereignly independent in all dharmas, still, he carried on with these endeavors and never fell into laxness in them.

如佛度众生已。于萨罗林中双树下卧。梵志须跋陀语阿难。我闻一切智人今夜当灭度。我欲见佛。阿难止之言。佛为众人广说法疲极。佛遥闻之告阿难。听须跋陀入。是我末后弟子。须跋陀得入问佛所疑。佛随意说法断疑得道。先佛入无馀涅盘。诸比丘白佛言。世尊。甚为希有。乃至末后怜愍外道梵志而共语言。佛言。我非但今世末后度。先世未得道时亦末后度。乃往过去无量阿僧只劫。有大林树多诸禽兽。野火来烧三边俱起。唯有一边而隔一水。众兽穷逼逃命无地。我尔时为大身多力鹿。以前脚跨一岸。以后脚。[5]距一岸。令众兽蹋[6]背上而[7]渡。皮肉尽坏以慈愍力忍之至

如佛度眾生已。於薩羅林中雙樹下臥。梵志須跋陀語阿難。我聞一切智人今夜當滅度。我欲見佛。阿難止之言。佛為眾人廣說法疲極。佛遙聞之告阿難。聽須跋陀入。是我末後弟子。須跋陀得入問佛所疑。佛隨意說法斷疑得道。先佛入無餘涅槃。諸比丘白佛言。世尊。甚為希有。乃至末後憐愍外道梵志而共語言。佛言。我非但今世末後度。先世未得道時亦末後度。乃往過去無量阿僧祇劫。有大林樹多諸禽獸。野火來燒三邊俱起。唯有一邊而隔一水。眾獸窮逼逃命無地。我爾時為大身多力鹿。以前腳跨一岸。以後腳。[5]距一岸。令眾獸蹋[6]背上而[7]渡。皮肉盡壞以慈愍力忍之至

简体字   正體字

The Buddha's Liberation of Subhadra

As another example [of the Buddha's unceasing dedication to carrying on with the practice of vigor], when the Buddha had finally finished with work of bringing beings across to liberation and lay there between the two trees in the Śāla-tree Woods, a brahmacārin named Subhadra arrived and declared to Ānanda, "I heard that the All-knowing One is preparing to pass into extinction this very night. I wish to have an audience with the Buddha."

Ānanda stopped him, saying, "The Buddha has fallen into a state of extreme exhaustion from extensively discoursing on Dharma for the members of the Community."

The Buddha heard this exchange from a distance and called over to Ānanda, "You must permit Subhadra to enter. He is my very last disciple."

After Subhadra gained entry, he inquired of the Buddha on the subject of his doubts. When the Buddha then spoke Dharma adapted to his mind, he was able to cut off his doubts, to gain realization of the Path, and to enter the nirvāṇa without residue even before the Buddha had done so.

The Bhikshus addressed the Buddha, saying, "Bhagavān. This is so extremely rare! Even in these very last moments, the Buddha has taken pity on a non-Buddhist brahmacārin and taken up a discussion with him."

The Buddha declared, "It is not only in this one life that there has been liberation even in the very last moments. In a previous life, before I had realized the Path, I also brought about his liberation in the very last moments. It was long ago in the past, innumerable *asaṃkhyeya* kalpas ago. There was a huge forest, the trees of which served as home for a multitude of birds and animals. A wildfire rose up, burning everywhere on three sides. There remained only one unaffected boundary, formed by a stream. The multitude of creatures were all driven there, attempting to escape for their lives, and then finding no more ground.

"At the time, I was a physically very large and extremely strong deer which stretched on across, planting its forelegs over on one bank while crouching its hind legs low on the other bank. It thus allowed the horde of creatures to make the ford by scrambling across its back.

"Although my skin and flesh were completely ruined by this, I endured it through the power of compassion right on through to

死。最后一兔来。气力已竭
自强努力忍令得过。过已[*]
背折堕水而死。如是久有非
但今也。前得度者今诸弟
子。最后一兔须跋陀是。佛
世世乐行精进今犹不息。是
故言精进无减。

死。最後一兔來。氣力已竭
自強努力忍令得過。過已[*]
背折墮水而死。如是久有非
但今也。前得度者今諸弟
子。最後一兔須跋陀是。佛
世世樂行精進今猶不息。是
故言精進無減。

简体字　　　　　　　　正體字

the very moment of death. At the very last, a rabbit came along. My strength had already been completely drained. Nonetheless, I pushed on with the power of perseverance and endured long enough to allow it to get across. After it had crossed, my back broke and I fell down into the waters and perished.

"And so occurrences of this sort have been going on for a long time. It is not the case that this has only happened just now. Those who made it across first are my present-life disciples. That very last rabbit was this very man, Subhadra."

In life after life, the Buddha has delighted in the practice of vigor. Even now, it does not cease. It is on account of this that his vigor is said to be undiminished.

复次萨遮只尼揵子铜鍱[16]络腹自誓言。无有人得我难而不流汗破坏者。大[17]象乃至树木瓦石闻我难声亦皆流汗。作是誓已来至佛所与佛论议。佛质问之皆不能得答。汗流淹地举体如渍。佛告尼揵。汝先誓言。无有闻我难者而不流[18]汗。汝今汗流淹地。汝试观佛见有汗相不。佛时脱欝多罗僧。示之言。汗在何处。复次有人言。或有头汗身不汗者。佛头虽不汗身必有汗。以是故佛脱欝多罗僧示其身。因是外道大得信向皆入佛法中。是智慧因缘身业随行。

復次薩遮祇尼揵子銅鍱[16]絡腹自誓言。無有人得我難而不流汗破壞者。大[17]象乃至樹木瓦石聞我難聲亦皆流汗。作是誓已來至佛所與佛論議。佛質問之皆不能得答。汗流淹地舉體如漬。佛告尼揵。汝先誓言。無有聞我難者而不流[18]汗。汝今汗流淹地。汝試觀佛見有汗相不。佛時脫欝多羅僧。示之言。汗在何處。復次有人言。或有頭汗身不汗者。佛頭雖不汗身必有汗。以是故佛脫欝多羅僧示其身。因是外道大得信向皆入佛法中。是智慧因緣身業隨行。

简体字   正體字

The Buddha's Imperturbability

Additionally, there was the case of Satyaka Nirgranthīputra who, with his belly girded in copper plate [lest it burst from all of his accumulated knowledge], boasted: "There is no one anywhere who, on being subjected to my challenges, fails to stream with profuse perspiration and then meet their destruction [in debate]. Everything from the great elephant on down to trees, tiles, and stones streams with perspiration on overhearing my challenges."

Having uttered these boasts, he arrived at the dwelling place of the Buddha to engage the Buddha in debate. The Buddha then interrogated him and, in every case, he was unable to reply. His own perspiration soaked the ground and his entire body was as if soaking wet.

The Buddha then announced to Nirgrantha, "Earlier, you boasted that there was no one who, on hearing your challenges, would not be reduced to streams of perspiration. But now it is you whose perspiration flows so profusely that it soaks the ground. Now, as you visually assess the appearance of the Buddha, do you notice any perspiration, or not?" The Buddha then removed his [upper] *uttarāsaṅgha* robe and instructed him further by asking, "So where is the perspiration?"

Nāgārjuna's Concluding Comments

Again, there might be others who would have said, "Since there are cases where one's head perspires and yet the body does not perspire, it must certainly be the case that now, although the Buddha's head is not perspiring, his body could be perspiring." It is for this reason that the Buddha proceeded then to take off his *uttarāsaṅgha*, revealing his torso. On account of this, those followers of non-Buddhist traditions gained great faith and were all thus enabled to enter the Dharma of the Buddha. This is an instance of [the Buddha's] physical actions according with wisdom-based causal factors.

问曰。入法位中过老病死。
及断诸结使。破三恶道等如
先说。何以但说过声闻辟支
佛地。亦住种种功德。何以
故。但说住阿鞞跋致地。答
曰。舍诸恶事得诸功德。后
当次第说及所住功德。[5]诸
法当须次第。不可一时顿
说。复次菩萨初发意时所可
怖畏无过声闻辟支佛地。正
使堕地狱无如是怖畏。不永
破大乘道故。阿罗汉辟支
佛。于此大乘以为永灭。譬
如空地有树名舍摩梨。舥枝
广大众鸟集宿。一鸽后至住
一枝上。其枝及[6]舥即时[7]
压折。泽神问树神。大鸟雕
鹫皆能任持。何至小鸟便不
自胜。树神答言。此鸟从我
怨家尼[8]俱卢树上来。食彼
树果来栖我上。必当放

問曰。入法位中過老病死。
及斷諸結使。破三惡道等如
先說。何以但說過聲聞辟支
佛地。亦住種種功德。何以
故。但說住阿鞞跋致地。答
曰。捨諸惡事得諸功德。後
當次第說及所住功德。[5]諸
法當須次第。不可一時頓
說。復次菩薩初發意時所可
怖畏無過聲聞辟支佛地。正
使墮地獄無如是怖畏。不永
破大乘道故。阿羅漢辟支
佛。於此大乘以為永滅。譬
如空地有樹名舍摩梨。舥枝
廣大眾鳥集宿。一鴿後至住
一枝上。其枝及[6]舥即時[7]
壓折。澤神問樹神。大鳥鵰
鷲皆能任持。何至小鳥便不
自勝。樹神答言。此鳥從我
怨家尼[8]俱盧樹上來。食彼
樹果來栖我上。必當放

简体字　　　　　　　　正體字

The Śālmalī Tree Sacrifices a Limb

Nāgārjuna's Introduction

Question: When one enters the [right and certain] Dharma position (*samyaktva niyāma*), one passes beyond aging, sickness, and death, cuts off all of the fetters, demolishes the three wretched destinies, and so forth, all as explained earlier. Why then does one only mention here the surpassing of the grounds of the Śrāvaka Disciples and the Pratyekabuddhas? One also abides in all sorts of different meritorious qualities. Why then does one only mention here the abiding at the [irreversible] ground of the *avaivartika*?

Response: The abandoning of unwholesome endeavors and the acquisition of meritorious qualities shall be discussed in proper sequence along with the meritorious qualities in which one comes to abide. One should hew to the appropriate sequence in the treatment of dharmas. One cannot just set them all forth simultaneously and in a precipitate manner.

Moreover, of those things which might be feared by the bodhisattva when he has first generated the determination [to become a buddha], there is nothing which surpasses the grounds of the Śrāvaka Disciples and the Pratyekabuddhas. Even the prospect of definitely falling down into the hells would not inspire such terror as this. This is because it would still not involve the eternal destruction of the Path of the Great Vehicle. Thus arhatship and pratyekabuddhahood are equated with the eternal destruction of the Great Vehicle.

Story: The Śālmalī Tree Sacrifices a Limb

By way of analogy, there once was a *śālmalī* tree growing out in an empty field with immense limbs and branches which spread out broadly. Many birds flocked together on it to roost for the night. A single pigeon came along afterwards and came to rest on a single branch. Suddenly that branch extending all the way back to the base of the limb split off and came crashing down. [Having observed this], the spirit of the marsh inquired of the tree spirit, "You have been able to endure holding up even the big birds such as eagles and vultures. Why then, when it came down to this little bird, you weren't able to bear up?"

The tree spirit replied, "This bird had come thither from roosting on my nemesis tree, the *nyagrodha*. Having eaten of the fruits from that tree, it had come to roost upon me. It was bound to excrete its

粪子堕地者恶树复生为害必
大。以是故于此一鸽大怀忧
[9]畏。宁舍一枝所全者大。
菩萨摩诃萨亦如是。于诸外
道魔众及诸结使恶业无如是
畏。如阿罗汉辟支佛。何以
故。声闻辟支佛。于菩萨边
亦如彼鸽。坏败大乘心永灭
佛业。以是故但说过声闻辟
支佛地。住阿鞞跋致地者。
从初发意已来。常喜乐住阿
鞞跋致地。闻诸菩萨多退转
故。发意时作愿。何时当得
过声闻辟支佛地住阿鞞跋致
地。以是故说住阿鞞跋致
地。

糞子墮地者惡樹復生為害必
大。以是故於此一鴿大懷憂
[9]畏。寧捨一枝所全者大。
菩薩摩訶薩亦如是。於諸外
道魔眾及諸結使惡業無如是
畏。如阿羅漢辟支佛。何以
故。聲聞辟支佛。於菩薩邊
亦如彼鴿。壞敗大乘心永滅
佛業。以是故但說過聲聞辟
支佛地。住阿鞞跋致地者。
從初發意已來。常喜樂住阿
鞞跋致地。聞諸菩薩多退轉
故。發意時作願。何時當得
過聲聞辟支佛地住阿鞞跋致
地。以是故說住阿鞞跋致
地。

简体字   正體字

stools. From the seeds which thus fell down to the ground, that detestable tree would grow up yet again [right here]. Thus the harm to be sustained would certainly be great. It was for this reason that, even with the presence of just this one pigeon, I was possessed by immense distress and fear. I would rather sacrifice one whole limb so that what is thereby preserved would be so great."

Nāgārjuna's Concluding Comments

The bodhisattva, mahāsattva is just like this. He does not have such great fear with respect to all of the heretical paths and hordes of demons, or with respect to the fetters and evil karmic deeds as he possesses with respect to arhatship and pratyekabuddhahood. Why is this the case? The implications for a bodhisattva of proximity to śrāvaka Disciples or pratyekabuddhas are just like those presented to the tree by that pigeon. They threaten to ruin the Great Vehicle mind and eternally destroy the karma of buddhahood. It is for this reason that the text only refers here to [the issue of] surpassing the grounds of the Śrāvaka Disciples and the Pratyekabuddhas.

As for dwelling at the [irreversible] ground of the *avaivartika*, from that very time when he generates the determination [to become a buddha] on forward to the present, he has always delighted in the prospect of dwelling at the ground of the *avaivartika*. Having heard that there are so many bodhisattvas who retreat, when he generates the determination, he formulates an aspiration wherein he wonders, "When might I finally be able to surpass the grounds of the Śrāvaka Disciples and Pratyekabuddhas and then come to dwell at the ground of the *avaivartika*? It is for this reason that the text refers here to the ground of the *avaivartika*.

无边故众生 [2]生厌生死长久。譬如波梨国四十比丘。俱行十二净行来至佛所。佛为说厌行。佛问比丘五恒河伽蓝牟 [3]那萨罗由阿 [4]脂罗婆提摩醯。从所来处流入大海。其中间水为多少。比丘言。[5]甚多。佛言。[6]但一人一劫中作畜生时。屠割剥刺。或时犯罪截其手足。斩其身首。如是等血多于此水。如是无边大劫中。受身出血不可 [7]称数。啼哭流泪及饮母乳亦如是。计一劫中一人积骨。过于鞞浮罗大山。（[8]丹注云此山天竺 [9]以人常 [10]见易信故说 [11]也）如是无量劫中受生死苦。诸比丘闻是已。厌患世间即时得道。

無邊故眾生 [2]生厭生死長久。譬如波梨國四十比丘。俱行十二淨行來至佛所。佛為說厭行。佛問比丘五恒河伽藍牟 [3]那薩羅由阿 [4]脂羅婆提摩醯。從所來處流入大海。其中間水為多少。比丘言。[5]甚多。佛言。[6]但一人一劫中作畜生時。屠割剝刺。或時犯罪截其手足。斬其身首。如是等血多於此水。如是無邊大劫中。受身出血不可 [7]稱數。啼哭流淚及飲母乳亦如是。計一劫中一人積骨。過於鞞浮羅大山。（[8]丹注云此山天竺 [9]以人常 [10]見易信故說 [11]也）如是無量劫中受生死苦。諸比丘聞是已。厭患世間即時得道。

简体字   正體字

The Buddha Inspires Renunciation in the Pāpīyaka Monks

Through the concept of limitlessness, beings are able to generate renunciation with regard to the long-enduring nature of birth and death.

As an example, we have the case of the forty bhikshus from the Pāpīyaka region, observers of the twelve pure practices, who came to where the Buddha dwelt. The Buddha explained for them the practice of renunciation. The Buddha asked them, "How much water is carried by the five rivers, the Ganges, the Yamunā, the Sarayū, the Aciravatī, and the Mahī, as they flow from their head-waters to the great ocean?"

The Bhikshus replied, "An extremely great amount."

The Buddha declared, "Even greater than all this water is the amount of blood lost by only one single person during the course of a kalpa in which, as an animal, he is butchered, sliced, skinned, and stabbed, and in which [as a human], on account of occasional criminal offenses, he has his hands and feet cut off or is subjected to decapitation. In this way, the amount of blood lost from bodies taken up throughout a limitless number of great kalpas is indescribably great in quantity. So too it is with the tears shed in weeping and the milk drunk from one's mothers. In reckoning the amount of bones piled up from a single person in a single kalpa, they would be even greater in mass than that huge Vaipulya Mountain. (The notes in red state: "This is brought up because people in India constantly see this mountain and so are easily moved to faith [through this description].") In this fashion, one undergoes the suffering involved in birth and death throughout an immeasurable number of kalpas."

After the Bhikshus had heard this, renouncing and abhorring the world, they immediately achieved realization of the Path.

菩萨满一切众生所愿。谓应可得者。然菩萨心无齐限。福德果报亦无有量。但众生无量阿僧只劫罪厚障故而不能得。如舍利弗弟子罗频[22]周比丘。持戒精进乞食。六日而不能得。乃至七日命在不久。有同道者乞食持与。鸟即持去。时舍利弗语目捷连。汝大神力守[23]护此食令彼得之。即时目连持食往与。始欲向口变成为[24]泥。又舍利弗乞食持与而口自合。最后佛来持食与之。以佛福德无量因缘故令彼得食。是比丘食已。心生欢喜倍加信敬。佛告比丘。有为之法皆是苦相为说四谛。即时比丘漏尽意解。得阿罗汉道。有薄福众生罪甚此者佛不能救。

菩薩滿一切眾生所願。謂應可得者。然菩薩心無齊限。福德果報亦無有量。但眾生無量阿僧祇劫罪厚障故而不能得。如舍利弗弟子羅頻[22]周比丘。持戒精進乞食。六日而不能得。乃至七日命在不久。有同道者乞食持與。鳥即持去。時舍利弗語目捷連。汝大神力守[23]護此食令彼得之。即時目連持食往與。始欲向口變成為[24]泥。又舍利弗乞食持與而口自合。最後佛來持食與之。以佛福德無量因緣故令彼得食。是比丘食已。心生歡喜倍加信敬。佛告比丘。有為之法皆是苦相為說四諦。即時比丘漏盡意解。得阿羅漢道。有薄福眾生罪甚此者佛不能救。

简体字   正體字

Losakatiṣya's Near Starvation

[When it is said] that the bodhisattva fulfills the wishes of all beings, this refers to those who, [by the nature of their karmic circumstances], should be able to gain [such fulfillment]. Thus, the bodhisattva's mind has no boundaries. Nor is it possible to measure the resultant retribution associated with their karmic blessings. It is only on account of thick obstacles [created from] beings' immeasurable number of *asaṃkhyeya* eons of offenses that they are unable to obtain [fulfillment of those wishes].

Take for example Śāriputra's disciple, the bhikshu named Losakatiṣya. He upheld the precepts and was vigorous. In going out in quest of alms, he once went six days and yet was not able to come by [any offerings]. When it came to the seventh day, his life was at the point verging on death. There was a fellow cultivator of the Path who acquired alms food and brought it to him. However, a bird suddenly took it away.

Śāriputra then told Maudgalyāyana, "Use your great spiritual powers to guard this food and cause him to succeed in getting it." Maudgalyāyana then took the food straightaway and gave it to him. When it was just about up to [Losakatiṣya's] mouth, it transformed into mud. Additionally, Śāriputra obtained alms food and took it and gave it to [the monk], whereupon his mouth spontaneously clamped shut.

Finally, the Buddha himself came and brought food and gave it to him. On account of the causes and conditions of the Buddha's immeasurable amount of merit, he was able to cause him to succeed in eating some food. After this bhikshu had eaten, his mind became delighted and he became doubly possessed of both faith and reverence.

The Buddha told that bhikshu, "Conditioned dharmas are all characterized by suffering." He then explained the four truths for his sake. The bhikshu then immediately gained the ending of outflow impurities and the liberation of his mind, whereupon he gained the path of arhatship. There are beings of only scant merit whose offenses are more extreme than this whom even the Buddha is not able to rescue.

Source Text Variant Readings

[0151005] 欲＝惟【宋】【元】【明】【宮】

[0151006] 曰＝言【宋】【元】【明】【宮】＊

[0151007] 〔語〕－【宋】【元】【明】【宮】【石】

[0151008] 次＝欲【宋】

[0151009] 全＝令【石】

[0151010] 免＝勉【石】＊

[0151011] 博＝搏【元】【明】，＝轉【宮】

[0151012] 〔船〕－【石】

[0151013] 板＝攀【宋】【元】【明】【宮】＊ ［＊ 1］

[0151014] 崖＝岸【宋】【元】【明】【宮】

[0151015] 免＝勉【宋】【宮】【石】

[0151016] 〔至〕－【宋】【元】【明】【宮】

[0151017] 垒＝齊【宋】【元】【明】【宮】下同

[0151018] （塗）＋泥【宋】【元】【明】，泥＝塗【宮】

[0151019] 三＝二【元】【明】【宮】【石】

[0151020] 〔王婦〕－【宋】【宮】

[0151021] 〔汁〕－【宋】【元】【明】【宮】【石】

[0152001] 諸＝珠【宋】【元】【明】【宮】【石】

[0152002] 歡＝欣【宋】【元】【明】【宮】【石】

[0152003] 念＝令【宋】【元】，＝憐【明】

[0152004] 〔此〕－【宋】【元】【明】【宮】【石】

[0152005] 抱＝挹【宮】

[0152006] 〔言〕－【石】

[0152007] 泰＝太【宋】【元】【明】【宮】

[0152008] 須＝願【石】

[0152009] 歙＝檢【宋】【元】【明】【宮】

[0152010] 殖＝植【元】【明】

[0152011] 樓＝樹【宮】

[0152012] 頗梨＝玻璃【宋】【元】【宮】下同，＝玻瓈【明】下同

[0152013] 大＝天【宮】【石】＊ ［＊ 1］

[0152014] 為＋（我）【宋】【元】【明】【宮】

[0153023] 考＝拷【宋】【元】【明】【宮】＊ ［＊ 1］

[0154001] 所＝何【宮】

[0154002] 自＝亦【宮】
[0154003] 物＝利【宋】【元】【明】【宮】【石】
[0154004] 〔周滿〕－【宋】【宮】【石】
[0154005] 行禪＝禪定【宋】【元】【明】【宮】【石】

The Merchant Who Lost All but the Most Precious Jewel — 105

[0155017] 兩＝後【宮】【石】
[0155018] 入＋（汝）【石】
[0155019] 〔罪〕－【宋】【元】【明】【宮】【石】
[0155020] 刑＝形【石】

The Butcher's Son Refuses to Kill — 109

[0155026] 全＝令【石】＊ ［＊ 1 2 3 4 5］
[0156001] 倍＝億【宮】
[0156002] 可＝以【宋】【宮】【石】

Kokālika's Slanderous Offense — 113

[0157005] 人＋（為）【石】
[0157006] 力＝為【宮】
[0157007] 洗＝浴【宋】【元】【明】【宮】
[0157008] 祇洹＝祇桓【宋】【元】【宮】【石】
[0157009] 故＝欲【宮】
[0157010] 野人＝人為【宮】＊ ［＊ 1］
[0157011] 此＝是【宋】【元】【明】【宮】
[0157012] 事＝意【宋】【元】【明】【宮】【石】
[0157013] 奈＝奈【宋】【元】【明】，＝奈【宮】
[0157014] 嘷哭＝號咷【宋】【元】【明】【宮】
[0157015] 獄＋（地獄）【石】
[0157016] 天＝王【石】
[0157017] 阿＝呵【宋】【元】【明】【宮】【石】＊ ［＊ 1 2 3］
[0157018] （五）＋百【宋】【元】【明】【宮】【石】
[0158001] 夫士之生＝夫世之士【宮】
[0158002] 毒苦＝苦毒【宋】【元】【明】【宮】
[0158003] 十＝千【石】
[0158004] 五＝三【宮】
[0158005] 形＝刑【石】

Rāhula's Lesson About False Speech — 123

[0158006] 槃＝盤【宋】【元】【明】【宮】＊ ［＊ 1］
[0158007] 語＝謀【宋】【元】【明】【宮】【石】

The Perfection of Patience 147
Devadatta's Ruination Through Affection for Offerings 149
[0164011] 名＋（為）【宋】【元】【明】【宮】

[0164012] 軟＝濡【宮】

[0164013] 瘡＝創【宮】＊［＊ 1］

[0164014] 淨清＝清淨【宋】【元】【明】【宮】

[0164015] 簡＝揀【宋】【元】【明】【宮】

[0164016] 戚＝族【宋】【元】【明】【宮】

[0164017] 曇＋（彌）【石】

[0164018] 汝＝以【宋】【元】【明】

[0164019] 敬＝以【宋】【元】【明】【宮】

[0164020] 〔受〕－【石】

[0164021] 旦＝怛【宋】【元】【明】【宮】

[0164022] 嬰＝瓔【宋】【元】【宮】

[0164023] 嗽＝嗽【元】【明】【宮】，＝［口＊束］【石】

[0164024] 奈＝李【宮】【石】

[0164025] 大立＝立大【宋】【元】【明】【宮】

[0165001] 爪＝［打-丁+瓜］【宋】【宮】

[0165002] 到＋（於）【宋】【元】【明】【宮】

[0165003] 應當＝當應【宋】【元】【明】【宮】

The Kashmiri Tripiṭaka Master 157
[0165004] 〔為人敬養〕－【宋】【宮】【石】

[0165005] 惟＋（便）【石】

Māra's Daughters and Buddha at the Bodhi Tree 161
[0165011] 玉＝王【石】

[0165012] 各＝名【石】

[0165013] 好黑好白＝好白好黑【宋】【元】【明】【宮】

[0165014] 一一＝二【宮】

[0165015] 睫孌娛＝［月＊妾］孌娛【宮】，＝［
月＊妾］［月＊（艮/安）］［目＊音］【石】

[0165016] 近＝迎【宋】【元】【明】【宮】

[0165017] 逼＝遍【石】

[0165018] 命＝帝【宋】【元】【明】【宮】

[0165019] 日＝月【宋】【元】【明】【宮】【石】

[0165020] 昱爍＝煜爐【元】【明】

[0165021] 傾＝輕【宮】

A Lazy Monk Discovers the Value of Vigor   193

[0174001] 是＝時【宋】【元】【明】【宮】

[0174002] 住＝立【宋】【元】【明】【宮】【石】

[0174003] 投＝救【宋】【元】【明】【宮】

The Buddha's Past Life as a Fiercely Vigorous Guide   197

[0174005] 以此五事為＝如是等名【宋】【元】【明】【宮】【石】

[0174006] 牟＝文【宋】【元】【明】【宮】【石】

[0174007] 以＝次【宋】【元】【明】【宮】【石】

[0174008] 休息＝首伏【石】

[0174009] 息＝伏【宋】【元】【明】【宮】【石】

The Buddha's Past Life as King of a Deer Herd   201

[0178008] 懈廢＝癈懈【石】

[0178009] 〔野〕－【宋】【元】【明】【宮】

[0178010] 牟尼＝文【宋】【元】【明】【宮】【石】

[0178011] 人＝又【石】

[0178012] 矢＝箭【宋】【元】【明】【宮】【石】

[0178013] 人王＝王言【宋】【元】【明】【宮】

[0178014] 輒當＝當自【宋】【元】【明】【宮】【石】

[0178015] 意＝言【宮】

[0178016] 〔送應次者〕－【宋】【元】【明】【宮】【石】

[0178017] 〔時〕－【宋】【元】【明】【宮】【石】

[0178018] 子＋（次至應送）【宋】【元】【明】【宮】【石】

[0178019] 當應＝應當【宋】【元】【明】【宮】

[0178020] 既＝明【石】

[0178021] 姐＝俎【宋】【元】【明】【宮】

[0178022] 併＝并【宋】【元】【明】【宮】

[0178023] 與＋（夫）【石】

[0178024] 無＝亦何【宋】【元】【明】【宮】，＝亦何以【石】

[0178025] 言＝曰【明】

[0178026] 獸＝生【宋】【元】【明】【宮】

The Brahmacārin's Great Sacrifice from Love for Dharma   207

[0178027] 愛法＝法愛【宋】【宮】

[0178028] 偈＝之【宮】

[0178029] 亦＝及【宋】【元】【明】【石】，＝乃【宮】

[0182021] 槃＝盤【宋】【元】【明】【宮】＊［＊ 1 2 3］

[0183001] （時）＋耶【宋】【元】【明】【宮】

[0183002] 遣＝進【宋】【元】【明】【宮】【石】

[0183003] 目＝自【宋】【元】【明】【宮】【石】

[0183004] 丘＋（汝欲聞不諦聽之）【元】【明】

[0183005] 婆＝波【元】【明】＊［＊ 1 2］

[0183006] 春＝秋【宋】【宮】【石】

[0183007] 娠＝身【宋】【元】【明】【宮】【石】

[0183008] 菴＝庵【宋】【元】【明】【宮】＊［＊ 1］

[0183009] 〔即〕－【宋】【元】【明】【宮】

[0183010] 鍾＝軍【宋】【元】【明】【宮】＊［＊ 1］

[0183011] 〔國〕－【宋】【元】【明】【宮】【石】＊［＊ 1］

[0183012] 官＝臣【元】【明】

[0183013] 〔曾〕－【宋】【元】【明】【宮】【石】

[0183014] 無雙＝巨富【宋】【宮】【石】

[0183015] 〔人〕－【石】

[0183016] 五百＝百五【石】

[0183017] 藥＋（草）【宋】【元】【明】【宮】【石】

[0183018] 眾彩畫之＝彩畫【宋】【元】【明】【宮】【石】

[0183019] 〔衣〕－【石】

[0183020] 以＝似【元】【明】

[0183021] 好＝妙【宋】【元】【明】【宮】【石】

[0183022] 〔皆〕－【宋】【元】【明】【宮】

[0183023] 淨＝清【宋】【元】【明】【宮】【石】

[0183024] 〔以〕－【宋】【元】【明】【宮】【石】

[0183025] 好果好水＝好水好果【宋】【元】【明】【宮】【石】

[0183026] 〔盛〕－【宋】【元】【明】【宮】【石】

[0183027] 〔美〕－【宋】【元】【明】【宮】【石】

[0183028] 喜＝樂【宋】【元】【明】【宮】【石】

[0183029] 已＝以【宋】【元】【明】【宮】【石】

[0183030] 果＝食【宋】【元】【明】【宮】【石】

[0183031] 〔婬女知〕－【宋】【元】【明】【宮】【石】

[0183032] 項＝擔【宋】【元】【明】【宮】【石】

[0183033] 足五所＝給足五【元】【明】

Mahākauṣṭhila, the Long-Nailed Brahman 293

[0061045] 爪＝抓【宋】＊〔＊1 2〕

[0061046]〔號〕－【聖】【石】

[0061047] 迦＝加【宋】【元】【明】【宮】

[0061048]〔等〕－【宋】【元】【明】【宮】【石】

[0061049] 惟＋（是）【宋】【元】【明】【宮】

[0061050] 言＝曰【聖】

[0061051]〔是〕－【聖】

[0061052]〔書〕－【宋】【元】【明】【宮】

[0061053]〔為〕－【聖】

[0061054] 唐突＝唐突【宋】【宮】，＝搪突【聖】

[0061055] 瞿＝衢【聖】＊〔＊1 2〕

[0061056]〔中〕－【宋】【元】【明】【宮】【石】

[0061057] 涯＝崖【宮】【聖】

[0062001] 而＝面【聖】

[0062002] 受＝忍【元】【宮】【石】＊〔＊1 2 3 4 5 6〕

[0062003] 所質義＝如是示【宮】，＝如是亦【石】

[0062004]〔今出是毒氣〕－【聖】

[0062005] 見＋（毒）【宋】【元】【明】【宮】

[0062006] 即覺＝覺畏【宮】【石】

[0062007] 二＝兩【聖】

[0062008] 多人＝多眾人共【聖】＊〔＊1〕

[0062009] 受＝言【宋】【元】【明】【宮】【石】

[0062010] 此是＝我受此【宋】【元】【明】，
＝我忍此【宮】【石】，＝此【聖】

[0062011]〔我〕－【宮】【石】

[0062012] 欲＝不【元】【明】

[0062013] 不多人知＝少有知者【聖】

[0062014] 受＝忍【宮】【石】＊〔＊1 2 3〕

[0062015] 受＝破【宮】【聖】【石】

[0062016] 自＝貢【宋】【元】【明】【宮】

[0062017] 彰＝鄣【聖】

[0062018] 濡＝軟【宋】【元】【明】【宮】

[0062019]（是）＋第【宋】【元】【明】【宮】

[0062020] 淨＋（處）【宋】【元】【明】【宮】【石】

[0062021]〔處〕－【宮】【石】

[0062022]〔大〕－【石】

[0062023] 是＋(最)【聖】

[0062024] 一＋(無過佛者)【元】【明】【聖】

[0062025] (於)＋諸【宋】【元】【明】【宮】

[0062026] (是)＋時【元】【明】【宮】【石】，〔時〕－【聖】

[0062027] 〔聞是語〕－【聖】

[0062028] 志＋(便)【宋】【元】【明】【宮】【石】

[0062029] 〔若〕－【聖】

[0062030] 〔佛〕－【宮】

[0062031] 引＝弘【石】

[0062032] (佛)＋說【宮】【石】

The Gods Request the Buddha to Speak the Dharma

[0063015] 佛＋(自念)【宋】【元】【明】【宮】【石】

[0063016] 袈裟＝衣【宋】【元】【明】【宮】【石】

[0063017] 〔者〕－【宋】【元】【明】【宮】【石】

[0063018] 〔以〕－【聖】

[0063019] 〔力〕－【聖】

[0063020] 請佛＝請曰【宋】【元】【明】
【宮】【石】，＝問佛【聖】

[0063021] 當說＝說諸【宋】【元】【明】【宮】【石】

[0063022] 是＝其【宮】

[0063023] 濡＝軟【宋】【元】【明】【宮】

[0063024] 〔者〕－【聖】

[0063025] 〔能〕－【宋】【元】【明】【宮】【石】

[0063026] 〔爾時世尊〕－【宋】【元】【明】【宮】【石】

[0063027] 如是＝言【宮】【石】

[0063028] 我＝法【宋】【元】【明】，＝我法【宮】【石】

[0063029] 〔法〕－【宋】【元】【明】【宮】【聖】【石】

[0063030] 猗＝倚【元】【明】＊［＊ 1］

[0063031] 〔為初信力〕－【宋】【宮】【石】

[0063032] 能＋(初)【宋】【宮】【石】

[0063033] 〔禪定智慧〕－【宋】【元】【明】【宮】【石】

[0063034] 說偈言＝偈曰【宋】【元】【明】
【宮】【石】，＝說偈【聖】

[0063035] 愛好＝猗著【宋】【宮】【石】，＝愛著【元】【明】

[0063036] 果報＝愛果【宋】【宮】，＝報果【聖】

[0063037] 因＝田【宋】【宮】【聖】

[0063038] 此＝是【宋】【元】【明】【宮】【石】

Ānanda's Final Questions of the Buddha 307

[0066044] （諸）＋弟子【聖】【石】

[0066045] 〔輩〕－【聖】【石】

[0066046] （而）＋臥【聖】【石】

[0066047] 阿泥盧豆＝阿尼盧豆【宋】【元】【明】【宮】，＝阿那律【聖】【石】

[0066048] 汝＋（是）【聖】【石】

[0066049] 人＝者【聖】【石】

[0066050] 法＋（皆）【聖】【石】

[0066051] 莫＝何以【聖】【石】

[0066052] 受＝愛【宋】【宮】

[0066053] 〔般〕－【宋】【元】【明】【宮】【聖】

[0066054] 初＋（首）【宋】【元】【明】【宮】【聖】【石】

[0066055] 〔佛〕－【宋】【元】【明】【宮】

[0066056] 後＝得【宮】

[0066057] 餘依止＝依止餘【聖】【石】＊〔＊ 1 2〕

[0066058] 於＝如【宮】

[0066059] 內觀＝觀內【宋】【元】【明】，＝觀由【宮】

[0066060] 當＝念【宋】【元】【明】【宮】【聖】【石】

[0066061] （以）＋除【石】

[0066062] 貪憂＝貪愛【宋】【元】【明】【宮】，＝憂貪【聖】【石】

[0066063] 經＋（所）【聖】【石】

[0066064] 梵＋（天）【元】【明】

[0066065] 伏＝復【宋】【聖】【石】，＝愎【宮】

[0066066] 刪＝那【元】【明】【聖】【石】

[0066067] 〔經〕－【宮】

[0066068] 〔復次〕－【宋】【元】【明】【宮】

[0066069] （是）＋我【聖】【石】

[0066070] 藏＋（中）【聖】【石】

[0066071] 〔初應作是說〕－【聖】【石】

[0066072] 〔土〕－【石】

[0066073] 〔樹〕－【宋】【元】【明】【宮】【聖】【石】

[0066074] 中＋（是我法門初應如是說）【聖】【石】

[0066075] 經初＝經法初首【聖】【石】

[0066076] 〔經初〕－【聖】【石】

The Buddha's *Parinirvāṇa* 311

[0067006] 〔廣〕－【宋】【元】【明】【宮】【聖】【石】
[0067007] 惡＋（戰）【聖】
[0067008] 天＝大【聖】
[0067009] 間＝聞【石】
[0067010] 葉＝華【聖】，＝菓【石】
[0067011] 崖＝峯【聖】【石】
[0067012] 嬈＝擾【元】【明】，＝繞【宮】
[0067013] 哽＝鯁【聖】
[0067014] 闍＝陀【聖】
[0067015] 漢＋（已過）【聖】【石】
[0067016] 夫＝人【宋】【元】【明】【宮】
[0067017] 流＝流【石】

Gods Distressed at Dharma's Decline 315

[0067018] 天＋（王）【聖】【石】
[0067019] 皆＝者【聖】
[0067020] 光＝先【宋】【元】【明】【宮】
[0067021] 滅＋（度）【宋】【元】【明】【宮】
[0067022] 〔有〕－【聖】【石】
[0067023] 〔大智〕－【聖】【石】
[0067024] 遂＝道【元】【明】
[0067025] 燈＝鐙【聖】＊〔＊ 1〕
[0067026] 目明＝明目【聖】【石】
[0067027] 〔大〕－【聖】
[0067028] （佛）＋法【宋】【元】【明】【宮】【聖】【石】
[0067029] 船＝般【石】

Mahākāśyapa Convenes a Dharma Council 319

[0067030] （如是）＋思惟【聖】【石】
[0067031] 尼＝泥【聖】【石】＊〔＊ 1 2 3 4 5 6〕
[0067032] 住＝往【明】
[0067033] 〔山〕－【聖】【石】
[0067034] 揵稚＝揵椎【宋】【元】【明】，＝揵槌【聖】【石】
[0067035] 稚＝極【聖】，＝槌【石】
[0067036] 神＋（通）【聖】【石】
[0067037] 學＝覺【聖】
[0067038] 善＝去【元】【明】，〔善〕－【宮】

Why Mahākāśyapa Chose One Thousand Arhats 323

[0067039] 〔故〕-【宋】【元】【明】【宮】【聖】【石】

[0067040] 正=止【宋】【元】【明】【宮】

[0067041] 頻婆娑羅=頻浮婆羅【宮】,＝
洴沙【聖】,＝洴娑【石】

[0067042] 時＋(洴沙)【聖】【石】

[0067043] 人＋(是時初度迦葉兄)【聖】【石】

[0067044] 貰=世【宋】【元】【明】【宮】

[0067045] 〔取〕-【聖】

[0067046] 多取=取多【聖】【石】

Ānanda's Banishment from the Dharma Council 325

[0068001] 〔曹〕-【宋】【元】【明】【宮】【聖】【石】

[0068002] 等＋(欲)【聖】【石】

[0068003] (以)＋汝【明】,汝＋(何以)【聖】【石】

[0068004] 〔佛〕-【聖】【石】

[0068005] 聽＋(使)【聖】【石】

[0068006] 是汝=汝應【聖】【石】＊ [＊ 1]

[0068007] 罪＋(讖悔)【聖】【石】＊ [＊ 1 2 3]

[0068008] 云何=豈可【聖】【石】

[0068009] 無＋(耶)【聖】【石】

[0068010] (般)＋涅【聖】【石】

[0068011] 脊=背【元】【明】

[0068012] 〔是汝突吉羅罪〕-【聖】【石】

[0068013] 以＋(故)【宋】【元】【明】【宮】

[0068014] 〔是汝之罪汝〕-【宮】

[0068015] 汝＋(人)【石】

[0068016] 〔去作突吉羅懺悔大迦葉復言佛問汝若有
人〕十八字-【石】,〔去作突吉羅懺悔〕-【宮】

[0068017] 是=應【聖】【石】

[0068018] 汝＋(之罪應)【聖】【石】

[0068019] 〔復〕-【聖】【石】

[0068020] 〔人〕-【聖】【石】

[0068021] 福德=諸善【聖】【石】

[0068022] 我示女人不=我以示之非【聖】【石】

[0068023] 罪＋(今)【聖】【石】

[0068024] 悔=海【聖】

[0068025] 屣=履【聖】

Gavāṃpati After the Buddha's Nirvāṇa　　　　　331

[0068026] （論）＋議【聖】【石】

[0068027] 〔言〕－【聖】【石】

[0068028] 阿泥盧豆＝阿那律【聖】【石】

[0068029] 佛＝師【聖】【石】

[0068030] 波提＝鉢提【明】，＝波題【聖】【石】

[0068031] 〔秦言牛呞〕－【宋】【元】【明】【宮】【聖】【石】

[0068032] 軟＝渜【聖】【石】＊〔＊ 1〕

[0068033] 心＝止【宮】

[0068034] 燕＝宴【宮】，〔燕〕－【聖】

[0068035] 樹＝林【聖】【石】＊〔＊ 1 2〕

[0068036] 中＋（華菓豐美）【聖】【石】

[0068037] 憍＝橋【聖】【石】＊〔＊ 1 2 3
　　4 5 6 7 8 9 10 11 12 13〕

[0068038] 波提＝鉢提【明】【宮】下同，＝波題【聖】【石】下同

[0068039] 語＝言【聖】【石】

[0068040] 下來＝來下【聖】【石】

[0068041] 〔覺生〕－【宋】【元】【明】
　　【宮】，覺＝即【聖】【石】

[0068042] 〔來〕－【宋】【元】【明】【宮】【聖】【石】

[0068043] 大＝太【宋】【元】【明】【宮】

[0068044] 〔輪〕－【聖】【石】

[0068045] 〔我〕－【聖】【石】

[0068046] 和上＝和尚【明】＊〔＊ 1 2〕

[0068047] 可奈＝奈之【聖】【石】

[0068048] 愍＝憐【聖】【石】

[0068049] 問＋（言）【聖】【石】

[0068050] 悶＋（倒錯）【聖】【石】

[0068051] 惱＝憹【聖】【石】

[0068052] 斷＋（是以）【宋】【元】【明】【宮】【聖】【石】

[0068053] 尸＝失【聖】【石】

[0068054] 下＋（至）【聖】【石】

[0069001] 提＝題【聖】【石】

Ānanda's Return　　　　　　　　　　　　　　　337

[0069002] 神通＝通神【宮】

[0069003] 共＋（八）【聖】【石】

[0069004] 敲＝撓【宮】【聖】【石】＊［＊ 1］

[0069005] 鑰＝籥【宋】【元】【明】【宮】＊［＊ 1］

The First Dharma Council　　　　　　　　　　339

[0069006] （眾）＋僧【聖】【石】＊［＊ 1］

[0069007] 〔復〕－【聖】【石】

[0069008] 法＝經【宋】【元】【明】【宮】【聖】【石】

[0069009] 泥盧＝那律【聖】【石】

[0069010] 弟子＋（中）【聖】【石】

[0069011] 唯＝惟【聖】，＝忖【石】

[0069012] 床＝座【宋】【元】【明】【宮】

[0069013] 空＝夜【元】【明】【聖】【石】

[0069014] 有宿而不嚴＝虛空不明淨【元】【明】【聖】【石】

[0069015] 現＝見【聖】

[0069016] 手＝掌【宋】【元】【明】【宮】

[0069017] 〔言〕－【宋】【元】【明】【宮】【聖】【石】

[0069018] 集滅＝習盡【聖】，＝集盡【石】

[0069019] 〔呪〕－【宋】【元】【明】【宮】【聖】

[0069020] 如＝此【宮】

[0069021] 根＝法【聖】【石】

[0069022] 為＝安【聖】【石】

[0069023] （此）＋偈【宋】【元】【明】【宮】【聖】【石】

[0069024] 免＝勉【聖】【石】

[0069025] 妬＝姤【石】＊［＊ 1］

[0069026] 憂婆離＝憂波利【宋】【元】【明】【宮】，＝憂婆梨【聖】，＝憂婆利【石】＊

[0069027] 〔說〕－【元】【明】

[0069028] 提＝鄰【宋】【元】【明】【宮】，＝［潾-米+羔］【聖】【石】

[0069029] 義＝議【聖】

[0069030] 婆＝波【宋】【元】【明】【宮】＊

[0069031] 十＝千【宋】【宮】

[0069032] 復更＝等復【宋】【元】【明】【宮】，＝等復更【聖】

[0069033] 中＋（誦持）【聖】【石】

[0069034] 〔義〕－【聖】【石】

[0069035] 〔起就師子座處坐〕－【聖】【石】

[0069036] （長老）＋阿【聖】【石】

[0069037] 〔師子座處坐〕－【聖】【石】

[0069038] 婆提＝衛【聖】【石】

[0069039] 〔復〕－【聖】【石】

[0069040] 〔於〕－【宋】【元】【明】【宮】

[0069041] 殺＋（生）【宋】【元】【明】【宮】【聖】【石】

[0069042] 名＋（為）【宋】【元】【明】【宮】

[0069043] 〔藏三法藏〕－【宋】【聖】【石】

[0070001] 集＝作【宋】【宮】，集＋（法）【聖】【石】

[0070002] 幡＝幢【宋】【元】【明】【宮】

[0070003] 世界＝世間【聖】【石】

[0070004] 藏法＝法藏【宋】【元】【明】【
宮】，＝法竟【聖】，＝藏竟【石】

Śāriputra's Unyielding Resolve 347

[0070053] 婆＝頗【宮】

[0070054] 〔人〕－【宮】

[0070055] 〔辟〕－【聖】

[0070056] 氣分不＝不了了【聖】【石】

[0070057] 出＝去【宋】【元】【明】【宮】，出＋（去）【聖】【石】

[0070058] 又＝有【石】

[0070059] 氣殘＝餘習【元】【明】【聖】【石】＊〔＊ 1 2〕

[0070060] 必＝畢【元】【明】【聖】【石】＊〔＊ 1 2 3 4〕

[0070061] 磋＝蹉【宋】【元】【明】【宮】

[0070062] 鎖初＝璅初得【聖】【石】

[0070063] 羸瘦＝瘦羸【聖】

[0070064] 酥＝蘇【宋】【元】【聖】

[0070065] 滓＝澤【聖】

[0070066] 〔誰為〕－【聖】【石】

[0070067] 座＋（為誰）【聖】【石】

[0070068] 〔轉〕－【聖】【石】

[0070069] 語＝言【聖】【石】

[0071001] 佛＋（說）【聖】【石】

[0071002] 〔舍利弗食〕－【聖】【石】

[0071003] 食＋（不應食）【聖】【石】

[0071004] 匿＋（王）【聖】

[0071005] 引＝說【聖】

[0071006] 〔為〕－【聖】【石】

[0071007] 諸＝請【聖】

[0071008] 嗽＝[口*數]【宋】【元】【明】【宮】＊ 〔＊ 1 2〕

[0071009] 心定＝定心【宋】【元】【明】【宮】

Pilindavatsa and the Ganges River Spirit 353

[0071010] 常＝當【元】【明】

[0071011] 〔水〕－【宋】【元】【明】【宮】【聖】【石】

[0071012] 告＝言【明】

[0071013] 懺謝＝謝懺【聖】

[0071014] 合＝又【聖】【石】＊ 〔＊ 1〕

[0071015] 之＝言【宮】

[0071016] 畢＝必【宮】

[0071017] 殘＝餘【元】【明】，＝習【聖】【石】＊ 〔＊ 1 2〕

[0071018] 〔若〕－【宮】

[0071019] 枏＝旃【宋】【元】【明】【宮】

[0071020] 木＝帶【宋】【元】【明】【宮】【聖】【石】

[0071021] 杅＝盂【元】【明】

[0071022] 娠＝身【宋】【元】【明】【宮】【聖】【石】

[0071023] 〔是〕－【石】

[0071024] 感＝戚【聖】

[0071025] 被＝服【宋】【元】【明】【宮】

[0071026] 無異也＝若干【聖】【石】

The Cowherds Test the Buddha's Omniscience 357

[0073040] 酥＝蘇【宋】【元】【宮】【聖】＊ 〔＊ 1 2 3〕

[0073041] 〔語〕－【聖】【石】

[0073042] 往＝住【聖】

[0073043] 等＝曹【聖】【石】

[0073044] 何能＝云何【聖】【石】

[0073045] 〔人〕－【聖】【石】

[0073046] 喜好＝好喜【宋】【元】【明】【宮】，＝喜【聖】【石】

[0073047] 故＝常【宋】【元】【明】【宮】

[0073048] 往＝住【石】

[0073049] 〔由是〕－【聖】【石】

[0073050] 種種＝[卄/(禾*魚)][卄/(禾*魚)]【聖】

[0073051] 違＝韋【宋】【元】【明】【宮】

[0073052] 陀＝大【聖】【石】

[0073053] 戰＝爭【聖】【石】

[0073054] 〔如〕－【宋】【元】【明】【宮】

[0073055] 伎＝技【元】【明】

[0073056] 於＝竹【石】

[0073057] 〔坐〕－【聖】【石】

[0073058] 下＋（坐）【石】

[0073059] 其炎＝焰煥【明】

[0073060] 融＝鎔【宋】【元】【明】【宮】

[0073061] 〔紫〕－【宋】【宮】【聖】【石】

[0073062] 〔大〕－【聖】

[0073063] 皆＝已【聖】【石】

[0073064] 纏＝繏【宋】【宮】

[0073065] 有＝得【聖】【石】

[0074001] 番息＝蕃息【宋】【元】【明】【宮】＊，＝
孜茂【聖】＊，＝牧茂【石】＊〔＊ 1 2〕

[0074002] 瘡＝創【聖】＊〔＊ 1 2 3 4〕

[0074003] 度＝淚【聖】

[0074004] 若＝谷【聖】

[0074005] 十一＝十二【宮】

[0074006] 〔知〕－【宋】【元】【明】【宮】

[0074007] 吉＝告【聖】＊〔＊ 1〕

[0074008] 為＝若【宮】【聖】【石】

[0074009] 虫＝蟲【元】【明】下同

[0074010] 則＋（住）【宮】

[0074011] 害＋（則悅澤）【宋】【元】【明】【宮】

[0074012] 〔若〕－【宋】【元】【明】【宮】

[0074013] 虻＝虻【宋】【元】【明】【宮】【聖】＊〔＊ 1 2〕

[0074014] 念＝以【宋】【元】【明】【宮】

[0074015] 〔觀〕－【宮】

[0074016] 遙＝這【聖】

[0074017] 如是＝爾【聖】【石】

[0074018] 〔如〕－【宋】【元】【明】【宮】

[0074019] 引＝弘【石】

[0074020] 牛＝中【聖】【石】

[0074021] 番＝蕃【宋】【元】【明】【宮】

[0074022] 知＋（度）【宋】【元】【明】【宮】

[0074023] 度＝渡【宋】【元】【明】【宮】【聖】

[0074024] 人＝入【石】

[0074025] 入＝人【宋】【元】【明】【宮】

[0074026] 好＝將【宮】

[0074027] 〔知〕－【宮】

[0074028] 犢子＝續有【宋】【元】【明】
【宮】，＝犢有【聖】【石】

[0074029] 磬＝都【宮】

[0074030] 諸＝護【宋】【元】【明】【宮】

[0074031] 特＝犢【宋】，明註曰犢南藏作牸

[0074032] 讚譽稱＝稱差【宋】【元】【明】
【宮】，＝稱美【聖】【石】

[0074033] 〔得〕－【聖】【石】

[0074034] 等＋（放牛人）【宋】【元】【明】【宮】

[0074035] 〔所知不過三四事〕－【聖】【石】

[0076003] 婆波＝波【宋】【元】【明】【宮】，＝婆婆【聖】

[0076004] 梨羅＝闍羅【元】【明】【聖】【石】

[0076005] 〔王〕－【聖】

[0076006] 〔宜〕－【宋】【元】【明】【宮】

[0076007] 〔諸〕－【石】

[0076008] （諸）＋仙【石】

[0076009] 〔入〕－【石】

[0076010] 羊＝生【明】＊，【石】 ［＊ 1］

[0076011] 頸＝頂【聖】【石】

[0076012] 令＝今【聖】

[0076013] 免＝勉【聖】

[0076014] 〔重〕－【石】

[0076015] 圍＝韋【明】【石】

[0076016] 催＝推【宋】【元】【明】【宮】，＝崔【聖】

[0076017] 以＝已【石】

[0076018] 藪＋（仙人）【石】

[0076019] 嗣＝福王【聖】

[0076020] 〔為王〕－【聖】

[0076021] 復不＝不復【石】

[0076022] 軟＝濡【聖】【石】

[0076023] 林木＝樹林【石】

[0076024] 涼＝浴【宋】【元】【明】【石】

[0076025] 應＝於【石】

[0076026] 是＝此【石】

[0076027] 元＝先【宋】【元】【明】【宮】

[0076028] 〔本起〕－【宋】【元】【明】【宮】

Mahākāśyapa and Mt. Gṛdhrakūṭa　　375

[0078059] 〔於耆闍崛山〕－【聖】

[0078060] 法藏＝藏法【聖】【石】

[0078061] 加＝跏【宋】【元】【明】【宮】

[0078062] 熏＝薰【聖】

[0078063] 人＋（語）【聖】

[0078064] 〔定〕－【宋】【元】【明】【宮】

[0078065] 諸＝說【宋】【元】【明】【宮】

[0078066] 〔我〕－【宋】【宮】＊　［＊ 1］

[0078067] 〔愁〕－【聖】

[0078068] 惱＋（應厭）【聖】【石】

[0078069] 世間＝世界【宋】【元】【明】【宮】【聖】

[0078070] 〔中心應厭〕－【聖】【石】

[0078071] 世界＝世間【石】

[0078072] 開導＝引導【聖】，＝道導引【石】

[0078073] 竟＋（即）【宋】【元】【明】【宮】

[0078074] 梨＝利【聖】

[0078075] 上昇＝上是【元】，＝昇【聖】【石】

[0079001] 作是＝直入山內【聖】

[0079002] 入＋（耆闍堀）【元】【明】【聖】【石】

[0079003] 頭石內＝內【宋】【宮】，＝石頭中【元】【明】，＝頭石中【聖】【石】

[0079004] 軟＝濡【聖】【石】

[0079005] 〔時〕－【聖】【石】

[0079006] 〔出佛〕－【聖】【石】

[0079007] 〔世〕－【宋】【元】【明】【宮】【聖】

[0079008] 隨＝遂【宋】【元】【明】【宮】

[0079009] 已＝以【聖】【石】

[0079010] 人＋（以此三會度人）【聖】

[0079011] 〔人〕－【聖】【石】

[0079012] 山＋（頭）【聖】

[0079013] 〔即於…槃〕十字－【聖】

[0079014] 〔而〕－【石】

[0079015] 文＝牟【聖】

[0079016] 漢＋（彌勒佛言）【聖】

[0079017] 以＝如【聖】【石】

[0079018] 眾＋（生）【宋】【元】【明】【宮】

[0079019] 〔是〕－【聖】【石】

[0079020] （（諸聖…次））二十三字＝（（吉處是故摩訶迦
葉於中集法亦於中般涅槃又諸聖人樂住是處佛為諸
聖人主以是故佛住耆闍崛山復次））四十三字【聖】

[0079021] 人喜住＝所樂【石】

[0079022] （是故摩訶迦葉於中集法亦於中般
涅槃又諸聖人皆住是處）＋佛【石】

[0079023] 主＋（以）【石】

[0079024] 住＝在【石】

[0079025] 山＋（中）【石】

Śāriputra Explains Pure Sustenance 381

[0079057] 〔為〕－【石】

[0079058] 〔時〕－【聖】

[0079059] 〔姊〕－【元】【明】【聖】【石】

[0079060] 耶＝那【聖】【石】＊〔＊ 1 2〕

[0079061] 說＋（云何為下口食）【聖】【石】

[0079062] 言＝答曰【石】，＝答言【聖】

[0079063] 〔穀〕－【石】

[0079064] 殖＝植【宋】【元】【明】【宮】

[0079065] 筮＝算【宋】【元】【明】【宮】

[0079066] 凶＋（小術不正）【聖】【石】

[0079067] 〔種種〕－【聖】【石】

[0079068] 〔清〕－【宮】

[0079069] 目聞說＝目因闍是故說【聖】，＝目聞是說【石】

[0079070] 〔舍利弗因為說法〕－【聖】

Subhadra, the Brahmacārin 385

[0080038] 墮＝崩【聖】【石】

[0080039] 知＝智【聖】

[0080040] 師＋（更）【聖】【石】

[0080041] 新＝親【石】

[0080042] 遙＝[這-言+(又/言)]【聖】

[0080043] 曰＝言【聖】

[0080044] 我年一十九＝我始年十九【宋】【元】
【明】【石】，＝我年二十九【宮】

[0080045] 已＝以【聖】

[0081001] 正＝聖【石】

On Viewing Mākandika's Corpse 389

[0082034] 輿＝舁【宋】【元】【明】，＝舉【宮】【聖】【石】

[0082035] 智慧功德乃為淨∞眼見求淨無
是事【宋】【元】【明】【宮】

[0082036] 智慧功德乃為淨∞眼見求淨無
是事【宋】【元】【明】【宮】

Why Ānanda was So Called 391

[0083025] 名＋（字）【聖】【石】

[0083026] 〔是〕－【宋】【元】【明】【宮】

[0083027] 目乾連＝目伽連【宋】【元】【
宮】【聖】，＝目犍連【明】

[0083028] 文＋（尼）【聖】【石】

[0083029] 〔佛〕－【宋】【元】【明】【宮】【聖】

[0083030] 名＋（字）【宋】【元】【明】【宮】【聖】

[0083031] 〔名〕－【宋】【元】【明】【宮】

[0083032] （阿難者秦言歡喜）夾註＝（阿難者秦言
歡喜）本文【宋】【元】【明】【宮】【聖】

[0083033] 〔有〕－【聖】

[0083034] 名＋（新韓阿[少/兔]秦言）【石】

[0083035] （其）＋第【宋】【元】【明】【宮】

[0083036] 佛＝悉達陀【宋】【元】【明】【聖】【石】

[0083037] 陀＝多【宋】【元】【明】【宮】，＝他【聖】

[0083038] 位＋（處）【石】

[0083039] 至＝往【宋】【元】【明】【宮】

[0083040] 〔欲知消息〕－【聖】【石】

[0083041] 死＋（欲知消息）【石】

[0083042] 耳＝身【宋】【元】【明】【宮】

[0083043] 微弱＝微少【宮】【聖】

[0083044] 尼＝㝹【聖】

[0083045] 座＝處【宋】【宮】【聖】

[0083046] 加＝跏【宋】【元】【明】【宮】

[0083047] 十八＝八十【明】

[0083048] （死）＋了【宋】【元】【明】【宮】

[0083049] 〔時悲〕－【宋】【元】【明】【宮】

[0083050] 〔說偈〕－【宋】【元】【明】【宮】

[0084001] 土＋（歡喜得大利, 解脫一切苦, 今得轉法輪, 無所不清淨）【宋】【元】【明】, 土＝國【聖】【石】

[0084002] 了＝死【宋】【元】【明】【宮】＊

[0084003] 違＝圍【聖】

[0084004] 〔又〕－【聖】

[0084005] 〔來〕－【宋】【元】【明】【宮】

[0084006] （死）＋了【宋】【元】【明】, 了＝死【宮】

[0084007] 〔王〕－【宋】【元】【明】【宮】【聖】

[0084008] 難＋（阿難者秦言歡喜）【聖】【石】

[0084009] 青＝清【聖】

[0084010] 大＝心【明】

The Bodhisattva Shakyamuni Encounters Puṣya Buddha　　　399

[0087029] 火＋（禪）【石】＊　［＊　1］

The King Śibi Jātaka Tale　　　403

[0088001] 羅＝隣【聖】【石】

[0088002] 〔盡〕－【宋】【元】【明】【宮】【聖】

[0088003] 墮＝終【宋】【元】【明】【宮】【聖】

[0088004] 念＝命【聖】

[0088005] 不＝都無【石】

[0088006] 疑＋（處）【石】

[0088007] 佯＝揚【宋】, ＝楊【聖】【石】

[0088008] 腋＝掖【聖】

[0088009] 作＋（大）【聖】

[0088010] 逐＝遂【石】

[0088011] 掖＝腋【宋】【元】【明】【宮】

[0088012] 底＝下【聖】

[0088013] 信＝護【宋】【元】【明】【宮】, ＝[言＊侯]【石】

[0088014] 作＝信【聖】

[0088015] 受＝愛【宋】

[0088016] 言＝曰【石】

[0088017] 熱＝血【聖】

[0088018] 無＝何【宋】【元】【明】【宮】

[0088019] 熱＝煖【聖】【石】

[0088020] 〔王〕－【宮】

[0088021] ［跳-兆+專］＝端【元】【明】

[0088022] 臗＝寬【宋】，＝［穴/日/（儿@厶）］【聖】【石】

[0088023] 項＝頸【宋】【元】【明】【宮】

[0088024] 戚＝［仁-二+鐵］【聖】

[0088025] 天人＝人天【聖】

[0088026] 求＝索【聖】

[0088027] 稱＝秤【石】＊ ［＊ 1 2］

[0088028] 物＝人【石】

[0088029] （力少不能得上）＋爾【石】，爾＝是【聖】

[0088030] 責＝情【聖】

[0088031] 度＝渡【宋】【元】【明】【宮】

[0088032] 怠＝迷【石】

[0088033] 〔一〕－【宋】【元】【明】【宮】

[0088034] 大＝天【宋】【元】【明】【宮】【聖】

[0088035] 振＝震【宋】【元】【明】【宮】

[0088036] 〔念我〕－【元】【明】【聖】【石】

[0088037] 終＝眾【宋】【元】【明】【宮】【聖】【石】

[0088038] 供養＝養護【宮】【聖】【石】

[0088039] 須我也＝如【石】

[0088040] 〔此〕－【聖】

[0088041] （一）＋心【宋】【元】【明】【宮】

[0088042] 〔是〕－【聖】

[0088043] 〔種種〕－【聖】【石】

[0088044] 是檀＝是為檀那【聖】【石】

King Sutasoma's Dedication to Truth   413

[0088045] 大＝天【石】

[0088046] 乃至捨＝欲棄身【聖】【石】

[0089001] 語＋（是王）【聖】【石】

[0089002] 匃＝自【宮】

[0089003] 王＋（語）【宋】【元】【明】【宮】

[0089004] 〔諾〕－【宮】

[0089005] 澡＝滲【聖】【石】

[0089006] 慟＝動【聖】

[0089007] 驚＝京【聖】【石】

[0089008] 止＝山【宋】【元】【明】【宮】【聖】【石】

[0089009] 〔諸〕－【聖】

[0089010] 〔王〕－【宋】【元】【明】【宮】

[0089011] 甚畏＝自根【宋】【元】【明】【宮】【聖】

[0089012] 已＝以【聖】

[0089013] （城）＋門【聖】

[0089014] 辜＝孤【宋】【元】【明】【宮】【聖】【石】

[0089015] 招＝貽【聖】

[0089016] 言＝語須陀須摩王【石】

[0089017] 〔兩〕－【元】【明】【宮】

[0089018] 物＝初【宋】【宮】

[0089019] 治＋（多）【宋】【元】【明】【宮】

[0089020] 忠恕＝中怒【聖】，＝中恕【石】

[0089021] 小而大＝為大人【宋】【元】【明】【宮】

[0089022] 〔壽〕－【聖】

[0089023] 有悔恨＝恨也【聖】

[0089024] 鹿＝麁【宮】＊［＊ 1］

[0089025] 赴＝起【聖】

[0089026] 〔實語〕－【石】

[0089027] 〔今相放捨〕－【聖】

[0089028] 汝既得脫＝汝得解脫【宋】【元】
【明】，〔汝既得脫〕－【宮】

[0089029] （九百）＋九【聖】

[0089030] 百＝九百九十九【聖】

[0089031] 〔本生中〕－【宋】【元】【明】【宮】

The Bodhisattvas Prasannendriya and Agramati   419

[0107005] 度＋（者）【宋】【宮】【聖】【聖乙】【石】

[0107006] 何以故＝二乘不能如所應度外道【聖乙】【石】

[0107007] 〔二乘雖有所度〕－【聖乙】【石】

[0107008] 如所應＝能如實【聖乙】【石】，如＝知【聖】

[0107009] 何以故＝二乘【聖乙】【石】

[0107010] 故＝是故不能巧度不以佛道而度眾
生以是故言不能巧度【聖乙】【石】

[0107011] 實＝法【聖乙】【石】

[0107012] 方＝舫【宋】，＝枋【聖乙】

[0107013] 病＝疾【宋】【元】【明】【宮】【聖】

[0107014] 〔坐〕－【宮】
[0107015] 佛＋（言）【聖】
[0107016] 〔能〕－【石】
[0107017] 佛＝國【聖乙】【石】
[0107018] 不＝無【石】
[0107019] 〔則〕－【宋】【元】【明】【宮】【聖】
[0107020] 求＋（為）【宋】【元】【明】【宮】【聖】
[0107021] 〔行〕－【宮】【聖】【聖乙】【石】
[0107022] 眥＝呰【宋】【元】【明】【宮】
[0107023] 欲＋（煩惱）【元】【明】【石】
[0107024] 滅＋（法）【聖乙】
[0107025] 〔相〕－【宋】【元】【明】【宮】
[0107026] （煩）＋惱【宋】【元】【明】【宮】【石】
[0107027] 〔所〕－【宋】【元】【明】【宮】
[0107028] 則＝便【聖乙】【石】
[0107029] 悅＝喜【石】
[0107030] 聞＋（說）【聖乙】
[0107031] 〔是人〕－【宋】【元】【明】【宮】【聖】
[0107032] 無＋（有）【石】
[0107033] 法＋（今）【石】
[0107034] 〔一〕－【宮】
[0108001] 〔即〕－【聖乙】
[0108002] 〔受〕－【聖乙】
[0108003] （（千萬…謗））十八字＝（（苦））一字【宮】
[0108004] （受）＋苦【聖乙】
[0108005] 三＝二【宋】【元】【明】【宮】【聖】【聖乙】【石】
[0108006] （國）＋土【聖乙】【石】
[0108007] 〔文殊師利言〕－【宮】【聖】
[0108008] 〔言〕－【宋】【元】【明】
[0108009] 〔復〕－【聖乙】【石】
[0108010] 曰＝言【宋】【元】【明】【宮】【聖乙】
[0108011] 深＋（法）【聖乙】【石】

Three Brothers Become Enlightened   433

[0110011] 煩惱＋（是名能斷種種諸見纏及煩惱）【石】
[0110012] 〔季〕－【宮】
[0110013] 婆提＝衛國【石】

[0110014] 曼＝蔓【宋】【元】【明】【宮】【石】

[0110015] 來＝求【宮】

The Buddha's Omniscience Converts a Brahman 435
(No variants recorded for this story.)

The Buddha, the Servant, and the Doubting Brahman 437

[0115003] 熙＝嬉【宋】【宮】

[0115004] 而＝微【元】【明】

[0115005] 光＋（明）【宋】【宮】

[0115006] 加＝跏【宋】【元】【明】【宮】＊［＊ 1 2 3]

[0115007] 似＝以【石】

[0115008] 眔生＝乃至【宋】【宮】

[0115009] 婆提＝衛【聖】【石】

[0115010] 人＝生【元】【明】【聖】【石】

[0115011] ［泳-永+(米＊番)]淀＝潘澱【元】
【明】，＝[米＊番]淀【聖】

[0115012] 毛＝毫【元】【明】

[0115013] （此）＋偈【聖】【石】

[0115014] 〔甚〕－【宋】【宮】

[0115015] 〔信〕－【聖】【石】

[0115016] 〔佛〕－【宋】【元】【明】【宮】

[0115017] 狀＝伏【石】

[0115018] 城＋（中）【宋】【元】【明】【宮】【聖】【石】

The Monk, the King and the Naked Ascetics 445

[0119004] 狂愚＝癡狂【石】

[0119005] 已＝以【石】

[0119006] 如＋（是）【宋】【元】【明】【宮】

The Arhat, the Elephant, and Causality 449

[0119008] 〔中〕－【宋】【元】【明】【宮】【石】

[0119009] 即＝既【宋】【元】【明】【宮】

[0119010] 呪＝術【石】

The Buddha Cares for a Sick Bhikshu 455

[0119011] 藏＝臟【明】

[0119012] 疹＝疾【宋】【元】【明】【宮】

[0119013] 塠壓＝堆壓【宋】【元】【明】【
宮】，＝堆[病-丙+甲]【石】

[0119014] 杖＝伎【宋】【元】【明】【宮】

[0119015] 婆提＝衛【石】

[0119016] 〔手〕－【宋】【元】【明】【宮】【石】

[0119017] 持＝特【石】

[0119018] 排＝俳【石】

[0119019] 盥＝與【石】

[0120001] 方＋（來）【石】

[0120002] 苦＋（痛）【元】【明】【石】

Gaṇḍaka's Miraculous Restoration 461

[0120003] 〔者〕－【宋】【元】【明】【宮】【石】

[0120004] 身＋（或）【石】

[0120005] 〔其〕－【宮】【石】

[0120006] 〔破〕－【宋】【元】【明】【宮】

[0120007] 致殘毀＝到形殘【石】

[0120008] 犍＝揵【宋】【元】【明】【宮】＊［＊ 1 2 3]

[0120009] （揵抵秦言續也）夾註＝（揵抵
秦言續也）本文【宋】【宮】

[0120010] 秦＝此【明】

[0120011] 〔也〕－【宋】【元】【明】【宮】

[0120012] 被＝狀【元】【明】

[0120013] 〔是〕－【宋】【元】【明】【宮】

[0120014] 復＝服【石】＊［＊ 1 2]

[0120015] 洹＝桓【石】＊［＊ 1]

The Buddha's Skillful Means on Behalf of Monastics 465

[0122004] 〔佛〕－【宮】

[0122005] 門＋（下）【宋】【元】【明】【宮】

[0122006] （佛）＋鉢【宋】【元】【明】【宮】

[0122007] 言＝曰【宋】【元】【明】【宮】

[0122008] 疾＝病【宋】【元】【明】【宮】

[0122009] 皆亦＝亦皆【石】

The Buddha Attempts to Connect with an Old Woman 469

[0125011] 〔國〕－【宋】【元】【明】【宮】

[0125012] 〔人〕－【宋】【元】【明】【宮】【石】

[0125013] 言＋（阿難）【宋】【元】【明】【宮】

Three Stories of Bodhisattvas and Buddhas Appearing in the World 473

The Leper Cured by Samantabhadra 473

Samantabhadra Appears to a Bhikshu Reciting the Lotus 473

A Monk Who Saw Amitabha and Whose Tongue Would Not Burn 475

[0126015] 〔一〕－【宋】【元】【明】【宮】

[0127001] 光明＋（色）【石】

[0127002] 手＝掌【宋】【元】【明】【宮】

[0127003] 自言＝白佛【宮】

[0127004] 誦讀＝讀誦【宋】【元】【明】【宮】

[0127005] 〔經〕－【石】

[0127006] 經＝或【宮】

[0127007] 普賢＋（也）【石】

[0127008] 〔有〕－【宋】【元】【明】【宮】

[0127009] 〔一〕－【宮】

Maudgalyāyana Seeks the Bounds of Buddha's Voice 477

[0127026] 聚＝眾【宋】【宮】

[0127027] 至＝去【宋】【元】【明】【宮】

[0127028] 世界＝國【石】

[0127029] 世界＝國土【石】＊ [＊ 1 2 3 4 5 6 7 8 9 10 11 12 13 14 15 16 17 18 19 20 21 22 23 24 25 26 27 28 29 30]

[0127030] 土＝界【宋】【元】【明】【宮】

[0127031] 度伽略子＝伽路子度【宋】【元】【明】【宮】【石】

Hastaka's Three Insatiables 479

[0128007] 〔此〕－【宋】【元】【明】【宮】【石】

[0128008] 〔諸〕－【宋】【元】【明】【宮】＊ [＊ 1]

The Limits of Mañjuśrī's Samādhi Power 483

[0129001] 紝＝衽【宋】【元】【明】【宮】＊ [＊ 1 2]

[0129002] 〔針〕－【宋】【元】【明】【宮】【石】

[0129003] 恩＝因【元】【明】

[0129004] 令＝今【宋】【元】【明】【宮】

[0129005] 尚＝向【宋】

[0129006] 翁＝公【宋】【元】【明】【宮】【石】＊ [＊ 1 2]

[0129007] 亦＝言【宋】【元】【明】【宮】

The Buddha's Love of Meritorious Deeds 485

[0129001] 紝＝衽【宋】【元】【明】【宮】＊ [＊ 1 2]

[0129002] 〔針〕－【宋】【元】【明】【宮】【石】

[0129003] 恩＝因【元】【明】
[0129004] 令＝今【宋】【元】【明】【宮】
[0129005] 尚＝向【宋】
[0129006] 翁＝公【宋】【元】【明】【宮】【石】＊［＊ 1 2］
[0129007] 亦＝言【宋】【元】【明】【宮】

The Arhat Upagupta Meets an Elderly Nun   487
[0129024] 狂＋（如賊）【石】
[0129025] 優＝憂【宋】【元】【明】【宮】
【石】＊［＊ 1 2 3 4 5］
[0129026] 小＝少【元】【明】＊［＊ 1］
[0129027] 儀＝貌【宋】【元】【明】【宮】，＝狼【石】
[0129028] 林＝床【宋】【元】【明】【宮】【石】
[0129029] 知＝如【宋】【元】【明】【宮】

The Life of Śāriputra   489
[0136005] 〔【論】〕－【宋】【宮】＊［＊ 1 2 3］
[0136006] （和）＋羅【宋】【元】【明】【宮】
[0136007] 言＝曰【宋】【元】【明】【宮】
[0136008] 告＝吉【宋】【元】【宮】，＝言【明】
[0136009] 告＝吉【宋】【元】【明】【宮】
[0136010] 重＝貴【宋】【元】【明】【宮】
[0136011] 最＝取【元】【明】【宮】
[0136012] 貴＝重【宋】【元】【明】【宮】
[0136013] 住＝坐【明】
[0136014] 情＝精【宋】【元】【明】【宮】
[0136015] 〔有〕－【宋】【元】【明】【宮】
[0136016] 語＝意【宋】【元】【明】
[0136017] 畢＝必【元】【明】
[0136018] 學日又＝受戒日【宋】【元】【明】【宮】
[0136019] 宣＝演【宋】【元】【明】【宮】
[0136020] 說＝言【宋】【元】【明】【宮】
[0136021] 弗＝佛【明】
[0136022] 師＝即【宮】

Subhūti and Floral Appearance Bhikshuni   501
[0136023] 〔多〕－【宋】【宮】
[0136024] 復＝後【宮】
[0137001] 磨＝摩【宋】【宮】

[0137002] 女＝惡【宋】【宮】

[0137003] 〔之惡〕－【宋】【宮】

[0137004] 〔應〕－【宮】

[0137005] 〔以〕－【宋】【元】【明】，以＝似【宮】

The Story Behind Śāriputra's Name 505

[0137006] 證＝說【宋】【元】【明】【宮】

[0137007] 議＝義【宋】【宮】＊ [＊ 1 2 3 4 5 6 7 8 9 10]

[0137008] 郗＝絺【元】【明】＊ [＊ 1 2]

[0137009] 秦＝此【明】

[0137010] 〔也〕－【明】

[0137011] 廢忘又不＝陳故不復【宋】【元】【明】【宮】＊ [＊ 1]

[0137012] 銅＝銅鍱【宋】，＝鐵鍱【元】【明】

[0137013] 者＝曰【宋】【元】【明】【宮】

[0137014] 羅＝國【明】

[0137015] 女＝妻【元】

[0137016] 被＝披【元】【明】

[0137017] 知＋〔姊〕【宋】【元】【明】【宮】

[0137018] 不剪指＝不暇剪【宋】【元】【明】，＝不翦指【宮】

[0137019] 爪＝抓【宋】【宮】＊ [＊ 1]

[0137020] 號＝名【宋】【元】【明】【宮】

[0137021] 疊＝[疊*毛]【宋】【元】【明】【宮】

[0137022] 波＝婆【宋】【宮】＊

[0137023] 逐＝豕【宮】

[0137024] 弗＋〔者〕【元】【明】，〔弗〕－【宮】
，明註曰北藏無弗者秦言子也六字

[0137025] 子＋〔也〕【宋】【元】【明】【宮】

Śāriputra, the Buddha, and the Pigeon 513

[0138032] 祇洹＝祇桓【宋】【元】【明】【宮】

[0138033] 戰＝顫【明】【宮】

[0138034] 戰＝顫【宋】【元】【明】【宮】

[0138035] 故＝初【元】【明】

[0139001] 〔無餘〕－【宋】【元】【明】【宮】

A Layman Witnesses Buddha's Concentration 519

[0220002] 〔生〕－【宋】【元】【明】【宮】【石】

[0220003] 蘇＝酥【元】【明】

[0220004] 〔問〕－【宋】【元】【明】【宮】【石】

[0225013] 若＝著【宋】【元】【明】【宮】

[0225014] 虫＝蟲【元】【明】＊

[0225015] 寶衣＝衣寶【宋】【元】【明】【宮】

[0225016] 〔言〕－【宋】【元】【明】【宮】，言＝欲【石】

[0225017] 師＝之【宋】【元】【明】

[0225018] 亦＝方【石】

[0225019] 是＝此【石】

[0225020] （於）＋無【宋】【元】【明】【宮】【石】

[0225021] 任＝住【元】【明】

[0225022] 僧＋（僧）【宋】【元】【明】【宮】

Two Brothers Throw Away Gold 543

[0226017] 〔是〕－【石】

[0226018] 尚＝常【宋】【元】【明】【宮】

[0226019] 〔而〕－【宮】

[0226020] 瞻＝占【宋】【元】【明】【宮】

[0226021] 〔更〕－【石】

[0226022] 〔故〕－【宋】【元】【明】【宮】

[0226023] 〔相〕－【宋】【元】【明】【宮】

[0226024] 危＝殺【石】

[0226025] 不＋（布）【宋】【元】【明】【宮】【石】

[0226026] 說＋（偈）【元】【明】【石】

[0226027] 名＝為【元】【明】【石】

[0226028] 終始＝始終【宋】【元】【明】【宮】

[0227001] 好＝善【石】

[0227002] 生福＝福生【石】

[0227003] 求＋（索）【石】

[0227004] 〔之〕－【石】

[0227005] 擯＝殯【宮】

[0227006] 〔慳〕－【石】

The Buddha Questions Monks on Mindfulness of Death 549

[0228001] 恃＝持【宋】【宮】

[0228002] （何）＋出【石】

[0228003] 〔保〕－【宋】【元】【明】【宮】【石】

[0228004] 老至時＝至時老【石】

[0228005] 免＝勉【宮】

[0228006] 怨之惡＝惡之怨【宋】【元】【明】【宮】

[0228007] 時捨＝捨時【宋】【元】【明】【宮】
[0228008] 相＝想【明】＊ ［＊ 1 2］
[0228009] 佛＋（言）【石】
[0228010] 相＝想【宋】【元】【明】【宮】＊ ［＊ 1 2］
[0228011] 是真＝真是【宋】【元】【明】【宮】

The Traveling Brahman's Quest for Pure Food   553

[0231015] 〔中〕－【宋】【元】【明】【宮】
[0231016] 思＋（惟）【石】
[0231017] 髓＝膸【宋】【宮】
[0231018] 耶＝邪【明】
[0231019] 問＝聞【石】
[0231020] 曰＝白【石】
[0231021] 得＝渴【石】
[0231022] 拳＝棒【石】，＝捲【宮】
[0231023] 搥胸＝推匈【石】
[0231024] 吁＝干【宋】【宮】，＝乾【元】【明】
[0231025] 好色＝色好【石】
[0231026] 四＝五【石】

The Buddha's Unceasing Zeal   557

[0249006] 厭＝猒【石】＊ ［＊ 1］
[0249007] 紙＝袟【宋】【元】【明】【宮】＊ ［＊ 1］
[0249008] 疊＝㲲【石】
[0249009] 更＝復【石】
[0249010] 得＝復【石】
[0249011] 嘗＝相【宋】【元】【明】【宮】【石】
[0249012] 佛＝人【宋】【宮】

The Buddha Praises Vigor   561

[0249017] 次＝以【宋】【元】【明】【宮】
[0249018] 襞＝辟【宋】【宮】，＝襞【元】【明】
[0250001] 病＋（時）【石】
[0250002] 遇＝過【宋】【元】【明】【宮】
[0250003] 食惡＝惡食【石】
[0250004] 聞＝問【宋】【元】【明】【宮】

About the Translator

Bhikshu Dharmamitra (ordination name "Heng Shou" – 釋恆授) is a Chinese-tradition translator-monk and one of the early American disciples (since 1968) of the late Weiyang Ch'an patriarch, Dharma teacher, and exegete, the Venerable Master Hsuan Hua (宣化上人). He has a total of 23 years in robes during two periods as a monastic (1969–1975; 1991 to present).

Dharmamitra's principal educational foundations as a translator lie in four years of intensive monastic training and Chinese-language study of classic Mahāyāna texts in a small-group setting under Master Hua from 1968–1972, undergraduate Chinese language study at Portland State University, a year of intensive one-on-one Classical Chinese study at the Fu Jen University Language Center near Taipei, and two years at the University of Washington's School of Asian Languages and Literature (1988–90).

Since taking robes again under Master Hua in 1991, Dharmamitra has devoted his energies primarily to study and translation of classic Mahāyāna texts with a special interest in works by Ārya Nāgārjuna and related authors. To date, he has translated more than a dozen important texts, most of which are slated for publication by Kalavinka Press.

Kalavinka Buddhist Classics Title List

Meditation Instruction Texts

The Essentials of Buddhist Meditation
A marvelously complete classic *śamathā-vipaśyanā* (calming-and-insight) meditation manual. By Tiantai Śramaṇa Zhiyi (538–597 CE).

The Six Gates to the Sublime
The earliest Indian Buddhist meditation method explaining the essentials of breath and calming-and-insight meditation. By Śramaṇa Zhiyi.

Bodhisattva Path Texts

Nāgārjuna on the Six Perfections
Chapters 17–30 of Ārya Nāgārjuna's *Mahāprājñāpāramitā Upadeśa.*

Marvelous Stories from the Perfection of Wisdom
100 Stories from Ārya Nāgārjuna's *Mahāprājñāpāramitā Upadeśa.*

A Strand of Dharma Jewels (Ārya Nāgārjuna's *Ratnāvalī*)
The earliest extant edition, translated by Paramārtha: *ca* 550 CE

Nāgārjuna's Guide to the Bodhisattva Path
The *Bodhisaṃbhāra Treatise* with abridged Vaśitva commentary.

The Bodhisaṃbhāra Treatise Commentary
The complete exegesis by the Indian Bhikshu Vaśitva (*ca* 300–500 CE).

Letter from a Friend - The Three Earliest Editions
The earliest extant editions of Ārya Nāgārjuna's *Suhṛlekkha*:

Translated by Tripiṭaka Master Guṇavarman	(*ca* 425 CE)
Translated by Tripiṭaka Master Saṇghavarman	(*ca* 450 CE)
Translated by Tripiṭaka Master Yijing	(*ca* 675 CE)

Resolve-for-Enlightenment Texts

On Generating the Resolve to Become a Buddha
On the Resolve to Become a Buddha by Ārya Nāgārjuna
Exhortation to Resolve on Buddhahood by Patriarch Sheng'an Shixian
Exhortation to Resolve on Buddhahood by the Tang Literatus, Peixiu

Vasubandhu's Treatise on the Bodhisattva Vow
By Vasubandhu Bodhisattva (*ca* 300 CE)

*All Kalavinka Press translations include facing-page source text.

CPSIA information can be obtained at www.ICGtesting.com
Printed in the USA
BVOW08s1013150216

436759BV00001B/68/P